Data
Communications
and Networks

Data Communications and Networks

Dave Miller

McGraw-Hill Irwin

Boston   Burr Ridge, IL   Dubuque, IA   Madison, WI   New York   San Francisco   St. Louis
Bangkok   Bogotá   Caracas   Kuala Lumpur   Lisbon   London   Madrid   Mexico City
Milan   Montreal   New Delhi   Santiago   Seoul   Singapore   Sydney   Taipei   Toronto

ISBN 0-07-296404-9

Editorial director: *Brent Gordon*
Publisher: *Stewart Mattson*
Senior sponsoring editor: *Paul Ducham*
Developmental editor: *Jennifer Wisnowski*
Senior marketing manager: *Douglas Reiner*
Senior media project manager: *Susan Lombardi*
Project manager: *Harvey Yep*
Production supervisor: *Gina Hangos*
Coordinator freelance design: *Artemio Ortiz Jr.*
Photo research coordinator: *Kathy Shive*
Senior digital content specialist: *Brian Nacik*
Cover design: *David Seidler*
Typeface: *10/12 Times New Roman*
Compositor: *Interactive Composition Corporation*
Printer: *Quebecor World Versailles Inc.*

Library of Congress Cataloging-in-Publication Data

Miller, David, 1960-
    Data communications and networks / David Miller.—1st ed.
      p. cm.
    Includes index.
    ISBN 0-07-296404-9 (alk. paper)
    1. Data transmission systems. 2. Computer networks. I. Title.
  TK5105.M553 2006
  004.6—dc22
                                       2004059743

www.mhhe.com

For Agnes & Lucia
One taught me to read. The other taught me to write.

—Dave Miller

Brief Contents

Contents

Chapter 5
Network Operating Systems   158

Chapter 6
Data Storage and Storage Networks   192

Chapter 7
Voice Networks   228

Chapter 8
Wide Area Networks   266

Chapter 9
Network Security   302

Preface

The world of data communications and networks incorporates many hardware and software components that are constantly undergoing upgrades and revisions or outright replacement. In this fast-paced environment, the conceptual knowledge that business managers must have in order to make effective decisions is paramount.

The underlying motive for the development of this text was to provide a building-block construct that not only introduces students to must-know terms and concepts but also provides the business reasoning behind the implementation of data communications and networking technologies. In addition, the development of this text was motivated by a passionate desire to incorporate a multisensory approach to the delivery of technical material; hence the inclusion of a digital supplement that provides real-world examples that reinforce the concepts that are presented in printed form.

And while there is no replacement for the conceptual knowledge introduced in this text, insight from a practitioner's viewpoint is essential for providing the student of data communications and networks with a complete understanding of the technologies that businesses implement in support of their data communications and networking needs. That's why this text includes real-world examples: tidbits that take a more in-depth look at technology, history, or business applications and case studies that are condensed from many years of work in the data communications and networking fields.

APPROACH

Data Communications and Networks has been developed with a building-block construct that begins with an introduction of basic data communications concepts and local area network concepts, and then builds on these concepts to introduce network operating systems, storage networks, voice networks, wide area networks, network security, and finally the Internet. Throughout the text, all concepts are related to real-world business applications and to the business drivers that support the implementation of various networking technologies. In addition, historical references are introduced to enhance the reader's conceptual knowledge and to link current data communications and network technologies to their historical roots.

Each chapter begins with a set of chapter objectives and a chapter outline that establish the concepts that are introduced and discussed throughout the chapter. Major and minor section headings delineate chapter concepts, and margin notes highlight key terms and definitions. Additional concept insights are also introduced throughout each chapter in the form of applied historical tidbits, applied business tidbits, and applied technical tidbits. These sections focus on specific examples that reinforce chapter concepts. In addition, the end-of-chapter materials provided with each chapter include a list of key terms, discussion questions, research activities, hands-on activities, and mini case studies.

As an added feature of this text, the online content provides real-world examples of people and hardware that are used in the data communications and networking professions.

INTENDED AUDIENCE

The building-block approach of this text is focused on students who need to develop a fundamental and practical knowledge base in data communications, networking technologies, and the impact that these technologies have on business functions. The intended audience is business students who are pursuing a career in data communications, network technologies, and management information systems.

ONLINE CONTENT

Data Communications and Networks has been designed to give students an added perspective that can only be gained from real world experiences. Since it is sometimes a significant challenge to coordinate field trips for large groups of students, the online content that supplements this text has been designed to bring the field trip into the classroom.

Each chapter has one or more video segments that address many of the major concepts that comprise the field of data communications and networks. You'll find footage of interviews with real-world data communications professionals as well as full-motion video segments that provide examples of and perspectives on numerous types of data communications and networking hardware. In addition, you'll find several video segments that demonstrate by example some of the major concepts that are discussed throughout the text.

The online content also includes digital images to supplement the content of each chapter. With these still images, you'll find examples of a range of networking hardware. Included are digital images of network interface cards, rack mount systems, chassis-based systems, wiring closets, servers, storage devices, cabling, hubs, switches, routers, voice network systems, and so on.

To view this and other additional student and instructor resources, visit the companion Web site for this text at www.mhhe.com/miller1e.

FOR THE INSTRUCTOR

Available to adopting faculty, the Instructor's Resource CD-ROM contains a variety of supplements in one convenient place: Instructor's Manual, Test Bank, PowerPoint slides for each chapter, and suggested answers to end-of-chapter questions and exercises as well as suggested solutions to the mini case studies. These resources are also available on the instructor's side of the Online Learning Center. There is also a lengthy case study that can be used as a building-block construct to reinforce the major concepts of each chapter, which also can challenge students to develop various phases of a network design and implementation project as they progress through the course. This case study is broad enough to either be introduced at the beginning of the course and used on a chapter-by-chapter basis, or it can be introduced midway through the course as a final project for submission at the end of the term.

About the Author

Dave Miller has been involved in data communications and networks since the early 1990s in capacities ranging from business and technical consultant to network trainer and college lecturer. His current academic and professional interests are focused on developing and improving courseware and instructional materials in the fields of data communications and networks as well as information systems. From a personal perspective, Mr. Miller enjoys restoring antique cars and pickup trucks.

Acknowledgments

I am forever grateful to the many individuals whose efforts and contributions were instrumental to the development of this book. Specifically, I would like to thank:

Dave McDowell, for providing me the opportunity to interview him and his staff.

Ann Marie Gizzi, for scheduling so many meetings.

Joe Ferrara, for his business and technical perspectives on large-scale technical services.

Patty Mabie, for her business and technical perspectives on data storage and administration.

Marcia LaManna, for her insight into data communications and network security.

Rick Paufve, for all the great interviews surrounding Novell, Microsoft, directory services, network attached storage, and network migration perspectives.

Tim Meyers, for his technical and business perspectives on wide area network services design, planning, and implementation.

Diane Vendel, for her detailed technical explanations of network attached storage and storage area networks and how they're implemented and maintained in a large network environment.

Al Atkinson, for his perspectives on monitoring systems.

Dave Yoder, for all of the technical interviews and insight regarding networks, network infrastructure, and network backbones.

Gary Johnston, for permitting me to use his school district as a case study.

Pat Lynch, for all of the technical telecommunications interviews.

Bill Grace, for guiding me through the telephone museum and for the detailed explanations of antique telephone equipment.

Bob Brentson, for putting up with my numerous phone calls and nearly endless questions.

Joe Sutorious, for discussing PBX design, implementation, and maintenance.

Peter Pappas, for paving the way to work with his school district.

John Grassi, for all the helpful suggestions about video hardware and software and for pushing me in the right direction with those development components.

Premier Maldonado, for assisting me with the production of numerous video clips.

Rick Indiano, for his technical tour of several wiring closets.

For all of their outstanding suggestions and clarifications, I would like to thank

Kamal Nayan Agarwal
Howard University

Bay Arinze
Drexel University

Greg Brewster
DePaul University

Steven M. Burleson
Milwaukee Area Technical College

Ann Burroughs
Humboldt State University

Jerry Carvalho
University of Utah—Salt Lake City

Q. B. Chung
Villanova University

M. Barry Dumas
Bernard M. Baruch College

Weiguo Fan
Virginia Polytechnic Institute and State University

Dennis Guster
St. Cloud State University

Margaret M. Hvatum
St. Louis Community College—Meramec/Kirkwood

Hassan Ibrahim
University of Maryland–College Park

Stuart Kaplan
Nassau Community College

Dana Ladd
Nichols College

R. Scott Lawyer
Hudson Valley Community College

Donna Lohn
Lakeland Community College

Scott Magruder
University of Southern Mississippi

Bruce J. McLaren
Indiana State University

Jerry Mefford
Hennepin Technical College

Abigail Lee Miller
Philadelphia University

Salim U. Mir
SUNY—Amherst

Pramod Pandya
California State University—Fullerton

Lynn Ray
University of Maryland—University College

Hendra Tandradinata
Iowa State University

Dan Turk
Colorado State University

Kent Webb
San Jose State University

Mark Weiser
Oklahoma State University, Stillwater

Judy Wynekoop
Florida Gulf Coast University

Samuel C. Yang
California State University—Fullerton

Sasithorn Zuge
University of Wisconsin—Stevens Point

    And I would also like to express my gratitude to the staff at McGraw-Hill/Irwin for their attention to detail and for making this project possible. I have really enjoyed working with all of you! Paul Ducham, thank you for your direction and for guiding this project. Jen Wisnowski, thank you for coordinating the development of this text and for keeping me on target in the final weeks of development. Harvey Yep, thank you for keeping me on track with copyedits and artwork reviews. D. J. Watt, thank you for meeting with me that very first time to discuss this project. Douglas Reiner, thank you for helping to promote this text. Alyson Platt, thank you for your attention to detail throughout the manuscript copyedit. Interactive Composition Corporation, thank you for developing such outstanding artwork. Art Ortiz, thank you for helping to create a wonderful design. Sue Lombardi, thank you for your assistance in creating the supplements for this text. You are a phenomenal team!

Data Communications and Networks

CHAPTER
One

Chapter Overview and Objectives

Data communications and networks touch all contemporary business functions in numerous ways. Marketing functions, accounting functions, distribution functions, and virtually all other business functions depend on data communications and networks for the transfer of information between any number of people, departments, and geographic locations. In other words, data communications and networks have become the infrastructure that supports the modern organization in information transfer. In this chapter, we examine a modern definition of data communications and discover several of the building blocks that make modern data communications possible. More specifically, by the end of this chapter, you will be able to

- Define data communications and its building blocks.

- Identify and describe three different types of data encoding.

- Describe the differences between analog and digital data.

- Describe the differences between analog transmission and digital transmission.

- Recognize the differences between parallel and serial transmission.

- Identify and describe asynchronous and synchronous transmission.

- Define and discuss simplex, half-duplex, and full-duplex data transmission.

- Identify and describe common data communications media options.

- Provide a simple explanation of data transmission security.

- List and discuss key data communications standards, standards organizations, and standards-making processes.

- Identify the layers of the OSI and TCP/IP models and describe the OSI and TCP/IP layered architectures.

- Identify two modern government regulations that have had a significant impact on the data communications industry.

Data Communications: An Introduction

AN OVERVIEW OF THE DATA COMMUNICATIONS INDUSTRY

The Data Communications Industry

The data communications industry is a big place that encompasses a multitude of manufacturing companies, service companies, consulting firms, political and regulatory agencies, standards-making organizations, research and development functions, and, of course, business and residential customers.

It has been marked by numerous periods of rapid growth, some of which date back to the mid and late 1800s with the development of electric telegraph and telephone communication. During the 20th century, we saw the introduction and development of computers as well as data communication within and across computer and data networks. In today's economy, we're witness to an unprecedented growth in wireless devices and wireless services combined with high-speed data networks that circumvent the globe. With all this growth and a world that continues to be drawn closer with every new communications link, it's little wonder that the data communications industry has such an impact on so many different organizations and aspects of our lives.

Political Influences in the Data Communications Industry

As far back as the optical telegraph in France in the 1700s, political influences were a factor in data communications advancement. The optical telegraph inventor, Claude Chappe, might not have found any interest at all in his optical telegraph had it not been for his brother's friendships with the political authorities in power at the time.[1] Samuel Morse was not exempt either. When it came to the development of his electric telegraph in the United States, his first funding came from the U.S. Congress.[2] Into the 19th and 20th centuries, telephone communication was observed and regulated by political agencies to assure fair practices and reasonable rate structures for consumers.

More recently, the political factors that affect data communications include the regulation and sale of radio frequencies for wireless communications technologies and the deployment of broadband (high-speed data network) technology to all markets. In many cases, new policies are enforced with the intention of improving competition and preventing monopolies. Policy makers can impose a set of rules on service providers that forces them to make investments in services with no guarantee of financial return or protection from competitors that enter the field after the heavy financial investments have been made. With modern wireless data communications, government regulation can provide the benefit of delineating frequency use across the data communications industry so that all wireless device technologies can be guaranteed unique frequency usage.

Other recent broad regulations, including the Telecommunications Act of 1996, provide for mass deployment and a virtual guarantee of universal access to newer data communications technologies. The intent of policy makers is to force communications companies and, in particular, telephone companies to provide high-speed access to public entities such as the public school system as well as to rural areas that might not otherwise get access for a number of years. In any event, the data communications industry has been historically linked to policy makers, for good or for bad, and will likely continue to be linked in a way that benefits some to the detriment of others. At the same time, policy actions will continue to assist in moving the data communications industry forward.

---

[1] For more information on the early history of the optical telegraph and Claude Chappe, see Appendix A, "A Brief History of Data Communications and Computer Networks."

[2] For more information regarding the early history of the electric telegraph and Samuel Morse, read Appendix A, "A Brief History of Data Communications and Computer Networks."

Employment Perspective

At any given time over the past 10 to 15 years, there have been thousands of unfilled jobs in the areas of data communications, information technology, information systems, telecommunications, and other fields directly related to the data communications industry. Job types include programmers, analysts, network engineers, telecom technicians, software security architects, network administrators, systems project engineers, carrier service designers and technicians, and the list goes on and on.

The key point is the journey you're about to take into the world of data communications is full of opportunity. You're going to examine the basics of data communications as well as numerous detailed topics within this text. And the whole reason for doing this is to prepare you for the kinds of business employment opportunities you'll encounter throughout your careers as well as define for you the components, strategies, and language that are common to the data communications industry. Even if you're a student of another discipline, the knowledge you'll extract from *Data Communications and Networks* will provide you with the techno-speak that you'll need to communicate in the modern business world.

A MODERN DEFINITION OF DATA COMMUNICATIONS

Data communications. We use it every day, whether we're talking on the telephone, our cell phones, accessing e-mail, or simply downloading files from the Internet. Banks depend on it for transactions and for timely and accurate account information. Manufacturers depend on it to remain competitive with customers and suppliers alike. Hospitals and medical professionals depend on it for events as important as saving lives and as mundane as structuring and cutting costs. Even widely followed sporting events have come to utilize modern data communications as a valuable necessity.

But what is data communications, and what can it do for us? If we start with a simple analysis, we can think of data communications in a very simplistic way as moving information from point A to point B.[3] If you download a file from the Internet, you're copying information from a remote location to your computer—from point A to point B. When you send an e-mail, you create it in one location and someone retrieves it at another location—once again from point A to point B. If you withdraw money from an automatic teller machine, you affect your account balance at the ATM, but the information is transmitted to your home bank's databases so that your account can be updated. Yet again, data communications moves data from point A to point B.

This definition, although convenient, isn't sufficient in today's modern world of data communications. After all, when you send information between points A and B, which we call *nodes* in network language, there's some type of communications medium in between. The medium can be anything you choose: copper wire, fiber-optic cable, or even radio waves. In addition, the data will have to be formatted in a way that is acceptable for transmission across the chosen medium. The data is encoded into a series of electrical pulses or optical pulses or radio frequency transmissions that allow the data to travel through a given medium from point A to point B. Along the way, computers will play a role, high-tech data transmission and control equipment will come into play, as will various vendors that supply the copper or optical transmission lines or wireless services that make data transmission possible. If we put this all together, you can think of **data communications** as the

data communications
the transmission of encoded data and information in a medium-specific format between two or more nodes, people, businesses, or entities

---

[3] Data communications can also mean moving information from point A to multiple points B through methods known as multicast and broadcast. In general, *multicast* involves transmitting information to groups of computers on a network and *broadcast* means transmitting to all computers on a network.

data encoding
the method by which data is represented in digital or binary format

pervasive
spread or diffused throughout

ubiquitous
present or existing everywhere at the same time

transmission of **encoded data** and information in a medium-specific format between two or more nodes, people, businesses, or entities.

What data communications can do for us is enormous. It plays a key role in supporting business needs. It facilitates the mobility of organizations' information. It links one business to another and extends the reach of many businesses to the public at large. It's truly **pervasive** today and supports every aspect of the modern business world. You could even say that without data communications our modern world of electronic business and electronic commerce couldn't exist. And tomorrow, data communications will allow for unsolicited interaction between people and technology, as business data communications becomes **ubiquitous**.

With this information in mind, let's take a look at some of the building blocks that make data transmission between two points possible. At first you'll be introduced to the concepts of bits, bytes, and data encoding. Then you'll have a look at digital and analog data combined with analog and digital transmission concepts. After that, you'll be introduced to some of the communications standards and data communications models that form the foundation for the design and manufacture of data communications products, services, and network data transmission.

Bits and Bytes and Data Encoding

For data to be successfully transmitted, it must be *encoded* into a format that both the sending and the receiving devices can understand. Humans understand language, letters, numerals, and other special characters, but machines need a language they can interpret. In the days of the telegraph, Morse code was the encoding scheme that converted letters and numbers into dots and dashes so that the resulting data could be successfully transmitted and received by electrical means (see Table 1.1). Both sender and receiver made use of the same encoding scheme. Because the encoding scheme was universal, a telegrapher receiving the transmission in San Francisco could understand a message sent from a telegraph in New York.

In much the same way, modern computers use the **binary number system** to represent letters, numerals, and other special characters. These numbers, letters, and characters are represented by a series of 1s and 0s that the computers can understand. Each one or zero is a **bit**, the smallest unit of encoding in the binary number system, and eight bits together comprise a **byte**. Bits and bytes are the data building blocks that allow computers to represent and convey digital information. Consider that the next time you're typing a term paper. Each letter or numeral or special character that you type is actually represented inside the computer as a series of 1s and 0s. If you zip the term paper file and send it to your professor in an e-mail, the e-mail along with the document are already in digital format. The entire message can then be transmitted by modem and across a phone line, which is digital data across an analog transmission line. Or, if you're sending the e-mail from a computer network on

bit
the smallest unit of encoding in the binary number system

byte
eight bits

TABLE 1.1
Morse Code

Human Readable	International Morse Code
A	• —
B	— • • •
C	— • — •
D	— • •
E	•
1	• — — — —
2	• • — — —
3	• • • — —
4	• • • • —
5	• • • • •

campus, the network devices that switch and route information to their intended recipients will service your digital e-mail transmission with digital data transmission services.

In today's data communications world, there are three major categories of encoding schemes, EBCDIC, ASCII, and Unicode, but only the last two, ASCII and Unicode, are commonly used.

Extended Binary Coded Decimal Interchange Code (EBCDIC) is an IBM proprietary encoding scheme that is used with **legacy** IBM mainframes and hardware. It is still a key data building block in today's IBM mainframe systems. EBCDIC utilizes a series of eight bits to represent letters, numerals, and special characters. Because it uses eight bits, EBCDIC can represent up to 256 different characters.

The **American Standard Code for Information Interchange (ASCII)** is an encoding scheme that is very common today. It is used with personal computers, computer networks, and many other kinds of hardware and software. It uses a series of seven bits to represent letters, numerals, and special characters.[4] Because it uses only seven bits for data, ASCII can encode only 128 different characters. You have probably used ASCII if you've ever used a word processing program or posted your résumé on the Internet. Most word processing programs have a feature that will allow you to convert your human readable file into an ASCII text file so that it is universally accessible by all computers. Table 1.2 provides a brief list of how human readable letters and numerals are represented by ASCII and EBCDIC.

Unicode allows encoded characters beyond the 128-character limitation of ASCII. Its first 128 characters are the same as ASCII so that it is fully compatible with ASCII characters. However, where ASCII uses seven bits to build characters, Unicode uses 16 bits. With 16 bits to represent letters, numerals, and special characters, Unicode can encode up to 65,536 different characters, including characters from Chinese, Greek, Hebrew, Japanese, Korean, Russian, and Sanskrit alphabets and other special characters such as technical and publishing symbols as well as various geometric forms.

For international businesses that communicate across boundaries in cyberspace, the Unicode character set is a required encoding scheme. Other encoding standards such as ASCII and EBCDIC are frequently converted to Unicode for data transmission purposes. One specific example is the Java programming language. It uses the Unicode character set and accommodates ASCII and EBCDIC by converting it to Unicode. Unicode is supported by all modern Internet browsers as well as in operating systems such as Microsoft Windows and Novell NetWare. Linux and UNIX operating systems utilize a modified version of Unicode known as UTF-8.[5]

legacy system
a computer system that has its roots in a previous generation of computing technology and which is generally retained and accommodated as new systems are implemented. The term *legacy system* generally implies a system that has been around for a long time, is not state of the art, but still provides business functionality.

TABLE 1.2
Examples of ASCII and EBCDIC Encoding

Human Readable	ASCII	EBCDIC
A	1000001	11000001
B	1000010	11000010
C	1000011	11000011
D	1000100	11000100
1	0110001	11110001
2	0110010	11110010
3	0110011	11110011
4	0110100	11110100
@	1000000	01111100
%	0100101	01101100

[4] ASCII traditionally used an eighth bit for error detection. In most modern systems, the eighth bit is set to zero for transmission, and error detection (for synchronous transmission) is done at the frame level only.
[5] To learn more about Unicode, you can visit http://www.unicode.org. Here you'll find information about Unicode as well as the consortium that supports its continued development.

Digital and Analog Data

Before you can proceed down the data communications road of understanding, you'll need to master two basic data communications terms, analog and digital. Speaking simplistically, analog is continuous as in waveform signals, and digital is discrete as in start and stop type patterns such as Morse code.[6] In terms of data types, the voice data created by the handset on a typical home phone is analog, whereas computer-generated data is digital. Your voice conveys a continuously variable series of pitches and tones as you speak, the basic characteristics of analog data. If you want to quantify **analog data** into a definition, you can think of it as the information that is represented and reproduced by a continuously variable level of sound, light, electricity, or other input. The information inside your computer, however, is created as a series of discrete voltage levels that are generated to represent 1s and 0s, the binary language that computers understand and use to represent data. Putting this into a definition, you can think of **digital data** as that information that is represented and reproduced by discrete levels of sound, light, electricity, or some other input. The music CDs you play are digital. Older style long-play (LP) records that your parents or grandparents played are analog. Figure 1.1 provides some additional representations of digital and analog data.

As a more in-depth example of digital data, consider the electric telegraph of the 19th century and the Morse code that was transmitted across it.[7] Morse code, the communications

analog data
information that is represented and reproduced by a continuously variable level of sound, light, electricity, or other input

digital data
information that is represented and reproduced by discrete levels of sound, light, electricity, or some other input

FIGURE 1.1

Analog and Digital Data

---

[6] Morse code is the telegraphic alphabet developed by Samuel Morse in the 1800s. You can learn more about Morse code and the history of data communications in Appendix A, "A Brief History of Data Communications and Computer Networks."

[7] See Appendix A, "A Brief History of Data Communications and Computer Networks."

encoding technique used by telegraph operators, is one of the earliest examples of digital data. Each letter of the alphabet and every number can be represented by a combination of two elements, a dot and a dash. The dots and dashes are analogous to the discrete voltages used to represent **binary data** (or 1s and 0s) in modern personal computers. In a computer, a discrete voltage change represents either a 1 or a 0, and in the appropriate sequence, the data you see on your computer's monitor is represented in the computer's circuitry as these binary digits, or digital data (1s and 0s). Similarly in the 1800s, Morse code represented a sender's personal message with a series of binary codes (the dots and dashes) combined by the telegraph operator to create a digital message for conveyance to a remote location.

Digital and Analog Transmission

Digital and analog transmissions have more to do with the way in which data is conveyed between points A and B than with whether the data itself is digital or analog. Analog data can be transmitted using analog transmission or digital transmission techniques. Likewise, digital data can be conveyed using either digital or analog transmission. The transmission type you choose is as much a function of the available technology as it is the business needs that drive a particular solution. You'll see more about business drivers in the next section.

digital transmission
a method of data transmission that utilizes discrete changes in electricity or light across a medium to convey data between two or more end points

First, let's look at **digital transmission** by reconsidering the electric telegraph example as a way of describing digital transmission. With the electric telegraph, and in particular Samuel Morse's telegraph, the signals that telegraphers sent and received were a series of dots and dashes encoded on an electric circuit. Whenever a telegrapher "keyed" a letter or number, he was transmitting data by placing a series of electrical pulses on the telegraph wire. A dot was a short pulse; a dash was a longer pulse. In either case, two or more distinct signals used in combination represented a message. By applying the dots and dashes of Morse code to close and open the electrical telegraph circuit numerous times, encoded messages could be sent to the receiving telegraph key at the other end of the wire. Close the circuit, data transmission takes place. Open the circuit, and there is no transmission. Close the circuit, another piece of the data transmission is sent. Open it, and once again there is no transmission. Electrical signal on, electrical signal off, on and off, on and off; each contact with the telegraph key was held for a discrete time interval so that the electrical signal could transmit the encoded message. Morse's invention used "current on" for a specific long or short burst combined with "current off" to separate characters in the transmitted messages. This was the primitive beginning of digital transmission using electricity—discrete changes in the electrical signal by turning it on or off to encode the data for transmission. Today digital transmission methods use discrete changes in voltage or light instead of pulses of current to convey data. Either way the process is digital transmission, one of the cornerstones of modern data communications. The top half of Figure 1.2 provides a graphical representation of digital transmission.

analog transmission
uses continuously varying levels of light, sound, or electricity across a medium to represent and convey data

Where digital transmission uses discrete signals to encode information between points A and B, **analog transmission** uses continuously varying levels of light or sound or electricity across a medium to represent and convey data. This was the marvel that Alexander Graham Bell and Thomas Watson discovered and which fostered the invention and

FIGURE 1.2
Digital Transmission and Analog Transmission

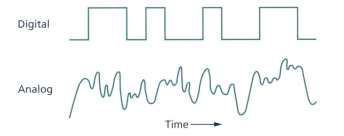

Digital

Analog

Time ⟶

development of the telephone. With analog transmission on a regular phone line, the electrical signal is continuously modulated into multiple and varying frequencies by the input of the human voice. By modulating a continuous electrical signal across a wire, Bell and Watson were able to convey human voice as it sounds—continuous—and with all of its varying pitches and tones. The bottom half of Figure 1.2 represents an analog transmission.

So which came first, digital or analog transmission? You could build a case for smoke signals as being discrete and lump them into digital data transmission. Naturally produced sound is by its nature continuous, so if you consider the sound produced from either yelling or whistling at your friends, or the beating of drums or logs in the forest or jungle, you could suggest that the earliest data transmissions were analog. Torches, semaphore signaling with flags, smoke signals, and early optical and electric telegraphs represent methods of digital data transmission because their encoded messages are not continuous; each "on" position of the sending device conveys a static and discrete portion of the entire message.[8] In contrast, the earliest telephones represent analog data transmission because they conveyed the human voice with a continuously modulated electrical signal. So if you think that analog data transmission came first, you're probably right. But it's not because of Bell and the telephone; it's because of the continuously varying levels of natural sounds as they travel through the air from point A to point B.

Modern Analog and Digital Transmission Devices

In the modern world of data communications, you're likely to use devices such as analog phones, digital phones, personal computers, Web servers, modems, cable modems, codecs, and Channel Service Unit/Digital Service Unit (CSU/DSU) to facilitate the transfer of data from your home or work environment through a **carrier service** to an intended destination. To make the data transmission connection between devices at point A and devices at point B, you're going to need an understanding of what these connectivity devices do. In this section, you get the 40,000-foot viewpoint. In later chapters, you'll explore the details of some of these connectivity devices and others, and you'll see from an up-close perspective how they facilitate connectivity between points A and B.

When you place a call from your home, your analog phone converts the acoustic properties of your voice into an analog signal that is then transmitted across a two-wire circuit, known as a local loop, that connects your home to a telephone company's central office. You don't need any special connectivity device to connect you to the central office other than a connection box known as a *demarc*.[9] This is the point at which the phone company connects to your house and to which you connect the telephone wires that run throughout your house. Your voice is converted to an analog signal within the phone's transmitter, which we know as a telephone mouthpiece, and the voice signal is sent as an analog transmission. This process is also an example of *analog transmission of analog data*. You can see a graphical representation in Figure 1.3.

A computer that you have at home or work, however, doesn't generate data the same way as your phone. The computer generates digital data. If you want to send this digital data across an analog telephone circuit, you'll need a device that conveys digital data onto an analog transmission medium. That device is a modem. A **modem** modulates (modifies) what is known as a carrier wave on an analog phone circuit at discrete intervals. At every interval, one or more bits of the digital data from the computer are transmitted across the analog

carrier service

a high-speed data transmission service that can be provided by a carrier company such as MCI, Sprint, AT&T, or other carrier company

---

[8] See Appendix A, "A Brief History of Data Communications and Computer Networks."
[9] In telephone vernacular, a *demarc* is the connection box. Technically speaking, however, the demarc is simply the demarcation point or transition point between the customer's premises and the telephone company's telephone network. The connection box can more accurately be referred to as the *network interface unit* or NIU.

FIGURE 1.3   Analog Transmission of Analog Data versus Analog Transmission of Digital Data

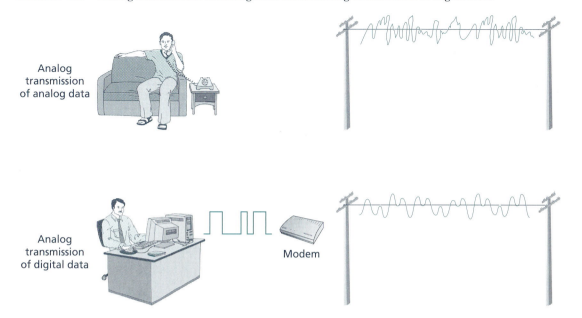

Analog transmission of analog data

Analog transmission of digital data

Modem

FIGURE 1.4   Digital Transmission of Digital Data versus Digital Transmission of Analog Data

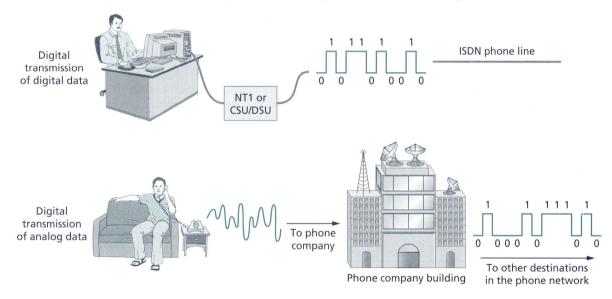

Digital transmission of digital data

NT1 or CSU/DSU

1 1 1 1 1
0 0 0 0 0 0

ISDN phone line

Digital transmission of analog data

To phone company

Phone company building

1 1 1 1 1 1
0 0 0 0 0 0 0 0

To other destinations in the phone network

phone line. The process continues until the entire digital data set is sent. This is an example of *analog transmission of digital data*. The bottom half of Figure 1.3 provides an example.

If you have a digital carrier circuit such as an Integrated Services Digital Network (ISDN) line or T1 line running to your home or business, you can connect your computer network or digital phone to the digital transmission line through a digital interface device such as an **NT1** or **CSU/DSU.** These digital connectivity devices interpret the digital data created by your computer or digital phone and format it for sending it across the digital circuit. The process of data transmission in this example is known as *digital transmission of digital data*. The top half of Figure 1.4 provides a graphic to match the preceding example.

Applied Technical **Tidbits**

Analog-to-digital conversion is also the principle by which music CDs are created. When a recording artist sings or plays a musical instrument (leave out synthesized music for now), the sounds that are created and transmitted through the air are analog. However, when you listen to a music CD, the sounds that are reproduced originate from the digital recording that is impressed on the music CD. The musical information on the CD is actually a vast number of discrete sounds (8,000 or more per second) sampled and recorded from the original analog musical inputs. Recorded end to end onto a music CD, these discrete sounds, or data elements of the music, can then be played and replayed through the use of a digital-to-analog converter that reads the discrete digital elements of the musical information and then converts them to an analog signal for playback through your favorite set of speakers. In principle, the analog-to-digital music recording and digital-to-analog music playback behave like the analog-to-digital and digital-to-analog conversions provided through a codec in the world of data communications.

You can also transmit analog data across a digital circuit. An example of *digital transmission of analog data* is the conversion of an analog phone call that you place from home into a digital signal so that it can be transmitted outside the phone company's central office and across the telephone network. Because modern phone company networks outside of the local loop are comprised of digital data transmission devices and services, all incoming analog signals from the local loop must be converted to digital signals before they can be switched to another central office and ultimately sent on to their destinations. A device that converts these analog signals to digital signals is known as a **codec,** short for coder/decoder. A codec works by listening to the analog signal, taking samples of the signal several thousand times per second, and then re-creating the data as a digital signal. Phone companies have an incentive to convert analog signals that arrive from homes and businesses via the analog *local loop* into digital transmissions at the central offices because digital signals provide greater data integrity, better capacity utilization, and better security within a phone company's communications network. The bottom half of Figure 1.4 matches the preceding example.

Parallel and Serial Transmission

Digital transmission and analog transmission indicate the two methods by which data bits can be transmitted across a medium. Encoding tells us which bits represent each letter, number, or special character and translates our human language and symbols into the EBCDIC, ASCII, or Unicode representations that the computer can understand. To further extend our data communications conceptual knowledge we need to discover how the data bits are sent across a given medium. To do this, let's take a look at parallel transmission and serial transmission.

Parallel transmission uses multiple parallel data paths to transmit multiple bits simultaneously, one bit per path, as shown in Figure 1.5. This is how data travels inside a computer, usually in 32-bit or 64-bit data paths, and it's the same method used to transmit data to any desktop printer that is connected to a physical parallel port connector.

Consider as an example several moving vans arriving at your house to pick up all your belongings to move you to another city. Each van is analogous to one data bit. Once all of the vans are full, they get on the freeway and travel side by side down the interstate, each van in its own separate lane. If the vans could continue along this multilane highway to your new home, they would all arrive at the same time, and they would even be sequenced in the proper order for unloading. You would be happy, and the trip would go by very quickly because of the multilane highway. Similarly, parallel data transmission is relatively fast. Practical

codec
short for coder/decoder is a device that converts analog data into digital data for transmission across a digital transmission medium and also converts the digital data back to analog data for transmission across an analog transmission medium. The term *codec* can also be used for compressor/decompressor when referring to removing bits from a data stream.

parallel transmission
uses multiple parallel data paths to transmit multiple bits of data simultaneously, one bit per path

FIGURE 1.5
Parallel Transmission
Bits travel in parallel across 8, 16, 32, or 64 wires or paths to their destinations.

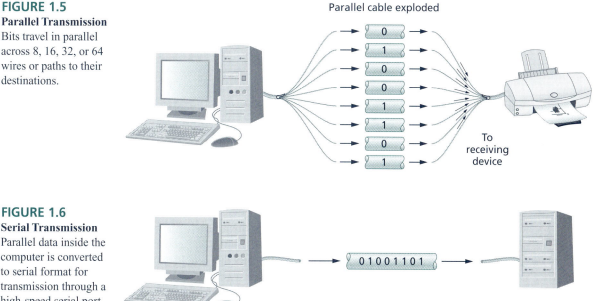

Parallel cable exploded

To receiving device

FIGURE 1.6
Serial Transmission
Parallel data inside the computer is converted to serial format for transmission through a high-speed serial port such as USB or Firewire to an external storage device.

implementations of parallel data transmission include data transmissions within a computer, printer connections to personal computers through a parallel port, and connections to other peripheral devices such as CD recorders/writers that connect through a parallel port.

But when was the last time you saw a multilane interstate that went door to door? That kind of highway might be nice when you are in a hurry to get from point A to point B, but from a practical standpoint, the costs to implement and maintain a multilane highway simply for reduced travel time are probably going to be prohibitive. Instead, you're most likely going to travel using one lane most of the time. This single-lane concept is what **serial transmission** is all about; the data bits travel in sequence across a single wire or data path (see Figure 1.6). The wiring cost is reduced at the expense of transmission speed.

serial transmission
a communications method that sequences data bits for transmission across a single wire or data path

A common implementation of serial data transmission exists with modem use. Data within the computer is formatted for parallel transmission. Analog phone lines utilize a two-wire pair that makes up a single communications channel. Transmitting the information from inside the computer across the analog phone circuit not only requires a conversion from digital to analog transmission, but the data must be formatted for serial transmission as well. This is the function of a **universal asynchronous receiver/transmitter (UART),** the component inside a modem that converts data being transmitted in parallel into a serial transmission.

Other practical implementations of serial data transmission include connections between older style terminals that connect to mainframe computers across serial cables as well as serial printers and plotters that connect to a serial port on the back of a personal computer. In the recent history of personal computers, a serial mouse was a commonly used serial device that connected to the serial port on the back of a personal computer.

Recent additions to serial data transmission technology include **Universal Serial Bus (USB)** and the **IEEE-1394** standard that is sometimes referred to as **Firewire.** Both USB and IEEE-1394 are newer technologies that support serial data transmission but at much higher speeds than standard serial connections. These technologies are replacing parallel cable connections to printers as well as older style serial connections to input devices such as keyboards and mice. Many of today's printers come with USB port communications capability, and some no longer support parallel communications. Other practical implementations of these USB technologies include add-on data storage devices that simply plug into a USB or Firewire port for additional storage capacity. Still other USB storage devices are portable and have replaced floppy disks as the preferred method of removable and portable data storage. Figure 1.6 provides an example of serial transmission from a computer through a USB or Firewire connection to an external storage device.

Asynchronous and Synchronous Data Transmission

If you look at the Morse code in Table 1.1, and if you envision a telegraph operator in the 1800s sending the word *HE* in a telegraph, it would consist of four dots for the letter H and one dot for the letter E. Now consider the numeral 5. With Morse code, it is represented by five dots, the same number of dots that represents the word *HE*. You might ask, How would the telegrapher at the receiving end of the transmission be able to distinguish between the word *he* and the numeral *5*? The answer is that the telegraphers at both the sending and receiving ends would know to include a timed pause between transmitted characters. With appropriate training and practice, skilled telegraphers could make the appropriate distinctions.

In much the same way that Morse code used appropriately timed pauses between characters, digital data transmissions require a timing or coding mechanism between bytes of data to distinguish one byte from the next or one set of bytes from the next set. **Asynchronous transmissions** add a **start bit** to the beginning of each byte and a **stop bit** at the end of the eight-bit transmission, as shown in Figure 1.7. The start and stop bits signal the receiving device to recognize each transmitted byte so the transmission is decoded accurately.

Synchronous transmissions are a little more efficient than asynchronous transmissions during large data transfers because **synchronous transmissions** send multiple bytes of data as one transmission without adding a start and stop bit to each byte. Instead, synchronous transmitting devices launch each multibyte bundle with a series of preceding **sync bits** that let the receiving device know it is about to receive data, as illustrated in Figure 1.8. Included with these sync bits is information about the rate of data transmission so that the receiving device can correctly adjust its receive rate to match the transmission rate of the

FIGURE 1.7   **Asynchronous Transmission**
Each byte of data is preceded by a start bit and followed by a stop bit.

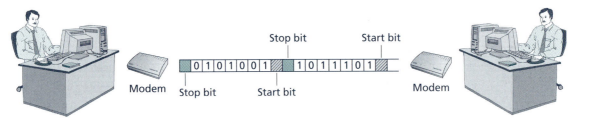

FIGURE 1.8   **Synchronous Transmission**

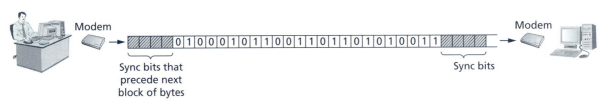

sending device. Other types of synchronous transmission devices use a separate communications channel instead of the preceding sync bits to announce the start of a data transmission and the transmission rate.

Simplex, Half-Duplex, and Full-Duplex Transmission

Simplex, half-duplex, and full-duplex transmissions, represented in Figure 1.9, are still other types of data transmissions about which you should be aware. **Simplex transmission** means that the data channel or path is one way only. There's a sending device and a receiving device, and the receiving device never sends back any data. An example of this is a kiosk in a mall that provides store information or directions or other one-way information. The computer in the kiosk transmits to the display, and that's the extent of the communication. Another example is an airline flight display. You can't interact with the display, but you do benefit from the information that is displayed there. The information flows one way from the computer that generates the display to you—there's no **bidirectional communication** with simplex data transmission.

Half-duplex transmission allows bidirectional communication between devices, but information flows in only one direction at a time. This method of communication was common to older style modem communication that took place over a single, two-wire circuit. With early modem technology, when one device was sending, the other could only receive. For bidirectional communication, the modems had to take turns sending and receiving.

Full-duplex transmission incorporates advanced communication technologies that allow simultaneous bidirectional communications. In data networks, full-duplex communications generally rely on two, two-wire pairs for full-duplex mode. One pair is used for sending, and the other two-wire pair is used for receiving. A common implementation is full-duplex communication across a data network using special network interface cards that support full-duplex communications. In data communications using modems, the breakthrough that allowed full-duplex transmission originally required two, two-wire pairs—two wires to

FIGURE 1.9
Simplex, Half-Duplex, and Full-Duplex Transmission

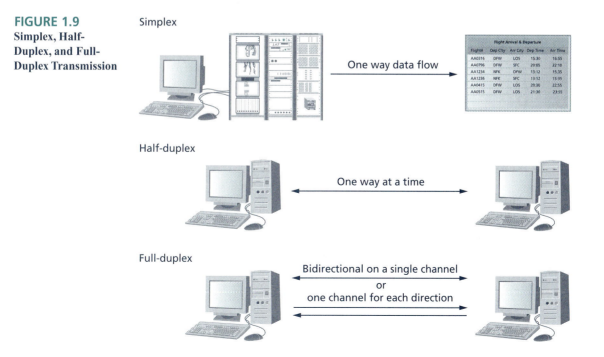

send and two to receive. However, with advances in detecting the noise on the communications channel and subtracting a device's own sending signal, a single two-wire pair can be used for full-duplex communications in data transmissions across analog lines. In either case, full-duplex transmission is a very efficient and fast way to ensure high-speed communications between points A and B when both devices can send and receive at the same time.

Common Data Communications Media Options

The devices you've discovered in this chapter represent only a portion of the components, services, and technologies that are available to build a data communications infrastructure. As you proceed through the book, you'll find more and more devices and technologies that will allow you to expand your repertoire of data communications terms and knowledge.

One other category of network components worthy of introduction in this chapter is **transmission media.** Whether you're connecting a computer to a cable modem or building a network of computers to support a companywide application, the data communications equipment such as phones, computers, modems and cable modems, and other analog and digital data transmission devices all require transmission media. The most common include **coaxial cable, unshielded twisted pair (UTP)** copper wire, **fiber-optic cable,** all of which fall into the category of **guided media**, and various forms of wireless, all of which can be categorized as **unguided media**. Guided media simply means that there are one or more wires over which data can be transmitted. In other words, there is a wire to physically guide the data transmission. Unguided media simply means that there is not a wired boundary to contain the communications channel—instead, other methods are implemented to contain the channel with unguided media. In this chapter, you're going to get only the briefest overview to introduce the basic media choices. In chapter 2 you'll explore the physical media types in greater detail, and you'll explore various wireless technologies throughout the text.

In its many forms, coaxial cable, or simply coax, has been around for a long time. In recent history, coaxial cable was used in local area network (LAN) installations but has since been supplanted by various forms of UTP copper wire and fiber-optic cables. Coax is still commonly used in residential and business installations that require high-speed access to the Internet through a cable service provider. Coaxial cable is made up of a core conductor that is surrounded by insulating material and a mesh of grounding metal fabric. You can see an example in Figure 1.10.

UTP is commonly used with small computer networks, and it is also used to connect your home to a phone company's central office. It is used as the connection between a computer or computer network and a cable modem, and it's commonly used as a practical media

guided media
a media type that uses one or more wires to convey data transmissions

unguided media
a media type that utilizes wireless communications channels to transmit data

FIGURE 1.10   **Coaxial, UTP, and Fiber Media**

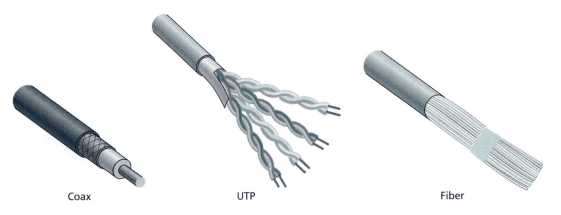

Coax   UTP   Fiber

A business might consider a terrestrial microwave solution when the cost of a high-speed carrier service is too high or if wired connections between remote locations are simply unavailable.

In one network installation with which I was involved, we contemplated using a terrestrial microwave solution to link two buildings that were on opposite ends of a large parking lot. The local phone service provider seemed unwilling to provide a high-speed carrier service solution at a reasonable monthly lease fee, so we looked into installing microwave. The microwave solution would have involved the installation of a rooftop antenna on each building along with the appropriate cabling and connectivity devices to connect the antenna to the network in each building. At the time, the fastest data-rate wireless solution we could find would transmit data at only 25 Mbps.

In the end, however, we chose to go with a cabling solution between the two buildings. We had a cabling contractor run fiber-optic cabling underground within a service tunnel owned and maintained by another business with which we negotiated a nominal usage fee. The reason we went with the cabling solution was because of the inherent data transmission problems that can be associated with terrestrial microwave in severe weather conditions such as heavy snow and rain. In addition, the cabling solution at the time proved much more cost effective when compared to the purchase and installation of the microwave solution.

choice for voice and data network communications within office buildings. It's comprised of one or more pairs of solid-core copper wires twisted together, and it's available in several different grades or categories. An example of UTP is provided in Figure 1.10.

Fiber-optic cables are another media choice in the world of data communications that can provide for higher levels of data traffic on a network or wide area network and which provides higher levels of security and connectivity over longer distances. Data transmissions over fiber-optic cabling use pulses of light across the glass fiber core that's at the center of the cable. Long distance telephone companies commonly use fiber in their communications infrastructures, and fiber is a medium of choice wherever security, high traffic requirements, and long-haul distances are business essentials. It's also the required media for fast transmission services such as synchronous optical network (SONET), which phone companies and carrier companies provide for customers who require transmission of vast amounts of data.[10] Fiber-optic cabling is available in a variety of formats, but its essential components are a glass core surrounded by one or more protective coatings and reinforcing fibers that provide added strength to the cable. An example of fiber-optic cabling is provided in Figure 1.10.

By far the fastest growing data transmission media type today is wireless. The roots of **wireless technologies** go back a long way with optical telegraphs and more importantly with the discovery of radio waves in the late 1800s. The electromagnetic waves that allow us to tune in to our favorite radio stations and listen to our favorite music "on the air" are the same types of waves that are driving cell phone communication, PDAs (personal digital assistants), wireless networks, and wireless Internet services. While our favorite radio stations use high-power levels and frequencies allocated specifically to radio broadcasts, the handheld devices we use every day for wireless data communication are much lower in power and use built-in antennas that transmit and receive frequencies that won't interfere with radio stations or other wireless data communications devices.

---

[10] You'll learn about carriers in chapter 8. For now a carrier is a company that provides the data communications services, such as T-carrier, optical carrier, and SONET, that connect remote networks.

If you ever work for a company that requires large-scale data transmission via wireless, you're going to have to consider two general types of wireless transmission services: **terrestrial microwave** or **satellite microwave.** Both types utilize directionally focused, high-frequency radio waves as the carrier for data transmissions. With terrestrial microwave, antennas must be installed at each location, the antennas must be within a "line of site" of each other, and each antenna must be properly aligned to send and receive the focused transmission signal. Figure 1.11 provides an example. Improper alignment as well as severe weather conditions can significantly affect the rate of data transmission or even stop it completely. Terrestrial microwave solutions can be practical wherever wired solutions aren't available, or if your business wants to trade the fixed costs of the terrestrial wireless implementation for the costs of a comparable wired service from a carrier.

With satellite microwave, as depicted in Figure 1.12, a ground-based transmitter/receiver is aligned with a communications satellite in **geosynchronous orbit** around the earth so that data can be sent from point A to point B via satellite.

Another form of wireless data transmission that is still in limited use today in some applications is infrared. **Infrared** technology uses light waves to transmit data over short distances from a few to several feet. At one point its use was very common in laptop computers for exchanging data in computer lab environments or among co-workers on a long airline flight. Today you're more likely to see infrared used for devices such as wireless computer mice.

FIGURE 1.11
Terrestrial Microwave

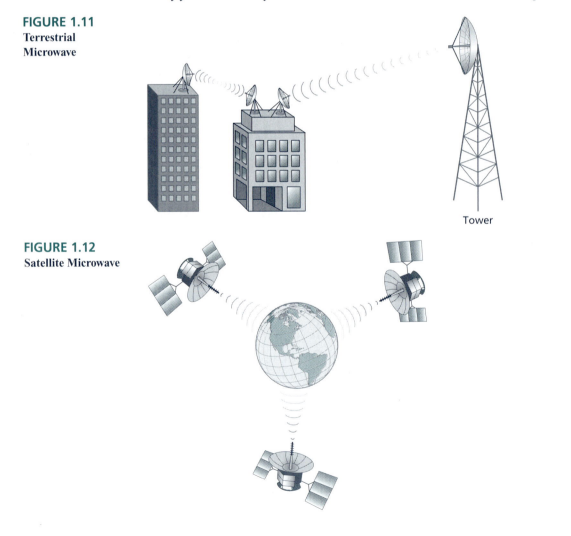

Tower

FIGURE 1.12
Satellite Microwave

Data Transmission Security

Data transmission security has become a very important hot button for data managers and data communications specialists. No one wants to inadvertently lose valuable data or worry about data theft while corporate information is being transmitted across a data communications circuit.

protocol
a formal set of rules that is used to define how data is transmitted between computing devices

Some of the methods that can prevent data loss and theft include the underlying **protocols** that are built into a transmission technology. For example, modems have error detection built in so that when an error is detected, the information can be retransmitted from the source. Other types of data transmission services provide error detection and correction within the transmission infrastructure so that the data is "scanned" at interim points located between points A and B. In this way errors can be stopped and retransmissions for correct data requested and sent prior to the data arriving at the final destination. Other types of services rely on the quality of the data transmission circuits. These transmission services perform error detection without any error correction at the interim locations so that error correction takes place only when bad data arrives at the final destination. This method makes sense if the data transmission circuit is highly reliable; that is, it typically experiences very few errors. And there are many other protocols that support and control transmission services in today's complex data communications networks. You'll discover many of these additional services in subsequent chapters.

Regarding data theft during transmission, various **encryption** schemes exist to keep data secure, and numerous hardware devices and software programs exist to keep your data safe while it's being transmitted. Examples include **digital certificates** and **digital signatures** to prevent unauthorized data access. Other examples include **virtual private networks (VPNs)** and **virtual local area networks (VLANs)** to create a private and secure data channel between one or more nodes or locations.[11]

DATA COMMUNICATIONS STANDARDS

According to the *Webster's Deluxe Unabridged Dictionary,* second edition, one definition of a **standard** is "anything recognized as correct by common consent, by approved custom, or by those most competent to decide; a model; a type; a pattern; a criterion." It's a definition that we can use with data communications as well. As early as the 1700s, Claude Chappe developed an "alphabet" by which trained station operators could decode messages transmitted between locations.[12] Chappe's alphabet became the standard for optical telegraphic communications in his native France. Similarly, the electric telegraph of the 1800s would have met with limited success had it not been for the standard encoding method known as Morse code. In the late 1800s and throughout most of the 1900s, the Bell service, pioneered by Alexander Graham Bell, became the standard for telephone technology and service. In each case, an ingredient within the technology or in the delivery of the technology provided the common criteria that made the product accessible and acceptable to a vast marketplace of businesses and consumers.

In today's data communications marketplace, the importance of standards is paramount. Standards provide a basic level of compatibility and interoperability among the devices and services supplied by the data communications industry. Without standards, products and services from any given communications vendor might not interface or work properly with

---

[11] You'll learn more about VLANs in chapters 4 and 9, VPNs in chapters 8 and 9, and encryption and other data communications security techniques in chapter 9.
[12] Claude Chappe and other data communications historical persons and events are examined in Appendix A, "A Brief History of Data Communications and Computer Networks."

the products and services from other vendors—a costly and limiting scenario. Because corporations spend billions of dollars annually on data communications and networking products, they want at least some level (preferably high) of assurance that the technology they purchase and implement will work with hardware and software from other vendors. Products and services that are developed based on accepted standards provide that assurance.

General Types of Standards

Standards for data communications products and services originate in a couple of ways. In some cases, a company launches a new product that fits a market need, and it gains rapid market acceptance; it might even be copied or licensed for copy by other vendors. As the product or service gains wide acceptance, it becomes the de facto standard. A **de facto standard** derives from a product that first gains market acceptance and by common use and implementation becomes the model or standard to which other suppliers of products and services conform. Examples of de facto standards are Microsoft Windows as a desktop operating system, Microsoft Excel as the commonly accepted spreadsheet software, and Microsoft Word as a widely and commonly used word processing application.

Dejure or formal standards, on the other hand, are developed by one or more committees or standards organizations, and vendors design their products for the marketplace based on the formalized standard. Dejure standards can be introduced to a standards-making organization by a single vendor, but typically there will be multiple vendors as well as one or more standards organizations that share in the creation of the formal standard. **Asynchronous Transfer Mode (ATM)** technology, used in long haul and wide area network data communications, is an example of a dejure or formal standard. Many companies participated in its development along with standards organizations and forums.

Standards Organizations and Standards-Making Processes

Many standards organizations develop and publish data communications standards. Some of these organizations are responsible for the establishment of formal standards that the data communications industry as a whole can follow in developing new products. Other standards organizations focus specifically on one type of data communications technology. Still others are more trade oriented and take an active role in standardizing and promoting the use of their members' products and services. In all cases, the overriding goal is the standardization of data communications products and services so that businesses can be assured of a basic level of compatibility and interoperability among the devices and services supplied by the data communications industry. Let's take a look at some of these organizations and see what their histories, primary missions, and standards-making processes are all about.

The **American National Standards Institute (ANSI)** (www.ansi.org) was founded in 1918 as the result of contributing efforts from the American Institute of Electrical Engineers, the American Society of Mechanical Engineers, the American Society of Civil Engineers, the American Institute of Mining and Metallurgical Engineers, the American Society of Testing Materials, and the U.S. Departments of War, Navy, and Commerce. Founded to promote standards in both technology-driven as well as nontechnology products to "halt user confusion on acceptability" (www.ansi.org), ANSI's first standard was issued for pipe thread. Today, ANSI is a private, nonprofit membership organization, supported by private and public-sector organizations to coordinate and administer a national standards system in the United States. Although ANSI doesn't develop standards per se, it does represent its approximately 1,000 member companies in the pursuit of national standards and oversees and supports the activities of the International Engineering Consortium (IEC) technical committees such as the Joint Technical Committee for Information Technology, a collaborative effort with the International Organization for Standardization, ISO. Through this joint effort, the interests of ANSI members, including companies and government agencies, along with established national standards are represented and promoted for adoption in the international community.

The **Institute of Electrical and Electronics Engineers (IEEE)** (www.ieee.org) origi- nated in an era when electric telegraphs and the first telephones were the pioneering data com- munications technologies of the day. In its original form in 1884 as the American Institute of Electrical Engineers (AIEE), its primary goal was to promote the development of standards in the electrical industry as those standards pertained to wired communications and light and power systems. Later, in the first two decades of the 1900s, a separate but kindred society of scientists and engineers whose work focused on electrical wireless communications formed the Institute of Radio Engineers (IRE) to foster the development of wireless communications. Across several decades in the first half of the 20th century, the AIEE and the IRE shared com- mon members as well as technological motivations, and in 1963, the two organizations com- bined to form the IEEE. Today, the mission of the IEEE is to foster the publication of electri- cal, computer, and control literature as well as develop and administer standards in these fields. It is comprised of nearly 400,000 individual members across some 150 countries.

Several well-known examples of IEEE standards are the **IEEE 802.*x* standards,** which specify local area and metropolitan area network performance (transmission rates) over various media types. For example, the **IEEE 802.3 series** of standards specifies Ethernet network transmission rates over various types of cabling while the **IEEE 802.11 series** specifies network transmission rates over infrared and radio frequency wireless. As another example, the IEEE 1394 standard, which is commonly referred to as Firewire and which you learned about earlier in this chapter, and 1394b specify data transmission rates over various media for a serial transmission connection between peripheral devices such as a digital camera and the computer to which the device is connected.

The next time you access the Internet and download a file that delivers voice, video, and data, or the next time you hear someone discussing voice over IP, or even the next time you make an electronic purchase using your credit card, you can thank the sector members and member states of the **International Telecommunications Union (ITU)** (www.itu.int) for assisting in the standardization of the technologies that make these modern-day services possible. ITU is a truly global standards organization that develops and coordinates inter- national communications standards and activities for nearly 200 member countries and 650 national and international companies.

ITU was originally formed as the International Telegraph Union in 1865 in Paris, France. Its history ties it to the international growth of the electric telegraph in Europe in the mid to late 1800s as well as the 19th century's business need to standardize telegraphic communications across national borders. Toward the end of the 19th century, with the development of the telephone, ITU grew its charter to include standards for telephone communication. As wireless began to grow in the early 1900s, ITU took an active role in international regulations related to wireless communications. As all three communications technologies expanded and prospered into the 20th century, ITU continued its role as developer and governor of communications standards. To more adequately reflect its role across all three communications areas, in 1934 ITU changed its name to the International Telecommunications Union, the name it retains today.[13]

In 1992, the ITU reorganized into three sectors: the **ITU-T,** chartered with telecommu- nications standardization and the "seamless interconnection of the world's communication networks and systems"; the **ITU-R,** charged with radio communications standards, coordi- nating international radio frequency use, and with "determining the technical characteristics

---

[13] There is more history regarding the ITU at http://www.itu.int/aboutitu/overview/history.html, including information about the International Telephone and Telegraph Consultative Committee (CCITT), a name under which the ITU operated from about 1947 until 1992.

and operational procedures for a huge and growing range of wireless services"; and the **ITU-D,** the sector that "promotes investment and fostering the expansion of telecommunications infrastructure in developing nations around the world" (www.itu.int). The activities of these sectors and their member companies work to set standards, adopt operational procedures, and design programs that will continually improve the global telecommunications infrastructure.

ITU standards are prefaced with a capital letter followed by a number. For example, the ITU Series H standards define rules and specifications for audiovisual and multimedia systems. One in particular, **H.323,** and its supporting standards define the rules and specifications for multimedia communications. As another example, **Series G standards** define transmission systems and media for digital systems and networks. One specific example in this series is the G.65x family that defines the characteristics of various types of fiber-optic cabling.

The **International Organization for Standardization** (www.iso.org), with headquarters in Geneva, Switzerland, is a nongovernmental, international organization with a primary mission to develop and publish standards for a broad spectrum of products and services ranging from agricultural and construction to standards that support the latest communications technologies. Its roots date to 1946 when a delegation comprised of 25 countries met in London to create an organization that would "facilitate the international coordination and unification of industrial standards" (www.iso.org). The organization became official in 1947 with the moniker **ISO,** and since its inception, ISO has published nearly 14,000 international standards.[14]

ISO membership is comprised of three categories: **member bodies, correspondent members,** and **subscriber members.** Member bodies are the national standards organizations that are "most representative of standardization in their countries" (www.iso.org). Member bodies participate in technical and policy committees and are the impetus behind standards development in ISO. For the United States, the member body is ANSI. Correspondent and subscriber members are the delegate organizations from countries that haven't yet formalized or developed a national standards agency. Correspondent and subscriber membership provides representation within ISO for those nations that wish to be kept informed of international standards as they're developed and voted upon by the member bodies. Subscriber members benefit from reduced membership fees due to the small economies of the countries included in this category.

The ISO standards-making process begins with a need in a particular industrial or technology market for a standard. The company or trade group that recognizes the need communicates its requirement to its national delegate to the ISO. The member organization, in turn, proposes the requirement to the entire ISO. If the request for a new standard is accepted, it's assigned to a technical committee for development. From there, the committee reviews and debates the proposal until committee members reach a consensus on a draft agreement and circulate a **Draft International Standard** to the ISO membership. ISO members then request feedback on the draft standard from their national constituents prior to taking a position on the draft standard. If the member bodies vote in favor of the draft standard, it is then circulated with any modifications as a **Final Draft International Standard** to all the ISO members. If the member bodies vote in favor of the final draft, the ISO publishes it as an **International Standard.**

Once they're published, ISO standards are categorized within an **International Classification for Standards (ICS)** code number. Of particular interest to data communications and networking are the **ICS code 33,** Telecommunications—audio and video engineering; and **ICS code 35,** Information technology—office machines. Both contain the ISO standards,

---

[14] *ISO* does not stand for International Standards Organization. Instead, ISO is derived from the Greek word *isos,* which means equal (www.iso.ch). ISO is a meaning, not an acronym.

generally published jointly with the International Electrotechnical Commission (IEC), that are relevant to the material you'll study throughout this book.[15]

ICS codes are further divided into groups and subgroups. For example, within ICS code 35, Information Technology—office machines, you'll find several groups, including 35.110, Networking. Within 35.110, Networking, you'll find all the ISO standards relevant to networking and information technology. These are listed with an ISO prefix followed by the standard's serial number and the year it was published. One particular example is standard ISO/IEC 8802-11:1999. This ISO standard, jointly published with IEC, defines certain characteristics of wireless local area networks. Notice how the serial number reflects the standard developed by the IEEE in IEEE 802.11. Other ISO standards of significant relevance are listed under the 35.100 group, Open Systems Interconnect (OSI). The standards within the subgroups of OSI define the standards of the seven layers of the OSI model, a layered framework for protocol development and definitions that you'll learn about later in this chapter.

Influence in standards development is not entirely limited to international standards-making organizations. Trade organizations, such as the **Telecommunications Industry Association (TIA)** (www.tiaonline.org), represent their membership in front of international standards organizations such as the ITU and are influential in the development of technical standards by contributing technical specifications to ANSI, which, in turn, is a member body of ISO.

Other agencies that are influential in the standards development process are **technical forums** such as the **ATM Forum** (www.atmforum.org), the **Frame Relay Forum** (www.mplsforum.org/frame), the **MPLS/Frame Relay Alliance** (www.mplsforum.org), and the **DSL Forum** (www.dslforum.org). Each of these forums operates as a technical committee whose major purposes are to facilitate the deployment of their technologies into the business community as well as to provide input to national and international standards-making organizations.

Standards and the Internet

So far in this section, you've examined several of the national and international organizations that are critical to the development and publication of standards for data communications technologies, products, and services. Just as important, the standards that have historically supported and continue to drive the Internet's expansion are coordinated and administered under the jurisdiction of the **Internet Society (ISOC).** Officially formed in 1992, the ISOC was created to expand financial support beyond government agency funding for the Internet standards development and publication activities of the **Internet Engineering Task Force (IETF).** Today, the ISOC continues its funding efforts for IETF activities as well as to provide ISOC members with current statuses on technical developments and IETF standards.

The three key organizations that do the standards development work are the **Internet Architecture Board (IAB),** the **Internet Engineering Steering Group (IESG),** and the IETF. The IAB has the responsibilities of defining Internet architecture and keeping the pulse of long-range Internet issues. The IESG handles technical management of IETF activities as well as the Internet standards process and approvals. The IETF, however, is the primary organization under ISOC responsible for Internet standards development.

The publication of an Internet standard is an involved process that by design proceeds through several stages including proposal, comment, review, and submission to the IESG.

---

[15] The International Electrotechnical Commission (IEC) is another international standards organization whose primary mission surrounds preparation and publication of electrical, electronic, and related technological standards.

If accepted by the IESG, the proposed standard culminates in the publication of a document known as a **Request for Comments (RFC).** Each RFC provides the accepted detail of an Internet standard. If you want to learn the excruciating detail of this process, you can check out RFC 2026, The Internet Standards Process—Revision 3 at www.ietf.org/rfc. If you want to look at the entire list of RFCs, look at the RFC Index link on the RFC page.

DATA COMMUNICATIONS MODELS

As you've already seen in this chapter, consumers of data communications equipment and services have a real demand for data communications standards. Businesses and individuals can buy standardized products and services with the assurance that those products and services will function with other products conforming to the same set of standards. Products from one vendor will interoperate with products and services provided by other vendors. Vendors design according to accepted standards, and compatibility is more or less assured.

It wasn't always this way. In the early 1970s, IBM, Digital Equipment, Honeywell, Burroughs, and other computer companies each developed proprietary computer-to-computer connection architectures that would allow their own computers to operate collectively in local computer networks but not necessarily interoperate with computers from other vendors, at least not without substantial translation software. If you were interested in a computer network during that era, and if you could afford it, choosing a solution from any of the computer network vendors locked you into their **proprietary architecture** that by design worked only with systems and devices from that vendor. Later on, if you wanted to purchase a computing device from one of the other manufacturers, either that device would be limited to stand-alone functions or you would have to purchase software or hardware or a combination of both to allow the two systems to interface. Clearly an architecture that was nonproprietary and which would assure **multivendor connectivity** was needed.

proprietary
patented, trademarked, or otherwise owned by one company

architecture
concept, plan, or framework

Layered Architectures and Protocols

During the early days of computer processing in the late 1950s and early 1960s, researchers at the Massachusetts Institute of Technology (MIT) as well as researchers at industrial giants such as IBM, Honeywell, and Digital Equipment Corporation, realized they could improve system utilization with minimal impact on performance by sharing a computer's processor across multiple interactive users. But expanding users' access to computing resources required that the application programs manage not only the processing of jobs but also the communications links between the computer and the interactive users sitting in front of the terminals. As more and more users simultaneously accessed a computer, the application program had to spend more time servicing the communication links between users and the computer at the expense of processing the actual job. It was evident that somehow the data communications function would have to be separated from the application program's logic—make it "modular" as the buzzword of the day indicated—or the newly developed method of shared interactive access would be severely limited.

At about the same time during the 1960s, researchers at the **Advanced Research Projects Agency (ARPA)** began experimenting with connecting multiple computers of different makes for resource sharing across vast geographic distances. Because these computers were of different types and would be sharing resources among multiple and various users who would be using various types of terminals to connect to these multiple and different computers, the researchers at ARPA very early on decided that their connectivity model, or communications architecture, would require a modular, or **layered,** approach to separate the machine functions from the data communications functions. They also realized that separate rules, or *protocols,* would be required at each layer to modularize or differentiate the hierarchical functions that take place when two or more computers and their related devices exchange data. And that's exactly what the Network Working Group (NWG) of the **ARPA network (ARPANET)** decided upon in the late 1960s; to separate machine functionality from process functionality as well as apply a layered approach to delineate the multiple and separate functions within the data communications process. This work and the progress made at MIT and the computer industrial giants of the era provided the beginnings of the layered approach to data communications.

An Introduction to the OSI Model

The late 1960s and early 1970s saw exploding interest in connecting computers from various vendors and connecting them across great distances. Layered architectures that would facilitate interconnectivity and compatible communications among different computer companies' systems were well recognized if not well documented. Many organizations, including ARPA, IBM, Honeywell, and Digital Equipment Corporation, were developing their own computer and data communications models based on layered architectures, but there was no internationally recognized standard for this layered approach. It was time for a common standard.

Enter ISO. In 1977, the ISO got involved and through the influential work of its U.S. representative, ANSI, work on an international standardized architecture for data communications was begun. The layered architectural model for data communications that the OSI published in 1978 and finalized with modifications in 1984 is the **Open Systems Interconnection (OSI) Reference Model.**

The OSI Reference Model, or simply *OSI model,* is an internationally recognized framework for the development of a standardized, data communications architecture. It uses a series of seven layers to define the communications functions that assure compatible communications among devices or systems. The layers are physical, data link, network, transport, session, presentation, and application, as presented in Figure 1.13.

By defining a layered architecture, the creators of the OSI model provided modularity to systems developers; that is, services and protocols can be developed to provide functions in one layer without impacting the functions and protocols and services in other layers. Within each layer, the model provides a standard set of rules that developers can use to create protocols and services that provide compatible data transmissions with the products and services of other vendors. Each layer has a specifically defined set of functions, protocols, and services that rely on the layer below and which provide support and services to the layer above. Overall it's a compartmentalized approach that corresponds to the various and multiple functions that facilitate data communications between two or more devices or systems.

Layers of the OSI Models

As you've already seen, there are seven layers that make up the OSI model. They are the physical, data link, network, transport, session, presentation, and application layers. An

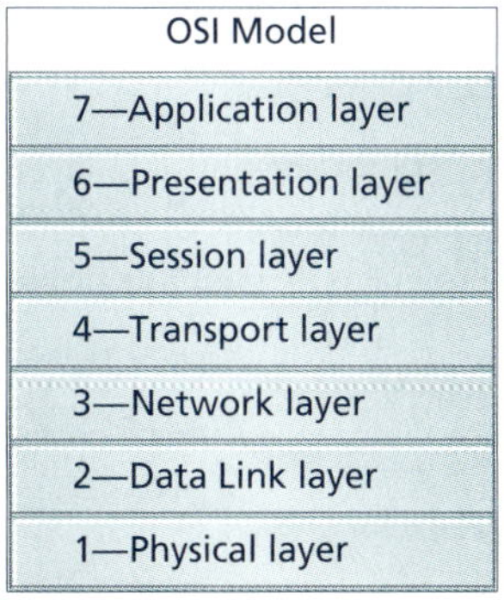

FIGURE 1.13
The OSI Reference Model

OSI Model
7—Application layer
6—Presentation layer
5—Session layer
4—Transport layer
3—Network layer
2—Data Link layer
1—Physical layer

As it turns out, the major U.S. computer corporations were using a layered approach in data communications prior to the publication of the OSI model. In the 1970s, IBM successfully linked its computers into networks by using its own proprietary seven-layer Systems Network Architecture (SNA). Honeywell accomplished the same thing with its Distributed Systems Architecture (DSA), a seven-layer architectural model that was very much like the IBM model. Digital Equipment developed Digital Network Architecture (DNA), but unlike the seven-layer approaches that IBM and Honeywell implemented, Digital's DNA utilized a four-layer model. Other computer vendors of the day, including Burroughs and Hewlett-Packard developed their own proprietary architectures for connecting the computer systems that they manufactured and marketed. With so many vendors in such a tight market space of the 1970s, and with computer equipment being so expensive relative to the cost of computers today, business owners would have been justified in worrying about what they would do if they had to switch to a different computer vendor after making a huge capital investment with their original computer vendor. This issue alone could have driven the demand for a data communications standard. As it turned out, the OSI model as adopted in 1978 looked very much like the seven-layer approach that both IBM and Honeywell had developed independently of each other earlier in that decade.

easy way to remember the names of each layer is to recall the first letter of each layer, starting with the lowest layer, and use the first letter of each layer in a sentence, such as, *p*lease *d*o *n*ot *t*hrow *s*ausage *p*izza *a*way. Another phrase that might help you recall the layers is, *a*ll *p*eople *s*eem *t*o *n*eed *d*ata *p*rocessing, although this phrase starts with the first letter of the top layer and works down to the lowest layer.[16]

Physical Layer

If someone asks you to describe the purpose of the **physical layer** of the OSI model, think cables and bits. The physical layer defines the characteristics of data bit transmissions across specific media. More technically, you can describe the physical layer, also known as layer 1, as the protocol that governs the physical connection and transmission of bits between two devices. Specifically, the physical layer defines

- Type of signaling method such as digital or analog.
- The electrical and optical characteristics of the transmission signal.
- Transmission characteristics such as asynchronous, synchronous, simplex, half-duplex, duplex.
- Data rate (**bandwidth**) such as 10 Mbps, 100 Mbps, or 1,000 Mbps.
- Network layout (*topology*) such as star, bus, ring, cellular, and other physical characteristics of the network.[17]
- Single or multiple communications channels over a given medium.

Data Link Layer

The **data link layer,** or layer 2, prepares data for the physical layer and provides services to the network layer above it. It organizes data bits received from the network layer into **frames,** which are nothing more than sequences of data bits defined by additional bits that

bandwidth
the amount of data that can be transmitted across a medium per unit of time. Bandwidth is also referred to as *data rate* and is commonly expressed in the number of bits per second, as in kilobits per second (Kbps) or megabits per second (Mbps) or gigabits per second (Gbps).

---

[16] Another way to remember the layers from the top down is with the phrase, *a*ny *p*erson *s*tanding *t*otally *n*aked *d*reads *p*ublicity.

[17] You'll learn about network topologies in chapter 3.

represent address and error correction information. Think of it this way. If you want to send an old-fashioned, snail-mail letter to someone, you write the recipient's address on the envelope. In much the same way, the data link layer is responsible for packaging a series of bits for presentation to the physical layer, and part of that package includes adding a series of bits that identify the physical address of the destination device. To facilitate error correction, the data link layer also adds **error detection** and **recovery bits.** If a frame gets corrupted during transmission, the error can be detected at the receiving location, and a request for retransmission can be issued to the sender instructing the sending device to resend that frame. In addition, layer 2 defines how data bits access the transmission medium, that is, how the bit sequence is timed for placement on the transmission medium so that it doesn't interfere with other data bits already on the medium. In summary, the data link layer is responsible for

- Organizing data bits into frames.
- Address information known as MAC addressing, or more commonly referred to as the physical address of a node or device.[18]
- Error correction and retransmission.
- How the data bits access a transmission medium.

Network Layer

Since data communications devices are not all connected to the same network, a set of protocols is required to facilitate the routing of data between networks. The **network layer** (layer 3) of the OSI model handles this function. Protocols at this layer are responsible for establishing, maintaining, and terminating end-to-end connections between two data communications devices located on separate networks.

Let's go back to the letter-writing example that we used in discussing the data link layer. If you wanted to write someone a letter, you could write it, put it in an envelope, and then deliver the letter personally to the other person, without the use of the postal system. You can probably imagine that this could be a costly delivery mechanism, especially if the person lives a great distance from you. However, if you place the letter in an envelope and then place the envelope in the mailbox, the postal carrier will pick it up. When the postal carrier picks up the envelope, he or she is acting as the network layer protocol that routes data from one location to another. In our example, the postal carrier looks at the city and street address information and routes your letter to its end location through the postal service. Continuing with our example, the postal service is acting as the network layer by providing services that establish, maintain, and terminate the communication connection (the letter) between you and the person to whom you wrote the letter.

Other services provided by the network layer include the following:

data packet
or simply packet, is data with source and destination address information attached to it for transmission through a network

- Adding network and node addressing information to a series of **data packets** prior to handing off the packet of information to the data link layer.
- Packet (or block) creation and packet sequence control.
- Support services to the transport layer and data preparation for the data link layer.
- Route discovery and determination of the best route for data between two separate network locations.

---

[18] Each device on a network has a hardware address that uniquely identifies that device on the network and to other computers. This address is known as the *MAC address* or *data link address, hardware address,* or even *physical address.* You'll learn about MAC addresses in more detail in chapter 2.

Transport Layer

As with all the layers between the physical layer and the application layer, the **transport layer** (layer 4) of the OSI model provides services to the layer above it. In support of the higher layers, the transport layer receives data in the form of *messages* (pieces of a file) from the upper layers. If the messages are too long for the underlying protocols in the lower layers, layer 4 breaks the messages into smaller segments that are more manageable for layers 3 and below. Some texts call this *segment development.*

For perspective and consistency, let's once again use the postal service example. You can think of a post office as a data communications device that has lots of data to send; if it's a big post office, not all of the letters intended for a destination location can fit on one truck. If all the packages taken as a whole represent one big data transmission, the shipment must be broken down into several truckloads to manage the shipment. In data communications, the transport layer of the OSI model handles the function of segmenting the data into manageable sizes.

connection-oriented data transmissions
data transmissions for which an acknowledgement is returned to the sending node to confirm receipt of data

The transport layer is also responsible for **connection-oriented,** or reliable, **data transmissions.** Connection-oriented protocols at layer 4 provide acknowledgement (or denial) that a segment has arrived at its intended destination. If we continue our post office analogy, you can compare certified mail that's sent with a return receipt request to connection-oriented protocols. If the letter with the return receipt request is received at its destination, the receipt is returned to you; it's your acknowledgement that the letter was received.

connectionless data transmissions
data transmissions for which no acknowledgement is returned to the sending node

Regular mail doesn't provide this service. In other words, regular mail is connectionless. In computer parlance the term **connectionless** means that a sending node doesn't receive a return receipt. When data is received at a destination node, no delivery acknowledgements are sent from the destination node to the sending node. The transport layer provides connection-oriented services for the end-to-end communications that are established in the network layer, by sending acknowledgements that data has been received.

Other functions that the transport layer supports include the following:

- Sequencing of the data segments so they can be reassembled at their destination.
- End-to-end control of data flow.
- Identification of service addresses (port numbers) at destination devices.

Session Layer

The **session layer,** layer 5, is responsible for establishing, maintaining, synchronizing, and terminating communications between two devices. For example, let's say that your company has a network management application that uses half-duplex communication. Protocols at the session layer would initiate and establish this method of dialog between the two devices. You might also want to download a file from another computer. The session layer establishes the connection. If you lose connection with the end device, session layer protocols step in to re-establish your connection. In turn when the download is complete, the session layer can release the connection with the remote device.

Presentation Layer

Protocols within the **presentation layer** (layer 6) provide data transformation services to the application layer. For example, the presentation layer is responsible for encoding. It establishes whether the transmission will use ASCII or EBCDIC to communicate with another device. Presentation layer protocols can also provide end-to-end encryption services within the data transmission.

Application Layer

The **application layer** (layer 7) provides the underlying services such as file, print, and e-mail services that support user applications such as word processing and spreadsheet applications. The actual user application programs, however, are not part of the application layer. **Remote access services** that allow connectivity to remote computers exist at this layer, as do **collaborative computing services** such as document management and group conferencing. In addition, service advertisement mechanisms that network operating systems use to let other devices know what services are available are categorized within layer 7.

The TCP/IP Model

The origins of the **TCP/IP "model"** date back to the early 1970s. **Vinton Cerf,** who at the time was an assistant professor of computer science and electrical engineering at Stanford, and **Robert Kahn,** who was working for ARPA, were trying to figure a way to get computers to send data packets across multiple networks without the computers knowing what the underlying network structure was.[19] During 1973, Cerf and Kahn conducted some of the first data communications protocol design work that would find its way into their architecture. They published their work in 1974. This was the beginning of the transmission control protocol (TCP) portion of TCP/IP. Shortly thereafter, as a result of experiments with sending voice conversations as data packets, another researcher provided Cerf and Kahn with a suggestion that led the two to separate out the functionality that ultimately became the Internet protocol (IP) portion of the TCP/IP protocol suite in 1978/1979. The TCP/IP model was born.

With simplicity, relative efficiency, and reliability built in, the TCP/IP family of protocols was ideal for the interconnection of national and international networks, including security-related computer networks in the United States, computer networks of colleges and universities, and private-sector companies under contract with the Department of Defense (DoD). The U.S. military adopted the TCP/IP suite in 1980, and in 1982, ARPA's network of computers known as the ARPANET was converted over from older protocols to the reliable and efficient TCP/IP suite.

Today, the TCP/IP suite of protocols is a de facto data communications standard. It provides a layered approach to data communications that loosely corresponds to the layers of the OSI model, albeit with fewer layers. Although it's not a formal standard, the TCP/IP "model," which is also referred to as the **Internet model** and sometimes as the **DoD model,** combines the top three layers of the OSI model into a single process/application layer. Host-to-host and Internet layers correspond closely to the OSI's transport and network layers, and the TCP/IP model's network access layer corresponds to a combination of the data link and physical layers of OSI. Figure 1.14 provides a graphical representation of the TCP/IP model in comparison to the OSI model.

FIGURE 1.14
The TCP/IP Model and the OSI Reference Model Compared

OSI Model	TCP/IP Model
7—Application layer	4—Process/Application layer
6—Presentation layer	
5—Session layer	
4—Transport layer	3—Host-to-Host layer
3—Network layer	2—Internet layer
2—Data Link layer	1—Network Access layer
1—Physical layer	

---

[19] See Appendix A, "A Brief History of Data Communications and Computer Networks."

Because of TCP/IP's efficiency, reliability, and early adoption by the U.S. military and the ARPANET as well as today's widespread acceptance and implementation, it's fair to say that most development work surrounding data communications compatibility follows the TCP/IP model rather than the OSI model. However, because of similarities between the two models, development for the TCP/IP model can generally be described in terms of the OSI model as well. That is, TCP is recognized as an OSI layer 4 protocol, and IP is recognized as an OSI layer 3 protocol.

You should also be aware that some texts and discussions of the TCP/IP layered approach define the TCP/IP model with five layers instead of four. That's okay, because those discussions have simply delineated the physical layer from the TCP/IP model's network access layer and have chosen to discuss it as a separate layer.

Data Encapsulation in a Layered Architecture

The layers of the OSI and TCP/IP models by themselves simply provide an architectural framework or a set of guidelines that describe how data communications should take place between similar processes, services, or functions running on two or more devices that are exchanging data. To facilitate this exchange of data between peer layers on these devices, researchers and standards organizations develop protocols that function according to the rules that describe each layer of a layered architecture such as the OSI model or the TCP/IP model.

Two of the data communications protocols that you have already seen are the transmission control protocol or TCP and the Internet protocol or IP. Each of these protocols defines a set of rules that governs processes and procedures at a given layer within a layered architecture. For example, TCP provides functionality that ensures reliability of data transmissions between devices, and it functions at the transport layer of the OSI model and at the host-to-host layer of the TCP/IP model. IP provides functionality at the Internet layer of the TCP/IP model and at the network layer of the OSI model. In the world of data communications and especially for data transmission across networks and the Internet, IP defines the rules for routing data across two or more networks.

As an example, let's look at what happens when you browse your favorite Web site on the Internet. If you want, you can think of browsing online for a piece of clothing or a book. To facilitate the transmission, more than TCP and IP are required; so for this example, you'll be introduced to a couple of additional protocols that function at different layers. You'll also discover the concept of **data encapsulation**, a process that adds an additional set of protocol information known as a *header* to a set of data bits for each layer of the OSI model. For illustration, this example uses the OSI model, although with little effort, the TCP/IP model could be utilized as well.

data encapsulation
the process of adding an additional set of protocol information to a set of data bits for each layer of the OSI model

In Figure 1.15, a communication session is set up between your computer and an Internet Web server that handles information and purchase transactions. When you initiate the connection to the Web site, your computer utilizes Hypertext Transfer Protocol (HTTP), a protocol that functions within the application layer of the OSI model to encapsulate the request data that is generated when you click on a hyperlink. To properly encode the transmission, protocols in the session layer encode the transmission in Unicode through the built-in Java functionality of the browser. In addition, if the sending computer is configured for secure communications across the Internet, the session layer provides the protocols and services necessary to establish a secure connection. At the transport layer, TCP adds another layer of encapsulation that identifies service addresses at the destination as well as sequencing of the data segments. This ensures that your request to access the chosen Web site is properly addressed and that you can connect to the appropriate services at the Web server. Your request is encapsulated yet again at the network layer to provide destination address information to the first router it will pass through on its way to the target Web server.

FIGURE 1.15 **Layered Approach to Data Encapsulation**

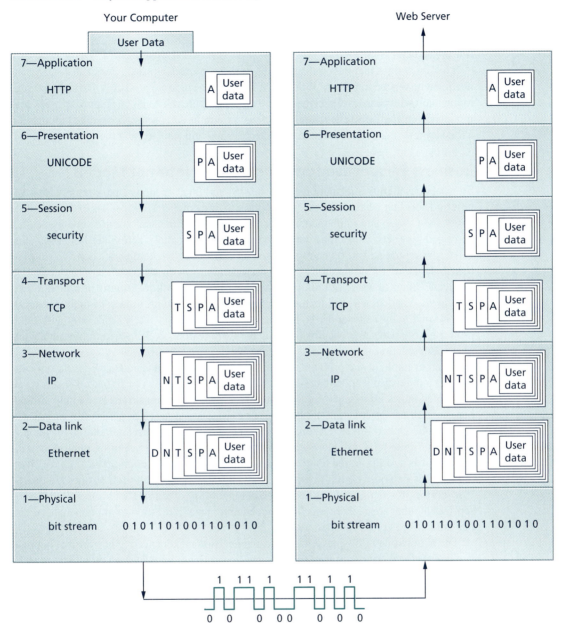

This time the encapsulation adds the IP address of the destination Web server. Once the address information is added with IP, your request is framed at the data link layer for presentation to the physical network over which it will travel. At the data link layer, the packet containing your request is framed with information that describes the type of connection you're using, such as Ethernet, as well as hardware address information and error correction information. Once all of these layers of encapsulation have taken place, your request is placed on the physical medium, and it travels to its destination where the encapsulated information is read, one layer at a time, until your request is received at the application layer of the destination device. Once your request has been received, the Web server generates a response in much the same way. That is, the Web server's response is generated as a sequence of packets, and each packet is encapsulated, layer by layer, for delivery across the transmission medium.

The key point is that data transmissions utilize a layered approach in establishing a connection with other computers. Within each layer are one or more protocols that support communication with peer-level services on the other computers. The layered approach produces modularity in application development so that programs and protocols designed to function at one layer do not need to include the rules and functions that exist at the other layers.

Business Perspective for Using OSI and Internet Models

So what does all this information about the OSI and Internet models have to do with business and deciding what hardware and software to implement? Mostly it has to do with standards, ease of use and implementation, competitive solutions that are not vendor specific, and a common set of rules for establishing data communications across dissimilar systems.

Hardware and software vendors as well as carrier service companies conform to published standards for compatibility and interoperability with other vendors' products and services. Things to watch out for, however, are **standards enhancements** or **nonstandard standards.** Vendors will add features that might improve the usefulness of their own products beyond published standards, but these features will very likely work only with other products from that same vendor. To enjoy the extra features, you'll need to buy into a single vendor solution.

As an example of the problems that can arise when products and services do not conform to a published standard, consider the original deployments of frame relay service in the United States. In its early deployment, frame relay communications technology did not benefit from consistency and conformity of products and services across the various regions of the United States. Different communications hardware manufacturers developed their own frame relay products based on their interpretation of yet-to-be published standards, and as a result, frame relay services at one time varied throughout the country, making a widely deployed commitment to frame relay service difficult for a business to justify. If a service provider could not guarantee compatibility of service with other frame relay services in other areas, there was little incentive for an organization to implement a service that couldn't be connected nationwide.

The bottom line is, business managers and decision makers need to be aware of national and international standards prior to implementing or upgrading data communications products and services. In an era of internationalized business practices and strategies combined with worldwide deployments of various technologies and vendor products, business managers must be able to distinguish between the sales hype of product features and benefits of a particular vendor, and the standardized products that will facilitate compatibility and interoperability across multiple business locations and diverse geographic regions.

GOVERNMENT REGULATIONS AND DATA COMMUNICATIONS

Some of the earliest government regulations in the United States surrounding communications technologies affected radio communications and the development and deployment of wireless telephony in the early 1900s. In 1910, the U.S. Congress passed an act that required certain seagoing vessels to carry radio equipment as a safety measure. This regulation quickly spawned additional regulations that placed radio communications of any kind under the Secretary of Commerce and Labor and further restricted airwave usage to distress signals between ships and from ship to shore. These regulations also apportioned specific airwaves for limited offshore usage to connect coastline islands via wireless to AT&T's land-based telephone lines. With these regulations and an insufficient number of wireless frequencies or the technologies to deliver them, it's little wonder that the burgeoning wireless communications industry of the late 1800s and early 1900s was quickly thwarted under government regulation. In addition, it's not inconceivable that AT&T, with its huge investments in wired infrastructure, must have been a formidable lobbying force for regulation against the apportionment of airwaves to companies that could have competed against AT&T in the wireless marketplace. Add to these factors a world war in the second decade of the 20th century and the concern over possible enemy interception of airwave communication most certainly enhanced efforts to enforce regulation in an early world of communications.

telecommunications
the classic term used to define the transmission of voice information across long distances using telephone lines and carrier services. In the modern era of computers and various data types, the term *telecommunications* is outdated because all information, including voice, can be reduced to binary bits of data for transmission across great distances

More modern government regulations have impacted the development of data communications in a much more positive way. The 1982 **Modified Final Judgment (MFJ)** regulated the AT&T monopoly out of existence. With the MFJ, AT&T was required to split into separate companies—a long-distance company and regional Bell operating companies (RBOCs) that provided local telephone service. The split took effect in 1984 with the divestiture of AT&T into these smaller companies. At the same time, the **telecommunications** industry was deregulated so that the RBOCs could compete in not only the telecommunications marketplace but also in markets such as information systems and computing. This deregulated marketplace was the cornerstone of much of the data communications technological and infrastructure development that the United States and the world have witnessed since 1984. In addition, deregulation fostered competition for long-distance service between the AT&T long-distance company and companies such as MCI and Sprint. Deregulation undoubtedly contributed to the growth of MCI as well as MCI's success in becoming the carrier of choice for the backbone that supported the National Science Foundation's network (NFSNET), the carrier service network infrastructure that preceded the commercial Internet we use today.

The most sweeping deregulation of the 20th century is undoubtedly the **Telecommunications Act of 1996.** With this single piece of legislation an entire industry was deregulated, opening the data communications market to anyone who wanted to venture into it. Of particular interest were the local competition section, the universal service and e-rate section, and the broadband facilities and services section. The local competition section required each carrier company to interconnect with other carriers. This regulation guaranteed that subscribers to a local telephone service provider would have access to a nationwide network of carriers. The universal service and e-rate section required the Federal Communications Commission (FCC) to enforce "the availability of basic communications services to the public at just, reasonable, and affordable rates . . . taking into account advances in telecommunications and information technologies." In addition, the e-rate portion of the section expanded the concept of universal service at subsidized rates to schools, libraries, and rural health-care providers that wanted Internet access. The broadband facilities and services section gave the FCC the power to induce the deployment of high-speed Internet access services such as digital subscriber line (DSL) and cable modems. Extending the effects of this act into today's data communications industry, these sections of the Telecommunications Act of 1996 are the foundation for universal Internet availability across the United States. As a package, these sections as well as the Telecommunications Act of 1996 as a whole provided the basis for the expansion of the Internet that we've enjoyed since this regulatory act took effect.

DATA COMMUNICATIONS INTO THE FUTURE

The concepts you've seen in this chapter have been constants in the data communications industry for decades. Into the future, the trend will be a continued application of these constants to evolving and new technologies. We're already witnessing the *convergence* of voice, video, and data communications into integrated networks and communications infrastructures made possible through the application of the concepts and technologies you've just studied and will continue to explore through this text. In the future, you'll see more use of Internet-enabling technologies that allow businesses to exchange and share information over the Internet via numerous media types, including wireless. You'll undoubtedly see new and evolving data communications technologies applied to nearly every electronic and mechanical device so that information can be collected and disseminated even more quickly, effectively, securely, and to more people and remote devices than ever before. Transmission speeds will increase. New standards and new technologies will continue to enhance interconnectivity and interoperability. And businesses will continue to seek new and viable data communications solutions that will solve the longer-term strategic problems as well as the shorter-term problems that organizations encounter on a daily basis.

Chapter Summary

- **Data communications and its building blocks.** Data communications is the transmission of encoded data and information in a medium-specific format between two or more nodes, people, businesses, or entities. It's pervasive throughout modern business enterprises, and in tomorrow's business world it's likely to allow for instantaneous if not unsolicited interaction between people and technology. Data communications will truly be ubiquitous in most if not all aspects of our personal and professional lives.

- **Different types of data encoding.** Data encoding is the method by which data is represented in digital or binary format. EBCDIC, ASCII, and Unicode are three common types of encoding schemes. EBCDIC is an IBM proprietary encoding scheme, represents characters such as numerals, letters, and special characters using a series of 8 bits, and is limited to 256 different characters. ASCII is a very common encoding method. It uses seven bits to represent up to 128 different characters, numerals, and special characters. Unicode extends the character set beyond the 128 ASCII limit by using 16 bits to represent numerals, letters, and special characters. Unicode can provide up to 65,536 different characters including characters from several different non-English alphabets.

- **Analog and digital data.** Analog data is continuous and digital data is discrete. Analog data is represented and reproduced by continuously variable levels of sound, light, electricity, or other input and is generally represented in wave format. Digital data is information that is represented and reproduced by discrete levels of sound, light, electricity, or other input, and can be represented by 1s and 0s, voltage changes, or changes in a magnetic field.

- **Analog transmission and digital transmission.** Analog transmission uses continuously varying levels of light or sound or electricity across a medium to represent and convey data whereas digital transmission is a method of data transmission that utilizes discrete changes in electricity or light across a medium to convey data between two or more end points. Either transmission type can be used to convey either analog or digital data. Which to implement is as much a business consideration as it is a function of the underlying technology.

- **Parallel and serial transmission.** Parallel transmission uses parallel data paths to convey multiple data bits simultaneously across a medium, one bit per path. Serial transmission is a communications method that sequences data bits for transmission across a single wire or data path. Parallel transmissions are common where data communications distances are short, such as within computer or between a computer and a printer. Serial transmissions are common where data communications distances are great or where transmission speed is critical.

- **Asynchronous and synchronous transmission.** Asynchronous transmissions add a start bit to the beginning of each byte of information and a stop bit at the end of each eight-bit data chunk. The start and stop bits indicate to the receiving data communications device when to recognize each byte so that the transmission can be decoded accurately. More efficient than asynchronous are synchronous transmissions. With synchronous transmissions larger data transfers are possible because start and stop bits are not added to each byte. Instead, multiple bytes are bundled together preceded by a series of sync bits with information pertaining to the rate of data transmission. With sync bits, receiving nodes can correctly adjust their receive rate to match the transmission rate of the sending device.

- **Simplex, half-duplex, and full-duplex data transmission.** Simplex transmissions have a one-way data path. Sending devices send to receiving devices, but the receiving devices don't reply or return any information to the sender. Half-duplex transmission provides for data communications in two directions, but information flows in only one direction at a time. Full-duplex transmission accommodates simultaneous, bidirectional communications between devices. This is accomplished either through two data channels or through advanced techniques that require only a single data channel for the bidirectional data flow.

- **Common data communications media options.** Coaxial cable, unshielded twisted-pair cabling, fiber-optic cabling, and wireless comprise the basic types of data communications media. Coaxial cable is still commonly used in residential and business cable TV and high-speed Internet access applications, while unshielded twisted-pair copper cabling is frequently used in local area network applications. Fiber-optic cabling is the choice for sending data across large geographic distances or even in campus networks, and wireless is a growing medium that eliminates the nuisance and impracticality of a wired network's tether.

- **Data transmission security.** Security is a critical business function in modern data communications, and companies employ many methods such as encryption, VPNs, and VLANs to secure their data during transmission.

- **Data communications standards, standards organizations, and standards-making processes.** Standards provide a basic pattern or foundation upon which data communications can operate, grow, and expand. Conformance to standards allows equipment and services from numerous different vendors to interconnect and interoperate without modification to the underlying technology. In today's data communications industry, standards originate from many sectors of the industry including trade organizations, software companies, hardware companies, carriers, and various service-oriented organizations. Some of the organizations that oversee standards development include ANSI, IEEE, ITU, and ISO. Others such as the ATM forum, the MPLS/Frame Relay Alliance, and the DSL forum also contribute to the standards process through their particular areas of expertise. The standards-making process generally involves technical committees and working groups that organize and coordinate new and existing standards.

- **Layers of the OSI and TCP/IP models and the OSI and TCP/IP layered architectures.** *All people seem to need data processing or Please do not throw sausage pizza* *a*way are easy-to-remember sentences that can help you recall the seven layers of the OSI model. In reality, those layers are the physical, data link, network, transport, session, presentation, and application layers, and collectively they provide an architectural framework for the development of layer-independent protocols and functions that vendors can reference in developing new products and services that must interoperate and interconnect with other vendor's products and services. Likewise, the TCP/IP layered architecture follows a similar layered approach, albeit with fewer layers. The layers of the TCP/IP model, which is also referred to as the Internet model or the DoD model, are process/application, host-to-host, Internet, and network access layers.

- **Government regulations that have had a significant impact on the data communications industry.** Government regulation of the communications has existed for a long time. You can even find examples of it with the optical telegraph in France in the 18th century. More modern examples, specifically in the United States, include the Act of 1910, which required seagoing vessels to maintain radio equipment for safety reasons. More recently the Modified Final Judgment of 1982 and the Telecommunications Act of 1996 spawned a new era of technology and business practices that have given rise to the pervasive use of data communications and networks.

Key Terms

Advanced Research Projects Agency (ARPA), *24*
Analog data, *8*
Analog data transmission, *9*
ANSI, *20*
Application layer, *28*
ARPA Network (ARPANET), *25*
ASCII, *7*
Asynchronous transfer mode (ATM), *20*
Asynchronous transmission, *14*
ATM Forum, *23*
Bandwidth, *26*
Bidirectional communication, *15*
Binary data, *9*
Binary number system, *6*
Bit, *6*
Byte, *6*
Coaxial cable, *16*
Codec, *12*
Collaborative computing services, *29*

Connection-oriented data transmission, *28*
CSU/DSU, *11*
Data communications, *5*
Data encoding, *6*
Data link layer, *26*
De facto standard, *20*
Dejure standard, *20*
Digital certificates, *19*
Digital data, *8*
Digital data transmission, *9*
Digital signatures, *19*
DoD model, *29*
DSL Forum, *23*
EBCDIC, *7*
Encoded data, *6*
Encryption, *19*
Error detection bits, *27*
Error recovery bits, *27*
Fiber-optic cable, *16*
Final Draft International Standard, *22*
Firewire, *13*
Frame Relay Forum, *23*
Frames, *26*
Full-duplex transmission, *15*

Geosynchronous orbit, *18*
H.323, *22*
Half-duplex transmission, *15*
ICS code 33, *22*
ICS code 35, *22*
IEEE, *21*
IEEE 802.*x* standards, *21*
IEEE 802.3 standards, *21*
IEEE 802.11 standards, *21*
IEEE-1394, *13*
Infrared, *18*
International Classification for Standards (ICS), *22*
International Standard, *22*
Internet Architecture Board (IAB), *23*
Internet Engineering Steering Group (IESG), *23*
Internet Engineering Task Force (IETF), *23*
Internet model, *29*
Internet Society (ISOC), *23*
ISO, *22*
ISO correspondent members, *22*

Questions

1. What is the origin of the OSI Reference Model?
2. What are the differences between digital data and analog data?
3. Why would a business use analog transmission?
4. How does analog transmission differ from digital transmission?
5. When would you use a codec?
6. How does the binary number system represent human words, letters, and numbers?
7. How many bits form a byte?
8. What is the purpose of encoding?
9. What are the differences between EBCDIC, ASCII, and Unicode? What purpose do they serve?
10. What is parallel transmission? How does it differ from serial transmission?
11. How does asynchronous transmission send data?
12. What makes synchronous transmission more efficient than asynchronous transmission?
13. How does full-duplex transmission function over a two-wire pair?
14. How does satellite microwave transmit data between two points?
15. What is a standard?
16. What are the differences between de facto standards and formal standards?
17. What is ANSI's role in the development of international data communications standards?
18. Are standards developed by IEEE of any value to ISO? How?
19. What are the differences among the three ITU sectors?
20. What numbering designation does the ITU use? What about ISO?

21. What are the steps that the ISO takes when developing a new standard?

22. What role do trade organizations play in the standards-making process?

23. What organizations are responsible for developing Internet standards? What are the roles of each?

24. Why does the OSI Reference Model utilize a layered approach to standards development?

25. What functions are generally associated with the OSI network layer? With the transport layer?

26. Which OSI Reference Model layer organizes data bits into frames for transmission?

27. How does the TCP/IP model correspond to the OSI Reference Model?

28. What business reasons would support development of a standard?

Research Activities

1. What kinds of data communications standards are used at your school? At your workplace? What business impact do you think these standards have on data communications at your organization?

2. What data communications methods are utilized at your school or workplace? If there are multiple methods, how are they linked together? Why can they be linked together?

3. Using the ISOC Web site, find out which RFCs relate to TCP/IP.

4. What kinds of wireless data communications devices are used in your school or organization? What standards are associated with the technologies being used?

5. Find out if your school or organization uses EBCDIC, ASCII, Unicode, or a combination of any of these, and then discover how these encoding schemes function together. Why would an organization choose to use two or more of these encoding schemes?

6. Where are digital and analog data transmission types being utilized in your school or workplace? Why were these methods chosen? Can you foresee a reason to change methods?

7. Access the ISO Web site at www.iso.org, and summarize the ISO standards development process.

Mini Case Study

METRO RADIOLOGY

Metro Radiology is a large provider of X-ray, ultrasound, CAT scan, and other imaging services. Within the past few years they have grown from a one-site facility to an organization that includes offices all over town plus offices in two separate cities that are nearly 50 or more miles from the home office. They use computers and digital phones for connecting all of the offices in the metro area, but the types of services that are available to connect the remote locations to the central location are limited. Assuming that the doctors who run the office are extremely interested in connecting the offices located outside of the city, what data communications technology that you've learned about in this chapter would allow the remote locations to connect? What standards are you aware of that will support your solution? Where could you find other standards to verify that your solution is adequate? What are these other standards?

DATACONNECT MANUFACTURING

DataConnect Manufacturing designs and produces products that are used in data communications equipment sold by the top vendors in the United States and Canada. During the 1980s and 1990s, company officers saw their business grow from less than $100,000 in sales to more than $25 million. However, they have always been an original equipment manufacturer (OEM), meaning that they build their products to be used as components in other manufacturers' products. Recently, they have hit upon an idea that they think would revolutionize data communications, and to support their thoughts, they haven't been able to find another manufacturer that is supplying the market with their technology. If DataConnect managers wants their product to ultimately become a standard in the industry, what avenues can they take in securing their technology as the standard?

Chapter
Two

Chapter Overview and Objectives

Local area networks (LANs) play a significant role in the world of data communications. In all major organizations and in a vast number of smaller organizations, local area networks have become a common, and often preferred, method of exchanging and accessing the numerous types of information that organizations create, disseminate, and store. In this chapter, we examine the basic building blocks of local area networks as well as several general types of LANs that are in use in the business world today. More specifically, by the end of this chapter, you will be able to

- Define server, LAN services, and client, and describe the role of each in a LAN.

- Provide a brief description of the mainframe and terminal LAN configuration.

- Define and discuss peer-to-peer, client-dominant, client/server, and distributed processing LAN configurations and identify their business purposes.

- Identify the requirements for connecting clients and servers to a LAN.

- Define coaxial cable, twisted-pair cabling, and fiber-optic cabling and identify a major business purpose for each.

- Define three types of wireless media and identify a business purpose for each.

- Provide a brief discussion of how network interface cards work.

- Identify four types of network interface cards (NICs) and their general business applications.

- Describe the role of NIC drivers.

- Define half-duplex and full-duplex NICs and identify a business purpose for each.

- Briefly describe the function of autosensing and high-performance NICs and identify their business purposes.

- Summarize a list of NIC vendors.

Local Area Networks: An Introduction

Chapter Outline

PROFESSIONAL PERSPECTIVE AND BUSINESS PURPOSE

When I first started in the networking field in the early 1990s, my primary goal was to change my career focus, learn a lot of new things, and then apply what I'd learned in the real world. But above all I wanted to have fun working in the networking field. So when I was asked to do my first local area network installation, I bid the job for the experience and challenge more than for any specific business purpose.

Having spent the previous 10 years in systems implementations and design, I was only too eager to get started with the hands-on installation of my first network but did not realize the importance of asking the owner some questions. And not technical questions, either: It was understood that it was my job to handle the technical aspects of the installation. Instead, *I had to ask the owner how he ran his business and what he intended to do with his new LAN once it was installed.* In fact, before installing a single cable at his company or configuring a workstation or server, I was right back in systems design mode, asking the kinds of questions that underscore any systems implementation or, for that matter, any local area network design and implementation; and that is, what are the underlying business issues that will support a LAN?

I was surprised to learn a very important lesson on my first job in the LAN field; local area networks have a purpose, and usually it's totally business motivated rather than technology driven. The people spending the money don't make purchase decisions because they're looking to buy cool technology. Playing with cool technology is for technicians and hobbyists. Businesspeople with real money to invest in their businesses want real results. And when you're dealing with owners and managers who have a vested interest in the ongoing success of the business, they won't spend money unless it's going to bring some kind of positive return. Local area networks aren't the business owner's hobby, and *I quickly realized that I could "sell" a local area network solution only if it provided a real solution to a business need.*

The kinds of questions I asked the owner of that small manufacturing company and the answers he provided taught me that for any local area network, the owner or business manager is looking for a direct benefit to the implementation. It sounds like a simple-enough concept, and in the case of my first network installation, the owner's needs were pretty simple. He had an accounting application that several people needed to access at the same time, and he wanted to be able to print reports without having to buy a printer for everyone in the company.

Over time, the theme of each LAN implementation with which I was involved resounded a similar echo—local area networks assist with a substantial number of business functions, and successful organizations and managers are interested in improving these business functions on an ongoing basis. To do that, they implement programs and technologies that make their businesses easier to manage, simplify business processes, and reduce costs and minimize or eliminate nonproductive capital outlays. In addressing the improvement of business functions, organizations will allocate financial resources to the implementation and support of a local area network only if they perceive a benefit or improvement in specific business functions. That is, a local area network must have a business purpose.

In terms of identifying and quantifying the business purposes of a local area network, you will find that one of the major purposes of a LAN is to facilitate the exchange of information among employees within an organization or business unit. Of course, this information exchange can take the form of stored files, printed reports, e-mails, centralized application usage, and so on, that employees use or create on a periodic, if not continuous, basis. And properly utilized, a LAN can enhance user productivity and extend the usefulness of computing resources.

Local area networks also extend user connectivity beyond the desktop. When a local area network is connected to other networks, users can then bring information from remote business units as well as general and business information from the outside world directly to their desktops.[1] With this extended connectivity, users can access competitive market information, business-to-business applications, and connectivity to vendors and customers. In today's business climate, local area networks have become a core means of information exchange within the organization along with facilitating access to the world of information outside of the organization.

To summarize, then, you'll find that local area networks assist specific business functions by allowing employees to

- Save files to a common, centralized location.
- Share files with other employees.
- Print to a common, centralized printer.
- Share printers with other employees.
- Exchange e-mails and other information.
- Simultaneously access centralized applications and databases.
- Maintain secure access to information and network resources.
- Access information that is external to the organization.

TECHNOLOGY OVERVIEW

You'll find lots of different technologies operating both at the surface and behind the scenes to make a local area network functional. For example, some of the tangible components that you'll need are specialized hardware and software: computers to act as servers and workstations, and operating systems to provide the necessary services on the servers and workstations in your LAN. Continuing in the hardware category, you'll need a piece of hardware known as a network interface card installed in each computer that you intend to connect to your network, and you'll likely use some type of cabling as the physical media that connects each network interface card to a centralized hardware device. In alternative local area network configurations, you might choose to use a wireless technology that's incorporated into your network interface cards so that you don't have to use physical cables.

As an example of a simple local area network configuration, refer to Figure 2.1. In the figure, you'll see a computer that has a network operating system installed and which will act as the local area network's server, several workstation computers that have local operating system software installed, cables, and a hub. Each cable is connected at one end to a network interface card in a computer, and the other end of each cable is connected to a centralized device such as a hub or switch.[2]

You can implement additional devices in a local area network to improve network performance and to link your LAN to other networks. Devices such as bridges, switches, routers, and other devices that combine these technologies provide additional levels of sophistication to a local area network. At the same time any increase in technology does not diminish the fundamental business purposes of a LAN, and that is to provide information exchange among employees and connectivity to computing and information resources.

---

[1] In this context, other networks implies wide area networks and the Internet. You'll examine wide area network topics in chapter 8 and Internet concepts in chapter 10.
[2] You'll examine hubs and switches in chapter 4.

FIGURE 2.1
Physical
Configuration of a
Simple Local Area
Network

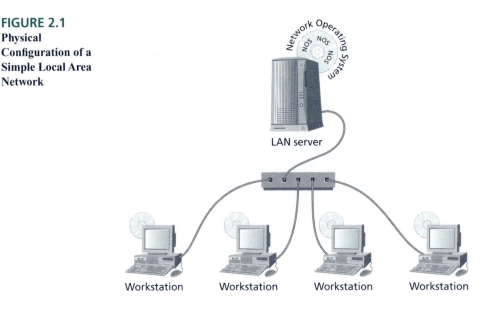

SERVERS, LAN SERVICES, AND CLIENTS

server
a computer that is
connected to the LAN
and that has specialized
network operating
system (NOS) software
installed and configured
to provide shared LAN
services to users and
devices on a local area
network

Servers, LAN services, and clients are three of the core components in any local area network. **Servers** are those local area network computers that run network operating system software. The **network operating system (NOS)** software provides the **LAN services** that allow users to perform functions such as store and retrieve files from a server, gain access to shared printers, and run shared network applications. **Clients** are the local area network computers that users use to connect to the LAN and access the LAN services that servers provide. In this section, you'll take a separate look at each of these core LAN components.

Servers and LAN Services

*network operating
system*
software that is installed
on server hardware to
interface with the server
hardware and to provide
LAN services such as
shared resource access
to users

When you hear or see the term **server**, you should think of more than a hardware device, as depicted in Figure 2.2. In the context of a local area network, a server is a computer that is connected to the LAN *and* that has specialized **network operating system** software installed and configured to provide shared **LAN services** to users and devices on a local area network. Some of these LAN services can be as simple as data storage and retrieval services and printing services. Or a server's NOS software can be configured to provide higher-end services such as shared application access and processing. The server's NOS can maintain a database of users and groups, provide centralized logon services, and coordinate centralized desktop management and control. When appropriately configured, servers can provide users with access to LAN services that can assist them with various work functions. For instance, users access logon services to access a server, and then they can save important data on a server hard disk and retrieve it later as needed. As another example, a user can access an available license for a software application that runs on the server. In either case, a server provides access to centralized and shared LAN services.

LAN services
the software
components of a
network operating
system that provide
users with access to
shared resources on the
LAN. LAN services
allow users to perform
functions such as store
and retrieve files from a
server, gain access to
shared printers, and run
shared network
applications

LAN Services

The original purpose of microcomputer-based local area networks was to share files from a centralized file server. Later, shared printing services were added so that users could print to printers that weren't connected directly to their local client computers.

Local area network services define the personality of your LAN environment. Default LAN services are the software components that are built into the network operating system

FIGURE 2.2
Local Area Network Servers

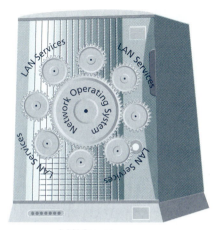

LAN Server

FIGURE 2.3
Basic Services on a Local Area Network

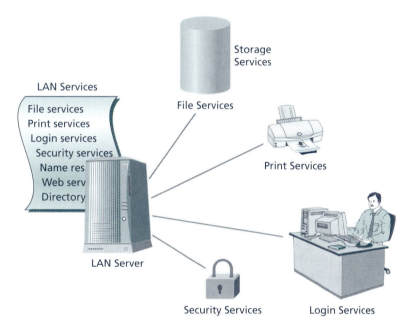

client
a LAN computer that has a workstation operating system (local OS) installed along with special software known as *network operating system* client software that provides the local OS with the additional functionality that is required to connect to the LAN services provided by a server's NOS software and the physical resources of the LAN

that has been installed on a server computer and generally include services such as file and print services, logon services, basic security configuration services, and name recognition/resolution services. Other services can be configured as needed to enhance your local area network's functionality, security, and performance. For example, you can restrict the hours during which users can log on, you can control what users can see on their desktops and what they can access from the network once they've logged on, or what they're allowed to view and download from the Internet, as in Figure 2.3.

Clients

In a broad sense, a local area network client connects a user to LAN services. More specifically, a client is a LAN computer with which a user connects to the LAN services provided by the server's NOS software and physical resources such as LAN printers and server disk drives. Refining the definition a little further, a **client** is comprised of a computer that has a workstation operating system (local OS) installed along with special software known as

FIGURE 2.4 **NOS Client Software and Access to Services**

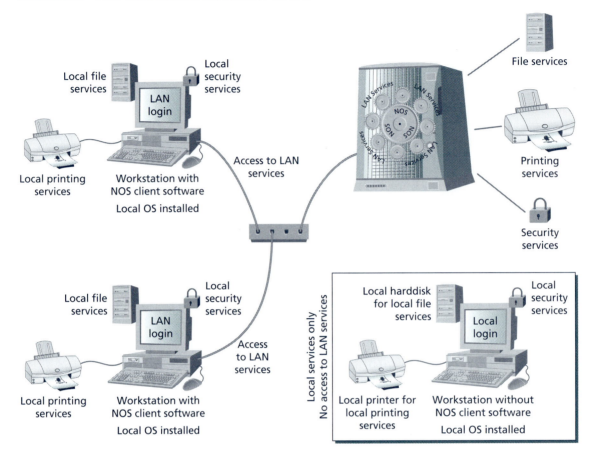

network operating system client software that provides the local OS with the additional functionality that is required to connect to the LAN services provided by a server's NOS software and the physical resources of the LAN.

Without NOS client software, a workstation can access only local OS services such as local file services for storing data files on the local hard drive, or local printing services for sending print jobs to a printer that is connected directly to the back of the computer, as depicted in Figure 2.4. In other words, without NOS client software, the local OS does not have access to LAN services. By including or installing NOS client software with the local OS, workstations that would otherwise have access only to local OS services are able to access LAN services from the network operating systems that are installed on servers. Workstations with NOS client software installed and configured can access resources such as server hard drives for saving and retrieving files, print devices that are attached anywhere on the local area network, and a myriad of LAN services such as security services, logon services, and application services to mention a few.

A client typically has a workstation operating system installed such as Windows 95/ 98/ME, Windows NT Workstation, Windows 2000 Professional, Windows XP Home/ Professional, Mac OS, or Linux. In addition, client computers generally have additional software known as *client software* or simply *the client* installed to allow the workstation operating system to connect to one or more servers on the LAN and thereby gain access to the LAN services provided by those servers' NOSs.

FIGURE 2.5

Importance of Different NOS Clients

Client A has access only to Microsoft server LAN services. Client B has access to both Microsoft and Novell LAN services.

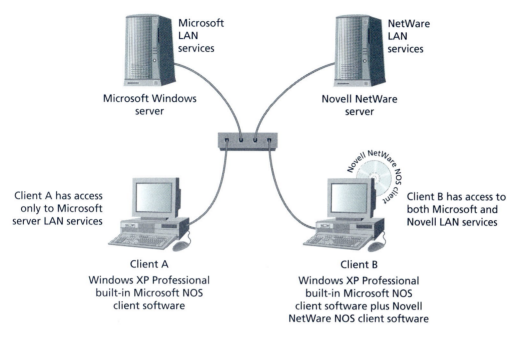

The client software can be bundled and installed by default with the local operating system, as is the case with the Windows family of products. This Windows client software allows for the seamless connection of Microsoft Windows client computers to Microsoft Windows servers. If you're trying to connect Windows client computers to servers that are running a non-Windows network operating system such as Novell's NetWare, you can install client software supplied by Novell, the network operating system vendor. For example, you would install Novell's NOS client software on a Windows client computer to allow the Windows client computer to connect to a server running Novell's NetWare.[3] Figure 2.5 provides an example.

In Figure 2.5, clients A and B can connect to each of the servers and gain access to the LAN services that are provided by the servers' network operating systems. Client A is a Windows XP Professional computer and because it's a Microsoft local OS, it has built-in NOS client software that a network administrator can configure to allow the client to gain access to the LAN services provided by the Microsoft server NOS.

Client B is a Windows XP Professional computer that is configured to access the LAN services provided by the Microsoft server NOS and the LAN services provided by the Novell NetWare server NOS. Client B gains access to the Microsoft server's LAN services the same way that client A does. The difference with client B is that it has the Novell NetWare NOS client software installed, too. The Novell NetWare NOS client software adds extra functionality to the Windows XP Professional operating system so that Windows XP can access the LAN services provided by the Novell NetWare server's NOS. In each case, client software gives local operating systems access to the LAN services provided by server network operating systems.

---

[3] You'll learn more about Novell's NetWare family of network operating systems in chapter 5.

Web-based NOS Client

NOS client software has traditionally provided its functionality in either of the following two ways:

1. The NOS client is incorporated into the local OS as an integral component, as with Microsoft Windows workstation operating systems.
2. The NOS client is installed as a separate software component as with Novell NetWare NOS client software being installed on Windows workstation computers.

With the latest versions of the Novell NetWare NOS, NOS client software does not need to be installed on a local OS such as Windows XP, Linux workstation, or Mac OS to provide users with access to LAN services. Instead, the NOS client functionality that would have traditionally been installed as an add-on to the local OS of each workstation is provided along with other LAN services for local operating system access. In other words, the NOS client software functionality is provided at the server by the Novell NetWare NOS that is installed on the server. With this functionality on the Novell NetWare server, network administrators do not need to install a separate Novell NetWare NOS client on each workstation computer that requires LAN services from the Novell NetWare server.

Because the client functionality is resident on the server in this scenario, and because this functionality is provided as a Web-based LAN service, local operating systems can gain access to LAN services on the Novell NetWare server through an Internet browser such as Internet Explorer or Netscape Navigator/Communicator. Figure 2.6 provides an illustration.

From a business perspective, the browser-based approach to accessing local area network services is advantageous in some situations. With networks that incorporate Novell NetWare servers, the configuration time associated with installing Novell NetWare NOS client software can be substantial in large networks with lots of workstations that require access to LAN services. Instead of installing and configuring a traditional Novell NetWare NOS client on each workstation computer, a network administrator can make LAN services on Novell NetWare servers available to users through the Internet browsers on their workstations.[4] This can add up to huge cost savings over time because Novell NOS

FIGURE 2.6
Access to LAN Services through a Web Browser

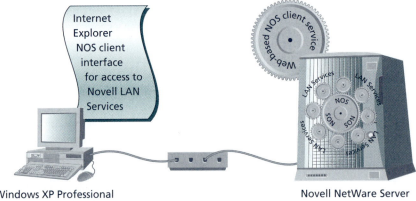

Windows XP Professional
without Novell NetWare NOS
client software installed

Novell NetWare Server

---

[4] Although simple LAN services such as file storage, printing services, and basic e-mail services on Novell NetWare servers can be accessed through an Internet browser, more advanced LAN services that provide functions such as workstation management are not currently available through the browser-based NOS client approach and require installation of the Novell NetWare NOS client software on each workstation computer that requires these advanced LAN services.

client software is frequently updated, and it's easier to manage updates on one or two or several servers rather than at hundreds or thousands of workstations.

LAN CONFIGURATIONS

The business needs and size of an organization determine the LAN configuration that network designers and administrators choose to implement. For instance, large organizations with significant investments in legacy mainframe computers might choose to continue this configuration rather than undergo the substantial resource investment to convert to a distributed processing environment. Other organizations with similar data communications requirements might choose to implement a modern LAN configuration that utilizes a client/server approach. And smaller organizations that have only modest requirements for information exchange among employees and minimal need for centralized LAN services might choose a peer-to-peer LAN configuration. In any case, the configuration that an organization chooses is based on the company's business needs and is supported by available LAN technologies.

mainframe
a computer that performs centralized computing functions such as running applications and processing data for an entire organization

terminal
an input device that transfers user input to the mainframe. Unlike modern personal computers, terminals of old did not run applications or process data. Those functions were reserved for the mainframe.

centralized processing
a system in which all data manipulation takes place on a single computer

Mainframes and Terminals

In the "old" days (1960s and 1970s), the primary types of computer networks used in businesses were mainframe/terminal configurations, sometimes referred to as host-based or terminal-host architectures. The servers (also called hosts) of this era were **mainframes**, which performed all of the computing functions such as running the applications and processing the data. The client was known as a **terminal**; an input device that was either a typewriterlike device complete with a roll of paper and configured for connection to a computer or a monitor terminal and keyboard. Users would sit in front of the terminal and keyboard, and keystrokes were transferred a screen at a time through a cable to the front-end processor and then to the mainframe for processing.[5] Since only minimal processing was done at the terminal, computer techs applied the *dumb-* prefix, referring to terminals as *dumb-terminals,* and hopefully not to the terminal users themselves. Figure 2.7 provides a representation of a mainframe network.

Mainframes were designed for **centralized processing**, centralized data access and storage, and centralized information management. This had tremendous benefits in the 1960s and 1970s with the recognition by business managers that corporate information was

FIGURE 2.7
A Mainframe Network

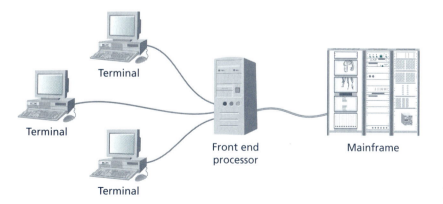

---

[5] A front-end processor (FEP) handles the communication function between terminals and the mainframe. This offloads the communications function from the mainframe processor so that the mainframe processor can be devoted to other tasks.

a very valuable asset, and centralizing it for data access and data manipulation through applications had great appeal on a cost/benefit basis. Even companies that couldn't afford to purchase their own mainframes could "time-share" or rent processing time from another company's mainframe computer and thereby obtain the benefits of computing power for data access and application processing without the huge capital outlay associated with a mainframe installation.

On a comparative basis, the disadvantage to using 1960s to 1970s mainframe computing technology in today's local area networks derives from simple economics. Mainframes of that era were designed to deliver a fixed amount of computing power for a given level of capital expenditure. With a fixed amount of processing power, any increase in demand on this centralized processing results in an increase in waiting time to users. As more and more users access the system simultaneously or as more applications demand processing power, the response performance of the computer decreases. Users have to wait, application performance decreases, and so forth. The fix for this is to upgrade the mainframe, but the cost of mainframe upgrades is not insignificant. Upgrade costs can range from tens of thousands to hundreds of thousands of dollars. In addition, the cost to develop mainframe-based applications is significantly more expensive than to purchase comparable software that is available for use on modern microcomputers—the types of computers we think about when we talk about servers in a LAN environment.[6] Once again, on a comparative basis, upgrades to a client server–based environment for both hardware and software are substantially less, ranging from hundreds of dollars to tens of thousands.

Mainframe-like architecture does, however, provide some benefits for today's local area network environments. Most notably, today's mass storage technologies utilize an approach that is very similar to the mainframe architecture of the 1960s and 1970s and can assist with the storage needs of a local area network. As was recognized in the early 1960s, information is a very valuable corporate asset, and accessing and archiving this information from a centralized data store has become a very popular addition to local area networks at a relatively reasonable cost per unit of storage. Companies that recognize this have several solutions available to them that look very similar to mainframe technology but with a state-of-the-art twist known as storage area networking.[7]

Peer-to-Peer Local Area Networks

peer-to-peer LAN
a local area network configuration in which each computer can be configured to act as both a server and a client

Peer-to-peer local area networks have been around since the mid-1980s. Their popularity stems from their simplicity as well as their ability to fill a business need for small organizations that don't have a substantial need for centralized computing power on a dedicated server. With a peer-to-peer LAN, each computer on the LAN acts as a peer to every other computer on the LAN. Each computer can request services of every other computer, and every computer on the LAN can be configured to provide LAN services to any computer on the LAN that requests those services. In other words, the local operating system has functionality built in to it so that each computer can be configured to act as both a server and a client. That is, the NOS client software is built in, and limited server NOS functionality is built in to provide limited LAN services.

If computer A requests services from computer B and computer B can provide those services, computer B performs the functions of a server by responding to computer A's

---

[6] In general, mainframe applications are more expensive because microcomputer-based software is produced for a larger market so that development costs can be distributed across a broader customer base. Mainframe software is generally proprietary to a specific hardware vendor and doesn't enjoy as broad an implementation base over which to amortize the cost of development. Fewer substitutes and steeper demand curves with mainframe-based applications are also likely causes.

[7] You'll explore data storage technologies and storage area networks when you get to chapter 6.

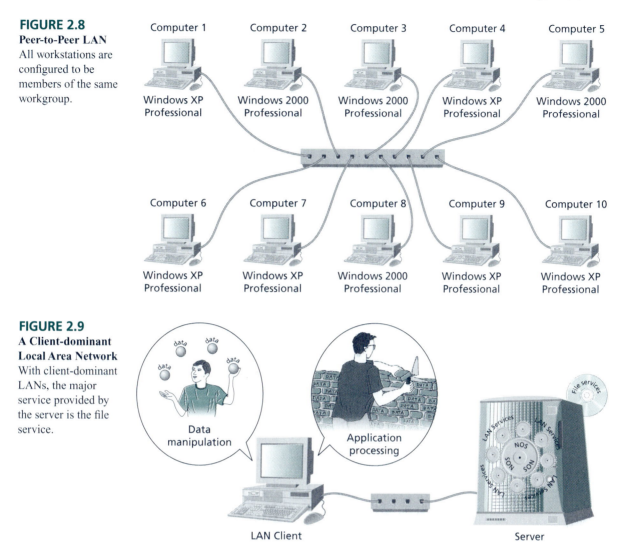

FIGURE 2.8
Peer-to-Peer LAN
All workstations are configured to be members of the same workgroup.

Computer 1 — Windows XP Professional
Computer 2 — Windows 2000 Professional
Computer 3 — Windows 2000 Professional
Computer 4 — Windows XP Professional
Computer 5 — Windows 2000 Professional
Computer 6 — Windows XP Professional
Computer 7 — Windows XP Professional
Computer 8 — Windows 2000 Professional
Computer 9 — Windows XP Professional
Computer 10 — Windows XP Professional

FIGURE 2.9
A Client-dominant Local Area Network
With client-dominant LANs, the major service provided by the server is the file service.

Data manipulation

Application processing

LAN Client

Server

---

workgroup
a collection of computers with similar resource requirements that act as resource-sharing peers in a LAN

client-dominant LAN
a LAN configuration in which most application processing and data manipulation take place on the client computer. Servers are relegated to storage and management functions in this configuration.

request. In Figure 2.8, 10 computers are each configured with either the Windows XP Professional local operating system or Windows 2000 Professional. Since both local operating systems support peer-to-peer networking, each of the computers is configured as a member of the same **workgroup**, a parameter that specifies which computers are peers, and each computer is configured to share resources with every other computer on the LAN.[8] When computer 1 needs a file that is stored on computer 8, for example, computer 1 functions as a client requesting services, and computer 8 acts as a server providing file system services to computer 1.

Client-dominant Local Area Networks

Client-dominant local area networks were quite popular from about the mid-1980s through the mid-1990s, and still are in many small businesses today.[9] With a client-dominant configuration, as illustrated in Figure 2.9, the local area network contained client

---

[8] Other operating systems such as Linux and Mac OS also support peer-to-peer networking.
[9] Client-dominant LANs are sometimes referred to as client-based or file-server architectures.

workstations on which most application processing and data manipulation took place. Servers were also connected to the local area network but in the client-dominant LAN environment, the primary purpose of the server is data storage and not supporting server-based applications and application processing. As a user needed to process or manipulate data through an application, the client workstation retrieved the data from the local area network file server, and then all application processing and data manipulation took place on the client computer.

The business motivation for client-dominant LANs was more evolutionary than revolutionary. During the early 1980s, businesses purchased many personal computers to obtain the benefits of spreadsheet and word processing programs such as Lotus 123 and WordPerfect. Departments or business units throughout a company would purchase numerous personal computers and the spreadsheet and word processing programs to make their employees more productive.

With so many personal computers being purchased by businesses and with no recognized need early on to connect them into any form of a network, applications were written for single users. The personal computer software companies in the early 1980s had not yet developed the multiuser approach for software applications because there weren't any servers to require such an approach. As a result, there were lots of personal computers with lots of single-user versions of spreadsheets and word processors.

At the same time, the cost of hard drives was relatively high in comparison with today's per-megabyte prices so that most personal computers came with two 5.25-inch floppy drives but no hard drive—a hard drive was a $2,000 to $3,000 option. If you wanted to save your data, you typically had to save it to a floppy drive that could hold only 360 kilobytes of information—tiny by today's standards.

Put these two components together—lots of personal computers running single-user versions of applications and no low-cost way to save the information to the local computer—

sneaker net
a network that involved users exchanging information by saving it to floppy disks and then carrying the disks to another user's work area for use on that user's computer

and suddenly there was a need to replace the **sneaker-net** networks that users had created by walking back and forth between co-workers with a diskette in hand to share information. This was hardly a productive way to share data, and with hard drive prices being high enough to preclude hard drive installation within all personal computers, several enterprising companies came up with microcomputer-based centralized storage devices that quickly became integrated into the first local area networks and came to be called *file servers,* the centralized storage devices of client-dominant networks.

Client/Server Local Area Networks

The performance loss to the file server and to the LAN as a whole is too great in a client-dominant local area network. When a client runs an application, more data is transmitted to the client than the client actually needs, and the application processing at the client is less than efficient due to the single-user version characteristics of the software application.

client/server LAN
a LAN configuration in which some of the processing is performed at the client and some at the server

With **client/server local area network** environments, some of the processing is performed at the client and some at the server. Data access and storage are processed primarily by the server, as depicted in Figure 2.10, but because of the way client/server application programs are written, an entire database does not have to be copied from the server to the client computer each time an application runs. Instead, the application program is typically written so that only the required information is copied to the client computer for data manipulation. Once the processing is complete, the updated information is sent back to the server where the server portion of the application program updates the database.

The clear business advantages to client/server environments are the reduced demands on the network media whenever multiple users access an application and the data associated with that application, and the sharing of application processing at both the client and the server. Neither the client nor the server has to handle all the processing. This results in better performance at both the clients and the servers.

FIGURE 2.10
A Client/Server Local Area Network

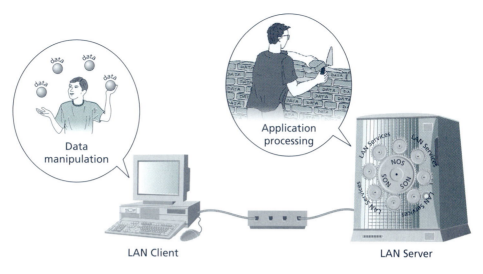

LAN Client   LAN Server

In addition, development of the client/server environment has resulted in several standards that provide application developers with an assurance of compatibility between client and server software components. For example, a software application developer could create a client computer version of a reporting software package that extracts data from a database application that runs on a server. As long as the application developer writes to the client/server standard, its client software will communicate correctly and effectively with the database on the server. Some of these standards include Common Object Request Broker Architecture (CORBA), Component Object Model (COM), Distributed Component Object Model (DCOM), Open Database Connectivity (ODBC), and Distributed Computing Environment (DCE).

Distributed Processing Local Area Networks

In more advanced LAN environments, where the demands on one server in a local area network might be too great to supply reasonable responses to application or service requests, distributed processing environments have become popular.

distributed processing LAN

a LAN configuration in which the data access and storage components of an application are separated out from the data processing component of the application, and the application processing itself can be shared across several computers

In a **distributed processing local area network**, the data access and storage components of an application are separated out from the data processing component of the application, and the application processing itself can be shared across several computers. For example, in a highly secure financial transaction-processing environment, multiple servers can be used for data storage and access, while the application processing might take place on one or more different servers. In addition, different components of the entire application could be installed on one or more servers. To use a simple example, an accounting application could have the general ledger component installed on one server, accounts payable on a different server, and accounts receivable on yet another server. To further the distributed environment, if the accounting application had a job-costing module, that module could be installed on still another server. The logic built into the application allows all the component modules to communicate with one another, and the client component of the application that would be installed on client computers would be indifferent as to where the processing actually took place.[10] Figure 2.11 provides an example.

In Figure 2.11, a user who needs to access the accounts receivable portion of an application does so by providing a URL through a Web browser. The Web server that responds

---

[10] With Web-based applications, there's no client component to install on client computers. Instead, users at client computers access the distributed applications by entering a URL in the address field of their Internet browser.

FIGURE 2.11
Distributed
Processing

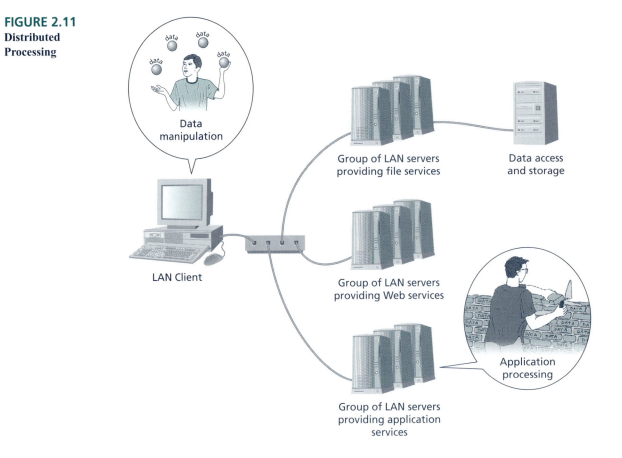

n-tier architecture
a distributed processing
model that separates the
logic of an application
from storage access and
processing and also
allows the application as
well as the data storage
to be distributed across
multiple and separate
computing devices

to the request redirects the request to the application so that the client can access the application's accounts receivable functionality. In this example, the accounts receivable function is installed on two different servers, either of which can respond to the client's request. When the user performs an operation within the application that requires access to accounts receivable data, additional requests are generated, but these requests are serviced by other servers that manage data storage and retrieval functions. Since applications such as these have multiple tiers, each of which provides different or redundant functionality, distributed processing is frequently referred to as **n-tier architecture**.

The biggest benefit to distributed processing environments is their ability to scale to new and increased processing demands. As more and more users access a distributed application, any decrease in performance at a server that is running the application can be augmented by an additional server running the same application or a portion of the same application. This results in load sharing and redundancy of the application and provides improved performance to application users and a reduced load on any single server running the application.

The flip side of this is that adding an additional server to a LAN increases the amount of communication going on across the local area network media. This is less of an issue, however, due to the availability of performance-enhancing network hardware such as switches and routers.[11]

---

[11] You'll learn about switches and routers in chapter 4.

Connecting Computers to a LAN

Connecting clients and servers to a LAN is a relatively straightforward procedure that is generally performed by a network administrator or network technician. Client computers require that a local OS be installed on users' computers, and the NOS client software must be configured so that the local OS can recognize one or more servers on the LAN. A network administrator or technician also configures the client software and other parameters such as TCP/IP, as well as hardware components such as network interface cards and the LAN media, both of which you'll learn about later on in this chapter.[12]

Connecting a server to a LAN is a little more complicated than connecting a client. First, a network administrator specifies the computer that will function as the server and installs and configures the server NOS. Setting up the NOS involves configuring numerous parameters such as TCP/IP settings, LAN services settings, and adding user accounts so that users can log in and connect to LAN services. The server is physically connected to the network through a network interface card that is installed in the server, and the LAN media connects the network interface card to one or more hardware devices that interconnect other devices on the LAN.

MEDIA TYPES AND CONNECTORS

Media refers to the environment through which communication or data transmission can take place. Until very recently, this environment has been limited to some type of cabling such as coaxial cabling or twisted-pair copper wire or even fiber-optic cabling. However, with the rapid development of wireless technologies, media doesn't have to be a physical cable for data transmissions to take place in a local area network.

Some of the features that business owners and managers look for are reliability, security, flexibility and adaptability, and longevity. Ease of installation is always a nice feature too, but not at the expense of other key features. In this section, you'll explore the various types of cabling and wireless communication types that can be implemented in a local area network as well as why businesses choose various types of communications media.

Coaxial Media and Connectors

Coaxial cable, more commonly referred to as "coax," was used in many early LAN installations. From a technology standpoint, it consists of two conductors separated by special insulating material. One conductor carries the signal and the other acts as a ground and as shielding for the conductor that carries the data signal. The center conductor can be made of solid or stranded copper; however, a solid center conductor is easier to work with and doesn't suffer the breakage problem associated with attaching connectors to the center conducting wire.

In early LAN installations, coaxial cable was a reliable, secure, and stable media choice for linking multiple computers together in a local area network, and in the early 1980s, it was the only choice for **Ethernet** networks. Today, coaxial cable is still implemented with cable TV installations, but this type of coaxial cable has different electrical characteristics than the coaxial cable used in early computer networks.[13]

Ethernet
an open standard developed jointly by Digital Equipment Corporation, Intel, and Xerox, which defines data transmission functions at the physical and data link layers of the OSI model

---

[12] You'll learn about TCP/IP classes and IP addressing in chapter 4.

[13] Early Ethernet networks that used coaxial cable used RG-58 coax cable. It had an electrical resistance index of 50 ohms. RG-62 was used in another type of early network known as Arcnet, and RG-62 had a resistance index of 93 ohms. Standard cable TV coaxial cable is designated as RG-6, which has a resistance index of 75 ohms. *RG* stands for radio guide, an obsolete military term used to designate signal transmission over a guided coax conductor.

FIGURE 2.12
Thick Ethernet Cabling

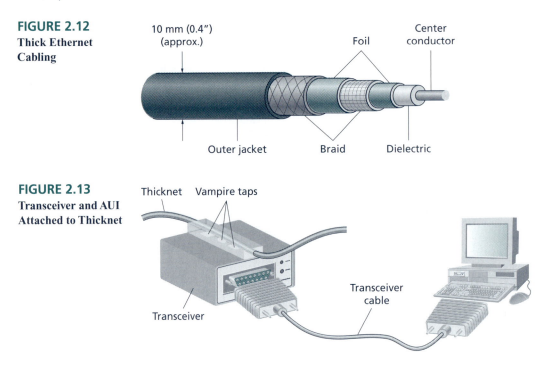

10 mm (0.4")
(approx.)

Foil

Center conductor

Outer jacket

Braid

Dielectric

FIGURE 2.13
Transceiver and AUI Attached to Thicknet

Thicknet   Vampire taps

Transceiver

Transceiver cable

network segment
any portion of the network in a local area network that's separated from other portions by a bridge, a switch, or a router

Thicknet

Thicknet or "thick" Ethernet cabling was a standard developed jointly by Digital Equipment Corporation, Intel, and Xerox in 1980. Using the first initial of each company's name, they labeled this new standard *DIX,* and it called for a thick cable with the two conductors mentioned previously in this section. From a technology standpoint, thicknet cabling would allow data transmission up to 10 Mbps over a distance of up to 500 meters and supported connectivity of 100 computers per local area **network segment**.[14]

From a business perspective, 10 Mbps was very fast for data transmission in 1980, and 500 meters and 100 computers would likely have met the needs of most local area networks of the time. As a result, thicknet became a popular choice, if not the only choice for businesses that were implementing a local area network based on Ethernet technology. It's rarely used today, however, because there are alternative methods that deliver higher performance, reliability, and security. Figure 2.12 provides an example of thicknet cabling.

Thicknet Connectors

Although thicknet cable is relegated to the archives of local area networking history, you might find the components and tools used to attach a local area network computer to a thicknet cable of passing historical interest. At 2.5 meter intervals, a device called a **transceiver** would be attached to the thicknet cable by using a device called a vampire tap. Using the vampire tap, you could bore a hole through the external protective jacket and shielding of the cabling until you reached the copper core. Then you would attach the transceiver to the cable. After installing the transceiver, you'd connect one end of an attachment user interface (AUI) cable to the transceiver and the other end to the network interface card. An example of a transceiver and AUI cable attached to a thicknet cable are displayed in Figure 2.13.

---

[14] Thicknet was also referred to as *10Base5*, where *10* refers to 10 Mbps, *Base* refers to baseband, or a single communications channel on the cable, and the *5* represents 500 meters, the maximum distance of a single cable segment.

FIGURE 2.14
Thinnet Cabling

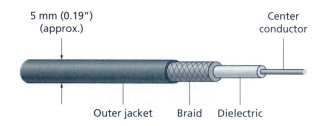

5 mm (0.19")
(approx.)

Center
conductor

Outer jacket   Braid   Dielectric

FIGURE 2.15
BNC Connectors Used with Thinnet Cabling

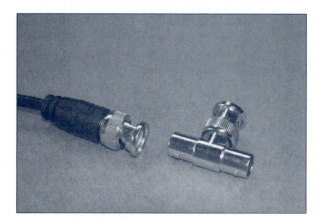

Thinnet

With both thicknet and thinnet, additional computers above the stated maximums could be connected to a local area network; however, an additional connectivity device such as a bridge or router must be added to the local area network before more computers can be added.

Thinnet or "thin" Ethernet is another form of coaxial cable, but it's thinner in diameter than thick coax. Arriving as an alternative to thicknet in 1985, it was frequently referred to as cheapnet, because it was cheaper per lineal foot and cheaper to install than thicknet.[15] From a technology standpoint, thinnet might have been cheaper, but it also had limitations that thicknet did not, namely distance and connectivity limitations. Thinnet would allow data transmission at the same 10 Mbps as thicknet, but the distance the transmission could travel on a single network segment was reduced to 185 meters, and only 30 computers could attach to the local area network.[16]

From a business perspective, thinnet became popular because it was extremely easy to implement and maintain for small local area networks. It's rarely used today because there are alternative methods that deliver higher performance, reliability, and security. Figure 2.14 provides an example of thinnet cabling.

Thinnet Connectors

In this day and age, the connectors used with thinnet to create a local area network are more of a historical footnote than anything, but they are of interest in that they have a peculiar name. These connectors are known as **BNC connectors,** and the *BNC* stands for bayonet nut connector.[17] The term grossly depicts the act of utilizing a bayonet at the end of a gun in military battle, or one can shorten this to "push and twist." Each end of a thinnet cable has a BNC, and two cables can be connected using a barrel connector or a T-connector as shown in Figure 2.15.

---

[15] Thinnet was also known as *10Base2*, where the *10* represents 10 Mbps, *Base* refers to a single channel on the cable, and the *2* represents a rounded up 185 meter distance limitation for a network segment.
[16] Thinnet's maximum length of 185 meters could be extended by using a repeater between segments.
[17] Other extractions of the BNC acronym include Bayonet Neill-Concelman and British Naval Connector, according to www.techweb.com/encyclopedia.

Twisted-Pair Media and Connectors

Twisted-pair cabling has become one of the most popular data transmission media used in local area networks. From a technology standpoint, twisted-pair cabling consists of several two-wire pairs enclosed in a synthetic sheath. Each of the twisted pairs is composed of two insulated 22- or 24-gauge copper wires twisted together; the twisting configuration reduces unwanted electronic and magnetic interference (**EMI**—electro-magnetic interference) from disrupting the existing data transmission on the wires.

EMI
electro-magnetic interference or signals that can be generated by electric motors, fluorescent lights, medical devices, and more, which interfere with data transmission

From a business perspective, twisted-pair cabling is very popular because it's relatively inexpensive and easy to install and maintain. It's highly reliable, supports high data rates, and it's a standard for Ethernet networks that has become pervasive in the business world for LAN data transmission. It's available in several different formats and various categories, as described in the following sections.

Unshielded Twisted Pair

Unshielded twisted-pair cabling, or **UTP** as it is commonly called, consists of two, three, or four unshielded twisted-wire pairs.[18] Each individual wire is coated in vinyl or other plastic derivative, and the entire bundle of wires is wrapped in a plastic sheath. The sheathing does not, however, provide any protection from EMI.

Category 1 UTP was originally specified for voice transmission. You can think of this as ordinary telephone wire. If an existing building is wired with this grade of UTP cabling, you should not use it for data transmission in a local area network. Category 2 UTP is also used in telephone voice applications, but it will support data transmission at speeds only up to 4 Mbps in a local area network. Category 3 UTP is considered data grade, as it supports data transmission at speeds up to 16 Mbps over a distance of 100 meters. At distances greater than 100 meters, degradation of the data transmission signal can result in data loss. Category 4 UTP is another data grade cable, capable of supporting data transmission rates up to 20 Mbps at distances of 100 meters.[19]

Category 5 UTP, as displayed in Figure 2.16, is data-grade, unshielded twisted-pair cable and was originally developed to handle 100 Mbps data transmission on local area networks at distances of up to 100 meters. The support for a greater transmission rate comes from twisting the cable more times per foot and using better materials than the lower categories. With any category 5 UTP installation, installation of connectors on the cable

FIGURE 2.16
Unshielded Twisted-Pair Cabling

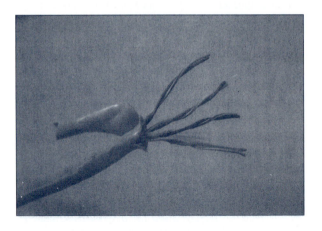

---

[18] Read this as four, six, or eight wires, but since they're in twisted pairs, the number of pairs is half the number of wires.
[19] Degradation of a data signal is technically referred to as signal attenuation.

TABLE 2.1
Common UTP Media Standards

Media Type	Maximum Data Rate	Where Used
Cat 1 UTP	less than 1 Mbps	Home telephone lines
Cat 2 UTP	4 Mbps	4 Mbps Token Ring networks, older POTs lines—1983–1993
Cat 3 UTP	100 Mbps[a]	4 Mbps Token Ring networks, 10 Mbps Ethernet LANs, some 100 Mbps Ethernet LANs, and POTs lines installed after 1993
Cat 4 UTP	100 Mbps[b]	4 or 16 Mbps Token Ring networks, 10 Mbps Ethernet LANs, some 100 Mbps Ethernet LANs
Cat 5 UTP	1,000 Mbps[c]	4 or 16 Mbps Token Ring networks, 10 and 100 Mbps Ethernet LANs, 1 Gbps Ethernet LANs—with four pairs ATM at 155 Mbps, FDDI
Cat 5e UTP	1 Gbps	10, 100, and 1,000 Mbps Ethernet ATM at 155 Mbps
Cat 6 UTP	10 Gbps	High-speed multimedia applications over future Ethernet LANs with speeds greater than 1 Gbps

[a] Category 3 can support 100 Mbps Ethernet LANs only if the NICs are 100BaseT4 NICs. The *100* means 100 Mbps, *Base* means a single communications channel, the *T* represents twisted pair, and the *4* designates four twisted pairs (eight wires total).
[b] Category 4 can also support 100 Mbps Ethernet only if the NICs are 100BaseT4.
[c] Category 5 can only support 1 Gbps Ethernet when implemented as 1000BaseT4. This means 1,000 Mbps (1 Gbps), single channel, twisted pair, four pairs.

ends is critical to supporting the high data transmission rates. Category 5 UTP was originally designed for bandwidths of up to 100 Mbps, and it will support 1,000 Mbps (1 Gbps) data transmissions according to the original IEEE 802.3z Gigabit Ethernet specifications, but for best results, category 5e UTP is recommended in Gigabit Ethernet environments. Category 5e UTP is much the same as Category 5 UTP, but with strict adherence to manufacturing and installation specifications. Category 5e UTP is designed to support data transmission rates of 1 Gbps and greater.

Category 6 UTP supports higher frequency transmission across the cable, which translates into higher data rates. Whereas Category 5 and 5e support signaling frequencies as high as 100 MHz, Category 6 UTP will support signal frequencies as high as 250 MHz. This category is also capable of data transmission rates as high as 10 Gbps. You can also expect newer categories that will support even higher signal frequencies with a resultant increase in data transmission rates.

UTP Connectors

The **UTP connectors** used to terminate the ends of unshielded twisted-pair cabling are properly called eight-pin connectors. Commonly, they're referred to as **RJ-45 connectors.** Terminating the ends of unshielded twisted pair requires skill and patience, because there is a standard ordering to placement of the wires within the connector. In addition, in order to support the high data transmission rates possible with UTP cabling, special care must be taken in attaching an RJ-45 connector so that there is no exposure of the twisted-pair wires between the external jacket of the cable and the connector itself. Examples of RJ-45 cable connectors are displayed in Figure 2.17.

Shielded Twisted Pair

Shielded twisted-pair (STP) cabling provides the same connectivity benefits as unshielded twisted pair, however, where unshielded twisted pair uses only a synthetic jacket to house

FIGURE 2.17
UTP Cable Connectors

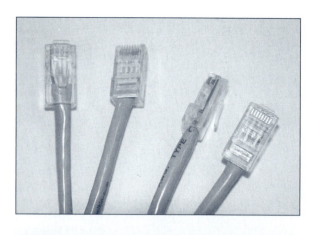

FIGURE 2.18
Shielded Twisted-Pair Cabling

FIGURE 2.19
STP Cable Connectors

the twisted pairs, shielded twisted-pair cabling adds two levels of shielding material to protect the data transmission from electromagnetic interference. Figure 2.18 provides an example of STP cabling.

In applications where your cabling might come in close contact with powerful electric motors, multiple banks of fluorescent lights, or high-voltage electrical cable runs. Each of these generate EMI that can interfere with your local area network data transmission. You might find it advantageous to budget for the extra dollar cost of STP cabling and the extra installation time associated with properly grounding the metallic shielding.

STP Connectors

RJ-45 connectors with a special ground casing are used for terminating the ends of STP cabling. Terminating the ends of shielded twisted pair is a little more involved than terminating unshielded twisted pair, because the installer must connect the shielding to the ground casing on the RJ-45 connector. STP cable connectors are displayed in Figure 2.19.

Fiber-Optic Media and Connectors

Fiber-optic media is another cabling option that provides very high reliability, security, and longevity. Unlike UTP and STP, which utilize copper wires to transmit data via electrical signals, fiber-optic cabling transmits data across a glass or plastic fiber using pulses of light. You probably won't specify fiber-optic cabling as the connection medium that connects each workstation to a LAN, because fiber-optic cabling installation is more expensive relative to unshielded-twisted-pair, and unshielded twisted-pair cabling can usually accommodate the bandwidth requirements of most workstations.[20] From a business perspective then, you'll install fiber-optic media where high data rates and large volumes of data transmissions are required. That is, you'll be more likely to see or specify fiber-optic cabling when you need to connect two or more LANs that exchange a lot of data.

Fiber-optic cable is also unlike copper in that the light pulses generated by a fiber-optic network interface card are unidirectional. To facilitate simultaneous two-way communication on a fiber-optic network, typical implementations include two fiber-optic cables between source and destination devices. One of the fiber-optic cables sends data and the other receives incoming data transmissions.

μ or micron
also called a micrometer, which is 1 millionth of a meter or about 1/25,000 of an inch. For comparison, a human hair is approximately 100μ to 200μ in diameter, and a human red blood cell is approximately 10μ in diameter

From a technology standpoint, fiber-optic cabling in LAN applications consists of a glass core that is commonly 50μ or 62.5μ in diameter surrounded by a reflective plastic coating called *cladding* that can range in diameter from 125μ to 150μ. The reflective coating is surrounded by additional components such as a synthetic woven sleeve made of aramid yarn and multiple strands of plastic tubing that protect the reflective coating and the core from damage due to bending, heat, moisture, and other stresses.[21] All of these components are then enveloped in a plastic jacket. See Figure 2.20.

One of the major advantages to using fiber-optic cabling is that it is not susceptible to EMI. Because all data transmissions across fiber-optic cabling use pulses of light, the data transmission is not disrupted by EMI generating devices such as electric motors, fluorescent lights, high-voltage electrical lines, and so on.

FIGURE 2.20   **Fiber-Optic Cable**

PhotoLink/Getty Images

CMCD/Getty Images

---

[20] The cost of the fiber-optic cable is not substantially more than the cost of UTP cabling, but the cost of installation is significantly more because fiber-optic cabling requires special tools to polish and splice the ends of the fibers to exacting specifications.
[21] Aramid yarn is the generic name for a high-strength and fire-resistant fiber that is the basis for trademarked products such as DuPont's Kevlar.

Another major advantage of using fiber-optic cabling is the distance the signal can travel. Fiber-optic cabling in local area network environments can support distances up to 10,000 meters between computers. Depending on the grade of fiber-optic cabling, data transmission rates can exceed 1 Gbps.

Multimode Fiber (MMF)

optical dispersion
the spreading out of a light signal as it is transmitted across a fiber-optic core

When fiber-optic cabling first became popular as a data transmission medium for local area networks, manufacturing and technical factors for both the fiber-optic cabling and fiber-optic network interface cards limited how small the diameter of the fiber core of the cable could be at an acceptable cost. However, with larger fiber core diameters, the light signals generated by the network interface card would enter the fiber core at multiple angles, which created a problem known as **optical dispersion**—or the spreading out of the light signal. With a more dispersed initial light signal, the different wavelengths of light traveled at different speeds along the fiber core, which resulted in the various parts of the data transmission signal arriving at the destination at different times. This imposed a performance restriction on the data transmission rate because the receiving end would have to wait for the various parts of the signal to reconstruct the data. Combining dispersion with another problem called **signal attenuation,** or the weakening of a signal over a given distance, and this early type of multimode fiber known as step-index multimode clearly needed some engineering improvements.[22]

signal attenuation
the loss in signal strength over distance

Later on, engineers developed **graded-index** multimode **fiber.** By changing the physical properties of the fiber core, engineers were able to reduce the effects of signal dispersion so that various parts of the data transmission signal arrived at the receiving end at the same time.

Multimode fiber cabling is still in use today, and you specify which type of MMF by the diameter of the fiber core. The two common core diameters for MMF are 50μ or 62.5μ, and the transmission wavelength of the light that carries the data signal is typically 850 nm. The reason it's important to know which core diameter you're using is because MMF has transmission distance specifications based on the core diameter and the transmission wavelength. In addition, the network interface cards you'll specify must be compatible with the MMF cable that's in your environment.

campus environment
the geographic area that comprises an entire business or office complex or college campus. When a LAN spans across a campus environment, the LAN is sometimes referred to as a campus area network, or CAN.

Single-Mode Fiber (SMF)

nanometer(nm)
a unit of measurement that defines wavelengths of light. A nanometer is one-billionth of a meter.

Introduced in the early 1980s, **SMF** cable is commonly used today in connecting local area networks across **campus environments** and in longer distance applications employed by telecommunications carriers for data communications between cities and over vast geographic distances. From a technology standpoint, SMF is available in core diameters ranging from about 4μ to 9μ, with 80μ of cladding used for the smaller core diameters and 125μ of cladding used with the thicker core diameters. In LAN campus environments, SMF transmits pulses of light at a wavelength of 1310 **nanometers**. Single-mode fiber that utilizes a 1310 nm wavelength is advantageous for connectivity in campus environments because the single mode of light that is transmitted across SMF at 1310 nm doesn't suffer the dispersion problems associated with 850 nm wavelengths that are transmitted across multimode fiber-optic cables. Because of the lack of dispersion with SMF, data transmission rates can be much higher—in the multi-Gbps range. In addition, signal attenuation is low enough at specified wavelengths to allow data transmission distances up to 10 kilometers.

---

[22] Weakening of the light signal over great distance was caused by light absorption and light scattering due to impurities in the glass fiber

Single-mode fiber is also used to transmit light pulses at a wavelength of 1550 nm. In order to support even greater transmission rates over longer distances without attenuation, engineers determined a way to capture the minimum dispersion characteristics of 1310 nm wavelength light across SMF and to combine those characteristics with the minimum attenuation characteristics of 1550 nm wavelength light across SMF. **Dispersion shifted fiber (DSF)** fiber-optic cable was the solution to combine these desirable attributes.

multiplexing
a method of combining multiple separate signals into a composite signal for transmission across a communications channel

DSF, however, caused irregularities with a high-speed, long-haul, carrier service technology known as Dense Wavelength Division Multiplexing (DWDM).[23] It seems that when engineers and the carrier service companies attempted to transmit DWDM signals over DSF cabling, the DWDM signal was effectively destroyed. The solution was a newer type of DSF cabling known as nonzero dispersion shifted fiber (NZDSF).

Fiber-optic Connectors

Several types of connectors are used to terminate the ends of fiber-optic cabling. Some of the most popular ones are listed here along with a brief description of each.

Connector Types

FC. The FC connector is one of the earliest examples of fiber connectors, originally developed in the 1980s. It uses a threaded nut, much like cable TV connectors, to connect to an interface such as a network interface card. It's available for both MMF and SMF applications.

ST. The ST connector works like a coaxial thinnet BNC. Simply push the connector into position with the interface, and gently turn the bayonet locking mechanism. It, too, is available for both MMF and SMF applications.

SC. The SC connector plugs into its interface and is readily adaptable to multifiber applications because of its interlocking ferrules. The SC connector is available for both MMF and SMF applications.

LC. The LC connector uses a housing that is similar to an RJ-45 twisted-pair housing, and the connector plugs into the housing using a latching mechanism that you push when you want to decouple the connection. This connector is available in both MMF and SMF configurations.

MT-RJ. The MT-RJ connector uses a modular plug and jack approach to fiber-optic cable termination. It's designed to terminate two fiber cores in the jack to accomplish what the SC connector does with two larger ferrules.

FDDI MIC. The FDDI MIC connector was originally designed for use with FDDI networking applications. It provides termination for two fiber-optic cables and uses a side-latching mechanism to snap into place. It is versatile beyond FDDI applications because it can connect with two ST-style connectors as well as with other FDDI connectors.

Small Form Factor. The small form factor is a connector type designed to use about the same amount of space per port as an RJ-45 jack that is used with UTP. This allows equipment manufacturers to maintain the same 24-port configuration in a 19-inch rack-mount system as is typically found with RJ-45 connection devices.

Terminating the ends of fiber-optic cabling has been described as both an art and a science. Attaching a connector requires special equipment, cable preparation, and attention to detail. An example of fiber-optic cable connectors are displayed in Figure 2.21.

---

[23] You'll learn about DWDM in chapter 8.

FIGURE 2.21
Fiber-optic Cable Connectors

CMCD/Getty Images

Wireless Media and Connectors

Wireless data transmissions do not require the physical cabling or physical connectors that wired connections do. Instead, a **wireless medium** can send and receive data transmissions without using an electrical or optical conductor. You can choose technology solutions based on radio frequency (RF) technology, infrared, and microwave, and from a business perspective, each has some advantages. With wireless networking, you can obtain access to your LAN and send information without being physically attached. This allows you to work from just about anywhere. You'll explore the basics in this section, and look at the world of wireless data transmission in much more detail in later chapters.

Radio Frequency

Radio frequency or radio wave technology has become very prevalent in wireless local area network implementations. The technology allows communication among wireless devices in your LAN by incorporating into each wireless device a tiny transceiver (transmitter plus receiver) and antenna. Wireless devices transmit and receive data using radio frequencies that don't interfere with other radio frequency users such as radio stations. Radio frequencies are allocated by the Federal Communications Commission (FCC), and these allocations are specific to each of the different types of radio frequency wireless transmission technologies. That is, different wireless technologies utilize different radio frequencies as allocated by the FCC.

For wireless LAN devices to communicate with other wireless devices on your local area network, you'll implement radio frequency **access points** such as wireless hubs, switches, or routers, as in Figure 2.22. Access points utilize tiny antennas and transceivers to receive and transmit data with the wireless devices. In addition, the access points act as a translation junction between the wireless devices and the "wired" devices on your local area network. This is achieved by connecting each of your access points with UTP or fiber-optic cabling to your "wired" LAN devices.

access point
a junction point that intercepts wireless transmissions from wireless devices and relays the transmissions between the wireless LAN devices and the wired devices on a local area network

Infrared

Infrared data transmission technology uses light frequencies that are invisible to the human eye and operate below the red band of the visible spectrum. Although incorporated into some laptops in the 1990s, this technology was limited to short distances and was susceptible to many types of interference such as rain and fog or someone standing between two computers that were trying to communicate.

Infrared is still available, and you can configure it for point-to-point transmission or broadcast transmission. With point-to-point, optical devices are incorporated to focus the light beam between devices. Practical implementations of this technology include wireless mice, keyboards, and some printers. For broadcast transmission, the infrared signal is spread out as it's generated making the signal less susceptible to direct interference; however, the signal is generally distance limited to a single room.

FIGURE 2.22
RF Wireless LAN Devices on a Local Area Network

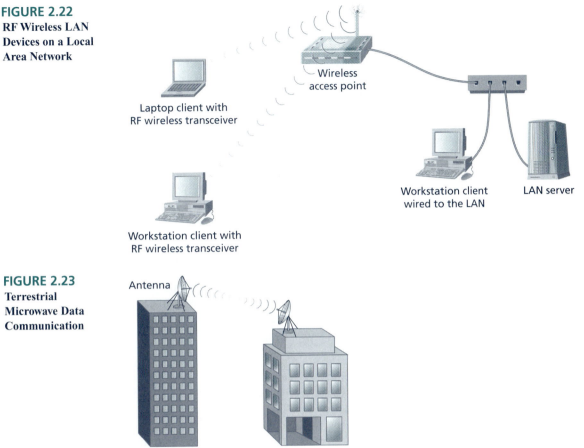

Laptop client with
RF wireless transceiver

Wireless
access point

Workstation client
wired to the LAN

LAN server

Workstation client with
RF wireless transceiver

FIGURE 2.23
Terrestrial Microwave Data Communication

Antenna

Building 1
LAN Segment

Building 2
LAN Segment

Microwave

Microwave data communication technology uses very high frequency radio waves to transmit and receive information between separate buildings or even distant geographic regions. The technology can be used in local area networks, generally between buildings, as shown in Figure 2.23, but it is more practical in campus or wide-area networking scenarios in which other connectivity solutions are either cost prohibitive or impractical.

One microwave technology, **terrestrial microwave,** utilizes parabolic antennas to generate and receive the microwave transmissions. Terrestrial microwave, as the name implies, is "earth-based" and requires a line-of-site path between antennas to ensure data transmission; in some cases this means building towers to which the microwave antennas are attached or installing microwave antennas on the tops of tall buildings.[24]

Wireless Connectors

Wireless devices don't really have physical connectors that correspond to the connectors used by coaxial, twisted-pair, and fiber-optic cabling. Instead, wireless devices use antennas and transceivers (transmitter plus receiver) to make connections between devices or locations.

---

[24] You'll learn more detail about cellular wireless technologies in chapter 7 and wide area network wireless technologies in chapter 8.

NETWORK INTERFACE CARDS

A **network interface card,** sometimes called a network adapter or network card or simply NIC, is the physical interface between a computer, or other device, and a local area network. Practically speaking, a network interface card connects your computer to the local area network cabling.

NICs come in various forms: some are built in to the computer's motherboard; others are in the form of an expansion card that "plugs into" your computer's motherboard; some are **PC cards;** and still others can attach to your computer's USB port.[25] Additional hardware specifications define whether a NIC will be used with coaxial cable, twisted pair, fiber optic, or even wireless. And you can also purchase cards that communicate at a designated data transmission rate, such as 10 Mbps, 16 Mbps, 100 Mbps, 1 Gbps, and so on.

You can purchase network interface cards from numerous vendors in various hardware configurations to support many different types of network architectures. If you have an Ethernet LAN, you'll need Ethernet NICs. If you have a Token Ring LAN, you'll need Token Ring NICs. And if you have a fiber-optic network, you're going to need network interface cards that support your chosen fiber technology.

With all these forms and combinations available to you, you'll need to understand how network interface cards work. And you'll need to have a fuller understanding of the types of cards available as well as who makes them.

How Network Interface Cards Work

The network interface card is a physical connectivity device that "translates" data from your computer and assembles it into an acceptable format for transmission across a network medium. Likewise, the NIC accepts information from the network medium and "translates" that information into a format the computer can understand.

When you want to send data such as a file from your computer to another computer through a local area network, it's a fairly simple process. If you're using e-mail, you click on Send. If you're accessing a file transfer protocol (FTP) or hypertext transfer protocol (HTTP) server, you click Upload. If you simply want to save a file to another computer such as a server on the LAN, you click File/Save, and then specify a filename and location on the other computer.

There's a lot of technology going on within the computer to help you convert your file into a format that is acceptable to the network medium. The data must exit the computer through the network interface card, but before it can do so, the NIC segments your data transmission into chunks, called **frames**, that the physical network can manage. In other words, an entire file might be broken into hundreds or thousands of smaller pieces and transmitted as frames as the file is being sent from your computer to another location across the local area network.

frame
a defined portion of a data transmission that includes data as well as source and destination address information

Each frame includes not only a portion of the data being sent, but also the address information of both the sending and the receiving network cards: Think of an envelope with a mailing address as well as a return address. Each frame needs to have this source and destination address information so that the data can find its intended destination as well as know where it originated. This address information is sometimes called the physical address of the network interface card, or simply the hardware address, because it's burned into a chip on the NIC. But this address is associated with the data link layer of the OSI model, so you could call the address of each network interface card a data link layer address. You will learn more regarding this nomenclature a little later on in the chapter.

---

[25] PC cards were formerly called PCMCIA cards, short for Personal Computer Memory Card International Association.

Every network interface card has a unique, 48-bit address known as a media access control (MAC) address. The MAC address is comprised of a 24-bit Organizationally Unique Identifier (OUI) that's assigned by the IEEE for a one-time fee of $1,650 to the manufacturer, plus a manufacturer-generated 24-bit code that is concatenated (appended) to the OUI. The address is represented as a series of six, eight-bit fields such as

af:00:ce:3a:8b:0c

MAC addresses are encoded, or "burned," into one of the integrated circuits on each NIC so that every computing device on a LAN can be uniquely identified. When devices generate requests or send information on the LAN, the MAC address of both the sending and destination computers is added to each packet of information that's placed on the network media. Computing devices on the LAN read the destination MAC address on these **data packets** and determine whether to receive or ignore these packets.

data packet
data with source and destination address information attached to it for transmission through a network

You can determine the MAC address of your computer by opening a command prompt and issuing a command that is specific to the operating system you're using. For example, if you're using Windows NT, Windows 2000, or Windows XP, you can open a command prompt and enter the command *ipconfig /all*. This command will display a MAC address in the format

00-03-47-8F-FF-8E

along with other pieces of information such as IP address information and information about various LAN services that support your configuration such as DNS and DHCP.[26] If you're using Windows 95/98/ME, you can run the graphical utility *winipcfg*. And if you're using a Linux system, you can open a session window and issue a command such as *ifconfig–a*. Depending on the version of Linux or Unix that you're using, you might need to consult your documentation for the exact command and command syntax that will display the MAC address information. Figure 2.24 provides an example of the *ipconfig /all* command at the command prompt of a Windows 2000 Professional computer.

FIGURE 2.24

Results of ipconfig/all Command on a Windows 2000 Professional Computer

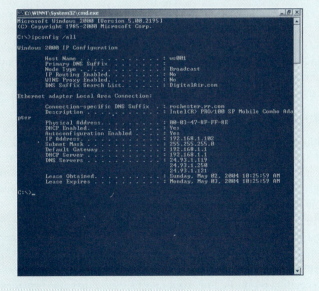

---

[26] You'll learn about DHCP in chapter 4 and DNS in chapters 5 and 10.

You learned in a previous Applied Technical Tidbit that each network interface card has a unique data link layer address assigned to the card, and you also learned that this address information is "burned" into the card on one of the integrated circuits on the network interface card as it's manufactured. In the course of business, NIC manufacturers will sometimes subcontract NIC manufacturing to a third-party vendor, and it's the vendor's responsibility to ensure that each NIC has a unique address.

Several years ago, a contract manufacturer that made network interface cards for one of the premier networking companies in the United States allowed two manufacturing runs of NICs to be coded with the same set of addresses. Imagine that both runs were shipped, and two cards with the same address were installed on the same network. It would be as if a postal carrier was trying to deliver mail on a street where two different houses had the same street number. How would the postal carrier know which house to take the mail to? Fortunately, the shift supervisor reviewed paperwork before the duplicate NICs ever shipped, and potential problems were avoided for both the contract manufacturer and the networking company.

As the NIC creates frames, it places them on the network medium as a series of electrical pulses, radio frequencies, or optical pulses that represent all the information in the frame. Because some of that information is data link layer address information, another NIC on the local area network that "owns" the corresponding destination address will recognize that the information belongs to it and will accept the data frames from the LAN medium. Other NICs that are connected to the network medium also "see" the same data frames, but upon examining the destination address and seeing that it's not for them, they discard all packets not intended for them.

And so we have a data transmission process that functions very much like the postal service. You send a letter, and (hopefully) it arrives. Similarly, you send a file, which is analogous to the letter, and it's recognized by the destination network interface card, which holds the destination address.

You might be wondering what happens if two network interface cards happened to have the same address. That's not allowed. Each manufacturer of network interface cards has a company code assigned by the IEEE, and this code represents one portion of the network card's address. The network card manufacturer generates the second part of the network card address. It's the NIC manufacturer's responsibility to never assign the same address to more than one network interface card.

Card Types

Depending on the type of local area network you've implemented, you'll need to specify network interface cards that match your LAN's topology, speed (bandwidth), access method, and the hardware type inside your computer. You'll learn more about topologies and access methods in chapter 3, but for now, we're going to focus on the types of NICs that you might implement with Ethernet, Token Ring, FDDI, and ATM.

In terms of the hardware compatibility within your computer, the network interface cards you specify must match the hardware configuration of your servers or workstations. For example, many modern Intel-based servers are configured with 64-bit **peripheral component interconnect (PCI)** slots. For the NIC to function with the server, you'll need to specify a 64-bit PCI network interface card that also provides you with the correct interface, which could consist of a twisted-pair connector, fiber interface, or wireless transceiver, and bandwidth rating, which could be 10 Mbps, 100 Mbps, or 1,000 Mbps, and more. Other common hardware configurations for Intel-based computers include ISA,

peripheral component interconnect
a high-speed data bus technology pioneered and advanced by Intel and used in most Intel-based server and workstation computers. It's now an industry standard for expansion cards such as network interface cards that plug into a computer's main system board.

data bus
the common pathway within a computer that is used to transfer data between devices and memory or between devices and the CPU

EISA, and 32-bit PCI.[27] Other hardware configurations include SBus for Sun Microsystems computers, NuBus for older Macintosh-based devices, USB for externally connected NICs that comply with USB technology, and PC card for laptop use. Many of today's workstations and servers even include built-in network interface cards on the main systemboard in the computer.

Ethernet

Ethernet NICs are used in computers that connect to Ethernet networks. They're one of the most common types of network cards being manufactured today because most local area networks use Ethernet as their data transmission architecture. Ethernet is frequently considered a network type, but it's more accurately defined as a network architecture or transmission technology. Ethernet has specific parameters and rules associated with devices that connect to an Ethernet LAN, and these rules define Ethernet network interface cards.[28]

autosense
a technology built into a networking device that allows the device to automatically determine the speed of the network and function at that rate without any manual configuration

Ethernet NICs are available with bandwidth ratings of 10 Mbps, 100 Mbps, 10/100 Mbps **autosense**, and 1,000 Mbps. With the 10 Mbps cards, you can choose the type of connector interface, such as AUI (used with thicknet), BNC (used with thinnet), or TP (short for untwisted pair). You can even specify Ethernet NICs for use with fiber-optic cables.

With 100 Mbps, you won't have the AUI or BNC connector choices, but you will find cards that are referred to as TP-only cards; that is, they support connection only to an RJ-45 twisted-pair connector. You'll also find 100 Mbps cards that have a fiber interface. With the fiber cards, you'll have to choose a connector type that is consistent with your network fiber-optic cable connectors. Figure 2.25 provides examples of several Ethernet NICs.

FIGURE 2.25
Examples of Ethernet NICs

---

[27] ISA is industry standard architecture, an older 8-bit or 16-bit databus technology. EISA is extended industry standard architecture. It was originally developed and pioneered by Compaq as a 32-bit databus that competed with IBM's proprietary 32-bit microchannel architecture.

[28] You'll discover a lot more about Ethernet rules and standards in chapter 3.

Token Ring

The types of network interface cards you can choose for Token Ring local area networks comprise a shorter list than you'll find for Ethernet NICs.[29] At one time Token Ring networks made up a much greater percentage of LAN installations than they do today. This was at a time when 16 Mbps Token Ring offered a substantial performance advantage over 10 Mbps Ethernet LANs. However, with the rapid market acceptance and continued development of Ethernet technologies, including Fast Ethernet and Gigabit Ethernet, Token Ring now makes up a much smaller percentage of local area network installations.

As with Ethernet NICs, **Token Ring NICs** are available in hardware configurations that will match your server or workstation hardware requirements. In addition, you'll need to specify the type of connector as well as the bandwidth required. In general, the bandwidth specification will be limited to 16/4 Mbps, which means the NIC can be configured to operate at either 4 Mbps or at 16 Mbps depending on your LAN's specified bandwidth. In addition, you might come across a 100 Mbps Token Ring installation that would require 100 Mbps Token Ring cards. However, with 100 Mbps Token Ring, the number of vendors will be extremely limited as this is a technology that only IBM has embraced.

FDDI

The **fiber distributed data interface (FDDI)** is an older technology that is still being used and supported in connectivity between LANs in campus environments. The connectors that FDDI uses include FDDI fiber-optic connectors and RJ-45 connectors. The RJ-45 connectors are used with an FDDI technology known as copper distributed data interface (CDDI). A CDDI allows FDDI data transmissions to be carried over unshielded twisted-pair cabling. You won't find various bandwidth ratings with FDDI or CDDI because these data transmission technologies are rated at 100 Mbps.[30]

ATM

You probably won't find a large number of **Asynchronous Transfer Mode (ATM)** LANs because when ATM was first released for LAN use, the network interface cards were relatively expensive compared to Ethernet NICs. Instead ATM has been implemented in LAN-to-LAN connectivity and in carrier service applications. If you do find a LAN deployment of ATM, the NICs that it will be using will be rated at either 25 Mbps or 155 Mbps.[31]

NIC Performance and Manageability

Many of today's network interface cards provide built-in features that allow network administrators and installation/support staff to tune the performance of their LANs. Software drivers, data transmission rate configuration, and NIC performance features all play into improving the performance of your LAN and making it more manageable.

The Role of NIC Drivers

To guarantee that a server's NOS or workstation's local OS can communicate with the NIC and vice versa, the network administrator must ensure that the appropriate software drivers are installed. Software drivers, or simply drivers, are the set of instructions that allow devices to communicate and function with one another. Every network interface card comes with a diskette or CD that has at least two sets of drivers: one to make the NIC that is installed in the server perform properly with the server NOS and one to make the NIC

---

[29] You'll learn more about the Token Ring architecture and the Token Ring access method in chapter 3.
[30] You'll learn more about FDDI technology and its business applications in chapter 3.
[31] You'll learn more about ATM technology in chapters 3 and 8.

that is installed in the workstation function with the workstation's local OS. Additional drivers are usually included as well: one for each version of local operating system and one for each NOS that could potentially be installed on a computer. Common drivers that might be included on a NIC's driver CD or diskette would include drivers for Windows 95/98, Windows 2000 Professional, Windows XP, Windows CE, Linux, and others. Drivers that might be supplied for use with a server's NOS could include separate drivers for the popular versions of each NOS software vendor's network operating systems. For instance, a NIC supplied by 3Com or Intel might include a driver for Novell NetWare version 3.12, version 4.11, version 5.1, and versions 6.0 and 6.5. The same CD or diskette would also include drivers for Microsoft Windows NT 4.0, Windows 2000 Server, and Windows 2003 server. Other drivers that might be included could be drivers for various versions of RedHat Linux and versions of Linux from other Linux vendors. If specific drivers are needed that aren't included on the manufacturer's CD or diskette, you can generally download them from the NIC manufacturer's Web site.

driver software
the software that provides the necessary instructions for devices to communicate and function together. The devices can be either hardware or software.

Frequently NIC drivers are included with the NOS or local OS installation software supplied by the NOS or local OS software manufacturer. This makes installation and configuration of the NIC driver software more convenient because it can be done during the installation of the operating system. If the NIC driver software is included with the operating system installation software, the operating system installation routine automatically recognizes the type of NIC and automatically installs the appropriate NIC driver software so that the NIC can communicate with the operating system. If the NIC driver software included with the operating system installation software is out of date or if it fails to recognize the NIC, you can usually continue with the operating system installation, obtain the NIC drivers from the NIC manufacturer's Web site, and install them later.

Half-Duplex and Full-Duplex NICs

Network interface cards send and receive data transmissions, but usually don't do both functions simultaneously. One-way-at-a-time transmission is commonly called **half-duplex**; while one computer is sending, the other is receiving, and the receiver has to wait until the sender has finished sending before the receiver can take its turn to send.

Many of today's network interface cards are configured to take advantage of **full-duplex** data communications so that computers configured with these NICs can simultaneously send and receive data. With full-duplex mode, the amount of data that can be transmitted per unit time between two devices is double that of half-duplex mode. That is, the bandwidth of the communications channel is effectively doubled with full-duplex mode. The only caveat is that the devices on each end of the communications link must be configured for full-duplex mode in order to take advantage of the doubled bandwidth between the devices. Figure 2.26 provides an example.

In Figure 2.26, a LAN is configured with a server and numerous workstations. Five of the workstations are configured with a half-duplex NIC, but two users with large data transmission requirements have full-duplex NICs installed. The server is also configured with a full-duplex NIC. The full-duplex NICs provide double the bandwidth capability of the half-duplex NICs but provide that doubled data transmission rate only between devices that are similarly configured for full-duplex mode. The client workstations that are configured with half-duplex NICs can also exchange information with the server and two workstations that are configured with full-duplex NICs, but the data rate for communications between half-duplex and full-duplex devices defaults to the half-duplex rate.

Another interesting advantage of full-duplex NICs is their ability to send data to one computer while receiving data from a different computer. Because a full-duplex NIC has two communications paths between it and the LAN, the server or either of the full-duplex clients in Figure 2.26 can be responding to a request from one of the half-duplex client

FIGURE 2.26
Using Full-duplex
Mode in a LAN

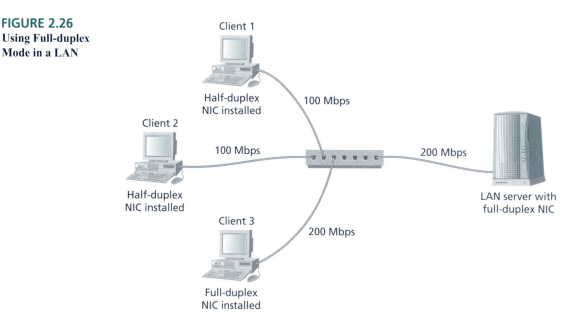

Client 1

Half-duplex
NIC installed

100 Mbps

Client 2

100 Mbps

200 Mbps

Half-duplex
NIC installed

LAN server with
full-duplex NIC

Client 3

200 Mbps

Full-duplex
NIC installed

computers while receiving information from a different half-duplex client computer. The effective data rate of the full-duplex NICs is still double that of any half-duplex device, because the full-duplex device is simultaneously sending and receiving data.

Autosensing NICs

Another feature that is common in modern NICs is their ability to autosense LAN conditions and adjust their configurations automatically based on the information received.[32] This feature reduces the amount of time that network administrators must spend manually managing and maintaining NIC configurations. With **autosensing**, the network administrator does not manually specify NIC configuration settings. Instead, the NIC self-adjusts to the conditions of the LAN. That is, if communications on the LAN are half-duplex, the NIC self-adjusts to accommodate half-duplex communication. If communications are full-duplex, the NIC self-adjusts to full-duplex mode. In addition, autosensing NICs can adjust their bandwidths according to conditions on the network. If a NIC is configured for 100 Mbps but detects a 10 Mbps transmission, it can self-adjust its receive rate to accommodate the 10 Mbps transmission.[33]

High-Performance NICs

High-performance network interface cards are designed to offload some or many of the processes that would typically be handled by the computer's central processing unit (CPU). For example, some new NICs are being touted as "secure" NICs, meaning they offload TCP/IP functions and encryption functions that are typically handled by the computer's CPU. When these types of processes are performed by the network interface card instead of the main CPU, the main CPU can service other requests faster, which results in higher performance on the computer and on the network.

Another popular feature that is available with some higher-end network cards is remote management capability. These manageable NICs can be accessed anywhere on the LAN

---

[32] The official technical term for autosensing is *auto-negotiation*, as defined by the IEEE.
[33] Bandwidth autosensing is more frequently accomplished at a connectivity device such as a hub or switch, rather than at the NIC itself. You'll learn about hubs and switches in chapter 4.

through a software program that runs on a client computer and which communicates with the NIC using a protocol known as simple network management protocol (SNMP). These cards and their associated management software program allow the network administrator or support staff to collect many different types of statistics such as the "health" or functional status of the card and the amount and types of information passing through the NIC. They're more expensive than network cards that don't have this feature, however, they're frequently cost-justified when used in LAN servers, through which much of a LAN's data exchange is conducted.

Wake-on-LAN is a recent feature built into many network interface cards that allows the network administrator to configure a network card so that it will turn on a computer's power. This is extremely helpful if computer support staff are deploying updates or additional programs from a central location on the LAN to a large number of client computers all across the local area network. If a computer is turned off, it can't receive the update. With **wake-on-LAN,** a signal on the network cabling instructs the NIC to "wake up" the computer so that a program can be run. By doing this, support staff don't have to physically access each computer on the network to turn on its power.

Other types of features that you can find with high-performance network interface cards include multiple ports for connecting multiple cables between the NIC and a device such as a LAN switch. With these types of network cards, a single data path that is typical for a standard NIC is multiplied by the number of ports. This speeds up data flow to the LAN as a whole. You'd be more likely to use this type of network card in a server than in a workstation so that the central point of data access can provide its data much more quickly to the LAN.

Network Interface Card Vendors

In Table 2.2 you'll find an extensive list of network interface card manufacturers. Many of today's manufacturers focus on the various configurations of Ethernet NICs because of the vast deployment and market acceptance of this technology. However, you'll find other vendors that offer a broader list of technologies including Token Ring and FDDI.

TABLE 2.2
Common Network Interface Cards from Various Vendors

Card Name	Manufacturer	Data Rate/Media Type/Functions
3c509b	3Com	10 Mbps Ethernet over UTP, no special functions
3cSOHO100B-TX	3Com	10/100 Mbps Ethernet over UTP, designed for small home offices, autosenses 10 or 100 Mbps LAN speeds
3c996B-T	3Com	Gigabit Ethernet over UTP, remote management, processor offloads, autosenses 10, 100, or 1,000 Mbps over cat 5 or cat 5e UTP
3c996-SX	3Com	Gigabit Ethernet over fiber, remote management, processor offloads
LNEPCI	Linksys	10 Mbps Ethernet, UTP and coaxial connectors, no management or high-end features
LNE100TX	Linksys	10 or 100 Mbps Ethernet, autosense, full-duplex capability, wake-on-LAN
WPC54G	Linksys	54 Mbps wireless, built-in security, designed for laptop use
Smart MK4 PCI	Madge	4, 16, or 100 Mbps Token Ring, autosense at 4 or 16 Mbps, full-duplex capability at 100 Mbps, wake-on-LAN, management functions
Pro/100 M	Intel	10 or 100 Mbps Ethernet, autosense, full-duplex, wake-on-LAN, management functions
Pro/10GbE LR	Intel	10 Gbps Ethernet for servers, single-mode fiber, management functions, full-duplex

Some of the major manufacturers that offer network interface cards as part of their networking solutions portfolio include 3Com, Intel, IBM, Compaq, Madge Networks, and SysKonnect.

Chapter Summary

- **Servers, LAN services, and clients.** Servers are the computers that are connected to the LAN and that have specialized NOS software installed and configured to provide shared LAN services to users and devices on a local area network. LAN services are the software components of a NOS that provide users with access to shared resources on a LAN. LAN services allow users to perform functions such as storing and retrieving files from a server, gain access to shared printers, and run shared network applications. Clients are the LAN computers that have local operating systems installed along with special software known as NOS client software. The NOS client software provides the local OS with the additional functionality that is required to connect to the LAN services provided by a server's NOS software and the physical resources of the LAN. With the combination of all three—servers, LAN services, and clients—organizations can share and access information and be more productive in the sharing of resources.

- **Mainframe and terminal LAN configuration.** Mainframes and terminals comprise one type of LAN configuration. Mainframes are the computers known as hosts that perform centralized computing functions such as running applications and processing data for an entire organization. The terminal is a client of sorts. It's an input device that transfers user input from the terminal to the mainframe. Unlike modern personal computers, however, terminals of old did not run applications or process data. Those functions were reserved for the mainframe. The business advantage of mainframes in the 1960s and 1970s, and even in some applications today is the centralized processing of organizational information.

- **Peer-to-peer, client-dominant, client/server, and distributed processing LAN configurations.** In a peer-to-peer LAN, each computer acts as both a client and a server. When a computer requests a service, it's acting as a client. When a computer provides services, it's acting as a server. This configuration might be advantageous for smaller organizations and at-home offices that don't require the LAN services of a dedicated server. With client-dominant LANs, most of the application processing and data manipulation is performed at the client, and the server stores files. These, too, are advantageous for smaller organizations or corporate departments that utilize local OS applications but require centralized storage of data files. In a client/server LAN, some of the application processing and data manipulation are reserved for the server while other processing takes place on the client. This configuration is common for applications that require multiple user access and data input. And a distributed-processing LAN separates the data access and storage components of an application from the data and application processing components. Organizations use this model to deploy large applications that require distributed access to various parts of an application and where the requirements for data access and storage are distributed across numerous locations.

- **Connecting clients and servers to a LAN.** To connect a client to a LAN requires a computer with a local OS installed, the NOS client software installed and configured, configuration of client parameters such as TCP/IP, a network interface card, and some type of communications medium. Connecting a server to a LAN requires a computer with a NOS installed and numerous parameters configured, such as TCP/IP settings and LAN services settings, and adding user accounts so that users can log in and connect to LAN services. The server requires a network interface card and some type of medium for connectivity with client devices on the LAN.

- **Coaxial cable, twisted-pair cabling, and fiber-optic cabling.** Coaxial cable was used in early LAN implementations as the medium of choice. Its structure consists of two conductors: one to carry the data transmissions and the other to act as a ground and shielding. Coax supported data transmission rates up to 10 Mbps and was relatively easy to install. Its application in LANs has disappeared because other media types provide greater bandwidths. Twisted-pair cabling is commonly used in LAN implementations because it is relatively inexpensive to install, configure, and maintain. The basic structure of twisted-pair cabling consists of several two-wire pairs of twisted copper wire enclosed in a protective synthetic jacket. Fiber-optic cabling supports higher data rates than either coax or twisted pair and is the medium of choice for connecting LAN devices that are significantly distant from one another. Fiber-optic cabling is composed of small glass fibers running through a protective jacket. Fiber-optic cabling is implemented where high data transmission rates and long distances are required and wherever there is an EMI or a significant chance of EMI.

- **Wireless media.** Wireless media in LANs is very common today. Choices include radio frequency (RF) wireless, infrared, or microwave. RF is the most common implementation of wireless in LANs and has the advantage of relatively simple implementation and configuration. RF wireless also integrates well with wired networks, utilizing access point devices to interface between wireless devices and wired LANs. Infrared is another wireless technology, but it's primarily used for transmissions between individual computers or in devices such as wireless mice and wireless keyboards. Microwave wireless is used for transmitting data between buildings that house separate network segments that cannot be connected with alternative methods. Its components include antennas at each location to send and receive the wireless signals.

- **How network interface cards work.** Network interface cards translate data from your computer to a format that is acceptable to the transmission medium of the LAN and vice versa. NICs build frames, which are manageable data chunks that the LAN medium can accommodate. NICs function at the data link layer of the OSI model, and their installation in a computer provides the computer with a unique data link layer address known as a MAC address. Utilization of the MAC address allows each device on a LAN to properly address information to other devices as well as identify information intended for itself.

- **Types of NICs.** Types of NICs include Ethernet, Token Ring, FDDI, and ATM. Ethernet NICs are used in workstations and servers on Ethernet LANs and can support data transmission rates of 10 Mbps, 100 Mbps, or 1,000 Mbps. They're relatively inexpensive and easy to configure. Some are even self-configuring. Token Ring NICs are used in Token Ring LANs and are available in 4 Mbps, 16 Mbps, and 100 Mbps configurations. FDDI NICs are generally reserved for connecting servers to high-speed campus networks, and their data rate is standardized at 100 Mbps. ATM NICs are generally used in applications similar to FDDI NICs and are available in a variety of data rates. In all cases, NICs provide the data translation between the computer or communicating device and the LAN medium, and vice versa.

- **NIC drivers.** NIC drivers are the software that provides the necessary instructions for devices to communicate and function together. That is, NIC drivers interface between NOS software and the NIC hardware or between the local OS software and the NIC hardware.

- **Half-duplex and full-duplex NICs.** Half-duplex NICs can send and receive data to a LAN but can only do one or the other function at a time. Full-duplex NICs can send and receive simultaneously. Half-duplex NICs are commonly installed in workstations because they're cheaper than full-duplex NICs, and, in general, workstations don't have the data transmission requirements that servers do. Full-duplex NICs are commonly installed in servers so that data can be transmitted faster between the servers and the

LAN. Full-duplex NICs also have the advantage of being able to simultaneously send to one device on a LAN while receiving from a different device on the LAN.

- **Autosensing and high-performance NICs.** Autosensing NICs configure themselves automatically depending on the conditions they sense on the LAN. The business advantage to this is it reduces the amount of time that network administrators must spend configuring NICs. High-performance NICs boost computer performance because these NICs off-load CPU-intensive functions from the computer. They also have management capability built in to provide network administrators with statistics about the network and the "health" of a particular NIC. Other features such as wake-on-LAN provide network administrators with a productivity tool that can turn on a computer that has been turned off so that diagnostics can be run or software can be installed from across the network.

- **Summarize a list of NIC vendors.** There are numerous NIC vendors in the network equipment marketplace. Some of the popular NIC vendors include Intel, 3Com, Linksys/Cisco, Madge, and others. Different vendors supply different types of cards, while most focus on Ethernet because of its broad market acceptance. Each vendor also provides its own set of functionality such as manageability and performance. In addition, each vendor supplies its customers with the appropriate driver software so that their NICs can be properly installed and configured.

Key Terms

ATM NIC, *70*	Graded-index fiber, *62*	RJ-45 connector, *59*
Autosensing NIC, *72*	Half-duplex NIC, *71*	Server, *44*
BNC connector, *57*	Infrared wireless, *64*	Shielded twisted pair
Category 5 UTP, *59*	LAN services, *44*	(STP), *59*
Category 5e UTP, *59*	Local area network	Signal attenuation, *62*
Category 6 UTP, *59*	(LAN), *40*	Single-mode fiber
Centralized processing, *49*	Mainframe, *49*	(SMF), *62*
Client, *45*	Media, *55*	Sneaker net, *52*
Client/server LAN, *52*	Micron, *61*	Terminal, *49*
Client-dominant LAN, *51*	Microwave wireless, *65*	Terrestrial microwave, *65*
Coaxial cable, *55*	Multimode fiber, *62*	Thicknet, *56*
Dispersion shifted fiber	Nanometer, *62*	Thinnet, *57*
(DSF), *63*	Network interface	Token Ring NIC, *70*
Distributed processing	card (NIC), *66*	Transceiver, *56*
(LAN), *53*	Network operating system	Unshielded twisted pair
EMI, *58*	(NOS), *44*	(UTP), *58*
Ethernet NIC, *69*	NIC drivers, *71*	UTP connector, *59*
FDDI NIC, *70*	Optical dispersion, *62*	Wake-on-LAN, *73*
Fiber-optic media, *61*	PC card, *66*	Wireless media, *64*
Frame, *66*	Peer-to-peer LAN, *50*	
Full-duplex NIC, *71*	Radio frequency (RF), *64*	

Questions

1. What are some of the business reasons behind mainframe computing being replaced by local area network computing?

2. What mainframelike architectures exist in today's local area networks?

3. In a client-dominant local area network, where does most of the application processing take place? Where is the data stored?

4. What were the business reasons behind the development of client-dominant local area networks?

5. What technology and cost-of-use issues are associated with a client-dominant local area network when the network grows large and users are storing and retrieving vast amounts of data from a centralized server to run on their local applications?

6. What advantages does a client/server local area network provide over a client-dominant local area network?

7. In terms of local area networks, what is a distributed processing environment? What business advantages can distributed processing bring to an organization?

8. What is a local area network client? How does it differ from the local operating system?

9. What benefit can be derived from using a browser-based client to connect to a local area network?

10. What is the purpose of local area network services? What are some services that you might commonly use in a local area network?

11. What are some of the business features that business owners look for when specifying media types for local area networks?

12. Describe the physical attributes of coaxial cable. Why do you suppose businesses chose coax cable for local area network installations?

13. Why did businesses choose to go with thin Ethernet cabling around the mid-1980s instead of thick Ethernet cabling? Were there any trade-offs when choosing thinnet instead of thicknet?

14. What are the physical characteristics of twisted-pair media? What attribute of this media type decreases the potential for EMI?

15. Why is twisted-pair media a popular cabling choice for local area networks?

16. What is the significance of the category ranking of unshielded twisted pair? What categories exist? Which should a business implement?

17. When might you choose to install fiber-optic cabling instead of unshielded twisted pair? What are the technical and business advantages of using fiber-optic cabling?

18. What are the technical differences between multimode fiber and single-mode fiber? Is one type better than the other?

19. When might a business choose to implement a wireless local area network? What type of wireless might you choose to implement for a local area network that was confined to one or two rooms in a building? How about for two buildings located close enough together to see either building from the top floor? How about for remote office locations located in separate cities? Why?

20. What is the technical purpose of a network interface card? What features are important from a business perspective?

Research Activities

1. Create a list of the functions performed by the local area network at your school or workplace. Does your LAN follow a client-dominant model or a client/server model? What attributes make it that way?

2. Using the search tools available to you, find two mainframe manufacturers and summarize their technical and marketing information regarding the intended purpose of their equipment. What are some of the intended markets into which modern mainframes are installed? What advantages do these computers provide to the businesses that buy them? Are modern mainframes compatible with modern LAN operating systems? Provide examples.

3. Access the Novell Web site (www.novell.com) and locate information about the company's client software. Identify and summarize the technical and business features of Novell's client software. In addition to its regular client software, how is Novell leveraging browser-based client features? How does Novell's NOS client software differ from Microsoft's NOS client software?

4. Discover the types of network media that are currently implemented in the local area network at your school or workplace. Briefly describe why these types of media were selected from both a technical and business viewpoint. Did your school or workplace ever use thicknet or thinnet? Provide a brief justification discussion for replacing thicknet and thinnet with one of the technologies that is installed at your school or workplace.

5. Using the various search tools available to you, provide a detailed list of technical specifications and intended uses of category 4, category 5, category 5e, and category 6 unshielded twisted-pair cabling. Is the local area network at your school or workplace using any of these UTP standards? What were the technical and business reasons for implementation versus another category level?

6. Using the search tools available to you, locate and list three manufacturers of fiber-optic cabling for local area networks. How expensive are the various types of fiber cabling that are used in local area networks?

7. Identify the types of network interface card technologies that are implemented at your school or workplace. Identify and describe the technological and business reasons for choosing these technologies.

8. Using the 3Com Web site, locate the higher speed NICs listed in Table 2.1. Specifically, access the product specifications pages and identify the connector type, operating distances, cabling grade, IEEE compliance, and drivers. Does any of this information correspond with the concepts you discovered in this chapter? (*Hint:* If you have difficulty navigating the 3Com site, try a Google search that specifies "network cards from 3Com," without the quotes, and then access the links.)

9. Repeat research activity 8 for Intel's high-end cards.

HANDS-ON ACTIVITIES

All hands-on activities require access to a computer lab that provides sufficient computers, hardware, media types, and software to perform these activities.

1. Within your lab environment, identify the server computers and workstation computers. What physical characteristics distinguish the servers in your lab from the workstations? What local operating systems are installed or are available for installation on the workstations? What server operating systems are installed or available for installation? If your lab has a LAN already configured, what is required for you to gain access to the LAN? Do you have printing and centralized data storage available to you? How would you classify the login, printing, and file storage functions?

2. If your lab has an active LAN already implemented, identify the components that facilitate data communications across the LAN. What is involved in connecting workstations and servers to the LAN?

3. Within your lab environment, identify the category of twisted-pair cabling that connects your workstations to the LAN. What types of connectors are used to terminate the ends of the cable segments?

4. If your lab uses wireless devices for data transmission, identify whether these devices are using infrared or radio frequency wireless.

5. Identify the types of NICs that you're using in your lab. Do the workstations have a different type of NIC than the server? If so, what are the differences? Are any of the servers or workstations using a full-duplex NIC? If you have access to a NIC with management capability, what kinds of management functions does it provide? How might you use this information? How about autosensing NICs—does your lab have any of these? What data communications characteristics do they provide and how are these characteristics identified? Can you find any other autosensing devices on your laboratory LAN?

Mini Case Study

LAKESIDE METAL STAMPINGS—PART 1

Lakeside Metal Stampings is a job shop that produces metal stampings for several local industrial giants, and they provide custom welding, metal fabrication, and design services for numerous business customers within a limited geographic region. Recently the owner has been considering a local area network so that he can have instantaneous access to information about the jobs in production as well as revenue and cost information and detailed financial reporting. In addition, the shop engineer has asked if he and his lead technical assistant can buy two computers and link them together so that they can share files back and forth for the jobs that they're working on now as well as jobs they'll be working on in the future. Based on the information provided here, list the business issues that support the owner's decision to invest in a local area network. If you were the consultant hired to implement a LAN for Lakeside Metal Stampings, how would you describe the advantages of a LAN to the owner? What LAN configuration would you recommend to them and why? If their shop has a substantial amount of electromagnetic interference generated by numerous motors and machines, what media types would you recommend and why? What kinds of factors would justify a wireless segment in this LAN? What kinds of network cards would you recommend for connecting workstations and servers to the LAN? Why? Based on what you know so far about local area networks, what configuration parameters will you need to go through in connecting the servers and workstations to the LAN?

CHAPTER
Three

Chapter Overview and Objectives

Local area network topologies and architectures drive the ways businesses design and implement their data communications infrastructures. The topologies that businesses choose represent not only the way in which data flows across a local area network but also the physical layout of the LAN. Architectures are the blueprints that define the way in which data access the network media and the structure of the data frames that are transported across a given medium. The architectures that businesses choose are functions of the business requirements such as types of data and data transmission rates. In this chapter, we're going to examine the LAN topologies and architectures that are common in modern organizations, and more specifically, by the end of this chapter you will be able to

- Define the term *LAN topology* and identify bus, star, ring, and wireless topologies.

- Describe the differences between physical topologies and logical topologies and relate these differences to bus, star, ring, and wireless topologies.

- Define the term *LAN architecture.*

- Describe the Ethernet LAN architecture, and identify common Ethernet standards.

- Describe the Ethernet access method.

- Discuss technical and business considerations of Ethernet.

- Describe the Token Ring LAN architecture, and identify common Token Ring standards.

- Describe the Token Ring access method.

- Discuss technical and business considerations of Token Ring.

- Describe the wireless LAN architecture.

- Provide a brief synopsis of wireless LAN and wireless PAN technologies and their histories.

- Identify and describe common standards and access methods for IEEE 802.11, Bluetooth, HiperLAN2, and HomeRF.

- Discuss technical and business considerations of wireless architectures.

- Identify and describe FDDI and ATM standards, access methods, and technical and business considerations.

Local Area Networks: Topologies and Architectures

LAN TOPOLOGIES

LAN topology
the map or layout of a local area network

logical topology
defines the conceptual network layout, which you can regard as the way that data travels or flows across the network

physical topology
defines the actual structure or configuration that you can see or touch. It's the configuration of cabling, computers, printers, and other devices on the network

If you were to become involved in a local area network design project, one of the key elements you would define is the **LAN topology**, or the basic map or layout of the local area network. A LAN topology can also be considered the way in which devices interconnect across the LAN.

In your LAN design, you would also identify one or more of four common topology types: bus, star, ring, and wireless.[1] When defining a topology for a network project, you'll also need to consider both the logical topology as well as the physical topology. The **logical topology** defines the conceptual network layout, which you can think about as the way that data travels or flows across the network. **Physical topology** defines the actual structure or configuration that you can see or touch, such as the configuration of cables, computers, printers, and other devices on the network. In some cases, the physical topology may differ from the logical topology, as you'll see.

Physical and Logical Topologies

Bus

A *bus topology* is comprised of a shared network medium, such as coaxial cable, to which various network devices such as printers, workstations, and servers are attached, and every connected device receives every data transmission on the network.

One of the oldest mediums used to implement a bus topology is coaxial cable. A bus topology that is implemented with coax cable is both a physical bus, as you can see in Figure 3.1, and a logical bus because of the way the data flows across it. In Figure 3.1 network devices can be attached to a single coaxial cable that acts as the "bus" for the delivery of data transmissions. Every device that is connected to the coaxial cable can send and receive data. Any data transmission that is sent is, in turn, received by every device attached to the cable. Coaxial bus topologies were very popular in the early days of local area networks, because it was easy to install and relatively inexpensive compared to other mediums such as fiber-optic cabling. Coax had one big drawback, however. A break, sharp bend, or kink anywhere in the coaxial cable would crash the network; data simply couldn't transmit across a broken bus.

Although coaxial bus topologies are specified in the original IEEE 802.3 standard, coaxial bus topologies are no longer implemented in modern LANs primarily because there are other topologies that significantly reduce the effects of a broken or damaged cable and because other technologies have been developed to provide significantly greater data transmission rates. You'll read about these improved topologies in the following sections.

Star

A *star topology* is comprised of network devices, data transmission media, and a centralized device that provides connectivity among all attached devices. In Figure 3.2 you can see how the network devices and transmission media emanate from a central device, such as a hub or switch creating the physical appearance of a star.[2]

One of the simplest star topologies can be assembled from a hub, unshielded twisted-pair cabling, and network devices such as workstations, servers, and printers. Many devices can be added to the network simply by connecting another network device to a patch cable and

---

[1] In this chapter you'll see wireless discussed as both a topology and an architecture. It's a topology from an implementation viewpoint and an architecture from a requirements standpoint. You'll examine architecture later on in this chapter.

[2] You'll learn about hubs, switches, and other connectivity hardware in chapter 4.

FIGURE 3.1

Simple Bus Topology
Logical and physical
bus implemented with
coaxial cable.

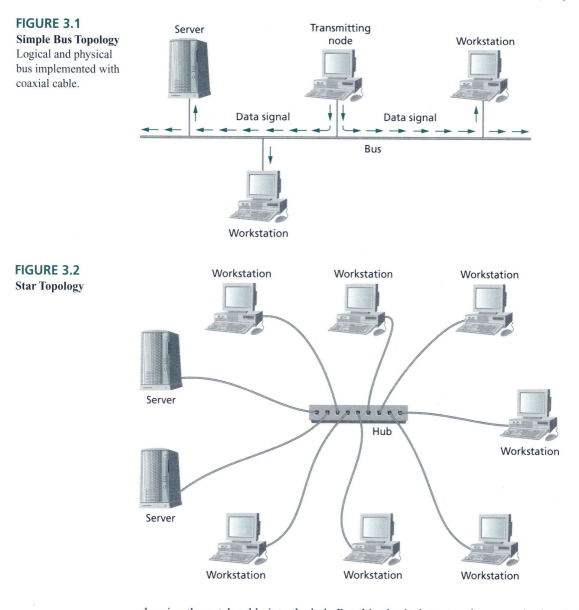

FIGURE 3.2

Star Topology

plugging the patch cable into the hub. But this physical star topology can also be a logical bus or a logical star in terms of the way the data flows. When a computer sends its data within a **physical star/logical bus topology**, all other computing devices that are connected to the hub immediately hear the data; that is, the topology is also a logical bus—the data travels in all directions across the LAN, and all devices hear all the data that flows across the LAN. Figure 3.3 provides a simple example of a physical star/logical bus LAN design.

The physical star topology/logical bus topology is specified in the IEEE 802.3 standard for use in Ethernet transmission architectures as a means of simplifying device connectivity to a LAN.[3] With the physical star/logical bus topology, network devices interconnect through cabling and a hub. The hub acts as an electronic grid through which all data transmissions travel, and all devices that are connected to the hub hear all data transmissions on the network. As you saw in Figure 3.3, the physical structure looks like a star, but the way

*physical star/logical
bus topology*
a LAN topology with
the physical
configuration of a star,
but the data flows in all
directions across the
LAN as if the topology
were a bus

---

[3] You'll learn about LAN architectures later on in this chapter.

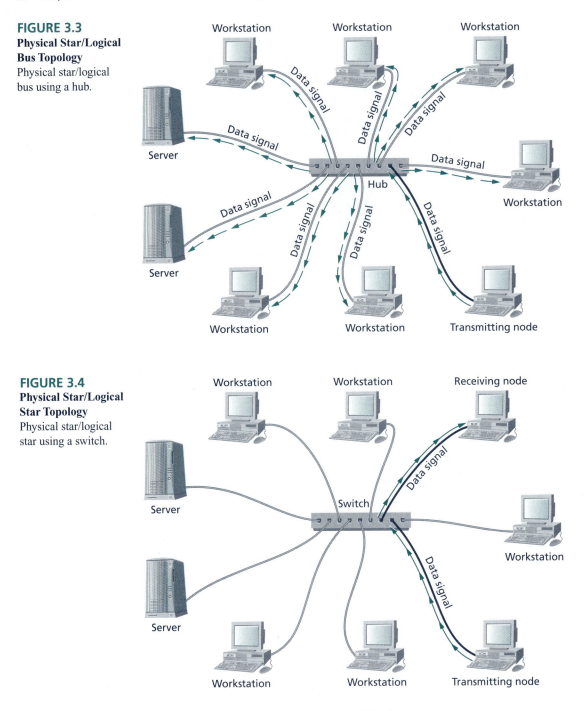

FIGURE 3.3
Physical Star/Logical Bus Topology
Physical star/logical bus using a hub.

FIGURE 3.4
Physical Star/Logical Star Topology
Physical star/logical star using a switch.

physical star/logical star topology
a star topology that has the physical configuration of a star, but the flow of data emanates only to intended recipients

in which the data flows is just like the bus topology you read about when considering coaxial buses.

Another type of star topology is the **physical star/logical star topology**. When a computer sends its data within a physical star/logical star topology, data flows only to the intended recipients; that is, the topology is also a logical star—the flow of data emanates only to intended recipients. This topology is the foundation of Ethernet LANs, whose computing devices are interconnected through a switch rather than a hub, as you can see in Figure 3.4.

With the physical star/logical star topology, network devices interconnect through cabling and a switch. When a computing device sends data, the switch filters the data flow to only those computing devices that are the intended recipients. That is, all devices that are connected to the switch do not hear all data transmissions on the LAN, as was the case with the physical bus/logical bus and physical star/logical bus topologies. As you can see in Figure 3.4, the physical structure looks like a star, but the way in which the data flows through the switch makes this configuration a logical star as well as a physical star.[4]

One major advantage to using any physical star topology is that device connectivity to the LAN can be achieved through a centralized device. It is this advantage that also provides a weakness to star topologies; if the centralized connectivity device such as a hub or switch fails, data transmission across the network will cease. At the same time, if any single cable segment fails in a star topology, the network continues to function; only the device that is connected by that cable segment will be unable to access the network. In addition, a physical star implementation requires cable to be run to each computing device on the LAN, resulting in significant amounts of cable being used to implement a star topology.

Ring

In a **ring topology**, all network devices are connected in a closed loop, or ring, and the data flows from device to device, in a unidirectional fashion, around the ring as illustrated in Figure 3.5.

Although the logical topology is a ring, the physical topology of ring networks can be either star or ring. With a **physical star/logical ring topology**, computing devices connect to a central hub.[5] The hub's ports connect to one another so that the data flows sequentially from port to port to port through the hub and around the ring. This is common in Token Ring networks and is represented in Figure 3.6.

With a **physical ring/logical ring topology**, there's no hub that acts as a central connectivity point. Instead, each computing device is connected to each adjacent device to form a physical ring, and the data flows sequentially from device to device. This was a

ring topology
a topology in which all network devices are connected in a closed loop, or ring, and the data flows from device to device, in a unidirectional fashion, around the ring

physical star/logical ring topology
a topology in which computing devices connect to a central hub, but the data flows sequentially from port to port to port through the hub and around the ring

FIGURE 3.5
Ring Topology

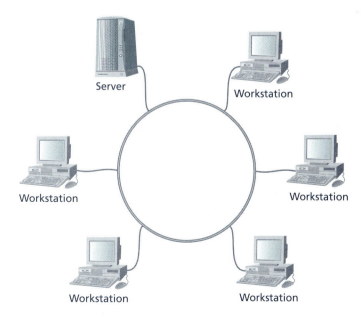

---

[4] You'll examine the details of Ethernet switching in chapter 4.
[5] The physical star/logical ring topology is sometimes referred to as a *star-wired ring topology.*

FIGURE 3.6

Physical Star/Logical Ring Topology

Closed loop of a Token Ring LAN. If you stretched out the closed loop, it would look like a ring.

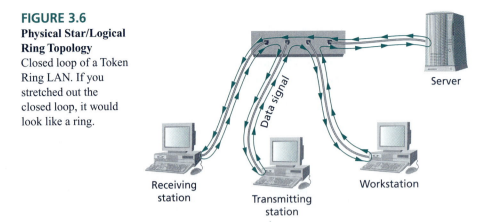

Server

Receiving station

Transmitting station

Workstation

Data signal

---

physical ring/logical ring topology
a topology in which each computing device is connected to each adjacent device to form a physical ring, and the data flows sequentially from device to device

common configuration in early Token Ring networks and can still be found in legacy fiber distributed data interface (FDDI) networks.[6]

Physical star/logical ring topologies have a distinct advantage over physical ring/logical ring configurations. With a physical star/logical ring topology, a damaged link between the hub and the computing device is automatically bypassed at the hub. That is, any port in the hub that detects a damaged connection is automatically bypassed so that the ring continues to function. In this scenario, the only computing device that is unavailable is the one with the damaged connection. At the same time, if the hub fails in a physical star/logical ring topology, the entire ring is unavailable for data transmissions.

Physical ring/logical ring topologies, on the other hand, do not share the potential single point of failure that is inherent in the central hub design of the physical star/logical ring topology. Because the physical ring does not utilize a hub, there is no single point of failure. At the same time, if there is a break in any of the cable segments between computing devices, the entire ring can crash. To circumvent a ring failure, physical ring/logical ring designs can include a redundant ring that provides fail-over protection if the first ring is damaged or broken. This dual-ring topology is possible with Token Ring as part of the IEE 802.5c standard, and when FDDI was in its heyday it was commonly configured with dual rings.

Wireless

wireless topology
a wireless topology uses radio frequencies instead of cables as the transmission media and wireless access points instead of hubs for connecting devices to the network

A **wireless topology** uses radio frequencies instead of cables as the transmission media and wireless access points instead of hubs for connecting devices to the network. Geographic areas are divided into cells, with each cell containing an access point, as illustrated in Figure 3.7.

Although the physical topology of a wireless LAN can be compared to a physical star and the data flow is similar to a logical bus, wireless topologies are different than bus topologies. That is, wireless devices that are part of a wireless LAN cannot always hear each other. In a wireless topology, every device can hear the access point but does not necessarily hear the transmissions from other wireless devices.

Advantages to using a wireless topology are numerous. One advantage is they're easy to install. You'll need wireless hardware, but you won't have to install any cables unless you're connecting to the wired part of your network. You don't have to drill holes in walls to run cabling or pull cabling through a ceiling to connect devices; network devices simply need to be located within range of an access point, which is generally within a few hundred feet.

---

[6] When FDDI networks are implemented with a physical ring/logical ring topology, two rings are generally implemented to form a dual-ring physical topology. The second ring provides redundancy in case the first ring is damaged. You'll learn more about FDDI later in this chapter.

FIGURE 3.7
Wireless Topology

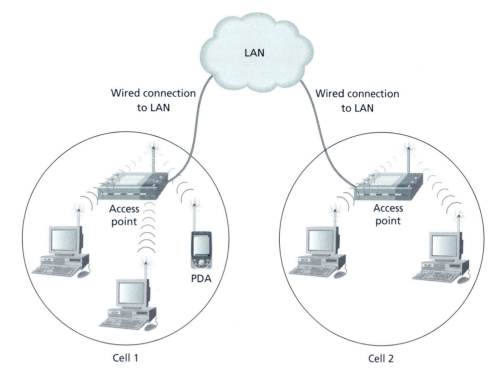

Network devices can move from one cell to another, with the only constraint being that the device must be able to receive a transmission signal from the new access point. This provides a huge mobility benefit for users who must move between rooms or offices while maintaining a network connection.

One drawback with wireless topology, however, is distance. Network devices must be located within a few hundred feet of the access point in order to receive data transmissions. Another disadvantage is security. Any wireless network device that is placed within close enough proximity to an access point can receive transmissions. In addition, if an unwanted recipient is intercepting your wireless transmissions, your network could be at risk.

See Table 3.1 for a comparison of topology types.

TABLE 3.1
Topology Comparison

Topology Type	Where Commonly Used	Business Considerations
Physical bus/logical bus	10Base5 and 10Base2 Ethernet LANs	Old technology that is no longer implemented. Provided 10 Mbps bandwidth in its day
Physical star/logical bus	10/100Base-T Ethernet LANs	Uses UTP cabling and hubs to link computers in 10Base-T or 100Base-T LANs
Physical star/logical star	10/100Base-T switched Ethernet LANs	Uses UTP cabling and Ethernet switches to link computers
Physical star/logical ring	Token Ring LANs and FDDI backbones	Uses STP or UTP cabling to link Token Ring devices through a MSAU. Uses fiber-optic or UTP cabling to link FDDI backbones through an FDDI hub
Physical ring/logical ring	Token Ring LANs and FDDI backbones	Uses STP or UTP cabling to link Token Ring devices in a ring. Uses fiber-optic or UTP cabling to link FDDI devices in either a single or dual ring

The history of Ethernet[7] and its use in data communications and local area networks is relatively new, dating back to the early 1970s with work done by a young **Bob Metcalfe**[8] at the **Palo Alto Research Center,** the scientific research arm of **Xerox Corporation** that is commonly referred to as PARC. In 1972, the two-year-old PARC was in the midst of developing a minicomputer for use in office automation, a business strategy Xerox had identified toward the end of the 1960s, and they needed someone to develop a communication system that would link Xerox's new "personal" computers into a network. Bob Metcalfe was that someone.

In 1972, Bob Metcalfe was finishing his Ph.D. when Xerox PARC hired him to undertake the development of their minicomputer communication system, a system that would become the earliest form of Ethernet. At the same time, Metcalfe maintained his previous ties to MIT, where he had worked on **ARPA**-funded projects while completing his Ph.D. work at Harvard. Through these previous ties and the ARPA projects at MIT, Metcalfe found himself traveling around the United States assisting various ARPA sites with connectivity to the relatively new **ARPANET.** During one of these trips, he read a paper entitled **"The Aloha System,"** which described the network system that ARPA had funded at the University of Hawaii.[9] It was the content of this paper that gave Metcalfe the idea to develop the communications architecture that would become Ethernet.

At the heart of the Aloha System was a radio frequency transmission methodology that allowed multiple terminals on the various islands to communicate with a mainframe on the island of Oahu. Just as the mainland ARPANET used **Interface Message Processors (IMPs)** to send and receive packets, the **"Alohanet"** used a radio frequency device known as the Menehune to facilitate wireless packet-switched transmissions between terminals and the mainframe. With the mainland ARPANET, the IMPs were connected to phone lines and could be regulated so that packet transmissions would not interfere with other traffic on the line or with other data transmissions. However, with the wireless data transmissions taking place on Alohanet, there was no way to regulate access to the transmission medium; any terminal device could send whenever it had data to transmit without the benefit of knowing when another terminal might be sending. As a result, Alohanet data transmissions were prone to colliding with the data transmissions from other terminals on the same network. To circumvent the problem, the Aloha System had a built-in mechanism to automatically retransmit information in the event that data from two terminals collided. Sending terminals would receive an acknowledgement when a data transmission was successfully received at the destination, but if no acknowledgement was received, it meant that a data collision or transmission failure had occurred. When that happened the sending devices would wait for a random amount of time and then retransmit their signals with the calculated "hope" that the subsequent transmission would not collide with data from another terminal's retransmission.

The data transmission method that Alohanet used became the foundation of Ethernet. Bob Metcalfe reasoned that accessing the wireless medium or "ether" the way the Aloha System did could be translated to coaxial cable. And because coaxial cable had better electrical properties than telephone wire, adapting the Aloha System's method of data transmission to coaxial cable would provide higher data rates than any other system had been able to support over existing telephone lines. Putting it all together, Metcalfe developed a method for data transmissions to randomly access a

---

[7] For more detailed information on the history of data communications, read Appendix A, "A Brief History of Data Communications and Computer Networks."

[8] Bob Metcalfe went on to found 3Com, the successful manufacturer of network interface cards and other network connectivity hardware.

[9] "The Aloha System," American Federation of Information Processing Societies Conference Proceedings, Volume 37, Fall 1970. Published by Norman Abramson.

coaxial cable's "ether," so that if two of PARC's new Alto computers happened to access the "Ether Network" at the same time, each device would then wait a random amount of time before retransmitting its data. Metcalfe detailed his Ether Network design in a memo to Xerox brass in May 1973, and so began the evolution of the network architecture that we commonly know today as *Ethernet.*

This earliest version of an Ether Network was deployed throughout Xerox during the 1970s and was good for a data transmission rate of 3 Mbps. It was also implemented at Boeing, the White House, and in various academic environments around the United States. Then in 1980, the first Ethernet standard was proposed by Digital Equipment, Intel, and Xerox. It became known as the **DIX standard** and had two versions (DIX 1.0 and 2.0) before being merged with developing Ethernet standards at the IEEE. The 1982 merger of the DIX and IEEE standards became known as the **IEEE 802.3** Ethernet standard and was good for 10 Mbps over thick **coaxial cable** (thicknet). Later adaptations standardized 10 Mbps Ethernet over thin coax, **unshielded twisted pair (UTP),** and fiber-optic cabling. There was even a version of 10 Mbps Ethernet specified for use over cable TV coax systems, but this **broadband** Ethernet technology never enjoyed widespread use.

The IEEE 10BASE-T standard, which is 10 Mbps **baseband** Ethernet transmitted over UTP, was adopted in 1990. Now Ethernet could be implemented with all the benefits of a logical bus topology but with the added advantage of a physical star topology; one break in the cable didn't crash the entire network. In addition, the relative simplicity of UTP cable installation, which installed much like regular phone cabling, combined with its low cost, accelerated the demand for connectivity and distributed processing. And so came the explosive growth in local area networks during the 1990s.

The year 1995 saw the adoption of the IEEE 100BASE-T or **Fast Ethernet** standard, which defined 100 Mbps baseband Ethernet data transmission over UTP cabling. Now data could be transmitted at 10 times the rate of **10BASE-T** networks. In addition, since the data frames for both 10BASE-T and 100BASE-T were the same, 100BASE-T Ethernet was backward compatible with the older technology. Business managers could make network expansion decisions without having to scrap previous investments in Ethernet technology; the two standards could work together in the same network environment with relative ease.

Today we have **Gigabit Ethernet,** which can be deployed over fiber-optic cable or over UTP. It provides 100 times the data transmission capacity of the original IEEE 802.3 standard, and 10 times that of 100BASE-T. In addition, newer standards have defined **10 Gigabit Ethernet** for use in network backbones, and 40 Gigabit and 100 Gigabit versions will likely be available in the not-to-distant future.[10]

---

[10] You'll be introduced to backbones in chapter 4. For now, think of a network backbone as a high-speed network link that connects two or more LANs.

broadband
a transmission medium that has multiple channels, as opposed to **baseband,** a transmission method in which the entire medium is devoted to a single channel

baseband
a transmission method that devotes the entire bandwidth of a medium to a single channel

baseband
in reference to Ethernet data transmission refers to the medium carrying only one transmission channel

LAN ARCHITECTURES

LAN architecture
the way in which data accesses network media. It is the structure of the data frames that are placed on the network media.

You could make a case for including the topologies you've already looked at within LAN architectures. However, **LAN architectures** pertain more to the way in which data accesses network media and the structure of the data frames that are placed on the network media than the physical or logical layout of the network. For example, you could configure a star physical topology and it could be a logical bus or logical ring in terms of the way the data flows around the network. But the way in which the data accesses the media and the types of frames that are placed on the media could include any of several types of LAN architectures. In this section, you're going to look at LAN architectures.

Ethernet

Overview

Ethernet in its many forms and configurations is by far the most popular architecture for use in modern local area networks. It's reliable, easy to implement, and fairly cost effective. It enjoys wide industry and technical acceptance; if you implement an Ethernet network, you'll never lack for support or continued technical innovation. But why is Ethernet such a darling of local area networks? Where did it originate, and how does Ethernet facilitate data transmission between points A and B? What standards support its historical, current, and ongoing technical popularity? And what media types and topologies support Ethernet networks? As you read through the next few subsections and the Applied Historical Tidbit on Ethernet history, you're going to find out that Ethernet is more than 30 years old. Its success is based in part on its ability to allow multiple devices to share access to the network media as well as support for many different types of media, network topologies, and standards. Ethernet is defined across a vast array of standards that support multiple classifications of data transmission; the IEEE that you learned about in Chapter 1 formalized the original Ethernet standards and continues to issue new ones as the technology continues to advance and improve.

Standards

The various types of Ethernet are defined primarily by the 802.3x standards of the IEEE. In general, Ethernet is a widely implemented network data transmission architecture because it is a mature technology, and because it is relatively easy and cost-effective to install, configure, and maintain. And because it's a mature technology with a vast number of supporting standards, there are many hardware vendors that supply the connectivity devices that businesses need to design and build local area network and data communications infrastructures. In choosing an Ethernet technology for your local area network, you'll never lack a choice of connectivity devices or supporting technologies to move your data from point A to point B.

In chapter 1 you learned about the importance of standards, and that importance is just as significant with Ethernet technologies. Many standards have been developed for Ethernet

TABLE 3.2
IEEE 802.3 Ethernet Standards

Ethernet Standard	Media Type(s) Supported	Description
10BASE5	Thicknet or thick Ethernet	10 Mbps Ethernet over thicknet with a maximum cable segment length of 500 meters
10BASE2	Thinnet or thin Ethernet	10 Mbps Ethernet over thinnet with a maximum cable segment length of 185 meters[a]
10BASE-T	Categories 3-6 UTP	10 Mbps Ethernet over UTP cabling, usually cat5. Uses two of the twisted pairs
100BASE-TX	Categories 3-6 UTP	100 Mbps Ethernet over UTP cabling, usually cat5 or cat5e. Uses two of the twisted pairs
100BASE-FX	Fiber-optic cable	100 Mbps Ethernet over fiber-optic cable
100BASE-T4	Category 3 UTP	Obsolete. Was designed to use all four of the twisted pairs of cat3 UTP cabling
1000BASE-T	Category 5-6 UTP	1 Gbps over cat 5 or greater. Uses all four of the cabling's twisted pairs. Generally implemented on cat5e or greater
10GBase-LX4	SMF or MMF	10 Gbps over SMF or MMF

[a]The 2 in 10Base2 is a representation of 200 meters, which is 185 meters rounded up.

over the years, and many of them are still in use today. In Table 3.2, you'll see a list of the common IEEE 802.3*x* Ethernet standards along with their common names, data transmission rates, and the types of media that can be specified for a given standard. Most popular among them are 100BASE-T standards and Gigabit Ethernet implementations.

Access Method

carrier sense multiple access with collision detection (CSMA/CD) the way in which data accesses a network medium in Ethernet networks. CSMA/CD attempts to avoid data collisions by first sensing a neutral carrier signal on the network medium. When a collision does occur, the sending stations wait a random amount of time before attempting retransmission.

Ethernet as we know it today uses an access methodology known as **carrier sense multiple access with collision detection (CSMA/CD)**, a fancy name for the way in which data accesses a network medium in Ethernet networks. CSMA/CD is also very much like the data communications method utilized by Alohanet and the communications methodology developed by Bob Metcalfe for Xerox's first minicomputer network back in the 1970s.

The **"carrier sense"** portion of the CSMA/CD refers to the computer or other network device listening for or sensing a neutral electrical signal on the network media. If the signal indicates that no other devices are accessing the media at that moment, then the network media is ready to receive a transmission. The **"multiple access"** part of this method specifies that all network devices have equal access to the network media so that two or more devices can attempt access to the media at the same time. However, if two or more devices sense the neutral signal and place data on the network media simultaneously, the data bits collide, and the **"collision detection"** portion of CSMA/CD comes into play. With collision detection, the sending device that first detects the collision sends out a signal to all other devices on the network indicating that a collision has taken place, and the network interface cards in these network devices then wait a random amount of time before attempting to retransmit the data. If collisions persist, the process continues until the media is available for a successful retransmission.

The biggest advantage to this method is its ease of configuration and widespread standardization and implementation. All you need to do is purchase the appropriate network interface card for the computer that you're going to attach to the network, provide the appropriate configuration, and connect the device to the network.[11] Disadvantages include increased rates of collision as the number of computers and network devices on the network increases. Also, if you have a computer that is transmitting huge amounts of data, other computers will find it increasingly difficult to access the network media because they will more frequently sense a busy carrier; that is, the chances of detecting a neutral electrical signal on the network media will be diminished when one or more computers is transmitting large amounts of information.

Technical Considerations

autosensing the ability of a network connectivity device to automatically determine the speed or bandwidth of the network signal and self-configure to accommodate devices that are operating at different bandwidths

You'll have numerous options in designing and building an Ethernet network. If you have the option to build it from scratch, you'll very likely implement 100BASE-TX utilizing network interface cards and UTP cabling that support the 100BASE-TX standard. You'll also include **hubs,** switches, and routers that conform to this standard as well, although the connectivity hardware and NICs that you purchase will very likely be of the 10/100 autosensing variety that accommodate older devices running at 10 Mbps.

A parameter that you'll need to consider in your design is the number of meters that the network will encompass or span, as well as the maximum segment length. Because of the signaling time that is required to notify sending stations of a collision, Ethernet has distance limitations to ensure that the sending devices know that a collision has taken place.

---

[11]Configuration parameters can include applying updated NIC drivers, setting up NIC management functions, or applying layer 3 addressing such as TCP/IP or IPX. You'll learn about TCP/IP and IPX in chapter 4.

FIGURE 3.8
Network Segment and Span Lengths in a 100BASE-T Ethernet LAN

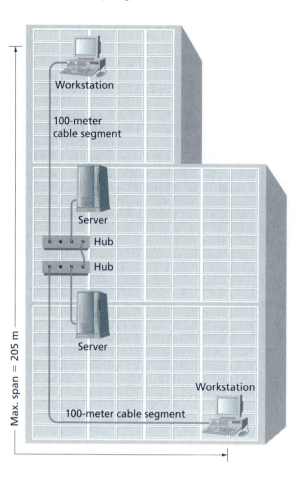

network segment
that part of a network on which all devices share the bandwidth and data traffic is broadcast to all devices that share the common bandwidth

Stretch that distance, and the affected computers would not know that a collision had taken place. For 100 Mbps Ethernet, the maximum length of a Category 5 UTP cable segment is 100 meters, while the network span is 205 meters.[12] What this means is the practical length for a Category 5 UTP cable is 100 meters between a LAN computer and a connectivity device such as a bridge, switch, or router. In real terms, that's something like a 30-story building or a factory floor that is a little longer than a football field. Likewise, the distance between any two computers on the LAN can be a maximum of 205 meters with Cat 5 UTP. An example is provided in Figure 3.8.

Business Considerations

network span or diameter
the longest distance along the cabling and through any intermediate hubs or repeaters between any two network end nodes such as clients or servers. Network diameter specifications are required to ensure that collisions can be detected and resolved.

The biggest benefit to implementing Ethernet is that it is a well-supported and scalable technology. Vendors continue to develop new products based on the IEEE 802.3x Ethernet standards. If you have an Ethernet network that is still utilizing 10BASE-T technology, you'll find numerous products that will allow you to connect 10BASE-T network to the newer and faster Ethernet technologies running at 100 Mbps or even 1,000 Mbps. It's advantageous to implement an Ethernet network because you do not necessarily have to replace older technology before incorporating new Ethernet technology. In addition, Ethernet is so widely implemented there is a plentiful supply of technical support; that is, there are many LAN technicians who are well-versed in Ethernet maintenance and support.

---

[12] Switched Ethernet eliminates the 205 meter span limit. You'll learn about switched Ethernet in chapter 4.

IBM is frequently referenced as the developer of Token Ring technology, and, in fact, much if not most of the Token Ring technology that came to market in the 1980s and throughout the 1990s and today is attributable to the research and marketing efforts of IBM.

However, the history of Token Ring dates back to the late 1960s and early 1970s with the research of **W. D. Farmer** and **E. E. Newhall** at the **Bell Telephone Laboratories,** and that of **David J. Farber** at the University of California, Irvine. In 1969, Farmer and Newhall were interested in transmitting bursty data traffic from sources such as credit card readers over existing telephone lines that were originally intended for more predictable voice traffic. To accomplish this task, they described a system of computers linked together that would sequentially transmit information around a closed loop or ring from machine to machine. If a machine in the ring didn't require transmission time, it passed control on to the next machine in the loop. These were the essential elements of Token Ring as this technology was later named.

Then in the early 1970s, David Farber, associate professor of information and computer sciences and of electrical engineering at the University of California, Irvine was running a National Science Foundation funded project known as the Distributed Computer System Research Project. This project ultimately delivered the **Distributed Computing System,** a computer network that pioneered ideas such as client/server processing and Token Ring technology. Both the work performed at the Bell Telephone Laboratories and at UC Irvine were instrumental in the initial development of Token Ring and are the direct forerunners to the IBM versions of Token Ring and published standards of the IEEE.

queuing theory
deals with problems
associated with waiting
for service or waiting
for a response or simply
waiting

By the late 1970s, much attention and research had been devoted to **queuing theory** as it applied to data flow through a computer and across transmission media, and IBM was interested in providing its customers with a method of connecting smaller networks of computers (LANs) to its mainframe networks. Because IBM's mainframe environments, especially those in automated factories and banking environments, required predictable delays in data traffic transmission, IBM poured money into a LAN transmission architecture that would provide deterministic data access and robust operation on a network connecting mainframes and LAN computers. The result was the development of Token Ring in the early 1980s and the standards as published by the IEEE beginning in 1984.

Token Ring

Overview

At one time, **Token Ring** technology and Token Ring networks provided a viable alternative to using Ethernet as a preferred LAN architecture. At the height of its popularity, Token Ring provided bandwidth of 16 Mbps as opposed to Ethernet's shared 10 Mbps bandwidth. What this meant to network users and technology and business managers alike was that an investment in Token Ring resulted in a substantially faster network. Because Ethernet utilized CSMA/CD, all users shared access to the network media. With shared access came collisions and retransmissions and less efficient and less reliable data transmissions.

Token Ring promised a substantial increase in performance with no collisions and more efficient, reliable, and faster data transmissions. With Token Ring access to the network bandwidth is deterministic; that is, the amount of time a device waits to gain access to the network bandwidth is predictable. In other words, only one user at a time would have access to the network. With deterministic access to the network media, there are no data collisions, data transmission is more efficient, and effective transmission rates on Token Ring networks were higher than (10 Mbps) Ethernet.

But Token Ring's bandwidth advantage disappeared almost overnight in the mid-1990s with the introduction of Fast Ethernet, which offered shared access to 100 Mbps of bandwidth. The transmission rate and cost advantage that Fast Ethernet provided over Token Ring initiated a steady decline in new Token Ring installations and maintenance of existing Token Ring networks. And with the introduction of switched Ethernet, Token Ring's continued decline was practically assured.[13] In today's LAN environments, the predominant player for new installations is Ethernet. Older Token Ring environments are still maintained, with IBM and Madge being the major suppliers of Token Ring NICs and connectivity devices, including 100 Mbps Token Ring components. However, even as support for existing Token Ring networks continues, recent articles have suggested that standards organizations will soon discontinue any further updates or support for Token Ring, leaving IBM as the only major player in the continuance of Token Ring technology.[14]

Standards

The IEEE specifications for Token Ring LANs originated out of the technologies developed by IBM in the 1970s and early 1980s and are generally defined under the **IEEE 802.5** set of standards. In the mid-1980s, the IEEE 802.5 standard defined Token Ring operation at 4 Mbps on a single ring. But by 1989, the 802.5 standard had been enhanced to include Token Ring operation across multiple rings connected by bridges and at an improved data transmission rate of 16 Mbps. In 1991, the dual-ring operation was defined so that Token Ring could operate with a redundant ring that could take over in the event of failure of the first ring. In 1997, the 802.5r standard defined **dedicated Token Ring (DTR),** which was really a full-duplex implementation of Token Ring that would allow the doubling of Token Ring data transmission rates between two computers over a point-to-point link.[15] Then in 1998, the 802.5t standard defined Token Ring operation at 100 Mbps. You can see a summary of the IEEE 802.5 standards in Table 3.3.

Access Method

Token Ring networks use a media access method known as **token passing.** In a token-passing network architecture, a special data frame called a **free token** circulates on the logical ring from computer to computer until a computer has data to send. When a computer has data to send, it takes possession of the token, modifies the token slightly, and places the data on the ring. After the data is successfully transmitted and the sending computer has received acknowledgement of a successful transmission, the token is set free on the ring for another computer to use. Because only the computer that possesses the token can access and place data on the ring, there are no collisions in a Token Ring network as there are in a network that uses the CSMA/CD access method.

TABLE 3.3 Token Ring Standards	
802.5-1998	Defines Token Ring access method and physical layer specifications at both 4 and 16 Mbps data transmission rates
802.5c	Defines Token Ring dual-ring operation
802.5r	Defines full-duplex Token Ring, also known as dedicated Token Ring (DTR)
802.5j	Defines the operation of Token Ring over fiber-optic media
802.5t	Defines 100 Mbps Token Ring
802.5v	Defines Gigabit Token Ring

---

[13] You'll learn about switched Ethernet in chapter 4.

[14] Even though IBM still supports Token Ring technology, in the majority of their product offerings you'll see Ethernet as the preferred transmission architecture.

[15] The point-to-point links defined by DTR implied token ring switching to establish point-to-point links.

FIGURE 3.9
Simple Token Ring Network

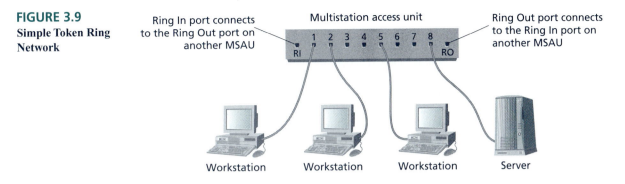

Ring In port connects to the Ring Out port on another MSAU

Multistation access unit

Ring Out port connects to the Ring In port on another MSAU

Workstation   Workstation   Workstation   Server

Technical Considerations

In the early days of Token Ring implementations, especially in smaller Token Ring networks, the connectivity device that was comparable to a hub in Ethernet was the ***multi station access unit (MSAU).*** In Figure 3.9, you can see a simplified Token Ring network. Although the MSAU acted as the center of the physical star topology, Token Ring architecture supported a logical ring topology. That is, the data flowed from computer to computer until the destination device accepted the data transmission. Later implementations of Token Ring utilized category 5 UTP, RJ-45 connectors, and hubs that looked very much like Ethernet hubs.

When a break occurred in a cable segment or when a network interface card was not functioning, Token Ring used a self-recovery mechanism known as **beaconing** to alert computers on the network that the ring was experiencing a failure. With beaconing, the problem area on the network could be identified, and the automatic reconfiguration process could attempt to bypass the malfunction so that the network could continue to transmit data.

Business Considerations

As you learned earlier in this section, the business advantages of Token Ring began to decline in the mid-1990s with the introduction of Fast Ethernet and switched Ethernet. Because Token Ring was capable of providing a maximum data transmission rate of only 16 Mbps, Fast Ethernet and Ethernet networks utilizing switching became the new network architectures of choice in the vast majority of network installations and upgrades. Even with the proposed introduction of 100 Mbps Token Ring in the late 1990s, Token Ring technology simply couldn't compete on a cost or performance basis with Fast Ethernet and the combination of switched Ethernet technologies.

Wireless

Overview

Wireless network technologies have made tremendous strides and have enjoyed substantial success in network implementations in recent years. In today's networking environments, it's not unusual for users to move from room to room with a laptop and expect on-the-fly connectivity without having to "plug in" a physical cable to connect to their client server networks. Building codes might impede or prohibit the installation of physical media such as UTP or fiber. In other cases, users might simply need to connect in a peer-to-peer connection to share data outside of the boundaries of their wired networks. In still other cases, devices such as personal digital assistants (PDAs) need to link up via wireless connection with laptops or servers. In any case, with the appropriate selection and configuration of wireless network technologies, users can gain access to their networks without wires.

Although wireless network technologies seldom constitute an entire network topology or architecture for a business, the incorporation of wireless technologies such as Bluetooth, Wi-Fi, HomeRF, and HiperLAN/2 in LAN environments has grown to the point where it would be remiss not to include a discussion of these technologies in a chapter on network topologies and architectures. Implementation of any of these technologies can provide the kinds of access that users might need to gain wireless access to their networks. While not all of these technologies conform to published IEEE standards, the most popular wireless network technologies are in general reliable, relatively easy to implement, and at the very least provide users with a convenience that is not possible with wired networks.

In this subsection, you're going to see that the wireless industry and the IEEE delineate wireless networks into **wireless personal area networks (WPANs)** and **wireless local area networks (WLANs)**. You're also going to take a look at the popular standards that support wireless data transmission in networked environments, examine the access methods they use, and learn about some of the technical and business considerations that you might have to watch out for if you need to implement and support wireless technologies.

WPAN and WLAN a wireless personal area network (WPAN) is technically distinguished from a wireless local area network (WLAN) by a specific wireless technology. The IEEE 802.11 standards define WLANs whereas the IEEE 802.15 (Bluetooth) standard and others such as HomeRF define WPANs.

History

Previously in this chapter you explored the history of the wireless Aloha network in the context of Ethernet's history.[16] Here, we're going to take a look at the development of more current technologies; namely those that fall under the **IEEE 802.11** series of standards, Bluetooth, HiperLAN/2, and HomeRF.

IEEE 802.11   The beginnings of **802.11 wireless** date to 1990 and the Wireless Local Area Networks Standards Working Group of the IEEE. The group was originally chartered with developing a global standard for WLANs, or wireless LANs, to operate in the unlicensed 2.4 GHz frequency spectrum.[17] 802.11 networks are sometimes called wireless Ethernet, and sometimes they're called Wi-Fi networks, short for wireless fidelity, depending on the implementation and who is doing the talking. Finally in 1997, the 802.11 Working Group released its first standard for wireless data transmission. It defined data transmission rates of 1 or 2 Mbps in the 2.4 GHz frequency range.

Moving data at 1 or 2 Mbps was good for wireless in 1997, but it was unacceptably slow for users who were used to 100 Mbps Ethernet or faster in their wired network connections. So in 1999, the IEEE issued **802.11a,** which defined transmission rates up to 54 Mbps in the 5 GHz frequency range; and **802.11b,** which defined transmission rates of either 5.5 Mbps or 11 Mbps in the 2.4 GHz range.

Then in June 2003, a subsequent 802.11 update known as **IEEE 802.11g** specified data transmission rates of up to 54 Mbps in the 2.4 GHz frequency range. Even before the final adoption of the standard, companies were offering products based on the **802.11g** standard.[18] The 802.11 standards are summarized in Table 3.4.

Bluetooth   **Bluetooth** is a WPAN technology that was originally conceived by Ericsson in 1994 as a short-range wireless transmission service that could interface between mobile phones and accessories. And because devices based on this technology would be limited in range, they would have low power requirements.

In 1998, IBM, Intel, Nokia, Toshiba, and Ericsson formed the Bluetooth Special Interest Group (SIG) to promote the use and development of Bluetooth technology, and in 2000, the first consumer product utilizing Bluetooth technology shipped.[19,20] It was a headset for

---

[16] For a broader-based history of wireless data transmission, read Appendix A, "A Brief History of Data Communications and Computer Networks."

[17] This is the same frequency range in which your microwave oven operates.

[18] 802.11b is frequently referred to in trade literature as Wireless-B, while 802.11g is referred to as Wireless-G.

[19] Motorola, Microsoft, Lucent, and 3Com have since joined the original five members of the Bluetooth SIG.

[20] The Bluetooth SIG works with the IEEE 802.15 working groups (WGs) and task groups (TGs) to develop the IEEE published standards and to solve any discrepancies between Bluetooth SIG's specifications and final IEEE standards.

In the 10th century, AD, **King Harald Blatand** successfully unified the two Scandinavian kingdoms of Denmark and Norway into a "network" of political and fiscal control. Since the Scandinavian region was relatively small, and since Ericsson is in the same geographic region, they adopted the name Bluetooth (*Blatand* translated) because it unifies very small networks within a limited area.

an **Ericsson** mobile phone. Today, Bluetooth wireless technology can be found in many types of portable devices, including laptops, mobile phones, and other portable devices. Connectivity is pretty much transparent to the user; Bluetooth devices simply link up on their own. You can find a summary of the **IEEE 802.15 Bluetooth standards** in Table 3.4.

HiperLAN2   **HiperLAN2,** or high-performance radio local area network (RLAN), is a wireless local area network technology based on low power and short distances between devices. It was developed by the **European Telecommunications Standards Institute (ETSI)** and published in 2000. It operates at 54 Mbps in the 5 GHz range, the same as 802.11a.[21]

Its primary technological advantage over the 802.11a standard is its ability to support voice and video as well as data. Its 802.11a rival was developed primarily as a data transmission standard. However, with the IEEE 802.11e standard, which supports quality of service (QoS)—a key ingredient for the real-time transmission of multimedia, the voice and video advantage held by HiperLAN2 could be overshadowed by 802.11e.[22]

TABLE 3.4
Wireless IEEE 802.11 Data Communications Standards

IEEE 802.11 Standard	Description
802.11	The basic standard with transmission rates up to 2 Mbps in the 2.4 GHz frequency range
802.11a	Extension to the basic standard with transmission rates up to 54 Mbps in the 5 GHz frequency range
802.11b	Extension to the basic 802.11 standard with transmission rates up to 11 Mbps in the 2.4 GHz frequency range
802.11e	Provides Quality of Service (QoS) functionality to allow voice, video, and data transmission over wireless
802.11g	Defines data transmission rates up to 54 Mbps in the 2.4 GHz frequency range
802.11h	Allows compatibility with European regulations in the 5 GHz frequency range
802.11i	Defines security protocols for 802.11 WLAN security
IEEE 802.15 (Bluetooth) Standard	
802.15.1	The basic standard for wireless personal area networks (WPANs) based on the Bluetooth v1.1 SIG specification, which includes data rate at up to 1 Mbps operating in the 2.4 GHz frequency range and at distances spanning less than 10 meters
802.15.1a	Update to the original standard to include the Bluetooth SIG v1.2 specs
802.15.2	Defines the coexistence of 802.11 WLANs and 802.15 WPANs within the 2.4 GHz frequency range so that the signals do not interfere with each other
802.15.3	Defines high-speed WPANs up to 55 Mbps for distances under 10 meters
802.15.4	Defines WPANs with data transmission rates between 2 Kbps and 200 Kbps in the 2.4 GHz and 915 MHz frequency ranges

[21] ETSI HiperLAN2 standards include TS 101 761-4, which defines home-use specifications and TS 101 761-3, which defines business-use specifications.

[22] You'll explore the concept of quality of service (QoS) in chapter 8. For now think of quality of service as a commitment to provide a quantified level of quality and bandwidth over a data transmission path so that various and different data types can be transmitted at predefined performance levels. QoS is important for the delivery of voice, multimedia, and other time-sensitive data types.

HomeRF **HomeRF** is a wireless technology developed by the HomeRF Working Group, a consortium of about 100 companies including Intel, Motorola, Siemens, and National Semiconductor. The HomeRF Working Group was formed in 1998, and its mission is to provide affordable WPANs for voice and data in the home using the Shared Wireless Access Protocol (SWAP).

In its initial version, HomeRF was capable of 1.6 Mbps transmission in the 2.4 GHz range; however, its latest version supports up to 10 Mbps, which is within close reach of the 11 Mbps of 802.11b. In addition, version 2.0 supports audio over wireless as well as streaming multimedia.

Standards

As the multitude of wireless LAN devices continues to grow and make technological improvements, you can be assured that the IEEE will continue to update and support wireless LAN specifications. So far, IEEE supports 802.11 and 802.15 (Bluetooth), while HiperLAN2 is supported by ETSI, and HomeRF seems to have support from a multitude of manufacturers as well as the HomeRF Working Group. However, from current indications, it looks as if the 802.11 and 802.15 (Bluetooth) specifications will be a primary focus for ongoing IEEE wireless standardization, while HiperLAN2 will likely continue in Europe as a wireless communication standard.

Access Methods

Wireless LANs that conform to the IEEE 802.11 standards use an access method to the wireless media that resembles Ethernet. However, where Ethernet uses collision detection (CSMA/CD) to listen to the media and then detect collisions when they happen, the 802.11 standards use a method of collision avoidance known as the **distributed coordination function (DCF)**. This method requires devices that are ready to transmit to first listen to the wireless channel to see if the airwaves are busy. If the channel is busy, the device will wait until the medium is clear. When the medium is available for a specified length of time, the device will send its data. The important feature of DCF in the world of wireless LANs is that it reduces the need for a full-duplex channel to communicate collision detection. This ensures that the maximum number of allowed frequencies is available for data communication instead of using some of those frequencies for collision detection transmissions.

Bluetooth uses a polling mechanism with controlled access to establish a connection to a Bluetooth WPAN, or **piconet**. When the first Bluetooth device is turned on, it uses its RF receiver to attempt detection of other Bluetooth devices. If none exist, then it establishes itself as the **Master** of the piconet. As other devices enter the piconet as **Slave** devices, they establish synchronization with the Master device, and data communication between any two piconet devices is then controlled by the Master. In this way, Bluetooth makes efficient use of the communication channel by preventing wasted data collisions.

When Bluetooth devices simultaneously join two or more piconets, the resulting group of piconets is called a **scatternet**. In joining two or more piconets, slave devices can exchange data with devices in other piconets.

HiperLAN2 uses a **time division multiple access (TDMA)** access method to convey data onto a wireless network. When a HiperLAN2 device has data to send, it notifies its **access point**, which in turn returns an acknowledgment to the HiperLAN2 device indicating when it can transmit and for what length of time it can add data to the transmission channel. By providing dynamic access to multiple devices on a time-sequenced basis, contention for media access is reduced and data transmission efficiency is increased.

HomeRF uses different media access methods depending on the types of data being sent. For example, for multimedia transmission where timing is critical, HomeRF utilizes a TDMA access method. For data transmissions that are less dependent upon time sequencing,

distributed coordination function (DCF)
the CSMA/CA (collision avoidance) access method utilized by the IEEE 802.11 WLAN standards

piconet
a collection of up to eight Bluetooth devices consisting of one Master and seven Slaves engaging in data exchange over a common media channel

scatternet
a Bluetooth WPAN that includes two or more piconets

TDMA
a media access method that dynamically allocates discrete units of time to devices that have data to send

access point
a device that facilitates communication among wireless communication devices. It is typically installed in a fixed location within a specified distance of where most users will access the network.

HomeRF uses a carrier sense multiple access with collision avoidance **(CSMA/CA)** access method that is similar to DCF.

Technical Considerations

One of the most important technical considerations you'll probably encounter with wireless technologies is frequency overlap among competing standards. For example, all four technologies discussed in this chapter utilize the unlicensed frequency bands in the 2.4 GHz and 5 GHz ranges. However, with recent proposals and published standards, some of the interference problems associated with frequency overlap have either gone away or are insignificant because of the ways the different technologies access the airwaves.

You'll also have to install access points in most situations to obtain optimal coverage for your users. Considerations include where to place access points to meet the range specifications of the manufacturer and ensuring that each access point uses a communication channel that does not overlap with an adjacent access point, as depicted in Figure 3.10. You'll want to ensure placement that delivers maximum access to your users. In addition, you'll have to consider whether you want to have a separate power source (wall plug) or have the power supplied by a **power injector** over an existing Ethernet cable.

Another technical consideration is security. Because others can eavesdrop on wireless data communications relatively easily, you'll want to consider implementing at least basic security to guard against accidental exposure of confidential information. For example, 802.11 networks can be configured with **Wireless Equivalent Privacy (WEP),** a wireless algorithm that provides basic encryption protection. While it's not even close to being the ultimate in encryption technology, WEP will protect transmission on an 802.11 WLAN from casual hackers looking to gain unauthorized access to your network.

Another security standard is the relatively new IEEE 802.11i standard. This standard defines enhanced security protocols for 802.11 WLAN security. For example, Wi-Fi Protected Access (WPA) enhances the basic wireless encryption protection of WEP. And

CSMA/CA
a collision avoidance media access method in which a transmitting station always broadcasts an "intention-to-transmit" signal prior to placing data on the network. The signal informs other nodes not to transmit in order to avoid collisions.

power injector
a device that provides power to an access point over an existing UTP cable. It is also known as Power over Ethernet (PoE).

Wireless Equivalent Privacy (WEP)
a basic encryption algorithm that is used to protect a wireless 802.11 WLAN from eavesdropping

FIGURE 3.10
Locating Access Points with No Channel Overlap

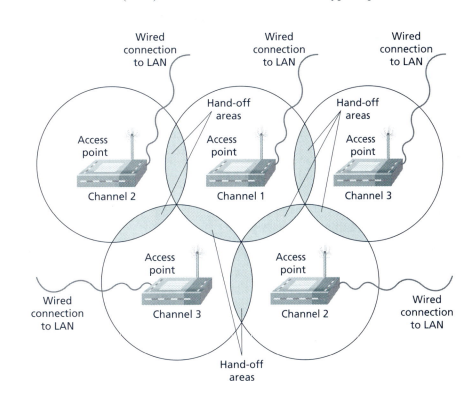

The WLANs you've learned about in this chapter use spread spectrum technology to transmit data across radio frequency waves. With spread spectrum technology, the digital data of a data transmission is spread across multiple analog frequencies to improve the performance and security of the data transmission. Specifically, spread spectrum minimizes the potential for

- Two wireless devices to attempt to communicate on the same frequency at the same time.
- Eavesdroppers to capture data from your transmissions.
- Data being lost owing to interference from other devices that use the same modulation technique in the same frequency range.

Two major types of spread spectrum technology are implemented in WLANs: frequency hopping spread spectrum (FHSS) and direct sequence spread spectrum (DSSS). With FHSS, digital data hops across numerous and pseudo-randomly generated analog frequencies at timed intervals.[23] The pseudo-random nature of the multiple frequencies combined with timed hopping to different frequencies prevents eavesdropping and data loss due to overlapping of communications with other FHSS-equipped transmitting devices. Both the sending and receiving devices know the pseudo-random sequence and the timing of the frequency hops so that receiving devices can always reassemble the sender's transmissions.

With DSSS, a string of data bits called a *chip* or *chipping code* is added to the original data stream and the data and chips are transmitted across several different frequencies. The added bits of the chipping code combined with data being spread across multiple frequencies significantly reduce the potential that eavesdroppers could reassemble the transmitted data. In addition, chipping and multiple frequencies prevent frequency overlap with other devices and associated data loss from interference from other devices. Both the sender and the receiver are aware of the chipping code as well as the transmitting frequencies so that receiving devices can always reassemble the sender's transmissions.

Robust Security Network (RSN) uses advanced authentication techniques to guarantee that users accessing the WLAN are legitimate, and it uses an encryption algorithm known as Advanced Encryption Standard (AES) to supplant the inadequacies of WEP.[24]

Other technical considerations surrounding security include using unsecured wireless data communications technologies inside an organization's firewall. This can provide an open pathway for unscrupulous hackers to access the entire network. Once connected to an unsecured WLAN, these unauthorized "users" can wreak havoc with a corporate network.

Business Considerations

If you haven't implemented a WPAN or WLAN in your network environment already, at some point you probably will. In making your decision, you'll need to consider not only the cost of wireless technologies, but which technology to choose as well. In general, it's safest from service, support, and cost viewpoints to specify products that follow an existing or soon-to-be-published standard. Right now, the IEEE 802.11 standards seem to have substantial support in the product marketplace, and enhanced standards are in process that will continue the 802.11 legacy and provide backward compatibility. In addition, the 802.11 standards can be fully and easily integrated with existing Ethernet networks, making data transmission throughout a heterogeneous network seamless to users.

---

[23] The Federal Communications Commission (FCC) regulates the number of frequencies to be at least 75 and the hop interval must not exceed 400 milliseconds.

[24] You'll examine more security topics, including expanded coverage of wireless security in chapter 9.

TABLE 3.5
Wireless Technologies Compared

Wireless Technology	WPAN or WLAN	Frequency Ranges	Data Rate (Mbps)	Common Operating Range
802.11	WLAN	2.4 GHz and 5 GHz	2 to 54	Up to 150 feet
Bluetooth	WPAN	2.4 GHz	Up to 55	Up to 10 meters
HiperLAN2	WLAN	5 GHz	Up to 54	30 to 150 meters
HomeRF	WPAN	2.4 GHz	Up to 10	Up to 150 feet

Bluetooth also looks promising. Recent work on coexistence with 802.11 standards makes this technology viable as well, especially since the need to integrate both Bluetooth and 802.11 technologies in the same networked environment will probably grow over time.

HiperLAN2, with its promise of smooth wireless delivery of data as well as multimedia, might also become a market reality in the United States. Although its specifications were developed for the European market, recent work by the IEEE to define coexistence with 802.11 standards could make this technology practical.

HomeRF is another story for the business marketplace. Developed for home use and supported by a consortium of companies rather than a standards organization, this technology may or may not flourish. Business users who are familiar with products that are based on the 802.11 or Bluetooth standards may be reluctant to implement separate technologies in their homes; instead they may prefer the same standards as they use at work.

FDDI

Overview

Fiber Distributed Data Interface (FDDI) rates discussion in a textbook about networks and data communications because it's an older network data transmission technology that is still being supported in various network environments. At one time FDDI was a common technology choice that would be implemented for its longer distance and high-speed connectivity capability between remote LANs. If you had multiple LANs in a campus environment such as a university campus or a business complex and if you wanted to link those networks together, you would very likely consider FDDI as your connectivity solution.[25]

Standards

FDDI standards fell under the auspices of the **ANSI X3T9** committee, and have numbering schemes such as X3.139-1987, the first FDDI standard. It defines the **media access control (MAC)** functions. Other standards such as X3.148-1988 define the physical layer (OSI model) specifications such as the types of media over which FDDI can function. One common media type for FDDI is 50-micron single-mode fiber (SMF).[26]

Access Methodology

FDDI uses a token passing access method that is much like Token Ring. For FDDI it's called timed-token token-passing. When a computer on an FDDI network needs to transmit information, it grabs the circulating token, transmits its data, and then reissues the token. The amount of time that a particular computer can monopolize the token for data transmission is known as the **token holding time,** usually 5 to 10 milliseconds.[27] The token holding time guarantees that in busy FDDI networks, every computer can gain access to the network at

---

[25] Another version of FDDI uses copper cabling to transmit FDDI frames. It's known as copper distributed data interface or CDDI.

[26] The ANSI X3T9.5 working group defined 50 micron SMF as an approved physical transmission medium for FDDI.

[27] The token holding time is configurable on a station-by-station basis.

FDDI is recognized as the first standardized 100 Mbps data transmission technology for local area networks.[28] Its roots can be traced back to work performed by **Robert Grow** at the **Burroughs Corporation** in the early 1980s. Burroughs was a manufacturer of mainframe computers as well as other mechanized and circuit-based calculating devices, and they needed a data communications solution that would provide a high-speed data transmission architecture between mainframe processing units and storage devices. Robert Grow first published his findings on this transmission architecture before the IEEE at their May 1982 conference held in Boston.

In today's networking world, FDDI technology would have been submitted to the IEEE 802 committee, because we now recognize FDDI as a LAN technology. However, in 1982, the intended purpose of the FDDI technology was to provide interconnection between mainframe computing devices such as processing units and storage units—not LAN technology—and this fell under the jurisdiction of the ANSI X3T9 committee.

The first standards for FDDI were published in 1987, and work continued throughout the rest of the 1980s and into the 1990s on FDDI and FDDI-II. However, with the improvements in Ethernet technologies throughout the 1990s, the choice of FDDI as a LAN architecture or even LAN-to-LAN connectivity solution began to evaporate. Today you'll find FDDI installations still in place where high-speed connectivity was once a priority, and perhaps still is, but where an upgrade to a new and faster technology is not yet cost justified.

a high-speed network link that connects two or more LANs

regular and frequent intervals. When a workstation has data to send, it will continue to transmit until it has either finished sending all of the data it needs to send or until the token holding time has expired, whichever is shorter.

Technical Considerations

FDDI uses a **dual-counter-rotating-ring topology** that has specific rules for device connectivity. That is, devices can be connected to either or both of the rings. The dual rings provide fault tolerance in case there is a device failure or a break in the fiber-optic ring. If a ring breaks, computers that are configured as **dual access stations (DAS)** reroute the information along the other fiber-optic ring so that data reaches its intended destination without interruption in service. You can see an example of a FDDI dual-ring configuration and network interconnectivity in Figure 3.11.

Other technical considerations for FDDI include a total fiber length that cannot exceed 200 km, including both rings. Inasmuch as an FDDI network utilizes dual rings, the effective length of a FDDI ring is 100 km. Each ring requires two fiber-optic cables, so FDDI installations can be expensive in terms of fiber-optic cabling alone.

With FDDI, you should also be aware that Ethernet network data transmissions can be transmitted across an FDDI interconnection. When Ethernet connects to FDDI, the data packets must be transformed from Ethernet packets to FDDI packets, and then the process is reversed at the receiving end. The translation is transparent to users. At the same time, you should be aware that in constructing a network that incorporates both technologies, you'll need to include a hardware device that can facilitate such a data translation between architectures such as Ethernet and FDDI.

Business Considerations

You wouldn't specify FDDI for a new network LAN-to-LAN connectivity solution. However, existing installations of FDDI might continue in service for years to come if there is no cost-justified reason to upgrade. When it's time to upgrade to a faster connectivity

---

[28] From the beginning, FDDI was conceived as an interconnection, or backbone, data transmission technology. You'll learn more about backbones in chapter 4.

FIGURE 3.11
FDDI Dual-ring
Configuration
and Network
Interconnectivity

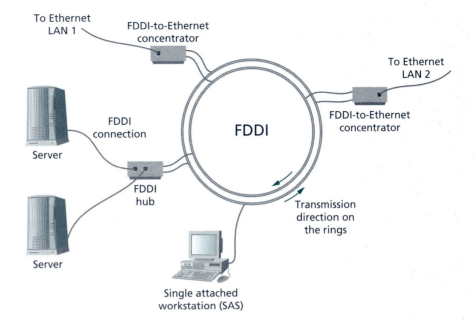

Single attached
workstation (SAS)

solution, Gigabit Ethernet is a common candidate to replace FDDI interconnections that are serving as network backbones, and other technologies such as ATM can be explored as well.

ATM

Overview

Asynchronous transfer mode (ATM) is a networking architecture that provides high-speed and low-latency information transfer on networks that require reliable and timely delivery of data, voice, and video transmissions. While ATM technology is generally reserved for **network backbones**, wide area networks, and carrier services, it's also a networking architecture that can be used to connect workstations and servers in a small- to medium-sized LAN. However, when ATM is implemented in a LAN, it's usually as a backbone architecture to connect remote networks.[29] ATM is also used in carrier service applications for high-speed data, video, and voice transmissions.[30]

network backbone
a high-speed network
link that connects two or
more LANs

Standards

Many organizations are involved in the development and support of ATM standards. Most notable are the ATM Forum, the DSL Forum, the Frame Relay Forum, the IETF, the ITU-T, and the T1 Committee. Each forum, group, or committee is chartered with its own set of standards and support issues for the continued development and deployment of ATM. There is also overlap in certain areas, and the various groups maintain communication to assure commonality. The most tangible historical standards for ATM include the fixed-length cell length of 48 bytes and the 3-byte virtual circuit identifier published in 1988. Other notable standards describe ATM interfaces with other technologies such as frame relay, DSL services, and ATM standards for physical media types and other protocols. In addition, the ATM user network interface (UNI) standards define how a user connects

---

[29] You'll learn more about backbones in chapter 4.
[30] You'll learn more about carrier services and how ATM is used in that capacity in chapter 8.

packet switching
a method of data communications that transmits data packets. Each data packet has a source and destination address and each data packet travels through the network from source to destination using the best available route.

The development of asynchronous transfer mode grew out of the need for AT&T to provide integrated services transmission, such as voice and data (and later video), to a growing base of customers that were exchanging computer-generated information over AT&T telephone circuits.

In the late 1960s, researchers at Bell Labs, and most notably **Alexander (Sandy) Fraser,** began working on a solution to more efficiently transmit voice and data traffic over existing AT&T telephone circuits. Combining **packet switching** theories advanced by **Paul Baran** at the **RAND Corporation** in the early 1960s with ARPA packet switching technology developed and implemented for the ARPANET in the late 1960s, Fraser suggested a high-speed packet switching scheme that would bundle fixed-length data packets and voice packets on the same telephone circuit. This high-speed packet switching scheme would also distinguish between the two different types of packets with a type-of-data identifier known as a **virtual circuit identifier.** The resulting switching and transmission technology was described as **asynchronous time division multiplexing (ATDM),** a technology that would efficiently bundle and transmit both data and voice (and later video) across a common communications channel.[31]

But in the late 1960s and early 1970s, the technology to implement fixed-length packets, or **cells,** as they became known, was insufficient to adequately develop and implement ATDM. Later on, with work performed at Bell Labs and with improvements in hardware technologies, practical demonstrations of ATDM technology (in the 1980s) became reality in the form of ATM. Several working prototype networks in both the United States and France were demonstrated and, in 1985, the **France-Telecom** laboratory in Lannion, France, unveiled the **PRELUDE** project, a network that demonstrated proof of concept. With the PRELUDE network, data, voice, and video could be transmitted across a high-speed network reliably and efficiently. By 1988, the European standards organization, **CCITT,** which is now known as **ITU-T,** issued its first recommendation on ATM. In 1991, the **ATM Forum** was established to develop and promote common ATM standards.

to an ATM network in order to use a specific service such as T1, T3, OC-3, OC-12, and so on.[32]

Access Method

For more information regarding approved and proposed ATM standards, have a look at the ATM Forum's Web site at www.atmforum.org.

ATM doesn't have a media access method in the traditional sense of the access methods you've learned about so far, because ATM sets up a switched point-to-point connection between end devices before any data transmission begins. In other words, ATM is a connection-oriented data transmission architecture that doesn't require shared access to the network medium. The access methods you've looked at so far are connectionless; data is transmitted and viewed by all attached devices without specific regard for the ultimate recipient. Second, ATM uses an addressing scheme known as virtual circuit identifiers that incorporate network address information as well as node address information, which is very different than the media access control or **MAC addressing** scenario used in the other architectures. Third, in an ATM network, computers, servers, and other network devices are connected to an **ATM switch,** a device that establishes connection-oriented communication

---

[31] The definition of multiplexing from chapter 2 described multiplexing as a method of combining multiple separate signals into a composite signal for transmission across a communications channel. With ATDM, both data and voice were multiplexed across a common communications channel. You'll learn more about multiplexing in chapter 8.

[32] You'll learn more about these services in chapter 8.

between ATM devices and, at the same time, maintains a table of the virtual circuit connections between remote computers. ATM devices do not randomly access the network media; connections are mapped, and then the switch intercepts and directs traffic from sending devices to the appropriate network locations attached to the other ports on the ATM switch.

In addition, ATM technology utilizes **Quality of Service (QoS)** to establish priorities on the virtual circuit connections between remote devices.[33] This allows data transmissions such as voice and video, which are time sensitive, to have transmission priority over another circuit that might be sending a lower priority transmission such as e-mail. The QoS priorities are generally configurable, and when a switch is experiencing heavy traffic loads, lower priority channels can store packets in favor of higher priority data transmissions. When traffic loads at the switch decrease, lower priority messages can then be forwarded.

As far as an access method, ATM devices generally transmit whenever they have data to send. Since each ATM device is connected directly to an ATM switch, there is no contention for bandwidth as in the case of (unswitched) Ethernet, nor is there a wait for a token as in the case of Token Ring and FDDI. Instead, ATM devices send at random, whenever they need to. The data transmissions are intercepted at the ATM switch, and then the ATM switch redirects the data traffic to its intended destination.

Technical Considerations

You'll probably never see asynchronous transfer mode deployed in small LAN environments due to the cost of connectivity components such as ATM NICs and switches. However, you will very likely see ATM deployed as a connectivity solution between LANs or LAN segments on the same network campus, as in a backbone connection. When ATM is implemented to connect remote LANs or LAN segments, you'll need to consider the interoperability issues associated with your LAN architecture. For example, in connecting one Ethernet LAN to another Ethernet LAN using ATM, you'll need to specify a LAN switch that can translate between Ethernet and ATM frames. You'll also specify the fiber media that connects one ATM switch to another remote ATM switch. In addition, the LAN switch on the remote network must also include an ATM module that performs frame translation.

In Figure 3.12, an Ethernet switch that is configured with an ATM interface converts Ethernet frames into ATM cells.[34,35] Once the Ethernet frames are converted into ATM cells, they're sent to the local ATM switch from which a virtual circuit is established with

FIGURE 3.12   **ATM LAN Emulation (LANE)**

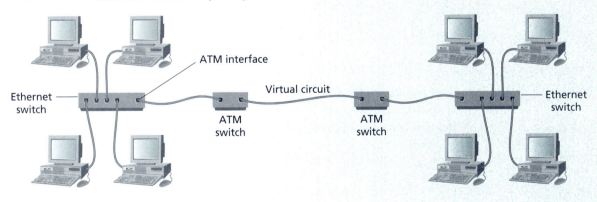

---

[33] You'll explore QoS in more depth in chapter 8.

[34] You'll learn about Ethernet switches in chapter 4.

[35] Token Ring and FDDI cells could be converted as well; however, you would need to add additional hardware devices to convert the Token Ring and FDDI frames into ATM cells.

an ATM switch at the remote location. Once the virtual circuit is established, the ATM cells can be transported across the ATM backbone to the remote location. At the remote location, another switch converts the ATM cells back into Ethernet frames.[36]

Business Considerations

In the mid- to late 1990s, there was talk that ATM might be widely deployed in LAN environments so that users of network services could take advantage of the high-speed, low-latency, and reliable delivery of voice, video, and data traffic at their desktop computers. But wide acceptance of ATM desktop connectivity found a substitute with less expensive switched 100 Mbps Ethernet. Even in LAN-to-LAN connectivity, ATM didn't gain the market acceptance that its promoters had hoped; instead Gigabit Ethernet provided a lower cost alternative for backbone connections.

ATM found its way into many corporate environments prior to the general acceptance of Gigabit Ethernet. In such installations, keep in mind that the technology devices that translate LAN-based 100 Mbps Ethernet frames into ATM cells carry substantial service contract and replacement costs. In addition, the frame translation from Ethernet to ATM introduces additional **latency** into the communications channel, so that your LAN-to-LAN connections with ATM might not be as fast as you could obtain with a Gigabit Ethernet implementation.

Although ATM can be deployed in a LAN environment, due to the cost of connectivity components such as ATM NICs and switches, you're not likely to see it implemented in smaller LAN environments. What you might see is ATM deployed as a connectivity solution between LANs on the same network campus, as in a backbone connection. In addition, ATM is offered as a carrier service by companies such as AT&T, MCI, Sprint, and others. ATM as a carrier has a lot more to it than can be covered in this chapter. For a more extensive look at ATM in wide area network (WAN) implementations, you'll have to wait until chapter 8.

TABLE 3.6
LAN Architectures Summary

LAN Architecture	Data Rates Supported	Topologies Supported	Common Usage
Ethernet	10, 100 Mbps, 1, 10 Gbps	Bus, Star	LANs, LAN Backbones
Token ring	4, 16, 100 Mbps	Ring, Star	Legacy LANs
Wireless LANs and WPANs	Up to 55 Mbps	Wireless	Short-range LAN connectivity
FDDI	100 Mbps	Ring, Star	Legacy LAN backbones
ATM	25, 155 Mbps	Star	LAN backbones

Chapter Summary

- **LAN topologies.** A LAN topology is the map or layout of a LAN. Types of topologies include bus, star, ring, and wireless.
- **Physical and logical topologies.** LAN topologies include logical topologies and physical topologies. Logical topologies define the conceptual layout of the network or the way the data flows across the LAN. Physical topologies define the actual structure or configuration that you can see or touch.

---

[36] ATM switches perform the translation between Ethernet frames and ATM cells using LAN Emulation (LANE) and MultiProtocols over ATM (MPOA). These two translation mechanisms use MAC addresses (for LANE) and network layer addresses (for MPOA) to direct traffic to the appropriate destination.

- **LAN architecture.** A LAN architecture is the way in which data accesses the network media, and it's the structure of the data frames that are placed on the network media. LAN architectures can take the forms of Ethernet, Token Ring, various forms of wireless, FDDI, and ATM, and they address business needs such as bandwidth, performance, and reliability.

- **Ethernet LAN architectures and common Ethernet standards.** Ethernet LAN architectures support specific business needs such as bandwidth and performance. There are various types of Ethernet architectures such as 10Base2, 10Base-T, 100Base-TX, 1000Base-T, and even fast versions such as 10GBase-LX4. Ethernet architectures and specifications are based on the IEEE 802.3 standards.

- **Ethernet access method.** Ethernet uses a CSMA/CD access method for data access to the LAN medium. CSMA/CD provides equal access for all connected devices to the shared LAN medium, and computing devices listen to the network medium to make sure it's not busy before placing data on the LAN. CSMA/CD uses collision detection to detect collisions and provides a framework for the retransmission of data after a collision occurs.

- **Technical and business considerations of Ethernet.** The biggest benefit to using Ethernet is that it's widely accepted in the LAN marketplace. Also, Ethernet products are readily available from a variety of vendors, newer versions are backward-compatible with older versions, and there are plenty of technicians who are well-trained in Ethernet functionality and maintenance.

- **Token Ring LAN architecture and common Token Ring standards.** Token Ring is an older LAN architecture that is still supported, primarily by IBM. It uses a deterministic access method to the LAN medium and generally operates at 4 or 16 Mbps. You might even find some newer versions that operate at 100 Mbps. Some of the standards include 802.5-1998, which defines the Token Ring access method and physical layer specifications at both 4 and 16 Mbps. The 802.5c standard defines Token Ring dual-ring operation, and 802.5t defines 100 Mbps Token Ring.

- **Token Ring access method.** The Token Ring access method is a token-passing method in which one device at a time has access to a special data frame called a free token. When a computing device has possession of the free token, the computing device can place data on the ring.

- **Technical and business considerations of Token Ring.** The technical and business considerations for Token Ring networks are primarily historical. Token Ring's performance advantage has long since given way to faster architectures. Token Ring networks are still highly efficient by design, but their lack of widespread industry support and slower network speeds has relegated their significance and business importance to the history books.

- **Wireless LAN architecture.** Wireless LAN architectures are important adjuncts to wired LAN architectures. Organizations can specify a wireless architecture where cost or building structure would preclude a wired architecture. In general, wireless LAN architectures in modern business settings utilize radio frequency wireless technologies for short-distance data transmissions.

- **Wireless LANs and wireless PAN technologies.** Wireless LANs and wireless PANs utilize radio frequency architectures and topologies to deliver wireless data transmissions in a LAN configuration. Primary differences between WLANs and WPANs include distance—WLANs have greater range and device interconnectivity—WPANs generally interconnect devices associated with a single user while WLANs interconnect multiple users. In addition, WLANs and WPANs are supported by different standards.

- **Standards and access methods for IEEE 802.11, Bluetooth, HiperLAN2, and HomeRF.** Standards for WLANs include the IEEE 802.11 standards and the Hiper-LAN2 standards as published by the ETSI. Standards for WPANs include the IEEE 802.15 standards and the work of the **Bluetooth SIG.** In addition, the HomeRF Working Group supports development of HomeRF WPAN technologies. Access methods for these wireless standards range from the distributed coordination function (DCF) that is used by the 802.11 architectures to the polling mechanism used by Bluetooth. Hiper-LAN2 uses time division multiple access (TDMA), and HomeRF uses either TDMA or CSMA/CA, depending on the type of data being transmitted.

- **Technical and business considerations of wireless architectures.** Technical and business considerations for wireless architectures include compatibility with existing LAN architectures and topologies as well as the data rates achievable with each wireless architecture. Many of the standards groups are working toward compatibility and interoperability, and data rates continue to increase as business demands faster wireless data communications.

- **FDDI and ATM standards, access methods, and technical and business considerations.** FDDI standards fall under the jurisdiction of ANSI and the X3T9 committee while ATM standards are developed and supported by numerous organizations such as the ATM Forum, the IETF, and ITU-T. FDDI uses a token-passing access method, while ATM uses a switched architecture that doesn't require media access control. Technical and business considerations for FDDI relegate it to legacy backbone implementations while ATM can be specified for more modern backbone implementations.

Key Terms

Questions

1. What is a LAN topology and how does a logical topology differ from a physical topology?

2. Historically, where were bus topologies implemented? What cabling type was used? What is a major disadvantage with bus topologies?

3. What components are required to create a star topology? Are the logical and physical topologies the same? What advantages and disadvantages exist with a physical star topology?

4. In a wireless topology, how would you divide geographic areas? What physical device do you need to allow portable devices to gain access to the wireless network?

5. Why would you implement a wireless topology? What disadvantages can you foresee?

6. What is a logical topology? Describe the flow of data on a network that is configured with a sequential topology.

7. How does a LAN architecture differ from a LAN topology? Provide an example.

8. What is Ethernet and why is it such a popular LAN architecture? When and where did Ethernet originate?

9. Who is Bob Metcalfe and what is his link to Ethernet? How does the Aloha System fit into the development of Ethernet?

10. What is the basic IEEE standard for Ethernet? What variations are there?

11. What is CSMA/CD and how does it work?

12. Would you ever choose to implement Token Ring instead of Ethernet? Why? Are there any advantages to the token-passing access method? What are they, and when might you choose token-passing over CSMA/CD?

13. Who are the people involved in the historical time line of Token Ring networks, and what are their contributions? What company is generally associated with Token Ring's market development?

14. If you had to support a Token Ring network, why would you choose to implement Token Ring bridging and switching?

15. What is the difference between a WPAN and a WLAN? Which wireless technologies fall into the WPAN category? The WLAN category?

16. Why might you implement a wireless LAN? What are the advantages of 802.11 Wireless over Bluetooth? Does Bluetooth provide any advantages over 802.11? Why might you choose to implement HyperLAN2? HomeRF?

17. What data speeds can be obtained with WLANs and WPANs?

18. How does the 802.11 DCF access method differ from Ethernet's CSMA/CD access method?

19. What does Bluetooth use as its method for data access to the airwaves? How does it work? What importance do piconets, scatternets, masters, and slaves have with Bluetooth devices?

20. What simple technical configuration would you make in an 802.11 wireless network to enhance security? What major benefit will you derive on your 802.11 wireless network by making this change?

21. How is FDDI typically implemented in a LAN? Are there any advantages to the built-in fault tolerance that FDDI's dual-ring technology provides?

22. Why is FDDI an ANSI standard instead of an IEEE standard?

23. What access method does FDDI use to access network media? How is it similar to Token Ring's access method?

24. What was the business driver behind the development of ATM? On what data communications technology is ATM based?

25. What organizations contribute to ATM standards?

26. How does data access an ATM network? Why might you consider implementing ATM as a LAN-to-LAN connectivity solution?

Research Activities

1. Find out if your school or workplace is using or has ever used Ethernet, Token Ring, FDDI, and/or ATM. What are the reasons for implementation or replacement of the chosen technologies?

2. Discover whether your school or workplace is using wireless technologies in its networks. Why did they decide to go with a wireless topology? What wireless technologies were chosen? What components were required to do the installation? What service (and other) issues have network administrators at these locations experienced with wireless networks?

3. Using the ATM Forum Web site (www.atmforum.com), develop a list of current ATM standards and proposed standards.

4. Using the search tools available to you, identify at least two ATM switch manufacturers. Provide a list of available models and describe the intended use or market for two ATM switches from each of your selected manufacturers.

5. Using the IEEE Web site www.ieee.org, prepare a list of recent news surrounding IEEE- supported wireless network technologies. See if you can do the same for the European Telecommunications Standards Institute (ETSI) at www.etsi.org.

HANDS-ON ACTIVITIES

All hands-on activities require access to a computer lab that provides sufficient computers, hardware, media types, and software to perform these activities.

1. Within your lab environment, identify Ethernet hubs and switches and Token Ring MSAUs. Using either the Ethernet hub or the Token Ring MSAU (and cabling), create a physical star/logical bus topology. Why is the physical star configuration also a logical bus? Using an Ethernet hub or switch (and cabling) create a physical star/logical star topology. Why is this physical star also a logical star instead of a logical bus?

2. Identify the topology and architecture that comprises the working LAN in your lab. What is its physical topology? What is its logical topology? What architecture is being used? What would you have to do to implement a new architecture in your working lab?

3. Using a wireless access point and wireless NICs, lay out a wireless topology. How do the wireless NICs communicate with the access point? How do the topologies and architectures of a wireless LAN differ from the topologies and architecture of a wired LAN? (*Hint:* Consider access method differences and technical considerations.) If you were to implement wireless access points, how would you connect them to your wired LAN? How do you ensure that multiple access points provide sufficient coverage for wireless users?

Mini Case Study

LAKESIDE METAL STAMPINGS—PART 2

Lakeside Metal Stampings is the case study first introduced in chapter 2. Using the information presented in this chapter along with the information presented in the case study from chapter 2, and assuming you're still the consultant who has been hired to help Lakeside Metal Stampings implement a LAN, what topologies would you consider recommending to Lakeside? Why?

After you've made your recommendation, the owner asks you to explain what a topology is. How do you describe the physical aspects of LAN topologies to him? If you decide to also discuss logical topologies with him, how might your answer change? How might it be the same?

As an integral part of the LAN implementation that you will ultimately provide Lakeside Metal Stampings, you need to advise the owner on the type of architecture you're going to select. In your meetings with the owner, you have always informed him about the technologies that you're considering, and now you need to discuss LAN architectures. If the company requires fast, reliable, and efficient data communications, what architecture might you suggest? Why? Describe the conversation you'll have with the owner to bring him up to speed on the technology of your chosen architecture. If during your explanation the owner informs you that there is one area of the main building in which he would like to try a wireless technology, what can you suggest regarding wireless architectures? What questions will you need to answer before you can firm up the exact wireless architecture that you'll recommend? How will you connect a wireless architecture to the wired architecture that you've decided upon for the rest of the building?

CHAPTER
Four

Chapter Overview and Objectives

Local area network connectivity provides one of the building blocks that allows network administrators to manage and control the flow of data across their networks. The connectivity components that network engineers specify and configure and that business managers approve for purchase can have a significant impact on the performance of a network as well as on the performance of data flow throughout an organization. In this chapter, we're going to examine LAN devices such as hubs, switches, routers, and gateways as well as protocols such as the Internet Protocol (IP) that allow networking professionals to interconnect the cables, NICs, servers, and clients on a local area network. More specifically, by the end of this chapter you will be able to

- Describe the purpose of a repeater and indicate where repeaters are used in a LAN.

- Discuss different hub technologies and indicate where hubs are used in a LAN.

- Identify the significance of adding a bridge to a LAN and discuss bridge technology.

- Describe what a switch is, how it differs from a bridge, why businesses implement different switch technologies, and discover the significance of VLAN switches.

- Discuss the differences between routing and switching and why businesses implement routers.

- List the functions of a gateway, and identify the reasons that gateways are implemented.

- Describe the three layers of network backbone design and identify how this layered approach can scale to the data flow needs of a business.

- Compare the differences between rack-mounted and chassis-based backbone hardware.

- Discuss network backbone data transmission architectures.

- Describe the Internet Protocol and provide examples of different IP address classes.

- Identify different methods of assigning IP addresses and the business impact of the dynamic host configuration protocol.

- List and describe other LAN communications protocols and their importance.

- Describe the network management protocol SNMP.

Local Area Networks: Connectivity

LAN DEVICES

LAN devices are the hardware components that provide the interfaces among the multitude of servers, workstations, and media types that are used in a local area network. These devices provide a variety of functions ranging from signal regeneration and media connectivity to advanced functions such as address identification and forwarding and protocol translation. In this section, you'll learn about repeaters, hubs, bridges, switches, routers, and gateways.

Repeaters

Data transmission signal strength degrades over distance on all kinds of media including copper, fiber optic, and wireless. It's a physical property known as **signal attenuation** or *signal loss* that engineers try to minimize because of the impact that signal loss can have on data communications. Even with the best and most efficient engineering, signal loss through media does occur over distance. To alleviate this problem, you can implement an OSI layer 1 networking device known as a **repeater.**

signal attenuation
also called signal loss, is the loss of data transmission signal strength over distance

You can implement a repeater at points on your network media where the data transmission signal starts to degrade. The repeater receives attenuated data transmission signals from a media segment, "cleans" the signals to remove extraneous noise, amplifies them, and then repeats, or sends, the signals onto the next media segment. This effectively extends the distance over which a signal can be transmitted.

Repeaters are commonly built into devices such as hubs or switches so that you'll have the functionality of the repeater combined with another device. Exceptions to this include repeaters that are used in thicknet or thinnet implementations and some fiber-optic implementations. In these cases, repeaters are separate devices that are physically placed at the locations where they're needed. When repeater functionality is built into a device such as a hub or switch, the location of the repeater will be where the hub or switch is placed, which is usually in a **wiring closet**.

wiring closet
a room or closet in which networking devices such as hubs, switches, and routers are implemented to connect different parts of a network. They're also referred to as distribution centers.

Hubs

A **hub** is an OSI layer 1 hardware device to which LAN devices such as servers, workstations, printers, and other computing devices can be connected in a local area network. Hubs don't interpret any of the data that flows through them. They're unaware of the source or destination of the packets flowing through them, and all packets flowing through a hub are broadcast to all other computing devices connected to the hub. Hubs generally have numerous **ports** so that many network devices can be interconnected. Figure 4.1 provides several examples of simple LAN hubs.

port
an entry point or connectivity point on a networking device such as a hub, a switch, a router, or even a network interface card to which a cable with a properly terminated connector can be attached

Hubs are commonly used in Ethernet and Token Ring networks as centralized connectivity devices. Any computer, printer, or other LAN device that regularly communicates with other computers that are configured with the same architecture can be connected to a hub port. Any devices that are attached to the hub can transmit data back and forth with any other device connected to that hub.

Hub Technologies: Stand-alone Hubs

Stand-alone hubs are available in a number of port configurations and generally include an **uplink port** that allows connectivity to another hub or to a switch or router.[1] Common

uplink port
a port on a networking device such as a hub or switch that provides connectivity to another hub or to a higher OSI layer device

---

[1] The uplink port on many stand-alone hubs includes a toggle that allows either cross-over mode or straight-through mode. These modes refer to the configuration of the wires within the UTP cabling. Hub-to-hub and hub-to-switch connections require the uplink port to be toggled to cross-over mode for use with a regular UTP patch cable, while hub-to-router connections through a hub's uplink port require the hub's uplink port to be set to straight-through mode for use with a regular UTP patch cable.

A publicly traded battery manufacturer for whom I did LAN support several years ago was having difficulty sending and receiving data from a single client workstation that was located in the back corner of the loading dock. Data transmission errors were occasional during the day and more frequent on second and third shifts. On second and third shifts there was no daylight entering the building, and workers turned on all the lights in the warehouse. These lights were a combination of both fluorescent tubes and high-intensity sodium vapor lamps. With a little investigation, we discovered that the thinnet cabling had been run very near the lights and when the lights came on, the data transmission problems increased. As a first attempt to correct the problem, we ran new cabling along the walls and away from the lighting. This improved the situation, but data transmission errors still occurred.

Thinking back to the Ethernet courses I had studied, I recalled that signal loss over distance on thinnet cabling can cause data transmission problems. We measured the distance between the server and the loading dock computer, installed a repeater, and the data transmission problems went away.

configurations for very small LANs include hubs with 6 ports or 12 ports, although other configurations with five ports or even eight ports are available.

Hub Technologies: Stackable Hubs

rack-mounted hub
any hub that can be mounted into a rack system, a series of vertically parallel brackets that function as a shelving unit for LAN devices

More common in business settings are **rack-mounted hubs** that have 24-, or 48-, or 60-port configurations. Frequently these hubs are stackable, a term used to define hubs that can be physically connected and stacked on top of each other in a rack system. **Stackable hubs** generally incorporate technology that allows data signals to pass from one hub to the next hub in the stack faster than data can flow between two or more interconnected stand-alone hubs. Stackable hubs frequently have built-in management capabilities that provide integration of management functions across all hubs in the stack. The added functionality of stackable hubs gives you the flexibility to grow the size of your LAN by adding more stackable hubs as more client workstations, servers, or other devices are added to the network. Figure 4.2 provides an illustration.

FIGURE 4.1
Simple LAN Hubs

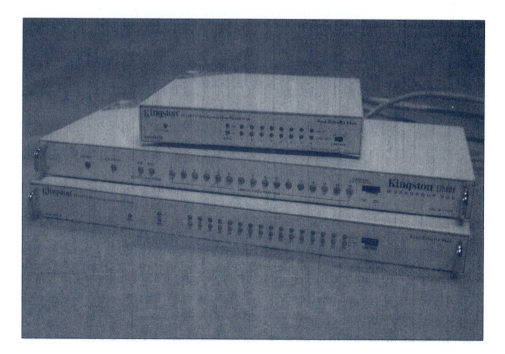

FIGURE 4.2

Rack-mounted Stackable Hub System
a. Rack system.
b. Same rack system as LAN grows.
c. Same rack system as LAN grows some more.

a. Rack system   **b.** Same rack system as LAN grows   **c.** Same rack system as LAN grows some more

Hub Technologies: Enterprise Hubs

stackable hub
a hub that can be physically connected to other hubs, usually in a rack-mounted configuration, and which incorporates technology that allows data signals to pass from one hub to the next hub in the stack faster than data can flow between two or more interconnected stand-alone hubs. Stackable hubs frequently have built-in management capabilities that provide integration of management functions across all hubs in the stack.

chassis design
a modular structure that can house multiple networking devices. The chassis provides shared and usually redundant power supplies, cooling fans, and a high-speed backplane through which multiple devices interconnect. Devices can generally be hot-swapped, meaning an individual network device can be removed from the chassis without shutting down the power supply.

Enterprise hubs provide functionality that goes beyond a small to medium-sized LAN. These types of hubs still provide the centralized connectivity associated with stand-alone or stackable hubs, however, enterprise hubs are a **chassis design** with separate modules that can function as centralized connectivity devices for multiple network architectures such as Fast Ethernet, Token Ring, FDDI, ATM, Gigabit Ethernet, and others. In an environment with this many network types, you would likely implement an enterprise hub solution that would contain separate modules known as **blades** that provide the ports for each network architecture type. Additional modules built into the chassis provide higher layer functionality such as the switching and/or routing functions necessary to provide connectivity between network types and among various departments or groups of users. Because enterprise hubs support multiple network types, they are more accurately defined as **concentrators,** but you'll more commonly hear them referred to as enterprise or backbone hubs.

Hub Technologies: Network Managed Hubs

Network managed hubs provide statistics gathering functionality combined with a software interface that is installed on an administrative workstation. The information that is available allows you to collect and view statistics about network performance, port usage, data throughput, potential network bottlenecks, destroyed data transmissions, and so on.

Bridges

In a very simple LAN environment, all computers can be connected to a single segment, and all of the computers on the LAN "hear" all exchanges of data between any two computers. As the number of computing devices on the LAN grows, the amount of traffic on the LAN grows as well, and all the newly attached devices as well as the previously installed devices must listen to an increasing number of data packets on the network.

From a practical viewpoint, not all of the computing devices on a LAN are constantly exchanging data with every other computer on the LAN. At the same time, there are computing devices that communicate with other devices on the LAN on a regular basis. Furthermore, if an organization has two LANs that aren't linked together and users on each LAN need to exchange information, overall data communications efficiency can be enhanced if the two LANs are connected through a common device. And overall, if there were a way to group the computers that need to communicate with each other on a regular basis and somehow separate that group from the other computers on the network while still allowing

FIGURE 4.3   LAN Bridge Connecting Two LAN Segments

The bridge and two LAN segments are all part of the same LAN.

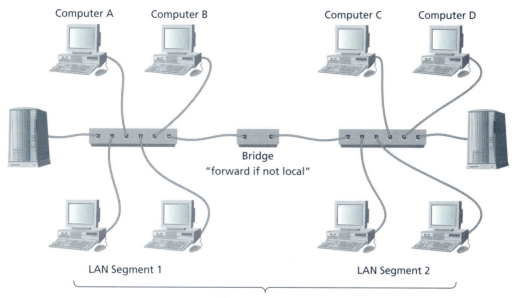

blade

a modular circuit board that can be inserted into a chassis-based LAN device that can hold multiple hub blades, switch blades, or even router blades. The chassis-based design that houses the blades provides integrated and expandable capacity.

concentrator

a device that functions as a central connectivity and collection point for network cabling and typically contains two or more port modules, each of which provides a central connectivity point for one type of network. Types of port modules can include Ethernet, Token Ring, FDDI, ATM, Gigabit Ethernet, and more.

communication between the two groups when necessary, then each computing device on a LAN would have to listen to fewer data packets, and the overall performance of the LAN could be improved. That was a lot to develop for early LANs, and in fact, that's where bridges came into play in early Ethernet networks under the 802.1D standard as published by the IEEE in 1990 and later on by the ISO in 1993.[2]

So what is a bridge, and what performance improvements can it bring to a LAN? Where is a bridge implemented, and how does it work? First of all, a **bridge** is a LAN device that connects two or more LAN segments while simultaneously **filtering** network data transmissions between those segments.[3] In a LAN that uses a bridge, data transmissions that originate on one LAN segment and that are destined for a computing device on that same segment stay on that segment. Data transmissions that originate on one LAN segment and that are destined for a computing device located on the other LAN segment are received by the bridge, stored in a buffer, checked for errors, and then a copy of the frame is propagated onto the other LAN segment. The LAN bridge connection is illustrated in Figure 4.3.

In Figure 4.3, two LAN segments are connected by a bridge. If computer A transmits to computer B, the transmitted frames stay on LAN segment 1. If computer A transmits to computer C, then the bridge forwards the packets to LAN segment 2. Because bridges filter the data transmissions and propagate only those frames destined for the adjacent segment, bridges are sometimes referred to as "forward if not local" LAN devices. LAN performance

---

[2] These standards have since been updated. You might want to check out the 802.1D standard on the IEEE Web site at http://standards.ieee.org/getieee802/download/802.1D-1998.pdf. You'll need to supply some limited information, and then you can download the standard.

[3] The bridges described in this section are also defined as transparent bridges. This name applies because transmitting computers are unaware that a destination computer is on another LAN segment or that one or more bridges exists between the source computer and the destination computer. That is, the bridge is transparent to the transmitting devices.

bridge
a LAN device that
connects two or more
LAN segments while
simultaneously filtering
network data
transmissions between
those segments

is improved because computing devices on opposite sides of the bridge do not have to listen to the local traffic that stays on the other side. In the absence of the bridge, and if the two LAN segments were connected as one big segment, then all computing devices would hear the data transmissions from all other devices. The trick for the network administrator, of course, is to establish the optimal location for the bridge. This can be accomplished by identifying the groups of computers that communicate most frequently and placing those computers on the same LAN segment.[4]

As a non-LAN example, think of a postal carrier delivering mail one letter at a time on any given street, and with each letter he runs down the street shouting the name on the letter and handing it to the household that responds to the shouting. For the next letter he does the same thing, and for the next letter, the same thing, and so on until there aren't any more letters to deliver. In this scenario, the street is analogous to a local area network, and every house on the street has to listen to every shout of the postal carrier to see if the letter is for that specific house. This is similar to how every NIC on a nonbridged LAN "hears" every piece of data on the network but reads only those pieces of information with the corresponding destination MAC address.

To continue the outrageous example, imagine the post office splitting the street into two sections and assigning two postal carriers, each of which runs down his or her own part of the street shouting only the names of the houses on his or her segment. The houses on one section would no longer hear the shouts directed at houses on the other section, so each house on each of the two sections hears less shouting.

If a house on one of the street sections has a letter to send and the name of the addressee happens to be on the other section of the street, the postal carrier on the source section picks up the letter and begins shouting the name. When none of the households on his section responds, he meets up with the other postal carrier, hands her the letter, and then the other postal carrier begins shouting the name on the letter as she runs down her own section.

The street and postal carrier example is analogous to placing a bridge in a local area network to create two network segments. When the street was divided into two sections in our example, receiving the mail became more efficient and less time consuming because each house no longer had to listen to as much shouting from the postal carrier. This is analogous to the inner workings of a LAN bridge. The bridge has a built-in algorithm that learns the MAC address of each network card in each computing device on each LAN segment that is connected to the bridge. The bridge learns the MAC addresses of individual computers as the computers transmit, the bridge links each MAC address to the bridge port that is connected to the originating LAN segment, and then the bridge saves the MAC addresses in a table, as shown in Figure 4.4.[5] When a bridge port hears a data transmission after the MAC address table is created, the bridge looks in the table for the MAC address, identifies the MAC address and the port it's linked to, and if the MAC address of the destination computer is local, the bridge drops the frame, preventing the local transmission from being propagated to the opposite side of the bridge. If the bridge identifies the MAC address of the destination computer as being on another LAN segment, the bridge forwards the frames to the other LAN segment. Local transmissions stay local, and all other transmissions are

---

[4] When bridges were used in the early 1990s, their implementation was based on the 80/20 rule. If 80 percent of LAN traffic would remain local and only about 20 percent would need to be forwarded to the other LAN segment, then performance improvements could be achieved by implementing a bridge.
[5] Remember that each device on the LAN segment, including the bridge port that is connected to the LAN segment, hears all data transmissions on the local LAN segment. Because the bridge ports hear these transmissions, the bridge can identify which MAC addresses are associated with which LAN segments and build a table that can be used to keep local traffic local and forward only the frames destined for the LAN segment that is attached to the other side of the bridge.

FIGURE 4.4

Different Views of a Simple MAC Address Table in a Three-port Bridge

Port 1		
MAC Address	Instruction	LAN Segment
b6 : 02 : ae : 09 : 4c : 2b	Bridge	Port 2
00 : 0a : bf : 4e : bd : 0a	Bridge	Port 3
06 : bf : 4a : 3e : ae : 2b	Local	Port 1
a8 : af : 2b : 5f : bc : 0c	Local	Port 1

Port 2		
MAC Address	Instruction	LAN Segment
b6 : 02 : ae : 09 : 4c : 2b	Local	Port 2
00 : 0a : bf : 4e : bd : 0a	Bridge	Port 3
06 : bf : 4a : 3e : ae : 2b	Bridge	Port 1
a8 : af : 2b : 5f : bc : 0c	Bridge	Port 1

Port 3		
MAC Address	Instruction	LAN Segment
b6 : 02 : ae : 09 : 4c : 2b	Bridge	Port 2
00 : 0a : bf : 4e : bd : 0a	Local	Port 3
06 : bf : 4a : 3e : ae : 2b	Bridge	Port 1
a8 : af : 2b : 5f : bc : 0c	Bridge	Port 1

propagated to the opposite side of the bridge. In this way, computing devices on each side of the bridge do not have to listen to all of the transmissions of both segments—only local transmissions plus those that are forwarded.

In Figure 4.4, the MAC addresses of four different computers are saved in the MAC address table of a three-port bridge. By referencing this table, each bridge port knows which addresses are local and which should be forwarded. For example, if port 1 hears a data transmission with the destination MAC address a8:af:2b:5f:bc:0c, port 1 discards the packet because its destination is on the local segment. When port 1 hears a data transmission with destination MAC address b6:02:ae:09:4c:2b, it forwards the frame to port 2. When port 1 hears frames with a destination MAC address of 00:0a:bf:4e:bd:0a, port 1 forwards those frames to port 3. When port 3 hears frames with a destination address of either 06:bf:4a:3e:ae:2b or a8:af:2b:5f:bc:0c, port 3 looks up the MAC address in the table and forwards those frames to port 1. Different bridges from different manufacturers display bridging table information in different ways, but Figure 4.4 shows one possibility for displaying the MAC table information—on a port-by-port basis. Because bridges function by utilizing data link layer MAC addressing, bridges are OSI layer 2 (L2) LAN devices.

flooding
the process of forwarding data frames from a receiving port to all other bridge ports if the bridge's MAC address table does not have a MAC address entry that corresponds to the destination MAC address of a received data frame

When a bridge is installed and first powered on in a LAN, it reads the data frames from all transmitting devices connected to it and forwards all frames to all bridge ports, except the bridge port from which the transmission originated. As the bridge receives frames from transmitting devices, the bridge records source MAC addresses in the bridge's MAC address table and links each MAC address with the port from which the frame originated.

Once the bridge has learned and stored a device's MAC address, the bridge can direct data transmissions received from any local segment to the specific bridge port that is connected to the LAN segment of the destination device. If the bridge reads the destination address of a frame and can't find that address in its MAC address table, the bridge forwards the frame to all bridge ports except the source port, in a process known as **flooding**.

FIGURE 4.5   Redundant Bridges between Two LAN Segments

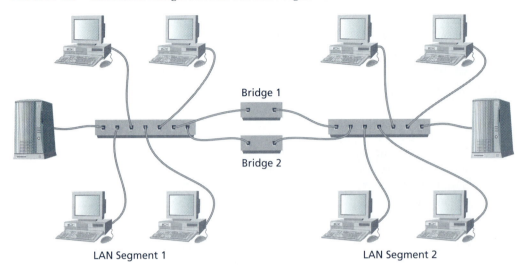

Bridge 1

Bridge 2

LAN Segment 1   LAN Segment 2

fault tolerant
the ability to recover from device or component failure

bridging loop
a condition on a LAN in which packets are forwarded between redundant bridges in an endless loop and never arrive at their intended destinations

spanning tree protocol
specifies that one bridge in a redundant pair be the designated bridge and the other be the backup bridge in order to prevent bridging loops. The spanning tree protocol also defines the communications between redundant-pair bridges so that the backup bridge can take over for the designated bridge if the designated bridge fails.

What happens if more computers are added to a LAN segment after the bridge has built its MAC address table? Or how about computers that are removed from a LAN segment? Or even computers that have a new NIC installed—what happens to their entries in the MAC address table? In reality, the MAC address table is not infinite. It will hold thousands of entries, and it is dynamically updated as new computers are added or removed from the LAN segments attached to the bridge.[6] Typically an administrator responsible for hardware infrastructure will specify the length of time, usually in seconds, that a MAC address entry should remain active in the table. The bridge will delete a computer's MAC address from the table if the bridge has not received any transmissions from that computer within the time interval. If a computer comes back online after the time interval, the bridge relearns the address and adds it back into the table. If the computer is moved to a LAN segment that is attached to a different bridge port, a new entry is added to the MAC address table linking the MAC address to its new port. The old entry is dropped after the time interval that is linked to the old entry expires.[7]

Bridges can also be implemented in redundant pairs between LAN segments so that data transmissions have a **fault-tolerant** path in the event that one bridge fails. Figure 4.5 provides an example of this configuration.

In Figure 4.5, the designers of the LAN illustrated have specified that two bridges connect LAN segment 1 to LAN segment 2. As part of this fault-tolerant specification, however, only one of the bridges can be actively forwarding packets at any point in time; otherwise a condition known as a **bridging loop** will occur. In a bridging loop, packets are forwarded between redundant bridges in an endless loop and never arrive at their intended destinations. To circumvent this problem, network engineers implement the **spanning tree protocol**, as specified in the IEEE 802.1D standard. The spanning tree protocol specifies that one

---

[6] The MAC address table is a design feature that should be considered at the time a bridge is purchased. A bridge's MAC address table must be large enough to hold an address for every device that is connected to the bridge including devices that can be reached through hubs and other bridges. Generally, the bigger the capacity of the MAC address table, the more expensive the bridge.
[7] Administrators can add static entries for MAC addresses and time intervals depending on the needs of the network.

Applied Technical **Tidbit**

When Token Ring networks were popular, they enjoyed a substantial implementation base, and in many cases, hundreds of workstations might be connected in a Token Ring network. A problem, according to the IEEE 802.5 specifications, was that only 250 nodes could be connected in a single Token Ring network. Even if you used IBM's implementation, you were allowed only 260 nodes per ring. To circumvent the node limitation problem, you could design your Token Ring network to include a source-routing bridge between two rings as illustrated in part **(a)** of Figure 4.6.

By implementing a source-routing bridge between two rings, you could effectively double the number of nodes in your Token Ring network. Add a third ring, and you connect that to either the first or second ring by implementing another source-routing bridge. As more and more rings were added and connected to an existing ring with a source-routing bridge, substantial delay or *latency* could result between the first and last rings on the network. Once again, technology provided assistance.

FIGURE 4.6 **Multiple Token Rings Connected by Source-Routing Bridges**
a. Multiple token rings are connected by source routing bridges. **b.** Multiple token rings are connected by a Token Ring switch.

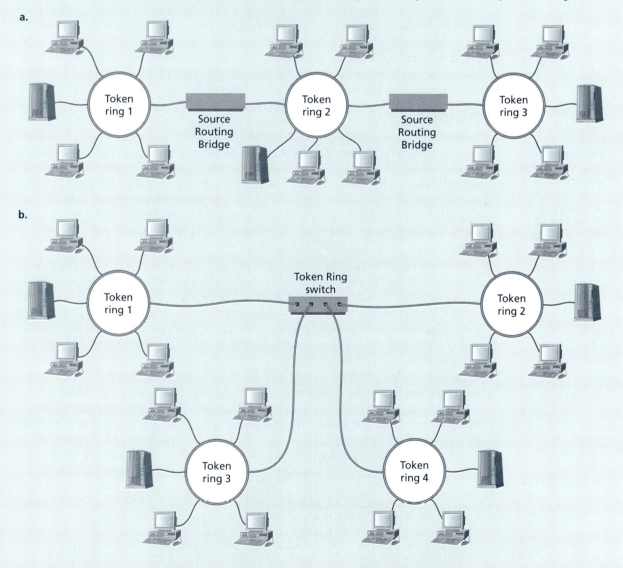

In part **(b)** of Figure 4.6, you'll see a representation of Token Ring switching. With a Token Ring switch, large Token Ring networks became more feasible and more reliable with lowered latency because data no longer had to travel across each ring to reach a destination on a distant ring. Token Ring switching provided a way to replace all of the source-routing bridges in a Token Ring network with a centralized device that acted as a source-routing bridge to each connected ring. Now each ring could be directly connected to every other ring in an entire Token Ring network with overall improved performance on the entire network.[8]

bridge in a redundant pair be the designated bridge and the other be the backup bridge. Only the designated bridge forwards data frames; the backup bridge does not. This prevents the redundant pair of bridges from generating bridging loops. In addition, the spanning tree protocol defines the communications between redundant-pair bridges so that the backup bridge can take over for the designated bridge if the designated bridge fails.

The benefit to the network and to the business environment from implementing a bridge is that the computers connected to each bridge port enjoy improved network performance and response times because local data transmissions are not propagated to the other bridge ports—only nonlocal traffic is forwarded to the other network segment. In addition, larger LANs with more computers are possible with the implementation of a bridge. Today bridges are generally considered obsolete because they have been supplanted by switching devices, which you'll discover later on in this chapter.

Switches

learning algorithm
functionality that is
programmed into a
bridge or switch that
allows these devices to
learn the MAC
addresses of all attached
network devices

Switches and bridges have a lot in common. Both can be multiport devices; both have **learning algorithms** that allow these devices to learn the MAC addresses of all attached network devices; both have filtering algorithms that allow data transmissions to be forwarded if the data transmission is not intended for a computer on the local segment where the communication originated; and both can be implemented with redundant links for fault tolerance.[9] In other words, both bridges and switches build MAC address tables; both perform frame flooding, forwarding, and filtering; and both implement the spanning tree protocol.

But there are differences between bridges and switches. In older networks, bridges were typically connected to hubs or other bridges. In modern networks, switch ports can be directly connected to individual PCs and servers or to hubs, bridges, other switches, and routers. Bridges usually had a single central processor that limited frame processing and forwarding to one frame at a time. Switches use special hardware components that can read multiple ports simultaneously and establish multiple and simultaneous forwarding paths, as in Figure 4.7.

In Figure 4.7, a multiport switch can read frames from computers A, C, and E at the same time and then make simultaneous forwarding decisions based on the MAC address information contained in the switch's MAC address table. For example, if computer A's information is destined for a computer on segment 2, computer C's information is destined for a computer on segment 4, and computer E's information is destined for a computer on segment 6, the MAC address table provides the information required for forwarding decisions and the hardware in a switch is capable of forwarding frames in parallel to all

---

[8] Additional performance was also available by installing full-duplex Token Ring network interface cards in the servers and connecting the servers directly to the token ring switch.
[9] The spanning tree protocol applies to redundant switches as well redundant bridges.

FIGURE 4.7   Data Propagation on a Multiport Switch

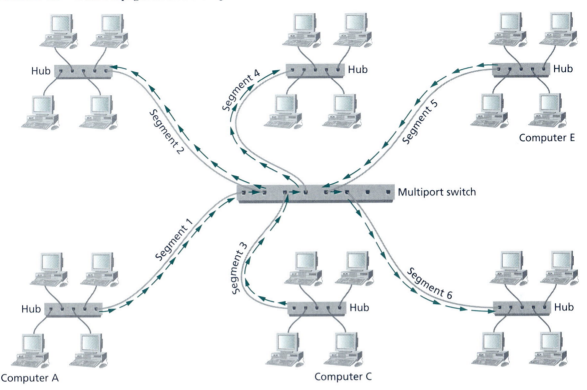

destinations simultaneously. This parallel capability gives switches a distinct performance advantage over bridges.

Switch Technologies: Store and Forward Switches

data transmission throughput
the amount of information, such as number of frames, passed through a device per unit time

LAN switch technology has evolved rapidly since the mid-1990s, and several types of switches have been engineered and marketed to meet varying business needs. Each major technology breakthrough has provided various and new levels of efficiency and **data transmission throughput**.

Store and forward switches were designed to do error checking on each frame after the entire frame has been received into the switch. If the error-checking algorithm determines that there is no error for a frame, the switch looks in its MAC address table for the port to which the destination device is attached, and then forwards the frame. This type of switching is highly reliable because it doesn't forward any bad frames. It is slower than other types of switches because it holds on to each frame until it is completely received to check for errors before starting to forward it.

Switch Technologies: Cut Through Switches

Cut through switches are faster than store and forward switches because the cut through switch doesn't perform error checking on frames. Instead, a cut through switch reads only the address information for each frame as frames enter the switch. After looking up the port that is linked to the destination device, the frame is forwarded to the appropriate port.

Two major performance issues are associated with cut through switches. First, cut through switches forward any bad frames that enter the switch. This imposes a performance penalty across the destination network segment because the switch forwards frames that the destination can't use. Second, each bad frame requires a replacement frame, which results in additional network traffic on the source network segment, additional traffic through the switch, and additional traffic across the destination network segment. If a source device on the source network segment continually generates errors, over time the increase in network traffic can slow your local area network's performance.

Switch Technologies: Error-Free Cut Through Switches

This is a preferred switching solution because an **error-free cut through switch** combines the fast throughput of a cut through switch with the error-checking functionality of a store and forward switch. An error-free cut through switch reads the address information of each frame that enters the switch and initially forwards all frames, both good and bad, to their intended destinations. If the error-free cut through switch determines that a particular port is receiving too many bad frames, it will reconfigure that port to store and forward mode so that bad frames are dropped. That is, bad frames are no longer forwarded to destination ports.

Switch Technologies: Intelligent versus Unmanaged Switches

In larger networks, network administrators track statistics on the amount of traffic and number of errors flowing through every port of every switch on the network. This lets network administrators identify problems and troubleshoot the problems before they become too serious.

unmanaged switch
a switch that does not have built-in management functions such as tracking and reporting of port performance and data transmission performance

When you decide to implement switching in your network, you can order unmanaged or intelligent switches. **Unmanaged switches** provide your LAN with all the benefits that switching can provide; however, you won't be able to keep tabs on port or data transmission performance. Whereas in small networks this might not be a big issue, in larger LANs you'll want an **intelligent switch** so that you can track performance information and make adjustments to your LAN or to your switches before smaller issues become major problems.

intelligent switch
a switch that tracks and reports LAN performance statistics

With intelligent switches, there is typically a database **application specific integrated circuit (ASIC),** which is nothing more than a semiconductor chip or series of chips that are designed based on a set of information gathering standards commonly called a management information base (MIB). The ASIC runs an internal program that collects the various performance statistics listed in the MIB and allows you to view and collect these statistics through a software interface that you'll load on a client or administrative workstation computer and manage.[10] Some of the types of statistics you might collect over time are error rate per port and data throughput per port.

Switch Technologies: Higher Layer Switches

When a device is referred to as a layer 2, layer 3, or layer 4 device, it indicates the corresponding layer within the OSI model where that device's functionality is represented.

By definition, a switch filters or forwards data frames based on the MAC address information that is part of the data frame. This makes a traditional switch an L2 networking device.

Within the past few years, switching devices that operate at OSI layer 3 (L3) and OSI layer 4 (L4) have become popular. Each of these types includes the data link layer data switching capability of traditional switching, but these newer switches add extra functionality. The L3 switches, for example, add routing functionality. If a data frame can't be switched, it is routed.[11] With L4 switches, requests for TCP port-level services can be directed to one or more service providers, such as applications running on a server, based on the TCP port number located in the data transmission.

---

[10] The protocol that is implemented to communicate with the MIB is known as the simple network management protocol (SNMP). SNMP is explained at the end of this chapter.
[11] You'll learn more about routing later in this chapter.

Applied Technical **Tidbit**   Switched Ethernet

broadcast
a method of transmitting data on a shared medium in which all nodes on the network hear every other station's transmissions but each station receives only those packets that are addressed to that station

collision domain
a CSMA/CD network segment that will experience collisions if two computers that are connected to the segment simultaneously attempt to send a transmission. With a switch located between the two computers, each of the two computers can simultaneously access the network, each on its own segment, without a collision taking place.

You learned about Ethernet's access method in chapter 3, and you also learned that with CSMA/CD and nonswitched Ethernet, all network devices compete for access to the shared network bandwidth. In addition, with Ethernet all network transmissions are **broadcast** throughout the network segment. That is, when one computer accesses the network and sends data, all the other devices on the network hear that transmission. But even though all the computers hear the transmitted packets, only the intended recipient receives the packets for further processing; the other computers simply discard the packets that aren't intended for them.

With nonswitched or traditional Ethernet, this process creates a problem as more and more computers are added to a network segment. If you have a network with relatively few computers, you'll enjoy faster transfer speeds. As more and more devices are added, however, the network can become congested with the network traffic created by the additional computers. Because the bandwidth is shared, each additional device that is added to the network makes the network less efficient, and users will complain with comments such as "the network is slow," or "it's taking too long to get my files."

To circumvent this network congestion problem on Ethernet networks, you can implement a switching device known as an Ethernet switch to divide an Ethernet network into two or more separate segments that function as separate **collision domains**. The switch receives traffic from each collision domain and filters the data transmissions between the two so that only the traffic that is supposed to be forwarded to the other segment will be allowed to pass through the filter. As a result, the switch reduces the number of collisions that would otherwise occur in an unswitched network. With fewer collisions, there is a reduced need for retransmissions, original transmissions access the network more efficiently, and overall network congestion is substantially reduced.

Because Ethernet switches have come down in price so much over the past few years, they have practically replaced hubs as the devices of choice for the physical layer as well as data link layer connectivity. Since hubs do not have the circuitry built in to them to filter network traffic as more devices are added to an Ethernet network, hubs do nothing to alleviate the added network congestion. However, when you replace an Ethernet hub with an Ethernet switch, the circuitry of the switch filters the data traffic. Upon powering up the switch, the switch learns the physical/media access control (MAC) address of each computer so that with any data transmission only the intended recipients receive the transmission, and the potential for collisions in this scenario is reduced to nearly zero.[12]

Switch Implementation

Switches can be used in various functions throughout a LAN environment. Some are implemented in place of hubs to connect client workstations within a department or specified group of users to improve network performance within the group. These are commonly referred to as workgroup, department, or access layer switches.[13]

Other switches are used to connect separate access layer switches. The workgroups that are connected to these access layer switches might be separated by floors in a building or be located in different buildings in a campus environment. Switches that link access layer switches are known as central switches or distribution layer switches.[14] Distribution layer switches provide connectivity between workgroups while ensuring the performance benefits of switching technology.

---

[12] Upon booting, a switch performs in the same capacity as a hub until the switch table is built.

[13] Access layer in this context does not have anything to do with the OSI model. Instead access layer as it refers to a switch is a Cisco Systems' term to define switches that connect department or workgroup computers to a network backbone.

[14] Distribution layer switch is another Cisco Systems' term that defines a type of switch that connects access layer switches to each other.

physical layer broadcast
a type of broadcast that is implemented by nonswitched Ethernet networks with the result that each bit transmitted by all nodes is physically received by every other node on the LAN

MAC-level Broadcasts
deal with how to handle MAC-level broadcast frames; that is, the data frames that are transmitted to all MAC addresses on a given network

There are two types of broadcasts with which you should be familiar in data communications and networks. There is the **physical layer broadcast** that is implemented by nonswitched Ethernet networks through shared cabling and hubs. With this type of broadcast, each bit that is transmitted by any station is physically received by every other station on the LAN.

Switches and VLANs don't do the physical layer broadcasts, which stands to reason because switches are OSI layer 2 devices. Instead, switches and VLANs are concerned with **MAC-level broadcasts**. MAC-level broadcasts deal with how to handle MAC-level broadcast frames; that is, the data frames that have a broadcast destination MAC address. In other words, MAC-level broadcast frames are addressed to all MAC addresses on a given network (not a network segment, but an actual network as that network is defined by its network address). A regular switch forwards all broadcast frames out all ports, but a VLAN switch forwards broadcast frames only to other ports that are part of the same VLAN.

So what is the purpose of MAC-level broadcast frames and how does this impact a network? Workstations use broadcast frames to (1) send dynamic host configuration protocol (DHCP) broadcasts to get IP addresses, (2) send Find Nearest Server broadcasts to locate local network servers, and (3) send address resolution protocol (ARP) broadcasts to determine the MAC addresses of other resources on the local network. Routers use MAC-level broadcast frames to advertise available routes and link status. Bridges and switches use MAC-level broadcasts to pass Spanning Tree data to other bridges and switches. Thus, using VLANs will (1) affect the IP network on which a computing device resides, (2) control which servers and network services a workstation hears when it boots up, and (3) control which network resources are accessible by a workstation without going through a router.

Still other switches connect various distribution layer switches together and provide access to centralized network services that are accessed by an entire company or organization. These types of switches usually have the higher-end bells and whistles such as built-in manageability and may contain separate blades that support connectivity among various network types such as Fast Ethernet, Token Ring, FDDI, ATM, Gigabit Ethernet, and so on. They're commonly referred to as enterprise switches, collapsed backbone switches, or core layer switches.[15]

VLAN Switches

broadcast domain
a collection of computer nodes that can receive broadcast packets. It's also a grouping of computers, each of which hears any data transmissions that are propagated on the broadcast domain.

Virtual local area network (VLAN) switches take switching a step further from what you've already learned about switches. With switched Ethernet, for example, each port on the switch defines a collision domain, and the entire switch forms a single broadcast domain.[16] VLAN switches, on the other hand, define not only specific collision domains, but they can define multiple **broadcast domains** as well. In simple terms, that means network traffic that is directed to all computers on the network can be segmented to transmit only on a specific VLAN. This improves network bandwidth on any given VLAN because each VLAN filters the network-to-network broadcast traffic as well as the collision traffic from other VLANs.

As an example, consider a VLAN switch that has been configured into three distinct VLANs. If it is an OSI layer 2 VLAN, none of the three VLANs can communicate unless each of the VLANs is connected to a router. That is because each VLAN is separating

---

[15] Core layer switch is yet another Cisco Systems' term that defines the type of switch that connects distribution layer switches and also provides access to wide area networking services and other high-end services such as mass data storage and high-availability application servers.

[16] See the Applied Technical Tidbit on switched Ethernet in this section.

collision traffic associated with MAC addresses *and,* and this is a big *AND,* each VLAN is separating the network-to-network broadcast traffic. In other words, each VLAN is behaving as a separate network, according to OSI layer 3. Without the use of an OSI layer 3 device such as a router, the configured VLANs will not communicate with each other.[17] To get the VLANs to communicate, you would need to connect each of them to a router, or you could implement an OSI layer 3 switch which would have the routing capability built in.

The flexibility of VLAN switches makes them a valuable addition to a local area network. Computers do not necessarily have to be in close proximity to share a network segment. Because VLAN switches are managed by software, a computer that is physically located in one end of a building can be part of the same VLAN as a computer that is physically located in another distant part of the building simply by reconfiguring the switch through its software interface. In addition, when you need to move a computer to another location, you can connect it to another port on the same switch or even to a port on another switch, and through software configuration make it part of its original VLAN.

VLAN Switch Types. VLAN switches follow the OSI model in terms of functionality and configuration capability. Some VLAN switches are port-based and follow the physical layer properties of OSI layer 1.[18] Computers that need to join a specific VLAN are connected to a port on the switch, and the switch port is configured to join the appropriate VLAN, as depicted in Figure 4.8. In the figure, multiple computers throughout an organization can connect to the switch, and groups of ports are configured through software to

FIGURE 4.8 **VLANs on a Port-based VLAN Switch**

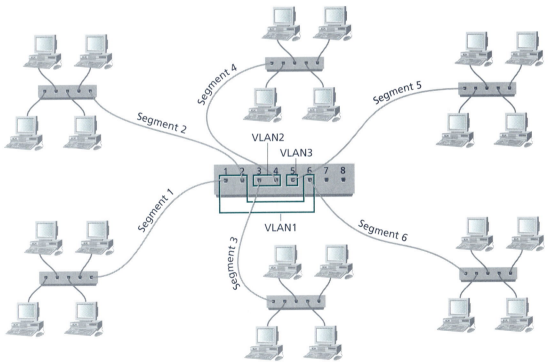

---

[17] Network administrators might implement a VLAN configuration like this for security purposes. That is, by forcing network traffic to pass through the router, the network administrator can control access to each VLAN through the router.

[18] Even though port-based switches are configured at OSI layer 1 via port assignment, the switching is still performed at OSI layer 2.

define the various VLANs. In Figure 4.8, ports 1, 2, and 6 comprise VLAN1, ports 3 and 4 form VLAN2, and port 5 is VLAN3. If a computer is moved to a different location and connects to a different port on the same switch, it can be rejoined to its original VLAN through software configuration; the network administrator simply reconfigures the newly connected port to be part of the desired VLAN. For example, if a computer is moved from segment 1 to a segment that is connected to port 7, port 7 can be added to VLAN1.

Another type of VLAN switch can be configured at OSI layer 2, based on the MAC address of computers connected to the switch. The switch learns and builds a table of the MAC addresses of the computers connected to it, and then the network administrator can customize the configuration of the switch to link specific MAC addresses to specific VLANs. Once the initial configuration is complete, MAC-based VLAN switches have even more flexibility than the port-based VLAN switches. With MAC-based VLAN switches, you can move a computer to another port on the switch, and you don't have to reconfigure the port to join the original VLAN. The switch automatically recognizes the MAC address, looks at the configuration table to see which VLAN the MAC address belongs to, and directs traffic from the computer according to the switch configuration.

Layer 3 and layer 4 VLAN switches function in much the same way as MAC-based VLAN switches, only they define each VLAN based on IP addresses and TCP port (service) addresses. With these types of VLAN switches, you obtain the typical benefits of port-based and MAC-based VLAN switching, plus you pick up the added benefit of routing and being able to define each VLAN based on layer 4 classes of service. For example, you could establish a VLAN within a specified IP address range (layer 3 functionality) and assign it to allow Internet access using the HTTP protocol on TCP port 80 (layer 4 functionality). On another VLAN, you might assign a different IP address range and allow it to use the FTP protocol on TCP port 21. In this way, you can refine your VLAN configuration to accommodate the specific access needs of your users and to enhance access security.

On the flip side, VLANs that operate at higher layers can impose a performance penalty because the additional functionality requires more processing. To address this performance penalty, many VLAN switch manufacturers have introduced higher-layer switches that operate at **wire speed**. That is, the manufacturer designs in more processing power and intelligence circuitry to delivery layer 3 and layer 4 switches that can handle continuous frame transmissions at the highest possible frame rate supported by the underlying medium. Nonwire speed devices by comparison do not have the processing power to continuously handle frame transmissions at the highest possible frame rate supported by the underlying medium and must buffer frames in order to compensate for the slower processing speed.

wire speed
the ability of higher layer networking devices to perform at the same speed as the underlying transmission medium to which the devices are connected

Multiple VLAN Switches. Multiple VLAN switches that are working together to provide campuswide VLANs need to be able to identify which VLAN any given packet belongs to. This is not a trivial task, as the VLAN switch has to read the packet information and direct it according to the VLAN identifier in the packet. Some manufacturers utilize their own proprietary protocols that encapsulate the packet with a VLAN identifier. Then as the encapsulated packet is directed across the network, the various VLAN switches know to which VLAN to direct the packet simply by looking at the VLAN identifier.

Other manufacturers have adopted the IEEE 802.1q standard for identifying VLAN packets. This standardized approach does not encapsulate the packet; instead it rebuilds the packet with its original information and adds a 16-bit VLAN identifier, in a process known as tagging. The idea is similar to the proprietary encapsulation approach, only the 16-bit identifier approach is standardized by the IEEE so that companies that want to implement VLAN switching have a high level of assurance that equipment from one vendor will work with VLAN equipment from another vendor. Proprietary protocols do not provide that assurance and generally limit you to using a single vendor's solution.

Switching Limitations

In a small LAN, L2 switching can segment the LAN into separate collision domains and provide valuable increases in network performance. In large-scale data networks, however, L2 switches are insufficient for interconnecting small LANs into a vast infrastructure. Why? After all, switched Ethernet has no distance limitations—in theory all LANs across the globe could be interconnected with switched Ethernet. And even if you accounted for the possibility of different LAN architectures such as Ethernet, Token Ring, FDDI, ATM, and others, there are OSI layer 2 LAN devices that can translate between these different architectures.[19] So why not just interconnect all the world's LANs via L2 switching?

address resolution protocol (arp)
the protocol that is used in IP networks to map an IP address to a MAC address

First, consider the impact of broadcast traffic on a large-scale network's performance. Some of the broadcast traffic is the result of **address resolution protocol (arp)** requests, but much of the broadcast traffic in a switched network is caused by the flooding of packets to all switch ports until the MAC address table is built and ongoing flooding as new computers are added to the network. If you consider a vast network interconnected by layer 2 switches, the MAC address tables of all the interconnected switches could conceivably be in a constant state of flux. All broadcasts would propagate across all switches and on to every LAN segment throughout the entire network, consuming bandwidth and requiring every computer on every LAN segment to read the broadcast packets. This scenario imposes a substantial performance penalty on the entire network as well as on each connected computer.

Second, consider the reliability and scalability of a layer 2 switched network infrastructure. If each switch is connected to the next switch in series, one failure could potentially disrupt data flow across a significant portion of the network. Even with redundant switches in place, the cost to scale this topology each time a new LAN segment is added would be staggering, not to mention the spanning tree protocol configuration required to prevent bridging loops.

Finally, consider one of the biggest limitations of switches—the scalability of their MAC address table sizes. Switches require a MAC address entry for every device that's connected to a network, and if an organization were to build a switched infrastructure of 500 LANs with 100 devices on each LAN, interconnection via switching would require every switch to maintain a MAC address table with as many as 50,000 entries to correctly deliver data to all possible **network nodes.** That would place an incredible amount of processing overhead on each switch every time a frame needed to be directed to its end location. As a comparison, if this infrastructure were built using 500 routers instead of 500 switches, and if all the routers were interconnected, each router would need to keep track of 500 IP networks in its routing table. And in reality, each router would not need to be interconnected with every other router, further reducing the amount of overhead on each individual router.

Any of these reasons is sufficient to preclude building a large-scale network infrastructure based solely on layer 2 switching. Instead, you'll need to implement switches in conjunction with routers to circumvent these limitations.

Routers

router
a layer 3 device that connects two or more networks, separates broadcast domains, and directs data packets to their destinations based on IP addresses and across the best possible path

We've already seen that a hub acts as a layer 1 LAN device that can be used to connect numerous computing devices in a local area network. A switch is a layer 2 LAN device that connects different LAN segments, workstations, and servers, directs data frames based on MAC addresses, and separates collision domains on the same network. But where a switch manages the flow of frames between computers within a network, a **router** is a layer 3 device that allows packets to flow between two networks. A router connects two or more

---

[19] OSI layer 2 LAN devices that translate between different architectures are generally known as translational bridges.

FIGURE 4.9
Two Networks Connected by a Router

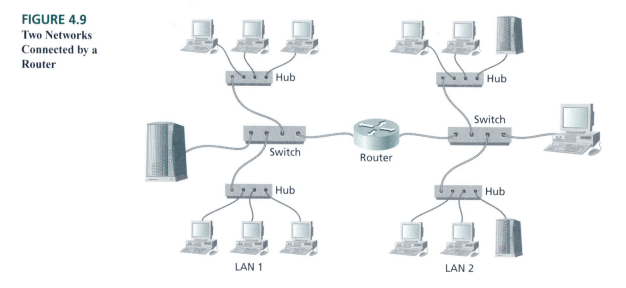

LAN 1   LAN 2

network
a logical grouping of computers and other devices that are defined by a common network address. The network address is a logical numbering scheme typically defined by the Internet Protocol.

networks, separates broadcast domains, and directs data packets to their destinations based on IP addresses and across the best possible route. When you want to send data transmissions to computers located on other networks, you'll need to implement a router, as shown in Figure 4.9.

Network designers implement routers for several key reasons. First of all, routers establish a path over which computers on one network can communicate with computers on another network. When a computer on one network needs to communicate with a computer on another network, the router reads the layer 3 destination information in the data packets and forwards the packets to the destination network.

Another reason network engineers and designers implement routers is to improve the security of a LAN. In the absence of a router, all computing devices on a LAN hear all packets that are broadcast across the network. Even a layer 2 switch does not filter broadcast transmissions. As a LAN grows in size, an increasing number of broadcasts to a growing number of network nodes increases the possibility that imposter nodes might listen to the broadcasts and illicitly capture valuable data. Routers control this problem with their ability to filter broadcasts. And in addition to filtering broadcasts, routers also provide general access list filtering for security purposes. This is often one of the primary reasons to implement routed versus switched interconnections.

Routers also provide scalability for growing networks by reducing the performance penalty associated with broadcast traffic. As more computers are added to a network, network bandwidth can become congested with broadcasts. If groups of users that utilize common resources and have common data sharing needs can be separated by a router to form their own network, those groups of users will no longer receive the broadcasts from the devices that are still connected on the other side of the router. In addition, as a network is divided into smaller networks that are interconnected by routers or as new networks are connected to an existing network, routers not only improve bandwidth efficiency, but they also direct data transmissions along optimal paths to the other networks. That is, routers have built-in intelligence that allows them to track the best paths to other networks so that data can be sent directly to a specific network along the best path without impacting traffic on other networks. With these capabilities, routers allow networks to grow in size beyond the limitations associated with layer 2 switched networks.

Routers can also be implemented at the "edge" or "border" of a LAN to connect the LAN to distant networks. In Figure 4.10, for example, network 1 is connected to network 2

FIGURE 4.10   Networks Interconnected by Routers

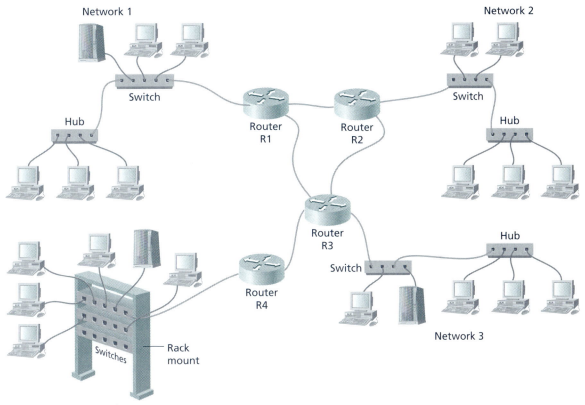

and network 3 through router R1. Network 2 is connected to network 1 and network 3 through router R2. Network 3 is connected to network 1 and network 4 through router R3. And network 4 is connected to network 3 through router R4. To allow data to flow between these networks, each network has its own unique **network address** that distinguishes it from the other networks, and each network is connected to at least one router. In addition, each router maintains a **routing table** that stores the addresses of other networks so that data from one network can be routed to the appropriate destination network over the best available path.[20]

In terms of the data flow between one network and another, here's how it works. To connect with other networks, a LAN is connected to a port on a router. That port has an assigned MAC address that workstations and servers and other computing devices can use to direct data frames to the router. When a router hears a data frame that is addressed to it, the router receives the frame, de-encapsulates the network layer address of the packet, and looks in its routing table to identify the best path for the packet to take to the destination network.

Sometimes a router can route a packet directly onto the destination network, as was the case in Figure 4.9, but other times data packets must be forwarded to another router before the packets can reach their destination network. In addition, the router that connects the

routing table
a list of networks and path criteria to other networks that a router maintains so that it can forward data to other networks

---

[20] The links between routers can be high-speed network backbone connections or high-speed carrier services designed to accommodate data packets. You'll discover network backbones later in this chapter, and you'll examine carrier services in chapter 8.

hop
a link between two routers in the path from source network to destination network

metric
a measurement of one or more properties that can be used to make a decision

route cost
the cost that is linked to a path between a source and destination network and which is based on one or more metrics

operating system
software that provides functionality to a networking device and services to other networking devices. Different operating systems provide different functionality and services, and they're generally specific to the type of networking device. For example, there are workstation operating systems, server or network operating systems, switch operating systems, and router operating systems.

gateway
hardware or software or a combination of both that connects two different network environments and operates at layers 3 and above

LAN to distant networks can be connected to more than one router, which creates more than one possible path to the destination network. In any case, each connection between routers along the entire path between source and destination network is known as a **hop**. In Figure 4.10 the path between a computer on network 1 and a computer on network 4 requires two hops if the data flows from network 1 through router R1, router R3, and router R4. The path would require three hops if it traveled from network 1 through router R1, router R2, router R3, and router R4 to network 4.

The possible paths between a source network and a destination network are determined based upon multiple **metrics**, or function measurements, that can be used to determine the **route cost** of each possible path between a source and destination network. The various metrics can include (1) path length as defined by the number of hops between source and destination network, (2) bandwidth of the connection between routers, (3) usage cost of communications links, and (4) routing delay—a metric that includes variables such as network congestion, physical distance between networks, and processing capacity of the routers in the path. Network administrators can use one or more of these metrics to manually configure routes and route costs to each destination network, or routers can be configured to use sophisticated routing algorithms that incorporate one or more of these metrics to automatically adjust routes and route costs.

So how are the routing paths created and information regarding those paths updated in the routing table of each router? Two fundamental approaches are possible: (1) static routing and (2) dynamic routing. With static routing, a network administrator defines the paths to other networks, creates an entry for each path, assigns metrics to those paths, and manually enters this information into the routing table. Static routing is effective when routing metrics are not expected to change over time.

Dynamic routing provides a mechanism for routers to automatically accommodate new routes and changing network conditions using sophisticated software known as a dynamic routing algorithm that is part of the router's **operating system**. When a change is detected along any of the paths between the source and destination network, such as a link being down or the addition of a new router, the routing algorithm recalculates optimal paths to destination networks and updates the router's routing table. In addition, the routing algorithm exchanges routing update messages with other routers so that the other routers dynamically update their routing tables with the new routing information.[21]

Gateways

A **gateway** is hardware or software or a combination of both that provides protocol translation or connectivity between disparate systems. Gateways can also establish service connectivity between disparate systems or from one network to another, and in these cases gateways can be functioning at the session layer, presentation layer, or application layer of the OSI model. Depending on the connectivity/conversion function a gateway needs to perform, it can handle data transmission frame size conversion from one environment to the other, it can perform protocol conversions, and it can make data format translations such as from ASCII to EBCDIC.

As an example, you might need to connect your LAN to a mainframe computer. To communicate between the two environments will very likely require a different set of protocols, different data frame sizes, and potential conversion from the ASCII character set to

---

[21] Examples of these dynamic routing algorithms include the link-state algorithm and distance vector algorithm. With link-state algorithms each router sends information about the links to which it is connected to all other routers. With a distance vector algorithm, each router shares routing information only with its neighboring routers. The pros and cons and detailed functionality of each of these algorithms is beyond the scope of this text.

FIGURE 4.11   **Connecting Client Workstations to a Mainframe through Novell's SNA Gateway Software**

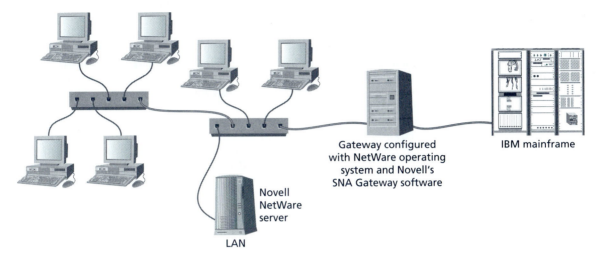

Gateway configured
with NetWare operating
system and Novell's
SNA Gateway software

IBM mainframe

Novell
NetWare
server

LAN

EBCDIC. If you were connecting to an IBM mainframe that utilized Systems Network Architecture (SNA), you would implement an SNA gateway between your LAN and the mainframe. Then users on the LAN would be able to transparently access and send information to the mainframe, as illustrated in Figure 4.11.

Some of the products that have been available over the past several years include the SNA Gateway product from Novell, which allowed users on a LAN running Novell's NetWare software to connect through a Novell NetWare server running the SNA Gateway software to an IBM mainframe. The Novell SNA Gateway software performed the protocol conversions as well as the data formatting and frame size translations. The product enjoyed modest success until the development of easy-to-implement and reliable terminal emulation software for workstations.

Because of the conversion processes that go on inside a gateway, a gateway can become a bottleneck to data transmission performance between the two environments. In recent years, this has led to the development of improved functionality within mainframes such as better LAN interfaces and improved processing of LAN protocols so that LAN nodes can access data from mainframes without the performance penalty imposed by gateways. That is, this improved mainframe functionality eliminates the need for a gateway to translate between the LAN and the mainframe. In addition, client-based software known as **terminal emulation software** can provide direct connectivity to a mainframe without the need for a gateway. Examples of terminal emulation software include VT-100 software for connectivity to legacy DEC computers and 3270 emulator software used for direct connectivity to legacy IBM mainframes.

You will find gateways in use in many areas of local area network functionality. Their implementation makes access to other networks and network services transparent to users. Some of the other types of gateways you might come across include

*terminal emulation
software*
software that can be run
on a computer to gain
direct access to legacy
mainframe systems,
without the use of a
gateway

- **E-mail gateways** Provide the necessary e-mail service translations between local area network e-mail systems and external e-mail providers.

- **Internet gateways** Provide internal networks that don't use TCP/IP with the protocol translation required to access an IP network or the Internet.

- **SAA gateways** Provide translation services between local area networks and Systems Application Architecture (SAA) networks from IBM.

Another example of a gateway product that provided a benefit to users several years ago, but which also created problems between two software manufacturers was the Gateway for NetWare product from Microsoft. Microsoft developed and released the **Gateway for NetWare (GNW)** product with Windows NT Server 3.5 and furthered the development and promotion with the release of Windows NT 4.0 Server. If you implemented GNW on a Windows NT Server, any Microsoft client computers on the network could access any Novell NetWare servers on your network through the Gateway for NetWare.

In traditional gateway fashion, the Microsoft GNW product performed all the data and protocol translations between Microsoft Windows clients and the Novell NetWare server, but a problem arose surrounding licensing of the NetWare server. Novell NetWare servers were supposed to be licensed for every connected user, but with the Microsoft GNW product installed on Microsoft Windows NT Server, users were no longer directly accessing the NetWare server. Instead they were directly accessing the Windows NT Server running the GNW product. Theoretically all you needed to purchase would be sufficient Windows NT Server connection licenses. As long as you had sufficient Windows NT Server licenses, you could provide virtually unlimited access to Novell NetWare services without having to purchase more than a five-user version of Novell's NetWare operating system. Novell was upset because the Microsoft gateway product had the potential to lower Novell's license revenue.

Novell's worry was short-lived, however, because the GNW product was not designed to be a "high-performance" gateway, meaning that if you implemented it and allowed too many users to connect, the users would experience performance issues in accessing and sending data to the Novell NetWare server. In fact, this was true. Direct access to a Novell NetWare server was indeed faster than passing the request through a Microsoft gateway. You just had to buy the Novell licenses to support the number of connections you needed to make.

Other Connectivity Terms and Devices

Other network connectivity terms and devices that you might come across include brouter, default gateway, and multiprotocol router. Each has a specific function in network connectivity, but their names can be a bit confusing. For example, a **brouter** is a LAN device that has built-in circuitry that gives it the characteristics of both a bridge and a router. That is, a brouter can bridge data frames within a given network based on layer 2 MAC addresses, and it can route data packets to other networks based on layer 3 IP addresses. Although it's not a term that is commonly used in LAN connectivity, the functionality exists, and you'll find devices that have both bridging and routing capabilities.

Another term that you'll encounter, especially if you look at the configuration of a Microsoft Windows workstation, is **default gateway**. It's really not a gateway at all, but the Internet community has historically referred to routers as gateways, and the term really means the default router that a workstation uses to communicate outside of its own network. You can see an example of the default gateway in Figure 4.12.

Another device that you might encounter is a **multiprotocol router.** If two networks were originally implemented with multiple layer 3 protocols, you can connect the two networks using a multiprotocol router. Multiprotocol routers can route data transmissions between networks that are using multiple layer 3 protocols, and frequently they have additional functionality built in that allows them to translate higher-layer services between networks that use different layer 3 protocols. If a multiprotocol router is implemented to translate these

brouter
a LAN device that has built-in circuitry that gives it the characteristics of a bridge and a router. That is, a brouter can bridge data frames within a given network based on layer 2 MAC addresses, and it can route data packets to other networks based on layer 3 IP addresses

default gateway
the router to which a workstation sends all transmissions that aren't intended for the LAN

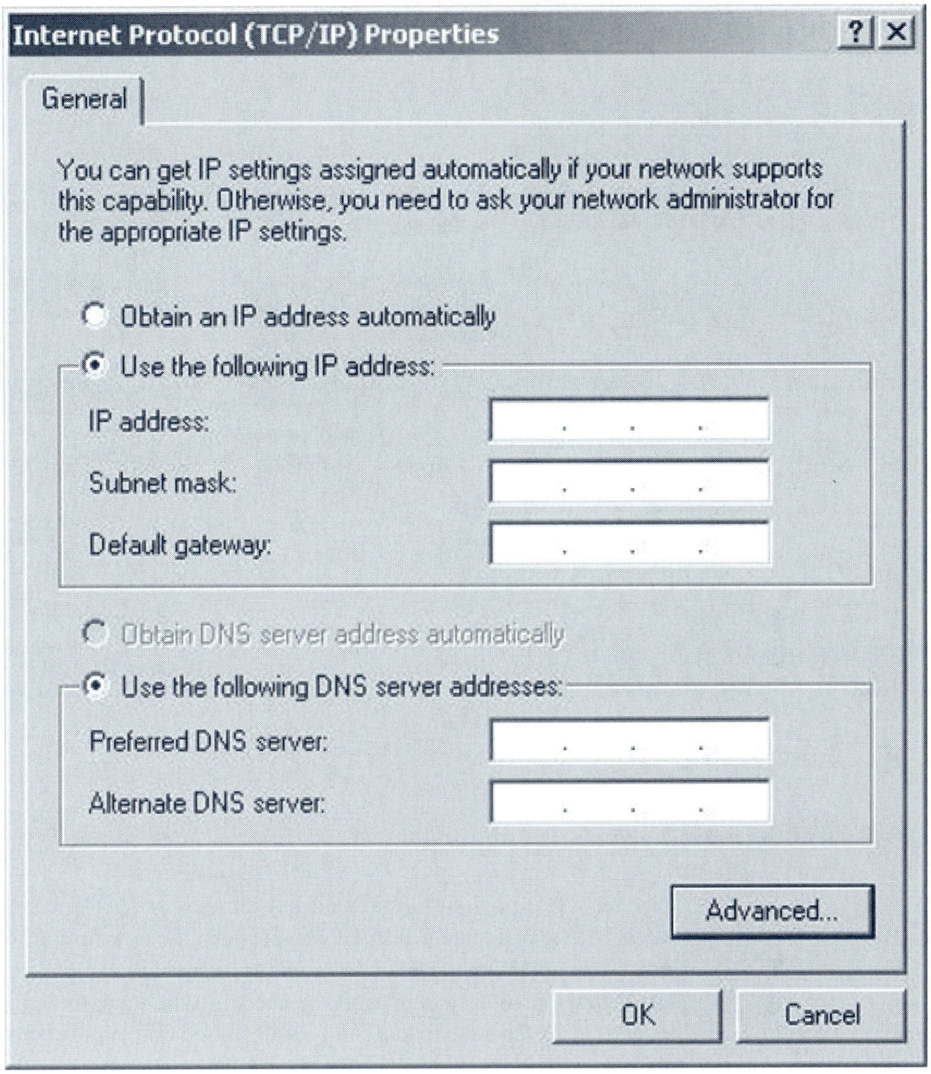

FIGURE 4.12
Default Gateway
Field in the TCP/IP
Properties Window of
a Microsoft Windows
Client Computer

higher-layer services, then it also has the functionality of a gateway. In either case, however, it's up to the network administrator or person specifying the device to ensure that the functionality meets the business and technological requirements.

A multiprotocol router is illustrated in Figure 4.13. In the figure, IP workstations on network A communicate with IP workstations on network B and vice versa. IPX workstations on network A communicate with IPX workstations on network B. If a computer that is configured for only IP on one network needs to communicate with an IPX computer on the other network, and if the multiprotocol router is configured to handle the translation between IP and IPX, then these two computers can also communicate through the multiprotocol router.[22]

---

[22] The multiprotocol router service that translates between IP and IPX or vice versa is sometimes referred to as a circuit gateway.

FIGURE 4.13 **Multiprotocol Router Connecting two Networks**

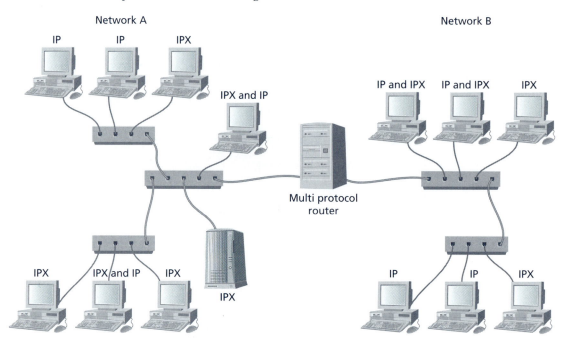

LAN BACKBONES

network backbone
the combination of
hardware, media,
protocols, and
architecture that form
the high-speed
communications link
between two networks

Whether it's to provide resource access on another LAN, enhance resource security between LANs, or separate distinct business functions across an organization, many businesses implement multiple local area networks within campus environments to meet their
data communications and networking needs. At the same time, these multiple LANs must
be interconnected so that data can be transmitted efficiently and cost effectively across the
entire organization. When an organization has such requirements, network engineers and
designers define and specify high-speed communications media and devices that link these
multiple networks together. These media and devices form links between LANs that are
known as **network backbones**. Figure 4.14 provides a conceptual illustration of a
network backbone.

Backbone Design: A Layered Approach

In today's world of networking, network designers and engineers speak of three different
layers when they discuss network backbones. Specifically, these layers include the access
layer, the distribution layer, and the core layer, none of which should be misinterpreted as
corresponding to the layers of the OSI or TCP/IP models. The three layers are industry
terms that have become somewhat generic in meaning within network design, but the origins of this terminology can be traced to the network design models developed and marketed by Cisco Systems for their switched network backbone designs.

access layer
the backbone network
layer at which users'
workstations physically
connect to a LAN

The **access layer** is the layer at which users' workstations physically connect to a LAN.
It is generally comprised of L2 switches to which users' workstations are connected via
Ethernet, Fast Ethernet, or some form of RF wireless. In network backbone design, you
can think of the switches that are implemented at the access layer as the end points of an

FIGURE 4.14
Simple Backbone

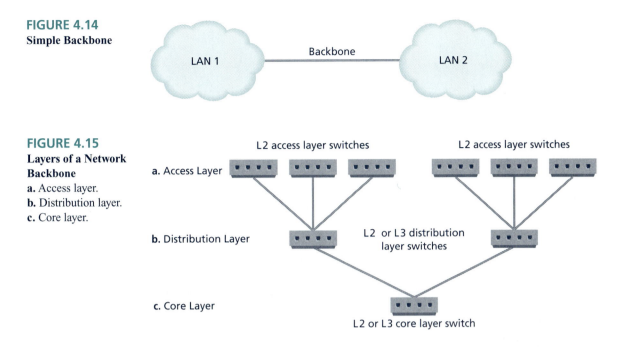

FIGURE 4.15
Layers of a Network Backbone
a. Access layer.
b. Distribution layer.
c. Core layer.

organization's network backbone.[23] In addition, you can refer to these switches as access layer switches.[24]

distribution layer
the backbone network layer at which different LANs in an organization are interconnected

The **distribution layer** of a network backbone is the layer at which different LANs in an organization are interconnected. That is, data from each LAN can be directed to other LANs through the distribution layer. The distribution layer is typically implemented using L3 switches that include both routing (OSI layer 3) and L2 switching capabilities. With both L2 and L3 functionalities built in, L3 switches can switch data frames between access layer switches, and if a data frame can't be switched, it's routed to the appropriate LAN. Switches that are implemented at the distribution layer are commonly referred to as distribution layer switches, regardless of whether the switch is an L2 or an L3 switch.[25]

core layer
the network backbone layer that provides high-speed L2 switching across the backbone between L3 switches in the distribution layer

The **core layer** of a network backbone is the layer at which switches in the distribution layer interconnect. Switches that are implemented in the core layer provide the high-end bandwidth needs and data throughput that support high-speed connectivity between distribution layer devices. The core layer is commonly implemented using L2 switches, but can also be implemented using L3 switches. Figure 4.15 illustrates the relationship among the core layer, the distribution layer, and the access layer of a network backbone.

Backbone Design: Access Layer Plus Distribution Layer

A network backbone that links a small number of LANs within a single building or even a small number of LANs across several floors in the same building can be configured using

---

[23] Some discussions of network backbones leave out the access layer as part of the backbone. Instead those discussions describe a network backbone as a combination of the distribution layer and the core layer. In still other discussions, only the core layer is referenced as the network backbone.

[24] Access layer switches are not limited to OSI layer 2. If an L3 switch is implemented at the access layer, it too is referred to as an access layer switch. Network backbone diagrams delineate the two OSI layers by either placing an L2 or an L3 next to the switch or by using a different graphic to depict each switch type.

[25] As with access layer switches, network backbone diagrams depict the distribution layer, and the figures that represent the switches are either labeled as L2 or L3, or a different graphic is used to delineate between L2 and L3 switches.

FIGURE 4.16   **Backbone Design: Access Layer Plus Distribution Layer**

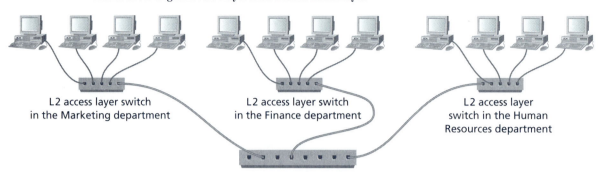

L2 access layer switch
in the Marketing department

L2 access layer switch
in the Finance department

L2 access layer
switch in the Human
Resources department

L3 distribution layer switch

access layer switches and distribution layer switches. In Figure 4.16, workstation computers in each of several departments in a small organization are connected to L2 switches at the access layer. Each L2 switch in each department provides connectivity among all network resources within that department. To form a backbone across all departments, each department's access layer switch is connected to an L3 distribution layer switch. The beauty of this network backbone design is that data can be switched between computers that are part of the same network or routed between computers that are on different networks.[26]

Backbone Design: Access Layer, Distribution Layer, and Core Layer Combined

When an organization is comprised of numerous departments and multiple buildings, a network backbone approach that includes the core layer is worth consideration. The core layer brings an extra layer of connectivity to the network backbone and provides the added scalability that larger organizations need. As Figure 4.17 illustrates, each L2 access layer switch in each department within each building is connected to an L3 distribution layer switch. As with the backbone design for small networks, data can be switched between computers that are part of the same network or routed between computers on different networks. What separates this design from smaller network backbone designs is the implementation of a core layer switch. In Figure 4.17, each of the L3 distribution layer switches is linked to an L2 core layer switch that handles the high-speed switching of frames between the L3 distribution layer switches. The distribution layer takes care of routing between the different department LANs and filters broadcasts from other LANs and from the core layer. That is, if a packet requires routing between buildings, the L3 distribution layer switches perform the routing function and use the core layer as their high-speed backbone.

The beauty of this backbone design is that it is modular and scalable. That is, as more buildings are connected to the backbone or as the network is further divided into additional distribution layers, new distribution layer switches can be directly connected to the core layer switch. In other words, connectivity between buildings happens through the core layer as opposed to connecting each individual distribution layer switch with every other distribution layer switch.

---

[26] This network backbone design is also referred to as a collapsed backbone, because some of the switching and all of the routing functionalities of the backbone are "collapsed" into a single device at the distribution layer using an L3 switch. Older and less efficient backbone designs interconnected multiple departments by using hubs and one or more routers to connect different networks.

FIGURE 4.17   Backbone Design: Access Layer, Distribution Layer, and Core Layer Combined

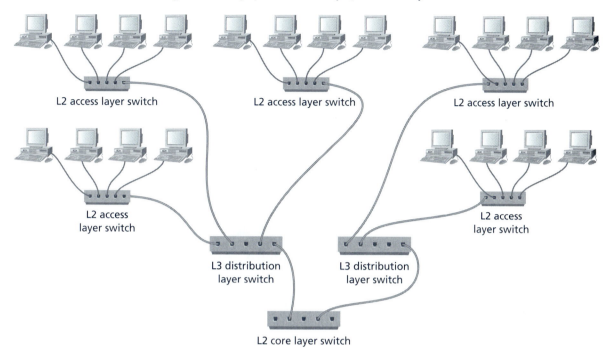

Backbone Design with Redundancy for Fault Tolerance and Load Balancing

Some organizations specify redundant network backbone devices and redundant data paths in their network backbones to provide fault tolerance and load balancing. Fault tolerance gives the organization the ability to continue transmitting data across the backbone in the event that a backbone device or data path fails. Load balancing provides the ability to transmit data going to the same destination across multiple paths simultaneously.

A redundant network backbone design requires the implementation of duplicate distribution layer switches and duplicate core layer switches along with the installation of redundant cabling for the extra data paths. In the access layer of Figure 4.18, each access layer switch has a duplicate connection to each distribution layer switch, and each distribution layer switch is connected to one of the redundant core layer switches. In this scenario, an organization can continue to transmit across the network backbone in the event of a loss or failure of one or more network backbone devices or paths, and in addition, data can be directed from one building to another simultaneously along multiple paths.

Rack-mounted Backbone Hardware versus Chassis-based Backbone Hardware

Network backbone hardware is available in two main types of physical configurations: rack-mounted and chassis-mounted. With rack-mounted backbone hardware, a self-contained rack unit provides a common location into which multiple access layer, distribution layer, and core layer switches can be mounted, as shown in Figure 4.19. As a network grows in size, additional access layer switches can be mounted into the rack and linked to other access layer switches to allow them to function in combination as a single access layer switch, or simply for connectivity to other departments. In addition, one or more

FIGURE 4.18
Backbone Design with Redundancy and Fault Tolerance
a. Access layer.
b. Distribution layer.
c. Core layer.

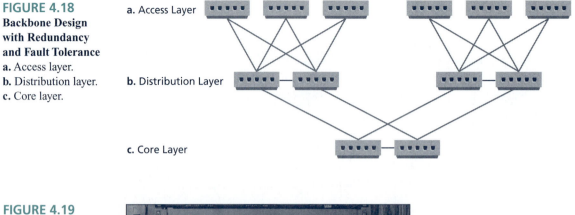

a. Access Layer

b. Distribution Layer

c. Core Layer

FIGURE 4.19
Rack-mounted Switches in a Distribution Facility

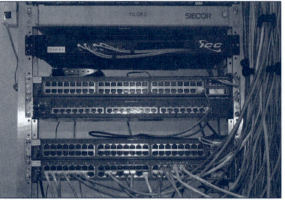

distribution layer switches can be bolted into the rack so that access layer switches from different departments can all be interconnected. If the organization has a need for a core layer switch, the core layer switch can also be bolted into the rack, and the distribution layer switch can be connected to the core layer switch using a high-speed link.[27]

Chassis-based switches can also be bolted into a rack system, but the difference with chassis-based hardware is that the chassis provides a metal frame with basic circuitry so that multiple devices can be plugged into it. The devices that plug into the chassis are commonly referred to as blades, and each blade can have the same or different functionality as every other blade in the chassis. For example, you could bolt a chassis-based access layer switch into a rack system and initially buy only one blade for the chassis. This blade might contain 48 ports, allowing 48 users' computers to connect to this blade in the switch. If your network grows beyond 48 users, you could buy another switch blade and install it into the switch chassis. The chassis provides a framework for expansion with built-in connectivity for other devices that are added later.

Chassis-based systems also provide the ability to add devices of different functionality. For example, you might choose to implement a core layer switch as a chassis-based system.

---

[27] These rack systems can be located in numerous wiring closets throughout an organization. Some wiring closets might contain only access layer switches, while others might contain access layer switches and distribution layer switches. Still other wiring closets might contain rack systems that house distribution layer switches and core layer switches. Whatever the topology, the design must meet the needs of the organization and be within the distance specifications of the network architecture such as Ethernet, FDDI, or Token Ring, etc.

FIGURE 4.20   **Chassis-based Hardware**

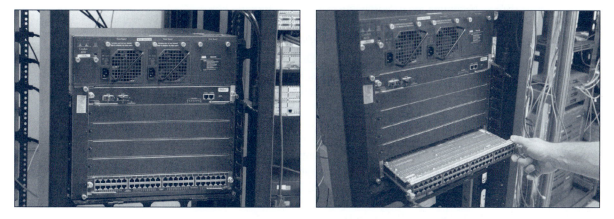

FIGURE 4.20   **Chassis-based Hardware**

One blade might accommodate fiber-optic connectivity with a distribution layer switch that is installed higher up in the rack system. Another blade might provide Gigabit connectivity to another distribution layer switch that is located in another building. A third blade might provide carrier service functionality so that you can connect your network backbone to the outside world. And a fourth blade might be a 10 gigabit distribution layer switch that connects storage servers and application servers to your network backbone. A chassis-based switch is illustrated in Figure 4.20.

Network Backbone Data Transmission Architectures

Business managers and network administrators alike want the fastest data transmission speed for each dollar spent on network switching equipment. In addition, they generally try to match network speed requirements to the specific business need. For example, an individual network user can probably be well served by a connection speed of 100 Mbps supplied by Fast Ethernet architecture. Similarly, it might be overkill to supply all but the most data-hungry users with Gigabit Ethernet to the desktop because the dollars spent on a Gigabit Ethernet connection to users' desktops would probably outweigh the marginal benefit delivered beyond that of slower 100 Mbps Ethernet connections.

At the same time, network backbone switches are constantly bombarded with data traffic from *all* users on the network. Here it makes sense to incorporate high-speed transmission architectures to maintain high levels of service to all users. Because network backbones have the potential of becoming a data traffic bottleneck, network backbone designs usually incorporate high-speed communications architectures. That is, the connections that link access layer switches to the distribution layer switches and the distribution layer switches to the core switches are generally faster than the links that connect individual users to department switches.

Gigabit Ethernet

In today's modern network backbones, it's very common to implement either or both Gigabit and 10 Gigabit Ethernet. You've already learned about Gigabit Ethernet and 10 Gigabit Ethernet in chapter 3, but it's important to keep in mind that both of these high-speed data transmission architectures are important components in network backbones. Users connect to the department switch using Fast Ethernet, but the connection between department switches and the central switch and between the central switch and the core switch is Gigabit Ethernet. For faster data transmission requirements, such as between centralized services and the core switch or connectivity between buildings, 10 Gigabit Ethernet is becoming the data transmission architecture of choice.

Fiber Distributed Data Interface (FDDI)

As you learned in chapter 3, FDDI is a network architecture that you might still find in older network backbone designs. It operates at 100 Mbps and was at one time commonly implemented as a high-speed network backbone architecture that connected remote networks between buildings. An access layer switch in one building could be connected via FDDI to a distribution layer switch located in a distribution facility in another building. The access layer and distribution layer switches require both Ethernet and FDDI technologies be built in so that users' data could be translated from Ethernet to FDDI for transmission across the FDDI network backbone. Since FDDI has not evolved, legacy installations of FDDI backbones are likely candidates for upgrade to faster Ethernet architectures such as Gigabit Ethernet or 10 Gigabit Ethernet, when the business needs of the organization justify the cost of an upgrade.

Asynchronous Transfer Mode (ATM)

You might find ATM as a network architecture in backbones that require extremely fast and time-sensitive data transmission rates. Delivering data at rates up to 622 Mbps in local area networks, ATM can provide an extremely fast network backbone, especially for networks

FIGURE 4.21   **Expanded Network Backbone**

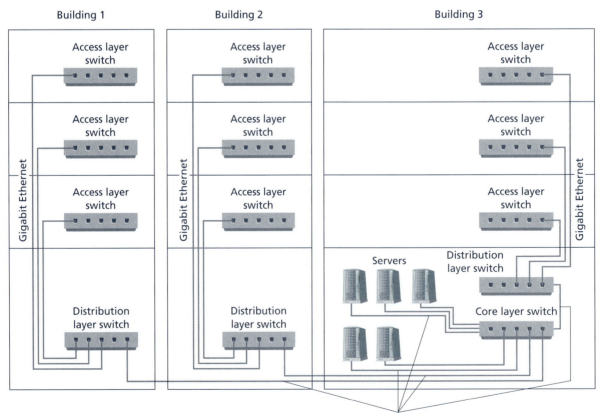

that require reliable delivery of multimedia information. Implementations of ATM in local area network backbones are not widespread, especially with alternatives such as 10 Gigabit Ethernet. Instead, it's much more common to find ATM implemented by carrier service companies as the transport for vast amounts of data between remote networks.

Expanded Network Backbones

It's not uncommon for an organization to have multiple wiring closets or distribution facilities, especially when there are multiple floors and buildings involved and all of those floors and buildings need to be connected. When multiple distribution facilities need to be linked together, it's fairly common to connect these facilities with Gigabit or 10 Gigabit Ethernet.

In Figure 4.21, an organization has three multistory buildings, and in general, it's likely that you'll find a wiring closet on each floor or every other floor within each building. Within each wiring closet is an access layer switch to which all users' computers on that floor are connected. Buildings 1 and 2 each have distribution layer switches to which the access switches are connected via Gigabit Ethernet, but building 3 has a core switch to which the access layer switch is linked via Gigabit Ethernet. Buildings 1 and 2 each connect via 10 Gigabit Ethernet to the core switch at building 3. In addition, central services such as network storage, application servers, Web servers, and voice servers can all connect to the core switch via 10 Gigabit Ethernet. In the example, the highest transmission rates are implemented wherever the biggest potential exists for data bottlenecks.

LAN PROTOCOLS

All communications on a local area network use protocols as the basis for creating, sending, and receiving data transmissions between two computers and across the LAN. Protocols define the ways in which data can be packaged to send across the network as well as the ways in which data can access the network, be transported, and even be reassembled at the destination host.

protocol
a set of rules

LAN protocols
the rules that specify how services and devices will exchange information among themselves

Simply defined, a **protocol** is a set of rules. In terms of data communications, **LAN protocols** are the rules that specify how services and devices will exchange information among themselves. Just as NASA has a set of protocols it follows in training astronauts and preparing for a launch into space and as the health care field has protocols for administering treatments and patient care, the data communications industry utilizes many protocols in the exchange of information between two or more end points.

Communication Protocols

Arguably the most important sets of data communications rules are those protocols that support the transfer of data between an information source and a user who needs to access that information. These protocols allow us to send information to and receive information from remote data sources located just about anywhere. In fact, they are the building blocks for information exchange around the world, and we refer to them collectively as communications protocols.

The Internet Protocol

By far the most commonly used addressing and network-defining protocol for local area networks, wide area networks, and the Internet is the **Internet Protocol (IP).** If you're connected to the Internet, you've felt the reach that your computer has to services such as e-mail, Web site content, streaming media, and perhaps even teleconferencing or Internet voice and phone services. All of these services use IP as their basis for communicating with your computer.

As you saw in chapter 1, IP has been around for quite a while; it was developed to allow communications among ARPANET-connected mainframe computers. Today, you're probably using it on a daily, if not minute-by-minute, basis to access the Internet, retrieve files from servers and other computers on a local area network, send print jobs to printers, e-mail your friends and business associates, and so on.

The entire process is transparent to users because so much configuration goes on behind the scenes to make it perform so effortlessly. To begin with, if you're using IP on your local area network, all the computers and possibly even the printers on your LAN will have an assigned IP address so that each device can be identified by every other device on the LAN. But, you might ask, I thought I could already do that with the data link layer address assigned to each network card? Of course, you'd be right about that—almost. Many services on your network utilize IP and other protocols in the TCP/IP suite of protocols to accept and deliver data to service requesters such as client computers. In addition, if you want to connect to other networks or to the Internet you can't use only the data link layer addressing you learned about previously in this chapter. Instead, each computer on your network will require an IP address in order to access a broad range of services and devices on other networks. By properly configuring each client workstation, each server, and every other device on your network with a unique IP address, you can provide communication and data transmission capability among thousands of devices on a single network, across multiple networks, and even across the Internet. Configured with a unique IP address, each device within and outside of a local area network can be located anywhere in the world so that source devices and destination devices can exchange information, as you can see in Figure 4.22.

IP Addressing

The most common implementation of **IP addressing** in today's networks is known as IPv4. With this version of IP addressing, each IP address that you assign to a networking device is comprised of a 32-bit binary address that is divided into four 8-bit octets, as illustrated in Figure 4.23.[28]

FIGURE 4.22

Internet Protocol and Data Communication LAN computers, each with a unique IP address.

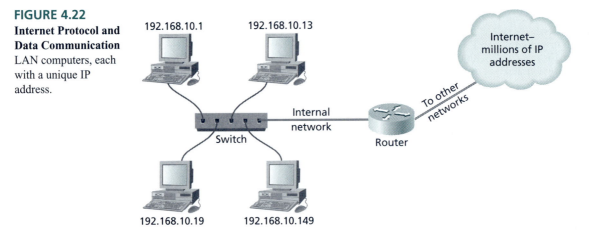

---

[28] Another version of IP, which will ultimately replace IPv4, is IPv6. IPv6 is comprised of a 128-bit addressing scheme that can provide over 340 trillion, trillion, trillion addresses. You'll discover the details of IPv6 in chapter 10.

FIGURE 4.23
IP Address for a
Network Device
Using IP's 32-bit
Binary Addressing

192.168.10.149
11000000.10101000.00001010.10010101

FIGURE 4.24   Binary to Dotted Decimal Conversion Grid

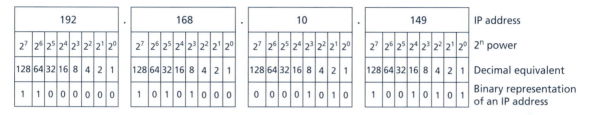

	192							.		168							.		10							.		149							IP address
2^7	2^6	2^5	2^4	2^3	2^2	2^1	2^0		2^7	2^6	2^5	2^4	2^3	2^2	2^1	2^0		2^7	2^6	2^5	2^4	2^3	2^2	2^1	2^0		2^7	2^6	2^5	2^4	2^3	2^2	2^1	2^0	2^n power
128	64	32	16	8	4	2	1		128	64	32	16	8	4	2	1		128	64	32	16	8	4	2	1		128	64	32	16	8	4	2	1	Decimal equivalent
1	1	0	0	0	0	0	0		1	0	1	0	1	0	0	0		0	0	0	0	1	0	1	0		1	0	0	1	0	1	0	1	Binary representation of an IP address

Since most of us prefer numerals to binary representations of those numerals, we need to know how to convert a binary number to dotted decimal and vice versa. The easiest way to do this is to create a binary-to-dotted-decimal grid that has four rows and four sets of eight columns, as illustrated in Figure 4.24.

In Figure 4.24, the first row represents the dotted decimal version of the IP address; the second row lists a series of columns labeled with 2^n power, starting with $n = 7$ and progressing down to $n = 0$; the third row shows the decimal equivalent of the 2^n directly above it; and the fourth row represents the binary equivalent of the IP address listed in the first row.

If you focus on the third row for a moment, the numbers listed here are the values of 2^n used in creating either the decimal representation of the IP address or the binary representation. So for the first **octet** in Figure 4.24, which is 192, you look for the biggest values in the third row that will add up to 192. In this case it happens to be 128 and 64. Then to create a binary representation, you put a 1 in each of the columns in the fourth row that correspond to 128 and 64 and zeros in the remaining columns, hence 11000000 as the binary representation of 192. For the second octet, look for the biggest numbers in the third row that add up to 168, and you'll figure out that 128 plus 32 plus 8 add up to 168. So you put a 1 in each of the corresponding boxes in the fourth row for the second octet and zeros in the other boxes. Do the same operation for the third and fourth octets, and voila, you have the binary equivalent of the IP address that is listed in the first row. If, on the other hand, you want to convert from binary to decimal equivalent, build this table, put the 1s and 0s in the fourth row, add up the corresponding values in the third row, and you'll have the decimal representation of the IP address.

Although the entire address respresented in either binary format or in dotted decimal format represents the address of the network device, some of the bits represent the address of your local area network while the rest of the bits represent the node or host, which is a device such as workstation or server. To determine which portion represents the network and which represents the node, we have to look at the subnet mask.

FIGURE 4.25   **Separating an IP Address into its Network and Node Portions**

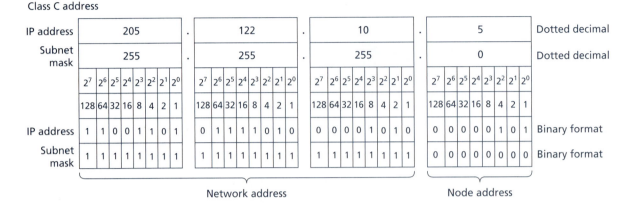

subnet mask

a combination of binary digits that identify which portion of an IP address is the network address and which portion is the node address

A **subnet mask** is a 32-bit combination of binary digits that identifies which portion of an IP address is the network address and which portion is the node address. But the subnet mask differs from the IP address in the following way. The 32 binary digits in the IP address uniquely identify a host on a network, while the 32-bit series of binary digits in the subnet mask separates the IP address into its network address and node address portions. Any binary 1 digit in the subnet mask indicates that the corresponding location in the 32-bit IP address is part of the network address. Likewise, if there is a zero digit in the subnet mask, the corresponding digit in the IP address is part of the node address.

For example, in Figure 4.25, a **network host** is assigned the IP address 205.122.10.5, with a corresponding subnet mask of 255.255.255.0. If you convert both the IP address and the subnet mask to binary format as displayed in the figure, the binary digits in the IP address that have a corresponding zero digit in the subnet mask represent the node portion of the IP address. Likewise, the binary digits in the IP address that have a corresponding binary 1 digit in the subnet mask represent the network portion of the address. In our example, the network address is represented by the first three octets or 205.122.10, but it would be written as 205.122.10.0. The node address is represented by the fourth octet. Note, however, that when referring to the node portion of an IP address, the entire IP address is typically written so that it isn't confused with a host on some other network. In other words, you would refer to the node address in our example as 205.122.10.5. For some additional examples, refer to Figure 4.26.

IP Address Classes

There are five different **classes of IP addresses** and all IP addresses can be identified as belonging to a Class A, Class B, Class C, Class D, or Class E address. Classes A, B, and C are the addresses you'll most likely use in implementing IP addresses in a local area network environment. You won't use any Class D addresses, because Class D addresses are reserved for IP multicasting, a process that allows communication from one device to reach many but not all devices on a network. You won't use Class E addresses, either, because these were originally set aside for future use. When they are used, their use is limited to broadcast messages that reach all hosts on a network.

Class A Networks.   In a Class A network, the first binary digit in the first octet is always a binary zero. As a result, the decimal format designation for Class A addresses can range

FIGURE 4.26

Network and Node Portions of IP Addresses

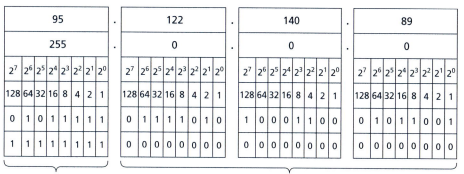

from 1 to 126 in the first octet, as in 1.0.0.0 or 119.0.0.0 or 126.0.0.0.[29] As another example, consider the binary notation 01111101 as the first octet. The first digit in this first octet is a binary zero, a requirement for a Class A IP network. Of course 01111101 translates to 125 in decimal notation, and the corresponding network would be 125.0.0.0. In a Class A network, you can have up to 126 possible networks, each of which can have up to 16,777,214 hosts or nodes. The default subnet mask for Class A networks is 255.0.0.0.

The default configuration for a Class A network uses the first octet to represent the network portion of the IP address and the last three octets represent the node, as in part **(a)** of Figure 4.26. An IP address assignment for a computer in a Class A network might look something like: 19.24.55.6, and if the default subnet mask is being used, you could see node addresses ranging from 19.0.0.1 to 19.255.255.254.

Class B Networks.   In a Class B network, the first two binary digits of the first octet begin with the binary digits 10, so that the dotted decimal representation can range from 128 to 191. In binary, that is 10000000 to 10111111—if you convert to decimal from binary, you'll get 128 to 191. In a Class B network, you can have up to 16,382 possible networks, each of which can have up to 65,534 nodes. The default subnet mask for Class B networks is 255.255.0.0.

---

[29] The address 127.0.0.0 is left out because it's used for the special purpose known as loopback, which is a diagnostic test that you can use in an IP network to verify that a node can send and receive IP data transmissions.

The number of hosts in an IP network is determined by $2^n - 2$, where n is the number of bits in the node portion of the IP address. For example, in the Class A networks, the first eight bits represent the network address while the remaining 24 bits represent the node portion of the address. To calculate the number of nodes in a Class A network, raise the numeral 2 to the power of 24, and that yields 16,777,216. Although that is a close approximation, it's not accurate because there are two addresses that can't be used on a particular Class A network X.0.0.0. Those two addresses are X.0.0.0, which is host 0.0.0 on this particular network, X; and X.255.255.255, which is the broadcast address to this particular network, X. So if we go back to our formula for determining the number of host addresses for an IP address class:

- Class A networks can have a maximum of $2^{24} - 2$, or 16,777,214, hosts per network.
- Class B networks can have a maximum of $2^{16} - 2$, or 65,534, hosts per network.
- Class C networks can have a maximum of $2^8 - 2$, or 254, hosts per network.

The default configuration for a Class B network uses the first two octets to represent the network portion of the IP address and the last two octets to represent the node, as illustrated in part **(b)** of Figure 4.26. An IP address assignment for a computer in a Class B network might look something like: 135.11.33.19, and if the default subnet mask is being used, you could see node addresses ranging from 135.11.1.1 to 135.11.255.254.

Class C Networks. In a Class C network, the first octet begins with the three binary bits 110. If you add the decimal equivalent of these first three digits, it yields a beginning value of 192 for the first octet. Then if you calculate the high end of the range by filling in the rest of the binary digits for the first octet with binary 1s, or 11011111, the high end on the first octet range for Class C is 223. Class C networks are very common, especially among Internet service providers. With a Class C address, it's possible to have up to 2,097,150 networks with up to 254 nodes per network. The default subnet mask for Class C networks is 255.255.255.0.

The default configuration for a Class C network uses the first three octets to represent the network portion of the IP address and the last octet to represent the node. Figure 4.25 provided an example of a Class C IP address. A typical IP address assignment for a computer in a Class C network might look something like: 218.10.42.103, and if the default subnet mask is being used, you could see node addresses ranging from 218.10.42.1 to 218.10.42.254.

Class D and Class E Networks. Class D is used for IP multicasts, and Class E is reserved and used in broadcast transmissions within a defined network. The first octet of a Class D network begins with 1110, and addresses range from 224.0.0.0 to 239.0.0.0. In Class E networks, the range is from 240 to 255 for the first octet.

Assigning IP Addresses

After you've designed your IP addressing scheme, you can begin making IP address assignments to the computers and other hosts, such as printers, in your network. Depending on the needs of your network, you can assign IP addresses manually, which is referred to as static IP addressing, or you can configure your network to have IP addresses assigned automatically. If you choose to assign addresses manually, your support staff will have to configure each host individually. If, however, you decide to assign IP addresses automatically, you can use a configuration protocol known as **dynamic host configuration protocol (DHCP).**[30]

Manual Assignment.   Manual IP assignments require technical support personnel to visit or "touch" each computer that requires an IP address, access the operating system's IP configuration program, and make an IP address assignment. This works fine in small environments, but in larger environments manually assigning IP addresses is a tedious process. A technician can make a mistake and assign an invalid IP address to a device or the same IP address to more than one device. In addition, if documentation is not current, then when hosts are taken off the network you might not remember to reenter that host's IP address for use on another computer. With enough changes over time, you'll either run out of IP addresses or be forced to redeploy or redesign your IP addressing scheme.

Assignment through Dynamic Host Configuration Protocol (DHCP).   Assigning IP addresses through a DHCP server is a much more efficient way to deliver IP addresses to host computers on your network. By using DHCP, you need not worry about duplicate IP address assignments or assigning an invalid IP address. Documentation is less of an issue because the DHCP service tracks the assignment of IP addresses on a host-by-host basis. And when a computer is finished using a DHCP-assigned IP address, the address is available for another computer to use: Running out of addresses because you don't know which addresses are assigned is no longer a problem.

DHCP is a service that you can choose to implement on your network either through a network operating system such as Novell NetWare, Linux, or Windows server, or through a DHCP service running on a router.[31] When a client computer or other host that is configured to use DHCP boots up, the host sends a general request for an IP address out onto the network. When a device that is configured as a DHCP server intercepts the request, it responds to the client computer's request in one of two ways. If the client computer is supposed to have the same IP address each time it boots up, the DHCP server will make the assignment from a table of static IP addresses where each address in the static IP address table is linked to a MAC address so that the DHCP server knows where to send the IP address. If the client computer or host doesn't need to have the same IP address assigned with each bootup, the DHCP server looks in its IP address pool to locate an available address and assigns that address to the client host.

To facilitate speedier DHCP-delivered IP address assignments and to ensure that IP addresses that are no longer under lease can be reclaimed by the DHCP service for reassignment to other nodes, DHCP maintains a time-configurable lease algorithm. This algorithm allows a host device to retain the same IP address assignment for some preconfigured period of time, for example, three days. If the host computer goes offline and returns online during the lease interval and if the IP address hasn't been reassigned to another host, then the original host device will obtain the IP address that it leased during the previous session. Similarly, if the host stays online during the entire time of the DHCP-leased IP address cycle, it will retain the address through the lease interval, after which the lease will be renegotiated between the host and the DHCP server so that the host may or may not retain the original IP address assignment after the lease period ends. On the other hand, if the DHCP lease expires while the host is offline, the DHCP service will assign a new IP address and lease when the host boots up the next time. Figure 4.27 illustrates a DHCP server making IP assignments to three different client computers on the same LAN.

---

[30] You'll discover more regarding DHCP later in this chapter.
[31] The operating system on most routers is multifunctional; that is, the router's operating system can be configured to provide services such as DHCP.

FIGURE 4.27   DHCP-Delivered IP Addresses

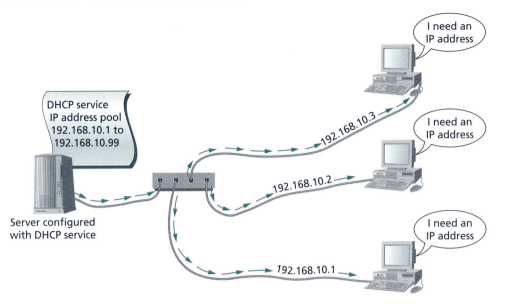

Other Communication Protocols

Before the vast popularity of the Internet, you were not as likely to see IP as the default protocol of choice in many local area networks. Novell provided the IPX communications protocol for Novell NetWare networks, and Apple Computer provided AppleTalk for Macintosh networks. Other communications protocols for small networks included NetBEUI, which was primarily used in Microsoft Windows peer-to-peer networks prior to the release of Windows NT.[32]

IPX.   IPX is the abbreviation for **Internetwork Packet Exchange,** and it is the communications protocol that was native to Novell NetWare networks prior to NetWare version 5.0. IPX was relatively popular in the 1980s through the mid-1990s because it was so easy to configure. Network administrators didn't have to manually assign addresses to each network node as they did with IP addressing before DHCP. Instead, IPX uses the MAC address of the network interface card in a host as the host's address. This had tremendous appeal for local area networks where there might not be sufficient human resources to maintain an IP addressing scheme on a node-by-node basis.

The disadvantage of IPX lies in its routing functionality. Although IPX is easy to set up and extremely reliable in small networks, its substantial use of bandwidth between servers to maintain routing tables in support of efficient data transmission frequently resulted in slower network performance. In addition, for routing to function in an IPX network, each Novell NetWare server required an assigned number known as an Internal IPX Address. This 32-bit address was assigned by the network administrator or by the person responsible for server installation and configuration. The internal IPX address was never required to be registered with any centralized network address authority, as were IP addresses. Not having these addresses registered precluded connectivity to other potentially "public" IPX networks, because there was no consistent addressing scheme or assurance that duplicate addresses could be prevented. With the popularity of IP and the

---

[32] You'll learn about network operating systems in chapter 5.

already established organization of IP addressing on the Internet through a centralized authority, IPX became a communications protocol that network administrators began planning into extinction. Today, although Novell maintains support for its nearly obsolete IPX protocol suite, Novell's native communications protocol for its Novell NetWare networks is IP.[33]

In terms of the OSI model, IPX is a communications protocol that has characteristics that overlap layers 2, 3, and 4 of the OSI model. For example, IPX utilizes a NIC's MAC address for device addressing, and MAC addressing is an OSI layer 2 function. In addition, IPX utilizes an IPX external address number, or network segment address, for network location, and this address functions at OSI layer 3. Other components of IPX make connection-oriented requests for application services in layer 4, thereby giving IPX the additional characteristics associated with OSI layer 4 protocols.

AppleTalk.   **AppleTalk** is the suite of communications protocols that Apple computers used to communicate in a networked environment. Specifically, Macintosh computers could use a protocol known as LocalTalk to communicate. LocalTalk dynamically assigned addresses to each node on the network so that each computer would have a unique identifier. Upon bootup, each computer would talk with the others to make sure there were no duplicate address assignments.

Apple also released EtherTalk and TokenTalk to provide networked communication across Ethernet networks and Token Ring networks, respectively. Each of these communications protocols made use of the network interface card address for the creation of unique computer addresses on an EtherTalk or TokenTalk network.

In terms of the OSI model, AppleTalk in and of itself is responsible, at least in terms of network functionality, for more service-oriented and formatting functions, which places it within the application and presentation layers of the OSI model. LocalTalk, on the other hand, is responsible for machine addressing and the bit-level transmission of data in a Macintosh network. This makes LocalTalk a protocol that spans both the physical and data link layers. EtherTalk and TokenTalk are more or less subsets of LocalTalk that define the bit-level communication across an Ethernet or Token Ring network, respectively. This makes both EtherTalk and TokenTalk layer 1 protocols.

NetBIOS Extended User Interface (NetBEUI).[34]   At one time, if you were running a small peer-to-peer Microsoft Windows network, and you didn't want to be bothered with address configuration issues, you could simply allow **NetBEUI** to be the default communications protocol on your network. NetBEUI uses the computer's name and MAC address as the unique identifiers on the network, and although it is fast and easy to set up, NetBEUI was not designed to make requests to other networks across a router.

As networks grew in size and required services outside of the local area network, NetBEUI's usefulness waned. It's not routable, so its performance and usefulness in larger networks is impractical. In addition, if it's installed on larger networks that are also using other communications protocols, NetBEUI can contribute to network congestion. If you need to remove it, you'll have to disable it at each workstation on the network.

Placing NetBEUI in perspective with the OSI model, NetBEUI is a session layer/transport layer protocol that establishes connection-oriented communications services between nodes on a network. It doesn't have the built-in capabilities of network layer protocols such as IPX and IP, which means that NetBEUI is not a practical solution for

simple network management protocol (SNMP)
an application layer protocol that is used to communicate with, monitor, and control network devices such as managed hubs, switches, and routers and even NICs. SNMP also works in conjunction with SNMP agents, SNMP manager software, and management information bascs to collect, store, and report various device and network statistics.

---

[33] In networks using IPX, not only does the server require an IPX address known as the internal IPX address, but the network requires an IPX address known as the IPX external address.

[34] NetBIOS stands for Network Basic Input/Output System, and it was developed by IBM in the early 1980s as a protocol for transporting data between network nodes.

SNMP agent
special software that runs on a managed device such as a managed hub, switch, router, or NIC, with the purpose of receiving commands from and communicating device statistics to the SNMP manager

SNMP manager
software that is installed on an administrative workstation computer and is used to configure and control managed devices as well as manage and maintain one or more databases of device statistics

management information base (MIB)
the database in which device and network statistics are stored

networks that require routers. However, because NetBEUI is designed to communicate with data link layer protocols, NetBEUI data transmissions can be sent across a bridge or switch, meaning it can be used in small local area networks.

Network Management

Networks are comprised of many different types of connectivity devices, such as hubs, switches, routers, and gateways, and each of these devices can provide valuable information that a network administrator can use to determine the status and health of the network or the status and health of a specific device. The protocol that is used to communicate this information is the **simple network management protocol (SNMP)**. SNMP is a standardized application layer network management protocol, developed by the IETF, that is used to communicate with, monitor, and control network devices such as managed hubs, switches, routers, and even NICs for the purpose of collecting network traffic statistics and performance statistics of managed network devices.

SNMP works in conjunction with SNMP agent software, SNMP manager software, and management information bases (MIBs), to collect, store, and report information about networking devices and the network traffic they process. The **SNMP agent** is special software that runs on a managed device such as a managed hub, switch, router, or NIC, with the purpose of receiving commands from and communicating device statistics to the SNMP manager. The **SNMP manager** is software that is installed on an administrative workstation computer and is used to configure and control managed devices as well as manage and maintain one or more databases of device statistics. The **management information base** *(MIB)* is one or more databases in which device and network statistics are stored.[35] Each device generally has its own MIB, and the SNMP manager issues commands to the SNMP agent to extract information from the MIB. Information stored in the MIB is used to monitor network and device operation as well as to manage and control performance of the device and the data traffic that the device processes.

Chapter Summary

- **Repeaters.** Network engineers implement repeaters to overcome signal attenuation over long cable segments. Repeaters are an OSI physical layer device and their functionality can be built into hubs or switches.

- **Hub technologies.** Hubs are OSI layer 1 hardware devices that act as a connection point for servers, workstations, printers, and other computing devices. Various types of hub technologies exist including stand-alone hubs, stackable hubs, enterprise hubs, and network managed hubs.

- **Bridges.** Bridges are networking devices that connect two or more LAN segments while simultaneously improving bandwidth performance. Bridges are OSI layer 2 devices that use MAC addresses to direct and filter traffic between LAN segments. When

---

[35] All modern device MIBs are more accurately defined as RMON MIBs, where RMON is an acronym for remote monitoring. RMON was originally developed in the early 1990s to provide a means of efficiently accessing device and network statistics from devices on remote networks without imposing significant data traffic congestion across the network connection. There are two versions of RMON: RMON1 and RMON2. RMON1 addresses traffic statistics at OSI layer 2 and below while RMON2 addresses network traffic at layers 3 and above, focusing primarily on IP traffic and application layer traffic.

used in pairs, bridges can provide fault tolerance, but redundant pair bridges must be managed by the spanning tree protocol to prevent bridging loops. Bridges are considered obsolete in today's LANs, but their technology has evolved into modern switch technology.

- **Switches.** Switches are OSI layer 2 devices that evolved from bridge technology. Switches can read frames from multiple ports and create simultaneous forwarding paths. Technologies to be aware of when comparing switches include store and forward, cut through, error-free cut through, intelligent versus unmanaged, higher layer switches, and VLAN switches.

- **Routers.** Routers are OSI layer 3 devices that can provide added dimensions of scalability, security, and manageability to a growing LAN. Routers can segment a network into smaller networks or join multiple networks into a larger enterprise network. Routers separate broadcast domains and direct packets to other networks using the best available path. Routers have various metrics that comprise the best path, and each link in the path is known as a hop.

- **Gateways.** Gateways provide connectivity between different network environments and operate at OSI layer 3 and above. Gateways perform functions such as service connectivity between disparate systems, conversion of frame sizes between different networks, protocol translation, or data format conversion. A common implementation of a gateway is between a LAN and a legacy mainframe network.

- **Layered network backbone design.** The access layer, the distribution layer, and the core layer comprise layered network backbone designs. The access layer connects department computers to the network backbone. The distribution layer interconnects access layer switches. And the core layer interconnects distribution layer devices. The layered approach to network backbone design provides numerous configurations that can meet the needs of differently sized organizations.

- **Rack-mounted and chassis-based backbone hardware.** Rack-mounted and chassis-based backbone hardware provides convenient and managed assembly and installation of layered network backbone components. With rack-mounted systems, numerous and separate switching devices can be bolted into the rack. With chassis-based systems, a modular chassis provides the framework for adding additional switching devices in a blade configuration to your network backbone.

- **Network backbone data transmission architectures.** Network backbones can be scaled to meet the data transmission needs of the organization. For example, small networks might function quite well with a Fast Ethernet network backbone, but a larger network with much greater data transmission requirements might require a Gigabit or even 10 Gigabit Ethernet network backbone. Other network backbone architectures include ATM and FDDI.

- **Internet Protocol and IP address classes.** The Internet Protocol is the most widely used OSI layer 3 communications protocol. Its origins date back to the 1970s, and it is the standard communications protocol of the Internet. IP is divided into five address classes: three address classes that are used to define networks and network hosts, and two additional classes that are used for special transmission types within networks.

- **Assigning IP addresses.** Every device on an IP network requires an IP address. IP addresses can be assigned manually or by using DHCP. Manual assignments are time consuming and error prone. Automatic assignments through DHCP are convenient and a big time saver for network technicians.

- **Other LAN communications protocols.** Other communications protocols that you might discover on older LANs include IPX, AppleTalk, and NetBEUI. IPX was used in LANs that supported Novell NetWare servers, and you might still find it implemented in legacy networks that use older versions of NetWare. AppleTalk was the protocol of choice for older LANs that supported Macintosh computers, and NetBEUI is a protocol that you might find installed in small LANs that don't require routing.

- **Network Management.** SNMP is used to communicate with, monitor, and control network devices such as managed hubs, switches, and routers and even NICs. SNMP also works in conjunction with SNMP agents, SNMP manager software, and management information bases to collect, store, and report various device and network statistics.

Key Terms

AppleTalk, *151*
Application specific integrated circuit (ASIC), *124*
Bridge filtering, *117*
Bridge, *118*
Brouter, *134*
Concentrator, *117*
Cut through switch, *123*
Data transmission throughput, *123*
Default gateway, *134*
Dynamic host configuration protocol (DHCP), *149*
E-mail gateway, *133*
Enterprise hub, *116*
Error-free cut through switch, *124*
Intelligent switch, *124*
Gateway, *132*
Higher layer switch, *124*

Hub, *114*
Internet gateway, *133*
Internet protocol (IP), *143*
Internetwork Packet Exchange (IPX), *150*
IP address classes, *146*
IP addressing, *144*
LAN protocols, *143*
Microsoft Gateway for NetWare (GNW), *134*
Multiprotocol router, *134*
NetBEUI, *151*
Network address, *131*
Network managed hub, *116*
Network Host, *146*
Network Node, *129*
Octet, *145*
Port, *114*
Protocol, *143*

Repeater, *114*
Router, *129*
SAA gateway, *133*
Signal attenuation, *114*
Simple network management protocol (SNMP), *151*
SAA gateway, *133*
Stackable hub, *116*
Stand-alone hub, *114*
Store and forward switch, *123*
Subnet mask, *146*
Switch, *122*
Terminal emulation software, *133*
Uplink port, *114*
Virtual local area network (VLAN) switch, *126*

Questions

1. What is a hub, and what benefit does it bring to a LAN?

2. What does the expression "forward if not local" mean in terms of local area networking and bridging?

3. How does a switch differ from a multiport bridge?

4. How does a switch distinguish one port from another? How does it obtain this information?

5. Where would you implement an access layer switch? A distribution layer switch? A core layer switch? A layer 2 switch? A layer 3 switch? Why?

6. For what reasons would you introduce a router into a local area network?

7. Under what circumstances would you implement a gateway in your local area network?

8. Why are communication protocols so important in local area networks?

9. When would you use a Class A IP address? How about Class B? Class C?

10. How do an IP address and its subnet mask function together?

11. What is the binary representation of the IP address 192.168.10.44? For 128.10.5.228? For 205.202.58.96?

12. Why would you implement DHCP in a local area network?

13. How does a DHCP server make an address assignment to a device on a local area network? For how long does the IP address assignment last?

14. What was the appeal of the IPX protocol in the 1980s and 1990s? What is a major disadvantage to using IPX as a LAN protocol?

15. What is AppleTalk? LocalTalk? When would you use EtherTalk or TokenTalk?

16. Would you use NetBEUI in a large local area network? Why? When would it be appropriate to utilize NetBEUI as the default communications protocol in a local area network?

17. What is the correlation between cabling, repeaters, and hubs, and the layers of the OSI model? What is the correlation between NICs, bridges, and switches? Routers and gateways? Communications protocols?

18. What is SNMP? What components are included with SNMP? What purpose does SNMP serve?

Research Activities

1. Identify the types of connectivity devices being used in the local area network at your school or workplace, and describe why they're being used. Are any of the devices network managed? How do your network administrators use the information collected from the managed devices?

2. Using the search tools available to you, identify three or more switch manufacturing companies and describe the features of two different switch types from each company. Based on what you know so far, how might you use the devices you've identified in a local area network?

3. Using the search tools available to you, identify two or more router manufacturing companies and describe the features of three different router types from each company. Based on what you know so far, how might you use the devices you've identified in a local area network?

4. Identify the network protocols that are used in the local area network at your school or workplace. Why were these protocols chosen for your network? Was IPX ever implemented in your local area network? Why? If your network is using IP, what address class(es) is being used? Why? See if you can find out if and how Class D and Class E addresses are used in your network.

5. Identify how IP addresses are assigned in the local area network at your school or workplace. Were any other methods used to assign IP addresses prior to the current configuration? Why was the current configuration chosen?

HANDS-ON ACTIVITIES

All hands-on activities require access to a computer lab that provides sufficient computers, hardware, media types, and software to perform these activities.

1. If you have a hub available to you, create a network of workstations and at least one server and connect all the workstations and servers to the hub. In bigger LANs, would you use a hub or a switch to connect servers and workstations?

2. If you have a switch available to you, replace the hub that you used in the previous activity with the switch. What does the switch do for the network?

3. If you have a VLAN switch available to you, configure a network that has at least two separate VLANs. Attempt to send some data from one VLAN to another. Are you successful? Given the rules associated with OSI layer 2 switching, what is required for the different VLANs to hear each other?

4. If you have a router available to you, connect your VLANs to the router. What is the purpose of making this connection? Can you now send data from one VLAN to another?

5. If you have managed switch and managed router hardware available to you, use the switch or router software interface to gather device statistics or create specific configurations. Consult the documentation for the device (either via paper documentation or online documentation) to verify whether the device is using SNMP or some other protocol to manage and make configuration changes to the device. What are some examples of other device management protocols?

Mini Case Study

THE BATAVIA CITY SCHOOL DISTRICT

The Batavia City School District (BCSD) has a large network that uses Ethernet architectures to connect elementary, middle school, high school, and administrative buildings throughout the city of Batavia. In developing their campus network, business administrators approved and network engineers specified and implemented the connectivity technologies and devices that would provide fast, efficient, and secure data transmission across the entire network. Taking into consideration that each classroom and each office uses one or more hubs to interconnect users within any given room, what kinds of connectivity devices could be implemented outside of the classroom to interconnect users across the entire BCSD campus? If you had designed this network, where would you implement these devices? If network engineers gathered network performance statistics and determined that too many collisions were taking place, what devices could you implement to reduce the number of collisions? What other benefits would be derived on the network from implementing these collision-reducing devices? If upon further analysis the network engineers discovered that too many broadcasts were circulating the entire network, what connectivity device types would you recommend to solve the broadcast problem? Where would you implement these devices? What other benefits would be derived on the entire network by implementing these devices? If you had designed the network backbone that interconnect the entire BCSD campus, what approach would you take, what devices would you specify, and what architecture or architectures would you have implemented to interconnect the backbone connectivity devices? What role do you suppose the Internet Protocol plays in the BCSD network? Would you choose a Class A, Class B, or Class C IP addressing scheme for the BCSD network? Why?

LAKESIDE METAL STAMPINGS—PART 3

Six months after you implemented a LAN for Lakeside Metal Stampings, the owner calls you to let you know that he has built another building adjacent to the existing building in which you implemented the LAN. He wants to extend the LAN to the new building and is interested in having you do this job for him. What connectivity options will you suggest to him? Will you need to make any changes to the LAN topology you recommended in chapter 3? If so, what changes will you suggest? What information will you require to assist in your recommendations regarding connectivity choices for this latest project?

CHAPTER
Five

Chapter Overview and Objectives

Network operating systems are another key ingredient in the modern world of data communications and networks. Network operating systems provide services such as network file storage and network printing that support many of the business activities we conduct on a daily basis, including real-time interaction with financial and production applications or real-time sharing of project data. In this chapter, we investigate the network operating systems that are commonly used in today's LANs and examine some of the network operating system management functions that support modern LANs. More specifically, by the end of this chapter you will be able to

- Identify the common features of network operating systems.

- Comment on the historical development of network operating systems.

- Provide business perspectives on network operating system implementations, upgrades, updates, service packs, maintenance, and system replacement.

- Describe the four major network operating systems and provide a brief discussion on their histories.

- Identify common network operating system management utilities and add-on products.

- Describe other network management tools.

Network Operating Systems

AN INTRODUCTION TO NETWORK OPERATING SYSTEMS

If you're a student or business professional, it's very likely that you use at least one network operating system (NOS) every day. Various versions of Novell NetWare, Microsoft Windows, Linux, and UNIX run on servers, generally located out of sight of regular users, in data centers or server closets, and they run in the background providing all the kinds of services and functions that users need to conduct their everyday tasks. You probably use one or more network operating systems to print documents, save files, send and receive e-mail, and access the Internet. And most of the time you probably don't even know that you're using them to access all the services you've come to expect in a networked computing environment, because network operating systems have become pervasive in the support of data communications and networks.

network operating system
the software that interfaces between server hardware and the network to which the server is attached while at the same time providing users with controlled access to shared services on the network

So what is a network operating system? In one sense, a **network operating system** is the software that interfaces between server hardware and the network to which the server is attached. Network operating system software contains programming code that communicates with server hardware such as random access memory, hard drives, CD-ROM drives, and various input/output ports such as printer ports and USB ports so that these hardware components can function with the network operating system as well as be shared with network users. In addition, network operating system software includes various programs that allow network administrators to manage and tune both the server hardware and the internal functions of the network operating system itself.

In a broader sense, a network operating system is the software that runs on server hardware and provides users with controlled access to **shared services** on a network. In simple terms, this means the network operating system allows network users to save and retrieve shared files on one or more servers, access shared printers anywhere on the network, and access application programs that are stored on network servers while at the same time regulating that access with various types of security. In Figure 5.1, users can access network resources that are controlled and managed by the network server.

FIGURE 5-1
Network Operating System—Access to Resources
NOS services on a network server.

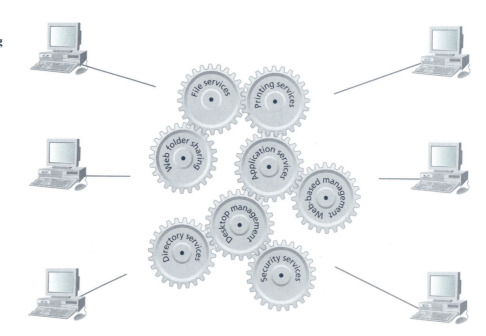

Common Features

In their original forms, network operating systems were relatively simple compared to today's NOSs and were limited in their service capabilities, providing controlled access to shared services such as file storage and printing, and later on, application services. With today's NOSs, however, your network can provide functionality that extends well beyond manipulation and control of server hardware and user access to shared resources. Many built-in features, in combination with add-on products from the NOS software vendors, provide a vast array of potential services that network administrators and business managers can no longer afford to overlook. Notably, features such as Web folder sharing, Web-based management tools, centralized desktop management, server clustering, directory services, metadirectory integration, open source technologies, advanced security services, Internet Web services, and Internet media services comprise the short list of built-in and add-on services that are available. In Table 5.1 you'll find a list of these common

TABLE 5.1
Network Operating System Features

Resource	Function
File system services	Secure access to and storage of files.
Printing services	Access to and maintenance of printing functions such as printing to one or more network printers, controlled access to printers, and letting users know when the printer is out of paper.
Application services	Manages and controls access to network-delivered applications and ensures the assignment of sufficient hardware resources to support application performance.
Web folder sharing	Enables users to share their data with other users anywhere on an internal or external network as well as across the Internet.
Web-based management	Gives network administrators the ability to manage network functions from anywhere using a Web browser and server-based Web management applications.
Desktop management	Provides network administrators the ability to control what users can see and access on their desktop computers.
Server clustering	Allows multiple servers to function as a collective unit to provide fault tolerance and load balancing for data, applications, and other NOS-delivered resources.
Directory services	Provides access to and maintenance of a central NOS database of network resources such as user accounts, group accounts, printers, applications, servers, etc.
Metadirectory integration	Supports access to resources located across multiple and different directories by storing and integrating the identity information of those resources in a central directory service. Frequently thought of as a directory of resource identity information from different directory services.
Open source technologies	Makes the network operating system's source code publicly available so that software developers can develop better programs and offer suggestions for improvement to the existing NOS.[a]
Advanced security services	Provides secure access services such as data encryption to ensure secure access to and transmission of data.[b]
Internet and Web services	Delivers access to and presentation of data using standardized Internet technologies such as IP, DNS, Web browsers, and advanced security techniques.

[a] Linux is the most widely deployed open source operating system.
[b] You'll explore the details of network security in chapter 9.

network operating system features as well as a brief description of the functions these services provide.[1]

Recent History

So what are the modern origins of network operating systems? Arguably they grew out of the 1960s and 1970s push to develop personal computing and the desire to distribute applications and data as well as the control of each, to a distributed population of users. However, if we take a more business-directed approach, you might find merit in the argument that network operating systems evolved because of the simple economic principle of substitution; that is, when there are scarce resources, people will find substitutes and use those alternative solutions. Such was the case in the early to mid-1980s when personal computers began to proliferate throughout corporate environments. In those early days of Personal Computers, most PCs came with dual 5¼-inch floppy disk drives and no hard drive; the hard drives were a $2,000 or $3,000 option which most financial managers couldn't or wouldn't justify and probably rightly so at that time in computing history. Equipping hundreds of PCs each with a $2,000 hard drive would add hundreds of thousands of dollars to a company's budget, not a trivial sum even in today's dollars!

At the same time that budgets were precluding the purchase of individual hard drives for each PC, users were developing a growing need to store an ever-increasing number of files, a number which very easily exceeded the 360-kilobyte capacity of the 5¼-inch floppy disks that were then available. In addition, various departments within organizations had taken to sharing information via **"sneaker net,"** or the process of copying files to floppy disks and walking with floppy in hand to deliver it to a user in another location—certainly not the most efficient form of data transmission, however practical. With the combination of these two major factors—storage needs and sneaker net—the time was ripe for a cost-effective solution that would give users the quantity of storage they required while at the same time filling the need for shared access to that storage.

The solution was found with a new type of software known as network operating system software, a group of programs acting together as a system that made shared access to high-cost hard drives a reality. Instead of configuring individual hard drives within each PC, a single shared server would be configured with one or multiple hard drives. The server would also be configured with a network interface card, and then it would be connected to a network—usually a bus or ring topology in those days. At the same time, the NOS would manage the connection of appropriately configured PC workstations allowing those workstations to connect to the server's hard drives. Since the broader intent of the NOS was to manage multiple simultaneous connections between workstations and the server, multiple users could share access to the server's hard drives at the same time—the problem of each user needing a hard drive to store a growing number of files was solved. The problem of sneaker net was also alleviated because now users could save their files to a central location, and authorized users at other computers could access those files, make changes, and then resave their modified files to the same server. Financial managers were happy because storing data on server hard drives spread the cost of data storage across multiple computers. Users were happy because they could save, retrieve, and share information more conveniently. The network operating system had solved two very real business problems of the early 1980s: data storage and data sharing.

---

[1] Other services can be implemented to run on network operating system software, such as e-mail and database services, but the services listed in Table 5.1 represent core services. That is, these are services that can be implemented and configured as part of the NOS without buying and implementing additional software.

In 1984, the Mobil Chemical Films Division headquarters purchased several AT&T personal computers at a cost of roughly $2,200 apiece to use in the finance, distribution, and information services departments. Each of the computers had dual floppy drives but no hard drive. The Films Division also had on loan from Wang Computers a personal computer with a 10-megabyte hard drive. Its cost would have been nearly $5,000 had the division decided to purchase it. The company also purchased several copies of Lotus 1-2-3 so that the analysts in the finance and distribution departments could develop cost projections for various raw materials, work-in-process inventory, and finished goods.

Because the distribution department was responsible for raw materials procurement, one of the analysts in the department became very adept at creating spreadsheets. At the same time, the finance department used Lotus 1-2-3 to develop cost projections for various other cost and revenue items used in financial statement preparation. Whenever the distribution analyst developed a raw materials cost spreadsheet, the controller always wanted to look at it and make his own adjustments. However, without a network installed, the only way to provide him with a copy was to sneaker net it to him. In other words, the distribution analyst would copy his cost spreadsheet to a 5¼-inch, 360-kilobyte floppy disk, and carry the floppy disk to the other side of the building where the finance department was located. The controller could then load the raw materials spreadsheet into his own computer for further processing.

But the key issue surrounds the inefficiency of the data transmission path and delivery mechanism. The distribution analyst made a copy of his data, walked it over to the controller, and undoubtedly stopped to talk to at least one person at each of the departments located between the distribution and finance departments. The process certainly supported the 1980s buzz term of *management by wandering around (MBWA)*, but it would certainly have been more efficient had there been a central computer acting as a server with a hard drive and network operating system installed. In that same year, 1984, Novell introduced a network operating system. But objects in the rearview mirror are frequently clearer than what is ahead of you, especially when the road is coming up quickly. And where today we take networks for granted and find it difficult to believe that anyone ever relied on ambulatory transmission of data, in 1984 the world of computer networks was relatively new, and the Films Division of Mobil Chemical wasn't considering connecting its PCs to a server via a network operating system. However, by the early 1990s, advances in networking technologies coupled with the business drivers behind efficient and fast data communications undoubtedly motivated many large organizations, like Mobil Chemical, to implement computer networks consisting of network operating systems, servers, workstations, and other peripheral devices.

Business Perspective

So what is the business purpose of network operating systems? Ten years ago someone might have suggested that they provide organizations' employees with shared access to expensive resources such as file storage and printers. But today, many of the devices that were once scarce are now relatively inexpensive. And beyond that, network operating systems have grown to support shared applications, e-mail, and Web services. Extend your thoughts for just a moment, and consider a world without the ability to chat or send documents via e-mail or create and send Web documents or even save files in a central location so that others can access those files; it wouldn't be a pretty picture. We have become so accustomed to network operating systems that to imagine a world without them is nearly impossible. Ask anyone who began a career prior to the mid-1980s if he or she would like to go back to a day without all the conveniences that network operating systems and pervasive computing have brought, and most likely you'll hear a resounding *no*.

It's true that as network operating systems evolved, hardware prices plummeted, making the cost of distributed computing extremely inexpensive. With more affordable hardware and the demand to place productivity enhancing software in the hands of employees, network operating systems proliferated throughout modern organizations. Today we use network operating systems to store vast amounts of information, to access shared software applications that integrate companywide business functions, to send and receive e-mails and documents, and to facilitate efficient workflow. So why do we implement network operating systems in our modern organizational cultures? Because they enhance the entire process of transmitting information between points A and B. Network operating systems improve data communications within the organization, allowing seamless transfer of data between network-connected business functions and processes. In addition, modern NOSs give business the ability to extend their reach beyond internal boundaries, to the world of shared information and transactions with customers, suppliers, and other organizations.

But there is a downside to the proliferation of network operating system installations; and that is they need to be managed and maintained. While the price of hardware has continued to drop like a stone over the past 20 years, and the productivity-enhancing software tools have continued to improve and add functionality, the cost of maintaining the distributed networks that are built upon network operating systems has continued to rise. Eighteen- to 24-month cycles for NOS updates have become the norm, and the wages to pay experienced technical personnel who install and manage these systems have continued to increase. New versions of a network operating system generally require hardware upgrades or replacements, and users must be trained in the new versions of the NOS. And when the network operating system is updated, application software programs frequently need to be updated or replaced. The costs are not insignificant and have even led some business decision makers to move away from the distributed network operating system model toward more centralized computing environments—hearkening to the days of mainframes and the centralized processing that mainframes supported, or to a business model that includes outsourcing of the support and maintenance of an organization's distributed networks.

local operating system
the software that is installed on a workstation computer to provide support for the workstation hardware and to provide services that are local to a specific workstation, such as local file storage, local printing services, local logon, among other services. Most local operating systems today also include functionality that allows these systems to share their services much like a network operating system, albeit in a capacity that is much reduced from that of a network operating system.

Network Operating System Implementations

Chances are, most large and medium-sized organizations that you'll come across today have some sort of network operating system that they're using for file storage, printer sharing, e-mail, and several other data communications functions. Many small businesses jumped on the bandwagon in the 1990s by implementing various versions of network operating systems that the major vendors developed specifically to assist smaller companies with their data communications needs. But whether it's a large organization or a small company with few employees, several characteristics of **network operating system implementations** are common across all organizations; specifically you'll need the NOS software itself and a server on which to install it, a software license, client computers and their **local operating systems**, and, of course, all the hardware and media components (network interface cards, cabling, hubs or switches, printers, etc.) that are necessary to facilitate data communication among users.

A company that doesn't already have a network operating system probably doesn't have a network infrastructure either. The company might have personal computers that they're using for data storage and printing, but they likely don't have the cabling and hubs or switches that will allow them to take advantage of the services provided by a network operating system.

Applied Business **Tidbit**

Once again the substitution effect comes into play whenever the costs of one good or service become expensive relative to the cost of another product or service. As distributed computing environments have pushed their way out to users so that users could have easy and cheap access to their files, shared printing, and other shared network operating system services, the costs of maintaining those environments has steadily increased. In attempts to reduce costs while providing users with adequate levels of access to shared resources, organizations have begun to centralize many network operating system functions. Today it is not uncommon to have many servers that are running NOS software located in a central location in what some have called **server farms**, or groups of several servers that are providing centralized network operating system functionality to users throughout an organization. Users see no difference in the level of services by having their servers and network operating systems located away from them, and at the same time, systems managers have been able to reduce costs by coordinating the management of servers and network operating systems within a single location. In addition, the NOS vendors themselves have in recent years provided tools that allow network administrators access to remote servers via Web interfaces; network managers seldom need to travel to a server to perform updates and maintenance services, they simply use one or more administrative tools in their Web browsers to make software fixes. The only time they need to physically touch a remote server is if there is a problem with a server's hardware.

A first step might be to contact a data network service organization and explain your business goals for your network. One of your goals might be to provide real-time access across departments to centralized customer data, which would result in a connectivity solution and network services for 25 users. You might also have several employees who work on colorful marketing communications copy and they need shared access to an expensive color printer and four high-speed black-and-white network printers. The data network service organization could develop a network services solution that included shared printing. Written and timely communications with customers and vendors is important, so they suggest e-mail and network faxing capability. You might also want to work from home occasionally and want an Internet connection that lets you remotely connect to the network. Security should also be another important issue to you, especially if you're going to allow company employees to exchange e-mail and other types of data communication with the outside world.

Once your business specifications are established, the service company develops a proposal specifying the type of cabling, network cards, server hardware, connectivity hardware, applications, and network operating system that will meet your needs. You have to be a little careful at this step and do some research on your own, because it's common for data services companies to specialize in a particular network operating system and not provide you with a choice of all competing vendors. The same goes for hardware, although hardware is more likely to conform to specific IEEE and other standards. The goal of the business owner should be to ensure the specifications in the proposal will suit the business needs of the organization while at the same time provide for potential expansion and network capabilities that might be needed later on.

Once an agreement has been made, the data network service company will install the cabling, network cards, and connectivity and server hardware, and then they'll install the network operating system. They'll set the appropriate installation parameters for the NOS and make configuration changes to facilitate efficient management of the network operating system once it's up and running and users have connected. Depending on the network operating system chosen, additional software might be installed on each workstation to allow workstation computers to take full advantage of the NOS services.

Finally, the network service organization will configure the workstation startup settings so that users have access to network storage and network printing. And if you specified e-mail and Internet connectivity as part of your network operating system implementation, they'll make the appropriate configuration settings to establish those types of connections as well.

Network Operating System Upgrades

A **network operating system upgrade** is the next generation of a network operating system vendor's NOS software. Its implementation process follows a different set of goals and specifications than the steps involved with a completely new network operating system installation. For instance, the original NOS was implemented to meet specific business goals. When an NOS upgrade is available, you have to ask the question, what does it do for the business as it exists today and what will it do for the business tomorrow? Does the upgrade have new and advanced features that will satisfy new business problems or goals that have emerged since the original NOS implementation or last NOS upgrade? Without the link between business goals and technology implementation, a NOS upgrade is wasted money. If the upgrade does have the potential to enhance business value in some way, then the NOS upgrade might be a project worth implementing.

What makes network operating system upgrades noteworthy is that they generally provide enhanced functionality developed to meet the needs of a changing business marketplace. For example, when the Internet became readily accessible in the mid-1990s and the drive to attract new customers and conduct business across the Internet became a substantial business driver, network operating systems evolved to accommodate organizations' desires to get connected to the outside world. In other cases, network operating system vendors have released NOS upgrades to provide a centralized database that stores users, groups, application objects, folders, printers, and other types of network objects. Other major releases have provided new functionality that provides revolutionary new tools that reduce the cost of managing and maintaining the network infrastructure. Lowering the total cost of ownership (TCO) has also been an ongoing business driver behind the implementation of any NOS upgrade.

In terms of planning the deployment of a network operating system upgrade, you'll first want to see if the new features of the NOS meet any current or future business goals. Sometimes new NOS versions require new versions of applications so that the applications will function properly once the NOS upgrade is installed. Examples include financial software or virus software that might need to be updated or replaced. You'll also need to verify whether the current versions of the local operating systems running on your workstations will need to be upgraded. You might even need to purchase new hardware to support the new upgrades—for both the server and possibly the workstations. All of these considerations add up to potentially significant expenditures.

But let's suppose that a network operating system upgrade is consistent with your business goals and the expense fits within budget constraints. Factors you should consider include integrity of your data and the potential disruption of network services and business processes. To plan for these issues, you should create two or more backups of the data that could be lost if the upgrade does not work and make sure you test those backups for data accuracy, and you need to plan the upgrade for nonpeak hours so that business processes and network services will not be disrupted if the upgrade fails. With these two key elements covered, follow the software vendor's upgrade procedures combined with your own professional experiences to smooth the transition to the new version of the NOS.

Network Operating System Updates, Service Packs, and Maintenance

New installations and upgrades are only part of the issues you'll face with network operating systems. The NOS software vendors continually receive feedback from their customers

Applied Technical **Tidbit**

Network operating system vendors are known to release both minor and major upgrades to their NOS software. Minor releases are different from major releases in that many times minor releases fix problems with previous versions of the NOS software and sometimes add new functionality, while major version changes usually add much new and improved functionality.

Novell, Linux, and UNIX distinguish their major and minor releases in numeral and decimal notation. For example, the current version of the software might be designated as version 7.1 and a minor release upgrade is designated as version 7.2. A major upgrade would be differentiated by the numeral to the left of the decimal; that is, version 8.0 would be a major upgrade with substantially new functionality. Microsoft, on the other hand, uses its company name and the year to designate major updates to its network operating systems; for example, Windows 2000 and Windows 2003. Minor upgrades haven't been a common practice for Microsoft; instead they release updates and fixes to their operating systems that are installed as **service packs.**

Minor releases generally provide installation instructions or training courses that walk administrators through upgrading the current version of the NOS on the same server on which the current NOS version is running. Although a same-server upgrade is achievable, most network administrators as a safety precaution against potential data loss generally install the minor or major release on a new server computer, migrate the old information to the new computer, adjust client computers as necessary, and then take the old server with the old version of the NOS offline.[2] This usually saves countless hours over upgrading the NOS on the existing server, only to see the upgrade choke—and, of course, risk the loss of existing data. Recovery time is substantial if problems occur with a same-server upgrade. With a NOS upgrade on new server hardware, the risk of data loss is virtually negated and business processes and network services can continue virtually uninterrupted.

and test sites about problems with the NOS software. Major problems are given first priority, and fixes to these problems are released on vendors' Web sites for customer download or perhaps even automatic installation over the Internet. Usually, several major fixes will be packaged together and released for installation as support packs, service packs, or **NOS updates.** Types of fixes can range from the simplest of issues that most customers might not ever notice to severe problems with security that must be addressed right away. It's good practice for network administrators to search a vendor's Web site on a scheduled basis for any new fixes or support packs that are available for download.[3] Common locations on vendors' Web sites for updates and service packs include "patches and fixes" sections (Novell), "downloads and updates" sections (Microsoft), and "errata" sections (Red Hat Linux).

One "gotcha" that you'll have to watch out for with updates or service packs is installing them before they've been thoroughly tested in the marketplace. Experience has shown that short of major security vulnerabilities in software, you should always wait to hear feedback from the field before deploying a NOS software patch or update. And the reason you should wait is that a patch or service pack can fix one problem but introduce another; for example, prior to implementing a service pack, all of your applications are functioning fine, but after the service pack one of the application programs quits working. By waiting a period of time

---

[2] A new server is not necessarily a requirement for a minor or major upgrade. As long as adequate data backups are performed and tested prior to an upgrade, the NOS upgrade can be performed on the same server. Then if problems do develop, the upgraded configuration can be deleted, and the previous version can be restored from backup.

[3] The schedule for looking at a NOS vendor's Web site for patches and fixes can be monthly, weekly, daily, etc., depending on the severity of the problem that the patch is supposed to fix and the proximity to the anticipated release date of the patch or fix.

after a vendor releases a service pack before implementing it, you can check on the vendors' Web sites to see what kind of feedback has been documented from network administrators in the field who have implemented the patch.

Network Operating System Replacement

In recent years, supporting multiple network operating systems within a single organization has become less common as companies work to consolidate costs and make network operating system support more efficient. In the past, one NOS might be implemented to deliver file storage and printing services while another might be added to better support distributed application programs. But in today's marketplace, companies keep an ever watchful eye on information system and technology budgets. With advances in NOS software so that there are fewer operational feature differences across NOS vendors, any environment with multiple network operating systems is a candidate for NOS consolidation.

However, replacing one vendor's network operating system with another is not without its own set of issues. For example, **NOS replacement** could mean replacing expensive application programs that used to run on the other NOS but which now need to run on the new NOS. You might also have to update existing hardware or even specify new server hardware if the specifications of the existing hardware don't meet the replacement network operating system's requirements. And you might need to reeducate users on login procedures and system use. From a management perspective, the decision to replace a NOS is more of a business decision than a technical decision. Reasons typically surround the cost of supporting multiple systems and are often supported by a directed business focus to standardize on one network operating system platform for simplicity, for ease of use, for ease of maintenance and upgrade, and, of course, for the seamless exchange of information across the organization.

As you've seen so far in this chapter, network operating systems provide a vast array of services and shared resources to network users. You've also seen several business factors that you might have to consider when implementing, upgrading, or replacing a network operating system. Each of the major NOSs that are available in today's marketplace provide many of the same features, and yet each is unique in its approach. As you move through the rest of this chapter, you're going to have a look at Novell's NetWare operating system and its several versions, Microsoft's Windows NT, Windows 2000, and Windows 2003 Server operating systems, Linux, and UNIX. When you're through reading the chapter, you'll have a pretty good overview and understanding of what a network operating system can provide, what it takes to install, upgrade, or replace a NOS, and the features that are built into the network operating systems of each of the top NOS vendors.

NETWORK OPERATING SYSTEMS IN TODAY'S MARKET

You've already had a look at the basic functions and services provided by a network operating system as well as some of the business issues that surround operating system upgrades, updates, and replacement. In this section, you're going to examine the NOS offerings from Novell, Microsoft, and Red Hat Linux, as well as look at some of the generic features of UNIX.

Novell NetWare

Novell NOS History

Novell started its early corporate life in 1979 as a hardware vendor under the name of **Novell Data Systems** but quickly shifted its strategy to network operating systems when IBM beat them to market with the first PC in 1981. Interestingly enough, Novell's redirected focus and first network operating system grew from a game that its inventors, **Drew Major, Kyle Powell,** and **Dale Neibour,** had created so that they could all play together using separate computers. The three young men and their game soon caught the attention of **Jack Messman,** a venture capitalist who was sent to liquidate Novell Data Systems in 1981. Messman realized that the software that allowed the game to be shared could also be adapted to the sharing of information in a business setting, and with an effective redirection of effort, Novell Data Systems was renamed **Novell**, and Novell's first network operating system, **NetWare,** was soon launched. The company went public in 1983, accelerated to market dominance in the late 1980s with a 70 percent market share of the NOS market, and continued its innovative development efforts, leading to directory services and NetWare 4 in 1992; open standards and Internet capability with NetWare 5 in 1999; and enhanced features and capabilities with its most recent NOS, NetWare 6.

NetWare 3

Novell's first widely implemented network operating system was NetWare 3, which was first released as version 3.10 in the early 1990s and soon thereafter was updated with the release of version 3.11. A later version included NetWare 3.12, and the final version of NetWare 3 was released in 1999 as NetWare 3.2 with enhancements to accommodate Y2K issues and to provide additional components for integration with Novell's newer NetWare 4 NOS. In the NetWare 3 world, the most common services were file and printer sharing, however, NetWare 3 was ideal as a platform for multiuser applications, and other services such as file system security, user authentication (verification of users' identities), and basic routing services such as those provided by hardware routers were also included.

All NetWare 3 versions were server specific; that is, if you installed more than one NetWare 3 server in your environment, users were required to log in to each server before they could gain access to the services provided by that server. In other words, network services were server specific, and logging in to one server did not provide you with access to the services provided by another NetWare 3 server, even if that other NetWare 3 server was on the same network. NetWare 3 servers used a linked-file system known as a **bindery** to store user and group accounts as well as information about the users and groups. When you created a user or group in the bindery, you could also provide specific information about the user or group such as when a user was allowed to log in to the NetWare server. For example, the network administrator might have configured a user account named Joe (user and group accounts were known as objects) with limited login hours (login hours was a property of the user object) of 8 AM to 4 PM (the time constraint was the value entered for the login hours property). For each server installed on the network, all of this information would have to be re-created on each server before a user would have access to the services provided by each additional server. That is, if you added a user account to just a single server on the network and if you had more than one NetWare 3 server, then the user would have access to services only on a single server. NetWare 3, while innovative for its day, required substantial administration in a multiserver network operating system environment.

NetWare 3 was also innovative in terms of memory usage. In the 1980s and early 1990s, random access memory was relatively expensive, and it was not uncommon to operate NetWare 3 servers with only 8 or 16 megabytes of RAM.[4] Because many different functions and services required RAM, and because RAM was expensive, Novell developed its NetWare 3 NOS with modular program components known as **NetWare Loadable Modules (NLMs).** These were compartmentalized programs that added functionality to a

---

[4] Compare this small amount of RAM to modern servers that operate with gigabytes of RAM.

NetWare 3 server. If you needed to provide additional services to your users or to the network as a whole, you could type in the commands to load additional NLMs. This concept is still in use today in Novell's most recent versions of NetWare.

In terms of data communications and network protocols, NetWare 3 existed long before the days of standardized and modern Internet technologies and used a communications protocol suite known as the **IPX/SPX protocol suite.** IPX, or Internet packet exchange was used for regular layer 3 data transmissions, and SPX, or sequenced packet exchange was used where reliability between communicating devices was required. SPX was a layer 4 protocol. However, as convenient as the IPX/SPX protocol suite was to configure, its popularity lost momentum in the early to mid-1990s as Internet technologies became mainstream. As Novell introduced later versions of NetWare, it began providing the option of using the TCP/IP protocol suite, and in today's versions of NetWare, TCP/IP has replaced IPX/SPX as the standard communications protocols suite.

As far as business use, Novell's NetWare 3 was not intended to be an enterprisewide solution for large businesses; instead, NetWare 3 was very adept at providing file and print services to millions of users worldwide through departmental deployments. In other words, lots of companies leased the NetWare 3 NOS and used it to provide basic shared services to users on a department-by-department basis. Novell's flexible NetWare 3 operating systems gained a tremendous following during its product life cycle, eventually growing into a near 70 percent market share in the late 1980s. And although it is no longer supported by Novell, it's still in use in many organizations that haven't found the need to jump beyond basic file and printer sharing services.

NetWare 4

NetWare 4 introduced business managers and network administrators to **NetWare Directory Services (NDS),** a hierarchical database that contains information about all network resources and that supplanted the NetWare 3 bindery.[5] NDS is based on a standard known as **X.500**, a standard for directory databases that is supported by both ISO and ITU. By conforming to the X.500 standard, NetWare 4 made a commitment to developing an NOS directory database that would simulate the structure of a typical business or organization. Within NDS, a network administrator can create user objects, group objects, printer objects, application objects, country code objects, organization objects, organizational unit objects, and other types of objects that mirror the types of resources indigenous to any organization. In addition, each of the objects has a related set of properties into which values can be placed to specifically identify the characteristics of each object.

NDS is similar to the bindery of NetWare 3 only in that it maintains a list of objects, properties of those objects, and property values. However, NDS differs from the bindery in that it tracks information for each network object or resource as opposed to the bindery's tracking of just user and group objects, properties, and values. NDS is a complete database of network resource information presented and stored within a hierarchical, or layered, database, which can be used to look up information by object name or searched to find the specific resource for which you're looking.

Many of the other distinguishing characteristics of NetWare 4 are also tied to NDS. NetWare 4 network resources are stored as objects within NDS independent of the physical location of the object. For example, you could create two printer objects in NDS and, depending on your NDS configuration, those two printer objects could be displayed adjacent to one another in the graphical utility used to create the objects. However, the physical

X.500

the ISO and ITU standard that defines the architecture for directory services that are accessed by enterprise or global resources

---

[5] Later called **Novell Directory Services,** and later still **eDirectory.**

FIGURE 5.2
Printer Objects and
Printer Locations
Network Administrator

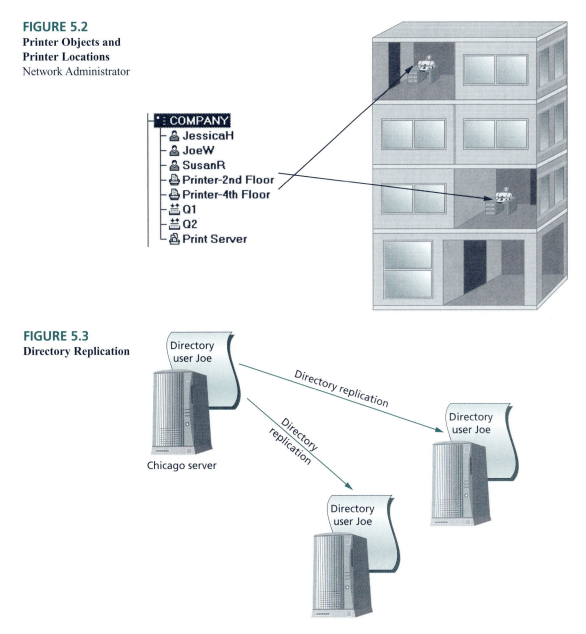

FIGURE 5.3
Directory Replication

locations of those two printers might actually be on different floors or at different ends of the building, as illustrated in Figure 5.2.[6]

NetWare 4 resources can be created on one NetWare 4 server in the network, and the objects representing those resources are replicated to other designated NetWare 4 servers to provide fault tolerance, redundancy, and improved accessibility. Depending on your NDS configuration and network design, a user object created on a NetWare 4 server in Chicago would be automatically **replicated,** or copied, to a designated NetWare 4 server in New York and perhaps even in Dallas. By copying the directory database to multiple remote servers, as is illustrated in Figure 5.3, you're not only protected from loss of your NDS

---

[6] Defining and creating objects within an NOS to represent physical network resources is common practice in today's network operating systems.

information in a given location, but resources are readily accessible locally instead of traversing a wide area network link to access those resources.

But the most significant, most distinguishing, and most time-consuming characteristic of NetWare 4 is the **tree** design. The tree of a NetWare 4 network should resemble the organizational chart or organizational hierarchy of a company or organization. Because NetWare 4 is based on the X.500 standard, the objects within NDS parallel the structure of a typical organization, from organization name to divisions, to departments, right on down to the users who need to log in to the network. And the corresponding NetWare 4 tree design that network administrators create and implement is simply a method to organize all the resources your network and your network users will need; suffice to say the tree design mirrors an organization's structure.

Other features of NetWare 4 are more general in nature. NetWare 4 can provide login access to thousands of users (up to the number of users specified in your license agreement with Novell), whereas NetWare 3 provided access to only 250 users per server. In the same vein, because NetWare 4 utilizes NDS, users are authenticated at login according to the property values stored in NDS. And because NDS information is stored on multiple servers within a NetWare 4 network, any of the servers can verify users' identities. This makes NetWare 4 network-centric; that is, users log in to the network to gain access to network resources and shared services. In NetWare 3, users were required to log in to any and all servers from which they required access to shared services. This is just another way in which NetWare 4 performance exceeds previous versions of NetWare. NetWare 4 also provides the ability to run Web server software, a feature that NetWare 3 didn't have, and NetWare 4 provides support for DNS and **DHCP.**[7]

NetWare 5

NetWare 5 continued the legacy of NetWare 4 with improvements to the NDS structure and a name change to **eDirectory** with the release of NetWare version 5.1. NetWare 5 also provided support for third-party database engines such as Oracle and SQL, and there were more options for Web server engines. Java-based utilities were added, and a new Java-based graphical interface for eDirectory and file-system management known as ConsoleOne was added. NetWare 5 made the jump from the IPX protocol to IP to make the NOS more compliant with Internet-based standards, and a new protocol known as **service location protocol (SLP)** was introduced to more efficiently facilitate the location of services and resources across a large network of NetWare servers. The other major feature addition for NetWare 5 was **Novell Storage Services (NSS),** a new file system that allows the NetWare 5 operating system to manage and maintain files up to 8 terabytes in size.

terabyte
1 trillion bytes or
8 trillion bits

In keeping with the strategy of fully supporting Internet technologies, with NetWare 5.1 Novell included FTP, News, Web Search, and Multimedia servers that could be installed as part of the initial NOS setup and configuration. Other special features of NetWare 5.1 included a browser-based network management utility that would allow network administrators to manage network functions from virtually anywhere.

NetWare 6

The most recent releases of the NetWare operating system are versions 6.0 and 6.5. One of the biggest functional additions is Novell's Native File Access Services, which allows client computers such as Linux, UNIX, Macintosh, and Windows to access data that's stored on NetWare servers without need of installing the Novell client software on the client computers; previous versions of NetWare required this client computer software to

---

[7] You'll learn more about DNS later in this chapter and in chapter 10. The details of DHCP were covered in chapter 4.

access files stored on NetWare servers. Users can gain access to files and basic NetWare services without client software being installed on their client computers. However, to obtain access to the complete set of NetWare services, the NetWare client software must still be installed on each client computer.

NetWare 6 has also added improvements such as **iFolder,** an application that maintains continuity of documents on multiple computers and the server. For example, if you create a file on your laptop, iFolder maintains an identical copy on a NetWare 6 server as well as on every other machine you log in to. Other improvements over NetWare 5 include **iPrint,** which is Novell's Internet printing services engine. With iPrint, users can select a topological map of their office environment and select an icon that represents the printer they want. In addition, NetWare 6 has added the Apache Web server and Tomcat to provide developers with the tools to create, deploy, and support Web-based technologies and Java applications.

NetWare 6.5 adds even more to the NetWare NOS. With NetWare 6.5, Novell has implemented open standards for Web application deployment so that more third-party software companies as well as Novell customers can take advantage of Internet technologies and e-business. With NetWare 6.5, many more network management functions have been converted to Web-based interfaces.

On another front, Novell's acquisition of SUSE LINUX in early 2004 affirms Novell's commitment to develop applications for and port existing applications to the Linux operating system. What this means to business managers is that Novell will be a major supporter of open standards in the Linux community and that future releases of the NetWare NOS will fully support Linux. With this merger of technologies within Novell, business managers can have a high level of confidence that Linux applications that are developed to solve evolving business needs will function in an enterprise environment built on Novell NetWare.

Microsoft's Network Operating Systems

Microsoft NOS History

Microsoft began development of a network operating system known as **Windows NT** in the late 1980s, with the intention of delivering this new server NOS to support client/server applications in the business world.[8] Initially released as Windows NT 3.1 in 1993 with both a workstation version and a server version, the server, or NOS, version was dubbed Windows NT Advanced Server, and it was marketed as an application server that could deliver multiuser client/server applications to users on Novell, Microsoft, and Banyan networks.[9] Since that initial release, Windows NT has been updated through several versions, including version 3.5 in 1994, which improved connectivity to Novell NetWare networks; version 3.51 in 1995, which provided management of client access licenses and support of Microsoft's Backoffice products; version 4.0 in 1996, which was faster and more reliable than previous versions, provided standards-based data communication protocol support, provided an integrated Web server, and had the look and feel of Windows 95; Windows NT 4.0 Enterprise Edition in 1997, which had expanded services, development tools for Internet-based application delivery, and better scalability for large corporations; the Windows 2000 Server Family in 2000, which provides policy-based management, the Active Directory directory service, and improved Web server functionality and features; and today's latest NOS from Microsoft, Windows Server 2003, which has more features, better security, and is more scalable across a wide range of business sizes.

---

[8] The NT in Windows NT stands for new technology.
[9] Banyan produced a network operating system known as Vines that competed directly with Novell's NetWare in the 1980s and early 1990s.

Windows NT Server[10]

As you've already learned, the Windows NT Server history began in the late 1980s, and the first Windows NT Server product was released to the public in 1993 as Windows NT Advanced Server; a server operating system designed to deliver client/server-based applications to network users. As Windows NT continued to evolve, it quickly outgrew its initial role of application server to become a full-featured network operating system providing many of the same services, such as file and printer sharing, as Novell's NetWare. While Windows NT 3.5 and Windows NT 3.51 were incremental improvements over the initial release of Advanced Server and were developed to better integrate Microsoft's application services with Novell networks, Windows NT Server 4.0 was really the first network operating system from Microsoft that the market accepted as a full-featured NOS product. As a result, business managers began to implement Windows NT Server 4.0 for its file and print services as well as its application server capability. In addition, NT 4.0 services provided the capability of managing multiple Windows NT 4.0 servers within the same network, a desirable feature to reduce server administration costs. But one of the large bonuses that network administrators and business managers discovered was the built-in Web server application known as **Internet Information Server.** This feature allowed organizations to take advantage of Internet technologies to deliver Web pages both within their organization as well as publish Internet-accessible Web pages.

Windows NT also introduced the concept of domains to the networking world. In Microsoft parlance, a **domain** is a grouping of network objects that share common resource needs. For example, a specific department within an organization might have its own computers and printers as well as users who log in to the network. If the resources within this department are generally accessible only to the users in this department, then the department would probably be represented as a domain within the context of a Windows NT NOS. In terms of comparison to Novell's NetWare, a domain would be roughly equivalent to an organization or organizational unit within NDS. However, where NDS allows subunits within other organization objects, Windows NT doesn't have the flexibility that **Novell Directory Services** provides. And so domains cannot have subdomains built within them; instead, if you need to represent another physical entity of your business within the structure of Windows NT, you would create another domain. If resources need to be shared across the network between domains, you simply configure the domains to trust one another. Then resources such as folders and printers can be shared between different domains.

If you look at Figure 5.4, you'll see representations of two different Microsoft Windows NT domain models. The first model is comprised of a single domain and is effective for small environments or single departments within larger environments that don't need to share resources with other departments or divisions. It's generally referred to as the Single Domain model. In an organization that requires centralized and shared resources, a Windows NT Server configured as a **Primary Domain Controller (PDC)** functions as the main server computer in the domain. The PDC provides shared services such as file and print services as well as the authentication services that allow users to log on to the server. The PDC also houses the Windows **NT Directory Services (NTDS),** a database of user accounts, group accounts, and computers that have been added to the domain.

Domain
a Microsoft Windows NT grouping of objects that share a common set of network resources

---

[10] Windows NT Workstation as well as the Windows 2000 Professional workstation (local) operating systems are not included in this discussion because they are commonly discussed as workstation or local operating systems, and the focus here is on network operating systems that provide services to an entire network. You should be aware, however, that Windows NT Workstation and Windows 2000 Professional operating systems do have built-in features that allow a computer configured with either of these two operating systems to provide shared services such as shared file and print services to up to 10 other computers simultaneously.

FIGURE 5.4 **Domain Models**
a. Single domain model. All resources are contained within a single domain.
b. Multiple domain model. Resources are distributed across multiple departments configured as multiple domains.

a. Single Domain Model

b. Multiple Domain Model

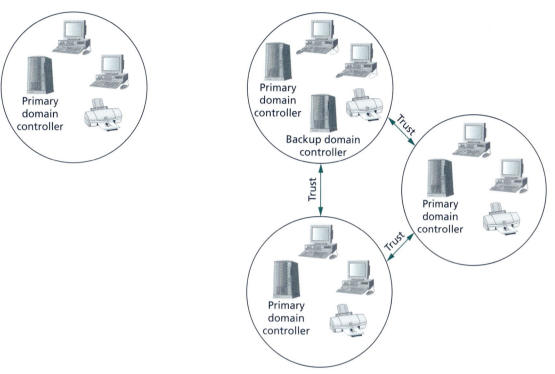

The second model is known as a Multiple Domain model and can be configured in a number of ways. For example, you might have multiple departments, each of which has its own set of users and computers and other resources such as printers and files. In this case, you could delineate network and NOS management responsibilities by creating a Windows NT domain for each department. Users log in to their respective domains and use the resources within their own "departmental" domains. But as users become more familiar with network use and sharing resources, they will probably require access to resources in other domains. With a multiple domain environment, you can provide access to shared resources across domains by establishing trust relationships between two domains that need to share resources. While having the potential of being an administrative nightmare in an environment that has numerous domains, trusts between large numbers of domains provides the flexibility to enhance resource access across departments and divisions.

Whether a Windows NOS environment is designed around a single domain model or multiple domain model, if a Windows NT Server 4.0 environment requires an additional level of fault tolerance and accessibility to users who need to log on, you can implement a second server with another licensed copy of Windows NT Server 4.0 installed to function as the **Backup Domain Controller (BDC).** On a BDC, the Windows NT Server software is installed and configured as a Backup Domain Controller. The BDC automatically stores and maintains a complete copy of all users, groups, and computers that were created and exist on the PDC. In addition, the BDC can also be configured to store files and provide print services, although these additional functions are not automatic; you have to configure the BDC to perform these services.

Applied Business **Tidbit**

Windows NT Server 4.0 did share one similarity with Novell Directory Services; that is, whenever you created a domain, it was created on a computer configured as a Primary Domain Controller. And for fault tolerance, the domain information created on the PDC was copied to another computer known as the Backup Domain Controller. In this way, Windows NT Server 4.0 provided a level of fault tolerance for domain information much like Novell replicated its directory to other NetWare servers throughout a Novell network. For this reason, Microsoft frequently referred to its domain capability as a directory service, and although it wasn't a directory in any standardized sense, Microsoft marketed it as NTDS, short for NT Directory Services.

Windows 2000 Server

active directory
Microsoft's version of a network operating system directory service

Domain Name System (DNS)
a service that translates, or resolves, Internet domains and computer names to IP addresses

Lightweight Directory Access Protocol (LDAP)
a protocol that provides access to directory databases

The Windows 2000 server introduced the computing world and data communications professionals to **Active Directory**, Microsoft's version of a directory service built on industry standards such as **Domain Name System (DNS)** and **Lightweight Directory Access Protocol (LDAP)**.[11] Active Directory is Microsoft's first true attempt to deliver a hierarchical directory structure of network resources. While the domain structure of Windows NT carries forward into Windows 2000, albeit substantially modified, Active Directory provides the organizational capabilities of a directory service. With Active Directory, a network administrator can create users, groups, and computer resources as well as printers and other network devices and organize these resources within container objects and hierarchical domains as shown in Figure 5.5. Groupings of domains form a tree, not unlike the tree structure in Novell's NDS, and groupings of trees can form a forest, to use Microsoft's terms.

One key aspect of the Windows 2000 Active Directory is its link to DNS.[12] When you create a Windows 2000 Domain, you name it with the same format that is used in creating Internet domain names. For example, if your organization's name is DataComm, and the organization has engineering, marketing, and finance departments, you could create a parent domain named datacomm.com; then you could create three subdomains with the names engineering.datacomm.com, marketing.datacomm.com, and finance.datacomm.com. By implementing Internet-based technologies and DNS, searching for resources can be handled through an Internet browser, and resources can be located within domains using the hierarchical search methods of DNS.

Another key aspect is Active Directory's link to LDAP. By designing the Active Directory around LDAP, Microsoft provided a common platform for other software vendors to develop software products that can readily integrate with Active Directory. For example, Novell could develop an LDAP-based interface product that allows NDS to integrate with Active Directory so that network administrators can manage both directory services with a common management program. Lotus could develop a collaborative groupware product that hooks into the Active Directory database so that the Lotus program would not have to re-create all the users and groups that were already created and being managed within Active Directory. LDAP makes Active Directory more extensible; that is, Active Directory can be extended or expanded because it's based on the LDAP standard.[13]

Windows 2000 Server is available in various versions to meet the needs of different size organizations. Microsoft categorizes the various versions as the **Windows 2000 Server**

---

[11] Although Microsoft's Active Directory is based on industry standards such as DNS and LDAP, Active Directory only loosely adheres to the X.500 standard for directory services.
[12] You'll learn more about DNS later in this chapter.
[13] The LDAP standard is defined by RFC 1777.

FIGURE 5.5   **Active Directory Hierarchy**

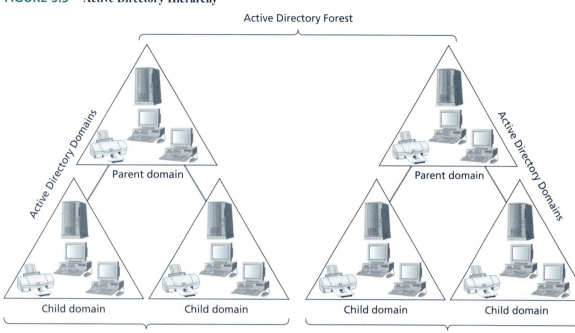

Family, and this family is comprised of Windows 2000 Server, Windows 2000 Advanced Server, and Windows 2000 Datacenter Server. Windows 2000 Server is the entry-level NOS version, and it provides all the regular services expected of a modern network operating system such as file and print services, Internet Web services, application services, networking services, and directory services. Windows 2000 Advanced Server provides all of that plus support for more and faster hardware as well as advanced services such as network server clustering and load balancing of applications. These advanced services translate into business services and functions such as Web hosting and high-availability online or in-house applications that must be available all the time to large numbers of users. The Datacenter Server is aimed primarily at large-scale enterprises that require data warehousing, scientific and engineering simulations and calculations, and online transaction processing. To handle these additional and power-intensive applications, the Datacenter Server accommodates substantially more processors and memory than the other versions within Windows 2000 Server family.

Windows Server 2003

In keeping with Microsoft's strategy of providing productivity enhancing software for business, the **Windows Server 2003** family generally provides faster performance over Windows 2000 in key service areas such as file services, Web services, networking services, and Active Directory. Security has been enhanced with the common language runtime software engine, functionality that Microsoft claims reduces the number of programming bugs and security holes, and within Internet Information Server (IIS) 6.0 to tighten and lock down Web-based security. Windows Server 2003 also expands Web-services functionality through XML Web services and the .NET Framework, matching Novell's deployment of XML-based technologies in NetWare 6.5, to satisfy organizations' needs to deploy substantial and robust enterprise Web-delivered applications both internally and for e-business. Multimedia services are also improved and include Windows Media Player, Encoder, codecs, and the Windows Media Software Development Kit (SDK).

Microsoft provides several editions of Windows Server 2003, including the Standard Edition, the Enterprise Edition, the Datacenter Edition, and the Web Edition. The Standard Edition provides services now common to network operating systems including file, print, and application services as well as more secure Internet connectivity and improved application deployment to workstation computers. Enterprise Edition provides enhanced support for Web services, eight-node server clustering, more processors and random access memory, and enhanced system management software. The Datacenter Edition provides software support for more processors and RAM than the Enterprise Edition and is intended for environments that require the highest levels of availability, which means there is no downtime. The Web Edition is new for the Windows Server 2003 Family. It is designed specifically to host Web-delivered applications and **XML services** through Microsoft's Internet Information Server version 6.0 and .NET Framework technologies.

Linux

Linux NOS History

Because **Linux** has evolved into a network operating system that on several levels competes with or complements Novell and Microsoft, it's not a bad idea to know its origins. And although it's an outgrowth of a smaller operating system named Minix, the series of events that ultimately led a 21-year-old computer science major named **Linus Torvalds** in 1991 to develop Linux are worthwhile to add to our descriptions of network operating systems.

We first have to go back to the 1960s, the decade of the space race, banana-seat bikes, and the humble beginnings of data communications through time-shared mainframe computers. In the 1960s, time sharing was a big deal with several universities under contract with the **Advanced Research Projects Agency** who were developing software and hardware that would allow multiple users to access a mainframe computer's central processing unit. Of notable interest and related to Linux history is the time-sharing system developed at MIT known as the **Compatible Time Sharing System (CTSS).** With the success of this early time-sharing system at MIT, joint efforts among researchers at MIT, General Electric, and AT&T Bell Labs led to work on a more substantial system that would supplant CTSS and function as a full-featured interactive operating system. Known as the **Multiplexed Information and Computing Service,** or **Multics** for short, this would-be operating system proved difficult to program and extremely costly in terms of the time commitment to the project. As a result, Bell Labs officially pulled out of the project in the late 1960s, but a Bell Labs employee who had been a key player in the Multics program with MIT turned to developing a watered-down version of Multics, incarnated as Unics in 1969 at **Bell Labs. Ken Thompson** programmed the **Uniplexed Information and Computing Service,** or **Unics** for short, using assembly language. But further collaborative work with another Bell Labs employee, **Dennis Ritchie,** resulted in a rewritten version in a programming language that would ultimately become C, and the first edition of **UNIX** was released in November 1971.[14] The second edition was released in December 1972; the third and fourth editions were released in 1973; and also in late 1973, Thompson and Ritchie delivered a paper about UNIX that garnered a great deal of attention from the computing community. Universities

---

[14] The beauty of UNIX was that it was an interactive operating system in the same spirit as Multics and CTSS before it, albeit much less expensive on a per-user basis than equivalent mainframe time-sharing systems of the day. If you would like the details of interactive computing and time sharing, refer to Appendix A: A Brief History of Data Communications and Computer Networks.

began asking for copies of UNIX along with the source code so that they could teach students of computer science how operating systems worked. And Bell Labs gave it away—*for free!* But toward the end of the 1970s, around the time of the release of the seventh edition of UNIX, AT&T finally realized that they were giving away something of significant value and discontinued the practice of giving UNIX or its source code away for free. Not only that, but universities were no longer allowed to use the source code to teach students about operating systems.

Enter **Andrew Tanenbaum,** a computer science professor in Amsterdam, the Netherlands. Without the availability of free UNIX and its source code, Tanenbaum no longer had the tools to teach his students how an operating system functioned. So he turned his attention to developing an operating system that would run on an Intel-based PC and which would restore the teaching tool that was lost when UNIX was no longer freely available. The system he developed was called **MINIX,** short for Mini-UNIX, and he released the first version and source code in January 1987. MINIX gained nearly instant credibility and interest in the academic and computing communities, and Tanenbaum's operating system book became a staple of an entire generation of computer science students. Among those students was Linus Torvalds, a second-year computer science student at the University of Helsinki in Finland.

In August 1991, Linus Torvalds posted a message to the MINIX news group stating that he was developing a new and free operating system for Intel-based computers. His new operating system didn't contain any MINIX code, but since MINIX had a wide following and the MINIX news group had an avid list of readers, he thought his announcement might garner some attention. And gather attention it did. By September 1991, Torvalds posted Linux version .01 on the Internet for free download. Subsequent releases through version .12 included suggestions and tweaks that came back to him from enthusiastic programmers, and then he made a jump to version .95. Version .96 was released in 1992 with a graphical user interface and 40,000 lines of code. Version .99 was released in 1993 with more than 100 programmers contributing to the effort and 100,000 lines of code.

But the big news came in 1994 with the release of Linux version 1.0. Not only did it have 170,000 lines of code and a user following of 100,000, but it was also the first version of Linux to have built-in network capability. Linux was on its way to the big time. It had a big user base, it was free, it was network ready, and it had attracted the attention of several for-profit vendors such as Red Hat, Caldera, Debian, and others that added features and support and marketed support of Linux to enterprise users for a fee.

Linux Today

Today, Linux celebrates more than a decade of development and is accepted in enterprise network environments as a useful tool where once it was dismissed because it was open source software without a big company backing a coordinated support effort. It provides most of the services expected of a modern network operating system, and can usually deliver these services with less-significant hardware requirements. Novell has affirmed its stance on Linux with its purchase of SUSE LINUX in early 2004 and has **ported** most of its applications, including eDirectory (also known as NDS), to work on Linux. IBM supports Linux and has launched numerous commercial applications that run on Linux. Many third-party software developers have jumped on board and provide applications to run on Linux. Even hardware vendors offer Linux as an option for their enterprise NOS solutions. And something like 80 or more percent of Internet Web servers are powered by Linux servers running the popular Apache Web-server application.

But even with all its advantages, Linux might still raise questions in the minds of enterprise network decision makers because of a perceived lack of adequate technical support and enterprise application development and availability. There are hundreds of thousands

ported
applications, services, and functions that are converted or modified to run on another system

So you think you want to implement Linux in your organization? You might want to think twice about it, at least in the short run. In March 2003, the SCO Group, one of the original licensees of UNIX and the current owner of UNIX technology, brought suit against IBM claiming that IBM has copied portions of the UNIX programming code into the Linux source code.[15] Because Linux is used in numerous corporate networks today and since the SCO Group claims that its UNIX source code has been illegally copied into the Linux source code, the SCO Group has also threatened to sue all organizations that use Linux or write applications that run on the Linux platform.

Where does this leave organizations with investments in Linux? It's hard to say currently because in March 2004, the SCO Group sued two major users of Linux, AutoZone and DaimlerChrysler, not for copying portions of UNIX programming code to Linux, but for merely using Linux in their networks. According to claims made by the SCO Group, the use of any versions of Linux that include portions of the UNIX code entitles SCO Group to remuneration, or some form of royalty for use.

Since SCO filed its initial claims, IBM has filed a counterclaim against SCO, and Red Hat has initiated a legal action seeking a permanent injunction against the SCO Group. What makes this truly interesting, however, is Microsoft's seemingly tangential involvement in the case. Microsoft licensed SCO Group's UNIX source code to supposedly make Windows products compatible with Linux and UNIX operating systems, and the fees paid to SCO Group were not insubstantial. You can construe this gesture as Microsoft's defense of intellectual property rights or as a financial foundation from which to attack the fast-paced growth of Linux in the operating systems marketplace. In any case, SCO versus IBM is a sticky and intricately interwoven legal battle that could be drawn out in the courts for years to come.

---

of Novell and Microsoft system engineers in the world, but only a fraction of that number are trained or certified as Linux technicians and administrators. Enterprise applications such as e-mail and Web servers have proven reliability on Linux, but other major network operating system services such as database engines and clustering are still not ready for prime time in the Linux world.

Still, the reluctance to implement Linux on a large scale should decrease over the next few years.[16] Development efforts from big players in the computing world such as IBM, HP, and even Novell in support of Linux will reassure business decision makers that Linux is a viable NOS alternative for use in enterprise solutions and that it will have the backing and support required to sustain longevity in the NOS marketplace.

UNIX

UNIX NOS History

You have already caught a glimpse of UNIX history in the "Linux NOS History" section previously in this chapter. However, what that section didn't point out was that UNIX evolved into several variants in the 1970s under the auspices of several different organizations. For example, at a November 1973 event at which Ken Thompson and Dennis Ritchie delivered their UNIX paper, a professor named **Bob Fabry** from the University of California at Berkeley was in attendance and requested a copy of the software to play with.[17] By 1975, two

---

[15] See the "UNIX NOS History" section for additional background on SCO Group.

[16] See the Applied Business Tidbit entitled "A Potential Legal Wrinkle for Linux Implementation" in this section.

[17] It's little wonder that Fabry requested a copy of UNIX. UNIX could provide interactive computing at a cost of about $5,000 per user whereas mainframe time sharing could run as high as $50,000 per user.

enterprising graduate students named **Bill Joy** and **Chuck Haley** were making modifications and improvements to the Bell Labs version of UNIX, and in 1977, Bill Joy distributed this updated UNIX version as the **Berkeley Software Distribution,** which was immediately dubbed **BSD.** Joy's later releases became known for useful feature additions, including the infamous **vi editor** in the second BSD release.

vi editor
the first onscreen text
editor/word processor
for UNIX-based sytems

In a sense, BSD UNIX was supposed to be a research version of UNIX, and AT&T Bell Labs UNIX was supposed to be the version that would be sold commercially. However, in 1979, Bob Fabry at the University of California at Berkeley contracted with the **Defense Advanced Research Projects Agency (DARPA)** to develop an enhanced version of 3BSD that would support the specific needs of the defense agency.[18] Among those enhancements were support of remote connections to facilitate data communications and networking among remote sites and the integration of TCP/IP protocols to provide a communications standard across the DARPA community and computers that were linked in the ARPANET. Although DARPA was required to obtain a UNIX software license from AT&T Bell Labs, an enhanced 3BSD was what DARPA implemented.

Other versions of UNIX became available to the market in the 1980s. A company named **SCO,** short for **Santa Cruz Operations,** started in 1979 as a consulting company that would port UNIX to other hardware platforms. A notable contribution from SCO in 1983 was a packaged UNIX variant named **XENIX** that would run on Intel-based processors. Today, SCO Group, as it is now called, owns the original SCO interests as well as **Caldera Linux,** one of the largest commercial variants of Linux.

Bill Joy left the Berkeley development efforts in 1982 to join Sun Microsystems and helped with tying BSD UNIX to the proprietary hardware developed by Sun. The roots of Sun Microsystem's **Solaris** operating system are based in BSD UNIX. Hewlett Packard maintains a variant of UNIX known as **HP-UX,** first released in 1986. IBM maintains a variant called **AIX** that is used in support of numerous commercial applications. And even the newest computers from Apple are based on UNIX; Apple's **Mac OS X** is a direct descendant of the work started by Ken Thompson and Dennis Ritchie some 30 or more years ago.

UNIX Today

portability
the ability of an
operating system to be
easily reconfigured for
different hardware
platforms

One of the major reasons for the early success of UNIX was its **portability**, or the ability of an operating system to be reconfigured for different hardware platforms.[19] Today, variants of UNIX can be found as host systems for commercial applications the world over. While not as commonplace as Novell or Microsoft in the world of network operating systems, UNIX in its many variant forms maintains the TCP/IP and data communications standards that made it such a robust network-ready and interactive operating system throughout the late 1970s and into the 1980s and 1990s. Its maturity, stability, and built-in security make it an ideal choice for networked databases and high-volume Web servers. Its only major drawback is its lack of an industry standard directory for managing network resources along the lines of Novell's eDirectory or Microsoft's Active Directory. With the continued growth of the Internet and database use, it's likely that you'll see UNIX and its variants integrated into business networks for years to come.

---

[18] 3BSD was the third release of BSD UNIX.
[19] Early on in the development of BSD UNIX, UC Berkeley had a need to run UNIX on a Digital Equipment Corporation (DEC) VAX computer. With modifications to the UNIX source code and feature additions such as virtual memory management and support for the VAX's 32-bit processor, BSD UNIX proved it could accommodate hardware platforms other than DEC's original PDP computers.

NOS MANAGEMENT UTILITIES AND ADD-ON PROGRAMS

Network management is an important consideration in the overall design, implementation, and ongoing maintenance of a local area network. There are utilities and add-on software programs that allow network administrators to control and manage workstations and servers, deploy applications and software to multiple users from a central location, collect detailed resource information for financial and physical inventory purposes, and simplify the broad range of tasks that network administrators face with network management. There are still other management services and products such as DHCP and DNS, and network protocol analyzers that enhance network management capabilities as well.

Utilities and Additional Products

The major network operating system vendors bundle numerous management utilities with their NOS software to assist network administrations with NOS and network management functions. Whether it's Novell, Microsoft, or a Linux or UNIX variant, numerous tools are available to manage these network operating systems.

Novell

Novell has included **NetWare Administrator,** a graphical interface utility for adding, deleting, and managing users and groups and other eDirectory objects and functions since the release of NetWare 4.10.[20] However, with the increased popularity of Web-based tools for network management, Novell has ported its NOS management utilities to Java-based applications to provide the flexibility in network management that derives from network management through a browser. Since the release of NetWare 5, Novell has included utilities such as **ConsoleOne,** a Java-based application designed to replace NetWare Administrator and which adds new functionality for managing the expanding functionality of eDirectory.[21] The newest versions of NetWare also include NOS management utilities such as **NetWare Remote Manager,** another browser-based application that allows network administrators to remotely monitor and configure NetWare servers and server applications, and **iManager,** a browser-based application that provides all the NOS management functionality of NetWare Administrator and ConsoleOne.[22]

Novell also provides additional products that enhance NOS management capability. Specifically, Novell developed **ZENworks,** a network management application that provides workstation management, server management, and handheld device management. It's fully integrated with eDirectory so that NOS configurations can be made through utilities such as ConsoleOne and iManager.

The major management functions that can be added with the installation of ZENworks are policy-based desktop and server administration and handheld device control and management, network-based application distribution and installation, and resource inventory collection and management. With **policy-based administration,** network administrators can specify the icons that appear and functions that are allowed on a user-by-user or workstation-by-workstation basis. Some users might be granted access to all desktop functions such as CD-ROM access, floppy access, My Computer, My Network Places, the Run

---

[20] NetWare 3 versions used a utility called SYSCON for user and group administration plus a utility called PRINTCON for printer services administration.

[21] NetWare's ConsoleOne runs as a server-based or client-based application. It is not a Web-based application.

[22] Security themes are prevalent in all modern NOS software. For example, NetWare Remote Manager uses Secure sockets layer (SSL) to encrypt passwords when remotely connecting to a NetWare server from a client workstation. You will learn more about network security in chapter 9.

and Search commands, and so forth, while other users might be restricted from all local peripherals and be granted access to only specified network storage locations and applications. Desktop preferences such as Microsoft Windows icon and desktop colors can also be administrator-specified and controlled so that users cannot change their desktop settings. Control can be user-specific or workstation-specific depending on the needs of your environment. Other policy-based functions include the ability to remotely control users' workstations and give users the ability to contact the help desk through e-mail when an application or network function isn't working properly. The latest versions of ZENworks are also fully integrated with Windows policy manager so that the look and feel of policy-based desktop administration is identical to Microsoft's policy-based administration. Figure 5.6 illustrates the types of policies that can be created with ZENworks for a Windows XP computer.

Network-based application distribution and installation is another feature of ZENworks that allows network administrators to manage applications through eDirectory. For example, if all users need to have a time-keeping application or the latest version of Microsoft Office installed, the network administrator can create application objects in eDirectory, set the configuration options, and push the application to users' desktops. The applications can be set to install automatically or, depending on the installation options selected, can require user involvement.

The **inventory collection and management** functionality of ZENworks provides network administrators with data and statistics about the hardware and software installed on workstations, servers, and handheld devices. With this information you can determine whether you need to upgrade hardware before you can install certain applications and whether certain applications are installed for which you don't have valid licenses.

Microsoft

Microsoft provides similar NOS management functionality through the implementation of the **Microsoft Management Console (MMC).**[23] Through this utility, Microsoft NOS administrators can add users, groups, printers, and computers; manage Microsoft domains and trusts; and manage a complete range of functions. These functions include system

FIGURE 5.6
ZENworks Policies for Windows XP Computers

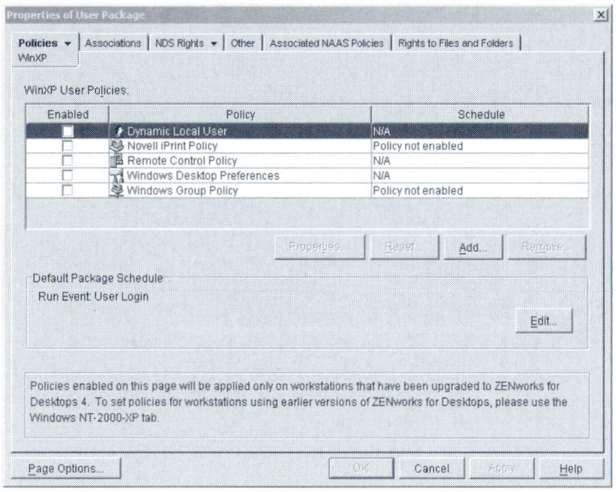

---

[23] MMC was first available with the Windows 2000 Server family. Windows NT Server provided a utility called Server Manager to manage the rudimentary functions of Windows NT Domain controllers and a utility called User Manager for Domains to manage users and groups.

performance of any computer on the network, shared folders, disk drives on workstations and servers, and policy-based administration. Many of these functions are fully integrated with Active Directory, while others are specific to local computers. An example of the Microsoft Management Console is illustrated in Figure 5.7.

The policy-based administration that is integrated with Microsoft's Active Directory is worth special mention here because of the power that it brings to network management and control. Similar to the policy-based management function of Novell's ZENworks, Microsoft's policy-based functionality is built into the base server operating system and Active Directory. You don't need to purchase a separate product to implement the power and control associated with policy-based administration. With it you can control something as simple as desktop color preferences or something as restrictive as desktop icon and menu item display. If you need to prevent users from accessing the Control Panel, you can. If you need to restrict access to the Run and Search commands on the Start menu, you can. If passwords need to be changed on a periodic basis, you can control this function. Microsoft policies are so flexible and powerful that you can configure and control nearly every aspect of every Microsoft computer in your environment.[24] Figure 5.8 provides an example of Microsoft's policy-based management.

FIGURE 5.7
Microsoft Management Console

FIGURE 5.8
Microsoft Policy-based Management

---

[24] Policy-based administration through Active Directory applies to desktop and server computers that belong to the Windows 2000 family, the Windows 2003 family, and Windows XP. For specific policy-based administration of Windows NT, Windows 98, and Windows 95, consult Microsoft's knowledge base on the Microsoft Web site.

Microsoft has add-on products such as **Systems Management Server (SMS)** that provide additional management functionality to a Windows NOS. SMS is similar to Novell's ZENworks in that it provides the engine for networkwide application distribution from a central source as well as full-featured resource inventory collection and management. And prior to the integration of policy-based administration into Windows 2000 and Active Directory, SMS was a key product for Microsoft networks if you wanted to implement policy-based administration.

The configuration of SMS is different from ZENworks, but the impact on network operating system management is the same; centralized control and administration of applications and resource inventory. With SMS you cannot only implement policy-based administration to control Windows computers, but you can configure applications to be delivered and installed on users' client computers and manage and collect hardware and software inventory from computers all across your network. It's not trivial to implement SMS, but the advantages in terms of reduced administration time can be significant.

Linux and UNIX

Linux and UNIX are a little different than Microsoft and Novell in their abilities to manage and configure resources across a network. Linux and UNIX have built-in utilities for adding users and groups and managing network services such as file and print services, remote connection services, and others, but Linux and UNIX do not have a specific utility such as MMC in Microsoft or iManager in NetWare, to manage network resources from a unified utility. Instead, Linux and UNIX can use **secure shell (SSH)** to manage remote computers using a command line interface from a single console and an X-windows GUI interface to run and execute commands on other Linux, UNIX, and many Microsoft computers.[25]

Other Management Services and Products

Other network management services and products include DHCP, DNS, and network traffic and protocol analyzers. Each of these services or products provides a valuable contribution to the overall reduction, simplification, or analysis of network management and problem diagnosis.

DHCP and DNS

The Dynamic Host Configuration Protocol and the Domain Name System play important roles within network operating system configuration and management. Most modern local area networks use the TCP/IP suite of protocols for data communication, which means that each workstation must possess an IP address assignment before it can communicate with other IP computers on internal and external networks, including the Internet. Because it's time consuming to manually configure all workstations in a network, network administrators generally implement tools that will automate time-consuming configuration tasks. DHCP is one of those tools. Network administrators can configure a device such as a router or switch or even a network operating system such as NetWare, Windows Server, or Linux with the DHCP service so that IP addresses can be automatically assigned to each computer in a network.[26]

DNS is another network management tool that facilitates access to resources on your internal network as well as the Internet. DNS works by matching IP addresses to friendly names that we can remember, generally called host names. For example, it's probably easier for you to remember a universal resource locator (URL) such as www.mcgraw-hill.com

---

[25] Secure shell (SSH) is covered in chapter 9.
[26] You learned about the automatic assignment of IP addresses through DHCP in chapter 4.

than it would be to remember the IP address of the computer associated with that URL. At the same time, however, for two computers to communicate, they need to work with the IP communications protocol, not the human-friendly host names that we like to use. To get the computer–human interaction to function well together, network administrators implement DNS.

When you enter a Web site address in a browser, your computer generates a request that is forwarded to a DNS server that has been configured or updated with a table of host names and corresponding IP addresses, as illustrated in Figure 5.9. If the URL can be located in the DNS table of this server, the IP address that corresponds to the URL is sent back to your workstation, and then the workstation uses the IP address of the URL you requested to contact the computer that has the resource you need. If the URL and IP address combination isn't found on the first DNS server, your request is forwarded to subsequent DNS servers in an iterative fashion to each successive DNS server in the DNS hierarchy until your request is resolved. Once your URL is matched (resolved) to an IP address, the IP address is returned to your machine so that your computer can direct packets to the target resource with the target resource's IP address.[27]

From time to time network administrators might need to troubleshoot various network problems about which the network operating system software and utilities can provide only limited information. When a NOS and its utilities can't provide sufficient diagnostic information, network administrators might make use of products such as network traffic and protocol analyzers, commonly called **sniffers.**[28]

Network Traffic and Protocol Analyzers

A **network traffic and protocol analyzer,** or **sniffer,** is a diagnostic application or device that a network administrator can purchase and install on a network workstation or attach to the network media to monitor and capture data packets for subsequent analysis. With the captured information, a network manager can determine performance problems such as network traffic bottlenecks and excessive traffic from specific protocols. The network administrator can also use the captured information to assist with network connectivity problems; that is, to assist in determining why certain traffic types aren't arriving at targeted

FIGURE 5.9
DNS Resolving a URL to an IP Address

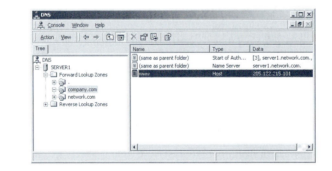

[27] Before the deployment of DNS in the early 1980s, early Internet users had to keep a list of host names and IP addresses in a "hosts" file on each local computer that needed to locate resources across the Internet. As the number of Internet hosts started expanding and later exploding, there wasn't enough time in a day to update these hosts files. DNS solved the problem by resolving host names to IP addresses through a hierarchy of DNS servers, each of which had at least a partial list of all Internet host names. If one DNS server couldn't resolve a host name to an IP address, a subsequent server would be able to.

[28] The term *sniffer* is a registered trademark of Network Associates.

destinations. Network analyzers can also be used to identify and isolate traffic from a network intruder or internal user who is using your network for illicit purposes. In general, it's not uncommon to implement a network analyzer by connecting it with a patch cable to a network hub or switch or to load analyzer software on a designated workstation to monitor all network traffic on a specific network segment. By configuring a network analyzer to send an alert if certain types of packets or protocols traverse a network, network managers can identify a problem quickly and implement a fix before the problem escalates or becomes a major security concern.

Chapter Summary

- **Common features of network operating systems.** Features that are common in today's NOSs include file system services, printing services, application services, Web folder sharing, Web-based management, desktop management, server clustering, directory services, metadirectory integration, open source technologies, advanced security services, and Internet and Web services.

- **Historical development of network operating systems.** Network operating systems evolved to support a growing business need to share distributed information across the organization. Their origins date to the 1980s and the need to provide a low-cost way of storing and accessing data from one or more server computers that housed network accessible hard drives.

- **Network operating system implementations, upgrades, updates, service packs, maintenance, and system replacement.** Network operating systems are implemented with the goal of supporting one or more major business functions such as access to and delivery of valuable organization information to a distributed population of users in an efficient and cost-effective way. Once a NOS is implemented, business goals might change and new NOS technologies evolve in support of a changing business climate. NOS upgrades provide a way to enhance the functionality of an existing NOS to meet the changing needs of the organization. Updates, service packs, and maintenance provide fixes to existing functionality that is already part of the NOS. And NOS replacement is a decision that supports the streamlining of an organization's NOS support function. Replacement is generally approved with the anticipation of lowered operating costs and improved efficiency of the network.

- **Four major network operating systems and their histories.** Novell's NetWare, Microsoft's Server products, various flavors of Linux, and UNIX round out the top choices in today's network operating system marketplace. Each has its own history and roots, with UNIX dating back to the 1960s, Novell and Microsoft dating to the 1980s, and Linux a product of the early 1990s.

- **Common network operating system management utilities and add-on management products.** NOS management utilities include graphical and Web-based utilities for adding, deleting, and managing users and groups and other network resources. There are also additional products to assist in desktop management, management of servers, and management of handheld devices.

- **Other management products.** Other management tools include protocols such as DHCP and DNS that can be implemented as a service with the NOS or as a service on a connectivity device. Still other management products that can assist in ongoing NOS and network management, such as sniffers, must be purchased separately from a vendor other than the NOS vendor.

Key Terms

Active directory, *176*
Advanced Research Projects Agency (ARPA), *178*
AIX, *181*
Andrew Tanenbaum, *179*
Backup domain controller (BDC), *175*
Bell Labs, *178*
Berkeley Software Distribution (BSD), *181*
Bill Joy, *181*
Bindery, *169*
Bob Fabry, *180*
Caldera Linux, *181*
Chuck Haley, *181*
Compatible Time Sharing System (CTSS), *178*
ConsoleOne, *182*
Dale Neibour, *169*
Defense Advanced Research Projects Agency (DARPA), *181*
Dennis Ritchie, *178*
DHCP, *172*
Directory replication, *171*
Domain Name System (DNS), *176*
Drew Major, *169*
eDirectory, *172*
HP-UX, *181*
iFolder, *173*
iManager, *182*
Internet Information Server, *174*
Inventory Collection and Management, *183*
iPrint, *173*
IPX/SPX protocol suite, *170*

Jack Messman, *169*
Ken Thompson, *178*
Kyle Powell, *169*
Lightweight Directory Access Protocol (LDAP), *176*
Linus Torvalds, *178*
Linux, *178*
Mac OS X, *181*
Microsoft Management Console (MMC), *183*
MINIX, *179*
Multiplexed Information and Computing Service (Multics), *178*
NetWare Administrator, *182*
NetWare Directory Services (NDS), *170*
NetWare Loadable Module (NLM), *169*
NetWare Remote Manager, *182*
NetWare Tree, *172*
Network management, *182*
Network operating system, *160*
Network traffic and protocol analyzer, *186*
Network-based application distribution, *183*
NOS implementation, *164*
NOS replacement, *168*
NOS updates, *167*
NOS upgrades, *166*
Novell, *169*
Novell Data Systems, *168*
Novell Directory Services, *174*

Novell Storage Services (NSS), *172*
NT Directory Services (NTDS), *174*
Policy-based administration, *182*
portability, *181*
Primary Domain Controller (PDC), *174*
Santa Cruz Operations (SCO), *181*
Secure shell (SSH), *185*
Server farm, *165*
Service Location Protocol (SLP), *172*
Service pack, *167*
Shared services, *160*
Sneaker net, *162*
Sniffer, *186*
Solaris, *181*
Systems Management Server (SMS), *185*
Uniplexed Information and Computing Service (Unics), *178*
UNIX, *178*
vi Editor, *181*
Windows 2000 Server Family, *176*
Windows domains, *174*
Windows NT, *173*
Windows Server 2003, *177*
X.500, *170*
XENIX, *181*
XML services, *178*
ZENworks, *182*

Questions

1. What is a network operating system and why might a business choose to implement a NOS?

2. What are some of the advanced features of modern network operating systems?

3. What are some of the business reasons behind the development and implementation of network operating systems in the 1980s?

4. What is sneaker net and how was the problem associated with it solved?

5. What are some of the modern business reasons for network operating system implementation? What are some of the disadvantages?

6. What is a server farm and what purpose does it serve?

7. What is a network operating system upgrade and what purposes does it serve? What components do you need to implement a network operating system, and what steps might you need to undertake if your organization does not already have a network infrastructure in place?

8. What are some specific reasons your organization might need to upgrade an existing network operating system? What issues will you need to be aware of and accommodate prior to implementing a NOS upgrade?

9. What is the purpose of a NOS service pack? What "gotcha" do you have to watch out for with a service pack?

10. What reasons substantiate the replacement of an existing network operating system? What issues are involved with replacing one NOS with another NOS?

11. In Novell's NetWare NOS, what is a bindery and what version of Novell's NetWare used a bindery to store user and group information?

12. What is a NetWare Loadable Module? What makes them important to the operation and functionality of NetWare?

13. What is the IPX/SPX protocol suite? How does it compare to TCP/IP?

14. What did Novell's NetWare 4 introduce to purchasers of the NetWare NOS? What is the significance of this functionality? Is it still implemented in modern versions of NetWare?

15. What is X.500? How does it relate to Novell's NetWare NOS? What is the significance of NetWare Tree Design?

16. What improvements did NetWare 5 provide over NetWare 4? How about versions of NetWare 6 over NetWare 5?

17. When did Microsoft release its first version of Windows NT? What was its intended function in the marketplace?

18. What was the significance of Windows NT Server 4.0?

19. What is a Microsoft Windows domain? Where might you use a single domain model? A multiple domain model? What might you configure in a domain if you want a redundant location for your network resources?

20. What is active directory and what major features did it introduce to the computing world and data communications professionals?

21. What NOS versions are available within the Windows 2000 and Windows 2003 Server families? What advantages does the Windows 2003 Server Family provide over the Windows 2000 Server NOS?

22. Who is given credit for the introduction of Linux and what was the motivation behind his development efforts? What year was Linux introduced to the Internet community?

23. Why might enterprise network decision makers be reluctant to implement Linux on a large scale in their organizations? What could lead to broader implementation of Linux in corporate settings?

24. What is UNIX? What company developed the first official version of UNIX? What differences did BSD UNIX provide? Where might you find implementations of UNIX today?

25. What tools do Microsoft, Novell, and Linux provide to assist in network operating system administration? What are the major functions of each tool?

26. What major functions do Novell's ZENworks and Microsoft's SMS provide? Why might these functions be important to an organization?

27. What is DHCP and how can it assist network administration?

28. What is DNS, how does it work, and what business purpose does it serve?
29. What is a traffic and protocol analyzer and how is it used?

Research Activities

1. Using the search tools available to you, create and compare a list of services provided by Novell's NetWare NOS, Microsoft's Windows 2003 Server NOS, and Red Hat's latest version of its NOS.

2. Using Novell's, Microsoft's, and one Linux Web site (use either Caldera or Red Hat Linux for convenience), find one "success story" company for each NOS and describe how that company has implemented the vendor's operating system and summarize the services being used.

3. Using the search tools available to you, find the latest service pack or update for Novell's latest version of NetWare, Microsoft's latest Server NOS, and either a Red Hat or Caldera's latest NOS release and describe the fixes that each update or service pack makes.

4. Using Novell's, Microsoft's, and one major Linux Web site, locate and print the upgrade instructions for the latest version of the NOS.

5. Using Novell's and Microsoft's Web sites, locate and print each vendor's instructions for converting from their competitor's NOS to their own NOS.

6. Using the search tools available to you, locate the X.500 directory standards and list up to 25 of the criteria specified in the standard.

7. Using Microsoft's Web site, identify and describe each of the major NOS editions of the Windows 2003 Server Family and identify and describe the intended business use or market for each.

8. Using Novell's and Microsoft's Web sites, identify a major implementation success story for ZENworks and SMS. Describe how these add-on products are being used.

9. Using the Novell, the Microsoft, and one major Linux Web site, describe how each vendor implements DHCP and DNS. For Microsoft, also describe how DNS is integral in the NOS and Active Directory.

10. Using the search tools available to you, identify three or more vendors that manufacture software and/or hardware network traffic and protocol analyzers, and then describe the top three to five features provided by each analyzer.

HANDS-ON ACTIVITIES

All hands-on activities require access to a computer lab that provides sufficient computers, hardware, media types, and software to perform these activities. In addition, hands-on activities for the installation of NOS software will require installation and configuration instructions from the vendors' Web sites or installation instructions from a certified training curriculum or other published installation instructions. You'll also find it helpful to have the vendors' Web sites open for doing searches on utility names and how to use the utilities.

1. Within your lab environment, install the latest versions of NOS software such as Novell NetWare, Microsoft Windows Server, and Red Hat Linux or other Linux variant. What kinds of differences are in the installation process for each NOS?

2. Once the network operating systems are installed, install additional products such as Novell's ZENworks on a Novell NetWare server and Microsoft's Systems Management Server on a Microsoft Server computer.

3. Open the graphical management utilities and Web-based management utilities identified in the chapter for NetWare, Microsoft Server, and Linux.

4. Open Novell's and Microsoft's DNS and DHCP services to identify configuration parameters.

Mini Case Study

LAKESIDE METAL STAMPINGS—PART 4

Lakeside Metal Stampings, the company to which you were introduced in chapter 2 and which appeared again at the end of chapters 3 and 4 must also consider options for implementing a network operating system to support their business needs. The owner of the company has discussed with you over the course of your interviews that he would like to be able to store information about new and existing projects as well as project designs electronically in a central location so that he, the engineers, and the shop forepersons can access the information and update it as needed. The owner has also requested that all of the company's financial information and records be available electronically so that he and numerous employees can access it. Your discussions have also revealed that the centralized desktop management will be important, and he would like you to be able to manage whatever NOS you recommend from wherever you are, just in case something needs to be tweaked and you're not able to get to the company location within a reasonable amount of time. He also reminds you that there will be a second building in the future and employees in that building will need to be able to share information with employees in the first building. In addition, he doesn't want any employees other than the engineers and shop forepersons sending print jobs between buildings, because he thinks that that would be a convenient excuse for employees to walk over to the other building to see their friends and waste work time.

Since this project has begun, you've figured out that the owner must be reading up on networking technologies, because he also asked you if it would be possible to implement open source technologies with the network operating system that Lakeside Metal Stampings will implement. You say sure, and you know that you're a little rusty on that topic, but you assure him that that topic will be included with your proposal. He has also asked you to put together a list of features from each of the major NOS vendors that will meet his business requirements.

Based on the business requirements that you've discussed with the owner, create a proposal that compares network operating systems from three different vendors as well as a comparison of add-on management products that will support the business needs of Lakeside Metal Stampings. In your proposal, make sure you provide a list and comparison of at least 10 services from each of the major NOS vendors that could support the major business functions within the company. Your proposal should also include a discussion of open source technologies and their significance in network operating systems. When you've completed the comparison of NOSs across the three vendors, summarize your findings and make a supported recommendation for a single network operating system that Lakeside Metal Stampings should implement.

CHAPTER
Six

Chapter Overview and Objectives

Data storage is a network function that has gathered widespread visibility in recent years. For a small organization, data storage may not generate a huge impact on their data communications or network needs. For large organizations, however, growing storage needs translate into large increases in transmitted data and a huge impact on network infrastructure; with large increases in storage come proportionate increases in data traffic. As a result business and technology managers alike are being forced to reevaluate the ways in which their organizations' data is stored, accessed, and maintained. Whether they are used to specify which data to store, used as a hardware device with adequate storage capacity, used to design a storage infrastructure to accommodate numerous and different types of users and client systems, or used to implement a carrier service to extend your data storage needs across vast geographic distances, data storage networks are an integral component of modern networks. In this chapter, we examine the network storage technologies that support this explosive growth in data storage as well as the changes that are required in network infrastructures to support these ever-expanding volumes of data. More specifically, by the end of this chapter you will be able to

- Define direct attached storage and identify practical implementations of direct attached storage.

- Identify network attached storage protocols, terminology, implementation, and management considerations, and several advanced network attached storage technologies.

- Provide historical and contemporary reasons for storage area networks.

- Describe the SCSI protocol.

- Define Fibre Channel and its topologies, configuration parameters, and security considerations.

- Describe IP storage network history and business drivers, topologies and protocols, iSCSI configuration, IP storage security, and other considerations with IP storage.

- Discuss storage area networks in terms of metropolitan area and wide area networks.

Data Storage and Storage Networks

Chapter Outline

BUSINESS PERSPECTIVE ON NETWORK DATA STORAGE

Information vs. Data
Information is the logical presentation of data to meet a business requirement or user requirement. Grouping data into something meaningful creates information. Data by itself is generally meaningless. That is, it is unprocessed information.

Users add to the amount of data traffic with each file accessed or saved. Applications, databases, and various other programs use stored data to create information, which is, in turn, transmitted across the network and saved as new and additional data. Data safety and security require regular data backups, which further adds to the amount of data being transmitted across a network infrastructure. In addition, government regulations require some organizations, especially health insurance organizations, to store vast amounts of data and provide special security configurations to protect the data.[1] With these added demands, valuable bandwidth can quickly become a bottleneck for data transmission.

Switched Ethernet networks have assisted in making bandwidth utilization more efficient, but with ever-increasing amounts of data being transmitted and saved across local area networks, switched Ethernet can only provide efficiency improvements. It directs data to the appropriate network segment, but by itself switched Ethernet cannot decrease the overall amount of data traffic being transmitted to and from storage devices across the organization's networks. Add to that the business impetus to consolidate distributed data for centralized management as well as the need to make data widely accessible and sharable across the entire organization, and you have a very strong business case for moving data storage off of the local network and onto a separate network designed specifically for storage. That is where network storage and storage area networks come into play.

In the following sections you'll examine three methods for network data storage: direct attached storage (DAS), network attached storage (NAS), and storage area networks (SANs). In addition, you'll discover why organizations are migrating away from DAS and toward hybrid data storage environments that merge NAS and SAN technologies.

DIRECT ATTACHED STORAGE

direct attached storage (DAS)

data storage such as hard drives and CD-ROM drives that are physically attached to a single server

In the simplest of network storage requirements, in which data sharing is limited to specific departments and centralized management is not an issue, business and technology managers can specify **direct attached storage (DAS)**. DAS is data storage such as hard drives and CD-ROM drives that are physically attached to a single server. DAS can be installed inside the server enclosure or it can be located within a separate enclosure that is connected via cabling to the server. Figure 6.1 provides an example of a server with an externally connected DAS device.

DAS works great for expanding the storage capacity of individual servers. It is easily installed and configured, and more drives can be added as capacity requirements grow. At the same time, capacity is limited by a couple of factors with DAS. The physical structure of the server and the external drive enclosures limit the number of drives that can be added, and the technical constraints of the drive technologies as well as the drive capacities

FIGURE 6.1
Direct Attached Storage

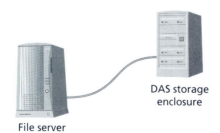

DAS storage
enclosure

File server

---

[1] The government regulations referred to here are governed by the Department of Health under the Health Insurance Portability and Accountability Act (HIPPA).

themselves limit the total storage capacity of DAS.[2] From a technical perspective, DAS is not a file system. Instead DAS simply adds storage space. Actual file-system functionality is provided by an operating system on the server to which the DAS storage is connected.

From a business perspective, DAS is best reserved for small or departmental networks, in which a fixed number of users require access to the same data and in which data sharing with other departments is uncommon. If users external to a department require access, a network administrator must provide secure access for these additional users. In addition, as more users are given access to an individual server, data-access performance can decline.

Other potential problems with DAS include the following:

- If the server crashes, the data is inaccessible.
- Any unused data-storage space is unavailable to other departments without additional storage configuration. If the manager of a department is reluctant to share this unused space with other departments, the space might remain unused.
- DAS requires data backups on each individual server or DAS device. This translates to increased data management as more individual servers and DAS devices are added, and managing distributed data is time consuming.
- With network backups, network data traffic can have a significant negative impact on network performance.
- DAS is not scalable to large organizations' needs. That is, it has capacity limitations.
- The total cost of ownership (TCO) can be higher than NAS or SANs as a long-term data-storage solution because of the factors listed here.

Practical implementations of DAS include several types of *redundant array of inexpensive disks (RAID)* technologies.[3] With RAID technologies, multiple disk drives work together to provide faster data reads and writes and levels of fault tolerance not achievable with a single hard disk. Table 6.1 provides a list of common RAID levels and their descriptions.[4]

TABLE 6.1
RAID Levels

RAID Level	Description
RAID 0	RAID 0 stripes data across two or more disk drives for improved Read/write performance. There is no data redundancy with RAID 0, which means that a single drive failure results in the loss of data from all drives in the set.
RAID 1	RAID 1 replicates and maintains identical copies of data on two sets of disk drives. The data is redundant and RAID 1 is fault tolerant. That is, the data can be recovered from the duplicate drive if the other drive fails. RAID 1 is commonly called **data mirroring.**
RAID 5	RAID 5 stripes data across three or more drives and also stripes error correction information known as *parity* across the drives, so that the data can be re-created if one drive in the disk array fails. RAID 5 is fault tolerant, but not redundant. This means that RAID 5 can recover from failure, but the data is not duplicated.
RAID 6	RAID 6 is RAID 5 plus an additional drive devoted entirely to parity. With the additional parity drive, RAID 6 can recover from the failure of two drives. Like RAID 5, RAID 6 is not redundant because the data is not duplicated across the drives.
RAID 1 + 0	RAID 1 + 0 mirrors two striped disk arrays. This configuration duplicates the data for redundancy—one array is the mirror of the other, and it's fault tolerant because any two nonadjacent drives can fail, and the data is still available.

---

[2] The drive technologies referred to here are Integrated Device Electronics (IDE) and Small Computer Systems Interface (SCSI). Each technology has its specific technical limitations on the number of drives that can be added to a specific channel. SCSI (in its various forms) has much greater capacity because it accommodates many more drives than IDE technology.

[3] The acronym *RAID* was originally coined from redundant array of inexpensive disks, but you might see it represented as redundant array of independent disks.

[4] Other RAID configurations exist, specifically RAID 2, 3, and 4, but they are not commonly implemented.

In general, DAS is considered a local data-storage solution, meaning that the data is attached to a single server. DAS is not designed to be an enterprisewide data-storage solution. Instead, you'll need to consider other types of data-storage techniques such as NAS and SANs.

NETWORK ATTACHED STORAGE

network attached storage (NAS)
a server computer that is optimized to provide fast and efficient shared data storage services to network clients

As users within an organization require shared access to any and all network files from anywhere and at any time, companies can introduce network attached storage to their networking environments. **Network attached storage (NAS)** is a server computer that is optimized to provide fast and efficient shared data-storage services to network clients. By adding one or more NAS servers to your network, you can significantly increase the shared storage capacity of your network while at the same time improving file-system performance. Figure 6.2 provides a simple example of NAS.

Sometimes called filers or NAS devices, NAS servers are different from other types of network servers. NAS servers don't include any network services other than file sharing. Services such as shared printing or application services or directory services that are common in modern network operating systems are not included. Instead each NAS server has a built-in operating system designed for optimum file-sharing performance. This makes NAS servers ideal for offloading the file-system tasks generally performed by regular network servers. With a focus on file sharing, NAS servers can provide much greater file-system performance than regular network servers. In addition, by transferring file-system services away from regular network servers and onto one or more NAS servers, the performance of regular network servers can be drastically improved in busy networks.

FIGURE 6.2
Network Attached Storage

NAS Protocols

NAS devices utilize standard file-sharing protocols to provide their file-sharing services to network clients. As a result, any client computer, including workstations and network servers, can save and retrieve files from a NAS server. The two major protocols typically implemented by NAS devices are CIFS and NFS.

CIFS

The **Common Internet File System (CIFS)** in its original form was known as **Server Message Block (SMB),** an OSI application layer protocol. SMB was developed by IBM in the early 1980s as a network naming and browsing protocol, but quickly became a file-sharing protocol in Microsoft operating systems. As Microsoft tweaked SMB for enhanced performance including file access across the Internet, the name was changed in 1996 to *CIFS* to reflect Internet file-sharing capability. In its latest incarnation, CIFS functions within the upper three layers of the OSI model.

CIFS is the file-sharing protocol common to Microsoft Windows operating systems and to Linux computers that have a program called *Samba* installed.[5] In either of these scenarios, CIFS allows clients and servers with this protocol installed to share files.

NFS

Sun Microsystems developed the **Network File System (NFS)** and made it available to the UNIX community in 1984. Within a very short period of time, it became the standard file-sharing service included with all versions of UNIX. In its original form, NFS, an OSI application layer protocol, was designed for encapsulation within User Datagram Protocol (UDP) packets for transmission across a network.[6] But NFS version 3 encapsulates NFS packets inside of transmission control protocol (TCP) packets.[7] This results in improved performance and more efficient use of network bandwidth.[8]

Other File Transfer Protocols

Some NAS servers provide the ability to transfer files using the HyperText Transfer Protocol (HTTP), the File Transfer Protocol (FTP), the Web-enabled version of the Network File System (WebNFS), the NetWare Core Protocol (NCP), and the AppleTalk Filing Protocol (AFP).[9] If your NAS implementation requires the functionality of these file-transfer protocols, verify these specifications with the NAS manufacturer.

So if CIFS and NFS can provide file-system services to network clients via regular network servers, why implement NAS devices? To answer this question, let's first look at a few of the problems that generally occur in networks requiring both file systems. First, as local

---

[5] A Linux or UNIX computer with Samba software installed can share files with Windows client computers in much the same way as one Windows client computer can share files with other Windows computers. Samba is simply a program that configures a Linux or UNIX computer with the SMB or CIFS protocol.

[6] UDP is a connectionless protocol that is part of the TCP/IP protocol suite and functions at the transport layer of the OSI model.

[7] TCP is a connection-oriented protocol that is part of the TCP/IP protocol suite and functions at the transport layer of the OSI model.

[8] NFS packages files into 8-kilobyte packets, which are then fragmented and encapsulated into six separate IP packets. If any of the six IP packets are lost in transit, all six IP packets must be retransmitted. UDP also has no flow control, which means the receiving computer can ask for more data than it can receive per unit time. Excess packets are dropped and must be retransmitted. With UDP, the potential exists for many dropped packets and lots of packets being retransmitted. In other words, NFS over UDP can choke a network.

[9] HTTP, FTP, and WebNFS are application layer protocols while NCP spans the transport, session, and presentation layers. AFP functions at the presentation and application layers.

FIGURE 6.3
File-Sharing
Protocols

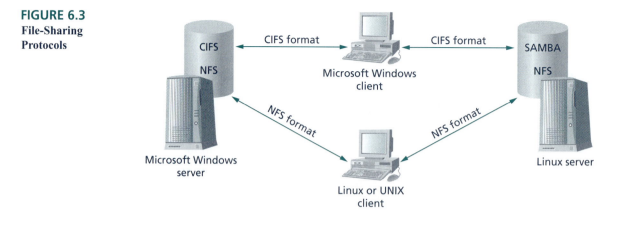

area networks grew to include more and different types of servers running different network operating systems, network managers found themselves managing one or more servers providing file services via CIFS and one or more servers providing file-system services via NFS. This required the network manager to have expertise with both types of file systems, not to mention managing the other services involved with at least two different network operating systems—NFS for UNIX and CIFS for Windows—and NetWare used its own file system, which represented yet another level of expertise.

Another problem arises in the form of file-system administration headaches if the network manager needs to configure different operating systems to accommodate both NFS and CIFS. For example, she could install NFS services on a Microsoft Windows computer. With NFS services installed, a Windows server looks like a UNIX or Linux computer to UNIX and Linux clients. Linux and UNIX clients can save files in NFS format to a Windows server while Windows clients can save files in CIFS format to the same Windows server, as illustrated in Figure 6.3. Similarly, a UNIX or Linux server with Samba software properly configured can act as a CIFS file server for Windows clients, while acting as an NFS file server for UNIX and Linux clients, also shown in Figure 6.3.[10] In both cases, the administration is not trivial. It requires the network manager to have expertise with both file systems as well as NFS services for Windows and Samba services on UNIX or Linux. Then, if the administrator really wants to stir the pot, she can add an older version of Novell NetWare to the mix and configure it to accept files from a UNIX or Linux client. Whereas older versions of NetWare would conveniently accept files from a Windows server or workstation, configuring NFS services on a NetWare server required the network administrator to install an additional product known as UnixWare on the NetWare server.[11]

The third problem in networks that support both NFS and CIFS is that the file systems provided by regular network operating systems are designed to provide suboptimal performance. Network operating system file-system services compete with all the other services that are built in to modern NOSs. With the extra overhead incurred with the other services, there is no way that a file system provided by a Microsoft Windows server, Novell NetWare server, or Linux server will be able to perform as well as a device that is configured specifically and solely for serving files. However, for small networks or with network servers that don't handle a significant amount of data requests, the impact on users due to this suboptimal performance is negligible.

---

[10] Linux servers do not need Samba installed to provide NFS file system services to Linux or UNIX clients.
[11] Newer versions of NetWare have Native File Access, a file system that accommodates NFS, CIFS, and AFP file systems.

Network attached storage solves the foregoing problems with improved data storage performance and consolidation of data locations.[12] The CIFS and NFS protocols are incorporated into each NAS device's operating system. This enables any computer that uses either or both of these protocols to save and retrieve files from a NAS server. With NAS, file-service functions can be offloaded from regular file servers and consolidated to one or more NAS devices. This results in improved file-system performance because there is a NAS device managing a single function: file services. Regular server performance improves because the other services no longer have to compete with file services for hardware resources. In addition, the file systems of many regular network servers can be transferred to a single NAS server resulting in a potentially significant reduction in data management requirements.

NAS Terminology

Network attached storage utilizes several terms that you might find helpful when discussing data storage and storage networks. In general, network attached storage is referred to as *NAS*, but other terms such as *NAS device, NAS appliance, NAS head,* and *NAS gateway* are frequently used for various implementations of NAS. Generically speaking, a **NAS device** is any computer that provides NAS capability. For example, a computer with a built-in operating system designed specifically to provide file-system services to network clients is a NAS device. The NAS device would have an Ethernet NIC installed and could be connected to a network hub or switch with UTP cabling or fiber-optic cable or even a wireless media type, as illustrated in Figure 6.4. Users can then access files on the NAS device for saving and retrieving files through an assigned drive letter that points to a specific folder location on the NAS device or by browsing network resources.[13]

NAS device
any computer that
provides NAS capability

FIGURE 6.4
Connecting to a NAS Device

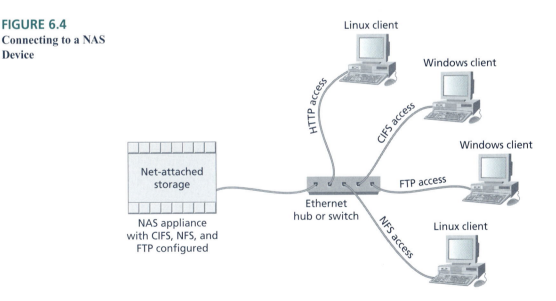

---

[12] Although NAS solves certain file-system performance problems and provides consolidation of data locations, NAS adds a layer of management complexity to the network. That is, there are implementation and configuration considerations that the network administrator must address. You'll learn about these in the "NAS Implementation and Management" section later in this chapter.
[13] Browsing in this context refers to using programs such as Network Neighborhood or My Network Places with Microsoft Windows workstation operating systems or one of the graphical file search tools on a Linux client.

FIGURE 6.5
NAS Storage Fabric

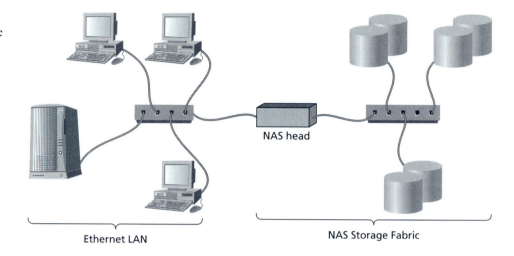

Ethernet LAN

NAS head

NAS Storage Fabric

NAS Appliance

NAS appliance
NAS device in which the file-system services and storage devices such as hard drives, tape drives, or CD-ROM drives are self-contained within a stand-alone computer that can be directly connected to your network

A **NAS appliance** is a NAS device in which the file-system services and storage devices such as hard drives, tape drives, or CD-ROM drives are self-contained within a stand-alone computer that can be directly connected to your network. NAS appliances are generally the easiest of the NAS devices to configure and implement for additional storage capacity.

NAS Head

NAS head
the file-system services portion of a NAS device to which users connect

A **NAS head** is the file-system services portion of a NAS device to which users connect. The NAS head is also the interface between the file-system services provided by the NAS device and the actual physical storage. The physical storage can either be directly attached to the NAS device as in a NAS appliance or the physical storage can be provided in one or more separate enclosures. In this case the NAS head accesses the physical storage through a network storage fabric. Figure 6.5 provides an example of a NAS head and a NAS storage fabric.

Network Storage Fabric

network storage fabric
a specialized network that communicates only with the NAS head for transferring data between the NAS head and the hard drives in the physical storage enclosures

The **network storage fabric** is a specialized network that communicates only with the NAS head for transferring data between the NAS head and the hard drives in the physical storage enclosures.[14] A NAS head in combination with this "backend" network storage fabric provides a data storage solution that is significantly more scalable than a self-contained NAS appliance. That is, as your networks storage needs grow, you can add more storage capacity to the network storage fabric.

NAS Gateway

NAS gateway
a NAS device that allows network users to connect to a storage area network and save and retrieve files from the SAN

A **NAS gateway** is a NAS device that allows network users to connect to a storage area network and save and retrieve files from the SAN.[15] A NAS gateway functions much like a NAS head in that the NAS gateway provides the file-system services to users and network client computers while at the same time acting as the interface between the NAS file system and the storage fabric of the SAN.

---

[14] NAS network storage fabric is also the foundation that is used in storage area networks, which you'll learn about later on in this chapter.
[15] Remember that gateways interconnect two different types of networks. The NAS gateway also connects two different types of networks, a LAN to a SAN.

Until early 2004, Excellus Blue Cross Blue Shield had been using DAS on 10 different file servers to store the Microsoft Excel and Microsoft Word documents that users generated in their Rochester, New York, location on a daily basis. Faced with increasing requirements for file storage, they considered several options, including an increase in DAS capacity as well as NAS and SAN solutions. They ultimately implemented NAS to accommodate their increasing file-storage needs.

DAS was ruled out because it would have required the continued support of multiple file servers as well as the backups for each of those file servers, and neither their existing DAS nor a new DAS solution would be scalable to their growing file-storage requirements. In addition, DAS couldn't provide the level of fault tolerance and data redundancy that is needed in an organization of approximately 4,500 employees.

Another option was to move all user data to their existing Fibre Channel SAN. Although this solution was scalable and provided the level of fault tolerance and redundancy they were looking for, the cost of the additional storage capacity for the SAN would have been approximately 10 cents per megabyte—or about $400,000 for the 4 terabytes of additional capacity that they estimated they would need. And the cost of the extra storage capacity didn't include the cost of reconfiguring the SAN to accommodate the new SAN nodes and data paths that would have been required.

They finally decided on a NAS solution that provided the required storage capacity and required level of fault tolerance and redundancy. With this solution, the technical staff was able to consolidate the file storage from 10 different servers to a single NAS device, and they accomplished this for about two-and-a-half-cents per megabyte, or about one-quarter of the cost of the SAN solution.

One of the interesting features of this particular NAS device is that it utilizes a RAID 4 configuration across each array of drives.[16] Each array consists of four disk drives, three for data striping, and one drive for parity. The next release of the NAS operating system for this device will feature support RAID 6. This NAS device also has two nodes built into it for redundancy so that if one node fails, the other takes over and can recognize any and all drive arrays. Data is accessed using CIFS, but FTP file access is also a configurable file-access option. In addition, this NAS device uses the Lightweight Directory Access Protocol (LDAP) for integration with Windows 2000 (or later) servers. This allows users' file storage to be managed with common Windows 2000 management utilities.

This NAS solution was not without its negative points. It utilizes the Network Data Management Protocol (NDMP) backup protocol, but the existing backup programs that Excellus Blue Cross Blue Shield had used for DAS backups are not fully compliant with NDMP. Ultimately this will require the purchase of a backup program that is fully NDMP-compliant so that data backups flow smoothly.

Another problem the company encountered was with virus scanning. They weren't able to use their existing antivirus software but instead were required to implement the virus-scanning software supplied by the vendor. The virus-scanning software was installed on a dedicated server, the operating system on the NAS device was configured to recognize the IP address of the virus-scanning server, and then the virus scanning was effective.

Overall, the implementation was a success. The NAS solution provided the capacity they needed and the level of fault tolerance and redundancy that Excellus Blue Cross Blue Shield required. They also were able to implement the solution for a fraction of the cost of an alternative SAN configuration.

---

[16] RAID 4 stripes blocks of data across multiple drives, but the parity data is always written to the same dedicated parity drive.

NAS Implementation and Management

Implementation and management of NAS include many facets about which business managers and network administrators must be aware. Before considering a NAS installation, you should be aware of issues surrounding configuration, device and data availability, fault tolerance, data backup capability, data migration from distributed servers to NAS, hardware and software updates, virus scanning, and management tools specific to NAS. In this section, you'll explore these NAS implementation and management issues.

Configuration

NAS devices are generally configured through a management interface such as a Web browser utility or Telnet. For example, in a small network environment comprised only of workstations, you could configure a NAS device to be part of the same workgroup as the workstations. Then when users browse their network resources for a place to save their data, they are able to select storage space on the NAS appliance. The NAS appliances utilize IP addressing, so they can be located on the network, and the NFS and CIFS protocols for sharing files.

For larger environments that contain one or more servers to which one or more NAS appliances are logically linked, the network administrator can configure the server to redirect file requests, such as saving and retrieving files, to the appropriate NAS device. The changes to the server's configuration that link it to the NAS device are transparent to users.[17] To users it looks as if files are still being saved to or retrieved from a folder on the server itself. As in smaller environments, IP addressing is used for network identification, and NFS and CIFS protocols provide the file-system services.

Availability and Fault Tolerance

fault tolerance
the ability to recover
from a loss

With the ever-increasing value of data and the expanding amounts of data that organizations store, data availability and **fault tolerance** are essential mission-critical data-management concerns for business and technology managers.[18] Modern NAS devices include numerous built-in capabilities that enhance data-storage availability and fault tolerance. Depending on the NAS manufacturer and the cost of the NAS device, you can specify a NAS device that will fit your organization's need to keep its data safe and available. The availability and fault-tolerance features you'll learn about here include high-availability NAS clustering, data mirroring, and NDMP backups.

High-Availability NAS Clustering   Some NAS manufacturers offer **high-availability (HA)** NAS systems that provide continuous access to data even if a NAS server crashes. With HA **NAS clustering,** sometimes called active/active failover, two or more NAS heads are linked together in a cluster to provide file system access, and the entire cluster is connected as a unit to a shared set of storage disks, as depicted in Figure 6.6. Any NAS head in the cluster can service any file-system request, which dramatically improves file-system performance. If one NAS head is busy, another can service the request. At the same time, if one of the heads in the cluster crashes, any other NAS server in the cluster can service incoming file-system requests.[19]

---

[17] These server configuration changes can take the form of dfs share points on Microsoft Windows servers or URL links that redirect file requests with Novell NetWare servers. With Microsoft's distributed file system (dfs), the network administrator creates a share point that links the Windows server to the NAS device's storage space. With Novell's NetWare, the network administrator creates a Web URL on the NetWare server that redirects file requests to the NAS device.

[18] Data availability also implies reliable accessibility of the data.

[19] In smaller organizations where the cost of NAS might preclude its implementation, some of the benefits of high availability NAS can be achieved through the implementation of RAID, especially RAID 1 + 0, where the data is both striped (RAID 0) and mirrored (RAID 1). Keep in mind, however, that a RAID system is not a substitute for HA NAS, nor does RAID provide fault tolerance in the event that the server that houses the disk drives crashes.

FIGURE 6.6
High-Availability NAS Clustering

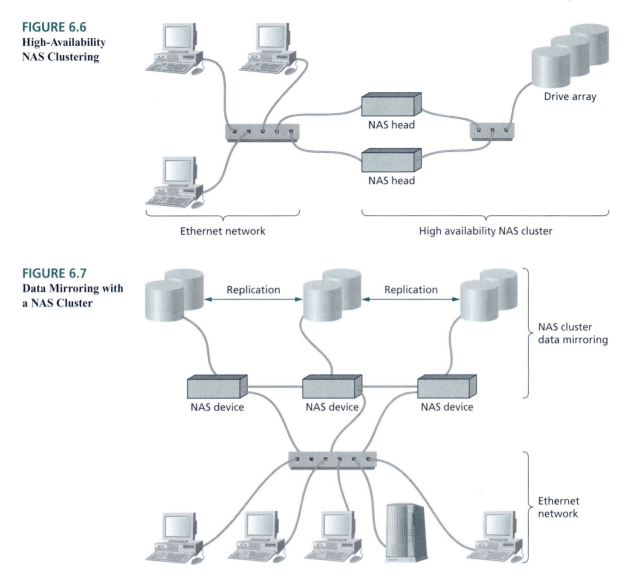

FIGURE 6.7
Data Mirroring with a NAS Cluster

These types of NAS configurations are much more expensive than stand-alone NAS appliances, but with the added expense comes continuous and uninterrupted file-system services. The downside of a HA NAS clustering configuration is that there is no redundancy with the stored data. The NAS heads are fault tolerant because there is more than one to take over in the event that one crashes. But the data is not fault tolerant because it is stored on a single set of drives that is shared by all of the NAS servers in the cluster. If the drives crash or the connection between the drives and the clustered NAS heads fails, data availability ceases. That is why data mirroring is so important.

Data mirroring   Data mirroring takes HA NAS clustering one step further. With data mirroring, sometimes called *data replication,* each NAS device in a cluster maintains an identical copy of the data, as shown in Figure 6.7. As changes are made to the data, those changes are replicated across all NAS servers in the cluster. If one of the NAS devices fails, any other NAS device in the cluster can provide file-system services as well as the data. The key benefit to data mirroring beyond the advantages associated with HA NAS clusters is that the data is available on any server in the cluster. That is, data mirroring eliminates the single point of failure associated with the HA NAS cluster's single shared set of storage disks. The downside is that a mirrored configuration is more expensive than simpler versions of HA NAS clusters.

NDMP Backups Most NAS devices include support for data backups through implementation of the Network Data Management Protocol (NDMP). With the implementation of this protocol, NAS servers do not require you to install backup software on the NAS device itself, providing a potentially significant savings in backup configuration, administration, and time. Instead, you can install and maintain NDMP-aware backup software on a separate backup storage device, and the backup storage device communicates with the NAS devices through NDMP. The major downside to **NDMP backups,** however, is that some programs that claim to be NDMP-aware are not fully compliant. That is, the backup software that was being used to back up DAS might not seamlessly back up data from a NAS device, even if it "says on the box" that it's NDMP-aware. It's best to confirm with the NAS vendor whether your existing backup program will function properly using NDMP.

Data Migration

After NAS has been configured on a network, data can be transferred from distributed network servers to the NAS device. Ways to perform **data migration** include

- Backing up the data on regular file servers to a backup device and then restoring the data to the NAS server.
- Copying the data across the network from regular file servers to the NAS server.

Choosing to migrate files with a backup and restore method will probably be slower, but it won't clog your network with backup data traffic. On the other hand, copying the files across the network is expedient, and it's a lot faster than the backup method. If you're going to migrate files across the network, consider copying the files outside of regular business hours to minimize the impact on network users. In addition, once the migration is complete, verify that users can still access their data. Data migration may not copy security features such as access control lists, and you might need to re-create these lists and associated permissions before users can access their files.[20]

Hardware Fixes and Software Updates

Hardware components can fail, so it's always a good idea to keep spares on hand for your NAS devices. Most NAS servers support hot-swappable hard drives, so that you can replace a damaged drive while the NAS server is still running. Other components such as power supplies, memory, and CPUs will require that you power off the NAS device before implementing the hardware fix.

NAS vendors update their operating system software periodically, and if you want to include the software fixes and feature improvements included with the updates, you'll need to perform the update. Fixes are probably more critical than feature updates, but in either case, you should back up the data before updating your NAS device's software and consider performing the update outside of regular business hours.

Virus Scanning

Virus scanning with NAS requires special attention because the virus-scanning software is specific to the NAS vendor, and you can't install the virus-scanning software on the NAS device itself. Instead the virus-scanning program is installed on a separate server that communicates with the NAS device. As part of the virus-scanning configuration, the operating

---

[20] Special care must also be taken with UNIX and Linux file migrations. UNIX and Linux use symbolic links in their file systems. Symbolic links allow a file or folder to be associated with another file or folder, and if the symbolic link is not copied, users will have difficulty accessing their data.

system on the NAS device must be configured to recognize the IP address of the virus-scanning server. Once this is accomplished, the virus-scanning server scans all files before they're written to disk on the NAS device.

Network Management Tools

Most NAS devices include monitoring tools that allow you to check on disk and file-system statistics, CPU utilization, and NIC statistics. For example, as NAS usage increases over time, you might find that the NIC statistics indicate less than satisfactory performance. If the NIC is approaching 100 percent utilization, you might find it advantageous to implement a higher performance NIC or move the NAS device onto its own switch port or VLAN. Likewise, if disk and file system utilization are being pushed to their upper limits, you might need to consider adding additional storage or even another NAS server to your network.

Advanced NAS Technologies to Consider

NAS continues to evolve and improve. Some technological advances that you should ask about when considering NAS include performance-enhancing hardware such as **nonvolatile random access memory (NVRAM),** faster file systems such as the **direct access file system (DAFS),** and alternative data transport protocols such as **iSCSI.**

NVRAM

Nonvolatile random access memory (NVRAM)
a type of random access memory that is connected to an alternate power source such as a battery so that data stored in NVRAM is not lost in the event of a system failure, crash, or loss of main power

direct access file system (DAFS)
a new file system that operates in conjunction with a transport protocol known as *direct access transport (DAT)*. With DAFS, the RAM in the NAS device performs as if it were an extension of memory in a client computer that is requesting file access or saving files

Random access memory (RAM) is a memory buffer, sometimes called a *memory cache,* or simply *cache,* that stores recently accessed data as well as data that needs to be written to disk. Since RAM provides faster file reads and writes than disk storage, NAS manufacturers have been able to offer significant performance improvements by using RAM in combination with disk storage in NAS devices.[21] Before NVRAM, dynamic RAM (DRAM) was implemented to improve data-access performance with caching. The problem with DRAM is that any data that is stored there is lost in the event of a crash, reboot, or power outage. On the other hand, NVRAM is nonvolatile, a feature made possible by connecting NVRAM to a battery or other power source that is independent of the main power supply in the storage unit itself. This means that the problem of losing data if there is a crash or reboot is eliminated. NVRAM gives a NAS device the same I/O performance improvement as DRAM with the added benefit of data recovery in the event of failure.

DAFS

The direct access file system (DAFS) is a new file system that operates in conjunction with a transport protocol known as *direct access transport (DAT)*. Combining the two significantly improves NAS performance. With DAFS, the RAM in the NAS device performs as if it were an extension of memory in a client computer that is requesting file access or saving files. With this "mapping" of memory on the client to memory on the NAS device, files can be accessed and retrieved much faster—almost as if the files were on the local workstation drive instead of across the network on a NAS device.

iSCSI

iSCSI is another technology to watch for in the new generation of NAS devices. iSCSI maps the SCSI data transfer protocols on top of TCP so that stored data can be transported across a typical Ethernet network without first being translated into file-level protocols such as CIFS and NFS.[22] The implementation of iSCSI has the potential to transform

---

[21] File reads and writes are commonly called *input/output (I/O)*.
[22] Instead, the translation from iSCSI to NFS or CIFS would take place within the operating system at a network server or workstation.

ubiquitous resource
a resource that can be accessed by anyone on the network at any time from anywhere

distributed data storage into a **ubiquitous resource**. Once iSCSI becomes the universal standard for data storage, anyone with an iSCSI-enabled workstation will be able to access iSCSI storage from anywhere in the world.[23] iSCSI has the potential to be to data storage what IP is to network and Internet communication—data communications anywhere in the world for IP, and data storage access from anywhere in the world with iSCSI.[24]

STORAGE AREA NETWORKS

You've already learned that one of the major purposes of a local area network is to facilitate the exchange of data, mostly in the form of files, among employees within an organization or business unit. Storage area networks are also used to transmit data, but the business purpose of SANs and the format of the data on a SAN are substantially different than they are for a LAN. Storage area networks have an underlying business purpose that is focused on the storage and retrieval of vast amounts of data—hundreds of gigabytes or even terabytes of data, and the format for transmitting that data is focused on physical blocks of data and a data transmission protocol that is not typically used in LANs.

So how should we formalize our definition of a SAN? Based on the business purpose, a SAN is a network that is connected to an organization's network infrastructure and which is used for storing and retrieving vast amounts of data. Looking at it from a technical perspective, a SAN is a network that uses a serial SCSI protocol to transmit blocks of data across a network infrastructure. Which to choose? A complete definition combines the two: a **SAN** is a network that is used for storing and retrieving vast amounts of data and which uses a serial SCSI protocol to transmit blocks of data across a network infrastructure.

The business part of the definition is pretty straightforward, but the technical part suggests two features of SANs with which you might not be familiar, serial SCSI and data blocks. To shed some light on these two features, the following section provides a brief technical lesson on the SCSI protocol and data transfer using data blocks. Then for a broader-based perspective on SANs, you'll consider their historical purpose followed by some contemporary reasons that business managers choose to include SANs in their enterprise networks. From there, you'll examine the two competing network storage architectures, Fibre Channel SANs and IP SANs, as well as their architectures, components, configurations, and management issues.

SAN
a network used for storing and retrieving vast amounts of data and which uses a serial SCSI protocol to transmit blocks of data across a network infrastructure

Historical Reasons for SANs

The original purpose behind SANs was to separate backup traffic from LAN traffic and provide shared access to backup tape libraries and centralized data storage by multiple computers. In the early days of local area networks, the amount of data generated and transmitted on a LAN was not a significant concern. All the data that users generated could be saved to disk drives in a LAN server and backed up on a floppy drive. As the amount of data expanded in those early days, extra drives could be added to a server for data storage and tape backup devices that could attach directly to a server or tape backup devices that connected directly to the LAN provided adequate backup capacity without substantial effect on LAN or server performance. Even as the amount of data and data traffic continued to increase, backups could run overnight to prevent congestion on the network during the day and ensure that users would have adequate network performance during regular business hours.

---

[23] iSCSI drivers are included with Windows 2003 operating systems and with NetWare 6.5
[24] iSCSI is discussed in terms of storage area networks later in the chapter.

That all changed as organizations began implementing large database servers that could store hundreds of gigabytes or even terabytes worth of data. Now backups could no longer be accomplished during night operations. As a result, backups had to be continuously performed throughout the day with a significant impact on network performance.

The introduction of SANs alleviated the performance hit that LANs would experience from the extra network traffic caused by making the data backups. With SANs, data backups and data storage could be moved off the LAN while still providing data-intensive applications and users on the LAN with shared access to data.

Contemporary Reasons for SANs

More contemporary reasons for SANs grew out of the need to have data available all of the time, 24 hours a day, 7 days a week, and 365 days per year without ever a moment of downtime. Not having data available due to a hardware failure was simply unacceptable, and not having data available to continue an organization's operations was unthinkable. With these criteria, SAN companies introduced hardware and software that would provide high-availability, disaster recovery, and business continuation.

High availability (HA) means that the data is always available, even in the event of a hardware or software failure. In general, HA includes multiple storage devices each with duplicate copies of an organization's data. If the hardware that is storing one copy fails, another storage device is immediately available. In addition, multiple servers are usually configured to act in concert for data access. If one server fails, another is immediately available to fulfill data requests.

Disaster recovery is the process of recovering from a catastrophic loss of data. The process includes backing up data to sophisticated tape libraries on a SAN as well as maintaining copies of data at off-site locations that are usually operated and maintained by another organization that specializes in off-site data storage. Modern SANs accommodate data transfer to tape libraries, and high-speed carrier services make SAN-to-SAN data transfer and replication an effective disaster-recovery mechanism. In the event of a catastrophic loss, the data can either be restored from tapes that are stored at the off-site data storage facility or the data can be restored back to the primary location across a high-speed carrier circuit.

Business continuation is another data availability strategy (and buzzword) that modern SANs support. With a SAN at one location and high-speed carrier services to connect to a SAN at another location, data can be continuously replicated to the remote SAN. If there is a catastrophic loss of data as well as damage to physical structures at the primary location, business operations can be immediately transferred to the remote location. Business continuation is possible because identical copies of all data are maintained at a remote site.

Historical and contemporary reasons aside, all of these SAN data storage and data availability strategies are made possible through the continued development of the SCSI protocol. In the following sections, you'll take a look at the SCSI protocol and data block data transfer, Fibre Channel—the serial SCSI protocol that ushered in the era of SANs, and you're going to examine the SAN implementation of iSCSI—the modern version of serial SCSI that runs on IP networks.

The SCSI Protocol

In a local area network, communications protocols such as IP or IPX facilitate the exchange of data between computing devices on a network. Data is assembled within a computer according to the protocols defined by various layers of the OSI or TCP/IP models, and the bits are framed for transmission across the network. In much the same way, the **Small Computer System Interface (SCSI) protocol** defines a method for transmitting data between a set of storage devices and a computer, as shown in Figure 6.8.

FIGURE 6.8
SCSI as a Data Interface

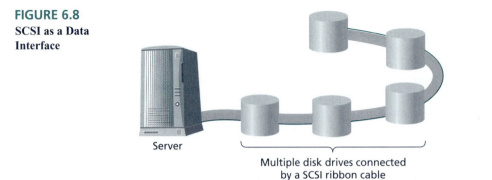

Server

Multiple disk drives connected
by a SCSI ribbon cable

In Figure 6.8, the SCSI protocol provides a parallel data transport mechanism for data delivery across a set of copper cables.[25] This transmission format, commonly known as *parallel SCSI*, provides a highly reliable and fast method of transferring data between a set of disk drives and a single computer.[26]

For environments that require more advanced data-storage capabilities such as SANs, parallel SCSI by itself has several limitations. First of all, parallel SCSI has practical limitations on the number of computers that can connect to a single set of shared storage devices. If you have a large network environment with the need for many computers to share individual storage devices, parallel SCSI is insufficient. Second, parallel SCSI is limited in terms of the number of storage devices that can be connected to the same cable, or databus. With a capacity for only 16 devices, the amount of storage space with parallel SCSI has finite limits. Third, parallel SCSI has limitations on the length of the cable between storage devices and computers that need access to the stored data. Each of these limitations precludes the development of parallel SCSI as a protocol to support SAN development.

So why even talk about parallel SCSI if it's not used in SANs? The answer is the technology behind parallel SCSI evolved into a serial data transmission architecture that has provided the foundation for modern SANs.[27] Serial SCSI extends the practical and theoretical distance of the SCSI databus. Computers that need access to stored data can now be located miles—instead of feet—from the storage devices. The number of devices that can be connected to a serial SCSI databus can be as many as 16 million, at least theoretically. And the number of computers that can connect to a shared data source can also be as many as 16 million. Serial SCSI is *the* data transmission protocol that facilitates the creation of storage area networks.

Data Block Data Transfer

Network attached storage and operating systems with embedded file systems have higher level services such as NFS and CIFS that facilitate data transfer between computers using filenames. If you need to retrieve a file, you access it from a folder, volume, or logical drive located somewhere on the network or on your computer and then copy it or move it to another location. With file system data access, you don't need to be concerned with where the actual data is stored on a storage device; the file system takes care of that for you.

With **data block data transfer,** actual blocks of data are transferred between storage devices or between a storage device and a computer without the assistance of a file system.

---

[25] You learned about parallel data transmission in chapter 1.
[26] By itself, a set of drives connected to a computer using the SCSI protocol could be considered direct attached storage, or DAS.
[27] You learned about serial data transmission in chapter 1.

FIGURE 6.9
Servicing Users' Data
Requests on a SAN

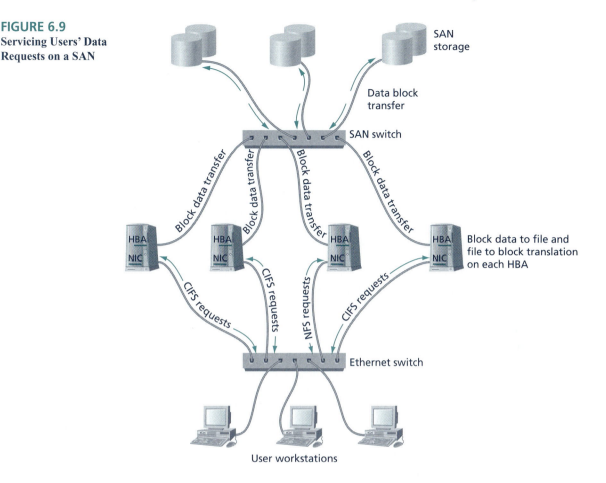

At the same time, some type of data transfer protocol is required to transfer data between physical devices, and that is where the SCSI protocol comes into play. The SCSI protocol has the ability to access and aggregate blocks of data and move them between physical devices. Block transfer is faster than file system data transfer. But at the same time, block level data transfer is not designed to assemble files: It's designed to move large amounts of data as quickly as possible between storage devices or between a storage device and a computer. If block level data is transferred to a computer, it can then be processed by a file system such as NFS or CIFS for presentation to a user. When data blocks are transferred between storage units, file system services are not required, because the blocks of data can simply be moved or copied to the physical disks at the new location. Figure 6.9 provides an example of a data block data transfer.

Figure 6.9 represents a small SAN that is connected to several file server computers. All data storage takes place on the SAN, and all file requests come from user computers. When a user makes a request for a file, the request is sent to a server that can respond to the user's file request. Within the server is an adapter card known as a *host bus adapter (HBA)* that connects to the SAN and translates the file request into a request for block data. As soon as the storage device on the SAN receives the request, the SCSI protocol transmits the data in block format to the server's HBA. The HBA passes the block data to the server's file system, which manipulates the data into file format. The file is then transferred across the LAN via IP to the user's workstation where the local file system presents the data on-screen. The key point is SANs do not service file system requests. Instead, SANs service data requests by transferring blocks of data via the SCSI protocol.

Fibre Channel SANs

Fibre Channel (FC) is a descendant of the original SCSI protocol and, in fact, is part of the SCSI-3 standards, which you can think of as the third generation of SCSI protocol development. Fibre Channel technology dates to the late 1980s and early 1990s and parallels the development of the SCSI-3 standards. ANSI issued the first FC standard in 1994, and by 1995 the first commercial products were available and were capable of supporting data transmission rates up to 1 Gbps. Two gigabit-per-second FC implementations have been in existence for the past few years, and now 4 Gbps and 10 Gbps FC technologies and equipment exist to build even faster FC SANs.

In essence, FC is a method of transmitting block data using SCSI protocols across a serial data transmission architecture instead of a parallel method. In other words, FC is a serial SCSI architecture. Consider the following example. At a server that stores and retrieves data from a FC SAN, upper-layer protocols in the network operating system will generate a file request, but before the request goes to the SAN, the HBA in the server converts parallel SCSI requests for block data into FC frames and transmits those requests across the SAN. A storage device on the SAN responds to the request, frames the block data for transmission, and sends it to the requesting server where the HBA performs a translation from FC back to parallel SCSI so that the network server can forward the data to upper-layer file-system services.

Topologies

Fibre Channel has three topologies: point-to-point, arbitrated loop, and fabric. A point-to-point topology is very simple, conveying storage data back and forth between a server that is configured with an FC HBA and a storage device, as illustrated in Figure 6.10. Data storage traffic is segregated from regular LAN traffic through the HBA, data requests are transmitted via Fibre Channel, and the underlying data transfer is in blocks rather than files.

Fibre Channel Arbitrated Loop (FC-AL) was developed to extend the capabilities of point-to-point FC while providing a lower-cost alternative to fabric topologies. FC-AL supports up to 126 storage devices, including the network server to which the SAN is attached. That means you could have an FC arbitrated loop topology with 125 storage devices connected to a single server or 124 storage devices connected to two servers, and so on.

The FC-AL topology can be configured in two different ways. One way is in a physical loop as portrayed on the left side of Figure 6.11. With the physical loop, storage devices and servers are connected to the loop by splitting the fiber-optic SC connectors so that the HBAs on devices in the loop are daisy-chained together.[28]

The right side of Figure 6.11 shows an FC-AL topology with a hub. The hub simplifies connectivity to the loop and at the same time provides fault tolerance to the loop. With a

FIGURE 6.10
FC Point-to-Point Topology

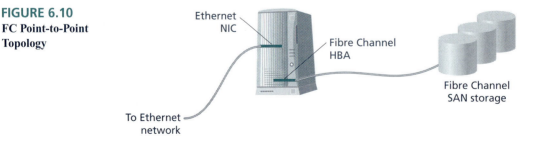

Ethernet NIC

Fibre Channel HBA

To Ethernet network

Fibre Channel SAN storage

---

[28] You learned about SC connectors for fiber-optic cabling in chapter 2.

FIGURE 6.11 **FC Arbitrated Loop Topologies**
a. Fibre Channel Arbitrated Loop. Physical loop topology.
b. Fibre Channel Arbitrated Loop. Logical loop/hub topology.

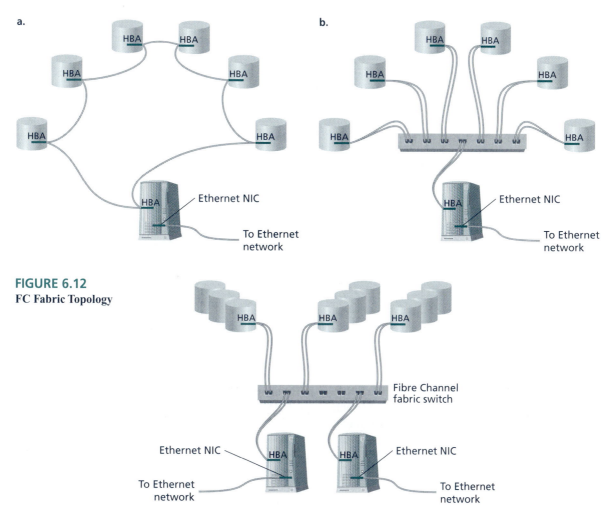

FIGURE 6.12
FC Fabric Topology

physical loop, as in the left side of Figure 6.11, one break in the fiber-optic cable or one malfunctioning HBA renders all storage devices on the SAN unavailable. With a hub-based loop, the internal components of the hub can automatically bypass a port or malfunctioning HBA connected to a port, thereby maintaining continuance of the loop and the remaining nodes on the SAN.

The **FC fabric topology** is differentiated from FC-AL or point-to-point by using FC switches to connect storage devices and computers to the SAN. By implementing FC switches, the number of nodes on an FC SAN can balloon to a theoretical 16 million devices. Figure 6.12 provides an example of an FC fabric topology.

Configuration

Fibre Channel SAN connectivity to a LAN can be configured in a couple of ways. You can have a network server that is connected to a LAN via its network interface card and to the FC SAN with an HBA. The HBA does the protocol conversion from FC to SCSI so that the server's operating system and file system can convert SCSI block data into filenames.

FIGURE 6.13

FC SAN through a Storage Router

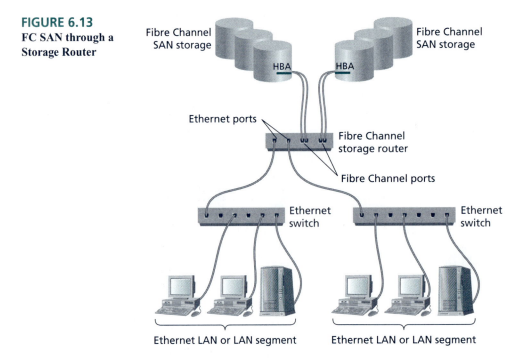

logical unit numbers (LUNs)
the identifiers that are assigned to logical portions of SAN storage space so that the storage space can be managed as if it were local hard disk drives

Simple Name Server (SNS)
a service that runs on an FC switch, registers the World Wide Name (WWN) of each SAN node as it logs in, and dynamically assigns a 24-bit port address to each node

World Wide Name (WWN)
a 64-bit identifier that uniquely identifies each node on an FC SAN. Each node registers its WWN with an FC switch and is dynamically assigned a 24-bit port address that is used in data transmissions across the SAN.

When you purchase the HBA from the manufacturer, you'll also receive driver software that configures the HBA to the specific NOS that you're using and management software that allows you to configure the storage space on the FC SAN. Storage space on one or more SAN storage devices is generally partitioned into **logical unit numbers (LUNs)** that can be managed as if they were parallel SCSI hard disk drives installed locally on the server. Once they're configured, the LUNs are displayed as drives on which users can create and store files and folders.

Another way to facilitate connectivity between a LAN and a FC SAN is with a specialized storage-to-LAN routing device. The FC SAN connects to a port on the storage router, and the LAN connects to an Ethernet port on the router, as in Figure 6.13. Now network servers can be connected directly to the LAN without the need of a HBA. As network users save and retrieve files, the storage router performs the necessary protocol conversions to make FC SAN storage devices appear as if they were storage devices attached directly to the network server.[29]

Simple Name Server (SNS) is another component of an FC fabric topology that provides FC nodes with a database of names and the locations of all other FC nodes on the SAN. Simple Name Server is a service that runs on an FC switch, and SNS registers the unique 64-bit identifier, or **World Wide Name (WWN),** of each node as a node logs in to the SAN.[30] When a node logs in, the FC switch dynamically assigns an additional 24-bit port address to the FC node, and it's this port address that is used for transmitting data

---

[29] This requires the implementation of the iSCSI protocol on your network servers. You'll learn about iSCSI later on in this chapter.

[30] Each World Wide Name is a 64-bit address that is encoded on the HBA by the HBA manufacturer. In order for the WWN to be truly unique, the HBA manufacturer must have registered with the IEEE, and the IEEE assigns a block of addresses to the manufacturer that the manufacturer can then use for address assignment on the HBAs.

across the FC SAN.[31] SNS also provides SAN administrators the ability to segregate SAN nodes into zones, the SAN equivalent to VLANs on Ethernet networks.[32] Zones are also known as **virtual storage area networks (VSANs),** and SAN administrators monitor the VSANs to modify traffic flow and congestion on the SAN.

Security

Security with a SAN is just as significant and important as the security of your LAN, MAN, or WAN. You don't want unauthorized persons accessing or harming your data. Within the world of FC SAN security, LUN masking, VSANs, and VLANs play an important role.

Logical unit number masking gives the SAN administrator the ability to hide specific LUNs from individual users or groups of users. Think of it as an access list that excludes unwanted users from gaining access. To implement LUN masking, the SAN administrator uses a LUN software interface to configure which LUNs should be hidden from whom.

Virtual storage area networks are another security measure with FC SANs. You already learned that VSANs are used for SAN traffic management, but they can also be used to restrict access. By grouping various storage devices and SAN nodes into several different VSANs, you can regulate access on a zone-by-zone basis.

Storage area network administrators must also consider the security ramifications of connecting one or more SANs to one or more LANs. Once a LAN is connected to a SAN, anyone with access to the LAN can potentially hack the data that is stored on the SAN. To circumvent this problem, consider connecting a SAN to a VLAN that is part of the LAN. The network administrator can restrict access to the VLAN, which, in turn, also limits access to the SAN to only those users who have VLAN access.

IP Storage Networks

Fibre Channel SANs gave network administrators the option to separate data storage traffic from regular network traffic, thereby improving the performance of both the SAN and the LAN. Internet protocol SANs take storage networking to its logical destination—implementing it on top of existing IP network infrastructures. In the following section, you'll look at IP storage networks, including a brief history and the business drivers behind IP SANs, the topologies and protocols that comprise IP SAN technologies, IP SAN components, and the configuration and management issues with which network administrators must contend on a regular basis.

History and Business Drivers

The development of IP SANs is relatively recent, dating to early 2000. The Internet Engineering Task Force (IETF) is the primary standards organization within which standards for **IP storage (IPS)** are published, and numerous organizations along with the IPS Working Group within IETF have worked to develop and enhance the standards surrounding IPS.[33]

The primary business drivers behind IP SAN development are the IP network infrastructures that have been maturing since the mid-1990s in combination with well-established SCSI storage device technology. By leveraging their IP infrastructures for data storage,

---

[31] The 64-bit address could have been used for source and destination addressing on SAN transmissions, but 64 bits for a source address and 64 bits for a destination address in the data frame would have consumed much more bandwidth than using a 24-bit source port address and a 24-bit destination port address. And there is no need to worry about running out of port addresses with a 24-bit address space. Even with the 24-bit addressing scheme, there are well over 16 million (2^{24}) potential port addresses available—more than sufficient for even the largest SANs.

[32] FC SAN zones can also be configured by linking ports on a FC switch to form "hard zones."

[33] You can access the IP Storage working group Web site at http://www.ietf.org/html.charters/ips-charter.html. The Web site for the Internet Engineering Task Force is www.ietf.org.

FIGURE 6.14
SAN-to-SAN
Connectivity Using
FCIP

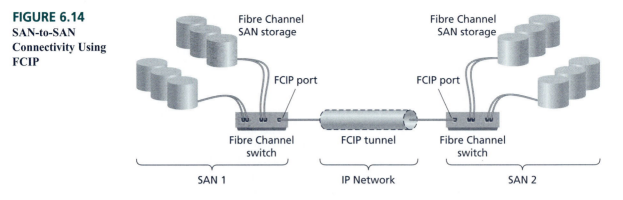

network managers can build SANs that don't require the extra administration, implementation, and support costs associated with Fibre Channel SANs, not to mention the high cost of FC SAN hardware.

Topologies and Protocols

There are three IP SAN protocols and topologies with which you should be familiar. FCIP attempts to perpetuate the existence of the Fibre Channel architecture while using an IP network to connect remote FC SANs. iFCP provides an alternative to Fibre Channel fabric architectures by delivering an IP storage fabric that can be fully integrated in an IP network while supporting connectivity with FC storage devices. iSCSI promises to deliver IP SANs on IP network infrastructures without the use of any Fibre Channel components. iSCSI makes storage devices ubiquitous with existing IP networks. In the following sections, you'll examine the details of the FCIP, iFCP, and iSCSI protocols and topologies.

Fibre Channel over IP (FCIP)
a protocol that defines the transmission of Fibre Channel data frames across a TCP/IP network

FCIP   **Fibre Channel over IP (FCIP)** is a protocol that defines the transmission of Fibre Channel data frames across a TCP/IP network. At the edge of each Fibre Channel SAN, an FCIP device encapsulates the Fibre Channel data frames into FCIP frames, as shown in Figure 6.14. This process creates an FCIP tunnel between the two SANs for the exclusive use of the two storage networks. For organizations with a substantial investment in Fibre Channel SANs, FCIP allows them to maintain their existing SAN infrastructure while taking advantage of the simplicity and extended distance capabilities of IP networks.

The FCIP device that performs the FC frame encapsulation can be a stand-alone device, a port in a Fibre Channel switch, or even a separate module (blade) in a router. The device, switch port, or router port links the FC SAN to the IP network and performs the protocol translation from FC to FCIP.[34] Note, however, that FCIP devices do not perform IP routing functions. Instead, an FCIP device is assigned an IP address on the IP network and behaves as any other node on an IP network—sending and receiving IP data frames, and in this case FCIP data frames, on the network medium.

Network managers might choose to implement FCIP because of the extended distances that an IP network can provide. Fibre Channel network architecture is generally limited to a distance of not more than 10 kilometers over single-mode fiber. IP networks do not have this distance limitation. They can extend for thousands of miles, literally traversing the world.

Typically, it's the Fibre Channel vendors that promote FCIP in order to perpetuate the installed base of Fibre Channel architecture. With FCIP, the Fibre Channel fabric remains intact: that is, it's not replaced by competing technologies such as iFCP or iSCSI. As a result, the FC vendor can potentially derive substantial future revenue growth through additional

---

[34] This translation is really an encapsulation of the FC frames within an IP packet, hence the name *FCIP.*

sales of FC storage devices, HBAs, fabric switches, and other FC components within the SAN—provided the customer doesn't make a strategic conversion to another technology such as iSCSI.

Before making an investment in FCIP devices for SAN-to-SAN connectivity, you should consider a few of the disadvantages to this technology. First, FCIP doesn't have built-in migration capability. That is, if your business strategy calls for adding iSCSI storage to your SAN or even replacing your FC SAN with iSCSI over time, FCIP is not equipped to communicate with native IP SAN technologies such as iFCP and iSCSI. Second, because the Fibre Channel SAN is unaware of the FC-to-FCIP protocol encapsulation, when a problem occurs it's difficult to determine whether the problem originated on the SAN or on the IP network. Third, FC SANs are generally implemented with 1 Gbps or 2 Gbps bandwidth. If you implement an IP network with bandwidth lower than the FC SAN bandwidth, you might experience unexpected disconnects or transmission errors that can affect data transmission performance between the two SANs or even stop it completely.[35]

iFCP The **Internet Fibre Channel Protocol (iFCP)** is different from FCIP and is used to create a different IP storage topology than can be created with FCIP. Whereas FCIP utilizes FCIP devices to encapsulate FC frames for bridging two FC SANs over an IP network, iFCP utilizes a gateway with an FC SAN to map an IP address to each FC device (servers and drive arrays) in the FC SAN, as illustrated in Figure 6.15. By creating this FC-to-IP mapping for each device, iFCP encapsulates FC frames within an iFCP frame for each FC SAN device rather than for the FC SAN fabric as a whole as with FCIP. With individual device address mapping, an iFCP topology can be used instead of the FC switching fabric to create a SAN infrastructure over an existing IP network.

In Figure 6.15, notice the absence of the FC SAN switching devices. Because the iFCP gateway maps each FC device to an IP address, each FC device can be identified as an

FIGURE 6.15
Fibre Channel SAN Using iFCP
With iFCP, Fibre Channel device addresses are mapped to IP addresses. The iFCP gateway performs the FC address-to-IP address mapping and stores this information in an iFCP lookup table.

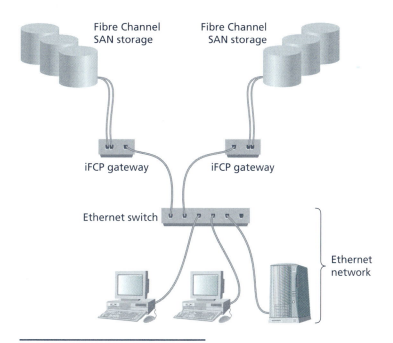

[35] The disruption caused by bandwidth mismatch is generally attributable to the time-out differences between TCP and Fibre Channel protocols. Time-out values have to do with how devices respond to one another in the event of an error. If significant differences exist between the time-out parameters for TCP and Fibre Channel, the FCIP devices might not be able to reestablish a communications link in the event of an error, and your two FC SANs can be disconnected.

IP node on an IP network. This means individual workstations and servers on an IP network can address frames directly to individual FC devices to request or save files, and FC devices can respond to file requests through the iFCP gateway. iFCP topology extends the usability of FC devices beyond the limits of an FC SAN. In other words, iFCP is not limited simply to connecting two different FC SANs using tunneling. Instead, iFCP makes FC storage accessible by individual devices on an IP network.

The **Metro Fibre Channel Protocol (mFCP)** is a variant of iFCP that implements the user datagram protocol (UDP) instead of the transmission control protocol (TCP) for the transport of data frames. In well-configured gigabit Ethernet backbones in a campus area network (CAN) or metropolitan area network (MAN), mFCP has the advantage of faster transmissions on dedicated backbones because UDP doesn't have the connection-oriented overhead associated with TCP.[36] mFCP does have the disadvantage, however, of requiring dedicated gigabit Ethernet backbones because UDP does not have the built-in control mechanisms to acknowledge data transmissions or lost packets. In other words, slower networks or congested networks will not be sufficient as a transport medium for data storage networks utilizing mFCP. As a result, if you want to implement mFCP outside of CAN or MAN boundaries or connect two or more mFCP storage networks across an IP WAN link, you'll need to connect your mFCP topology through one or more iFCP switches.

Probably the biggest benefit to iFCP is that it provides a migration path from a pure FC SAN solution to a pure IP-based SAN solution such as iSCSI. If an organization's business and technology strategies require the continued support and maintenance of existing FC devices while at the same time requiring any new storage devices to be purely IP-based, iFCP can provide the data storage topology that will allow both FC storage and pure IP-based storage technologies to coexist on the same IP network. That is not to say that FC devices can communicate directly with iSCSI devices via iFCP—that would require a specific multiprotocol device to convert the FC frames and data within iFCP frames into iSCSI format. Instead, with iFCP an existing FC SAN can be attached to an organization's IP network to give users direct access to FC SAN storage, and at the same time users can also directly access any new iSCSI devices that are attached to the IP network. Because iFCP makes FC storage accessible on an IP network, users will continue to have access to FC SAN data until a complete migration from FC to iSCSI is accomplished.

iSCSI   **Internet SCSI (iSCSI)** is a relatively new protocol that began as a cooperative effort between IBM and Cisco Systems in 1999 and became a formal IETF standard in February 2003. iSCSI defines the serial transmission of SCSI data blocks over IP networks and from the beginning was designed to be an IP SAN solution.[37] Where FCIP defines a SAN-to-SAN connection strategy for remote FC SANs and iFCP provides a migration path from FC SANs to IP-based SANs, iSCSI does not attempt to bridge non-IP storage technologies onto an IP network. Instead, iSCSI provides the native IP support that allows IP storage devices to attach directly to an IP network, as shown in Figure 6.16.

In Figure 6.16, two servers and two IP storage disk arrays are connected to a Gigabit Ethernet switch to form an iSCSI SAN. In addition, numerous client computers are connected to the iSCSI SAN through access layer and distribution layer Ethernet switches. When a user at a client computer wants to retrieve a file, the request is intercepted (serviced) by one of the servers, which, in turn, sends a request to the appropriate IP storage array. The IP storage array transmits the data in block format to the server, and the

---

[36] You'll learn about CANs and MANs in chapter 8. For now think of CANs as local area networks that span a number of buildings in a business office complex or campus. You can think of MANs as networks that interconnect an organization's LANs within the geographic confines of a city, or metropolitan area.
[37] Remember from the Fibre Channel section of this chapter that SCSI provides block-level data access as compared to file-level data access with NAS and through a network operating system.

FIGURE 6.16
A Simple iSCSI SAN

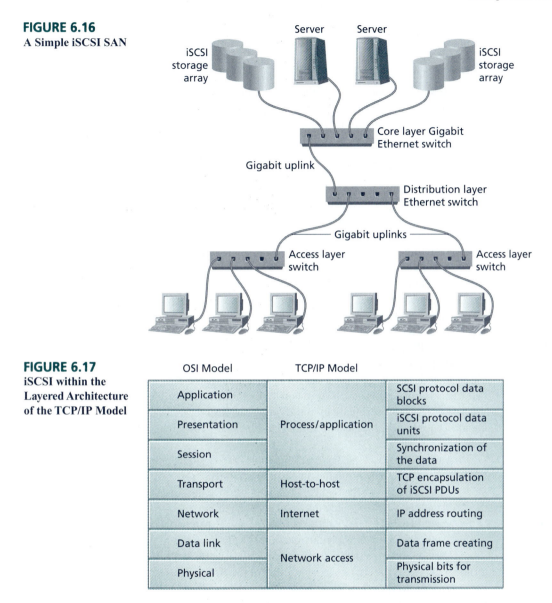

FIGURE 6.17
iSCSI within the
**Layered Architecture
of the TCP/IP Model**

OSI Model	TCP/IP Model	
Application	Process/application	SCSI protocol data blocks
Presentation		iSCSI protocol data units
Session		Synchronization of the data
Transport	Host-to-host	TCP encapsulation of iSCSI PDUs
Network	Internet	IP address routing
Data link	Network access	Data frame creating
Physical		Physical bits for transmission

network operating system on the server provides the high-level services that transform the block-level data into file-system format using NFS, CIFS, NCP, or WebNFS, among others for transmission to the client workstation. The beauty of this process is that it all takes place over an Ethernet network with existing Ethernet components. No Fibre Channel frames have to be translated and no iFCP gateways have to be implemented to perform protocol conversion from FC to an IP-compatible format. Instead, the iSCSI protocol supports the transmission of block-level data from storage devices across an IP network using TCP.

iSCSI Configuration

To connect to an IP network, iSCSI storage devices, iSCSI servers, and iSCSI client computers must support the iSCSI protocol. Conceptually, this support for iSCSI follows the OSI and TCP/IP models' layered architectures that you studied in chapter 1. In Figure 6.17, SCSI data blocks are formatted into iSCSI protocol data units (PDUs), and then the iSCSI

PDUs from the application layer are encapsulated into TCP packets. From there, packets are routed to the appropriate destination, such as a server or workstation, via IP address assignment. Frame creation takes place at the data link layer, and finally, the bits are transmitted according to the access methods and protocols of the physical layer.

The actual implementation of the iSCSI protocol occurs either through iSCSI software that is installed on servers and workstations or by installing specialized network interface cards (NICs) that support IP storage. If you choose a software implementation, you'll download the appropriate iSCSI driver software from the operating system vendor's Web site and install it according to the vendor's specifications. If you choose a hardware implementation of iSCSI, the functionality that would otherwise be accomplished with software drivers and the server or workstation operating system will be built into specialized NICs known as either IP storage adapters or iSCSI **host bus adapters (HBAs).**

iSCSI HBAs are preferred over software implementations of iSCSI because the iSCSI HBAs can improve iSCSI SAN performance in a couple of ways. First of all, TCP encapsulation and other TCP processes that are built into server and workstation operating systems consume a substantial amount of CPU processing power. An iSCSI HBA equipped with a TCP Offload Engine (TOE) can offload the TCP processes from the operating system. This allows the operating system to devote the processing power that was previously allocated to TCP functions to other services and processes. In addition, the SCSI-to-iSCSI application level process can also be offloaded to the HBA, further reducing the overall impact on CPU processing power.

In addition to iSCSI software drivers and iSCSI HBAs, other configuration issues with iSCSI include assigning LUNs, VLANs, storage resource discovery, and data storage access. You learned about LUNs previously in this chapter in the Fibre Channel section. iSCSI uses the same terminology for dividing physical disk-storage space into logical segments. These logical segments can then be allocated to different departments or functions within an organization.

VLANs are more of an Ethernet function than a storage function, but the effect of VLANs is the same as you studied in chapter 4. With VLANs, you can segment iSCSI SAN data-storage traffic from the regular LAN and improve the bandwidth performance of both the SAN and the LAN to which the SAN is attached.

In the world of SANs, initiators request data and targets supply data. To facilitate this exchange, initiators need to know the location of targets on the IP network. This is the function of storage resource discovery. For small IP networks with minimal IP SAN storage, a protocol known as the service locator protocol (SLP) can be used to identify IP storage devices to the network. When an initiator requires access to data storage on the IP SAN, SLP provides the location either by direct communication between initiator and target or between initiator and a storage-routing device or server that maintains a table of storage device locations that is continuously updated via SLP. For larger networks, a newer protocol known as the Internet Storage Name Server (iSNS) can be implemented to track storage devices on an IP SAN. iSNS works very much like the DNS protocol that you discovered in chapter 5 and the Fibre Channel SNS you looked at previously in this chapter. iSNS consolidates storage device locations to a central location so that initiators can contact one central source for IP storage device locations on an IP network.

In addition to SLP and iSNS, data-storage access requires configuration of IP storage devices as well as workstations and servers. If an iSCSI HBA isn't implemented on an initiator such as a workstation or server, then iSCSI device drivers must be installed on the operating system. Once that is completed and the IP storage devices are in place and configured, workstations and servers will require additional configuration—either through a graphical interface in the case of Windows computers, or, in the case of Linux and UNIX, modifications to the iscsi.conf file. Novell requires the network administrator to load iSCSI-related NLMs on the NetWare server and establish initiator configuration through a graphical interface, in addition to the configuration of the iSCSI software drivers. In any case, once the LUNs are active and recognized by a server or workstation operating system, the network administrator can then allocate these LUN drives to various departments by assigning permissions to different groups of network users.

The iSCSI storage devices themselves are configured by connecting a workstation computer to the network and using protocols such as the simple network management protocol (SNMP) or Telnet to connect to the storage device. The actual configuration is accomplished with scripting language that is specific to the device manufacturer, and the completed script is saved to nonvolatile memory on the storage device.

Security

Internet protocol storage security takes advantage of SAN security features as well as the security features typical of IP networks. Included in this security feature set are LUN masking, discovery domains, VLANs, IPSec, and access control lists (ACLs).

Logical unit numbers masking simply hides selected LUNs from selected departments or users for security purposes. LUN masking can either be achieved through an iSCSI HBA that has that capability built in or through the controller card that manages the hard disk storage. In either case, a software interface would allow the storage administrator to configure the HBA or controller card and specify the groups of initiators that could have access to different LUNs.

Discovery domains segment IP storage networks into defined groups of target devices. The storage administrator creates these domains by manually assigning IP storage devices to a specific domain. In Figure 6.18, discovery domain 1 might include two iSCSI storage arrays associated with one or more Microsoft Windows servers, discovery domain 2 might include a single iSCSI storage array that is associated with a NetWare server, and discovery domain 3 might include an iSCSI tape storage device connected to a Linux server. Through the creation of discovery domains, storage device access can be restricted by discovery domain to specific initiators or groups of initiators.

VLANs provide the same kinds of security provisions that you learned about in chapter 4. In the case of IP storage, initiator and target storage devices can be assigned to a specific VLAN so that only the initiators on that VLAN will have access to the target devices on that VLAN.

Depending on the level of security required with an IP SAN, you could choose to implement IPSec. IPSec is a security protocol that provides authentication and encryption protection of data that is transmitted across an IP network. You'll learn a lot more about IPSec in chapter 8, but for now keep in mind that IPSec can be implemented to enhance security across your IP network and IP SAN environments. One way to implement it would require an IPSec firewall that encrypts data as it is being transmitted from an organization's internal network to an unsecure external network. This implementation would encrypt all data traversing the firewall, not just the IP SAN data. Within the internal network, however, data would not be encrypted. Another way to implement IPSec would be to configure IPSec on network switches that linked internal IP network segments to internal IP SANs. This implementation would encrypt data as it passed between an IP SAN and the IP network. Still a third way would be to implement IPSec on every end device in the IP network, including initiators and targets. This configuration would serve environments in which the highest levels of data security must be maintained.

Access control lists (ACLs) are another great way to enforce security on an IP network or an IP SAN. With ACLs, a storage administrator can specify which initiators can access

FIGURE 6.18
**Discovery Domains
and IP Storage
Security**

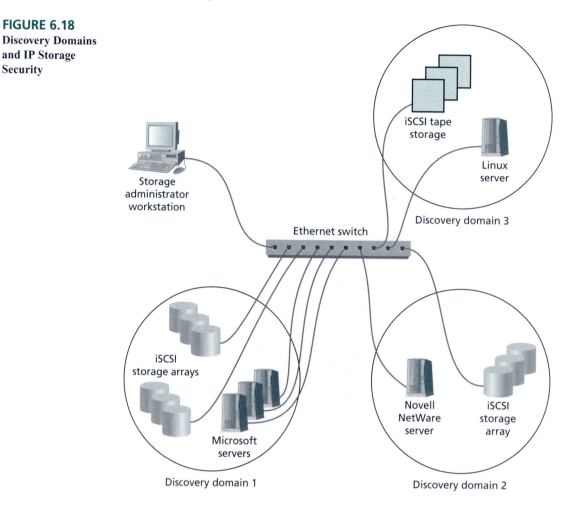

target storage devices. If an initiator is not on an ACL for a particular device, the initiator will be denied access.

Additional Considerations

With large investments already in place for FC SANs in many large organizations, FC will likely be supported for some years to come. At the same time, most organizations have standardized their data communications strategies based on IP networks, which means that there is substantial potential for iSCSI SAN technology to coexist if not supplant existing FC SAN infrastructures. With IP, organizations can take advantage of a large pool of technicians and administrators experienced in IP technologies. Fibre Channel is still relatively specialized and requires a separate talent pool to implement it and provide ongoing support and maintenance.

In the near term, iSCSI technology makes perfect sense as an incremental addition to an organization's SAN requirements. In addition, incremental implementations of iSCSI combined with other IP storage technologies such as iFCP devices pave the way for seamless migration from FC to IP storage technologies. As vendors ramp up their product offerings and support of iSCSI and at the same time gradually begin the discontinuance of FC support, it's quite possible that iSCSI will be the SAN technology that replaces Fibre Channel SANs in the not-to-distant future.

METROPOLITAN AREA AND WIDE AREA NETWORK SANs

Every data network has a business motivation behind it, and storage area networks are no exception. SANs provide massive amounts of data storage and remove a large percentage of data-storage traffic from regular LAN segments for improved LAN performance and traffic management. Storage area networks also facilitate business continuation, a crucial organization strategy that ensures data availability under any potential disastrous circumstance. Included within this strategy are efficient and high-performance data backups and high availability of data—two substantial business drivers for SAN implementation. SAN integration with IP networks can provide a migration path that improves overall data access and availability as well as reduces the overall costs of managing and maintaining data storage. If we extend these business drivers and the SAN technologies you've studied in this chapter beyond the boundaries of a LAN and into larger networks that span broader geographic distances, data storage and SANs can support the business continuity planning that most modern organizations now require.

Fibre Channel versus IP Storage in Metropolitan Area Networks and Wide Area Networks

Both FC SANs and IP SANs can be linked to remote SANs, but there are some limitations and technology factors to consider before connecting SANs in a metropolitan area network (MAN) or wide area networking (WAN) configuration.[38] Without piggybacking on top of IP, FC by itself has technical limitations that limit FC links to distances of 30 or fewer miles.[39] Metropolitan area network and WAN FC backbones require dedicated bandwidth of either 1 or 2 Gbps, and that is bandwidth that cannot be shared with other network traffic while FC storage traffic is using the connection.[40] Other network applications might require bandwidth that can be serviced by slower connection speeds, making the communications costs of connecting remote FC SANs an expensive proposition for even some large organizations.

IP SANs, on the other hand, can utilize existing IP network infrastructures and shared bandwidth across MANs and WANs. For organizations with large investments in FC SANs, FCIP and iFCP can be used to create MAN and WAN SANs. FCIP provides IP tunneling across an IP network so that FC frames can be transmitted across an IP network. As long as a 1 or 2 Gbps (or faster) IP network infrastructure is available, an FC SAN can be expanded to MAN and WAN capability with FCIP. Keep in mind, however, the potential for disconnects between remote FC SANs if the bandwidth of the IP network is lower than that of the FC SAN.[41]

iFCP removes the tunneling and high bandwidth requirements of FCIP, and both iFCP and iSCSI provide integrated IP SAN access with other IP devices on an IP network. As a

---

[38] You're going to learn about metropolitan area networks (MANs) and wide area networks (WANs) in chapter 8, but for now, you can think about MANs as networks that interconnect an organization's LANs within the geographic confines of a city or metropolitan area. You can think of WANs as networks that interconnect an organization's LANs across geographic boundaries that extend beyond the confines of a city or proximate region. WANs can circumvent the globe.

[39] Fibre Channel was designed for data centers and not MAN or WAN distances. Data and control messages generally require microsecond responses with FC SANs, but when distances between SANs exceed 30 miles these response times grow into the millisecond range. Without the use of substantial memory buffers to store data, FC-to-FC SAN links (without IP) are distance limited.

[40] Recall from earlier in the chapter that older FC SANs were implemented with Gbps speeds and newer FC SANs utilize 2 Gbps bandwidth.

[41] You looked at this briefly in the "Topologies and Protocols" section previously in this chapter.

FIGURE 6.19   **Remote Storage Spanning a Wide Area Network**

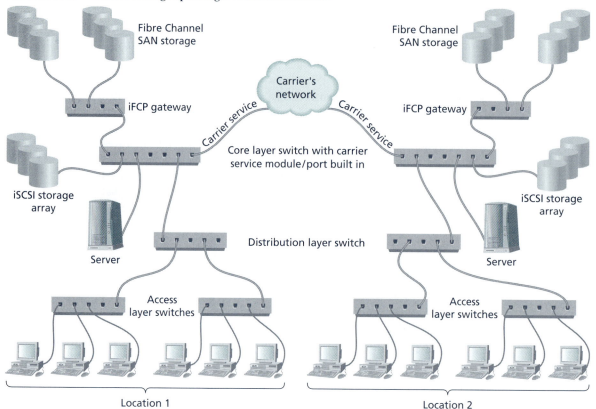

carrier's network

the network provided by a carrier such as MCI, Sprint, AT&T, or other carrier. It's a network of high-speed transmission circuits that can be used to create MANs and WANs.

result, iFCP and iSCSI protocols support MAN and WAN SANs. iFCP and iSCSI devices can be directly connected either to a **carrier's network** or to an internal IP network for eventual routing across the carrier's infrastructure. Figure 6.19 provides an example of a MAN or WAN SAN.

In Figure 6.19, remote FC SANs are connected across a WAN using iFCP and a high-speed carrier service. In addition, each location has an iSCSI SAN that leverages the existing Ethernet LAN infrastructure. No separate protocol switch is required to convert SAN protocols prior to routing storage data onto the carrier's infrastructure.

SAN Backups

A major benefit to MAN and WAN SANs is consolidated remote data backup capability. With sufficient carrier-service bandwidth, the data stored on remote SANs can be backed up to one or more centralized locations. For example, data can be backed up to an organization's corporate offices while simultaneously being backed up to another site managed by an off-site data-storage company.[42]

In addition to the reduced administrative costs associated with consolidated backups, organizations can benefit from implementing high-performance tape backup devices, or tape libraries as they're frequently called. In Figure 6.20, an organization with three SAN

---

[42] The offsite storage site is commonly referred to as a *data vault*.

FIGURE 6.20
Remote SAN Backup to Two Locations

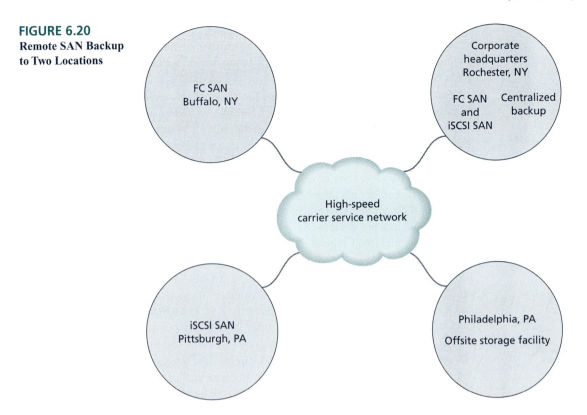

locations can back up its remote SAN data to a corporate data center as well as to an offsite storage facility.

High Availability

High-speed carrier services have made high availability possible across remote locations. Sometimes referred to as *data mirroring* or *remote mirroring,* high availability across remote locations is a strategy that involves data replication at multiple sites. With identical data at multiple locations, organizations can provide the users at those locations with quicker access to data because the data is locally available. Multiple copies of an organization's data can also provide continued access to the data for all locations in the event of a disaster at any one site. In addition, data mirroring provides instantaneous access in the event of a disaster at one site—data backups take time to restore, and that time is precious when it comes to continuing the operations of an entire organization.

Chapter Summary

- **Direct attached storage.** Direct attached storage (DAS) provides data storage such as hard drives and CD-ROM drives on single servers. It's a satisfactory data-storage solution for smaller organizations, but doesn't scale well to larger organizations' needs. Practical implementations include RAID configurations installed in file servers.

- **Network attached storage.** Network attached storage (NAS) provides optimized file-system services to network users. NAS storage scales well to the growing needs of organizations and can be integrated with SANs. NAS utilizes file-sharing protocols such as CIFS and NFS, but can also deliver file-sharing capabilities through HTTP, FTP, WebNFS, NCP, and AFP. Some of the different NAS terms include filer, NAS server,

NAS device, NAS appliance, NAS head, network storage fabric, and NAS gateway. Each term applies to specific NAS functionality or NAS device types. NAS can be configured for high availability and fault tolerance, which can include NAS clustering and data mirroring.

- **Historical and contemporary reasons for SANs.** SANs were originally implemented to remove backup traffic from regular LAN traffic, provide shared access to backup tape libraries, and provide centralized storage to multiple computers. More contemporary reasons include high availability, disaster recovery, and business continuation.

- **The SCSI protocol.** Parallel SCSI provides a highly reliable and fast method of transferring data between a set of disk drives and a single computer. But parallel SCSI has limits on the number of supported drives, the number of computers that can connect to a single set of drives, and the distance between storage devices and the computers that access those storage devices. Serial SCSI overcomes these limitations and is implemented through Fibre Channel technology.

- **Fibre Channel.** Fibre Channel is a serial SCSI technology that is used in SANs. It provides data transmission speeds of 1 Gbps, 2 Gbps, 4 Gbps, or 10 Gbps. It can be configured in three different topologies: point-to-point, arbitrated loop, and fabric. It uses logical unit numbers (LUNs) to identify logical portions of SAN storage space, and it's a scalable data storage solution for large organizations with large data storage needs.

- **IP storage networks.** IP storage networks implement storage networking on top of existing IP network infrastructures. It can be implemented using the FCIP, iFCP, or iSCSI protocols, each of which is used under specific configurations.

- **MAN and WAN SANs.** Moving SAN data across geographic distances that span beyond a local network is possible with SAN technologies. While Fibre Channel is limited in transmission distance, the various IP storage technologies support the kinds of distances available through a carrier network.

Key Terms

Simple Name Server, *212*

Small Computer
System Interface
(SCSI) protocol, *207*

Storage area
network (SAN), *206*

Virtual storage area
network (VSAN), *213*

World Wide Name
(WWN), *212*

Questions

1. Why might an organization choose to implement direct attached storage?

2. What potential problems exist with direct attached storage?

3. Why might an organization choose to implement network attached storage? What distinguishes NAS from DAS? What kinds of problems does NAS solve? What protocols are used for file transfer in a NAS configuration?

4. What are CIFS and NFS? Where are they implemented? What are the configuration issues associated with CIFS and NFS with Novell, Microsoft, and Linux network operating systems?

5. What are the major components of a NAS configuration? What does each device contribute to a NAS implementation? What tools are available for configuring NAS devices? Is NAS fault tolerant? Why or why not? How would you provide continuous access to data using NAS?

6. After adding a NAS configuration to a network, how would you migrate data from existing servers to the NAS devices?

7. What are the business reasons for implementing a SAN? What differentiates a SAN from NAS or DAS?

8. Describe Fibre Channel and iSCSI in terms of storage area networks. What are the advantages and disadvantages of each? Why might an organization choose one of these SAN technologies over the other? Why might an organization choose to utilize both technologies?

9. Compare iFCP to FCIP. What are these two protocols used for? What are the advantages of each? What are the limitations? Why might an organization choose to implement just FCIP? Why might it implement both iFCP and FCIP? How do these two protocols integrate with iSCSI?

10. What are the key components of SAN security? How does each component assist in the protection of stored data?

11. How does block data transfer differ from file transfers?

Research Activities

1. Identify three major manufacturers of direct attached storage devices. How do these vendors package their systems? What features does each vendor provide? How much storage capacity is available? How does each vendor's products conform to standards such as CIFS and NFS?

2. Identify two NAS vendors. What terminology do they use to define the various components of their NAS solutions? What are the installation and configuration instructions that each vendor suggests? Do their products integrate with Novell, Microsoft,

and Linux? What configuration information do the vendors provide for each network operating system? What software management tools are included with each vendor's product?

3. Using the search tools available to you, research the details of WebNFS and DAFS. How are NAS configurations implementing these technologies? Are WebNFS and DAFS available for Novell, Microsoft, and Linux network operating systems? (*Hint:* In addition to google.com, see what information you can find out on the Novell, Microsoft, and RedHat Linux sites.) Why might an organization choose to implement WebNFS, DAFS, or both?

4. Using the search tools available to you, research NAS clustering and identify the hardware and software components required to design, build, and configure a high-availability NAS cluster. (*Hint:* In addition to google.com, consider searching the Novell, Microsoft, and RedHat Linux sites for software NAS solutions and the Intel, Dell Computer, Hewlett-Packard, Network Appliance, and Sun Microsystems Web sites for hardware NAS components.) Also discover whether these high-availability NAS clusters utilize the NDMP backup protocol, and discuss any data migration and network management tools that the various vendors provide. Of the vendors you've examined, are any of them implementing Fibre Channel with their NAS clusters? How about iSCSI?

5. Identify three SAN vendors and discuss their SAN products. Make sure you include a discussion of their Fibre Channel and iSCSI solutions. What components does each vendor include in its SAN systems? What configuration issues can you discover to integrate each vendor's SAN systems with existing Ethernet networks? (Make sure you discuss this in terms of how each vendor integrates Fibre Channel SANs with Ethernet networks and how each vendor integrates iSCSI SANs with Ethernet networks.) Do any of these vendors provide a detailed migration plan from Fibre Channel to iSCSI? Does each vendor provide a design and installation team for a fee?

6. Using the research tools available to you, discover and report how SAN vendors provide data storage fault tolerance and data-storage security.

Mini Case Study

RADIOLOGY ASSOCIATES

Over the past 18 years, Radiology Associates has grown from an office with two radiologists and a small clerical staff to 28 radiologists, five nurses, and a clerical staff of seven. The services they provide range from simple X-rays to the latest MRI, nuclear, and CAT scan imaging. The number of images created and stored per year generates between 10 and 25 terabytes of imaging data, and health care regulations and insurance companies require that the images be stored for several years. This places a significant data storage requirement on Radiology Associates.

When Radiology Associates was a small office, the network that supported the clerical staff also provided the data storage for patient imaging. As the practice has grown, more hard drives have been added to existing file servers, and as file server–storage capacities have peaked, additional file servers have been added to support the growing data-storage requirements. Some attention has been given to fault tolerance with the implementation of RAID solutions, but an overall plan for data growth has so far been neglected. In addition, the partners in the practice have considered expanding to a second and perhaps a third location within the same city, which will increase the amount of data-storage requirements and potentially generate a requirement to link offices and share images electronically between locations.

With these considerations in mind, Radiology Associates has requested a consultation with you so that you can describe new technology alternatives that will fit their growing business need for image storage. Based on the facts presented here and the information in the chapter, what solutions will you suggest? Why? What advantages and disadvantages does each of your alternatives present? What data storage technology(ies) will allow Radiology Associates to share images across a high-speed connection between offices, if, in fact, they open additional offices and have a need to transmit images between offices?

CHAPTER
Seven

Chapter Overview and Objectives

Voice networks have gained increasing visibility over the past few years because of the tremendous potential for reduced administrative costs through voice and data network convergence. With modern technologies, the parallel voice and data infrastructures that organizations maintain can be combined into a single unified network. Network support and maintenance costs as well as the capital outlay for maintaining two separate network infrastructures can be substantially reduced. That is, by combining voice communications and data communications into a unified network, organizations can realize substantial maintenance and support cost reductions as well as increases in network management efficiencies.

In this chapter, we explore how modern organizations implement and use voice networks. You'll examine several different voice network technologies, and you'll discover the business and technology drivers that are pushing voice and data networks onto the same infrastructures. In other words, you'll see how both business and technology are motivating the convergence of voice and data networks. More specifically, by the end of this chapter you will be able to

- Identify the business purpose of voice networks.

- Describe how data is transmitted over a plain old telephone system local loop.

- Identify the business purpose and features of a private branch exchange.

- Define PBX technology and discuss PBX switching topologies and design considerations.

- Identify the business purpose of an IP-PBX.

- Describe the converged and packet-switched topologies of an IP-PBX.

- Define and describe Voice over IP.

- Define computer–telephony integration and identify its business purpose and features.

- Discuss cellular wireless voice networks and describe the anatomy of a cellular wireless connection.

- List and describe three cellular wireless access methods.

- Identify and describe three cellular wireless topologies and connectivity to the public switched telephone network.

- List and discuss cellular wireless data services.

Voice Networks

Chapter Outline

VOICE NETWORKS: A BRIEF INTRODUCTION

Voice networks convey the human voice between remote locations. If you think that sounds similar to what a data network does with data, you're right. Both convey information between remote locations, and both use electrical transmission techniques to transmit that information. Differences between them have been both historical and technical; voice networks were in existence long before modern data networks, and voice networks have traditionally used analog transmission techniques where data networks generally use digital methods. In addition, voice networks have traditionally been constructed and maintained separately from data networks. Each has relied on its own unique technologies and infrastructure as well as separate management and support costs.

Throughout their first 80 years of existence, from the late 1870s to the late 1950s, voice networks were specifically used for the analog transmission of the human voice. In the 1960s and 1970s, that began to change as organizations with large mainframe computers began using the telephone companies' analog voice networks to share computing resources and transmit digital data between those mainframe computers. Today, voice networks are still used to convey voice traffic, but the method of voice transmission is changing. Voice networks can be based on analog or digital techniques or a combination of both. They can be as simple as a pair of wires that connect your home to the phone company or as state-of-the-art as an IP service that uses a LAN or WAN infrastructure.

The earliest voice networks started to appear shortly after Alexander Graham Bell and Thomas Watson introduced the first commercial telephone in the late 1870s. These early telephone networks connected a person's home directly with another person's home to create a **point-to-point connection.** Subsequent connections from a person's home to others' homes required the installation of additional point-to-point connections—one for each person with whom you might wish to talk.

The maze of wires created by such point-to-point networks soon became unmanageable, resulting in the development of the first **telephone exchange** in 1878.[1] The telephone exchange, which later became known as the telephone **central office (CO),** was a physical facility owned by the telephone company, and it acted as a hub to which all telephone subscribers (customers) in a specific geographic location connected. Whenever a subscriber made a call, the call first connected to the exchange, and then the call could be connected, via the exchange, to another subscriber.

Today, the connection between your home or office and the CO is provided by a **local exchange carrier (LEC)** and is known as a *local loop.*[2] The local loop consists of a pair of twisted copper wires that are like the UTP cabling you learned about in chapter 2.[3] Local loops in combination with one or more local central offices form the basic voice network for local calls, linking all local subscribers. Local loops and COs in combination with the technologies that facilitate long-distance telephone calls comprise a voice network that is commonly referred to as the **plain old telephone system (POTS),** or more formally as the **public switched telephone network (PSTN).** POTS provides the basic foundation for the voice network that spans across the United States and the entire world and is technically

---

[1] For a detailed historical account of the development of wired voice and data communications, take a look at Appendix A, "A Brief History of Data Communications and Computer Networks."
[2] Local exchange carriers can be either incumbent local exchange carriers (ILECs) or competitive local exchange carriers (CLECs). ILECs were simply called local exchange carriers before local telephone service deregulation allowed competition in the local loop. After deregulation, anyone with enough capital and sales ability could provide local loop service. The competitors became known as CLECs.
[3] Although the local loop consists of UTP cabling, the connector that is used is known as an RJ-11, a narrower connecter than the RJ-45 connectors that are used in data networks connected by UTP.

FIGURE 7.1   Plain Old Telephone System (POTS)

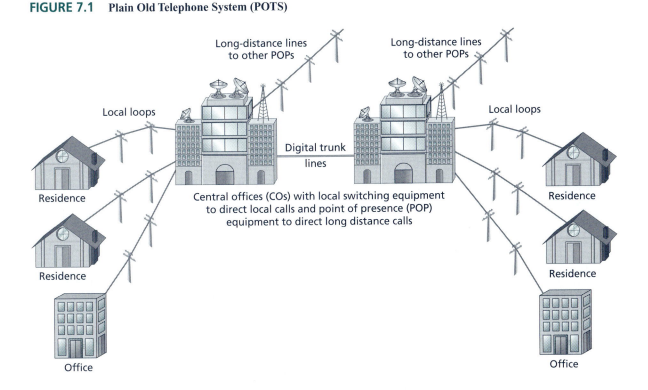

that part of the PSTN that services regular analog telephones. PSTN refers to the entire network of analog and digital equipment and services that provide telephone service to subscribers. Figure 7.1 provides a simple example of POTS.

In Figure 7.1, several home and business telephones are connected to a telephone company's CO facility via local loops. The central office is analogous to a data network switch, and the local loop can be compared to a UTP cable that is used to connect a computer to a switch in a data network. Once a call is received at the CO, it can be switched to another telephone subscriber who is also connected to the same CO. If the call needs to be routed to another local CO, digital **trunks** that connect local COs **multiplex** multiple calls from one CO and transmit them across high-speed circuits—the trunks—to other local COs.[4] For comparison purposes, trunks are analogous to the high-speed data network backbones that you learned about in chapter 4. If the call is long distance, **point of presence (POP)** equipment owned by an **interexchange carrier (IXC or IEC)** transmits the call along the appropriate long-distance communications path so that the call can be received at a remote POP, handed off to the destination subscriber's LEC, and ultimately received at the destination subscriber's home or office.[5]

multiplexing
a method of combining multiple separate signals into a composite signal for transmission across a communications channel

Business Purpose

So what is the business purpose of voice networks? As with data networks, the business purpose is to transmit data between point A and point B, except historically, voice networks

---

[4] These high-speed circuits can be T1 circuits, T3 circuits, Optical Carrier circuits, or other types of high-speed carrier services that you will learn about in chapter 8.
[5] The point of presence (POP) equipment is analogous to data network routers, except it's equipment used for routing data through the PSTN. In addition, the POP described here is not the same as the POP3 protocol with which you might be familiar in e-mail systems. The POP3 in e-mail is the post office protocol, version 3.

trunk or trunk line
a high-speed
multiplexed circuit that
connects two switching
systems. Trunks can
exist between CO
switches, between
switches in a PBX
system, between a PBX
system and a CO, or
between mobile
switching centers
and a CO switch.

*private branch
exchange (PBX)*
a private version of a
PSTN central exchange
that can be implemented
by an organization to
control and manage
voice network use,
functionality, and costs

have primarily been engaged in transmitting the human voice. More recently, voice networks have transmitted data as well as voice. And in today's world of data communications, the business purpose of voice networks is still to convey voice transmissions, but the technology is driving voice networks into convergence with data networks.

Data over POTS

So how do organizations utilize POTS and the PSTN for voice and data communications? They use them for practically everything from simple analog voice and data communications over POTS local loops to switched digital services such as ISDN. The PSTN services voice and data transmissions across **trunks** connected to organizations' **private branch exchange (PBX)** systems, and even the cellular wireless infrastructure that you'll learn about shortly relies on the PSTN for connecting voice and data transmissions between points A and B.

In the 1960s and 1970s, organizations with large mainframe computers began using the analog POTS network to share computing resources and digital data with remote users. What made this possible was the development of technologies that could modulate a simple carrier wave into different frequencies, amplitudes, and phases. Then at the other end of the transmission circuit, the modulated wave could be demodulated so that the data could be received. The device that performed these modulation and demodulation techniques was called a **modem,** which is short for *mo*dulate/*dem*odulate, and modem development spawned the beginning of data communications over regular analog telephone lines.[6]

By the 1980s, the growth of the personal computer coupled with modem technology and connectivity to other computers was fostering the continued growth of data communications over voice networks. Then in the 1990s, faster modems and the Internet accelerated the transformation so that by the mid-1990s, more data was being transmitted over analog voice lines than regular analog voice traffic.

But how does digital data transmission take place through a modem and over an analog voice network? Practically speaking, a modem in the sending computer places data bits on a modulated carrier wave, and the digital data travels across the analog local loop to the telephone company's CO. If the intended recipient of the data "conversation" is connected to the same CO, the data is switched to the recipient's analog local loop, and the data is transmitted to the destination computer's modem where it can be demodulated into a file or message or document. If the intended recipient is connected to another local CO, the CO that is connected to the sender's local loop digitizes the analog "data conversation" and uses various digital **carrier services**—the trunk lines—to multiplex the analog "data conversation" with other analog and digital conversations for transmission across the telephone company's PSTN. If the destination requires a long-distance call, then the multiplexing and data transmission process is similar to the digital connection between COs. The major difference is, the "data conversation" must be handed off through a POP to other carriers until it reaches its destination.[7] In any of these cases, the destination computer has a modem that demodulates the signal and turns the data bits into a file or message or document that is readable.

From the preceding discussion, it's relatively straightforward to see that digital data can be transmitted through a modem, across an analog local loop, and then through the telephone company's PSTN. From a technology perspective, however, getting data to hitch

carrier service
a high-speed data
transmission service
that can be provided by
a carrier company such
as MCI, Sprint, AT&T,
or other carrier
company

---

[6] Earlier implementations of data communications over voice networks existed in the 1950s, but these were reserved primarily for military projects such as radar defense. Appendix A covers this and other network and data communications technology history in much greater detail.

[7] If you dial up an Internet service provider (ISP) through your modem instead of your local phone company, the "data conversation" is still transmitted across the local loop. The difference is that your "data conversation" is routed through the ISP's network, which very likely uses some of the PSTN for its infrastructure.

a ride across an analog local loop is not as simple as the preceding discussion. For a technical perspective, you'll need to understand some terms that are critical to data communications across an analog voice network. Those terms are carrier wave, modulation, amplitude modulation, frequency modulation, phase modulation, baud rate, and bit rate.

Modulation and Carrier Wave

POTS was originally designed to convey the continuously varying pitches and tones of the human voice between two remote locations. If you represented the human voice and its continuous variations graphically, it would look like a sound wave with numerous peaks and valleys. You would also see the sound wave continuously changing as a person spoke to accommodate every variation in the person's voice. Each change in tone or speed conveys specific meaning to both the talker and the listener, and as long as both parties understand the nuances of speech, the vocal information is transmitted and understood.

carrier wave
a "neutral" or non-data-carrying wave that a modem generates prior to a data transmission session

Data communications across POTS works in much the same way. The difference is computers by themselves don't generate any sound waves to convey information. That's the job of a modem. A modem generates a sound wave known as a **carrier wave** that initially doesn't convey any data. If you were to view a carrier wave graphically, it would look like Figure 7.2. When a computer has data to send and that data will be transmitted through a modem and onto an analog local loop, the carrier wave is modulated in numerous ways. With each modulation of the carrier wave, bits of data are transmitted, and as long as both the sending and receiving computers understand the nuances of the modulation techniques, the receiving computer can always understand the data being transmitted.

Amplitude Modulation

There are different ways to modulate a carrier wave so that data bits can be transmitted. One way is amplitude modulation. With the human voice, **amplitude modulation** refers to changes in loudness. Amplitude modulation of a carrier wave refers to changes in height of the wave. In Figure 7.3, the taller sections of the modulated carrier wave represent binary 1s and the shorter sections represent binary 0s. When a computer needs to transmit a binary 1, a modem that uses amplitude modulation modifies the carrier wave with a higher amplitude. When a binary 0 needs to be transmitted, the carrier wave is modulated with a shorter amplitude wave. Because higher amplitudes also represent higher energy in an electrical wave, amplitude modulation is more susceptible to external interferences such as high-voltage lines, electric motors, and electrical storms.

FIGURE 7.2
Carrier Wave

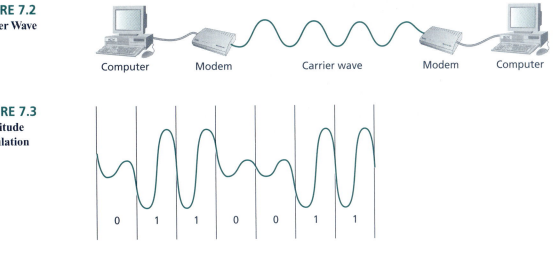

Computer   Modem   Carrier wave   Modem   Computer

FIGURE 7.3
Amplitude Modulation

0   1   1   0   0   1   1

FIGURE 7.4
**Frequency
Modulation**

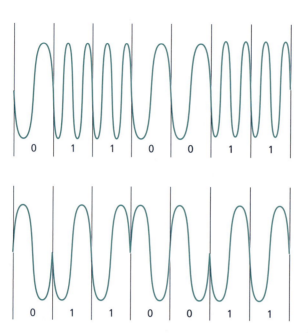

FIGURE 7.5
Phase Modulation

Frequency Modulation

Also referred to as frequency shift keying, **frequency modulation** changes the frequency, or number of waves per second, of a carrier wave. In Figure 7.4, the higher frequency sections of the modulated carrier wave can represent binary 1s and the lower frequency sections can represent binary 0s. Shifting frequencies with the electronic capabilities of a modem thousands of times per second can allow thousands of binary 1s and 0s to be transmitted in a very short period of time.

Phase Modulation

Phase modulation, or phase shift keying, interrupts the continuous flow of the carrier wave by changing the direction of the wave, as you can see in Figure 7.5. When the direction of the wave is down and to the right, this is known as a phase of 180 degrees. When the direction of the wave is up and to the right, it's known as a phase of 0 degrees. Phases of 180 degrees can represent binary 1s and phases of 0 degrees can represent binary 0s. Changing the phase of the carrier wave thousands of times per second results in many thousands of bits being transmitted per second across a voice circuit.

Baud Rate and Bit Rate

Baud rate and *bit rate* are two terms that are frequently, yet incorrectly, interchanged most of the time. **Bit rate** defines the number of bits per second (bps) that can be transmitted across a circuit. A baud is a signaling event, or the change in the amplitude or frequency or phase of the carrier wave.[8] **Baud rate** refers to the number of signaling events that a modem can generate in a one-second interval. Most modern modems include special modulation technologies such as quadrature amplitude modulation (QAM) or trellis-coded modulation (TCM) that allow multiple bits to be transmitted with each baud. The only time bit rate equals baud rate is if only a single bit is transmitted with each baud. Since QAM and TCM provide for the transmission of multiple bits per baud, the bit rate is always higher

---

[8] The term *signaling event* is also referred to as a *symbol,* and the *baud rate* is also known as the *symbol rate.*

than the baud rate in modern modems. As an example, a modern analog modem can create 3,429 changes in the carrier wave per second for a baud rate of 3,429. This modem will also use TCM, which can generate 9.8 bits per baud. Multiplying the baud rate by the number of bits per baud yields a modem with a data transmission rate of 33,600 bits per second.

Today, modems that combine both analog and digital transmission techniques can provide much faster bit rates than traditional analog modems. For example, the V.90 standard for 56 Kbps modems uses analog transmission of digital data for upstream data rates of 33,600 bps and digital transmission of digital data for downstream data rates that approach 56 Kbps. Still newer standards such as V.92 provide for digital transmission of digital data in both directions over an analog local loop. Upstream rates approach 48 Kbps and downstream rates compare with the V.90 standard.

Additional Comments on Modems and Analog Local Loops

If you use a digital telephone or digital communications line to connect your computer with other computers or to the PSTN or to the Internet, you don't need a modem to generate a carrier wave or modulate your computer's digital data onto an analog voice network. In fact, all you need to be concerned about is how fast and accurately you can transmit your data and the types of digital transmission equipment and services you require to establish the connection. Since most home phone lines and some business phone lines are still analog, analog local loops are still required to connect to the PSTN.

It's also important to keep in mind that while data communications over voice networks is generally devoted to modem usage on the analog local loops of the PSTN and in some PBX systems, voice communications over data networks is becoming increasingly coincident with the drive to lower network infrastructure, administrative, and support costs.

PRIVATE BRANCH EXCHANGE

A **private branch exchange (PBX)** is a private version of a PSTN central exchange that can be implemented by an organization to control and manage voice network use, functionality, and costs. With the implementation of a modern PBX, the control, management, and cost of a substantial part of an organization's voice network passes from the telephone company to the organization itself. The only parts of the voice network that aren't internalized are those hardware components and services that connect an organization's internal voice network to the PSTN or to a metropolitan area or wide area carrier service. All other costs, functionality, and configuration are borne by the organization.

Business Purpose and Features

Private branch exchanges have been in existence for over a hundred years. The first PBXs were simple switchboards installed at business locations in the late 1800s and early 1900s, and their exclusive business purpose was to reduce the cost of telephone service to organizations that had multiple telephones. Without an internal switchboard, each telephone within an organization required its own local loop. Anytime a call was placed it would traverse the local loop to the telephone company's central office exchange, and the customer would be billed for the connection time plus monthly or annual service fees, even if the call was placed to another person within the same building. If an organization had a large number of phones, the cost of telephone service using unique local loops for each phone was something that captured the attention of both the business owner and the telephone company. An example of an early telephone switchboard is shown in Figure 7.6.

Business owners wanted to reduce the costs associated with renting multiple local loops that weren't being used all the time, and telephone companies wanted to reduce the expense

FIGURE 7.6
Early Telephone Switchboard

of installing additional local loops each time a new telephone line was added within a business subscriber's premises. The solution was a private branch exchange: a smaller version of the central office's exchange that could be installed at the subscriber's location, and trunk lines that connected the private exchange with the telephone company's central exchange, as illustrated in Figure 7.7.

In reality early PBXs were manually operated switchboards, and they were installed, owned, and maintained by the telephone company for a fee. The business subscriber would enjoy the benefits of internal call switching and control as well as a cost structure that was offset by reduced local loop charges. The telephone company benefited by reducing the number of local loops it had to install and maintain. Of course the business would be charged for the trunk lines that connected the PBX to the central office exchange, but the number of trunk lines could be significantly less than the number of local loops required prior to PBX installation. The business subscriber needed only enough trunk lines to service the maximum number of outgoing calls, a number that was generally substantially less than the number of internal calls.[9]

As an example, an organization that didn't have a PBX might require 25 to 50 local loops to support 50 employees. The telephone company would have to make the capital

---

[9] In the late 1800s and early 1900s, trunk lines were the same as local loops; that is, one call per two-wire twisted-pair line. By 1910, methods such as phantom circuits allowed three calls to be transmitted across two lines and ghosting allowed for four calls to be transmitted across two lines under certain conditions. In 1918, Type A carrier circuits were introduced, and they provided for five calls per two-wire twisted-pair line—one call in the regular voice frequency range and four multiplexed calls that were transmitted on separate frequencies above the regular voice frequency range.

FIGURE 7.7
Connectivity to Central Office Exchange

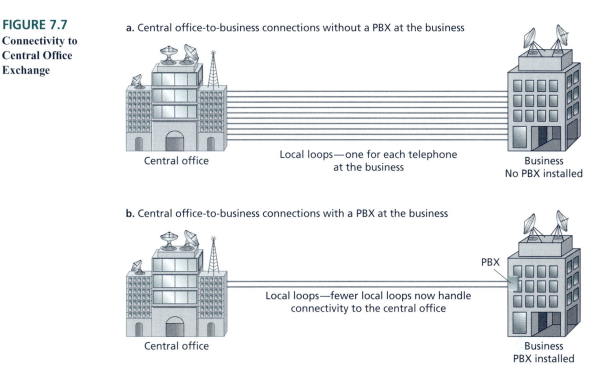

a. Central office-to-business connections without a PBX at the business

Central office

Local loops—one for each telephone at the business

Business
No PBX installed

b. Central office-to-business connections with a PBX at the business

PBX

Central office

Local loops—fewer local loops now handle connectivity to the central office

Business
PBX installed

investment to install these 25 to 50 local loops, and the business would have to pay the rental fees and usage charges for each of the lines installed. With a little preplanning, a PBX could be installed, and the number of local loops required to connect the business to the telephone company central office could potentially be reduced to 10 or maybe even 5. In this scenario, the telephone company conserves capital for other uses, and the overall fees charged to the business are reduced by a significant percentage.

While the features of "ancient" PBXs were focused on the efficiencies of internal switching of telephone calls and cost savings, modern PBXs include those features and a whole host of newer services designed to improve voice network performance and communications efficiency.[10] Table 7.1 provides a list of some of the common features found in modern PBXs.

PBX Technology

Prior to the mid-1970s, PBXs were either operator-attended switchboards or electro-mechanical devices that automatically serviced analog telephones. Since the mid-1970s, analog PBX technologies have faded and the emphasis has been on digital PBXs. Digital PBX technologies have paralleled the development and implementation of digital switching equipment in telephone company COs, and software-based features have paralleled the development of computers and programming tools.

call processing
the services that establish, maintain, and terminate a call session between end locations

You can think of modern PBX technology as sophisticated computers running software that handles **call processing** and switching as well as software that provides the services

---

[10] Because early PBXs were stationed by an operator, the operator could switch a call to the intended recipient even if the intended recipient was in an office other than his or her own. This ability to identify a caller's exact location without having to try multiple different numbers in a sequenced path is known as *hoteling,* and is a feature that was lost with the first automatic switchboards but has since made a comeback with modern PBXs.

TABLE 7.1
Common Features of Modern PBXs

Feature	Description
Automated attendant	Answers incoming calls and instructs callers how to dial to reach an internal extension.
Voice mail	Storage location on the PBX for incoming callers to leave messages.
Call coverage	Allows users to program their phones to direct calls to one or more alternative phones connected to the PBX system. A user's voice mail answers the call only if no one in the call coverage path answers.
Hoteling	Allows users who move from desk to desk to access the phone system and forward their regular phone numbers to their temporary phones as well as associate their regular phone preferences with their temporary phones.
Find-me	Allows users to program their phones to redirect calls sequentially to one or more external telephone numbers.
Interactive voice response	Initiates calling actions within the PBX system based on a caller's telephone Touch-Tone inputs.
System administration	The PBX system administrator sets overall system calling parameters using PBX system commands.

FIGURE 7.8
Modular PBX that Accommodates Digital and Analog Devices

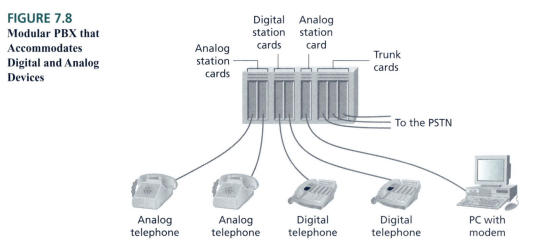

you saw in Table 7.1. In addition, today's PBXs are based on digital transmission technologies. They're also sophisticated enough to service analog signals from analog telephones and computers equipped with modems—all you need to do is specify these requirements with the PBX vendor. Modern PBXs are also modular in design so that expansion ports can be added to accommodate additional telephones. Figure 7.8 provides an example of a modular PBX.

In Figure 7.8, the voice network includes digital telephones, analog telephones, fax machines, and computers with modems. The PBX itself is comprised of several internal components including the common control complex, a switching matrix, station cards, and trunk cards as illustrated in Figure 7.9. The common control complex, or simply common control, is a computer within the PBX that controls call processing and switching functions. Call processing functions include dial tone and station number receipt and analysis.[11] Switching functions include the control of station-to-station call connections and station-to-trunk connections.

---

[11] The term *station* refers to the telephone handset.

FIGURE 7.9
PBX Components

The switching matrix provides the circuitry that supports station-to-station or station-to-trunk connectivity. Each time a user takes a telephone handset off hook, common control issues orders to deliver dial tone to the off-hook phone. When the user makes a call, the call is connected through the station card, which is connected to the switching matrix. If the call is internal, based on the number the user enters, the call is switched to another station card for delivery. If the call is external, usually defined by the user first pressing a 9, the user receives an external dial tone, and then the call is switched from the user's station card to a trunk card for delivery across a trunk line to the PSTN.[12]

The technologies embedded in PBX design include some of the same technologies used in the PSTN, specifically **pulse coded modulation (PCM)** and **time division multiplexing (TDM).** PCM uses a **coder/decoder (codec)** to sample analog voice signals at a rate of 8,000 times per second and converts each sample into an eight-bit data value.[13] In digital telephones, the codec is designed into the circuitry of the phone so that a person's voice is converted from analog to digital at the phone before transmission across the line to the station card. With computers that are connected via modem to a PBX, analog phones, and fax machines, the signals are sampled and encoded at the station card before being transmitted digitally through the PBX's switching matrix.

Once an analog signal is digitally encoded, the station card can occupy a talk slot on the TDM bus for transmission across the switching matrix. Time division multiplexing combines the digital signals from multiple station cards and trunk cards onto a shared circuit known in PBX terminology as the **TDM bus.** The available bandwidth of the TDM bus is divided into time slots, measured in milliseconds, to create a multiplexed signal. When a call is made through the PBX, the sending and receiving station cards are each allocated a time slot, also known as a **talk slot,** according to the TDM bus sequencing mechanism designed into the PBX. That is, the TDM bus sequentially polls each active station card and trunk card in the PBX for a short interval of time. During a call between internal phones, the sending station card and the receiving station card each occupy a talk slot on the TDM bus. With a call that originates from an internal phone to an outside line, the sending station

---

[12] Modern trunk lines can be BRI ISDN, PRI ISDN, T1, or combinations of these and other digital carrier circuits.
[13] You learned about codecs in chapter 1.

FIGURE 7.10
Digital and Analog Devices Occupying a TDM Bus

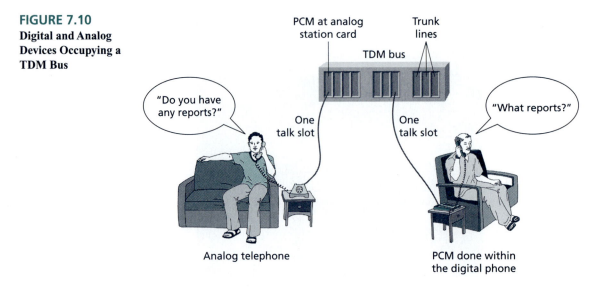

card and the trunk card each occupy a talk slot on the TDM bus. Figure 7.10 provides a graphic representation of a TDM bus.

Another technology that voice network administrators must be concerned with is wireless communication. Regular cellular phones can be partially integrated with PBX systems meaning that users' cell phone numbers can be programmed into the PBX database to take advantage of features such as call coverage, hoteling, and find-me. At the same time, regular cell phones don't receive their dial tone, call processing, or switching functions from the PBX. Instead, a cellular service company provides those functions. Wireless PBX phones, on the other hand, can be programmed much the same as wired PBX telephones. Wireless PBX phones connect via radio frequency to one or more radio controller cards in the PBX, and they receive all of the same functions that are generally programmed for hard-wired PBX phones. The disadvantage is that the wireless PBX phones typically sell at a significant premium over regular cellular phones making them difficult to justify on a cost/benefit basis, although this cost differential may diminish over time.

PBX Switching Topologies and Design Considerations

centralized PBX switching topology
with this topology, a call from any PBX station to another PBX station must pass through the central switch, even if the communicating stations are on the same TDM bus

One of the most important considerations in a PBX installation is the design of the **PBX switching topology.** Depending on the size and structure of an organization, voice network users can be located in a central location, distributed between two or three locations, or remotely located in numerous locations. There can be many employees or few employees in the organization. In any of these cases, there is a PBX switching network topology that will fit the needs of an organization's physical layout. The three basic PBX switching topology designs are centralized, distributed, and dispersed.

highway bus
a high-speed link that connects remote station card enclosures to the PBX switch. It can be a T-carrier circuit such as a T1 or multiple T1s or even a T3 or other carrier type.

Centralized PBX Switching Topology

In a **centralized PBX switching topology**, a call from any PBX telephone to another PBX telephone must pass through the PBX switch, even if the two phones are on the same TDM bus. As an example, take a look at Figure 7.11. In the figure, the PBX switch is located in one enclosure, and the station and trunk cards are located in another enclosure. When a caller at station A calls another employee at station B, the call is multiplexed on the local TDM bus, transmitted across a high-speed link known as a **highway bus** to the PBX switch, and then switched back to the local TDM bus for delivery to station B. Each call placed in this topology requires the services of the central switch; local TDM buses do not

FIGURE 7.11
Centralized PBX
Switching Topology

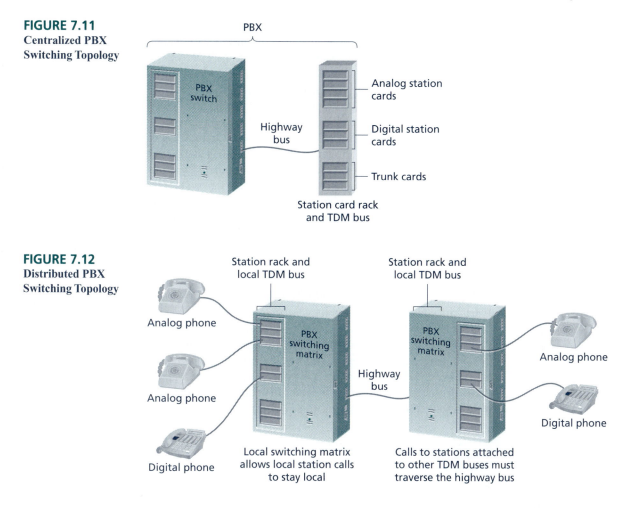

FIGURE 7.12
Distributed PBX
Switching Topology

have built-in switching capability. In other words, calls cannot travel from station to station on any local TDM bus without first passing through the central switch, because the local TDM buses do not have the circuitry to perform the call-switching operations.

This design is relatively simple and adequate for a small organization at one location because the central switch and the station card enclosure can be adjacently installed or can be configured as a single cabinet. Where this design runs into problems is with remote location connectivity. If an organization implements this design and later opens a remote office, the remote TDM bus will need to be connected to the PBX switch, and that connection might require a carrier service such as a T1 circuit. If the number of employees at the remote location grows, the organization might need to install additional T1 circuits to provide adequate levels of service or even consider another complete PBX system at the remote location.

Distributed PBX Switching Topology

distributed PBX switching topology
with this topology, each local TDM bus has switching circuitry built in so that each TDM bus does not need to access a central switch

The **distributed PBX switching topology** is suited to organizations with multiple business locations. With the distributed topology, each local TDM bus has switching circuitry built in so that each TDM bus does not need to access a central switch. Figure 7.12 provides an example.

In Figure 7.12, local stations can call each other without having to traverse the highway bus. Switching and call processing capability within each TDM bus make this possible.

Since most calls will likely be local within each TDM bus, this design can be a big cost saver in terms of the communications links needed to support the highway bus. The highway bus is utilized only when stations from one TDM bus need to communicate with stations on another TDM bus. Once again, the highway bus can be comprised of one or more T1 circuits through the PSTN, or if the distributed TDM buses are close enough, fiber-optic cabling can connect them.

The disadvantage to installing a distributed switch topology is that it doesn't scale efficiently once the number of local TDM buses exceeds three. That is because each local TDM bus must be connected with each additional TDM bus that is added to the PBX voice network. If your voice network has three locations and you need to add a fourth, three new highway buses must be implemented to connect the new TDM bus to the original three. If you then add a fifth TDM bus at a new location, four new highway buses must be installed. Add a sixth, and you'll need highway bus connections to the previous five TDM buses, and so on. The cost of the additional local TDM buses can be significant, but the costs of the highway buses can be very expensive, especially if you need to use carrier services through the PSTN to establish the links.

Dispersed PBX Switching Topology

The third common design topology is a *dispersed PBX switching topology*. This design includes local TDM buses with built-in switching capability at each remote location and a central switch to which the local TDMs connect, as shown in Figure 7.13.

In Figure 7.13, each local TDM bus in the PBX is connected via a highway bus to the central switch. Local station-to-station calls are switched within each local TDM bus, but calls that need to connect with nonlocal stations are switched to the appropriate station through the central PBX switch. The advantage to this design is that you only need to build

FIGURE 7.13
**Dispersed PBX
Switching Topology**

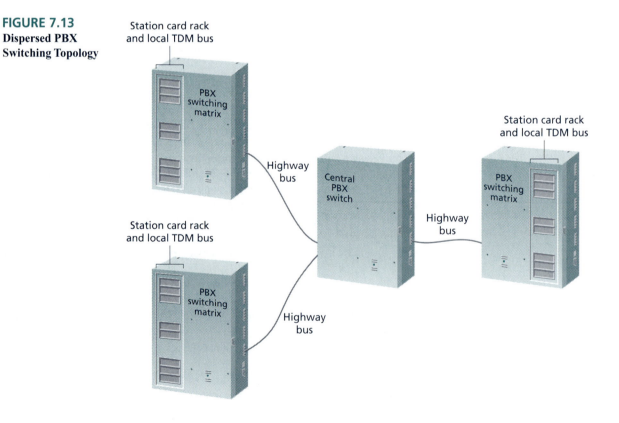

one highway bus with each new local TDM bus installation. Because the central switch can transfer all calls that aren't local to any local TDM bus, there is no need for each local TDM bus to be directly connected to every other TDM bus. This can provide huge cost savings over the long term with reduced need for multiple highway bus installations with each new local TDM, as well as the potential savings on carrier service charges if those carrier services are needed to create the highway bus communications link. The only downside is that the upfront cost of implementation can be more expensive than the upfront costs of other switched designs.

IP-PRIVATE BRANCH EXCHANGE

converged voice and data network
a unified network in which voice communications and data communications technologies are combined and presented via a single delivery system

Private branch exchange systems that incorporate IP technologies are the latest evolution of PBX design and functionality. In this section, you'll discover two different types of PBX systems that incorporate IP technologies. One type provides the capability of integrating existing circuit-switched PBX infrastructures with packet-switched Ethernet IP networks to create a **converged voice and data network**. The other type replaces the traditional circuit-switched PBX infrastructure with a packet-switched voice communications architecture running on an Ethernet IP network.[14] In this section, you're going to look at the business drivers behind converged **IP-PBX** systems and IP packet-switched PBX systems, example topologies that support these two types of IP-PBX systems, and the underlying protocols that facilitate time- and quality-sensitive voice transmissions in an Ethernet IP network.

Business Purpose

When deregulation hit the monopolistic telephone industry with full force in 1984, organizations found it much more cost effective to implement and maintain their own PBX voice networks rather than lease enterprise central exchange **(CENTREX)** systems from the telephone company.[15,16] During that same period, data networks were beginning to evolve with their own separate infrastructures, resulting in separate capital and operational costs. With voice and data being such integral parts of the organization and no single communications technology available at the time to combine the two into a single network, business managers were forced to build and support two separate network infrastructures—one for voice and one for data.

As data networks continued to evolve throughout the 1980s and 1990s, the costs of transporting data over data networks continued to decrease making data networks highly attractive for transporting voice traffic as well. The only problem was figuring out a way to do that. That is where the voice and data engineers and product developers made their mark: providing IP-PBX solutions that could integrate voice traffic onto highly efficient and cost-effective data networks.

---

[14] Packet switching was defined in chapter 3. Circuit switching and packet switching are covered in more detail in chapter 8.

[15] The telephone industry was deregulated in 1984. The major business changes that resulted allowed AT&T and its regional bell operating companies (RBOCs) to enter new markets such as computer hardware and compete without price regulation in markets such as cellular telephone service. Deregulation also allowed companies such as MCI and Sprint to compete with AT&T in the long-distance service market.

[16] Enterprise central exchange systems, or CENTREX systems are similar to PBX systems, but they're owned and maintained by the telephone company. Generally they're leased by companies that need the extra voice network features of a PBX system but can't afford the purchase price and maintenance fees of a PBX. CENTREX systems are still available in today's competitive voice network marketplace.

Topologies

We've already seen the traditional PBX topologies that use PCM and TDM for analog-to-digital encoding and digital transmission in a voice network. IP-PBX topologies include two additional PBX topologies: the **converged PBX topology,** which combines the best of traditional PBX systems with Ethernet IP networks; and the IP packet-switched topology, which uses the existing infrastructure and protocols of an IP Ethernet network to process, switch, and transport voice traffic.

Converged Topology

With the converged IP-PBX topology shown in Figure 7.14, PCM and TDM are utilized to maintain the existing voice network infrastructure, but the Ethernet data network infrastructure is used to switch and transport IP voice traffic as well as transport voice traffic between PBX card cabinets.

In Figure 7.14, analog and digital telephones continue to be serviced by analog or digital cards. A call made from a digital or analog handset is connected to the IP-PBX just as it would be in a legacy PBX system. If a call is connected to another digital or analog PBX telephone, the call processing and switching functions are performed through the PBX's legacy call processing and **circuit switching** functions. PCM services the analog-to-digital encoding and TDM provides the transport through the PBX.

circuit switching
a communications method that creates a dedicated communications path between points A and B for the exclusive use of points A and B for the duration of the connection

Traditional digital trunk lines can still be used to link the IP-PBX to the outside world, but a PCM-to-IP gateway can provide connectivity across an organization's LAN and WAN. In Figure 7.14, a PCM-to-IP gateway card is connected to the circuitry of the IP-PBX and to the organization's IP network. Any calls that must be transported between remote TDM buses or to other IP-PBX systems within the organization pass through the

FIGURE 7.14
Converged PBX Topologies

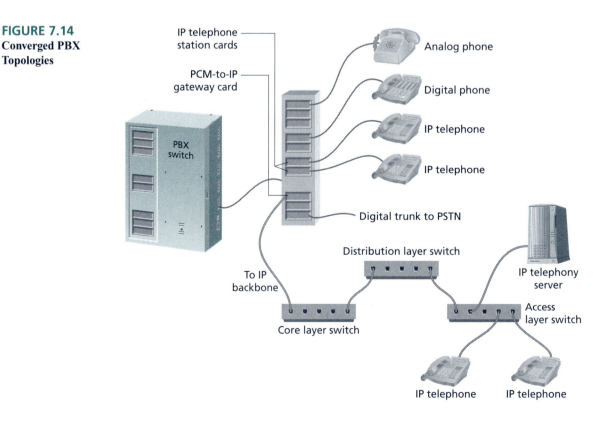

PCM-to-IP gateway.[17] In this scenario, call control and processing are still handled by legacy PBX functions, but the IP Ethernet network services call transport between remote PBX locations. If the data network is busy, such that call quality would be affected by passing through the gateway, the intelligence of the PCM-to-IP gateway can direct the call to the PBX trunk lines for connection with the PSTN.

The switched Ethernet network also supports call switching and other internal call services between IP telephones that are directly attached to the IP network. In Figure 7.14, several IP telephones are connected to an Ethernet switch. Calls placed between these IP handsets receive their call processing and control instructions from an IP telephony server that is also connected to the Ethernet data network. Call switching for IP-to-IP calls takes place through the Ethernet switches that are part of the data network infrastructure. Calls that connect between IP handsets and legacy digital and analog PBX handsets are serviced by the **PCM-to-IP gateway** in the PBX.

IP Packet-Switched Topology

An **IP packet-switched IP-PBX topology** is also referred to as *client/server IP-PBX*.[18] With this topology, one or more telephony servers provide PBX call processing and control, and the existing IP Ethernet data network infrastructure performs the call switching. Special IP telephones are connected directly to the Ethernet network and voice traffic is encoded for transmission across the IP Ethernet data network. Calls are processed as packets so that both voice and data can be serviced by a single network infrastructure. Client/server IP-PBX systems can be integrated into legacy PBX voice networks, but an implementation of an IP packet-switched IP-PBX topology does not need to rely in any way on legacy PBX architecture. Figure 7.15 provides an example of a client/server IP-PBX system.

FIGURE 7.15   **Client/server IP-PBX System**

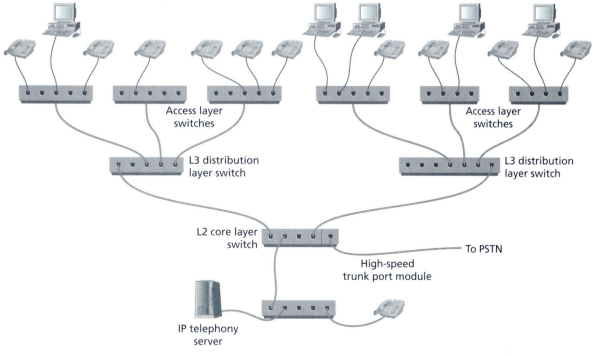

---

[17] Each remote TDM bus would need to be equipped with a PCM-to-IP gateway.
[18] Client/server IP-PBX systems are also referred to as *VoIP systems*.

In Figure 7.15, a data network infrastructure supports a client/server IP-PBX through the use of a telephony server and IP telephones. All voice traffic is transported across the data network infrastructure so that even remote LAN segments can be configured for voice traffic without the use of remote PBX equipment. Branch offices in an organization that might find it difficult to justify the capital expense of a PBX can minimize their voice network expenditures with the purchase and implementation of IP telephones. The IP telephones use the existing data network infrastructure for call switching and the organization's telephony server for call processing and control. When an IP telephone user needs to make a call, an IP telephony server, which is comprised of both hardware and software, identifies the IP telephone by its IP address and provides dial tone. Once the user dials a number, the telephony server or a voice gateway can establish a path for the call. If the call is internal, the Ethernet network switching hardware switches the IP voice packets to the destination IP telephone. If the call is external, the call can be switched to a router for transfer across a WAN link or to a PSTN trunk line according to the configuration established on the telephony server or voice gateway. Telephony servers and gateways can even have the intelligence to route external calls to the PSTN in the event that the data network is too busy.

It is very likely that legacy PBX systems will continue in service for years to come because their utility can be extended and enhanced through convergence with IP technologies. At the same time, installations of client/server IP-PBX systems are becoming much more common in organizations that have outgrown their existing PBX voice networks and are looking to migrate to newer technologies. With client/server IP-PBX systems, organizations can more efficiently utilize the bandwidth of their existing data networks, consolidate voice and data network capital expenditures, reduce support and maintenance costs to a single data network, expand voice connectivity to any IP device with telephony capability such as wireless PDAs, and install IP telephones in any remote LAN location without the cost of an additional IP-PBX or TDM bus. In addition, packet-switched IP-PBXs don't require the specialized skill set associated with PBX hardware support and maintenance. Because data network technicians are already familiar with support and maintenance of IP networks, it's likely that fewer people will be needed to support a data network that includes a packet-switched IP-PBX system than were required to support both a data network and a legacy voice network.

Voice over IP

Voice over IP (VoIP) is the combination of hardware, software, and protocols that support voice communications over IP networks. You learned about some of the hardware and software components of VoIP in the previous section when you examined the client/server IP-PBX topology. Protocols make up the other major component of VoIP, and in this section you'll identify several of the major VoIP protocols and examine the roles they play in support of voice communications over an IP network. You can also see how these protocols fit within the structure of the OSI model in Figure 7.16.

VoIP Protocols

VoIP requires the coordinated effort of numerous protocols to accommodate the transmission of voice, video, and data across IP networks. These protocols have been in constant development since the mid-1990s and in their current versions support a wide array of communications services that range from simple voice calls across a LAN to involved multimedia conferencing across a WAN or the Internet. These protocols conform to the hierarchy of the OSI model and include two basic levels of functionality: call signaling and call transport.

Call Signaling   In VoIP networks, **call signaling** is the process of exchanging information across an IP data network with the purpose of establishing, monitoring, maintaining, and

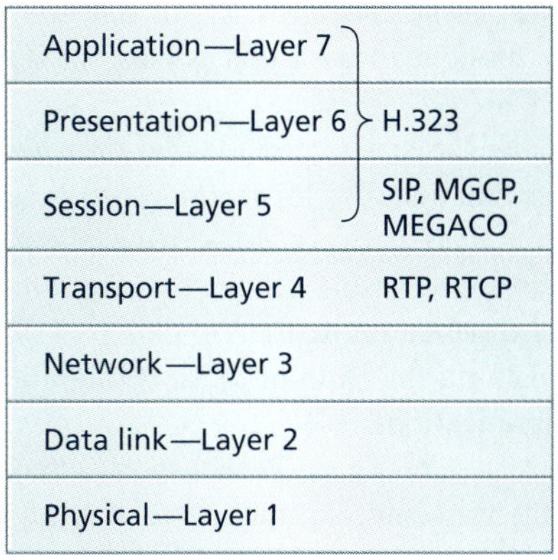

FIGURE 7.16
**VoIP Protocols and
the OSI Model**

Application—Layer 7	
Presentation—Layer 6	H.323
Session—Layer 5	SIP, MGCP, MEGACO
Transport—Layer 4	RTP, RTCP
Network—Layer 3	
Data link—Layer 2	
Physical—Layer 1	

terminating connections between communicating devices.[19] In other words, when you make a call from an IP telephone, call setup, monitoring, maintaining, and terminating information has to be exchanged between communicating devices. This information exchange connects your call, maintains and monitors the call while you're communicating with the destination device, and then terminates the call when you hang up. These are the functions of VoIP signaling protocols such as H.323 and Session Initiation Protocol (SIP).

H.323 is actually a suite of protocols that was originally developed under the auspices of the International Telecommunications Union (ITU) in the mid-1990s.[20] In its original form, H.323 was designed to provide videoconferencing capability on Ethernet LANs; it wasn't designed specifically for VoIP. In VoIP networks, the H.323 suite of protocols provides functionality such as call setup, codec specifications, and call control mechanisms on Ethernet LANs that don't provide guaranteed **quality of service (QoS)**.

quality of service (QoS)
a commitment to provide a quantified level of quality and bandwidth over a data transmission path so that various and different data types can be transmitted at predefined performance levels. QoS is important for the delivery of voice, multimedia, and other time-sensitive data types.

The H.323 protocols operate throughout the upper three layers of the OSI model. For example, call setup is a session layer function; codec specifications are defined at the presentation layer; and audio and video applications and certain types of call signaling fall within the application layer. Microsoft's NetMeeting software is a simple implementation of H.323. More advanced implementations include high-end voice network application software running on IP telephony servers and switching and routing hardware that support H.323.

Session Initiation Protocol is another call signaling protocol that was developed specifically for VoIP by the Internet Engineering Task Force (IETF).[21] SIP functions at layer 5 of the OSI model, performing call setup, maintenance, and termination. SIP has a simpler structure and fewer built-in functions than H.323, which allows it to provide faster call setup and simpler call control functions. Its simplicity is accomplished through modularity, meaning that more complex features are left to other applications.

SIP was designed for scalability in newer and expanding IP networks that have the need for VoIP services. It uses addressing that is similar to Web-based URLs so that callers can use either a telephone number or a person's name in combination with the domain or network location of the destination telephone. For example, on an IP telephone, you could create a telephone URL entry named destinationcaller@calldomain.net. Each time you

---

[19] Call signaling takes place over PSTN networks also. For the PSTN, a protocol known as Signaling System 7 (SS7) is a common signaling protocol.

[20] Specifically, H.323 falls under the ITU-T sector of the ITU. You learned about the ITU and its sectors in chapter 1.

[21] You can find more information regarding the SIP protocol on the SIP forum Web site www.sipforum.org.

needed to call this person, you could use the URL to dial the person named "destinationcaller" in a DNS domain associated with that person, in this case a domain named calldomain.net.[22]

SIP does not have built-in mechanisms to provide real-time delivery of voice and video packets. Instead it leaves this functionality to other protocols and mechanisms, namely efficient routing and QoS within the IP network. For voice packets, you would configure the IP network hardware and software to ensure efficient routing of network traffic, and you would assign a higher priority to voice traffic than to data packets because voice traffic is more sensitive to delay than data traffic. Both of these configuration options facilitate the timely delivery of voice communications.

Signaling and media differences between IP packet-switched voice networks and the PSTN require gateways and gateway control protocols to connect these two dissimilar networks. For example, H.323 is designed for LAN and WAN multimedia conferencing, but when it needs to interface with the PSTN for packet transmission, its signaling and media formats must be converted through a gateway. Similarly, SIP is designed for call signaling across a WAN environment but doesn't convert automatically to a PSTN-compatible format.

For interoperability between H.323 and the PSTN or SIP and the PSTN, two other protocols—the **Media Gateway Control Protocol (MGCP)** and its more evolved progeny, **MEGACO**—support the protocol translations that are required for packet-switched VoIP information to transmit across the PSTN. In other words, MGCP and MEGACO are the gateway protocols that allow SIP-based and H.323-based VoIP networks to communicate with the PSTN.[23]

So which do you choose in support of your organization's VoIP network, H.323 or SIP? H.323 was designed from the start with a bias toward packetized communications across the PSTN. Its heritage derived from an older ISDN videoconferencing standard, known as **H.320,** and so contained elements that favored interoperability with the PSTN. If your organization uses primarily PSTN services for WAN support and connectivity, an H.323 VoIP approach might be the right choice. On the other hand, if your organization has developed an IP-based WAN infrastructure, SIP might be the better choice for a VoIP implementation.

Call Transport   Voice traffic is very sensitive to delays, packet loss, and packet sequence upon arrival. If any of these sensitivities is not accommodated, VoIP voice communications will very likely be unacceptable and perhaps even unintelligible. Routing protocols assist in the timely delivery of packets, and QoS ensures priority delivery based on packet type, but a set of transport protocols that work in conjunction with the User Datagram Protocol (UDP) is also required to assist in the timely and sequenced delivery of voice traffic.[24]

The **Real-Time Transport Protocol (RTP)** and the **Real-Time Transport Control Protocol (RTCP)** assist in addressing the issues of delay, loss, and sequencing of voice packets on an IP network. RTP time-stamps each voice packet so that the packets can be sequenced in the appropriate order upon delivery at the destination. Reassembling the packets in sequence at the destination will indicate if there is a lost packet, and any packet-loss information can be passed on to the upper-layer protocols such as codec functions. Because RTP assists in packet loss detection, the receiving codec can determine how best to reconstruct the remaining voice packets for playback. In addition, these upper layer codec protocols can communicate between source and destination to determine if the voice packet flow needs to be adjusted for better transmission.

---

[22] You learned about DNS in chapter 5, and you'll explore it again in chapter 10.

[23] These VoIP-to-PSTN gateways can be located either at the customer premises or at the service provider's central office.

[24] The User Datagram Protocol (UDP) is an OSI layer 4 protocol that is used for connectionless transport between end devices.

Applied Technical **Tidbit**

The Process of Making a
Call from an IP Telephone
on a Data Network

The steps involved in making an IP telephone call on an IP data network are similar to the steps in all data transmissions across data networks. That is, there is some information at point A, such as your voice on the IP telephone. It needs to get to point B, which is likely to be the receiving party's ear, and in between lots of technology processes get involved to establish, maintain, and then terminate the call. The major difference is the type of data and how it starts its journey. Here's how VoIP sets up a call and transmits a conversation across an IP network.

When you take an IP telephone that is part of a VoIP network off hook, it sends a signal across the data network to the VoIP server. The server recognizes the off-hook signal as well as the specific telephone that generated the signal, provides dial tone to the telephone, and makes available any features and functions that are specific to that phone when it is off hook.

When you dial the number of your destination party, the number is transmitted across the data network to the VoIP server. The server's voice application reads the destination telephone number and determines whether the number is on network, that is, on the VoIP network, or an outside call. Then the server compares the caller's configuration profile to the number dialed and enforces any calling restrictions.[25] If the call is on network, the VoIP server connects (switches) the call to the destination telephone, where the call is either answered or transferred to another phone or to voice mail.

Once the call is connected and you start speaking, many steps come into play to encode and transport your voice to the receiving telephone. Figure 7.17 provides a numbered sequence of this process as it corresponds to the layers of the OSI model.

1. OSI layer 5, 6, and 7 protocols provide application services, encoding, call setup, and control functionality. The VoIP server provides the application, call setup, and control functions, but the encoding takes place at the IP telephone. Sophisticated codec hardware within the telephone mouthpiece sample your voice's analog sound waves up to 8,000 times per second and encode the analog signal into digital data bits. Concurrently, the codec's compression algorithm filters out any nonspeech noise as well as nonessential digitized voice bits so that the resultant transmission will be an efficiently compressed signal. The bits are buffered until they exist in sufficient number to create packets, and then the lower layer protocols come into play.

2. The buffered packets are encapsulated with an RTP header at layer 4 for end-to-end reliability and for timing and sequencing of the voice packets. Layer 4 also encapsulates RTP within UDP to provide the transport services.

FIGURE 7.17
Making an IP Voice Call

Application	(1) VoIP server provides application services and call setup and control functions. Codec converts analog voice to binary and compresses the bits. Bits are buffered until sufficient in number to form a packet. SIP or H.323 monitor and maintain the session.
Presentation	
Session	
Transport	(2) Packet encapsulation in an RTP header for end-to-end reliability and for timing and sequencing of packets. Further encapsulation in a UDP header for transport services. RTCP monitors the session.
Network	(3) IP header added for routing.
Data link	(4) Packets are framed with Ethernet header.
Physical	(5) Bits placed on network medium.

[25] Caller configuration profiles are call restriction filters that can be implemented on a user-by-user or phone-by-phone basis. The VoIP network administrator creates and maintains the configuration profile database that stores the configurations.

3. After that, an IP header is added to each packet for routing across the network.
4. The packets are framed with an Ethernet header.
5. Finally the bits are placed on the network medium for transmission across the network to the destination phone. At the receiving end, the process is reversed so that the called party or the called party's voice mail can hear what you're saying.

When it's an outside call, the server compares the caller's configuration profile to the number dialed. If the number dialed is allowed according to the caller's configuration profile, the call will be connected through the organization's WAN or through the PSTN depending on the external network the organization has implemented.

RTP uses UDP for its underlying transport across an IP network. The **User Datagram Protocol** is a connectionless protocol that doesn't provide delivery notification, error detection, retransmission requests, or packet sequencing. As a result UDP is faster than TCP for transport, a critical consideration for voice packet transport. While RTP does not reduce the overall delay of voice packet delivery, its time stamp and packet sequencing operations provide the error detection and packet loss functionality that make RTP a suitable adjunct for UDP in the transport of VoIP packets.

RTCP is a control protocol that establishes and monitors RTP sessions. RTCP provides feedback to upper layer protocols on the quality of the transmission with information such as the number of RTP packets that have been lost, packet delays, and jitter.[26] With this information, upper layer protocols can adjust packet flow and reassembly to circumvent playback problems attributable to loss, delay, and jitter.[27]

COMPUTER–TELEPHONY INTEGRATION

Computer–telephony integration (CTI) is a combination of hardware and software that is designed to integrate the capabilities of an organization's voice network with the information on the organization's data network. Its roots date back to the early 1990s with the introduction of hardware and software that could be added to a PC to integrate PCs with an existing telephone system.

CTI does not provide data and voice network convergence, nor does it replace a voice network system. Instead, CTI facilitates information access from a data network by running one or more computer applications that can service caller requests that originate on the voice network. CTI also makes network call information available to applications running on the data network.

Business Purpose and Features

In its simplest form, CTI can be an application running on a desktop computer that has a telephony card installed, and the telephony card is connected to the voice network and to a telephone as you can see in Figure 7.18.[28]

---

[26] *Packet delay* is the elapsed time, typically measured in milliseconds, that it takes a packet to travel from source to destination. *Jitter* is the time variance between arriving packets.

[27] Delays and *jitter* are typically solved through packet buffering at the source and destination locations.

[28] Another very simple form of CTI is a computer softphone, in which a desktop computer equipped with a microphone, speakers (or a headset with the same components), and a CTI card runs a telephony application, which allows the computer to function as a telephone. The application and telephony card can provide services such as voice mail, outbound faxing, fax-on-demand, and more without the use of a telephone handset.

FIGURE 7.18
Simple CTI Configuration
Ethernet NIC may also be required if telephony card is connected to a legacy station card on the PBX.

Telephony card

To voice network PBX, IP-PBX, or VoIP/data network

TABLE 7.2
CTI Applications

Application	Description
Interactive voice response	Initiates transactions in response to telephone touch tones or even callers' voice commands.
Voice recognition	Recognizes and responds to voice commands for access to data.
Fax-on-demand	Faxes documents from a network storage location to a caller-specified telephone number.
Outbound faxing	Allows the computer user to fax documents directly from the computer.
Speech/text conversion	Stores callers' voice messages on a network hard drive or other network storage system as text. Can also deliver stored text messages in voice format from data storage to a requesting caller.
Conferencing	Sets up conference calls based on Touch-Tone or voice commands.
Outbound dialing	Allows a user at a CTI-configured computer to make a call using point-and-click dialing from an on-screen list of numbers.
GUI call control	Users can control incoming and outgoing calls with graphical commands and icons on their desktops.

The CTI card illustrated in Figure 7.18 can provide features such as outbound faxing, fax-on-demand, outbound dialing, voice mail, and other services that are generally associated with modern PBX and VoIP voice network systems. Table 7.2 provides a more complete list of CTI applications and their descriptions.

In more sophisticated implementations of CTI, voice networks pass along call information to the data network so that applications on the data network can deliver information to callers across the voice network. For example, an organization can provide internal data to external callers using databases and CTI servers that are connected to the organization's data network. Figure 7.19 provides an example of this configuration.

In Figure 7.19, a database server and a CTI server running a Web-based application are connected to a data network. The data network and the voice network are also connected to each other in either a converged or client/server configuration. When an external caller calls in for information, the voice network intercepts the call and provides signaling and call control functions and other functions such as voice mail and call switching depending on how the caller responds to recorded directions from an automated call attendant supplied by the VoIP server or PBX. If the inbound caller presses a numeric key or speaks a phrase that indicates an information request, the call is forwarded from the PBX or VoIP server to the data network where applications on the CTI server can service the data request. Applications on the CTI server respond to callers' requests either through numbers dialed, through speech recognition, or even by recognizing a caller's telephone number. Once the CTI server has received the call, it can direct an information request to a database server or fax server, which can, in turn, provide the information that the caller requested. Response information is either spoken to the caller, or if the caller chooses an electronic document, the document can be faxed to a number that the caller enters.

FIGURE 7.19 **Sophisticated CTI**

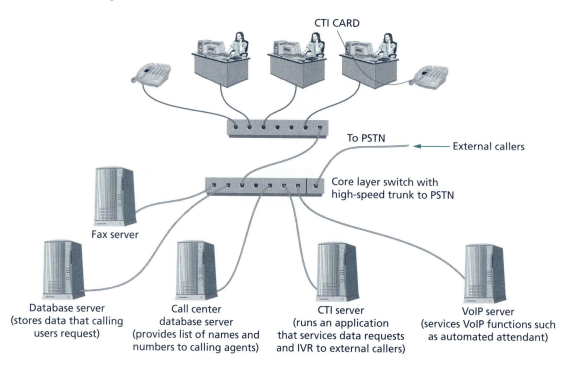

A significant business use of CTI occurs within large call centers. Call centers provide **integrated voice response (IVR)** systems that service incoming caller requests very much like the preceding discussion of Figure 7.19. Requests are serviced through integration of voice and data networks in conjunction with CTI servers, database servers, Web servers, and media servers.

For outgoing calls, CTI applications can provide automated outbound calling programs that link databases of customer information, including customer telephone numbers, with a dialing application. Service agents are connected to the CTI server application through a Web browser interface, and database servers on the data network provide the customer information that is displayed on the agent's computer screen. When a service agent places a call to a customer, the call is either automatically dialed by the CTI application, or the agent can click on an on-screen dial button to initiate the call. The data network supplies the customer database information to the agent, and CTI facilitates the outbound call through the voice network.

CELLULAR WIRELESS VOICE NETWORKS

In recent years, cellular wireless voice networks have provided subscribers with services that previously were available only with land-based telephones connected to the PSTN. Mobile and land-based users alike can talk, send faxes, receive text messages, and exchange data with wireless cell phones and devices from virtually anywhere. While they began as wireless networks designed to transmit only voice, cellular wireless networks have quickly evolved into an infrastructure that combines both voice and data. For example, high-speed Internet connections are available across cellular wireless networks that have implemented high-speed wireless technologies.[29] But the technological innovations that

---

[29] You'll learn about high-speed wireless technologies later on in this chapter.

allow the transmission of both voice and data via wireless across mobile-to-mobile, mobile-to-land, and land-to-mobile connections do not rely on wireless technologies alone. Instead, these vast cellular wireless networks rely on connectivity with the PSTN.

Anatomy of a Cellular Wireless Connection

When a cellular wireless device is turned on, it transmits its identity signal over radio frequency (RF) to the nearest cell tower and receives cell network information on another radio frequency to establish an RF **control channel** between it and the cellular network. The control channel facilitates the exchange of administrative messages such as call initiation, which is the dialing of a number and pressing the Send button; and paging, which is the notification to wireless devices of an incoming call or text message; sleep mode, which tells the cellular device to go into power save mode; caller ID; roaming mode; and there are more.[30]

After a cellular wireless device's identity has been verified and the user has dialed a number and pressed Send, the number is transmitted across the control channel to the cell tower. The cell tower relays the call to the **mobile switching center (MSC),** which then performs two key functions: it instructs the cellular device that is making the call to use a specific set of frequencies known as the **traffic channel** for voice and data communication between the cellular device and the cell tower, and the MSC scans its database to see whether the number being called is within the MSC's cellular network or part of another wireless system. If the call is a mobile-to-mobile call that is within the same cell or within a group of cells that is connected to the same MSC, the MSC switches the call to the destination mobile subscriber, as shown in part **(a)** of Figure 7.20. When the call must connect to a land-based phone or to a cell phone that is part of another cellular network, the MSC routes the call to the PSTN so that the PSTN can connect the call to the appropriate destination. Part **(b)** of Figure 7.20 provides an example.

When cellular wireless subscribers are truly mobile, as in changing locations frequently, the signal strength between the subscriber and a given cell tower fades as the subscriber moves further away from the cell tower. When this happens, new control channels and traffic channels must be established between the wireless caller and an adjacent cell tower to maintain call quality and signaling. This process is known as **call handoff**, and it is performed by the MSC.[31] With call handoff, the MSC monitors the signal strength between subscriber devices and cell towers and transfers control and traffic frequency settings to an adjacent cell tower at the instant the adjacent cell tower can provide a stronger signal. Once call handoff is complete, the resources that were in use in the previous cell are available for other callers.

Cellular Wireless Access Methods

Just like various data network architectures use different methods for accessing data network media, cellular wireless voice networks have implemented different methods of accessing radio frequencies for voice and data transmissions. Sometimes these access methods are referred to as **air interfaces**, and the most common methods in use today are Time Division Multiple Access (TDMA) and Code Division Multiple Access (CDMA). An

control channel
two frequencies working in combination to send and receive administrative information between a cellular device and the cell tower. The control channel is also used to initiate a mobile cellular call or receive a paging message that a call or text message is about to be received.

traffic channel
the set of frequencies that comprise the communications path between the wireless cellular device and the cell tower

call handoff
the process of establishing new control channels and traffic channels between a mobile wireless caller and an adjacent cell tower to maintain call quality and signaling

air interface
another name for a cellular wireless access method. It's the way in which voice and data from a cellular device access the airwaves.

[30] Cellular devices that are serviced by a given cellular provider are part of that cellular company's home location register (HLR). Devices that aren't recognized in the MSC database are known as visitor location register (VLR) numbers, or simply VLRs. HLRs can include the entire national customer base of a cellular provider or they can be segmented by geography. These designations are used for billing purposes.
[31] The cellular world is gradually moving to the term *handover* instead of *handoff*. You might see either term in cellular discussions.

FIGURE 7.20   Anatomy of a Cellular Wireless Call

a. Mobile-to-mobile calls within the same group of cells

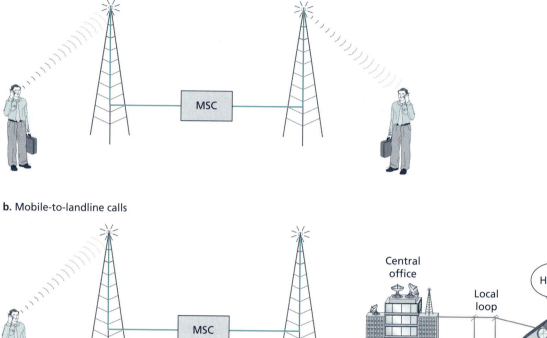

b. Mobile-to-landline calls

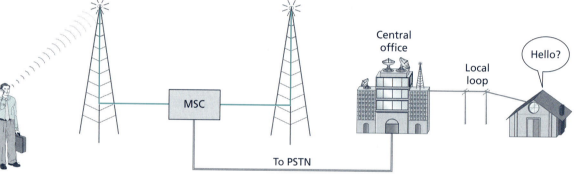

older access method known as Frequency Division Multiple Access (FDMA) was prevalent in the 1980s.

FDMA

Frequency Division Multiple Access (FDMA) is an analog cellular wireless access method that was implemented in test markets in the late 1970s in the United States and became the access method for the first widely deployed cellular wireless network in the early 1980s. This early analog cellular network became known as the Advanced Mobile Phone Service (AMPS).

With FDMA, multiple radio frequencies are available in any given cell of the cellular network, but each cellular call is allocated a specific frequency for the duration of the call. This method worked fine when there weren't a significant number of cellular callers making calls within a given cell, but FDMA could become overloaded and unable to provide calling service if the number of callers equaled or exceeded the number of available frequencies in a given cell. In other words, on busy cells in an FDMA cellular network callers might occasionally have to wait for service until other callers hung up. In addition, adjacent cells could not use the same set of frequencies, which reduced the number of frequencies that any given cell could maintain.

FDMA was not bandwidth efficient. Any silence during a call was wasted bandwidth that potentially could have been used for another voice call or for data. These are two of the reasons why TDMA evolved as a new cellular access method in the late 1980s and early

1990s. Today, FDMA functions as a backup access method on cellular devices that by design implement newer technologies such as TDMA and CDMA as the primary access method.

TDMA

Time Division Multiple Access (TDMA) adds a time dimension to FDMA to make more efficient use of radio frequency bandwidth. Instead of each cellular call being allocated a specific frequency for the duration of a call, TDMA shares a given frequency with a number of callers, and each caller's voice is sampled and digitized and then transmitted for a few milliseconds. Then the next caller's voice is sampled and digitized and transmitted for a few milliseconds on the same frequency. The same process occurs for the third caller on a shared frequency. With TDMA, multiple calls are multiplexed across the same frequency so that each caller shares that frequency with other callers. The calls don't "bump into each other" because the individual calls are separated in time. Deployed in cellular voice networks in the early 1990s, TDMA offered three time slots per frequency, which increased the calling capacity for cellular systems by a factor of three. In addition, the digital nature of TDMA required less power consumption than FDMA so that TDMA phones could operate at 600 milliwatts instead of the 1 to 3 watts required by FDMA phones.[32]

Like FDMA, TDMA had its own inefficiencies. Like FDMA, TDMA wasted portions of the bandwidth, albeit smaller portions than FDMA, such that any silent moments during a call were still wasted portions of the available bandwidth. TDMA also requires that adjacent cells not use the same set of frequencies to prevent call interference. In addition, with TDMA a caller is allocated a time slot for the duration of the call. If the caller initiates a call in one cell but travels outside of the cell calling area so that the call must be handed off to another cell, the call is not guaranteed a time slot in the other cell. If all time slots are being used in the other cell, the call is terminated, and the caller will have to initiate a new call. If no time slots are available when the caller attempts to redial, the caller won't get a connection and will have to try again later.

TDMA by itself is offered by some carriers as a cellular service, but it's becoming more common to see TDMA deployed as the underlying air interface for the **Global System for Mobile Communication (GSM),** one of the major cellular systems in use in the United States and Europe. AT&T, Cingular Wireless, and T-Mobile implement TDMA as the air interface for their GSM networks.

CDMA

Code Division Multiple Access is a wireless access method developed for the U.S. military in the 1960s. CDMA eliminates some of the inefficiencies associated with FDMA and TDMA by spreading a call or data transmission across multiple frequencies. This **direct sequence spread spectrum (DSSS)** encoding technique virtually eliminates the potential for frequency overlap in adjacent cells, so that more frequencies are available per cell across a CDMA cellular network than in FDMA or TDMA cellular networks.[33] In addition, because DSSS spreads a transmission across multiple frequencies, the bandwidth efficiency of each frequency is increased. That is, the number of callers that can simultaneously use a range of radio frequencies for call transmission is increased with CDMA.[34] In addition, CDMA offers an improved method of call handoff and **call signal reflection**

call signal reflection takes place when a transmitted signal is reflected off of an object such as a building or other large physical object

---

[32] In an analog cell signal, any noise introduced during the call could not be filtered out. This required higher wattage in order to deliver acceptable levels of voice quality.

[33] You learned about direct sequence spread spectrum (DSSS) in chapter 3.

[34] CDMA adds overhead to each transmission because the DSSS encoding technique requires additional "chirping" bits with each portion of the transmission on each frequency.

FIGURE 7.21
Cellular Ring Topology

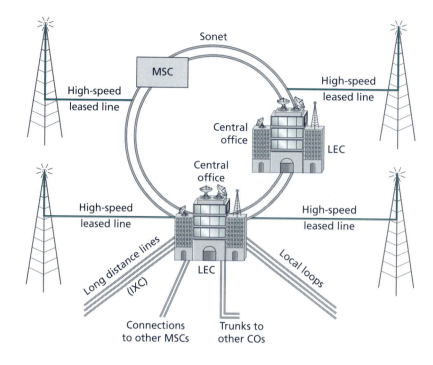

management so that cell phones based on CDMA technology can consume less power.[35] Carriers that offer CDMA cellular service include Verizon and Sprint, and it's commonly deployed as CDMA2000 1x, which is also known as 1xRTT.

Cellular Topologies and Connectivity to the PSTN

In general, the design of a cellular wireless network topology depends on whether **synchronous optical network (SONET)** carrier services are available.[36] In most urban areas SONET rings can be leased from a LEC (generally an ILEC), and the cellular provider installs its MSCs on the SONET rings, as illustrated in Figure 7.21.

Ring Topology

In terms of a cellular wireless network configuration, Figure 7.21 represents a **cellular ring topology** or ring configuration. SONET provides the high-speed transmission characteristics needed for large volumes of voice and data traffic, and the redundant rings associated with SONET deployments provide fault-tolerance if one of the rings is damaged, fails, or otherwise suffers signal degradation.

In Figure 7.21, each cell tower in the wireless cellular network is connected to the leased SONET services via high-speed leased lines such as T-carrier services.[37] The MSC is connected to the LEC CO through the SONET ring, and the LEC CO is connected to other COs in its market and to one or more IXCs that are colocated within the CO. When a cellular subscriber makes a call, the call is time division multiplexed with other cellular calls in the

---

[35] In FDMA and TDMA networks, call signal reflection can result in the call being canceled. CDMA uses a special device called a *rake receiver* to detect and coordinate signal reflections into a single, more powerful signal.

[36] You'll learn the details of SONET technology in chapter 8. For now you can think of SONET as a high-speed optical data transmission service that is provided by a carrier.

[37] You'll learn about T-carrier services in chapter 8. For now, know that T-carrier is a family of high-speed transmission services that are provided by a carrier such as MCI, AT&T, or Sprint. On an order of magnitude, SONET provides transmission rates that are much faster than T-carrier.

FIGURE 7.22   **Cellular Daisy-Chain Topology**

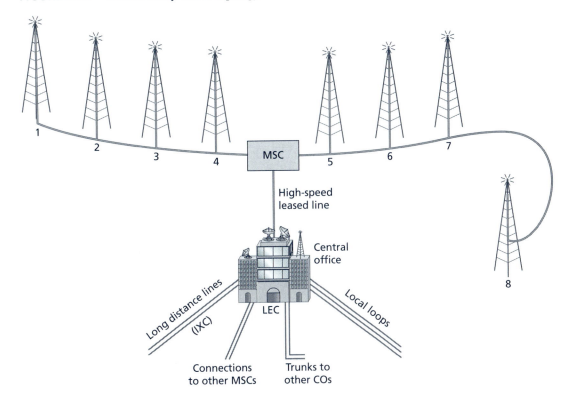

cell tower's base station, transmitted across the high-speed leased line to the SONET ring, connected to the MSC, and then either switched to another cellular user connected to the same MSC or routed to the LEC's central office for transmission through the PSTN. Connections through the PSTN provide connectivity to land-based phones and connections to other cellular networks. From the central office, calls can be connected to their destinations either through a local loop, to another CO, across the IXC's long-distance lines, or through a point-to-point connection with another cellular network.

Daisy-Chain Topology

For geographic regions in which SONET is unavailable, a **daisy-chain topology** can be created. With a daisy-chain configuration, calls received at each tower are multiplexed and transmitted across the high-speed trunks from tower to tower, as shown in Figure 7.22. As a result, the high-speed trunks closest to the MSC service the largest volume of multiplexed calls and require the greatest capacity for call transmission. For example, in Figure 7.22, trunk capacity between tower 4 and the MSC should be greater than the trunk capacity between towers 3 and 4, which should be greater than the trunk capacity between towers 2 and 3. In addition, trunk capacity should be scalable to accommodate the addition of new towers.

Microwave Topologies

For environments that cannot provide SONET or the land-based trunks that create a daisy-chain configuration, cellular providers can design and implement **microwave topologies.** Microwave topologies can be implemented either as a ring or as a daisy-chain configuration. With the microwave ring, as illustrated in Figure 7.23, calls received at each cell tower are multiplexed and transmitted via microwave to a hub site. The hub site maintains a microwave connection with the two adjacent hub sites in the ring as well as a microwave connection with the MSC.

FIGURE 7.23
**Cellular Microwave
Ring Topology**

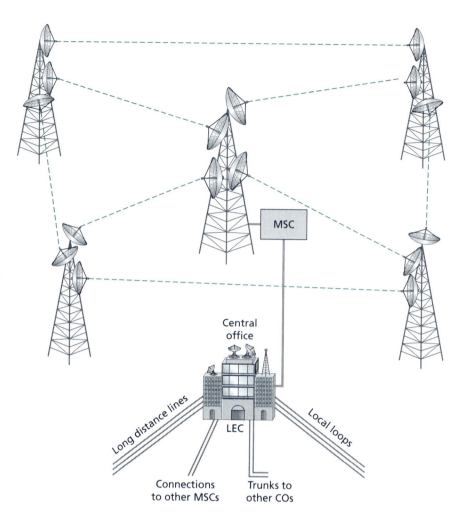

With the microwave daisy-chain configuration, calls received at each cell tower are multiplexed and transmitted via microwave to the next tower in the chain until the signal reaches the MSC. As with the land-based daisy chain, each successive link in the microwave daisy chain requires a higher capacity circuit, only with this configuration it's a microwave circuit instead of a leased carrier circuit.

In both the ring and daisy-chain configurations, the MSC is connected to the PSTN through a LEC CO. The connection between the MSC and the CO can be microwave or a physical media high-speed carrier service.

Cellular Wireless Carrier Services

Wireless carrier services for wide area network connectivity can be divided into two major categories: wireless data services and wireless metropolitan area network (MAN)/wireless wide area network (WAN) services. Here you'll discover wireless data services, while a discussion of wireless MAN and wireless WAN services is reserved for chapter 8.

Wireless Data Services

wireless data services provide a wireless carrier connection between individual remote users and parent organization networks

Wireless data services provide a wireless carrier connection between individual remote users and parent organization networks from virtually any location. Until recently these services have been able to provide only minimal data rates in the range of 25 to 40 Kbps,

TABLE 7.3
Wireless Data Services

Service Type	Bandwidth	Description
GPRS	Typical is 32–40 Kbps; Theoretical is 171.2 Kbps	**General Packet Radio Service (GPRS)** is a radio frequency packet-switched data service that uses the existing Global System for Mobile Communications (GSM) digital cellular communications system for data transmission. In its higher bit rate format, GPRS is considered a step beyond second-generation wireless data communications technology, or 2.5G.
CDMA	Up to 64 Kbps	Code Division Multiple Access (CDMA) is a radio frequency voice and data service that uses spread spectrum techniques to transmit voice and data, with data transmission rates up to 64 Kbps. It's considered a second-generation (2G) wireless data communications technology.
EDGE	Typical is 100–130 Kbps; Theoretical is 384 Kbps	**Enhanced Data Rates for GSM Evolution (EDGE)** increases data rates in Global System for Mobile Communications (GSM) networks. With its initial data rate of under 144 Kbps, EDGE is considered a second-and-a-half generation, or 2.5G wireless data communications technology.
CDMA2000 1X	Typical is 60–80 Kbps; Up to 614 Kbps	**CDMA2000 1X,** or simply CDMA2000, is the third-generation (3G) wireless data communications version of CDMA. Also known as 1xRTT.
CDMA2000 1xEV-DO	384 Kbps–2.4 Mbps	**CDMA2000 1x Evolution-Data Optimized.** An enhancement to CDMA2000 1X that provides for higher data rates. CDMA2000 1xEV-DO is also a 3G wireless data communications technology.
WCDMA	Up to 2 Mbps	**Wideband CDMA (WCDMA)** will likely replace EDGE in the evolution of data networks that ride on top of the GSM digital cellular communications system. WCDMA will also be used in the European wireless data communications network known as the Universal Mobile Telecommunications System, or UMTS. WCDMA is a 3G wireless technology.

but now they're capable of data transmission rates ranging from about 100 Kbps up to 2.4 Mbps, depending on the type of service you need and the amount you're willing to pay. In Table 7.3, you'll see a list of several wireless data services.

Wireless data services are classified in terms of second-generation **(2G),** second-and-a-half-generation **(2.5G),** third-generation **(3G),** and fourth-generation **(4G)** wireless data communications technologies.[38] Second-generation communications technologies incorporated digital encoding for wireless voice and data traffic along with various levels of encryption. Examples include CDMA and GSM. Second-and-a-half-generation wireless technologies extended the 2G systems by providing increases in data rates over existing 2G cellular networks without the implementation of new hardware. Common 2.5G wireless data services include GPRS and EDGE, which are listed in Table 7.3. Third-generation cellular wireless systems provide data transmission rates that meet or exceed 144 Kbps. Wireless data services in the 3G camp include CDMA2000 1X, CDMA2000 1xEV-DO, and WCDMA. Fourth-generation wireless systems are on the horizon and should provide high-speed wireless data rates that meet or exceed 20 Mbps.

---

[38] First-generation (1G) wireless was simply analog, circuit-switched mobile telephony. 1G systems were not designed specifically to accommodate wireless data traffic.

Chapter Summary

- **Business purpose of voice networks.** As with data networks, the business purpose of voice networks is to convey data between points A and B. In some instances voice networks convey only voice traffic while in others they convey data traffic. The trend is toward convergence between voice networks and data networks.

- **Data transmissions over POTS local loops.** Data transmission over POTS local loops is possible with the use of a modem. A modem generates a carrier wave and modulates that carrier wave with the purpose of transmitting data from a computer. Different modulation techniques are applied including amplitude modulation, frequency modulation, and phase modulation. Each modulation presents a signaling opportunity known as a baud, and with each baud, one or more bits can be transmitted on the modulated carrier wave. A higher baud rate, expressed as the number of signaling events per second combined with the number of bits per baud result in the rate of data transmission, represented as bits per second.

- **Business purpose and features of a PBX.** The implementation of a PBX has two major financial implications. One is to reduce the capital outlay of the telephone company for local loop installations to the business that installs the PBX. The other is to reduce the installation and recurring charges to the subscribing organization. Features include automatic attendant, voice mail, call coverage, hoteling, find-me, interactive voice response, and system administration.

- **PBX technology, switching topologies, and design considerations.** PBX technologies can be analog, digital, IP-based, integrated with CTI, or a combination of all of these. PBX designs use PCM and TDM much like local exchange carriers provide in their central offices. The switching topologies include centralized, distributed, and dispersed, with each fitting a specific business need. Design considerations accommodate the size of an organization and generally follow a specific topology to meet an organization's requirements.

- **Business purpose of an IP-PBX.** IP-PBX meets the business needs of reduced capital expenditures on two different network infrastructures—voice and data, and the reduction of voice network administrative cost by merging voice traffic onto highly efficient and cost effective data networks.

- **IP-PBX converged and packet-switched topologies.** An IP-PBX converged topology utilizes an existing Ethernet data network infrastructure to transport IP voice traffic to IP telephones connected to the data network and to transport IP voice traffic between IP-PBX systems. An IP packet-switched topology, which is also known as a client/server IP-PBX or VoIP system can be integrated with legacy PBX voice networks or can operate on an IP Ethernet data network without the traditional PBX cabinets or infrastructure.

- **Voice over IP.** VoIP is the combination of hardware, software, and protocols that support voice communications over IP networks. Hardware generally includes servers, data networking connectivity components, and IP telephones. Software includes the programs that provide the services common to PBX voice networks. Protocols include the H.323 suite, SIP, MGCP, MEGACO, RTP, and RTCP.

- **CTI business purpose and features.** CTI is the combination of hardware and software that integrates the capabilities of an organization's voice network with the information on the organization's data network. It can provide many of the same features as PBX and VoIP systems, but does not provide voice and data network convergence. Instead CTI is designed to provide information access from a data network by running one or more computer applications that can service caller requests that originate on the voice network.

- **Cellular wireless voice networks and the anatomy of a cellular wireless connection.** Cellular wireless voice networks provide subscribers with the kinds of services that previously were available only with land-based telephone systems connected to the PSTN. With cellular wireless calls, voice and/or data traffic is transmitted from a cellular wireless device to a cell tower, which relays the data to the mobile switching center, or MSC, which, in turn, relays the voice or data to either another cellular device within the same cell or group of cells or to a land-based phone or other cellular network through the PSTN.

- **Cellular wireless access methods.** Access methods for cellular wireless include FDMA, TDMA, and CDMA. FDMA is an older analog technology that originally supported the AMPS cellular network. Today, it functions as a backup access method for newer technologies such as TDMA and CDMA. TDMA can transmit multiple calls across each radio frequency by time sequencing the transmissions. TDMA is implemented as the air interface for GSM networks owned by AT&T, Cingular Wireless, and T-Mobile. CDMA uses direct sequence spread spectrum technology to transmit voice and data across numerous frequencies. It's very bandwidth efficient and offers improved call handoff and call signal reflection management for reduced power consumption by cellular devices.

- **Cellular wireless topologies.** Cellular wireless topologies include ring, daisy-chain, and microwave. A ring topology has MSCs connected to a SONET ring. SONET provides the high-speed transmission required for large volumes of network traffic. Daisy-chain topologies link cell towers together in a chain using high-speed trunks. A microwave topology utilizes high-speed microwave transmission technologies to create either a ring or daisy-chain of towers connected via microwave transmission.

- **Cellular wireless carrier services.** Cellular wireless carrier services provide wireless cellular connections between individual remote users and their parent organizations from virtually any location. Wireless data services are represented as 2G, 2.5G, 3G, and 4G services and can provide data transmission rates from low Kbps to 2 or more Mbps.

Key Terms

Questions

1. What was the original business purpose of the telephone exchange?

2. Describe the relationship among local loop, telephone exchange, central office, local exchange carrier, and the plain old telephone system. How are calls transmitted between central offices? How are long-distance calls handled?

3. Discuss how digital data from computers can be transmitted across analog phone lines.

4. What is a private branch exchange? What business purpose does it server? What kinds of services are available with a PBX? How can a traditional (non-IP) PBX be integrated with a data network?

5. Discuss the relationship of time division multiplexing and pulse-coded modulation as it relates to voice transmission through a PBX system.

6. From a business perspective, is it practical to incorporate wireless voice and data communications with PBX systems? Why or why not?

7. Compare and contrast the three main PBX switching topologies. Be sure your discussion integrates the terms *TDM bus, highway bus,* and, of course, *centralized, distributed,* and *dispersed topologies.*

8. Describe and discuss converged PBX topology. Make sure you include a discussion of design and configuration issues.

9. What is voice over IP? What are the business drivers behind it? What are the protocols involved with VoIP and what are their functions? Why is it important to integrate a high quality of service (QoS) with VoIP?

10. What is computer telephony integration? Describe one major business driver in support of CTI. Are there any similarities between CTI and VoIP? Are there any differences?

11. Describe three cellular wireless access methods and list the carriers that implement two of these methods.

12. In your own words, describe three cellular topologies. Where would it make sense to use each of these topologies?

13. What are wireless data services? Which service types are 2G technologies? 2.5G? 3G? Why are they ranked as they are?

Research Activities

1. Using the search tools available to you, identify three modem manufacturers and describe the technologies behind their highest speed modems. Is the quoted transmission rate truly achievable over a local loop? Why or why not?

2. Using the search tools available to you, identify three major PBX companies and describe their PBX product lines, including brand names, models/types, features, and target markets for which these systems are intended. Do these companies offer traditional PBX as well as IP-PBX systems? Do their systems support analog as well as digital telephones? Can any of these PBX systems support data transmission across the PBX infrastructure? Do any of these vendors sell and support VoIP and/or computer telephony? What are their VoIP and CTI product offerings and what features are available with these systems? Do any of these vendors provide technical documentation for their products? Describe examples of this documentation and summarize the contents.

3. Using the search tools available to you, identify at least three different real-world examples of PBX implementations, and summarize the business and technology case. What benefits did the customer derive from the implementation?

4. In a follow-up to Research Activity 3, identify at least three different real-world examples of PBX and/or VoIP systems that were integrated with a data network, and summarize the business and technology case. What benefits did the customer derive from the implementation of a converged network?

5. Using the search tools available to you, identify at least two different real-world examples of VoIP systems that have implemented H.323 as the upper-layer protocol of choice. Why did they choose this technology? What benefits has it delivered to the customer? Were there legacy telephony issues that forced them toward an H.323 solution?

6. In contrast to Research Activity 5, identify two different real-world examples of VoIP systems that have implemented SIP as the upper-layer protocol of choice. Why did these companies favor SIP over H.323?

7. Using the search tools available to you, identify two major reasons that organizations implement CTI, and then identify at least two real-world examples of companies that have successfully implemented CTI. How do they use it and why? What benefits have these companies derived from the implementation of CTI?

8. Using the search tools available to you, identify three cellular service providers and identify the access methods and service types that they provide to their customers. Have any of these providers recently upgraded their nationwide cellular service to a new access method? To a new service type? What benefits does this new method or service provide to their customers?

9. Using the search tools available to you, identify an application other than Microsoft NetMeeting that utilizes H.323 or SIP for audio- and videoconferencing.

HANDS-ON ACTIVITIES

1. Identify the type of phone system that your school or workplace is using. Is it a PBX? Is it a VoIP implementation? Is it a combination? Is CTI involved in any way? How did the system evolve? Are there any plans for expansion or conversion of the system to another technology? Are there any plans for convergence of the voice and data networks? What business drivers are motivating the decision to converge or keep the two networks separate?

2. Identify a LEC (either ILEC or CLEC) or cable company that provides VoIP service in your area. What requirements must be met for you to subscribe to this service? How would you connect to this service? What charges can you expect? What voice quality does the service provider guarantee with their VoIP service?

Mini Case Studies

LAKESIDE METAL STAMPINGS—PART 5

The owner of Lakeside Metal Stampings is convinced that there is a market for the company's products outside of the company's regional market and has recently hired three additional sales reps to develop new territories. The reps will be based out of their homes and each of them will be responsible for a substantial geographic distance that will keep them on the road from four to five days a week. To keep up to date with the new business that the reps are certain to develop, the owner wants the reps to have immediate communication access to the home office. In addition, the owner wants the new reps to be able to transmit drawings and purchase orders directly from their cars, so that the shop can respond to engineering requests and new orders as promptly as possible.

Once again, the owner has contacted you to ask your opinion on what the company should do. Based on the information presented in this chapter, how would you advise the owner on a technology solution to meet the the company's current business needs?

SCHOOL DISTRICT PBX DESIGN

A suburban school district in the Rochester, New York, area has a high school building, a middle school building, an elementary school building, and a district office that is attached to the elementary school, and all of these facilities are interconnected by a Gigabit Ethernet data network. In addition, the district has legacy PBX systems at the district office/elementary school location, the middle school, and the high school that are interconnected using high-speed trunks that they lease from their local exchange carrier.

As part of their spending plan for the next school year, the district is contemplating converging their voice network onto their data network. Based on the information presented in this chapter, how would you advise the school district board members on a course of action? What benefits can they expect if they decide to merge their voice and data networks? What technology options are available to them? What are the disadvantages of convergence?

Based on further conversations with the district's director of information technology, you and she have decided to develop two plans to present to the district business officer. One plan will allow them to integrate their existing PBX systems with their IP Ethernet data network. The other plan will eliminate their existing PBX system in favor of a VoIP system that runs on their existing data network. Describe each of these plans in detail. Your written plan should include (1) drawings that represent the current PBX systems and the existing data network, including PBX equipment and data network equipment; (2) drawings that represent a PBX system integrated with the data network, including PBX and data network hardware; (3) drawings that represent a converged voice and data network, including voice network hardware and data network hardware; and (4) a detailed description of each of the two proposed systems with benefits of each. (*Hint:* Make an assumption regarding the existing PBX topology. That is, choose one of the topologies you learned about in this chapter, and use that as your existing PBX system. For the data network, assume that the district has implemented a three-layer network backbone like the ones you learned about in chapter 4.)

CHAPTER
Eight

Chapter Overview and Objectives

Wide area networks (WANs) provide the services and connections that allow organizations to interconnect their local area networks into a unified data communications infrastructure that can span vast geographic distances. With modern wide area network technologies, data that is stored halfway around the world can be accessed instantaneously, and employees at different and distant offices can exchange ideas, share information, and collaborate on projects as quickly and efficiently as the business need requires.

In this chapter we explore the wide area network services and technologies that support the business need for data communications between distant locations. More specifically, by the end of this chapter you will be able to

- Define circuit switching, describe circuit-switched architecture, and identify and describe different types of circuit-switched carrier services.

- Define dedicated circuit, and list and describe dedicated-circuit carrier services.

- Discuss packet-switched networks, and list and describe different types of packet-switched carrier services.

- Identify how the Internet can be used as a wide area network backbone.

- List and describe other high-speed carrier services.

- Identify and describe different types of multiplexing.

- Discuss wide area network management in terms of quality of service, circuit capacity, and circuit upgrades.

Wide Area Networks

Chapter Outline

Connectivity to Remote Networks

Data Communication through the Carrier

WAN Management Issues

CONNECTIVITY TO REMOTE NETWORKS

When data needs to travel beyond the boundaries of a LAN, organizations implement **campus area networks (CANs), metropolitan area networks (MANs),** and **wide area networks (WANs).** Figure 8.1 provides a simple example of each.

Although technically not a WAN, a CAN extends the reach of each individual LAN in an organization's office complex. With a CAN, all the buildings on a common office campus, business campus, or university campus, are interconnected using the same kinds of hardware and networking technologies that you would use in a LAN. In addition, all the components, including switches, routers, and cabling are owned and maintained by the organization.

Metropolitan area networks and wide area networks can be designed to extend the reach of individual LANs and can serve to interconnect multiple LANs and CANs that are owned by the same organization. An organization might have several LANs distributed across multiple buildings that the organization may or may not own, and the proximity of the buildings

FIGURE 8.1   Campus Area Network, Metropolitan Area Network, and Wide Area Network Examples

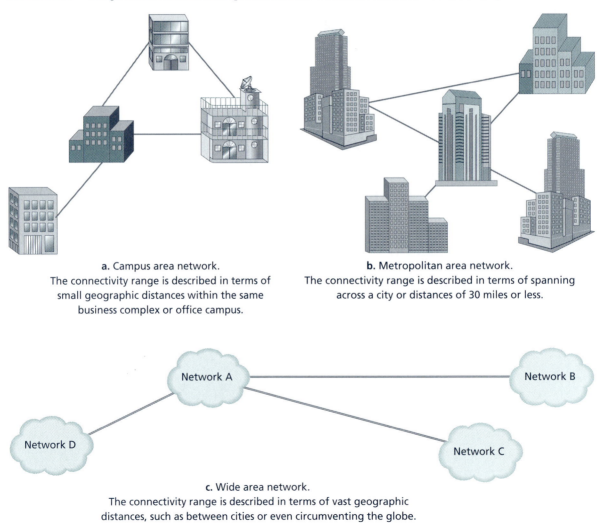

a. Campus area network.
The connectivity range is described in terms of small geographic distances within the same business complex or office campus.

b. Metropolitan area network.
The connectivity range is described in terms of spanning across a city or distances of 30 miles or less.

c. Wide area network.
The connectivity range is described in terms of vast geographic distances, such as between cities or even circumventing the globe.

might vary from a several yards to several miles. Regardless of whether the organization owns the buildings, the distances between buildings might be substantial enough to prevent the organization from installing its own cabling.[1] Instead, organizations contract with a carrier such as MCI, Sprint, AT&T, Global Crossing, Verizon Wireless, SBC Communications, or any of a long list of other carriers for one or more **carrier services.** The carrier services provide the media and delivery mechanism for transmitting data across vast distances between the organization's LANs.

Network administrators and business managers must always be vigilant of the amounts and types of data that need to be exchanged between remote locations as well as the cost of transmitting that data across a MAN or WAN. If your organization has an office in Boston and another in Chicago, each location is likely to have one or more LANs that handle the exchange of data within each office. If you need to exchange information between the two offices, the distance between the two cities would prevent you from installing your own connections between your LANs, and the cost of establishing a satellite wireless link would probably be prohibitive. Instead you would contact a carrier and describe the types and volume of data that you send and receive on a regular basis. If the volume of data is light enough and the type of data is fairly simple, you might be able to use a computer and a modem on each end for the data transfer.[2] On the other hand, if your organization needs to transmit large volumes of data between different locations, or if the types of data are complex and time-sensitive, or if you need to interconnect an entire network so that network operating systems, applications, and numerous types of data can be interconnected between the two locations, you will need to implement some type of high-speed link. That is where carrier services come in to play.

carrier service
a high-speed data transmission service that can be provided by a carrier company such as MCI, Sprint, AT&T, or other carrier company

Circuit-Switched Carrier Services

Many types of carrier services are available in our modern world of data communications, including **circuit-switched services,** dedicated circuits, wireless solutions, and several newer services that are rapidly gaining momentum in the data communications marketplace. One of the major categories of services you might choose in connecting two remote LANs is circuit switching. **Circuit switching** is a communications method that creates a dedicated communications path between points A and B for the exclusive use of the end nodes for the duration of the connection. In general, circuit switching doesn't offer extremely high-speed connectivity between remote locations, but it does offer data transmission rates that range from modem dial-up speeds of 28.8 Kbps to 56 Kbps, to low-end broadband data rates of 1.544 Mbps.

circuit switching
a communications method that creates a dedicated communications path between points A and B for the exclusive use of points A and B for the duration of the connection

You might choose to implement a circuit-switched service for your organization if you're looking for a low-to-medium-cost data transmission service through a carrier or if your data transmission requirements between remote networks are mostly text-based and don't require a continuous connection.

circuit
the connection between two points. In data communications, a circuit provides connectivity between two communicating devices, and a switched circuit provides a temporary pathway between remote networks that lasts for the duration of the data transmission.

Architecture

First of all, a **circuit** is nothing more than a connection between two points. In the case of data communications and networks, a circuit is the electrical, optical, or wireless connection

---

[1] In a city, especially, it's difficult for organizations other than municipalities and carriers to obtain the necessary easements and rights-of-way to install their own cabling through underground tunnels let alone get the permits to dig up streets or sidewalks to install their own cabling.

[2] Simple in this context implies text and perhaps small graphics files. Modems do not scale well to data types such as streaming media, large graphics files, or any types of data that require real-time interaction between points A and B.

FIGURE 8.2

**LAN-to-LAN
Connectivity through
the PSTN**

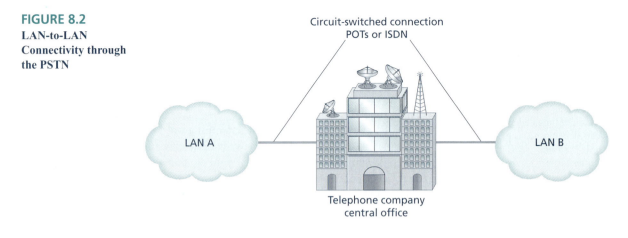

between two users or two LANs. To say that a circuit is switched means that the connection between two remote locations might follow one path today and another path tomorrow. Switched circuits are temporary and last for as long as the users remain connected.

All circuit-switched services use the **public switched telephone network (PSTN).** The PSTN is comprised of the telephone networks that are operated by carriers such as MCI, Sprint, AT&T, and others. When you implement a circuit-switched service, the PSTN provides the infrastructure that allows you to make a connection between locations. Figure 8.2 provides an example of this infrastructure.

In Figure 8.2, users in LAN A dial a telephone number of a computer in LAN B to make a temporary connection. Within the PSTN, the telephone company establishes the circuit that connects the two networks, users transfer their data, and the call is then completed. Upon completion of the call, the circuit is disconnected, and further data cannot be transmitted until the next time users dial the number and a new connection is established.

One advantage of a circuit-switched connection is its flexibility. You can establish a connection simply by dialing the number of the computer or network to which you want to connect and your computers can continue to exchange information until you disconnect the call. Another advantage is that the circuit-switched architecture shifts the burden of LAN-to-LAN data transmission to the carrier; you don't have to build a WAN infrastructure to facilitate data transmission across vast distances.

The major disadvantage to most circuit-switched connections as a LAN-to-LAN connectivity solution is that most network operating systems (NOSs) and network applications are not designed to wait for the **call setup** associated with circuit-switched connections. If your data transmission requirements are infrequent or can be batched together for transfer at various times throughout the day, then circuit switching can work for your data transmission needs between remote LANs. However, with modern network operating systems that utilize directory databases such as e-Directory with Novell or Active Directory with the Microsoft Server Family, the network operating system is configured so that various remote locations must stay in constant contact with each other. NOSs are not designed to accommodate call setup times.[3] Instead, modern NOSs require a continuous connection that is free of the wait time associated with call setup in circuit-switched carrier networks.

call setup

the process of waiting for a dial tone when a phone is taken off hook, dialing the telephone number of the remote location, waiting for the call to be answered, and ultimately the answering of the call at the remote location

---

[3] Circuit-switched connections can be used as backup connections to dedicated circuits. If a dedicated circuit goes down, the circuit-switched service establishes a temporary dedicated connection between remote networks. Once the connection is made, the NOS can exchange information interactively between locations. This switched service is expensive, however, because you'll pay based on time connected rather than a flat-rate per month associated with dedicated circuits.

Another disadvantage to circuit-switched carrier services is that you're charged for every minute you're connected, even if you're not transferring information. That is one of the reasons that circuit-switched networks are generally used for sporadic and infrequent data exchange. If you use a switched circuit to maintain a constant connection between remote locations, the costs associated with that connection could become exorbitant. Instead and, if your data transmission needs warrant it, you might be better served by implementing an alternative connectivity solution such as a dedicated circuit or a packet-switched service.[4]

The Plain Old Telephone System

The **plain old telephone system (POTS)** is the dial-up analog telephone service that you might be using to connect to the Internet or to connect to another computer located in a remote location of your organization. POTS was originally designed for voice traffic, but through the use of modems and other analog-to-digital data conversion devices, computers at one location can use regular telephone lines to connect to computers at other locations.

POTS uses the PSTN for both voice and data transmission, and if you're using POTS in your organization, you'll pay a fee for use based on the time the circuit is connected and the distance between locations. POTS is convenient for simple data transfers between computers, but its low bandwidth capability (up to 56 Kbps) is generally insufficient as a wide area network connection between LANs.

ISDN

Integrated Services Digital Network (ISDN) is a digital circuit-switched service that you can obtain through a telephone company or carrier. Although not appearing in commercial business use until much later, ISDN was originally conceived in the 1960s as a digital replacement for the analog phone lines that connect your home or business to the phone company's central office facility.[5] ISDN has many of the same features as a regular telephone line; that is, you hear a dial tone, dial a number, wait for the call to be answered, and so on. The early appeal of ISDN over regular analog phone lines was its ability to accommodate multiple types of communication traffic such as voice and data, text, graphics, video, audio, and any other source material that can be converted into a digital signal for transmission over existing phone lines. In addition, an ISDN line could accommodate the connection of several devices to the line without interference among those devices. The problem was early telephone switches from competing companies didn't implement the ISDN standard in the same way, which made it nearly impossible to deploy ISDN nationally as a replacement for analog phone lines.[6] In addition, digitizing the connection between people's homes and the telephone company's central office facilities would have meant replacing every telephone in every home across the United States. Since AT&T owned all of the phones in that era, the costs of replacing all analog telephones with digital phones, or adding analog-to-digital converters for existing analog phones, most likely prevented ISDN from evolving into a mass-market service.

Today, ISDN is available as a digital circuit-switched service from telephone companies, Internet service providers, and other carriers. Implementation generally requires additional connectivity hardware to connect to the PSTN, although you can purchase ISDN-ready devices. For starters, there are two types of equipment that can connect to the ISDN network: digital devices such as ISDN telephones, computers, scanners, faxes, and other equipment,

---

[4] You'll learn about dedicated-circuit networks and packet-switched networks later in this chapter.
[5] You might recall from chapter 7 that these twisted-pair telephone wires that connect a residence or office to the telephone company's central office is known as a local loop.
[6] The differences between analog and digital data transmission were discussed in chapter 1.

FIGURE 8.3
ISDN Connectivity

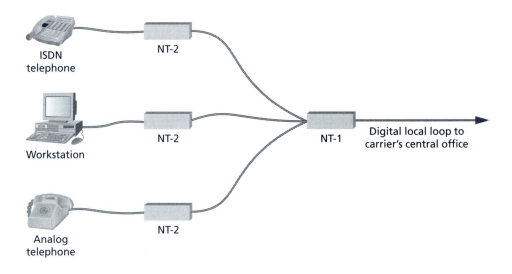

and non-ISDN devices such as regular analog telephones. To connect these devices, you'll need to install two types of network terminators. Also, for analog equipment you'll need a terminal adapter that converts analog signals into a digital signal that ISDN can understand.

In Figure 8.3, you'll see a computer, an ISDN-ready telephone, and a regular analog telephone. The computer and the ISDN telephone require network terminators (NT-2 and NT-1) to connect to the ISDN switch at the carrier's central office facility, and the analog telephone requires network terminators as well as a terminal adapter. The NT-2 network terminators manage ISDN protocols that handle call setup, control, status, and disconnect information.[7] NT-1 terminators allow multiple devices to connect to the ISDN circuit. Terminal adapters provide the circuitry that converts analog information to digital ISDN signals. From a practical standpoint, terminal adapter and NT-2 functions are often consolidated within a single device or on a single circuit board that can be installed in a computer or included in an ISDN phone's electronics. The NT-1 can function as a stand-alone device into which numerous ISDN devices can be connected.[8]

ISDN is available as **basic rate interface (BRI)** or as **primary rate interface (PRI).** Basic rate interface provides an organization with two 64 Kbps digital transmission channels known as B or bearer channels, and one 16 Kbps channel that is known as the D or delta channel. The bearer channels are used to carry data, voice, and video. The delta channel is used for call setup, phone number identification, and other signals specific to ISDN network management. With basic rate interface, each bearer channel has its own phone number, but you can choose to bond the two bearer channels so that the two channels are collectively identified as one telephone number. Bonded together in this way, an organization can implement BRI ISDN for an effective bandwidth of 128 Kbps.

Primary rate interface is designed for higher bandwidth requirements. It is comprised of twenty-three 64 Kbps bearer channels and one 64 Kbps D channel, giving it an effective bandwidth that is nearly comparable to a T1 circuit.[9,10]

---

[7] Call setup, status, and disconnect information are managed across an ISDN channel known as a D channel, which you'll learn about shortly.

[8] In European countries, the function of the NT-1 network terminator is included in the carrier's service to the customer. In the United States, the NT-1 is an electronic device that is owned and installed at the customer's premises.

[9] In European countries, PRI ISDN is comprised of 30 bearer channels and one D channel.

[10] You'll learn about T1 circuits a little later in this chapter.

In general, ISDN is not used extensively by businesses as a primary WAN connection because of competing technologies that offer comparable or faster service for the same or lower cost. At the same time, ISDN has found a home as a data-communications medium where alternative services such as cable and digital subscriber lines are unavailable.[11] In addition, ISDN is sometimes implemented as a backup to higher speed WAN services such as dedicated carrier services in the event that the higher speed service is unexpectedly interrupted or unavailable.

Dedicated-Circuit Carrier Services

dedicated circuit
an exclusive communications channel provided by a carrier between two remote locations

One of the types of carrier services you can consider when your organization's data transmissions between remote locations are relatively continuous is a dedicated circuit. A **dedicated circuit** provides an exclusive communications channel between two remote locations. Sometimes called a point-to-point connection, a dedicated circuit provides dedicated bandwidth per your requirements and specifications, and the carrier charges you an installation fee plus a flat monthly rate regardless of how much you use the circuit.

For organizations with large and continuous amounts of data exchange between remote locations, dedicated circuits can provide a cost-effective data communications solution. Because dedicated circuits are always on, data transfer is immediate; that is, no dial-up is required to make a connection. A dedicated circuit can be an analog voice-grade line with a modem at each end, but this type of dedicated circuit will generally be limited to a bandwidth of 56 Kbps or less. For higher capacity dedicated circuits, you'll need to specify a digital services circuit, such as a T-carrier connection or an optical carrier circuit such as SONET.

multiplexing
a method of combining multiple separate signals into a composite signal for transmission across a communications channel

Note, however, that dedicated circuit does not mean that the carrier installs a new line or cabling throughout its facilities specifically for your organization's use. Instead, dedicated circuit means that you are guaranteed an exclusive communications channel through the carrier's existing communications infrastructure, usually over existing cabling, and your dedicated circuit will in all likelihoosd be **multiplexed** with other circuits throughout the carrier's and other carriers' networks.[12]

T-Carrier Circuits

T-carrier circuits have been in existence since the early 1960s. They evolved as high-capacity circuits that telephone companies used for transmitting multiple telephone calls across twisted-pair copper wires between central offices.[13] As the role of computers grew in the business world in the mid-1960s and demand arose for the electronic transfer of information between business locations, telephone companies began offering **T-carrier service** to external organizations. Over time, different levels of T-carrier circuits provided businesses with data rates that would suit specific requirements.

Two common implementations of T-carrier services are T1 and T3 circuits, frequently referred to as *T1 lines* and *T3 lines*. A T1 line is a digital circuit that provides bandwidth of 1.544 Mbps. Also defined as a **digital signal 1 (DS1) circuit,** a T1 line can be used exclusively for data, or it can be divided into twenty-four 64 Kbps digital channels, also known as *DS0 circuits* or *DS0 channels,* to accommodate voice transmissions.[14] Depending on the

---

[11] You'll learn about several digital subscriber line services and cable services later in this chapter.

[12] You'll discover the details of multiplexing later in this chapter.

[13] The European equivalent of T-carrier is E-carrier, although comparable E-carrier circuits have different transmission rates than T-carrier circuits. For example, E1 circuits provide 2.048 Mbps and E3 circuits provide 34.368 Mbps.

[14] Although the bandwidth of a T1 line is 1.544 Mbps, if you add up the 64 Kbps bandwidths across all 24 channels, the sum will be 1.536 Mbps, not 1.544 Mbps. The 8 Kbps difference is attributable to circuit overhead applied by the carrier to provide control signals.

TABLE 8.1

T-Carrier Services

T-Carrier Type	Data Rate	Digital Signal Designation
FracT1	64 Kbps per channel up to a full T1	Multiples of DS0
T1	1.544 Mbps	DS1
FracT3	1.544 Mbps per channel up to a full T3	Multiples of DS1
T3	44.736 Mbps	DS3

Note: T-carrier services are frequently described in terms of their digital services level, or DS level. These DS levels correspond to the T-carrier type so that DS1 = T1 = 1.544 Mbps, DS2 = T2 = 6.312 Mbps, and DS3 = T3 = 44.736 Mbps.

needs of the organization, you can configure a T1 circuit with several DS0 channels allocated to voice and the remaining channels allocated to data.

If your organization's data and voice requirements don't add up to a full T1 line, you can usually lease a specific number of channels, known as fractional T1 service, or simply FracT1, or even FracT, from your local exchange carrier (LEC). Pricing for FracT1s is generally less than the cost of a full T1 because there is less bandwidth, but the installation and setup costs could run about the same. Common implementations of FracT1s are 128 Kbps, 256 Kbps, 384 Kbps, 512 Kbps, and 768 Kbps, but other combinations are possible. At some point the cost between the FracT1 service and a full T1 becomes so close that it makes sense to implement the full T1. The LEC can provide the details of cost break points for each level of FracT1 service.

T3 lines, which are also designated as *DS3 circuits,* provide a digital transmission rate of 44.736 Mbps, or the equivalent of 28 T1 circuits. If required for voice transmissions, T3 circuits can be divided into a maximum of 672 different DS0 circuits, or you can order FracT3 services, which are generally offered in increments of 1.544 Mbps (T1 equivalents), such as 3 Mbps, 6 Mbps, 9 Mbps, 12 Mbps, 15 Mbps, and so on, although other FracT3 data rates are available depending on the needs of your business and how the carrier segments its T3 services. Table 8.1 provides a list of common T-carrier services.

If you decide to implement a T-carrier service, you can expect to pay a one-time installation charge for the connection and an ongoing monthly flat-rate fee. There is no restriction on the amount of data transmitted; you'll pay the same flat rate per month regardless of how much data is transmitted across the circuit.

So why would you choose a T-carrier circuit to connect remote LANs? For starters, the capacity of the circuit might be necessary to support the volume of data transmitted. Your business might require a dedicated digital communications channel that's always available.[15] You want your organization to have exclusive access to the circuit, which enhances the security of your data transmissions. You don't have to worry about being billed for the amount of connection time. In addition, with a T-carrier service you can allocate one or more 64 Kbps chunks of the circuit to voice transmission between locations. Or if you're using some type of digital voice service within your organization, you can transmit voice traffic along with the data traffic. And generally with a T-carrier circuit, the carrier provides constant monitoring of the circuit 24 hours per day, seven days per week so that you don't have to worry about the condition of the circuit.

To connect a LAN to a T-carrier circuit, you'll need to purchase a CSU/DSU.[16] A **CSU/DSU** is the device that interfaces between your local area network's router and the

[15] Always available in this context means you don't have to dial a telephone number to establish the connection.
[16] *CSU* is short for channel service unit and *DSU* is short for data service unit. It is fairly common, however, to refer to a T1 CSU/DSU as simply a CSU.

FIGURE 8.4
CSU/DSU Interface

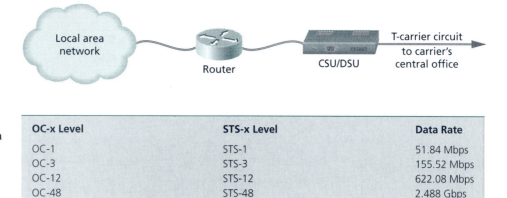

TABLE 8.2
Optical Carrier Data
Rates

OC-x Level	STS-x Level	Data Rate
OC-1	STS-1	51.84 Mbps
OC-3	STS-3	155.52 Mbps
OC-12	STS-12	622.08 Mbps
OC-48	STS-48	2.488 Gbps
OC-192	STS-192	9.953 Gbps
OC-768	STS-768	38.486 Gbps

T-carrier circuit that the carrier brings to your organization's offices. In Figure 8.4, you'll see a CSU/DSU sitting between a router and the T1 line that connects an organization to the carrier's central office.

A CSU/DSU is usually one device, but it provides dual functionality. The CSU is used for line (channel) testing by the carrier as well as for transmitting the T-carrier digital signals between the T-carrier circuit and the DSU. The DSU does the actual data conversion between your network and the digital T-carrier circuit and vice versa. In other words, the DSU reformats data from your LAN into T-carrier frames for outbound transmissions and reformats T-carrier frames into LAN data for inbound transmissions.

SONET

SONET is short for **Synchronous Optical Network,** an ANSI standard for high-speed data communication over fiber-optic cables.[17] Data rates for SONET networks are defined in terms of their multiples of the standardized **Optical Carrier** (OC-*x*) levels or in terms of their Synchronous Transport Signal (STS-*x*) levels as listed in Table 8.2.[18]

SONET is deployed as a system of rings throughout the United States, as depicted in Figure 8.5. With this ring format, SONET is able to provide businesses with a redundant data path that can act as a backup data communications channel in the event that the primary pathway is damaged or unavailable. In the event of a primary SONET circuit failure, transition to the secondary pathway is virtually immediate, occurring within millionths of a second, so that there is no downtime in the subscriber's data communications channel.

To access a SONET ring, your organization's offices must be within range of a carrier's SONET serving office. If your office is within a specified distance, the carrier can connect you as a node on the SONET ring. If you're not within the specified distance, the carrier can connect you to the SONET ring with an alternative dedicated circuit, such as a T1, T3, or even a packet-switched service. In this latter case, your connection to the SONET ring will be limited to the digital signal (DS) data rates that you lease from the carrier, but your

---

[17] The European equivalent of SONET is Synchronous Digital Hierarchy (SDH). Data rates correspond one for one with the optical carrier data rates of SONET making optical links between U.S. and European standards seamless.

[18] *STS* actually refers to the electrical component of SONET; that is, the framing and multiplexing of data from the electronic or digital world in preparation for transport as an optical carrier signal. A detailed technical explanation of STS is beyond the scope of this book.

FIGURE 8.5
SONET Ring
Infrastructure

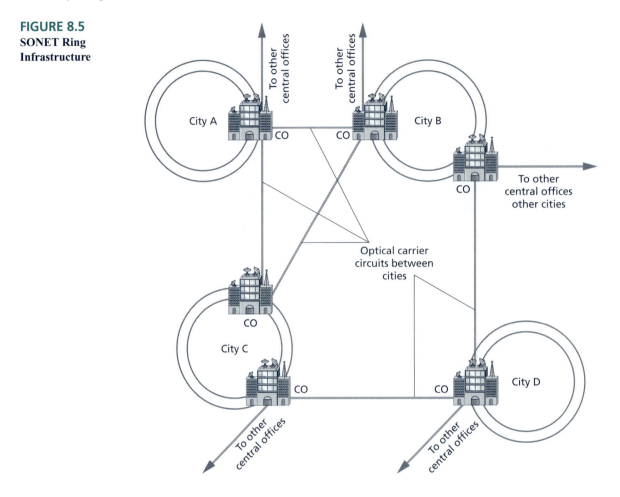

backbone between business locations will be provided by the SONET infrastructure and will benefit from the scalability of bandwidth that SONET offers.

Packet-Switched Carrier Services

The types of carrier services that you've learned about so far include circuit-switched services and dedicated circuits. With each of these types of carrier services, an organization has exclusive use of the communications channel between remote locations. Data packets flow from point A to point B, and any data that is sent across the circuit belongs only to the subscriber organization. There is no sharing of the circuit; it's a private data highway for the sole use of the subscriber.

From a historical perspective, the switched and dedicated circuits that provide these private data channels were originally designed to carry only voice traffic. With the increasing use of computers in the 1960s and 1970s, however, businesses began to use the PSTN for data transmissions. As the demand for data communication continued to grow, telephone companies began adding circuit capacity in the form of switched circuits to accommodate lower end data transmission needs and T-carrier services for businesses that had higher speed needs.

The resulting need for expanded capacity in switched and dedicated circuits was a capital-intensive solution. Each time a business wanted to establish data communications between two remote locations, either total switched-circuit capacity had to be increased, or the telephone company had to install one or more new, dedicated circuits. These solutions were expensive not only because of the investment in the physical infrastructure, but there

Applied Historical **Tidbit**

equal access
required AT&T to provide access to its long-distance circuits for all long-distance companies on terms equal to AT&T's access. Equal Access was one of the requirements set forth in a Department of Justice (DOJ) judgment against AT&T known as the 1982 Consent Decree or more commonly known as the Modified Final Judgment (MFJ). Equal Access took effect in the deregulated telecommunications industry in 1984.

When the first major deregulation of the telecommunications industry forced AT&T to break apart in 1984 into seven Regional Bell Operating Companies (RBOCs) and one long-distance company, competition was thrust upon the telecommunications industry. Two additional long-distance telecommunications companies—MCI and Sprint—were also allowed to compete in the long-distance marketplace.

As part of the newly allowed competition, AT&T was required to provide **equal access** to its long-distance circuits by the other long-distance companies, specifically MCI and Sprint, with the result that consumers would have a choice of three long-distance carriers: MCI, Sprint, or AT&T. The only problem with equal access at the time, however, was that AT&T had built the infrastructure, and the AT&T switching equipment was a proprietary design. Since AT&T was the exclusive producer of equipment that could communicate with other AT&T equipment, MCI and Sprint were forced to purchase AT&T long-distance switches if they wanted long-distance switches that would interoperate with AT&T's proprietary infrastructure.

To standardize a solution to this new interoperability issue, an optical communications system known as Metrobus that was developed at AT&T's Bell Labs was introduced to several standards organizations, including the American National Standards Institute (ANSI) and the International Telecommunications Union's Telecommunications Standardization Sector (ITU-T), which was then known as the International Telephone and Telegraph Consultative Committee (CCITT). These organizations committed to developing a standard by which long-distance switching equipment from different vendors would interoperate. The resulting standard, much of which was based on Bell Lab's Metrobus technology, developed over the next several years following the 1984 breakup of AT&T and became known as the Synchronous Optical Network, or SONET.

was a tremendous opportunity cost associated with any new capacity that was added. That is, no matter how much data an organization had to send, there were always times when there wasn't enough data being transmitted to fill up the new capacity, and that idle time represented a forgone opportunity for AT&T.

To circumvent this idle capacity problem, in the late 1960s researchers at Bell Labs, and most notably **Alexander (Sandy) Fraser,** began working on a solution that would more efficiently transmit voice and data traffic over existing AT&T telephone circuits. Combining packet-switching theories advanced by **Leonard Kleinrock** in his 1962 Ph.D. thesis and research performed in 1964 by **Paul Baran** of the RAND Corporation with ARPA packet-switching technology developed and implemented for the ARPANET in the late 1960s, Fraser suggested a high-speed packet-switching scheme that would multiplex data packets and voice packets on the same telephone circuit.[19] This high-speed packet-switching scheme would meet the data transmission needs of business and leverage existing capacity by reducing the opportunity cost associated with idle time on communications circuits.[20]

Packet-switched networks ultimately provided the efficiency increases that AT&T was looking for on its circuits. With packet switching, data and voice traffic from one organization could be combined with data and voice traffic from other organizations onto the same physical circuit while maintaining the data transmission speeds required by multiple and different organizations. In other words, the data and voice traffic from your organization can share one or more physical communications circuits with other organizations through the carrier. As a result, carrier circuits are more efficiently utilized, and your data arrives at

---

[19] This concept was first introduced in the "ATM History Applied Historical Tidbit" in chapter 3.
[20] The results of this research ultimately led to the development of asynchronous transfer mode.

the appropriate destination despite the fact that packet-switched networks combine data transmissions from different organizations on the same physical circuits.

So why would you choose a packet-switched service over dedicated circuits or circuit switching? One reason is the amount and nature of the data an organization transmits. If the nature of your data transmissions is relatively infrequent or if the data your organization sends is transmitted in sporadic bursts of various amounts, a dedicated circuit could handle the task, but you'll be paying for the circuit even when you're not using it. A circuit-switched connection might be able to accommodate the volume of data, but the transaction program that creates the bursts of data might not be able to wait for the required call setup time associated with circuit-switched services. Packet-switched services provide a viable alternative because they're always on and ready to transmit. No excess capacity is wasted when the connection is not in use, and no call setup is involved.

Architecture

Packet-switched networks are different from circuit-switched and dedicated-circuit networks in terms of their architectures, as illustrated in Figure 8.6. In circuit-switched and dedicated-circuit networks, computers or LANs on each end of the circuit have a point-to-point connection with dedicated bandwidth that is reserved specifically for their use. In the case of a circuit-switched connection, the dedicated bandwidth is reserved for the duration of the connection, and with a dedicated circuit the bandwidth is always available. With packet-switched networks, however, packets are transmitted across the network from packet switch to packet switch. The path that each packet takes as it travels from source to destination can be different from the path taken by other packets, and the network is shared with other LANs that use the same packet-switched network.

Packet-switched networks are generally represented as a cloud in diagrams, and they're also referred to collectively as the **public data network (PDN)**. For a packet to enter the PDN, it must first pass through a device that is known generically as a **packet assembler/ disassembler (PAD)**.[21] At the source end of a data transmission, the PAD prepares data packets from a LAN into the appropriate format for the carrier's packet-switched network. The PAD adds address and sequence information to the packets so that the packets can find their way through the PDN to their destinations and be reassembled in the proper sequence at the destination. In part **(b)** of Figure 8.6, you can see an example of how four LANs might be connected to a packet-switched network. In the figure, each customer's LAN is connected to a PAD, also located at the customer site, and the PAD is connected to a dedicated circuit that, in turn, connects to a carrier's central office facility. LAN A sends packets A1 and A2 into the network and LAN C sends packets C1 and C2 into the network. As you follow the paths of the packets through the network, you'll notice that all of the packets from the two LANs enter the network at the same central office, but in the example they don't follow the same path across the network. In addition, packets from LAN A and packets from LAN C sometimes share the same circuit through the network.

Datagrams and Connectionless Services   Once packets are inside the carrier's packet-switched network, it's up to the switches within the "cloud" to direct the packets from source to destination. This can be accomplished in a couple of different ways. One way simply places packets on the network with the destination addresses and sequence numbers supplied by the PAD, and the switches within the PDN direct each packet toward its destination based on network metrics such as the available bandwidth of various paths and line conditions

public data network (PDN)
another name for the packet-switched networks provided by carrier companies

packet assembler/ disassembler (PAD)
a device that prepares data packets from a LAN into the appropriate format for the carrier's packet-switched network

---

[21] If you're connecting your LAN to a frame relay carrier service, you'll implement a FRAD, short for frame relay access device or frame relay assembler/disassembler. For connectivity to an ATM carrier service, you'll specify an ATM access device that's appropriate for the type of LAN to carrier connectivity you're looking for; that is, either ATM LAN to carrier ATM or Ethernet LAN to ATM carrier, and so on.

FIGURE 8.6 Circuit-Switched and Dedicated-Circuit Networks versus Packet-Switched Networks

a. Circuit-switched and dedicated-circuit networks. With switched-circuit or dedicated-circuit networks, you have exclusive use of the communications channel. **b.** Packet-switched network. With packet-switched networks, packets can travel different paths, and the physical circuits between the source and destination are shared with other LANs that use the same packet-switched network.

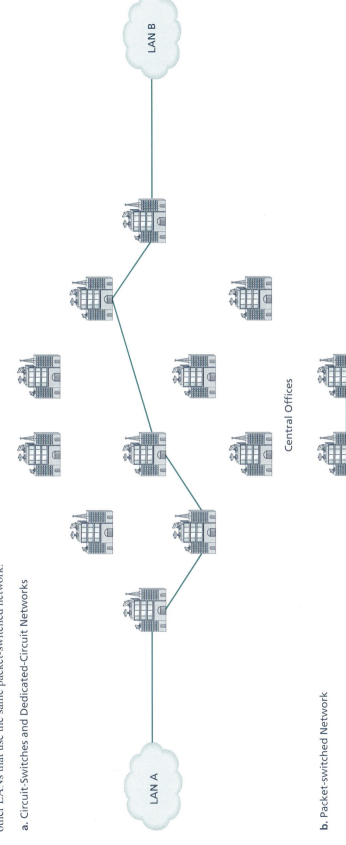

a. Circuit-Switches and Dedicated-Circuit Networks

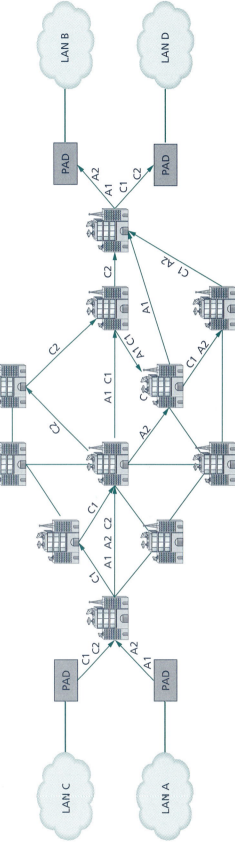

b. Packet-switched Network

datagram

a packet that contains sufficient information to direct it from source to destination without a prior connection being established between the source and destination

connectionless service

a data transmission service in which the source and destination locations do not set up a specified path along which packets will travel, prior to the data transmission

connection-oriented service

a data transmission service in which a connection is established between source and destination LANs prior to the transmission of packets across the network

virtual circuit

a connection-oriented method of directing packets through a packet-switched network

virtual circuit identifier (VCI)

an identifier that specifies the path along which all packets from a particular transmission will travel from source to destination

permanent virtual circuit (PVC)

a virtual circuit that establishes a permanent path or set of paths through the PDN and which an organization can use for data transmissions that require a specific and consistent bandwidth

through the PDN.[22] Packets in this scenario are referred to as **datagrams**, because they contain sufficient information to direct them from source to destination without a prior connection being established between the source and destination. This method of directing packets from source to destination using only address and sequencing information is considered a **connectionless service**. It's considered connectionless because the source and destination locations do not set up a specified path along which packets will travel, prior to the data transmission; that is, there is no dedicated circuit or connection. Instead, with connectionless services each packet can take a different path through the network.

Virtual Circuits and Connection-Oriented Services Another method for directing packets through a packet-switched network is a **connection-oriented** approach known as a **virtual circuit (VC)**. With a VC, a connection is established between source and destination LANs prior to the transmission of packets across the PDN. Once the VC is established, packets are assembled with not only address and sequence information, but they receive an identifier known as a **virtual circuit identifier (VCI)** that specifies the path along which all packets from a particular transmission will travel from source to destination. In other words, with a VC, all packets in a data transmission follow the same path for the duration of the connection. Figure 8.7 provides an illustration of a virtual circuit.

A VC behaves much like a circuit-switched connection. The VC is established prior to data transmission so that switches along the path between the source and destination are aware of what to do with packets marked with a specific VCI. In addition, the same VC is used for the duration of the transmission, and upon completion of the transmission, the VC is terminated. To the source and destination locations, the VC looks like a point-to-point connection. The major difference between a VC and a circuit-switched connection is the following: The physical circuit that carries a VC can be shared with packets from other transmissions, whereas a circuit-switched connection carries only those packets that are transmitted between the source and destination LANs that are connected to the circuit.

A common type of virtual circuit is the **permanent virtual circuit (PVC)**. With PVCs, a carrier uses software to create and manage a permanent path or set of paths through the PDN that an organization can use for data transmissions requiring a specific and consistent bandwidth. This allows PVCs to provide organizations with data transmission functionality that's very much like dedicated-circuit networks. The difference is, with PVCs multiple transmissions from different LANs can traverse the same physical circuit. In contrast, a dedicated circuit carries only those packets that are transmitted between the source and destination LANs that are connected to the circuit.

Reliable versus Unreliable Data Delivery Services **Reliable data delivery services** provide guaranteed delivery and error control of packets through the PDN.[23] This means that for reliable data delivery service, a connection must be created between points A and B prior to data transmission, and there must be some type of error control within the network. This makes connection-oriented services that provide error control within the network reliable data delivery services. On the other hand, data delivery services that do not create a connection between end devices prior to data transmission and which do not perform error control within the network are considered **unreliable data delivery services**.

Several traditional **packet-switched carrier services** are in common use today. Included among them are X.25, frame relay, asynchronous transfer mode (ATM), and

---

[22] These kinds of metrics are similar to the metrics associated with routing in a local area network. You learned about routers and network metrics associated with routing in chapter 4.

[23] Some discussions of reliable and unreliable data delivery services focus on error control within the network as the primary delineator of reliability. That is, if error control is performed within the network, the data delivery service is considered reliable. If error control is left up to the end devices, then the data delivery service is said to be unreliable.

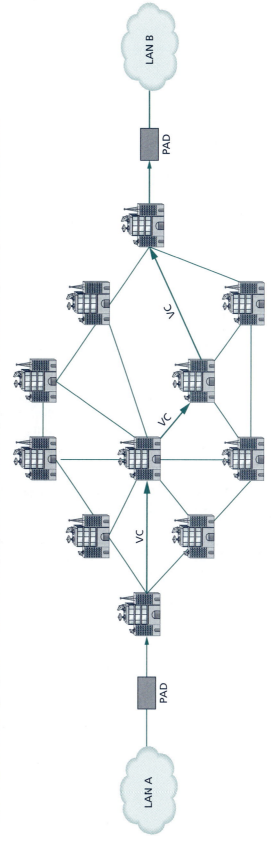

FIGURE 8.7   Virtual Circuit through a Packet-Switched Network

With a virtual circuit through a packet-switched network, all packets travel the same path. The VC is terminated upon completion of the transmission.

switched multimegabit data service (SMDS). Others such as Metropolitan Ethernet and Multiprotocol Label Switching (MPLS) are relatively new and are discussed in a later section of this chapter.

X.25

X.25 is an ITU-T standard dating back to the 1970s that specifies data communications across the PSTN between remote computers. Its data rate in most applications is limited to 64 Kbps or less. One of its early advantages was that it provided a standard for communication between remote computers across the PSTN while at the same time providing for high levels of reliability. This meant that error correction was handled at each switch in the carrier's cloud. X.25 was defined at about the same time as the OSI model, and its underlying architecture corresponds to the first three layers of the OSI model.[24]

While X.25 is an older technology that doesn't provide for high data transmission rates, it's still an available carrier service that you might come across. For example, in data transmission scenarios that don't require real-time data exchange, such as in some mainframe-to-mainframe data transmissions, X.25 is a viable solution. In addition, X.25 is still used in credit card validations, financial transactions, and bank ATMs.[25]

Frame Relay

Frame relay is a packet-switched service operating at the physical and data link layers of the OSI model. Originally developed for use on ISDN networks in the early 1980s, frame relay was proposed as a standard to the CCITT in 1984 but didn't see major deployment until several technology giants formed a consortium in 1990 to develop the technology.[26]

Frame relay provides data rates ranging from 56 Kbps up to 45 Mbps. And aside from its higher data rate capability, another characteristic that sets frame relay apart from X.25 technology is its end-to-end error control. Where X.25 is considered reliable because error correction is administered at each switch within the carrier's infrastructure, frame relay is considered an unreliable packet service because error correction is not performed within the network.[27] Not that unreliable is bad in this context. Quite the opposite—moving error correction to the end points of the communications channel facilitates the faster data rates associated with frame relay.

committed information rate (CIR)
a minimum bandwidth that the carrier will guarantee per your organizations' data rate requirements

If you subscribe to a frame relay service, the carrier will very likely define a **committed information rate (CIR)** and a **committed burst size (CBS)**. The CIR is a minimum bandwidth that the carrier will guarantee per your organization's data rate requirements. The CBS provides you with dynamic bandwidth as long as you don't exceed your CIR over a defined time period. All this means is the traffic you transmit onto the frame relay network can be released in bursts that on average can't exceed the CIR. This gives you the flexibility to send large bursts of data that exceed the stated data rate of the frame relay service as long as you don't do it all the time and stay within your CIR.

Committed Burst Size (CBS)
specifies that the bursts of traffic released onto a frame relay network on average cannot exceed the CIR

Asynchronous Transfer Mode

Asynchronous transfer mode (ATM) is the widely accepted standard of **cell relay technology**, a switching technology that uses fixed-length cells for faster switching of

cell relay technology
a switching technology that uses fixed-length cells for faster switching of packets. Cell relay is the foundation of ATM.

[24] Many OSI model research papers in the late 1970s suggest that the OSI model was structured based on the X.25 standard.
[25] This type of ATM refers to *anytime money*, and not the data communications' acronym for ATM—asynchronous transfer mode.
[26] The companies in the consortium included Cisco Systems, Digital Equipment Corporation (purchased by Compaq and both now owned by Hewlett-Packard), Northern Telecom (now Nortel), and Stratacom (now owned by Cisco Systems).
[27] Since error correction is not performed within the network, error correction is left up to the end points.

packets.[28] ATM can provide organizations with high-speed packet-switched WAN connectivity.[29] Common data rates for ATM are 155 Mbps and 622 Mbps, although other rates that correspond to multiples of OC-x rates are available. In addition, most carriers provide ATM services over T1 and T3 at data rates of 1.544 Mbps and 44.736 Mbps, respectively.

In terms of error correction, ATM functions much like frame relay. It is an unreliable packet service, meaning that error correction is not performed in the network but is instead left up to the end points of the ATM network. ATM differs from frame relay, however, in that it provides *quality of service (QoS),* a set of built-in capabilities that provides different levels of service quality depending on the type of data you need to send. For example, voice and video need to be coordinated for streaming media, which requires a higher level of service priority for data packets in the stream than might be required for data packets within a simple text message that is being delivered across the network. With ATM, you can specify a quality of service priority for different types of data.

Switched Multimegabit Data Service

Switched multimegabit data service (SMDS) is another packet-switched carrier service that competes directly with frame relay and ATM. Although SMDS provides data rates equivalent to T3 circuits, it is a data-only service; its architecture makes it unsuitable for transporting voice and video in multimedia applications.

Multiprotocol Label Switching

traffic engineering
the ability to manage network traffic characteristics and qualify network traffic types for more efficient routing and better data delivery performance

virtual private network (VPN)
a secure point-to-point connection between two private networks or between two network devices that uses a public network instead of a private communication channel as a backbone for data transmission

Multiprotocol label switching (MPLS) is a packet-switching technology that you might be hearing more about from carriers in the very near future. MPLS technology provides an integrated carrier platform that has the potential to blur the boundaries between technologies such as SONET, ATM, frame relay, and IP, integrate standard LAN architectures such as Ethernet, and provide other advanced services such as **traffic engineering** and **virtual private networks (VPNs)**.

For example, most carriers define SONET as a physical layer, or OSI layer 1, transport technology. ATM is defined within OSI layer 2, and IP is defined within layer 3. With MPLS, carriers will be able to migrate SONET and ATM functionality into a single layer—layer 3, through the use of specialized data routing and prioritization software in MPLS IP routers. In addition, MPLS will provide a seamless carrier transport for high-speed Ethernet traffic without the overhead currently associated with converting Ethernet frames into ATM cells. Theoretically, this functionality will reduce the complexity of the carrier network and simplify the carrier network system to a single platform—MPLS.

MPLS has the potential to bring sweeping changes to the way carrier services are delivered and managed. For example, MPLS has the capability to provide advanced traffic engineering and security. In addition to defining traffic routes, MPLS will be able to define performance characteristics, as in quality of service, for various classes of traffic. Security could be simplified because MPLS allows carriers to create VPNs without requiring encryption software or end-user security applications. Several MPSL standards are already finalized, and many draft standards are in development and should be adopted in late 2004.[30]

---

[28] The "Applied Historical Tidbit" in chapter 3 that covered ATM history discusses the development of fixed-length cell technology in the evolution of ATM.

[29] You also learned about ATM's use as a high-speed LAN architecture in chapter 3.

[30] For more information regarding MPLS development, access the Internet Engineering Task Force's Web page at www.ietf.org, click on the Working Groups link. Then, in the table of contents, click on the link for Routing Area, and then click on the mpls link. Also, try the MPLS Forum at www.mplsforum.org.

The Internet as a WAN Backbone

Whereas large and medium-sized organizations will likely continue to utilize the WAN services provided by carriers, small and work-at-home businesses might find using the Internet as a WAN backbone cost effective and relatively straightforward to implement.

To utilize the Internet as a WAN backbone, you'll still need to obtain a high-speed connection between your home or office location and your Internet service provider (ISP). Digital subscriber line (DSL), cable television (CATV), or even T-carrier services provided by your local carrier can give you the speed you're looking for. You'll also need a VPN device such as a router or switch with built-in VPN capability to establish the secure connection between your business location and your ISP.[31] As an alternative, you could purchase VPN software that installs on a workstation. In either case, you'll have secure VPN access from your location through the carrier and then across the Internet via your ISP, as represented in Figure 8.8.

Trusted VPN
an ISP-controlled VPN that no one other than the customer can use for data transmission and that only the ISP can modify

The major drawback to using the Internet as a WAN backbone is reliability and transmission speed once your information has passed from your ISP to the Internet. To circumvent this problem, some ISPs provide VPN services known as trusted VPNs. With a **trusted VPN**, the customer trusts the ISP to set up the communications pathway between the customer's remote locations so that no one other than the ISP can modify the data path or the data that is transmitted across the VPN. This provides a level of assurance that the VPN will provide and maintain a specified bandwidth as well as a secure channel for data transmission across the Internet.

FIGURE 8.8   **Using the Internet as a WAN Backbone**

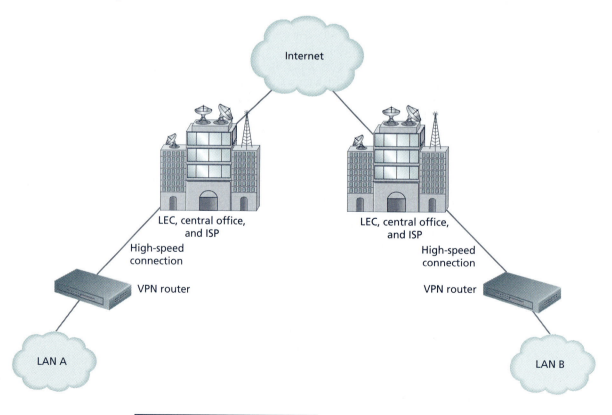

[31] You'll discover more detail regarding VPNs as they apply to network security in chapter 9.

Hybrid VPN
a trusted VPN that adds QoS to ensure timely delivery of time-sensitive data across the Internet

Beyond trusted VPNs, some ISPs can provide hybrid VPNs that support time-sensitive data transmissions such as voice and multimedia. The feature to look for if you have these types of data communications requirements is QoS capability across the VPN provided by your ISP. With a **hybrid VPN**, QoS guarantees that your time-critical data transmissions can be transmitted across the Internet without disruptive delays.[32]

Other High-Speed Carrier Services

You might find several other high-speed carrier services interesting in developing a plan for a MAN or WAN. Most common among these newer services are DSL, cable TV, metropolitan Ethernet, passive optical networking, and wireless MAN/WAN services.

Digital Subscriber Line Technologies

Digital subscriber line technologies, more commonly known as DSL, provide home users and businesses with an alternative high-speed connection that utilizes the existing telephone lines between your home or business and a telephone company's central office facility. Digital subscriber line is relatively fast for both upload and download speeds with the priority generally being placed on download speed. Download speeds range from roughly 1 Mbps to 52 Mbps depending on the DSL technology chosen, and upload speeds range from 16 Kbps up to 8 Mbps, depending on the distance between the subscriber and the local exchange carrier's central office. Although data transmission across DSL circuits is relatively fast and home offices and small businesses have adopted it for Internet access, DSL is not generally intended to be or implemented as a WAN connectivity solution.

DSL modem
CPE that converts Ethernet 10BaseT packets from the computer into DSL signals that can be sent across the phone line to the carrier's central office

DSL requires additional equipment at your home or office and special DSL equipment at the carrier's central office facility. The equipment at your home is known as customer premise equipment (CPE) and is generally comprised of a **DSL modem** and a **line splitter**. When you're trying to send information from a computer within your LAN or simply from a single computer, the DSL modem converts Ethernet 10BaseT packets from the computer into DSL signals that can be sent across the phone line to the carrier's central office. The splitter CPE separates regular analog voice traffic from the digital computer traffic.[33]

DSL line splitter
CPE that separates regular analog voice traffic from the digital computer traffic

At the carrier's central office, thousands of incoming lines from thousands of customers connect to a special wiring panel known as a main distribution frame (MDF) or main cross-connect (MC).[34] The MDF separates the incoming voice traffic from the data traffic and routes voice traffic to the PSTN and DSL data traffic to the **digital subscriber line access multiplexer (DSLAM)**, which is located at the carrier's central office. The DSLAM converts DSL data streams into ATM cells, and the ATM traffic is either routed through the carrier's own network or forwarded to another carrier's switching equipment for transmission through the other carrier's "cloud." Figure 8.9 illustrates a DSL configuration from customer premise to a carrier's central office.

digital subscriber line access multiplexer (DSLAM)
a device at a local exchange carrier's central office that receives and processes DSL data traffic. It is pronounced *D-slam*.

Ongoing development and standardization of DSL technologies continue under the guidance of the DSL Forum, a consortium of nearly 200 organizations whose mission is the continued market development of DSL technologies. At the time of publication of this text, ITU-T standards exist for ADSL, ADSL2, and SHDSL, while work continues on standards for other DSL technologies such as VDSL. Other organizations such as ANSI and ETSI also support ADSL and SHDSL standardization.

Asymmetric Digital Subscriber Line DSL is available in several formats, but by far the most widely deployed version is **asymmetric digital subscriber line (ADSL)**. ADSL

---

[32] For more information on VPNs, check out the VPN Consortium Web site at www.vpnc.org.

[33] If the DSL line does not carry a regular analog telephone channel along with it, you can implement splitterless DSL.

[34] The term *main distribution frame* is still used, but the more modern term is *main cross-connect*.

FIGURE 8.9 DSL Configuration

a. Customer's premises. b. Carrier's central office.

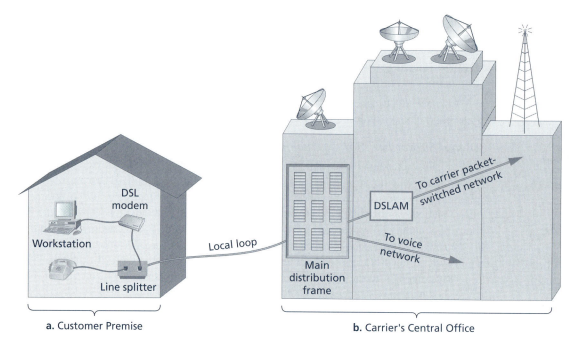

a. Customer Premise   b. Carrier's Central Office

utilizes three distinct channels across the twisted-pair telephone wires that connect your residence or office to the telephone company's central office. One channel is used for regular voice traffic. Another is used for data downloads with data transmission rates ranging from 1.5 Mbps up to 9 Mbps, depending on distance from the carrier's central office. The third channel is used for data uploads with data rates hovering in the 16 Kbps to 640 Kbps range.

ADSL2 is the successor to ADSL. In general, ADSL2 provides faster data transmission rates for a given distance between your business location and a carrier's central office. Specifically, users can expect data download rates of up to 12 Mbps, depending on the distance from a carrier's central office, and upload speed improves to approximately 1 Mbps. In addition, an extension to the ADSL2 standard, ADSL2+, provides for download speeds of up to 20 Mbps if your network or computer is within 5,000 feet of the carrier's central office.

Symmetric High Bit Rate Digital Subscriber Line **Symmetric high bit rate digital subscriber line (SHDSL)** is the business-class version of DSL. Unlike ADSL, SHDSL provides the same data transmission rates for both uploads and downloads. Data transmission rates are distance dependent just as they are with ADSL. For SHDSL running on a single copper-wire pair, those data rates range between 192 Kbps if your location is 20,000 feet from the carrier's central office, and 2.3 Mbps if your location is 10,000 feet from the carrier's central office. There is also a specification for implementing SHDSL over two copper-wire pairs with data rates ranging between 384 Kbps and 4.6 Mbps.

Very-High-Data-Rate Digital Subscriber Line **Very-high-data-rate digital subscriber line (VDSL)** is designed to provide upload speeds of up to 16 Mbps and download speeds of up to 52 Mbps, but the distance between customer and carrier must be 4,000 feet or less.

For a given amount of money, security, and reliability, business managers will always choose faster over slower when selecting data transmission speeds. So it stands to reason that VDSL should surpass implementations of ADSL. But that hasn't happened. And that's because there's one major problem with implementing VDSL, and that is competing standards.

In one camp is the VDSL Alliance, whose members include Texas Instruments and Alcatel. The VDSL Alliance has based its VDSL equipment design and carrier systems on a technology known as Discrete MultiTone (DMT). DMT divides the carrier signal into 247 separate channels. If all the channels are clear, meaning there is an absence of line noise or interference, then data can be transmitted across all of the channels. If a channel happens to intercept some type of interference, then the data is shifted to another channel, and the transmission continues uninterrupted on another clearer channel. It's a good system, perhaps more difficult to deploy than other carrier technologies, but fairly robust when line noise gets in the way. If you want to look at it another way and boil it down for simplicity, you can think of DMT as one technological method of sending and receiving the ones and zeros of a digital data signal, and one group of vendors has put their money behind DMT.

In the other camp is the VDSL Coalition. Members of this group include Broadcom and Lucent Technologies, and their VDSL equipment design and carrier technology is based on quadrature amplitude modulation (QAM) and carrierless amplitude phase (CAP). CAP divides the line between the customer and the carrier into three distinct channels. One channel is used for voice, a second for high-speed downloads, and a third for slower uploads. At the same time, QAM is responsible for placing the bits on the data channels. QAM is a relatively sophisticated technology that accomplishes fast data transmission by substantially increasing the number of bits sent per unit time.

It's unclear which standard will win the technology battle between the Alliance and the Coalition. It might even play out that both technologies survive, albeit with some sort of translation hardware or software to ease compatibility issues. Whatever the result, debates such as this one reinforce the need for adherence to standards and the implementation of standards-based technologies that fit the business need. If a technology is popular and widely implemented, it might very well become the de facto standard from which you can gather some assurance that it will survive because of its market acceptance and widespread implementation.

For competing products that are not yet standardized, the decision of which to implement is not as clear. This is where the ability to assimilate information from standards organizations such as IEEE and ITU-T takes on heightened value. You don't want to rush into an implementation of a technology that might not become standardized. Money spent on these kinds of technology solutions might meet an immediate business need but at the expense of a solution that will provide longer term scalability and industry support.

Currently, VDSL suffers from competing standards.[35] In the future as a singular standard is adopted, VDSL will provide substantial bandwidth for short-distance data transmission between businesses or homes and carrier's central offices.

Cable Television

Cable television (CATV) circuits have become another alternative for digital data transmission service in recent years. Primarily marketed to home users, CATV systems can be used by small businesses for Internet connectivity, e-mail, and data exchange between

---

[35] See the Applied Business Tidbit entitled "Competing Standards Slow VDSL Deployment" in this section.

FIGURE 8.10
**Cable TV
Network for Data
Transmission**

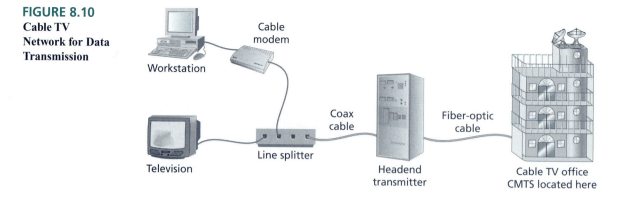

remote locations. Typical CATV download speeds fall into the 27 to 56 Mbps range and upload speeds approach 3 Mbps. That data rate is shared with others who are connected to your circuit so that actual transmission rates decline as more users access the data portion of the cable circuit.[36] Although data transmission across CATV circuits is relatively fast and business-class CATV data transmission services are available, CATV is not generally intended to be or implemented as a wide area network connectivity solution.

Cable television data transmission services require special equipment at both the customer premises and at the CATV operator's location. Customer premise equipment includes a cable modem that converts your computer's digital data into signals that can be transmitted across the CATV circuit. In addition, your computer will require either an Ethernet NIC or a USB port to connect your computer to the cable modem.[37]

The CATV company provides connectivity to your home or business through a hybrid fiber coax (HFC) network, the cable headend transmitter, and the cable modem termination system (CMTS). In Figure 8.10, customers' cable modems are connected via coax cable to a cable *headend transmitter,* a device that converts electrical signals from the coax cable to light signals on the fiber-optic cables and vice versa. The cable headend transmitter is connected via fiber to the cable company's main office facility.

At the main office facility, the cable company maintains the CMTS, a device that's comparable to the DSLAM used with DSL technology. The major function of the CMTS is to route upstream data traffic via high-speed circuits to an Internet service provider, which could even be the cable TV company, and route downstream data traffic from the Internet to CATV data service customers. Other functions of the CMTS include accounting, so the customer can be billed for service, and automatic assignment of IP addresses to subscribing customers.[38]

Metropolitan Ethernet

Metropolitan Ethernet is a relatively new carrier service that provides high-speed Ethernet connectivity between your organizations' LANs or to other organizations' networks using a carrier's infrastructure. For example, your organization might want to establish a

---

[36] Although overall data download speeds for CATV connections are 27 to 56 Mbps, individual customers are typically rate-limited to something much lower, such as 1.5 Mbps or even as low as 512 Kbps or 256 Kbps. With rate limits, customers cannot exceed the rate limit regardless of how light the network traffic load.

[37] An alternative connection between your computer and the cable modem can include various wireless solutions, but these wireless solutions involve the connection of a wireless hub between the computer and the cable modem.

[38] The automatic assignment of IP addresses occurs through DHCP, a TCP/IP protocol that you learned about in chapter 4.

FIGURE 8.11 **Metropolitan Ethernet Networks**
a. Point-to-point metropolitan Ethernet network. **b.** Multipoint-to-multipoint metropolitan Ethernet network.

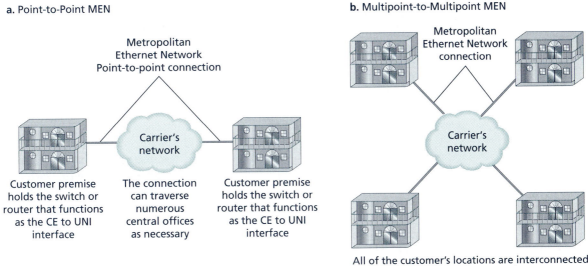

a. Point-to-Point MEN

b. Multipoint-to-Multipoint MEN

metropolitan Ethernet connection to several buildings in a carrier's service area. To make this happen, the carrier might install fiber-optic cable to each of the buildings your company occupies, and you would connect a high-speed Ethernet interface, such as a Gigabit Ethernet switch or 10 Gigabit Ethernet switch to connect your LAN to their fiber as illustrated in Figure 8.11. Part **(a)** of Figure 8.11 depicts a point-to-point metropolitan Ethernet network (MEN) using a carrier's infrastructure, and example B shows a multipoint-to-multipoint MEN. Other ways to connect to the carrier's infrastructure include **passive optical networks,** which are referred to as Ethernet PONs or EPONs, and business-class DSL circuits such as VDSL.[39]

Whatever the connection to the carrier, once your organization has established this link to the carrier's metropolitan Ethernet service, the carrier can transmit your Ethernet packets across its existing infrastructure. This infrastructure might include SONET rings or Ethernet PONs or some form of high-speed WDM or even MPLS. With any of these, the underlying technologies providing the data transmissions might be different, but the end result is the same: a metropolitan Ethernet network.

The Metro Ethernet Forum (MEF), the organization that oversees metropolitan Ethernet development and standards, has defined two types of Ethernet MAN services.[40] E-line defines point-to-point MENs and E-LAN defines multipoint-to-multipoint MENs, which are also known as any-to-any MENs. Figure 8.11 provides you with an example of each. MEF has defined the high-speed Gigabit or 10 Gigabit Ethernet interface as the customer equipment (CE)-to-user network interface (UNI). This interface is simply the high-capacity switch or router that incorporates the Gigabit or 10 Gigabit Ethernet connections.

Under the MEF's guidelines, a metro Ethernet carrier will also provide several classes of service (CoS) to its customers to guarantee various bandwidth profiles as well as various

---

[39] You'll learn about passive optical networking later in this chapter.
[40] The Metro Ethernet Forum is the organization that facilitates the development of metropolitan Ethernet network standards. You can learn more about the Metro Ethernet Forum at www.metroethernetforum.org.

levels of service performance. Since the carrier's infrastructure is shared with other customer organizations, the amount of data that a customer sends must be monitored and defined within specific parameters. To meet this goal, the MEF has defined specifications for committed information rate (CIR), committed burst size (CBS), excess information rate (EIR), and excess burst size (EBS). By categorizing data in terms of the average rate at which a customer can send information and the peak amount of information that can be sent and still fall within the average rate, the carrier can maintain a promised level of service throughout its infrastructure to all customers using the metro Ethernet service.[41]

According to the Metro Ethernet Forum, implementing a metropolitan Ethernet connection can offer large cost savings over other traditional carrier services such as frame relay and ATM. Ethernet hardware costs are lower, and the cost of metropolitan Ethernet service is significantly less than ATM or dedicated T1 service. Other advantages include excellent scalability. With traditional carrier technologies, incremental bandwidth additions were not possible without migrating to a different technology platform, such as a move from T1 to T3 or frame relay to ATM. This type of traditional service upgrade would require the installation of new equipment and a potential increase in bandwidth that might not be used for years to come. With metropolitan Ethernet, you can add or delete bandwidth in 1 Mbps increments to match an organization's changing needs without the need of expensive equipment or service upgrades.

Other features that business managers might find appealing include the 30 or more years of Ethernet knowledge that exists in the marketplace. Ethernet is a well-understood and widely adopted data communications architecture. You can do all of the things with metro Ethernet that you can do with Ethernet in the LAN, including managing the network, creating VLANs, and securing connections with VPNs.

Passive Optical Networking

A **passive optical network (PON)** is a fiber-optic network in which all active components—those components that require a power source as well as memory chips and processors—have been removed between the carrier's central office facility and the customers' premises.[42] Replacing these active components are passive optical devices such as optical splitters, which can distribute optical signals to multiple customers. By removing the active components and replacing them with passive devices, carriers can reduce installation and maintenance costs and, in turn, provide PON carrier services at rates that are comparable to or lower than traditional carrier services.

The components of a passive optical network include an optical line terminator (OLT), which is located at the carrier's central office facility. Optical network terminals (ONTs) are located at customers' premises to provide the connection interface between the customer's LAN and the PON. The fiber-optic network that links customers to the carrier's central office is known as the optical distribution network (ODN), and the ODN consists of fiber-optic cables and passive optical splitters. An example of a PON is represented in Figure 8.12.

In Figure 8.12, fiber-optic cables run from the carrier's central office facility to a fiber splitter that is installed in a convenient distribution location. From the splitter, other fiber-optic cables are run to individual businesses and to other distribution locations that can connect the ODN to a copper-based or wireless medium. The fiber that is run from a splitter

---

[41] CIR and CBS are associated with information that is time sensitive, such as multimedia files whose audio and video must be in sync. EIR and EBS are associated with data delivery that is not time sensitive.
[42] In comparison, SONET is a fiber network that is comprised of fiber-optic cables and active devices such as optical repeaters, optical relays, and sophisticated electronics that require a power source and which are more susceptible to failure that are passive devices.

FIGURE 8.12
Passive Optical
Network

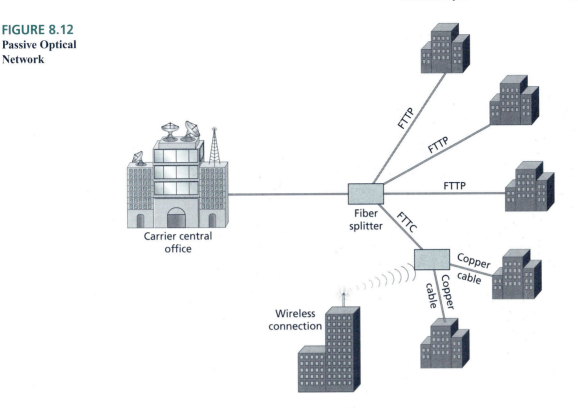

to a business location is known as **fiber to the premises (FTTP),** and the fiber cable that is run from a splitter to a fiber-to-copper or fiber-to-wireless distribution point is known as **fiber to the curb (FTTC).**[43] By installing the PON in this hub (splitter) and spoke (FTTC and FTTP) configuration, carriers circumvent the costs associated with running an individual fiber link to each individual customer. Instead, each customer shares the PON's available bandwidth with every other customer connected to the PON.

Depending on the standard that a carrier chooses to deploy, the main fiber that runs to the splitter can supply shared bandwidth of 155 Mbps, 622 Mbps, 1.25 Gbps, or 2.5 Gbps. **ATM-based PONs (APONs)** can supply 155 Mbps or 622 Mbps downstream and 155 Mbps upstream.[44] Ethernet-based PONs are still in the standards development process with the IEEE but should support shared bandwidth capability in the 1 Gbps range. **EPONs** will also likely provide competition for wireless metropolitan Ethernet in the last mile. **GPONs,** or gigabit PONs, will provide 1 Gbps and above bandwidth and will be able to accommodate many types of carrier services including ATM, Ethernet, T1 technologies, SONET, and others. Some GPON standards are already published under the ITU while other GPON standards are under development.[45]

Wireless

Wireless MAN/WAN services can provide a very high-speed carrier connection between an organization's remote LANs and the carrier's central office facility. Shared bandwidth of up

---

[43] When the fiber is run from a splitter to a home-use customer, that fiber segment is known as *fiber to the home (FTTH)*.
[44] *Downstream* refers to data delivery to the customer and *upstream* refers to data delivery from the customer to another location.
[45] Generically, high-speed PONs can be referred to as broadband PONs (BPONs).

FIGURE 8.13   **Wireless MAN/WAN Service**

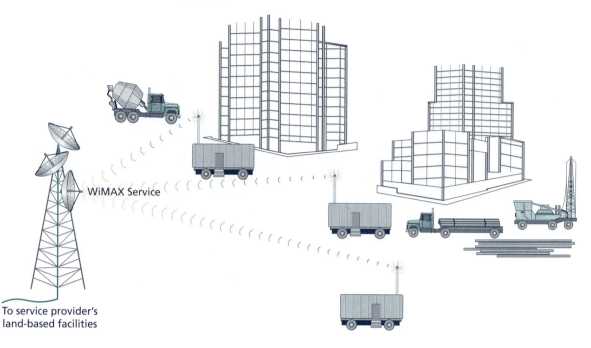

WiMAX Service

To service provider's
land-based facilities

to 70 Mbps is achievable over a 30-mile non-line-of-sight range. The bandwidth and range will allow carriers to provide what the industry is calling "last mile broadband" connectivity for remote LANs. That is to say, for locations that don't have a copper or fiber-optic cable connection to a carrier's central office facility, wireless MAN/WAN service can provide a high-speed wireless connection between a customer and the carrier. Examples of potential customers include trade show participants who need high-speed connectivity to the Internet or to their parent organizations' networks, construction sites that have high-speed data communications needs only while the job is in progress, and rural homes and businesses that don't have a wired alternative such as cable or DSL. Figure 8.13 shows a potential connectivity scenario between a remote LAN and a parent organization's LAN using a wireless MAN/WAN service.

Wireless MAN/WAN services are commonly known in the wireless data communications industry as WiMAX, and they follow the IEEE 802.16 series of standards.[46] A temporary but stationary network site that requires high-speed access can implement WiMAX equipment to connect to a carrier's cell tower network. In addition, recent revisions to IEEE 802.16 provide for roaming access to a carrier's WiMAX wireless network. Using this roaming feature, traveling users and mobile LANs can obtain high-speed access to a carrier's WiMAX service without maintaining a stationary location. Once data is received via wireless data transmission at the carrier's central office facility, the information is transmitted via the carrier's infrastructure, which can be a high-speed transmission service such as ATM over SONET.

---

[46] WiMAX is a nonprofit corporation comprised of several corporations that produce communication equipment and components. The goal of WiMAX is to promote the development and implementation of WiMAX wireless technologies and equipment.

DATA COMMUNICATION THROUGH THE CARRIER

Once your data gets to the carrier, the carrier is responsible for routing and delivering it to its intended destination. To make that happen, carriers have complex infrastructures of circuit-switched, packet-switched, and dedicated-circuit networks that are continuously receiving data from thousands of organizations at any given moment.

Imagine for a moment that you needed to connect your organization's home office to several remote offices and that you needed a high-speed carrier service to fit your needs. The carrier could install new cabling just for you, from the home office to each of the remote locations, but the charges that you would incur to have the carrier create such a connection would probably keep you from building your WAN. Instead, the carrier uses its existing infrastructure as efficiently as possible through a process known as *multiplexing*.

Multiplexing

multiplexing
a method of combining multiple separate signals into a composite signal for transmission across a communications channel

To make the cost of bandwidth more palatable for organizations that require WAN connectivity through a carrier, carriers share the circuits within their infrastructures by using various forms of multiplexing. **Multiplexing** combines multiple signals from multiple sources into a single, composite signal, as shown in Figure 8.14. Each carrier customer produces a signal that is received at the carrier's central office facility, but once these signals arrive at the carrier's central office, the carrier combines the numerous signals into a multiplexed signal that, in turn, traverses the carrier's (and other carriers') networks. This process makes more efficient use of a carrier's available infrastructure and allows delivery of high-speed WAN services at affordable rates.[47]

FIGURE 8.14 **Multiplexing at the Carrier**

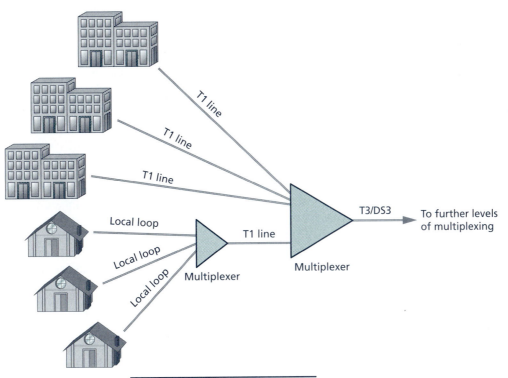

---

[47] Multiplexing can be implemented at any organization that has multiple input signals that will share a single circuit. It is presented as a function internal to a carrier simply to demonstrate data transmission from a single LAN to a carrier and then through the carrier's network. Multiplexing could just as easily be demonstrated at a customer site where telephony is one input and data from a LAN is a second input.

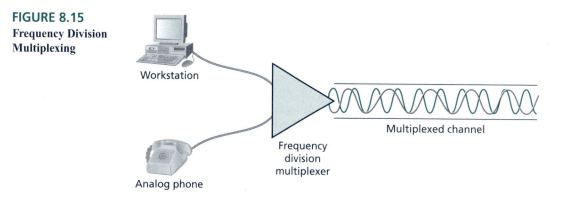

Several types of multiplexing can be used to create these combined, complex signals. In this chapter you're going to learn about frequency division multiplexing (FDM), time-division multiplexing (TDM), statistical time-division multiplexing (STDM), wavelength-division multiplexing (WDM), dense wavelength-division multiplexing (DWDM), and inverse multiplexing (IMUX).

Frequency Division Multiplexing

Frequency division multiplexing (FDM) combines signals from multiple sources onto a shared circuit by utilizing a different frequency band for each source signal, as you can see in Figure 8.15. Within the multiplexed signal, each source signal occupies a portion of the total available bandwidth for the duration of the transmission.

When two or more signals are multiplexed into an FDM signal, guardbands are implemented to keep the different frequencies from overlapping. The guardbands are nondata-carrying portions of the composite signal that prevent the source signals' frequencies from interfering with one another.

In today's data communications marketplace, FDM is used in CATV systems to transmit multiplexed signals that are comprised of numerous television station signals, each transmitted across a separate frequency, and a high-speed data signal for network or computer data transmission, which is transmitted as another separate frequency. In addition, DSL services use FDM to multiplex the separate data and voice signals that are used with DSL connections.

Time-Division Multiplexing

Time-division multiplexing (TDM) combines digital signals from multiple sources onto a shared circuit by dividing the available bandwidth of the shared circuit into time slices. To create a multiplexed signal, each source is allocated a time slice, measured in milliseconds. During its time slice a source can occupy the entire bandwidth for a short interval of time. Figure 8.16 provides an example of a multiplexed signal using TDM.

One of the advantages of TDM is that it's more bandwidth efficient. Each input device is allotted the full bandwidth during each time slice, and bits are added to the composite signal in time sequence. Since there is no chance of interference between time slices as there is between frequencies in FDM (that is, the time slices sequence the data), the allocation of bandwidth between sources is more efficient.

At the same time, TDM does have a potential inefficiency built into it. If a source has no data to send during its allotted time slice, the composite signal is created with a null place-holder for that source's time slot. The null placeholder maintains the sequence of the inputs on the circuit for reassembly of the message at the destination. Whenever sources do not have information to send, valuable bandwidth is wasted with these null time slices.

FIGURE 8.16   Time-Division Multiplexing

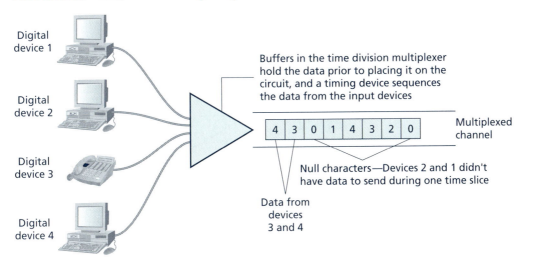

Digital device 1

Digital device 2

Digital device 3

Digital device 4

Buffers in the time division multiplexer hold the data prior to placing it on the circuit, and a timing device sequences the data from the input devices

| 4 | 3 | 0 | 1 | 4 | 3 | 2 | 0 |

Multiplexed channel

Null characters—Devices 2 and 1 didn't have data to send during one time slice

Data from devices 3 and 4

Statistical Time-Division Multiplexing

Statistical time-division multiplexing (STDM) is a more sophisticated type of time-division multiplexing that dynamically allocates time slices to source devices based on their transmitting activity over time. Active devices are allotted longer time slice intervals, and less active devices are allocated shorter time slices. If a less active device suddenly becomes more active, the statistical multiplexer dynamically allocates more time to that source. On the other hand, if an active device becomes less active, it will be allocated less time. Inactive devices are skipped.[48]

Because source devices will vary in the amount of data they have to send over time and because STDM dynamically allocates time slices based on activity, the multiplexed signal does not have the sequencing characteristics, meaning the null placeholders, associated with TDM. Instead, an STDM multiplexer adds control bits to the data of each source device. These control bits identify the source device as well as the number of bits being transmitted from the source device. Of course, the control bits consume some of the circuit's bandwidth, but even with control bits STDM is typically more efficient in terms of bandwidth utilization than TDM.

Wavelength-Division Multiplexing

In **wavelength-division multiplexing (WDM),** multiple and different wavelengths of the visible light spectrum are used to generate multiple and different data transmission signals across a fiber-optic circuit. Each wavelength is capable of producing very high data rate signals, so when multiple wavelengths are transmitted simultaneously in a multiplexed signal the data rates across a single fiber-optic cable can reach hundreds of gigabits or even tens of terabits per second.

Dense wavelength-division multiplexing (DWDM) is a version of WDM that incorporates eight or more wavelengths into a composite signal. Extremely high data rates are possible with DWDM because it multiplexes optical carrier signals such as OC-48, OC-192, and even OC-768 signals, which are already achieving significant data transmission rates

---

[48] Statistical time-division multiplexers incorporate sophisticated microprocessors that are capable of dynamically computing the duration of a time slice for any given source.

FIGURE 8.17
Inverse Multiplexing

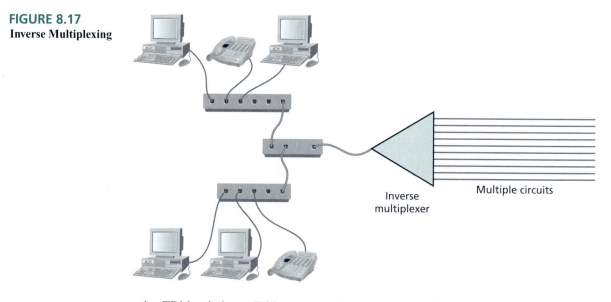

Inverse
multiplexer

Multiple circuits

using TDM techniques. With current technology capable of multiplexing up to 160 signals across a single optical circuit, data rates into the low terabits are possible using DWDM.[49]

A major benefit of DWDM is that it can multiplex source signals of different bandwidths and different formats. For example, OC-12, OC-48, and OC-192 signals can each be assigned a distinct wavelength for transmission across a single multiplexed circuit. At the same time each of the different OC signals can carry a different data format, such as ATM, frame relay, or metropolitan Ethernet. DWDM enhances capacity over existing circuits without regard for the type of data being transmitted.

Inverse Multiplexing

With the types of multiplexing you've just learned about, multiple signals are transmitted across a single, multiplexed circuit. This efficiently allocates the entire bandwidth of a single circuit to multiple source devices. **Inverse multiplexing (IMUX),** in comparison, divides a single data stream across several individual circuits, as illustrated in Figure 8.17.

In Figure 8.17, an organization's LAN is connected to an inverse multiplexer. The inverse multiplexer receives a continuous stream of data from the LAN and divides the data stream sequentially across multiple T1 circuits. To the LAN, the multiple T1 circuits behave as one aggregated data channel. That is, the data flows as if it were connected to a single 12.352 Mbps circuit.

IMUX provides organizations with an efficient and flexible solution for growing bandwidth needs. As bandwidth requirements increase, more T1 circuits can be connected to the inverse multiplexer until the total cost approaches the cost of a T3 circuit, which is about eight T1 circuits. At that point, you could make the switch to a full T3. IMUX is a cost-effective way to scale your circuit capacity to your expanding bandwidth needs on a gradual basis without making a static jump from single T1 to full T3 service.

WAN MANAGEMENT ISSUES

So far in this chapter you've examined several types of carrier services that you might implement to extend your data communications needs beyond the LAN and into a MAN or WAN. In extending your LAN into the realm of MANs and WANs, you should also be

---

[49] Multiplexing 160 OC-768 signals (38.486 Mbps each) would produce a multiplexed data rate of 6 million Mbps, or 6 terabits per second.

aware of two key management issues that affect the quality of your data transmissions. One is called quality of service, and the other involves circuit capacity and circuit upgrades.

Quality of Service

Quality of service **(QoS)** can be defined as a commitment to provide a quantified level of circuit quality and bandwidth so that various and different data types can be transmitted at predefined performance levels. For example, text messages might require a relatively low priority for bandwidth and circuit quality because the text doesn't have to synchronize with voice or video. In comparison, if you're sending a data transmission that includes voice and video such as in teleconferencing, it's pretty important that a person's voice synchronize with the video recording. If it doesn't, the quality of the reproduced transmission will be poor or even unacceptable.

In either of these examples, QoS levels can be assigned to different types of traffic or network devices. In practice, it's common to assign QoS levels based on IP addresses, TCP and UDP port numbers, MAC addresses, or even time of day, to guarantee that specific data is handled properly across the WAN.

To implement QoS, you'll need to incorporate LAN switches and routers that accommodate QoS configuration. In addition, you'll need to notify your carrier that your WAN connections require QoS so that an appropriate carrier service can be installed.

Circuit Capacity and Circuit Upgrades

When you're examining various carrier services that can support your WAN requirements, one of the criteria that you'll need to meet will be circuit capacity. You might initially contract with your carrier to implement a circuit that has modestly higher capacity than you need. This will provide adequate bandwidth for your current needs and provide a little room for growth as the amount of data you transmit increases.

If your company is growing, but you don't want to pay for more circuit capacity than you need right now, make sure you discuss the scalability of the service with your carrier. For example, IMUX can provide one alternative for future circuit capacity expansion with costs that scale to your increased bandwidth needs.

At the same time, you should also discuss with the carrier the types of data you expect to send. For example, today you might need to transmit only text at sporadic time intervals, but within the near future your data communications needs might include voice and video synchronization. Make sure your carrier can provide you with a migration path that will allow you to maximize the return on equipment and installation investment that you make today.

Chapter Summary

- **Circuit switching and circuit-switched carrier services.** Circuit switching creates a dedicated communications path between two end locations for the exclusive use of the end nodes for the duration of the connection. Circuit-switched services use the PSTN and are generally used only for temporary connection needs and when bandwidth requirements can be met with 1.544 Mbps or less.

- **Dedicated circuits and dedicated-circuit carrier services.** Dedicated circuits provide an exclusive communications channel between two remote locations. Dedicated circuits can be implemented when an organization has large and continuous amounts of data to exchange between locations. Types of dedicated-circuit networks include T-carrier, FracT, and SONET.

- **Packet-switched networks and packet-switched carrier services.** In packet-switched networks, packets are transmitted across the network from packet switch to packet switch, and the path that each packet takes as it travels from source to destination can be different from the path taken by other packets. In addition, the network is shared with other LANs that use the same packet-switched network. Types of packet-switched networks include X.25, frame relay, ATM, SMDS, and MPLS.

- **The Internet as a WAN backbone.** Using the Internet as a WAN backbone involves a carrier connection to an ISP. The ISP, in turn, provides you with a connection to the Internet. WAN backbones across the Internet generally require the implementation of VPNs—one between your office location and another to protect your data and ensure sufficient bandwidth as the data traverses the Internet.

- **Other high-speed carrier services.** Other high-speed carrier services include digital subscriber line technologies such as ADSL, ADSL2, SHDSL, VDSL, cable TV, metropolitan Ethernet, passive optical networking, and WiMAX.

- **Multiplexing through the carrier.** Various types of multiplexing are implemented to create complex composite signals across carrier circuits. The result of these multiplexing methods is faster data transmission speeds and more efficient use of existing circuit capacity. Multiplexing types include FDM, TDM, STDM, WDM, and IMUX.

- **WAN management.** WAN management issues include sustained circuit quality and bandwidth to provide adequate data transmission performance for various types of data. This is generally referred to as quality of service. If an organization is growing, it's also important to have a WAN connectivity solution that is scalable.

Key Terms

Alexander (Sandy) Fraser, *277*

Asymmetric digital subscriber line (ADSL), *285*

Asynchronous transfer mode (ATM), *280*

ATM-based PON (APON), *291*

Basic rate interface (BRI), *272*

Cable television (CATV), *287*

Call setup, *270*

Campus area network (CAN), *268*

Carrier service, *269*

Channel service unit/data service unit (CSU/DSU), *000*

Circuit, *269*

Circuit-switched services, *269*

Committed burst size (CBS), *282*

Committed information rate (CIR), *282*

Connectionless services, *280*

Connection-oriented services, *280*

Datagram, *280*

Dedicated circuits, *273*

Dense wavelength-division multiplexing (DWDM), *295*

Digital signal 1 (DS1) circuit, *273*

Digital subscriber line access multiplexer (DSLAM), *285*

Digital subscriber line (DSL), *285*

Ethernet PON (EPON), *291*

Fiber to the curb (FTTC), *291*

Fiber to the premises (FTTP), *291*

Frame relay, *282*

Frequency division multiplexing (FDM), *294*

Gigabit PON (GPON), *291*

Hybrid VPN, *285*

Integrated Services Digital Network (ISDN), *271*

Inverse multiplexing (IMUX), *296*

Leonard Kleinrock, *277*

Metropolitan area network (MAN), *268*

Metropolitan Ethernet, *288*

Multiplexing, *293*

Multiprotocol label switching (MPLS), *283*

Optical carrier, *275*

Packet assembler/disassembler (PAD), *278*

Questions

1. What is the major purpose of a campus area network? A metropolitan area network? A wide area network?

2. When might you consider implementing a carrier service? When might you choose to use circuit-switched services? What is a major reason not to use a circuit-switched service for WAN connectivity?

3. Why might you choose a dedicated-circuit service? Are there any disadvantages to implementing dedicated-circuit services?

4. What was the early appeal of ISDN? Are there any good business reasons for implementing ISDN? What prevented ISDN from gaining wide acceptance? Where might you use it today?

5. What role can T-carrier technologies play in modern organizations? Can you implement more than one T-carrier circuit in an organization? How would you scale growing data communications needs with T1 circuits?

6. What is SONET and what role can it play in a modern organization? Why might a business choose to implement SONET? Where is SONET commonly implemented on a wide scale?

7. What are packet-switched carrier services and how do they work? When would you choose to implement these types of services? What are some examples of packet-switched carrier services?

8. What constitutes a connectionless service? A connection-oriented service? A reliable data delivery service? An unreliable data delivery service?

9. What is MPLS? What potential benefits could MPLS bring to carriers?

10. When might you consider using the Internet as a WAN backbone? What factors would you need to consider? How can your ISP guarantee the integrity and security of your data? Are there any issues to consider if you send and receive data that is time sensitive?

11. What is DSL and how does it work? Describe three or more variants of DSL and how each could be effective as a WAN connectivity solution.

12. Is CATV a viable carrier service? How does it work? When might you consider using CATV as a carrier service for a business?

13. What types of wireless WAN services are available today? What standards are involved with wireless WAN services? When might you consider implementing a wireless WAN service?

14. What is metropolitan Ethernet? When might you consider implementing it as a WAN carrier service?

15. What is the main technological difference between passive optical networking and SONET? What are the components of a PON? Would you consider PON service a dedicated circuit? Why?

16. Define multiplexing. What kinds of carrier services use FDM? TDM? WDM?

Research Activities

1. Identify the carriers that are providing WAN or MAN services to your school or organization. What types of carrier services are your school or organization currently using? Are there plans to change to a different service? What is the business purpose, and how will this be accomplished?

2. Using the search tools available to you, including the telephone and the Internet, list the types of carrier services that your local service provider offers. Find out if your local carrier can provide VPN connectivity over the Internet and whether their VPN connectivity includes QoS.

3. Using the search tools available to you, find two or more carriers that provide metropolitan Ethernet and describe the connectivity equipment and installation issues associated with a metro Ethernet implementation. If possible, provide pricing information.

4. Using the search tools available to you, find two or more carriers that provide scalable data communications services using IMUX T-carrier service. If possible, provide pricing information.

5. Using the search tools available to you, locate two or more business applications for SONET technologies. If possible, provide real examples of the business reasoning these companies used to justify the use of SONET.

6. Using your favorite browser, visit the Frame Relay forum and the ATM forum. Describe any recent and proposed standards that could affect these two carrier technologies.

7. Using the search tools available to you, locate at least two carriers that are still providing X.25 service and identify the charges associated with X.25 service. If possible, identify customers of the carriers who are still using this service and describe the business reasons that these companies continue to use X.25.

8. Provide a detailed technological and business discussion of DWDM. Describe how the technology works and discuss how carriers have implemented this technology into their infrastructures. See if you can identify and describe any new or proposed standards and technologies that will deliver even faster data transmission rates using DWDM.

9. Using the search tools available to you, locate at least three carriers that provide DSL services. Specifically, find out who is deploying VDSL, ADSL2, and SHDSL and how these technologies are implemented to the customer.

10. Using the search tools available to you, identify at least three carriers that have implemented passive optical networks. Specifically, find out who is offering APON, EPON, and GPON services and then see if you can discover why particular customers subscribe to a PON service versus some other carrier service.

Mini Case Study

LAKESIDE METAL STAMPINGS—PART 6

Lakeside Metal Stampings recently purchased another metal fabrication company based out of Raleigh, North Carolina. When the owners of Lakeside were first considering the purchase of the Raleigh-based company, they liked the way the Raleigh company's product line complemented their own, and the two companies were soon working on the details of a buyout arrangement. During the purchase negotiations, the owners of Lakeside soon discovered that in addition to the manufacturing plant in Raleigh, there was also a small sales office in Asheville, North Carolina, and another in Charlotte, North Carolina. Both sales offices contributed significantly to the company's sales, so Lakeside's owners were pleased with the discovery and planned on keeping the offices in those two locations.

Within a very short period of time after the purchase, the owners of Lakeside Metal Stampings found that they were spending a significant amount of time on the phone with the shop foreman in the Raleigh facility and with the reps in the two sales offices. Most of the discussions were centered on design specifications, customer requirements, and pricing. Much of the follow-up on these topics was handled by fax, but that wasn't well coordinated—important documents could sit in the fax for hours, and many times the fine details of prints and sketches simply didn't transmit well. In addition, important financial data was sent by overnight delivery once a month, and this created a problem with maintaining timely federal and state withholding-tax deposits and reconciling employee wages with unemployment insurance payments to the State of North Carolina.

And then there was the network that was installed in their new Raleigh company. It had been installed at about the same time as the network in the Rochester location, but every time a service call was required, the network service company that handled the Raleigh location either was not timely in fixing the problem or sent a new technician who had to learn the network from the ground up before fixing the problem.

With their new purchase beginning to seem like it was worlds away instead of just a few states away, the owners of Lakeside realized that they needed a more efficient method of conveying important data between the locations and decided to contact you once again to help them match technology requirements to their business needs.

Based on what you've learned so far in this text and with an emphasis on the wide area network technologies presented in this chapter, develop a list of business issues now facing Lakeside Metal Stampings, and create a WAN design proposal that will provide the owners of Lakeside with a comprehensive set of technical solutions that could meet their current business needs. In creating this proposal, make sure you define and describe each suggested technology solution in your own words so that the owners will have a clear understanding of what they need to do to address their new data communications and networking needs. In addition, for each proposed technical solution, provide a diagram or sketch that maps your written discussion to a physical design specification.

CHAPTER
Nine

Chapter Overview and Objectives

Network security continually attracts attention from business managers and technology managers alike. Information has value and, in the modern era of data communications and networks, potential exposure and loss are critical business considerations. As businesses become increasingly vigilant for security threats and breaches, managers will need an enhanced understanding of the kinds of tools available to them to make their networks less vulnerable. In this chapter, we examine the kinds of security practices and devices you can implement to guard against unauthorized access and information loss. More specifically, by the end of this chapter, you will be able to

- Identify and describe the components of a comprehensive security plan.

- Define social engineering.

- Explain eavesdropping and data interception.

- Describe different types of security attacks.

- Define dial-in security and discuss its importance.

- Describe various types of malicious programs.

- Define and describe physical network security.

- Identify and describe several types of firewall devices.

- Define network address translation and describe its significance.

- Describe proxy servers and their functions.

- Discuss perimeter networks and provide examples of perimeter network design.

- Explain intrusion protection and its components.

- Explain how VLANs add to network security.

- Discuss wireless LAN and MAN/WAN security concepts.

- Identify ways to physically secure data.

- Describe the security implications of virtual private networks.

- Define encryption and discuss encryption techniques.

- Identify and describe security protocols.

Network Security

Chapter Outline

Business Perspective on Network Security

Potential Vulnerabilities

Securing Your Network

Securing Your Data

BUSINESS PERSPECTIVE ON NETWORK SECURITY

The motivation behind protecting networks and the data stored on them derives from the value associated with an organization's data and the potential for exposure or loss of that data. This seemingly simple business driver results in security planning, technology design and implementation, and ongoing maintenance and support of an organization's security infrastructure.

Components of a Comprehensive Security Plan

Network and data security generally follow a formal plan in large organizations, and even in smaller organizations there is usually some level of planning associated with network and data security even if it's as simple as deleting all e-mails that arrive from unrecognized sources. But no matter what the size of the company or organization, a comprehensive **security plan** for any organization should include at least some level of commitment to risk analysis, data and network protection planning, business continuity planning, and incident response planning. Figure 9.1 provides a conceptual representation of security planning.

Risk Analysis

Risk analysis defines the value of an organization's network and data assets, examines the potential vulnerabilities of those assets, determines the potential exposure caused by the identified vulnerabilities, computes the expected cost of network and data asset loss or misuse, and defines the controls that are required to mitigate risk to an acceptable level.

Organizations that don't conduct a risk analysis have no **baseline** for the value of their network resources and unfortunately are unlikely to realize the true value of their data until it is lost, stolen, damaged, or otherwise unavailable or irretrievable. And with no baseline from which to define a network's current security status, an organization cannot define its security vulnerabilities or the methods required to secure their networks from potential attack. Risk analysis is crucial to comprehensive security planning.

Data and Network Protection Planning

Data and network protection planning is a major component of a comprehensive security plan, and it generally includes development and implementation of **security policies**,

baseline
a benchmark that an organization can use to measure changing conditions over time

security policies
define an organization's security objectives, specify persons responsible for the various components of the security plan, provide assurance of ongoing support for network and data security, and delineate levels of access to resources

FIGURE 9.1
Security Planning

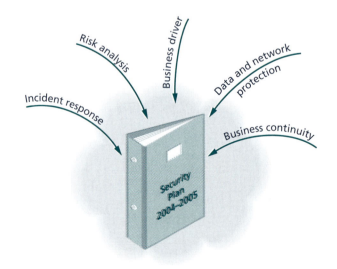

security controls
the actions of employees
and the technology that
is implemented to
reduce security
vulnerabilities

*security
documentation*
records the policies,
procedures, responsible
persons, levels of access
that should be
administered, and the
security controls of a
security plan

*Ongoing security
monitoring and
enforcement*
provide feedback
regarding the
performance of an
organization's security
and whether
modifications might be
necessary. Monitoring
and enforcement also
acknowledge an
organization's ongoing
commitment to the
security plan.

The Centers for
Medicare and
Medicaid Services
(CMS) oversees
HIPAA regulations
including information
technology
specifications for
health care providers.
Two of their sites are
of particular interest
for information
technology–related
disciplines. Those sites
are the Security
Architecture page
at http://www.cms.hhs.
gov/it/security/docs/IT
Av6.pdf, and the
Acceptable Risk
Safeguards page at
http://cms.hhs.gov/it/
security/docs/ars.pdf.

implementation and configuration of the controls specified in the risk analysis, documentation of the security plan, and ongoing security monitoring and enforcement.

Security policies define an organization's security objectives, specify persons responsible for the various components of the security plan, provide assurance of ongoing support for network and data security, and delineate levels of access to resources. **Security controls** are the actions of employees and the technology that is implemented to reduce security vulnerabilities. **Security documentation** records the policies, procedures, responsible persons, levels of access that should be administered, and the security controls of a security plan. **Ongoing security monitoring and enforcement** provide feedback regarding the performance of an organization's security and whether modifications might be necessary. Monitoring and enforcement also acknowledge an organization's ongoing commitment to the security plan.

Security policies can also be regulated, as in the case of the Health Insurance Portability and Accountability Act (HIPAA) of 1996. HIPAA specifies procedures and security policies that health care providers and other organizations should implement for the protection of sensitive subscriber (customer) data.

Business Continuity Planning

Business continuity planning is a subset of an organization's comprehensive security plan, and it includes all of the business functions and processes that must be continued for the business to carry on in the event of a network disaster or catastrophic loss of data at an organization's primary business location. These kinds of catastrophic events are known to happen and include events such as floods, fires, extended loss of power, or any other event that would render a primary business location inoperable.

At a minimum, business continuity planning should include an alternative physical location from which business functions and processes can be run in the event of a catastrophic network failure or loss of data that is unrecoverable at the primary business location. Business continuity planning should also require offsite data backup storage that is deliverable to the alternate location within an acceptable time frame so that data can be restored to an equivalent network configuration.[1] In addition, business continuity planning should include contingencies for the human factor. That is, in the event of a disaster at the primary business location, an organization will require trained staff to operate mission critical business functions at the alternative location.

Incident Response Planning

Incident response planning is another subset of an organization's comprehensive security plan. But where business continuity planning focuses on the successful restoration of business functions and processes in the event of a disaster, incident response planning focuses on solving an immediate security problem, or incident. For example, an organization might be under a denial of service attack, and a properly executed incident response plan provides the guidelines for handling the problem. That is, the incident response plan includes a list of employees to notify and their contact information, the equipment and data to isolate for various types of attacks, documented configuration changes to implement on various security devices to defeat an attack, and any other identified steps that assist in restoring technical functionality as quickly as possible. Incident response planning might also include a selected list of law enforcement and technical agencies to notify in case of an incident, and

---

[1] In large organizations the offsite backup storage might include or be replaced by real-time replication of data onto a network configuration that is as close to identical as possible to the primary business location. A real-time data replication configuration at an alternative location significantly reduces the amount of time to recover from a catastrophic network or data loss at the primary business location, but it also costs more to implement and maintain.

the incident response plan should also include what to do after an incident. That is, document and enact steps that can make future incident responses more productive and less likely to occur for similar future incidents.

POTENTIAL VULNERABILITIES

network vulnerabilities
define how exposed an organization's network and data are to security threats

Network vulnerabilities define how exposed an organization's network and data are to security threats. For example, an employee might disclose a user name and password over the phone or through e-mail to an imposter pretending to be one of the organization's network security technicians. A network technician might forget to update a virus definition, leaving a network exposed and open to infiltration. A denial of service attack might crash a server, leaving all of the information on that computer inaccessible. Employees who are not authorized to access certain files might install rogue programs that collect user names and passwords with the intent to disclose confidential information.

At the very least, attackers, hackers, and unauthorized information seekers target organizations' information to leave their personal mark—call it the graffiti of the 21st century. In the most diabolical of security breaches, valuable information is copied, stolen, or severely damaged, leaving the information's owners to undertake expensive and time-consuming recovery measures as well as implement reinforced security. At the very worst, your valuable information can be sold to other entities, including corporations or persons, potentially negating its value to you and causing you great expense to recover.

Although the following vulnerabilities are by no means comprehensive, they provide a good start toward building a list of some of the more common vulnerabilities that can affect the security planning of an organization. This list includes social engineering, eavesdropping, security attacks, dial-in security, user and computer policies, and malicious programs. Table 9.2, at the end of this section, provides a summary list of these vulnerabilities with brief descriptions and safeguards.

Social Engineering

social engineering
a method of exploiting the people component of the security equation rather than the hardware or software components to gain access to computer networks and valuable data

One of the easiest and most straightforward methods that attackers use to gain access to organizations' networks and data is social engineering, which is illustrated in Figure 9.2. **Social engineering** is a method of exploiting the people component of the security equation rather than the hardware or software components to gain access to computer networks

FIGURE 9.2
Social Engineering

"Good morning, this is Rick in systems. We're doing a quick security check on everyone's system. I'll need your IP address to get started ..."

"My IP address? I get that how? ... command prompt? ... as long as you walk me through it. What did you say your name is?"

Another good Web site for security-related information is the SANS institute at www.sans.org. The name doesn't stand for storage area networks. It's an acronym for SysAdmin, Audit, Network, Security.

and valuable data. Examples include phone calls from individuals who pretend to be a fellow employee while urgently and politely requesting your assistance in gaining access to your organization's network or data. The request could be something as simple as asking for a user name and password to get logged in, to something more involved such as asking the user to access a command prompt, execute the ipconfig /all command, and then requesting the IP address of the computer. This type of vulnerability preys on the general willingness to help someone in need, especially when the requester generally poses as someone from the IT department or even a high-ranking company official.

The best methods of defense against this vulnerability are employee training and on-going awareness. New employees should be trained and coached on proper procedures for dealing with requests for security information, and existing employees should be reminded of procedures and policies on a scheduled and consistent basis. In addition, employees should also be trained to *always* report any requests they receive to the IT department, regardless of whether the employee knew the true identity of the caller. This includes requests for security information solicited via e-mail, instant messaging, or over the phone.

Eavesdropping and Data Interception

In addition to social engineering, attackers frequently eavesdrop and illicitly intercept data to discover user names, passwords, MAC addresses, IP addresses, and other information, with the intent of gaining access to an organization's network resources. **Eavesdropping** is the act of secretly listening in on voice and data communications channels, and **data interception** involves recording the eavesdropped data without modifying the data in any way. Eavesdropping and data interception frequently go hand in hand.

eavesdropping
the act of secretly listening in on voice and data communications channels

data interception
involves recording the eavesdropped data without modifying the data in any way

One of the simplest methods of eavesdropping is to watch someone enter a user name and password. Watching is eavesdropping. Remembering or recording the user name and the keystrokes used for the password constitutes data interception. More involved methods of eavesdropping include keystroke loggers, which are programs that can be delivered through e-mail viruses and which track all of a user's keystrokes and mouse movements. Another method is using spyware, a modern version of a keystroke logger designed for both legitimate and illegitimate uses. Spyware is commonly installed by file-sharing applications, and can be used as a data-recording service that tracks users' Web site accesses, user names and passwords used for those sites, and keystroke entries for bank accounts and credit card numbers.

Still other methods for listening in on an organization's data include network traffic analyzers that read packets on an organization's network. Eavesdroppers can use these "sniffing" devices to collect the packets that flow across an organization's network and over time collect enough user names and passwords to gain access to network resources. Physical installation of a sniffing device might be difficult on a wired network, unless, of course, the attacker gains access to physical facilities. But collecting packets on unsecured wireless networks offer unscrupulous eavesdroppers a tremendous opportunity to secretly listen in and record all of the packets transmitted across the wireless network.

strong passwords
passwords that are at least eight characters in length and include both uppercase and lowercase letters plus numerals and special characters

Ways to protect against eavesdropping and data interception include the frequent changing of passwords; the use of **strong passwords**, that is, passwords that are at least eight characters long and include both uppercase and lowercase letters plus numerals and special characters; and training users not to give out their passwords or to allow onlookers to watch the user enter his or her password during logon. Protection against more sophisticated attacks include antispyware software and the implementation of various types of data encryption techniques.

Security Attacks

Attacks against major Internet commerce sites, major software vendors, and Internet search engines garner plenty of media attention these days. Most of these highly publicized

TABLE 9.1

Common DoS Attacks

An interesting site for detailed descriptions of different types of security advisories is http://www.cert.org/ advisories. One specific advisory that CERT published in 1996 regarding TCP SYN floods is located at http://www.cert.org/ advisories/CA-1996-21.html. Another interesting and recent cyber security alert is located at http://www .us-cert.gov/cas/ techalerts/TA04-111A.html. It was published in April 2004 by the U.S. Computer Emergency Readiness Team (US-CERT).

Attacks	Description
Ping storms	Flood a service-providing computer with a barrage of ping commands. The volume of incoming pings prevents the computer from responding to other legitimate requests.
Smurfing	Floods a network with responses to the ping command. An attacker impersonates a legitimate computer on the network by using that computer's IP address (this is called *spoofing*), sends a ping to all network devices using the spoofed address, and every device on the network replies to the ping.
TCP SYN floods	One or more attacking client computers bombard a server computer with requests for service, but the clients never finish their connections with the server so that the service request can be fulfilled. This results in a growing number of half-open connections with the server. The server maintains a database of these partially filled connections, and eventually this database fills up and halts the server's ability to respond to any service requests.
E-mail cluster bombs	Attackers flood a victim computer with e-mail messages. The messages are generally large and flow continuously with the aim of consuming a computer's resources so that it cannot provide services to other computers.
Buffer overflow	Attackers take control of processes on victim computers by exploiting the vulnerabilities of the programming language on which the process is built. Then they run their own programs on victim computers to deny service to that computer or launch additional programs that can attack an entire network.
TCP reset (RST)	Attackers send TCP reset packets to target network hosts and devices, which terminates TCP sessions between communicating end points. Network routers are especially vulnerable, losing their connections with other networks.

Denial of Service Attack
an attack in which hackers disrupt the normal flow of network and business activity by bombarding an organization's network with specific patterns or types of traffic designed to harm or halt network and business functions or data flow

Distributed Denial of Service Attack
an attack against hundreds or thousands of networks in which rogue programs are distributed and installed on thousands of computers and then the rogue programs simultaneously attack targeted sites with one or more denial of service programs

attacks are some form of **denial of service (DoS)**. In a denial of service attack, hackers disrupt the normal flow of network and business activity by bombarding an organization's network with specific patterns or types of traffic designed to harm or halt network and business functions or data flow. The organization's publicly accessible servers, such as Web servers or e-mail servers, attempt to respond to all the incoming traffic, but the sheer volume overloads the computers' response capacity and makes it impossible for inside users to send their data or legitimate external users to gain access.[2] Unfortunately there isn't any way to prevent a coordinated attack effort from launching a DoS attack against your organization. However, various intrusion detection and alert solutions can warn you of an attack in process and thereby allow you to take appropriate actions to contain the attack and reduce its associated impact. Some companies have even taken the extreme measure of taking their Web servers offline for a period of time once the attack is discovered. Some of the common DoS attacks are listed and described in Table 9.1.

Distributed denial of service (DDoS) attacks can cause even more far-reaching disruption, because these attacks distribute rogue programs to thousands of computers on the Internet. Once the rogue programs are running on their unsuspecting hosts, they initiate a coordinated effort of denial of service attacks against targeted sites. This magnifies the amount of network traffic bombarding a site and can bring business and network functionality to a standstill.

---

[2] Three great sources of information about DoS and DDoS attacks and related links are the CERT Coordination Center at Carnegie Mellon University (www.cert.org), the Denial of Service Attack Resource Page at www.denialinfo.com, and the list of links at http://staff.washington.edu/dittrich/misc/ddos.

Trojan horse attacks
attacks that hide
malicious programs
inside of a seemingly
harmless e-mail or
program

spoofing
attempts to gain
unauthorized access by
utilizing one of the
legitimate IP addresses
on your network to trick
other computers on your
network into allowing
access to network
resources and
information

port scanners
constantly monitor the
actions of unprotected
computers connected to
the Internet and search
for open ports on these
computers that will
allow the attacker to
gain access to various
services on an internal
network through these
open ports

security holes
unfixed or unpatched
bugs in an operating
system, which are
susceptible to security
attacks

Still other types of attacks attempt to gain unauthorized access to internal resources. Notorious among these types of attacks are Trojan horse attacks, spoofing, and port scanning. **Trojan horse attacks**, described in more detail in the virus section of this chapter, attempt to gain access and damage files. An attacker who uses **spoofing** attempts to gain unauthorized access by utilizing one of the legitimate IP addresses on your network to trick other computers on your network into allowing access to network resources and information. Even more diabolical are **port scanners** that constantly monitor the actions of unprotected computers connected to the Internet and search for open ports on these computers that will allow the attacker to gain access to various services on an internal network through these open ports. Once an open and unsecured port is found, the attacker can gain access to unsecured computers in your network and launch rogue programs that can damage files or provide access to confidential information. These types of attacks are the major reason that security measures such as firewalls, packet filtering, port filtering, and virus software are so important.

Network administrators are not alone in combating these attacks. Various organizations, including the Department of Defense, the FBI, and other nonprofit organizations such as Carnegie Mellon University's **CERT** Coordination Center collect information about network and Internet security problems and publish the vulnerabilities and attack information. The CERT Coordination Center is an extremely informative site on DoS attacks and many other network security issues.[3]

Security holes are nothing more than unfixed or unpatched bugs in an operating system. However, the potential security exposure due to security holes is very real if left unprotected. External security threat barriers such as firewalls, proxy servers, network address translation devices, and, to a certain extent, virus software, can minimize the exposure of unresolved security holes. But you still need to plug these holes with the latest updates from the operating system manufacturer as soon as they become available.

As an example, Figure 9.3 shows a security hole fix for Windows XP. The Microsoft Automatic Update service automatically notified the user that there was a security vulnerability in Windows XP and, if left unresolved, the computer would be susceptible to denial of service attacks. For a machine connected directly to the Internet, the fix was applied automatically; the user simply clicked the Install button, and the fix was applied automatically.

FIGURE 9.3
Fixing a Security Hole with Microsoft Automatic Update

---

[3] You can access the CERT Coordination Center's Web site at www.cert.org.

In the fall of 2002, a friend needed additional disk space on the computer that she used for Internet access at home and figured it would be an ideal time to upgrade the workstation operating system as well as install additional hard drive capacity. She set about the reconfiguration on a Friday afternoon.

During the installation of the operating system, she inadvertently installed Windows 2000 Server instead of Windows 2000 Professional. Since she had valid licenses for both operating systems, and since both operating systems have the same graphical interface, she made an expedient decision to continue with the Windows 2000 Server installation. In the business world, this would have raised an immediate flag because of all the vulnerabilities that exist within Windows operating systems, especially for a computer that is connected to the Internet. But at home, in a little more comfortable environment, it's easy to let one's guard down. Not to mention that she had already installed a physical security device that translated IP addresses between the cable service and her computer. I suggested to her that she not leave the computer on and connected to the Internet for any length of time until the security patches were applied, but apparently she figured it would be safe to wait until the following week to apply the Microsoft updates to her Windows 2000 Server installation. Little did she realize at the time the problems that this little miscalculation would cause.

Late Monday morning I received a call from her with a worried tone. She had received an e-mail from her ISP informing her that her computer was acting as a host for the distribution of the Wklez32 virus that had been circulating the Internet. The ISP also recommended that she access a specific site to download the software that would rid her system of this destructive program. She installed the program and ran it to quarantine all instances of the virus, but it indicated that thousands of files had been infected. She attempted to clean the files one by one, but the damage was too severe. Since all of her data was backed up, she decided it was easier to reinstall the operating system and restore the data.

The discovery of how this happened in such a short span of time came with the installation of a personal firewall security program once the operating system was reinstalled as Windows 2000 Professional. (Windows 2000 Professional doesn't have the same vulnerabilities as an unprotected Windows 2000 Server, but it does have its own vulnerabilities.) Once the security program was configured and activated, it indicated that there was an automated program running on a computer somewhere in Washington state that was scanning the ports on her computer. The malicious scanner continued the attempted attacks against the computer for the next few days, but the personal firewall software continued to defeat the attacks, and after a few days the attacks stopped. Chances are the attacker's efforts were redirected to other devices that provided less resistance.

What can we learn from all this? First of all, no computer is totally safe. Patches and fixes are critically important, even at home, and security is best applied in layers—it's not sufficient to rely on security that applies to only one layer of the OSI model, as in the security device that translated IP addresses between her service provider and her computer.[4] And most importantly, recovery is time consuming and costly—the more valuable the data, the more emphasis and investment that should be placed on securing that data.

In a large network environment in which this computer was only one of many computers with the same potential vulnerability, the network administrator would distribute the fix to all affected computers during nonpeak business hours or schedule it to run after business hours.

---

[4] The translation of IP addresses occurred through a network address translation, or NAT, device. You'll learn about network address translation later in this chapter.

Dial-in Security

Many companies still allow remote users to connect to their internal networks via regular analog phone lines. **Dial-in security** should be an area of concern for network administrators and business managers alike as anyone with the phone number to an internal server can potentially gain access to the network. To circumvent potential security exposure with dial-in users, you should always keep dial-in telephone numbers unlisted and confidential and require any dial-in users to authenticate with a user name and password. These steps will keep most unauthorized users out.

For added security, you can implement callback functionality. With this feature, dial-in users dial the number of a computer's modem, and once the call is answered and the user has entered a user name and password, the computer hangs up and dials the user's number to make the connection. However, this functionality is generally limited to remote users who always call from the same number. The computer at work knows that one number to dial back when you call in, so it can reestablish the connection.

If you travel a lot and you need to dial in, there are other ways to ensure a secure connection without having the work computer call you back. For example, you might keep a pass code generating device that is about the size of a key fob or credit card, and which gives you a specific pass phrase or code at the time you're attempting to dial in. The computer at work that you're dialing in to also has one of these devices, and it generates the same pass code at the same time your device does. When you dial in, you enter the pass code and you're allowed to log on because your pass code matches the one at work. For an unauthorized person to gain access, he or she would require the dial-in phone number as well as your pass code generator.

Malicious Programs

virus
programming code that attaches itself to other files or programs and is designed to cause damage to files on local computer systems. Viruses can replicate and transfer themselves to files and programs on other computers, spreading their destructive code to numerous computers throughout a network

worm
a computer program that is self-propagating; it doesn't attach itself to other programs or files. Worms are also self-replicating across a network. They make copies of themselves with the intent of choking the network or even causing it to crash.

Malicious programs such as **viruses** and **worms** represent another important security threat that can devastate your company's operations. These programs come in many forms and can be introduced through many different channels. They're commonly introduced through e-mail attachments or programs downloaded from untrusted Web sites. Other methods of introduction include files copied to floppy disk or CD-ROM; however, these can be readily controlled with hardware policies that limit access to these physical devices. Malicious programs introduced through e-mail or from the Internet pose a more immediate threat. To counter malicious programs, most network administrators implement antivirus software on their network servers that constantly scans for malicious programs on the servers as well as the workstations. When a malicious program's profile is detected, the suspected file is quarantined or, if possible, repaired.

Boot Sector Virus

Boot sector viruses are some of the original viruses, as they were spread by floppy disk. This type of virus functions by placing its program code in the boot sector of a hard disk or floppy disk. By doing so, the functionality of the virus is launched when the computer boots up, often with devastating results.

Macro Virus

A **macro virus** is a piece of code that is embedded within a data file. In legitimate usage, a macro is a feature of a software program that causes something such as spell-checking to be done or file minimization to the system tray, each time the file is opened or saved. When this feature is embedded in a data file and the unsuspecting user opens the file, whatever program functionality is built into the macro virus will be unleashed on your computer system. Macros are a little sneakier than Trojan horse viruses because they don't look like an executable program file. You might be trained not to run any unknown program executable files, but you might not be as wary of a word processing file that contained a macro. As soon as you open the file, the damaging effects of the virus are unleashed. One famous macro virus that attacked computer systems and networks in the 1990s was the Melissa virus.

Trojan Horse

Named after the giant wooden horse that held invading Greek soldiers in the ancient city of Troy, **Trojan horse** viruses are frequently distributed through e-mail in the form of an attachment with a seductive name; one that is nearly irresistible to the unsuspecting user, and many an e-mail reader has succumbed to launching a Trojan horse program.

Once launched, the Trojan horse program can be something as simple as a humorous motion file, for example, the Internet snowball fight, or it can be something much more diabolical like a program that claims to be a patch for a computer's operating system. Once you've opened it and it's inside your computer, the damage can be severe, making changes to files and registry databases. Fortunately, antivirus software can quarantine these files before they unleash their damage, as displayed in Figure 9.4. However, for those viruses that manage to get past the virus software, nothing can be better than user education to alert them to the dangers of viruses and instructing them not to open any file that they're unsure of or that arrived via e-mail from an unknown source.

Virus Hoax

A **virus hoax** is not really a virus but a false report of a virus generally propagated through a massive e-mail distribution. The real damage is not caused by a virus but by the extra e-mail and Internet traffic generated by unsuspecting and unknowledgeable users propagating the hoax by informing all their friends and work buddies.

Worms

Three of the best-known worms are the ILOVEYOU worm that spread to millions of computers a few years ago, Code Red that circulated in 2001, and MSBlast, which had widespread effects throughout 2003. All three wrought havoc with networks all over the world in a very short period of time.

FIGURE 9.4   **Firewall**

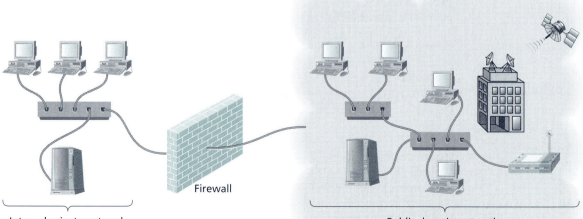

Internal private network   Firewall   Public domain networks

TABLE 9.2
Potential
Vulnerabilities

Vulnerability	Description	Safeguards
Social engineering	Method of exploiting the people component of security to gain access to computer resources	Employee training, and reporting of any requests for security information
Eavesdropping and data Interception	Act of secretly listening in on communications channels and then recording the data without modifying it	Strong passwords, employee training, antispyware software, data encryption
Security attacks	Disruption of network and business activity by infiltrating a network or host's defenses	Firewalls, intrusion detection systems, intrusion prevention systems, honeypots, perimeter networks, antivirus software, security patches, physical security and user and computer policies, network address translation, proxy servers, VLANs, VPNs, WEP, WPA, RSN, 802.16e, encryption
Dial-in security	Secure access over a telephone line to network resources	Unlisted telephone numbers, required authentication, required passwords, callback functionality, pass code generating devices
Malicious programs	Viruses and worms	Employee awareness, antivirus software

Technically speaking, **worms** are not viruses because they don't attach themselves to other programs or files. However, because they can spread throughout a computer network, worms are frequently categorized with viruses. What makes worms so potentially damaging is that they are self-replicating, meaning they copy themselves to their initial target computer and then replicate to other computers connected to your network. If a worm has some destructive functionality built into it, the damage to your network computers can be severe.

SECURING YOUR NETWORK

As part of any well-designed and comprehensive security plan, security of an organization's network includes everything from identifying and managing the potential security vulnerabilities that you've already examined to the physical security of network devices and the implementation and configuration of devices that protect your network from external threats. In this section, you'll examine physical security concepts, firewalls, network address translation, proxy servers, perimeter networks, security through VLANs, and wireless security.

Physical Security

Physical network security implies the safeguarding of all networking assets including servers, connectivity devices, cabling, and points of access to the network such as workstations and portable devices. Physical security is often one of the easiest and least costly methods of security that an organization can implement. Examples of physical security include locked doors, locked airflow vents, locked windows, and electronic sentries or human guards that monitor access to and egress from computing centers, server rooms, and wiring closets.

Other physical security practices include not leaving portable devices such as laptops and PDAs or any other portable computing resource unattended for even brief periods. This can reduce the potential for unauthorized access to the network or theft of the portable access device. If a portable computing device must be left unattended, it should be secured within a locked enclosure, whether that is a locked office or a locked drawer of a desk.

Because devices such as workstations, laptops, and PDAs can store vast amounts of an organization's data as well as provide access to an organization's networks, it's crucial that user and computer policies be implemented as part of a physical security plan. **User and computer policies** control access to each computer in your network and to network functionality on a user-by-user or computer-by-computer basis, and they're generally enforced through software such as Novell's ZENworks or Microsoft's Systems Management Server and other Microsoft security policies.

For example, users can be restricted from logging on to the network during specific hours of the day and be forced to log out after a certain time of day. Users can be restricted to a certain number of unsuccessful logon attempts before their accounts are locked. Users might be required to supply updated passwords on a periodic basis or even supply a thumbprint, palm print, voice sample, or retina scan to gain access to their computers or the network. In addition, user and computer policies can be configured to automatically display a password-protected screensaver if the computer is left unattended for a defined period of time.

Policies can also restrict access to certain applications and files. Still other policies audit network activity to alert network managers of potential security violations. All user and computer policies are configured to prevent unauthorized access to various computer and network functions. The policies mentioned here are just a few of the restrictions that a knowledgeable network administrator can apply.

These measures might seem trivial in an environment in which all users trust each other. With the increasing transition to Internet technologies, combined with frequent use of temporary help in the workplace, and constant threats from hackers and virus propagation, simple measures such as these can significantly reduce an organization's exposure to attacks against physical network resources and the network as a whole.

Firewalls

In today's valuable LAN environments, managers and administrators must constantly be on guard for unauthorized network access and network security risks at every level. That includes securing valuable hardware, software, and information within locked rooms, providing access control through unique user names and passwords, implementing routers that provide **network address translation (NAT)** to secure private networks from public networks, and configuring **proxy servers** to provide application-level security functionality. In addition, modern networks require **firewalls** to protect trusted private network environments from public domain networks and to provide a focused point of security administration. Figure 9.4 provides an example.

A firewall is any device comprised of hardware, software, or a combination of the two that protects your LAN from unauthorized access and reduces potential security risks. Like bulkhead hatches on a ship or submarine that allow the boat to continue operating in the event of damage caused by an attack, firewalls provide organizations with the ability to isolate their networks or sections of their networks from unauthorized access and still allow the network to function. In recent years, firewalls have become highly specialized devices that can regulate access across the various layers of the OSI or TPC/IP models. For example, firewalls can limit data transmissions between networks according to MAC address

user and computer policies
control access to each computer in your network and to network functionality on a user-by-user or computer-by-computer basis

Network Address Translation (NAT)
the process of translating private network IP addresses into one or more registered IP addresses for transmission across an external network

proxy server
a computer or network device that acts on behalf of client computers to provide access to remote resources

firewall
any device comprised of hardware, software, or a combination of the two that protects your LAN from unauthorized access and security risks

information (OSI layer 2), by IP address (OSI layer 3), by IP port (OSI layer 4), and even by type of service (upper layers).[5]

Even as you're reading this book, firewalls are evolving to accommodate a constantly changing security environment. In the very early days of firewalls, routers configured with access control lists provided limited security between external networks and private local area networks. If you were an external user, you could gain access to a private network as long as your IP address and type of service you wanted to use were included on the access list; any external users that did not have their IP addresses on the access control list were denied entry to the internal network.

LAN security became a lot more complicated, however, once the Internet became readily accessible and administrators began connecting their private networks. With that, simple access control lists became obsolete overnight because access control lists that allowed or denied entry by IP address and type of service couldn't guard against anonymous access by protocols such as the File Transfer Protocol (FTP). Private networks were no longer safe based on access control alone; a simple anonymous FTP connection could compromise a LAN and its information in a matter of minutes if not seconds. And security threats didn't stop there. Port-level access breaches soon followed, and now LANs must include constant vigilance against service-level attacks that could temporarily or even permanently damage a private network.

But a firewall is not the only solution that you can use to keep your network safe. You could implement security policies at each and every computer in your LAN and forget about the firewall. However, the problem with this approach is that there is much configuration and monitoring time and cost associated with maintaining high levels of security on every computing device located within a LAN. In addition, administration consistency over time and across large numbers of computers is a difficult task, and potentially devastating mistakes can happen inadvertently; the more devices that require constant configuration, monitoring, and updating, the higher the potential for unauthorized access and disastrous security breaches. To circumvent the time and cost issues as well as the security issues associated with maintaining security policies on multiple computers, you can implement firewalls at the key points on your network that connect to the outside world or to other external networks. With this configuration strategy, you can narrow your security focus to a few points of administration.

Packet-level Firewalls

packet-level firewall allows or denies access to a network based on the source and destination address included with each packet attempting to traverse the firewall

You can define firewall functionality at two major levels: packet level is one, and application level is the other. **Packet-level firewalls** have the ability to deny or allow access to an internal network based on the source and destination addresses included with every packet that attempts to pass through the firewall, as illustrated in Figure 9.5. As an external computer attempts to send data to your internal network, the firewall reads the transport layer and network layer addresses on each packet for comparison with a set of filtering rules. The filtering rules are established by the network administrator and are configured on the firewall. These rules generally limit which source addresses will be allowed to send packets through the firewall and which will be denied. The filtering rules also define which protocols, such as TCP or UDP, are allowed to traverse the firewall. In addition, destination addresses can be configured in the firewall filtering rules to allow or deny access to various services such as HTTP or SMTP. This has the effect of controlling access to Web servers and e-mail.

---

[5] Telnet, for example, follows the functionality defined by the upper layers of the OSI model or the application layer of the TCP/IP model.

FIGURE 9.5 **Packet-level Firewall**

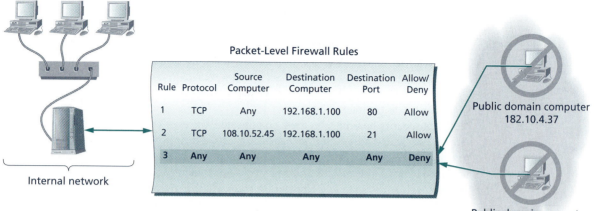

Packet-Level Firewall Rules

Rule	Protocol	Source Computer	Destination Computer	Destination Port	Allow/ Deny
1	TCP	Any	192.168.1.100	80	Allow
2	TCP	108.10.52.45	192.168.1.100	21	Allow
3	Any	Any	Any	Any	Deny

Internal network

Public domain computer
182.10.4.37

Public domain computer
139.2.45.11

In Figure 9.5, a network administrator has configured the packet-level firewall to allow and deny access under certain sets of circumstances. For example, in the first rule, the TCP protocol is allowed from any external computer to access an internal Web-server computer that has an IP address of 192.168.1.100. The destination port of 80 that is associated with this Web server indicates that this internal computer will service HTTP requests as long as the source computer is in the source list. As a second example, rule 2 allows FTP access from an external computer with an IP address of 108.10.52.45; port 21 signifies the service port associated with FTP. Finally, rule 3 denies access to all other external computers for any services residing on internal computers by denying packets containing any other protocol, source address, destination address, or port address.

Packet-level firewalls can also be configured to allow or deny internal-to-external data transmissions. In many cases, the flow of data from inside a trusted network to an external network is quite permissive; however, for higher levels of security, this outward flow of data should also be restricted to operate within the security policy defined by your company or organization.

Stateful Packet Inspection

Let's say you get your packet-level firewall configured so that the security rules for external-to-internal as well as internal-to-external data transmissions are very strict. This keeps your network very secure by limiting the inflow of data traffic as well as limiting the types of connections that internal computers can make with computers in the outside world. Sounds great, doesn't it? Only it's not as secure as you think it is. Hackers who want to get into your internal network can use spoofing to trick your packet-level firewall into letting them in. With spoofing, an external computer changes the source IP address on its packets into a source IP address that is valid on your internal network. Because all internal IP addresses are trusted by the packet-level firewall, the hacker gets in to do whatever it is he or she wants to do on your network.

Stateful packet inspection can solve this problem. With **stateful packet inspection**, the configured packet filter rules still apply, but in addition, each incoming packet is examined to see if it is part of an existing connection between an internal and an external computer. If it is and it passes the existing filter rules, the packet is allowed to traverse the firewall, as illustrated in Figure 9.6.

stateful packet inspection
firewall functionality that includes not only packet filter rules but also includes connection information about packets traversing the firewall

FIGURE 9.6 Stateful Packet Inspection

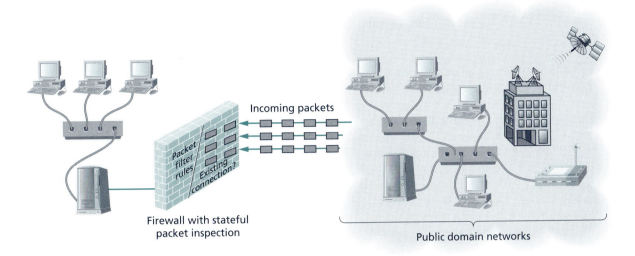

Firewall with stateful
packet inspection

Public domain networks

Incoming packets

Stateful packet inspection reduces the potential for spoofed packets to gain entry into your internal network. If an incoming packet has a spoofed internal IP address, there is no way it could be part of an existing connection. In addition, stateful packet inspection can be configured to examine data contents of specified protocols such as FTP and SMTP. Since both of these protocols can transmit commands that you might not want communicated to internal FTP or SMTP computers, the stateful inspection process can read each packet's contents and drop those incoming packets that harbor unwanted FTP or SMTP commands.

Stateful packet inspection functionality is common in most modern firewalls. It provides a level of security that is a cut above simple packet-level firewalls but it's not as secure as an application-level firewall. The trade-off is speed. Because application-level firewalls inspect more information on each data packet, their performance is slower; stateful packet inspection foregoes that extra level of packet examination in favor of increased data transmission performance.

Application-level Firewalls

application-level firewall
a firewall that filters traffic between networks at the service level

Application-level firewalls are another method of protecting internal networks from the security exposure caused by connection to an untrusted external network. When a firewall functions as a gateway to internal computers that are hosting applications that external users access, we refer to the firewall as an *application gateway* or *application-level firewall*. Under this functionality, it is common for the application firewall to require authentication by user name and password. Application-level firewalls can also filter by type of service such as FTP, HTTP, or Telnet.

Because application-level firewalls are filtering at the service level as opposed to the packet level, they are slower than packet-level firewalls because of the extra overhead associated with examining upper-layer protocol information. In addition, if the authentication requirement is configured, transaction time is increased by the amount of time required to perform the authentication.

Firewall Software versus Firewall Appliances

firewall software
a firewall solution that is comprised of a software program that runs on top of an operating system

Once you've made the decision to implement a firewall, the next step will be to choose your approach; you can install firewall software or a firewall appliance. The **firewall software** solution generally involves installing a configurable application on top of an existing operating system, but it might involve reconfiguring the operating system itself to provide the additional firewall functionality. The major network operating system companies, Microsoft and Novell, provide application-based firewall solutions that install on top of their operating systems. Linux and UNIX operating systems also include firewall functionality, but you have to add this functionality by installing it as part of the core operating system. All of the common software-based firewalls generally include packet-level as well as application-level firewall services. You can then choose your level of configuration to meet your security needs.

firewall appliance
a firewall solution that includes a combination of hardware and software designed for optimum data transmission performance based on the security configuration you establish

Firewall appliances, on the other hand, are a combination of hardware and software designed for optimum data transmission performance based on the security configuration you establish. Firewall appliances offer the same levels of security that you can obtain in packet-level or application-level software firewalls, but you won't have the added overhead of a full-featured operating system. That is, with software-based firewalls, you'll probably need to tweak the underlying operating system to make it more secure prior to installing the software firewall and the operating system will still be providing other services such as file and printer sharing. With firewall appliances, the appliance's operating system is designed specifically for security duty; all you need to do is establish your security policy and implement the configuration.

Network Address Translation

Network address translation (NAT)
the process of translating private network IP addresses into one or more registered IP addresses for transmission across an external network

Network address translation (NAT) is another method that can be employed in a LAN environment to enhance network security. NAT translates the internal network IP addresses of the **stub domain**, which is NAT-speak for your internal LAN, into globally recognized and registered IP addresses for transmission across external networks including the Internet. With this translation, the IP addresses of your organization's computers are hidden from the outside world so that the risks associated with IP data communications across the Internet and other outside networks is substantially reduced. Would-be hackers see only the registered address of the device that is connected to the outside world and not the individual IP addresses of the computers on your network. Generally speaking, external users can gain access through the NAT device only if the connection originated from a device on your internal LAN.

stub domain
the term used to describe your local area network when it is connected to the outside world through a NAT device such as a NAT router

Network address translation is typically implemented through a **router** designed to perform address translation in addition to its normal routing functions. Here's how it works from a technical viewpoint. In Figure 9.7, a computer on a LAN has information to send to another computer somewhere on another network. As the packets from the source computer reach the NAT router and are forwarded to another network, the NAT router strips off the source computer's IP address and port information from each data packet, and replaces the address and port information with the IP address of the NAT router along with a unique port address. The NAT router stores this address translation information in a table known as a *port mapping table* so that when the receiving device on the remote network responds, the NAT router can look up the translation information, repackage the incoming packets with the source computer's IP address and port information, and send the response back to the computer that originated the communication.

NAT router
a routing device that connects your internal network to an external network while providing both routing and NAT functionality

inbound mapping
sometimes referred to as Static NAT allows external computers to initiate connections with computers such as Web servers on the internal network

Although NAT generally restricts connections that originate outside of the stub domain, you might have devices such as Web servers on your LAN that need to service requests from external computers. In cases like that, you can configure NAT to provide **inbound mapping**. With **inbound mapping**, specific port addresses are configured in the NAT table and are mapped to specific internal addresses so that outside requests directed at specific internal devices such as Web servers can be satisfied.

FIGURE 9.7
Network Address
Translation

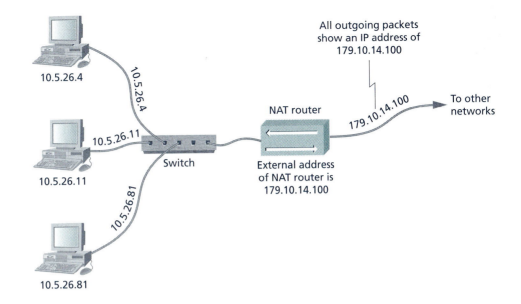

Proxy Servers

Ari Luotonen is credited with developing the first Web proxy server in 1994 at **CERN**.[6] His goal was to improve network security by providing an intermediate device that could act on behalf of internal network computers and which would intercept all network traffic that passed between an internal network and the Internet. The Web proxy would limit the amount of direct traffic between internal client computers and computers on external networks so that outside computers would not have direct access to corporate data. **Proxy servers** provide a level of security between local area network users and remote networks such as the Internet or other corporate networks. By acting as an intermediary between client computers and remote networks, proxy servers are able to reduce security exposure while at the same time providing other services that benefit network and data access performance.

proxy server
a computer or network device that acts on behalf of client computers to provide access to remote resources

A **proxy server** is a computer or other network device that acts on behalf of client computers to provide access to remote resources. This computer intercepts requests from client computers and repackages and forwards the request to a computer on a targeted remote network. The remote computer sees the proxy server as the originator of the request, thereby shielding the client computer from the remote computer. All responses are directed back to the proxy server, which, in turn, forwards the response back to the client computer. Using a proxy provides a level of secrecy for client computers that make requests for services located on other networks.

But client secrecy is not the only security feature bundled into proxy servers. Proxy servers can be configured to block access to specified Web pages; they can restrict access to remote services based on client-user ID, workstation ID, type of service requested, IP address of the client computer, and so on. For example, as represented in Figure 9.8, you can configure your proxy server to allow one user to have Internet access and make HTTP requests, while at the same time denying that user FTP access to the Internet or other remote network. You might configure a second user to have both FTP and HTTP access but restrict

---

[6] CERN is the acronym for Conseil Européen pour la Recherche Nucléaire. It was established in the 1950s and is the world's largest particle physics lab.

FIGURE 9.8
**Proxy Server Access
Restrictions**

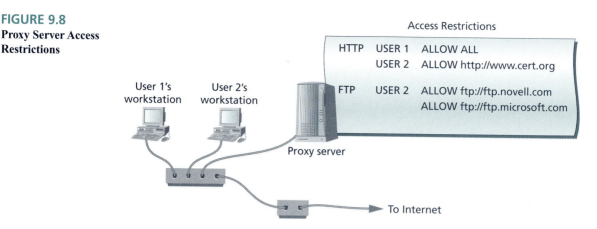

access to certain URLs. Still other users might need access to services that supply multimedia files and presentations, and due to the amount of traffic on your LAN, you configure your proxy server to allow only specific users or workstations to have this type of access. You can also configure FTP uploads but not downloads or vice versa, restrict access to remote network services based on time of day, and log the types of traffic traversing your network.

reverse proxy
a computer or network device that acts on behalf of external client computers to provide controlled access to internal resources

Reverse proxy is another way to improve LAN security, especially when you want to provide information to external users. External users who do not have direct access to content-delivering Web servers on your LAN can be granted controlled and restricted access through a reverse proxy configuration. In this scenario, the proxy server acts on behalf of the external users to direct requests to the Web server located on your LAN. The reverse proxy controls access to the Web server so that external users do not have direct and unrestricted access to your Web server's content. In fact, you can place control parameters on the reverse proxy to restrict access so that only certain external users or specific external networks can gain access to your Web server's content.

For enhanced security, proxy servers are generally implemented in conjunction with firewalls. Specifically, a firewall can be installed and configured to be very restrictive, so restrictive, in fact, that direct client access to outside networks is not allowed. To provide outside access, one or more proxy servers is configured to service client computer requests, and the firewall is configured to allow only the proxy server to pass requests to the outside world, as presented in Figure 9.9.[7]

Web caching
a process that stores frequently accessed Web content on the proxy server so that LAN clients can access the information faster

Security and access control are not the only built-in services that proxy servers provide. Proxy servers also provide **Web caching**, a process that stores frequently accessed Web content on the proxy server so that LAN clients can access the information at faster network data transmission rates instead of at slower Internet data transmission rates.[8]

Web caching, also referred to as *proxy caching,* works like this. When a client computer makes a remote network request that is serviced through a proxy server, the proxy server retrieves the information on behalf of the client, responds to the client's request by delivering the content to the client, and at the same time saves a copy of the content on the proxy server. The next time someone accesses the same remote site, the information is retrieved from the copy that is stored on the proxy server. Information access is faster because the data can be transferred from the proxy server at LAN speeds instead of at Internet speeds,

---

[7]The proxy server software can be installed on the same device as the firewall software, or it can be run on a separate device, depending on the software and hardware being used.

[8] Static content, meaning content that doesn't change over time, requires a less sophisticated caching application than dynamic content, which is content that changes frequently over time.

FIGURE 9.9   **Proxy Server Working in Conjunction with a Firewall**

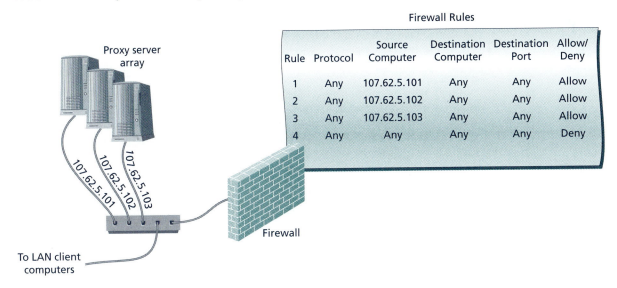

Firewall Rules

Rule	Protocol	Source Computer	Destination Computer	Destination Port	Allow/ Deny
1	Any	107.62.5.101	Any	Any	Allow
2	Any	107.62.5.102	Any	Any	Allow
3	Any	107.62.5.103	Any	Any	Allow
4	Any	Any	Any	Any	Deny

which are limited by the data transmission rate of the carrier service you lease and are generally slower than the speed of your internal network.

Another feature of caching that is important in terms of network performance and content access is read-ahead caching. With **read-ahead caching** a proxy server is configured to automatically download content from commonly accessed Web sites without a client request triggering the download. This can improve network performance and data accessibility because frequently accessed sites will always be stored locally on the proxy server for fast access. Read-ahead caching is not necessarily a security-enhancing feature other than it reinforces the intermediary role that a proxy server plays in controlling client access to remote networks.

In contemporary LAN environments that require controlled access and cached content, you might find proxy arrays or hierarchically configured proxy servers. With **proxy arrays**, multiple proxy servers are configured and linked to provide load balancing of client requests and fault tolerance in the event that one or more proxy servers crash. In addition, the proxy array can be configured to act as a giant cache for Web content; with more proxy servers in the configuration, there is also more capacity to store commonly accessed Web pages.

With hierarchically configured proxy servers, each department in an organization is configured with a proxy server, and client computers within the department are configured to direct their requests to the department's proxy server. If there is a request for Web content from an internally configured Web server, the department-level proxy server acts on behalf of the client computer in the department to fulfill the request. If, however, a client computer in one of the departments requests external Web content, the request is first reviewed by the department's proxy server, which, in turn, forwards the request to another proxy server that interfaces with the corporate firewall. This higher level proxy server packages the request for passage through the firewall, and the firewall is configured to allow only the requests from this higher level proxy server to pass to the outside world. Generally speaking, the proxy server that communicates with the firewall is configured with much tighter restrictions than department-level proxy servers. This ensures tighter security for your LAN.

Proxy arrays and hierarchical proxy configurations also provide enhanced caching capability over a single proxy server configuration. Specifically, when a client computer makes a request for Web content, the proxy server that intercepts the request will first look

read-ahead caching
the process of automatically downloading content from commonly accessed Web sites without a client request triggering the download

proxy array
provides multiple proxy servers configured and linked to provide load balancing of client requests and fault tolerance in the event that one or more proxy servers crash

If you've already studied the previous sections of this chapter, you might be wondering what the differences are between NAT and a proxy server. With NAT the sending and receiving devices have no knowledge of an intermediate device; the translation is transparent to both devices. In addition, because NAT performs address translation on a layer 3 protocol, that is, IP, it's a service that is also defined by layer 3 of the OSI model.

Proxy servers, on the other hand, require configuration at the client computer so that requests are specifically directed to the proxy server. This is not transparent to the client computer. In addition, since proxy servers generally perform security on protocols such as HTTP and FTP, proxy servers provide functionality at OSI layer 4 and above.

in its cache to see if the Web page is available there. If it is not in its local cache, the proxy server will redirect its request to another proxy server in the array or hierarchy to see if the Web content is located on one of these "upstream" proxy servers. The search continues from proxy server to proxy server until the content is found; if it's not cached anywhere in the array or hierarchy, the request is forwarded to the outside world.[9]

Perimeter Networks

In today's networking environments, using a single firewall with very strict access controls is hardly sufficient to both deny access to unauthorized external users as well as allow access to friendly external users. If you configure your corporate firewall so that it is very secure, you won't be able to provide high levels of information access to authorized users sitting outside the firewall. On the other hand, if your firewall's configuration is too permissive, then management won't believe that vital information is sufficiently protected. The goal, then, is to implement a solution that satisfies both needs—high security and adequate access. That dual-purpose solution can be found in a perimeter network. Figure 9.10 provides an illustration of a perimeter network.

perimeter network
a LAN that sits between the outside world and your internal network and is designed and configured to improve overall network security

A **perimeter network** is a LAN that sits between external public networks and your internal network. Perimeter networks frequently contain devices such as Web servers, e-mail servers, DNS servers, and other types of servers that contain the types of information that external users might need to access on a regular and relatively unrestricted basis. Often called a **demilitarized zone (DMZ)**, a perimeter network is generally configured with other security technologies as well; it is common to see a firewall at each border of the perimeter network and one or more proxy servers to provide access to remote resources.

demilitarized zone (DMZ)
another term used to describe a perimeter network

DMZ with Firewalls

In Figure 9.10, the perimeter network is connected to the outside world through a firewall configured to allow HTTP and FTP traffic. Within the DMZ is a Web server configured to deliver content and files via HTTP and FTP. Any users outside the perimeter network can use a Web browser to gain access to this DMZ Web server. However, at the internal border of the DMZ, an "internal" firewall denies incoming HTTP and FTP traffic so that external users cannot use the ports associated with HTTP and FTP to gain access to the internal network. The firewall that connects to the outside world is less restrictive while the firewall that protects the internal network is very restrictive. Access to unrestricted content is provided where it's needed without compromising the security of internal corporate information. The

---

[9] More modern proxy arrays use a protocol known as Cache Array Routing Protocol or (CARP) to locate the other proxy servers with cached content. In older hierarchical proxy configurations, the Internet Cache Protocol (ICP) is used to route cache searches throughout the proxy hierarchy.

FIGURE 9.10 Perimeter Network

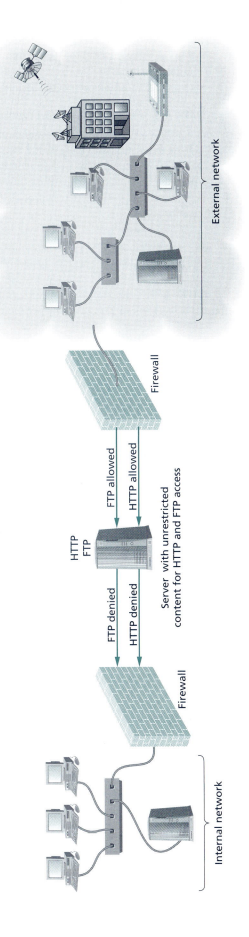

intrusion protection
the set of policies,
procedures, and systems
within an organization
that work to detect,
prevent, and respond
to network and host
intruders

audit logs and alerts
the reporting
mechanisms for
intrusion protection.
Audit logs record
suspicious and
inappropriate network
traffic or host activity
in a database for
subsequent review by
security administrators.
Alerts are the thresholds
for suspicious and
inappropriate activity
above which security
administrators are
notified by e-mail,
pager, telephone, etc.

*honeypots and
honeynets*
decoy computing
devices and networks
that are open to
attackers

Interesting Web sites
for honeypots and
honeynets include
www.honeypots.org
and www.honeynet.org.

intrusion detection
the hardware, software,
and human factors
that passively detect
suspicious and
inappropriate activity on
a network or network
host

intrusion prevention
the hardware, software,
and human factors
that actively detect,
intercept, and stop or
redirect suspicious and
inappropriate activity on
a network or network
host

internal network is safer this way because external users will not have unauthorized access to corporate information located behind the perimeter network.

DMZ with Proxy Servers and Network Address Translation

In a perimeter network, the firewall devices will generally incorporate proxy and network address translation services. At the internal border, the proxy server will act on behalf of internal LAN computers to provide access to remote application services located both within the DMZ and outside of the firewall on the DMZ's external border. In addition, the internal firewall will also likely provide NAT services so that a single IP address represents the internal network.

At the external border of the DMZ, the firewall won't be configured to provide NAT services; however, any proxy service built into the firewall will very likely be configured to provide Web-caching services for external users. While the proxy service at the external border firewall doesn't provide any additional access restrictions, implementing a proxy service at this external location can significantly improve the access response to Web server requests originating outside the perimeter network.

Intrusion Protection

Intrusion protection has become popular in recent years, providing services that function as the eyes and ears of perimeter networks. **Intrusion protection** is the set of policies, procedures, and systems within an organization that work to detect, prevent, and respond to intruders. While intrusion protection has traditionally functioned as an attack detection service known as intrusion detection, more recently, intrusion protection has expanded into actively preventing intruders from attacking an organization's networks through a process called intrusion prevention. Another component of intrusion protection is intrusion response, which can include policy-based responses that dictate how specific networking devices should respond in the event of an intrusion; **audit logs and alerts**, which generate database records of suspicious or anomalous behavior and send electronic messages to network security administrators; and **honeypots** or **honeynets** that serve as decoys to lead would-be attackers away from production networks.

Intrusion Detection **Intrusion detection** is the hardware, software, and human factors that passively detect suspicious and inappropriate activity on a network or network host. Intrusion detection systems (IDS) monitor network and host activity according to a set of rules known as pattern matching, which simply means that IDS continuously looks for patterns that correspond to known attacks, such as TCP SYN floods, ping storms, or buffer overflows. When IDS recognizes an attack, it can instruct the firewall to shut down the affected TCP ports and deny access to the intruder's IP address. In addition, IDS can send *TCP reset packets* to the target host computer instructing the host to kill the session that is underway between the attacker and the target host. IDS software can reside on a firewall device, or it can be a separate device that works in conjunction with the firewall. Part **(a)** of Figure 9.11 provides an example of where IDS might be placed relative to a firewall and how it interacts with both the firewall and the target host.

Intrusion Prevention **Intrusion prevention** is the hardware, software, and human factors that actively detect, intercept, and stop or redirect suspicious and inappropriate activity on a network or network host. The goal of intrusion prevention systems (IPS) is to detect and defeat attackers in real time. Intrusion prevention systems detect known attacks much like IDS, but IPS can also detect unknown attacks based on unusual traffic patterns and protocols that vary from the standards set forth in Requests for Comment (RFC).[10]

---

[10] You learned about RFCs in chapter 1.

FIGURE 9.11 Intrusion Detection and Intrusion Prevention Systems

a. Intrusion detection system. **b.** Intrusion prevention system

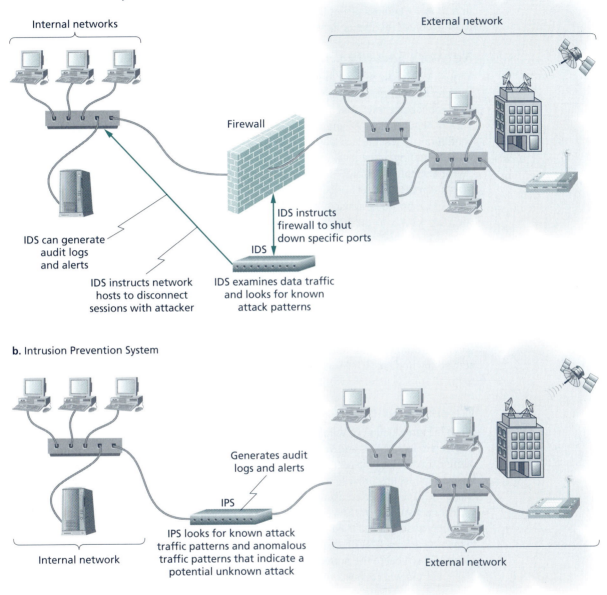

a. Intrusion Detection System

Internal networks

External network

Firewall

IDS instructs
firewall to shut
down specific ports

IDS

IDS can generate
audit logs
and alerts

IDS instructs network
hosts to disconnect
sessions with attacker

IDS examines data traffic
and looks for known
attack patterns

b. Intrusion Prevention System

Generates audit
logs and alerts

IPS

IPS looks for known attack
traffic patterns and anomalous
traffic patterns that indicate a
potential unknown attack

Internal network

External network

Other differences between IPS and IDS allow IPS to stop all attacks automatically without having to update rules on other filtering devices such as firewalls. Intrusion prevention system devices sit inline with other network devices, as represented in part **(b)** of Figure 9.11.

intrusion response
the set of methods that can be implemented in response to intrusion detection or intrusion prevention

Intrusion Response **Intrusion response** is the set of methods that can be implemented in response to intrusion detection or intrusion prevention. Intrusion response can automatically push more restrictive settings to a firewall when an attack is suspected. Intrusion response can result in audit logs and alerts being generated when suspicious network activity is detected. Intrusion response can redirect suspicious activity to a honeypot so that suspicious activity and attack patterns can be studied and stored for future reference or so that suspicious traffic can be directed away from the production network. Or intrusion response can simply drop all suspicious packets and defeat the attack in real time, which is the expected goal of intrusion prevention systems. The desired activity is as much a function of the overall security plan of the organization as it is a function of the intrusion protection technology that is implemented.

Network Security with VLANs

Virtual LANs can be used to separate collision domains and broadcast domains in a LAN and can be configured to separate groups of computers according to TCP port address.[11] This application-level functionality has implications for network security. Because layer 4 VLAN switches can discriminate based on TCP port addresses, network administrators can configure application-based VLANs and then isolate these VLANs with one or more firewalls according to the level of service the VLAN provides.

For example, you might have a number of Web servers that you want to make available to users on external networks. You could configure those servers to provide only HTTP services (TCP port 80), connect your Web servers to a specific VLAN, and then connect the specified VLAN to the Internet through a firewall. Allowing only HTTP traffic affords a level of protection to your Web servers, but making these servers available only through a VLAN isolates your other internal network computers as well as other VLANs from external network traffic in much the same way as application-level filtering. It may not be as discriminating as a DMZ implementation, but application-based VLANs are another method of enhancing internal network security.

VLANs also provide a level of internal security for corporate environments that include highly secure network segments. For example, if part of your business works with highly secure government contracts or other highly sensitive information, you can segment your network by implementing one or more VLANs to separate the network traffic on the secure segment from general network traffic.

Wireless LAN and MAN/WAN Security

Since the introduction of wireless LANs in the 1990s and more recently with the introduction of wireless MANs and WANs, wireless security has been a major concern for network administrators who are requested to implement and manage wireless networks as well as for the vendors that provide wireless products to the networking marketplace. Wireless networks are easily detected using any number of wireless network scanning devices, and if a wireless network operates without any form of security, packets can just as easily be intercepted by attackers and used to gain access to the data transmitting across the airwaves and to the network itself. With this relative ease of detection and interception, wireless network security is critical to the protection of organizations' networks and data.

To address wireless network security concerns, three technologies assist with reducing the potential exposure of wireless LANs, and another standard deals with the security of wireless MANs and WANs. For wireless LANs, a security standard known as Wired Equivalent Privacy (WEP) is built into the 802.11 wireless standard. Another, which was driven by the Wi-Fi Alliance, is known as Wi-Fi Protected Access (WPA). And a new wireless LAN technology that is in development but which hasn't been officially published as of this writing is called **IEEE 802.11i**.[12] For wireless MANs and WANs, commonly known as WiMAX, there is a security standard called **IEEE 802.16.**

---

[11] You learned about VLANs in chapter 4.

[12] The IEEE 802.11 standards were introduced in chapter 1 and discussed in more detail in chapter 3. IEEE 802.11i was first introduced in chapter 3.

The WEP authentication process uses MAC addresses to filter unauthorized wireless stations, but the problem with WEP authentication is that an attacker can scan a wireless network, intercept one or more valid MAC addresses, and then change his or her station's MAC address to match one of the valid addresses in order to gain access to the network.

The encryption algorithm was updated in early 2002, which eliminated the weakness that attackers exploited to defeat encryption with older versions of WEP, but much of the damage to WEP's reputation had already been done in the trade press. And the problem with authentication still exists. Overall, WEP is not considered a secure protocol and will not prevent a skilled attacker from accessing a wireless network. At the same time, WEP does provide basic encryption and authentication services that can ward off casual attackers.

Wired Equivalent Privacy (WEP) the original security protocol for IEEE 802.11 wireless networks. It uses authentication so that wireless stations and the access point can initially identify one another, and it uses encryption to provide confidentiality of the data being transmitted.

Wi-Fi Protected Access (WPA) a security protocol for IEEE 802.11 wireless LANs that uses the Temporal Key Integrity Protocol (TKIP) to make 802.11 wireless networks secure

There are several interesting commentaries on WEP security on the Web. For current results, do a Web search on "WEP cracking," and take a look at some of the postings.

Wired Equivalent Privacy

Wired Equivalent Privacy (WEP) uses authentication so that wireless stations and the access point can initially identify one another and encryption to provide confidentiality of the data being transmitted.[13] Wired Equivalent Privacy was the original security service for 802.11 wireless LANs and can still be implemented, but since it was cracked in 2001, it is considered secure enough only to forestall casual attacks. Subsequent revisions to the WEP encryption algorithm have supplanted the weaknesses of the original versions of WEP, but there is a new generation of security services that provides greater levels of security for wireless LANs than WEP.

Wi-Fi Protected Access

Wi-Fi Protected Access (WPA) is the current generation of wireless LAN security that uses the **Temporal Key Integrity Protocol (TKIP)** for enhanced encryption and the Extensible Access Protocol (EAP) for improved authentication. The combination of TKIP and EAP make WPA a much more formidable security service than WEP for IEEE 802.11 wireless LANs.[14]

Although WPA is a widely accepted industry standard, it is not an official IEEE standard. Instead, WPA is a transitional security service whose TKIP protocol is a subset of the forthcoming IEEE 802.11i standard. Since 2003, WPA has gained substantial industry support, and in many cases it can be implemented as a software upgrade to older Wi-Fi NICs.

The TKIP encryption protocol that drives WPA was developed under the direction of the IEEE 802.11 Task Group I, an IEEE group chartered with developing enhanced security for IEEE 802.11 wireless LANs and the Wi-Fi Alliance, an industry alliance that promotes the development and implementation of 802.11 products.[15]

IEEE 802.11i

The IEEE 802.11i standard will provide a new and secure wireless LAN standard known as the **robust security network (RSN).** With RSN, wireless access points will allow RSN-enabled stations as well as WEP-enabled stations to connect to the wireless LAN, but only the RSN-enabled stations will benefit from the enhanced security services of RSN. The

---

[13] You'll learn about encryption later on in this chapter. For now think of encryption as the scrambling of data so that only the intended receiving device can read the sender's information.

[14] You first learned about Wi-Fi as wireless fidelity in chapter 3. It is used synonymously with the IEEE 802.11 standard.

[15] The "I" in Task Group I is pronounced "eye."

You can discover more information regarding Task Group I on the IEEE Web site at www.ieee.org. Information regarding the Wi-Fi Alliance can be found at www.wi-fi.org, and information regarding WPA can be found at www.wi-fi.org/wpa.

802.11i standard includes support for WEP to provide a transition period for consumers to upgrade to newer RSN-capable devices.[16]

The difference between RSN under IEEE 802.11i and WPA is the addition of the Advanced Encryption Standard (AES) with RSN. Both RSN and WPA can be implemented with TKIP, but TKIP was promoted to provide a secure solution for 802.11 LANs once WEP was cracked. The addition of AES within the 802.11i standard provides organizations with a security standard that is both highly secure and highly scalable to large wireless LAN implementations.

IEEE 802.16

IEEE 802.16 is the standard for wireless MANs, commonly referred to as WiMAX. IEEE 802.16 has built-in authentication and data encryption according to the 802.16 standard, but the security features of the base 802.16 standard have several of the same shortcomings as WEP, namely inadequate authentication and insufficient encryption. To address this problem, the IEEE is revising the 802.16 set of standards. One revision that is expected to be published in 2005 is the 802.16e standard, which will include enhanced encryption based on AES. And although 802.16e doesn't currently specify an enhanced authentication method, the work being conducted within the IEEE 802.11i standard could migrate, with modifications, into the 802.16 standards to provide both the authentication and encryption requirements for a robust security specification within wireless MANs.

SECURING YOUR DATA

Securing an organization's data includes everything from the physical security of networking hardware and data resources to the implementation of advanced encryption and security protocols. Data security is generally part of an organization's comprehensive security plan and is crucial to business continuity in the event of a disaster as well as day-to-day business functionality. In this section, you'll examine physical security measures, virtual private networks, encryption, and security protocols.

Physical Security

Physical security with data assets is much the same as physical security with network assets. Once again, examples of physical security include locked access points such as doors, vents, and windows, and electronic sentries or human guards that monitor access and egress to computing centers and wiring closets. And as with physical security of a network, portable devices such as laptops and PDAs should be constantly monitored and policies for their safety enforced to prevent unauthorized access to an organization's data.

Regarding the physical protection of the actual data, one of the simplest and most practical methods employed is a data backup with offsite storage. With a systemwide backup combined with offsite storage, an organization stores its valuable corporate data on alternative media in its own location and maintains a copy of the stored data in one or more offsite locations. Since information can be lost from even the simplest of mistakes, such as inadvertent file deletion or spilling a cup of coffee on a laptop, ensuring that important files are saved to a central location that is backed up frequently is critical. In addition, storing one or more copies of the backed-up data at an offsite location will significantly reduce the risk of data loss.

---

[16] The encryption algorithm associated with RSN will preclude Wi-Fi hardware from being upgraded to RSN capability. Instead, devices will need to be replaced with the newer RSN devices.

Virtual Private Networks

virtual private network (VPN)
a secure point-to-point connection between two private networks or between two network devices that uses a public network instead of a private communication channel as a backbone for data transmission

A **virtual private network (VPN)** is a secure point-to-point connection between two private networks or between two network devices that uses a public network instead of a private communication channel as a backbone for data transmission.[17] A VPN extends the security of your internal network to the data packets that travel outside of your network and across the Internet or other external networks. Virtual private networks have become increasingly popular in recent years because of the importance of providing secure communication across public networks such as the Internet.

Typical VPNs utilize encryption and encapsulation technologies to create a secure communication channel between two networks or networking devices. In a mode of transmission known as *tunneling,* illustrated in Figure 9.12, data packets are encrypted and then encapsulated with the IP address of the device that interfaces with the public network, usually a firewall. The encapsulation hides the IP address of the true source device from any would-be Internet snooping sleuths (this is the tunnel), and the encryption scrambles the data so that only the intended receiving device can decrypt and read the sender's information. In another mode known as *transport mode,* only the data portion of each packet is encrypted; the source and destination IP address information remain intact.

You'll need to give special consideration to individual workstations that need to connect via VPN to your internal network. Unless you're providing a corporate firewall at the user's remote location of the type and configuration you're using for your local network, remote workstations generally don't have the built-in security features to provide a sufficiently secure VPN between the remote workstation and your internal network. The potential security exposure is that any open security holes on the workstation can allow an Internet hacker to gain access to the workstation and then remotely access your internal network through a VPN that connects the workstation to your internal network. Once connected to the workstation, the VPN will provide the hacker with an open door to your internal network. To guard against such a security exposure, you can obtain special client firewall software that provides the same kinds of protection as a corporate firewall, and you can implement special configuration options on the client computer's operating system such as system hardening, a process that enhances the security of a computer's operating system.

The business reasoning behind VPNs is cost; using the Internet as a backbone is cheaper than leasing a private carrier service. Whereas the carrier service would theoretically provide a secure channel for data transmission that would be used only by your organization, similar results can be achieved at much lower cost by utilizing virtual private network technologies.

FIGURE 9.12   **VPN with Tunneling Technology**

---

[17] The private communication channel mentioned here would be a carrier service such as T1 or T3 or frame relay, etc. Carrier services were discussed in chapter 8.

In an effort to reduce the cost of distributing forms and reports and to facilitate information updates, many companies have implemented online reporting of employee information. The information is readily accessible to employees who are logged onto the network from within the corporate firewall; all they have to do is provide a user name and password to access the database, and they have all their personal information available for review and modification in a Web browser window.

If you're a remote employee, you don't get quite the same easy and simple access. When you attempt to access that information from outside the corporate firewall, there's a security exposure that doesn't exist when you log on from the inside. That's where VPN software comes into play. The firewall will be configured to allow only certain types of remote access from the outside world. That means only certain protocols are allowed and only certain ports will be open to gain access to internal services or applications, such as the employee database. If the firewall has also been configured for VPNs, the first time you attempt to connect from a remote computer to the internal network, you will receive a message that the service couldn't be found. Generally this will prompt a call to the information services team to find out what's going on, and they'll instruct you to access the required VPN client on a corporate Web server that sits outside the firewall.

With very little effort, you download the VPN client software, install it, restart your computer, and then run the VPN application. Once the VPN application is running, you can open your Web browser, enter the URL you wanted to get to in the first place, and then you'll be prompted for a user name and password just like users who are inside the firewall. During your remote communication session the VPN client is very likely performing services such as IP address translation and tunneling as well as encryption of the communication session with a popular symmetric encryption program like 3DES or maybe even AES.[18]

---

encryption
the process of turning plaintext into ciphertext

plaintext
also known as *cleartext,* is data in its original and readable character and numeric format

ciphertext
encrypted cleartext

encryption key
the sequence of bits that controls how strong the encryption is

encryption algorithm
the sequence of mathematical instructions that performs the encryption

decryption
the reverse of encryption; it's the process of unencrypting data

Encryption

So far in this chapter, we've explored ways to keep unauthorized users from gaining access to your internal networks and the valuable information stored there. But what happens if someone can actually gain access to your data, or in some way eavesdrops on the information you're sending over a communication channel? In a case like this, you had better have a method of storing and sending your information so that prying eyes can't read it even if they gain access to it. That method is encryption.

Actually, **encryption** is the process of turning **plaintext** or **cleartext**—two synonymous terms that define data in its original and readable character and numeric forms—into scrambled information known as **ciphertext**. Encryption is accomplished through software or hardware by applying an encryption key to an encryption algorithm. The **encryption key** is a sequence of bits that controls the level of encryption. That is, the more bits in the encryption key, the stronger the encryption. The **encryption algorithm**, also known as a *cipher,* is the sequence of mathematical instructions that performs the encryption. **Decryption** is the reverse of encryption. Decryption turns the scrambled information into plaintext—words and numbers that a person can read.

The encryption/decryption process goes on behind the scenes and you won't even be aware of its existence once you've enabled it within a software program or on a hardware security device. However, because of the security exposure of plaintext data transmissions, you should be familiar with the two major types of encryption that will help you protect your data. They are secret key encryption and public key encryption.

---

[18] You'll learn about encryption and encryption methods later in this chapter.

Secret Key Encryption

Secret key encryption, which is also known as *single key encryption, conventional encryption,* or *symmetric encryption,* uses a single shared key along with an encryption algorithm at both ends of the communication channel to encrypt or decrypt data transmissions. The algorithm can be public knowledge, but only the communicating devices on either end of the transmission channel share the encryption key. Because the key is a secret shared only by the end devices, eavesdroppers on the communications channel will not be able to decipher the encrypted transmission unless they somehow steal the key.

The encryption key itself is a series of bits, and as more bits are added to the key the safer will be the resulting encryption. With more bits in the key, your encryption will be less susceptible to unauthorized parties who want to crack your encryption. Common examples of key length include 40-bit, 56-bit, 64-bit, 128-bit, and 256-bit keys. More bits mean more secure data transmissions. If you prefer, you can think of it like this. If you have a combination lock that requires only three numbers to open, and if two people have the combination, each can open it quite rapidly. Any other person without the combination will be sitting there a while trying to figure out the combination. Increase the number of digits in the combination to four, and the time frame required to figure out the exact series of numbers in the combination increases by a huge factor; probably longer than someone will want to take to figure it out. Such is the case with encryption keys; more bits in the key means more secure encryption because of the time factor and expensive computer hardware and software required to figure out the exact combination.

Several secret key encryption standards exist, with the primary differentiator being the number of bits used in the encryption key and the complexity of the encryption algorithm. The ones you'll learn about in this chapter are the Data Encryption Standard (DES), Triple DES (3DES), the International Data Encryption Algorithm (IDEA), RC4, and the Advanced Encryption Standard (AES).

Data Encryption Standard   The **Data Encryption Standard (DES)** was developed by IBM in the 1970s and was published in 1977 by the National Bureau of Standards, which has since become the National Institute of Standards and Technology (NIST). It uses a 56-bit encryption key to encrypt 64-bit blocks of data. Since it can be deciphered relatively quickly (in under a day) in what are known as **brute-force attacks**—attacks on encrypted data that run through all the potential bit combinations of the secret key in a relatively short amount of time—DES is no longer considered secure and is not recommended for environments that require secure encryption. However, it is still commonly used for data encryption that requires only modest levels of encryption protection.

Triple DES   The **Triple Data Encryption Standard (3DES)** performs triple encryption on 64-bit data blocks using two secret keys. The first encryption uses the first key to encrypt the 64-bit data block. The second encryption uses a different secret key to perform decryption on the encrypted 64-bit block, resulting in a further scrambling of the data.[19] Finally, a third encryption uses the first secret key to encrypt the result of the second encryption. The overall encrypted result is more secure than the standard DES because it's using two secret keys for a total of 112 keying bits. Other implementations of 3DES utilize three distinct secret keys but it's not common to see that with 3DES.

Blowfish   **Blowfish** is a symmetric encryption algorithm invented by Bruce Schneier in 1993. It encrypts 64-bit data blocks using keys that range in size from 32 bits to 448 bits. In its 448-bit configuration, it is a highly secure encryption alternative. Designed to be faster than DES or IDEA, Blowfish can be found as an encryption choice in numerous applications. Its inventor didn't seek patent protection, which makes Blowfish available without personal or commercial license constraints.

---

[19] It's not decrypted back to its original plaintext form because it's a different key doing the decrypting.

RC4   **RC4** is another single key encryption method that first entered the public domain in 1994 after being a proprietary technology of RSA Data Security. It can encrypt data using secret keys of 40 bits up to 256 bits, although the 40-bit keys are most common. Because it is generally implemented with 40-bit keys, it is readily cracked using brute-force attacks. In addition, RC4 is the encryption security standard utilized by Wired Equivalent Privacy (WEP).

International Data Encryption Algorithm   The **International Data Encryption Algorithm (IDEA)** was first published in 1991. Using an as yet uncracked 128-bit encryption key to turn plaintext into ciphertext, to date it is still a secure method of data encryption.

Advanced Encryption Standard   The **Advanced Encryption Standard (AES)** is a true 21st century encryption technology that began as a contest proposed by the National Institute of Standards and Technology (NIST). NIST was looking for a new encryption algorithm that would provide speed as well as security, and Drs. Joan Daemen and Vincent Rijmen answered the call. Their algorithm, known as **Rijndael** (pronounced *Reign Dahl*), now a Federal Information Processing Standard (FIPS 197), provides for 128-, 192-, and 256-bit encryption keys in combination with data blocks of 128-, 192-, or 256-bits.[20] This standard should be sufficient to withstand brute-force attacks because it would take about 150 trillion years to crack a 128-bit AES encryption key. The IEEE 802.11i standard that is proposed for wireless LANs specifies AES as the encryption algorithm.

You'll find some interesting information about AES if you search the NIST Web site at www.nist.gov, or go to http://csrc.nist .gov/CryptoToolkit/aes or http://csrc.nist.gov/ CryptoToolkit/aes/roun d2/aesfact.html.

Practical Considerations for Secret Key Encryption   In addition to being practically "uncrackable" or unhackable when using 128-bit or greater encryption keys, secret key encryption is also fast, a feature that makes it attractive as a security solution. However, a big issue with implementing conventional encryption systems is the management of the encryption keys. Two computers will always share a key, which opens the door for unauthorized access to the key at each of the two computers that hold the key. In addition, once a secret key is generated at the source computer, it has to be delivered to its peer computer; that is, the one with which the source computer will be exchanging encrypted information. To keep the secret encryption key secret, you could create it through a software program that you purchased from a vendor that specializes in secret key encryption, copy it to a floppy disk, and then physically deliver it and install it on the destination computer. With one or two computers, this might be practical, but in a widely distributed computing environment with hundreds or thousands of users, physical delivery of secret keys for every two computers that need to exchange encrypted information would not be practical.

To solve the key management problem, software vendors that support secret key encryption provide a method for encrypting the secret key for delivery across the network to the two peer computers that need to exchange encrypted data. This way the secret key remains a secret without the necessity of physical key delivery. Secret keys can easily be distributed between computers while at the same time being managed by the encryption software application.

Public Key Encryption

public key encryption also known as *asymmetric encryption,* is a very secure way to encrypt your data transmissions across public networks without having to share a secret key with another computer. Public key encryption makes use of two keys: a public key and a private key.

Public key encryption, also known as *asymmetric encryption,* is a very secure way to encrypt your data transmissions across public networks without having to share a secret key with another computer. Public key encryption uses two encryption keys: a **public key** that is available for the entire computer world to use when exchanging encrypted information with your computer, and a **private key** that is known only to a single computer. Either key can be used to encrypt data, but for typical encrypted transmissions, the sending computer

---

[20] Other key and block lengths are achievable in 32-bit increments with appropriate configuration of the encryption program.

Next time you're faced with a decision about whether to encrypt data, consider the business problem you're trying to address. If you participate in a gaming network across the Internet, the need to encrypt a transmission that results in a series of moves that destroys your opponent might not be as crucial as the need to protect your bank account number the next time you pay bills online. The important questions to ask are how important is the data, what are the consequences if the data is lost or stolen, and can the data that might be illicitly captured be used in any way to gain access to other, more valuable data on an organization's network?

Sending the latest joke file via e-mail to a friend at another company or requesting the latest gossip news from the Internet are probably not substantial enough to warrant data encryption or an encrypted channel between locations. Banking transactions across a public network such as the Internet, however, should require the highest levels of encryption and authentication.

retrieves the public key of the intended recipient's computer and uses that key to encrypt the data transmission. When the target computer receives the transmission, it uses its own private key to unlock the information.

In Figure 9.13, when computer A needs to send a secure data transmission to computer B on another network, the encryption program accesses the intended recipient's public key from a directory of public keys located on a computer server somewhere—either within your organization or at a third-party location that provides such a directory service. Computer A then uses computer B's public key to encrypt the data packets. Once computer B receives the encrypted data transmission, it uses its own private key—it's a different private key than the private key used by the sending computer—to perform the decryption.

Sounds a bit complicated, but the advantage over secret key encryption is one of key management. With secret key encryption, keys are shared between two computers. If a computer communicates with 100 other computers using secret key encryption, then 100 keys must be managed along with 100 copies; that is, each key is saved in a file on at least two computers. With that many shared keys to manage, the possibility of key theft is always present. But with public key encryption, a computer need manage only one private key, and that key is stored on a single computer generally in an encrypted file.

digital signature
a process that is also known as *authentication* and which guarantees to the recipient that the data transmission came from the sender

Digital Signatures   Public key encryption can also be used to create a **digital signature**, a process that's also known as **authentication** and which guarantees to the recipient that the data transmission came from the sender. Public key encryption can create a digital signature using the sender's private key to encrypt the data transmission instead of using the intended recipient's public key. When the data transmission arrives at its destination, the

FIGURE 9.13
Public Key
Encryption

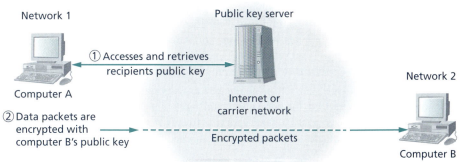

recipient computer uses the sender's public key to decrypt the transmission. Because a data transmission that has been encrypted with the sender's private key can only be unlocked with the same computer's public key, the recipient knows that the data transmission came from the sending computer.

But what if someone stole the sender's private key, and the recipient didn't know it had been stolen? Any data transmissions utilizing the private key for encryption would look authentic, but they would be coming from a stolen source. The thief could use the stolen key to encrypt and send any number of transmissions to various recipients. These recipients would still have access to the sender's public key and could decrypt the transmissions. The digital signature would look authentic. But the reality of our stolen key example is, an imposter was sending the transmissions. So how do you protect yourself and your organization from fraudulent digital signatures?

For comparison, would you accept via post office mail, a check signed by someone you had never met, as payment for an expensive item you were about to ship back to him? Probably not. Could that person be an imposter claiming to be the owner of the checkbook and sign the check anyway? Sure he could. So what would you do? Well, you'd get verification. And how would you obtain such verification? Most likely through a third party that you trusted, someone who lived close to the sender so that you could verify the identity of the person sending you payment. Once the verification was made, you would accept the sender's check and signature, and you'd send your expensive merchandise on its way.

In much the same way as our check verification example, you can prove authenticity of data transmissions and senders on large public networks like the Internet by using **public key infrastructure (PKI)**. PKI utilizes public key encryption plus digital certificates, certificate authorities, centralized storage and management of public keys, and the software to generate private keys. By supporting all these components, companies that provide PKI services to other companies for secure data transmission give their customers a level of trust that facilitates the kinds of business commerce we've come to expect in today's "online" world.

A **digital certificate** is a public network identity that can be verified by a trusted third party. The digital certificate might contain information such as the certificate holder's name, organization name and address, Internet domain name, expiration date of the certificate, the certificate's serial number, and other higher levels of detail according to the level of security you wish to convey. Digital certificates are created and stored on a **certificate authority (CA)**, a network server that provides digital identity verification services and that both senders and receivers trust for identity validation in data communications across large public networks.[21]

In addition to storing digital certificates, the CA also stores a public key for each organization that subscribes to the CA's services. Because public keys can be used for digital signatures, a public key is frequently referred to as **certificate signing request (CSR)** when discussing digital certificates and certificate authorities. The certificate authority will also provide you with the software to create your private key.

Combining Public Key and Secret Key Encryption

One shortfall of public key encryption is that it requires significant computing power to perform the encryption, and another is that it's slower than secret key encryption. So whenever possible, encryption software vendors provide solutions that combine the two technologies. Here's how the combined approach works.

PKI
the public key encryption implementation on public networks such as the Internet. PKI uses public key encryption as well as digital certificates, certificate authorities, and centralized storage and management of certificate signing requests.

digital certificate
a public network identity that can be verified by a trusted third party

certificate authority
a network server that provides digital identity verification services

certificate signing request (CSR)
the public key that is stored on a certificate authority

---

[21] Verisign is a name that has become familiar to users of PKI. They act as the certificate authority to thousands of businesses.

Computer A wants to communicate with computer B, but you want the process to be as secure as possible while at the same time you want the fastest encryption performance possible within the desired level of security you choose. To accomplish this, the encryption software on computer A creates a secret key and then forwards it to computer B using public key encryption. Once the secret key arrives at computer B and is decrypted, the two computers begin communicating using secret key encryption. However, to maintain security once the data exchange is finished, both computers delete their secret keys. The next time computer A and computer B need to initiate an encrypted data exchange, they'll repeat the same process, but this time they'll have a new secret key to share.

Security Protocols

Now that you've learned about encryption, it's time to take a look at some of the security protocols that make encryption a reality in data communication. Whether you're sending e-mails, transmitting data files, or logging on to your LAN, security protocols are another level of defense to protect your information from unauthorized electronic surveillance.

PGP

Pretty good privacy (PGP) is a public key encryption protocol that has become a de facto standard for data encryption, e-mail encryption, and digital signatures. It was invented by Phil Zimmermann in the early 1990s and is freely distributed for personal use; however, commercial versions are available from Network Associates. When you begin using PGP, you'll need to install your distribution copy to obtain the encryption algorithm and create your private key, and you'll need to post your public key on a public PGP server. Other users to whom you send encrypted data files or e-mails can then retrieve your public key and decrypt your transmissions. Interesting sites that discuss PGP include the International PGP home page at www.pgpi.org, the MIT Distribution Center for PGP at http://web .mit.edu/network/pgp.html, and the OpenPGP Public Key Server page at http://pgpkeys .mit.edu:11371.

Kerberos

Kerberos is a secret-key encryption technology that is used in client/server environments for secure authentication between computers. It allows client and server computers to prove their identities to one another while at the same time ensuring the secrecy of data transmissions through secret-key encryption techniques. Common implementations of Kerberos include encrypted communication between clients and servers for applications like TELNET and FTP, which would otherwise be unsecured.[22] Kerberos also provides a secure mechanism to distribute the shared secret key between computers. As with PGP, free versions of Kerberos are available from MIT at http://web.mit.edu/kerberos.

SSL

Secure Sockets Layer (SSL) is an industry-standard public-key encryption technique developed by Netscape Communications that is used for secure Web-based communications and transactions, and it's activated in your Web browser when you create a digital certificate with a certificate authority. Within your browser, you can configure SSL for either a 40-bit key or a 128-bit key, and as you've learned already, a 128-bit key provides for greater security. An interesting characteristic of SSL is that it provides its encryption capability between the application and transport layers of the OSI model. You may have used SSL and not even known it. The next time you make a Web-based purchase or banking transaction,

---

[22] Kerberos is also implemented as a security protocol for remote procedure call communication between two devices.

look in the URL after you've made the connection. If the URL has changed from http:// to https://, then the connection has been secured using SSL.

S-HTTP

Secure HTTP (S-HTTP) is an extension of the Hypertext Transport Protocol (HTTP) and is designed to provide for secure Web transactions. It's another Web-based public-key encryption technology that is similar to SSL. The difference is, S-HTTP adds its encryption functionality specifically at the OSI application layer. This means that S-HTTP is linked directly to HTTP and is not application-independent as is SSL. In addition, SSL is designed to encrypt the entire connection channel between a client and a server; S-HTTP encrypts the data transmission itself. In other words, with SSL, once the secure connection is established between two computers, any amount of information can be sent securely over the communications channel. With S-HTTP, each data transmission is separately secured from the previous transmission. However, both SSL and S-HTTP are standards supported by the IETF.

SSH

Another data communications security protocol is **secure shell (SSH).** By design, SSH utilizes public-key encryption to exchange a secret key for the current session, and then the data is encrypted using the shared secret key.[23] SSH is available as SSH 1 or SSH 2; the two are not compatible. When SSH 1 was first released, it used patented technology that could only be used under a license agreement, and later on, several technical problems, which have since been fixed, were discovered. SSH 2 was developed to avoid the patented encryption technology used in SSH 1 and to fix the technical issues associated with SSH 1. Both are available for free now, as patent protection for the underlying encryption algorithm in SSH 1 has long since expired. Originally developed to encrypt passwords during remote login (rlogin), telnet, and FTP sessions, SSH is also used in Kerberos security between remote computers.

IPSec

The **IP security (IPSec)** protocol is used to provide secure IP data transmissions across a wide variety of applications; it's not limited to securing Web-based HTTP traffic as in SSL technology. Using a standard technology known as *Internet Key Exchange (IKE),* IPSec can automatically negotiation a common encryption scheme between communicating computers; no preconfiguration of encryption types at each computer is required.

Another feature of IPSec allows it to be configured for transport mode or tunnel mode. In **transport mode,** the data packet is encrypted and encapsulated. Eavesdroppers on the communications channel can intercept the packet and find the source and destination IP address information, but won't be able to decipher the encrypted data. In **tunnel mode,** the entire IP packet is encrypted, and IP tunnel identifiers for source and destination addresses are added. If an eavesdropper intercepts an IPSec tunnel packet, the most he or she will be able to gain are the source and destination locations of the tunnel and not the actual source and destination of the communicating computers.

In some ways, the address translation feature of IPSec in tunnel mode is similar to NAT (network address translation); however, NAT and IPSec tunneling are not compatible protocols. If you are using VPN with IPSec as the tunneling protocol, the NAT functionality on a firewall will either interfere, causing you to disable it, or with newer firewalls, the NAT functionality will be dynamically set aside while the IPSec tunnel is in effect.

---

[23] SSH uses RSA public-key encryption for key exchange and then 3DES or Blowfish for data encryption.

Chapter Summary

- **Components of a comprehensive security plan.** A comprehensive security plan includes risk analysis, data and network protection planning, business continuity planning, and incident response planning. Crucial subcomponents include defining security baselines, establishing controls, setting security policies, and documentation.

- **Social engineering.** Social engineering is a method of exploiting the people component of the security equation rather than the hardware or software components to gain access to computer networks and valuable data. Constant attention must be given to this vulnerability to reduce the chances that employees will be caught off guard and divulge secret information such as user names and passwords.

- **Eavesdropping and data interception.** Eavesdropping is the act of secretly listening in on voice and data communications channels, while data interception involves recording the eavesdropped data without modifying the data in any way. Each of these vulnerabilities must be guarded against with a password policy that includes strong passwords and software that prevents eavesdroppers from gathering critical data that will allow them to access network resources.

- **Security attacks.** Security attacks include denial of service and distributed denial of service attacks, Trojan horse attacks, spoofing, and port scanning are other types of attacks. Defenses against attacks include patching security holes, firewalls, intrusion detection, intrusion prevention, honeypots, perimeter networks, antivirus software, physical security, user and computer policies, network address translation, proxy servers, VLANs, VPNs, WEP, WPA, RSN, 802.16e, and encryption.

- **Dial-in security.** For companies that allow dial-in access to network resources, dial-in security is a must. Dial-in telephone numbers should be unlisted, callback functionality should be implemented, secret pass codes should be used, and data encryption should be required.

- **Malicious programs.** Malicious programs include viruses and worms. These potential vulnerabilities can be mitigated through employ awareness and antivirus software.

- **Physical network security.** Physical network security involves locking equipment in safe areas such as data centers, wiring closets, and server rooms. With laptops and other portable devices, physical network security means never leaving these devices unattended, or locking them in an office or desk when they are unattended. User and computer policies can assist with controlling physical access to network resources by enforcing password changes, automatic logout times, and restricted access to data and applications.

- **Firewall devices.** A firewall is any device that is comprised of hardware, software, or a combination of the two that protects a LAN from unauthorized access and security risks. Firewalls are generally implemented within perimeter networks and are used in conjunction with other security technologies such as network address translation, proxy servers, and intrusion protection devices and services. Types of firewalls include packet-level firewalls, packet-level firewalls with stateful packet inspection, and application-level firewalls.

- **Network address translation.** Network address translation is the process of translating private network IP addresses into one or more registered IP addresses for transmission across external networks. NAT is used in conjunction with firewalls and perimeter networks as part of the controls used to mitigate security risk.

- **Proxy servers.** A proxy server is a computer or network device that acts on behalf of client computers to provide access to remote resources. Proxy servers assist in maintaining client secrecy, blocking access to specified Web pages, and restricting service access. Proxy server can also be used to enhance network performance through Web caching.

- **Perimeter networks.** A perimeter network is a LAN that sits between the outside world and an internal network and is designed and configured to improve overall network security. Devices that are used in a perimeter network include firewalls, NAT devices, proxy servers, and various devices that perform intrusion protection. Another term for perimeter network is DMZ.

- **Intrusion protection.** Intrusion protection is the set of policies, procedures, and systems within an organization that work to detect, prevent, and respond to network and host intruders. Types of intrusion protection include intrusion detection systems and intrusion prevention systems. Other intrusion protection components and services include audit logs and alerts, and honeypots, both of which can be used in effective intrusion response.

- **Network security with VLANs.** VLANs can assist at OSI layer 4 with network security by isolating network segments according to service requirements. VLANs can also assist with lower layer LAN segmentation to promote internal network separation and security.

- **Wireless LAN and MAN/WAN security.** Wireless LAN security includes Wired Equivalent Privacy, Wi-Fi Protected Access, and robust security network technologies. WEP is part of the original specification for IEEE 802.11 LANs, and is not as secure as WPA or RSN. WPA includes TKIP for enhanced encryption and EAP for improved authentication. RSN is part of the forthcoming and official IEEE 802.11i standard. Wireless MAN/WAN security is based on the IEEE 802.16 series of standards and is undergoing changes to make it more secure.

- **Physically securing data.** Physical security of data includes many of the same components as physical network security. Additionally, data backups combined with offsite storage are very effective against data loss.

- **Virtual private networks.** Virtual private networks add to network security by creating secure point-to-point connections between private networks. VPNs use encryption and encapsulation technologies to create secure communications channels. Encapsulation hides the IP address of the originating device and encryption scrambles the data.

- **Encryption.** Encryption is the process of turning plaintext into ciphertext. Encryption is accomplished through software or hardware by applying an encryption key to an encryption algorithm. Major types of encryption include secret key encryption and public key encryption. Secret key encryption standards include DES, Triple DES, RC4, IDEA, AES, and Blowfish. Public key encryption uses public keys and private keys to encrypt and decrypt data. Public key encryption implementations also include digital signatures, digital certificates, and public key infrastructure technology.

- **Security protocols.** Security protocols are the building blocks upon which encryption is delivered for use in data communications and networks. Examples include PGP, Kerberos, SSL, S-HTTP, SSH, and IPSec.

Key Terms

Advanced Encryption Standard (AES), *332*
Application-level firewall, *317*
Ari Luotonen, *319*
Authentication, *333*
Blowfish, *331*
Business continuity planning, *305*
CERN, *319*
CERT, *309*
Certificate authority (CA), *334*
Certificate signing request (CSR), *334*

Questions

1. What is a major business driver behind network security?

2. What are the components of a comprehensive security plan?

3. What is a network vulnerability and how is it identified?

4. What is a security attack? What kinds of attacks can cause partial or total disruption of network services? How can you defend your network against such attacks? Are there any agencies or Web sites that can assist in attack prevention? What are they?

5. What are some of the major types of computer viruses? How can you defend against them?

6. What is the purpose of user and computer policies? When would you implement these policies?

7. What is a firewall and what are some ways that a firewall can assist with network security?

8. How do OSI layer 2 firewalls differ from layer 3 firewalls?

9. What is a packet-level firewall? How does it differ from a firewall that is configured with stateful packet inspection?

10. When would you choose to implement an application-layer firewall?

11. What are some of the differences between firewall software and firewall appliances?

12. What is network address translation? On what network device is it generally implemented? Why would you want to use NAT in a LAN? When would you be able to justify the use of inbound mapping?

13. For what purposes would you implement a proxy server in a LAN environment?

14. How does reverse proxy differ from regular proxy server services?

15. Why would you choose to implement Web proxy services? How about a proxy array?

16. What is a perimeter network and why do most networks need its associated functionality? Where is intrusion protection and how does it fit in with perimeter networks?

17. What is a VLAN, and what benefits could VLAN functionality bring to a local area network?

18. What kinds of security are available for wireless LANs? For wireless MANs? What are some of the deficiencies of these technologies? What do some of the newer wireless security technologies offer?

19. What is a virtual private network? How would you incorporate VPN technology into your overall network security plan? What are some reasons you would implement VPN technology?

20. What is encryption? How does symmetric encryption differ from asymmetric encryption? What benefits does public key encryption offer over secret key encryption?

21. What are some of the common symmetric encryption standards? What differentiates one standard from another?

22. What is a digital signature? Under what circumstances would you require digital signatures? How can you ensure that a digital signature is legitimate, and what technology and components of that technology assure the receiver that senders are legitimate?

23. What security protocols are available for public key encryption? When would you use each one?

24. With IPSec, what is the difference between transport mode and tunnel mode?

Research Activities

1. Identify three major backup software suites. What are the features of each? Do any of these suites include antivirus software?

2. Using the search tools available to you, identify three proxy server manufacturers and their proxy server products. Make sure that you describe whether the proxy server products are software-based or hardware-based. What differentiates each product from the other? What features does each provide? In general, are proxy server services built into other products such as firewalls? What implementation success stories do these manufacturers provide?

3. Using the search tools available to you, find three commercial firewall products, and describe the features of each. Make sure you locate firewall examples that include the topics covered in the text, such as packet filtering, stateful packet inspection, application-level functionality, network address translation, and proxy services. How do enterprise-level products differ from home-use firewall products?

4. Identify whether your organization or school is using virtual private networking. Describe how it's being used and the steps that were taken in its implementation. If your workplace or school is not using VPN, what other security measures have they implemented for remote users who need to gain access to internal information? Using the search tools available to you, find one or two successful implementations of VPN technologies.

5. Identify whether your organization or school is using VLAN technology. Why did network administrators choose to implement a VLAN-based network? What advantages and disadvantages have they discovered since its implementation? Using the search tools available to you, discover one or two successful implementations of VLAN technologies.

6. Using the search tools available to you, discover and describe the origin of public key encryption. What other people and companies have been instrumental in the development of public key encryption technologies?

7. Using the search tools available to you, find three applications that implement one or more of the encryption technologies discussed in the chapter. What encryption standards do these applications implement? Which ones use both public key and secret key encryption?

8. Using the search tools available to you, discover and describe the historical development of the Rijndael algorithm. Can you find a reason that it was chosen as the U.S. government encryption standard over several other competing encryption methods?

9. Using the search tools available to you, discover and describe how public key infrastructure is being implemented in the corporate world. If your own organization or school is using PKI, describe how it's being used.

10. Describe three virus horror stories that have happened in recent years. You can discuss organizations known to you, or you can use the search tools available to you to discover and describe two or three large-scale virus infections. Address the following questions: How were the viruses detected? What damage was caused? How was the virus eliminated? How was the data repaired or retrieved?

11. Using the search tools available to you, locate at least one representative company that implemented a wireless LAN and used WEP. What problems did the company run into? What problems arose with WEP in the summer of 2001? How would you solve this problem with WPA? With RSN?

12. Using the search tools available to you, locate and list five recent vulnerabilities and summarize the significance of each one to organizations' networks.

Mini Case Study

LAKESIDE METAL STAMPINGS—PART 7

Lakeside Metal Stampings has finally implemented the WAN recommendations that you created at the end of chapter 8, and now the owners are concerned that the order information and financial data that the two locations share back and forth regularly might be vulnerable to eavesdropping. They're also concerned that their networks at each location are overly exposed to data loss, damage, or theft from the kinds of attacks they've heard about on the news. Based on what you've learned in this chapter, develop a security plan for Lakeside Metal Stampings that will address their security needs. For your proposal, you can assume that the information that Lakeside transmits back and forth needs to remain confidential, and you can assume that you haven't previously implemented a security plan or any security devices to protect the data on their networks.

CHAPTER
Ten

Chapter Overview and Objectives

The Internet has been described as a network of networks that links homes, businesses, government agencies, and academic institutions in the pursuit of information exchange, knowledge sharing, and commerce. For more than 30 years the Internet has provided a network backbone for connectivity between distant computers, and since the mid-1990s it has interconnected millions of networks and computers all around the world. In this chapter we examine the Internet from several perspectives. You'll look at its history, where it is today, and where it will be in the future. More specifically, by the end of this chapter you will be able to

- Identify and describe important historically significant events in the development of the Internet.

- Discuss the topology of the Internet.

- Provide a list of organizations that govern the Internet and describe their functions.

- Define the Domain Name System and describe the purpose of Name Servers.

- List and describe the original top-level Internet domains and new top-level domains and their purposes.

- List and describe common Internet protocols and applications.

- Discuss Internet2, the Abilene Project, and Internet2 working groups.

- Describe IPv6 business drivers, addressing, and address types.

- Summarize the impact that Internet2 might have on organizations.

The Internet

AN INTRODUCTION TO THE INTERNET

The Internet is comprised of virtually countless computers and a seemingly limitless maze of interconnected networks. And like so many of the technological innovations that we've come to take for granted, the Internet has a history that defines it, a structure that allows us to access and share data from virtually anywhere and at any time, and a collection of supporting organizations that oversees its maintenance and continuously works toward the Internet's continued development.

Brief History

The earliest origins of the Internet span several decades of the 20th century. Its conception was the product of the thoughts and efforts of many scientists, professionals, and political figures over many years.[1] The Internet was "born" on September 1, 1969, under the auspices of the **Advanced Research Projects Agency (ARPA).** Dubbed the ARPA network, or **ARPANET** for short, this infant Internet began its incredible journey with the connection of one computer at the UCLA college campus to an AT&T carrier service network. By year's end, the ARPANET connected computers at four locations, and by the end of 1970 the number of connected sites that were exchanging information had grown to 13. In 1971, the number of ARPANET sites exceeded the original 16 that had been part of the ARPA network plan, and by August 1972 nearly 30 sites were connected. A little over a year later, the ARPANET had grown to 40 sites and was international in scope. By September 1973, Norway and London were connected to the ARPANET.

At about the same time as the ARPANET went international, ARPA was funding a project that would allow multiple and different types of networks to interconnect and exchange information with a common protocol.[2] Under the collaborative efforts of **Vinton Cerf** and **Robert Kahn** and supported by ARPA, an Internet architecture began to take shape in June 1973 with the specification of the **transmission control protocol (TCP).** TCP could establish communications sessions between computer hosts and acknowledge the safe arrival of packets. If a packet didn't arrive, it was subsequently retransmitted. In addition, TCP regulated the flow of traffic between computer hosts. These attributes made TCP ideal for internetwork (Internet) communications among the different networks that ARPA had been funding.[3] Then in January 1978, with the need to simplify the identification of individual computers on different networks, Cerf and his codevelopers reengineered TCP into two parts: one part for connecting computer hosts and ensuring the reliable delivery of packets and the other part for identifying individual hosts by address. These two parts became known, respectively, as TCP and **IP,** with TCP responsible for sequencing of packets and delivery reliability and IP responsible for host addressing. To guarantee support of a unified communications architecture, ARPA required the transition from an older transmission protocol called **network control protocol (NCP)** to TCP and IP in 1981, completing the migration by year end 1982. By January 1983 all networks wishing to communicate across

---

[1] For a more extensive history of the events that fostered the development of the Internet, check out Appendix A, "A Brief History of Data Communications and Computer Networks."

[2] ARPANET used a point-to-point transmission protocol that maintained a constant connection between two communicating computers. This transmission technique was incompatible with the broadcast transmission protocols used by two other ARPA-funded networks, PRNET and SATNET. PRNET was a radio frequency military network that used packet technology, and SATNET was a Defense Department network that used radio frequency broadcasts tuned specifically for communications with a space satellite.

[3] These other ARPA-funded networks included PRNET and SATNET.

the ARPANET were required to utilize the TCP and IP protocols for their data transmissions.

Protocols alone, however, do not complete the historical perspective of the Internet. Supervision of the ARPANET was transferred from ARPA to the **Defense Communications Agency (DCA)** in 1975 because of the potential military importance of a packet-switched data communications network. That is, in the event of catastrophic wartime communications failures in the circuit-switched AT&T telephone network, the packet-switched ARPANET could have been used to maintain military command and control. But the transfer of supervision to a purely military agency had repercussions for both the academic researchers who comprised the pre-DCA ARPANET stewardship and the military personnel who were now in charge of the ARPANET. Academic researchers were used to an unsecured data access policy. When someone needed a file, the file was simply transferred to that person—academic and research communities were comfortable with the open sharing of information and knowledge. Under military control, however, the potential for compromised security was real and immediate, especially with the introduction of personal-use computers and modems in the late 1970s and early 1980s. To reduce this potential threat, in 1982 the DCA decided to split the ARPANET into two networks with the separation effective in April 1983. **MILNET** became the military network, and the ARPANET returned to its research roots.[4]

Although both MILNET and the ARPANET remained under military jurisdiction after the split, the ARPANET became more and more civilian-dominated with each passing day. While it still wasn't available for commercial use, the ARPANET experienced significant growth after its split from MILNET for a couple of reasons. First, the **National Science Foundation (NSF)** began funding connectivity to a network known as **CSNET,** a network that connected computer science departments at universities that had not been part of the ARPANET's creation and development. CSNET was connected to the ARPANET, thereby providing access to computers on either network. Second, the early 1980s saw the introduction and explosive growth of the personal computer. With this growth came the demand for data sharing between these personal computers and the introduction of local area networks (LANs). If a university or organization had a LAN as well as access to a "public" network such as CSNET or the ARPANET, all of the computers on the LAN could be interconnected to a growing network of networks. The only requirements were that the connecting computers be configured with TCP/IP, LANs were required to connect through a router, and usage was restricted to research functions, that is, noncommercial pursuits only.[5]

The success of the ARPANET and the NSF's CSNET prompted the NSF to continue funding computer-related research and networking. In 1984, the NSF began building five regional supercomputing centers across the United States to provide computing resources to researchers and academia and, in 1985, began linking them together in a network known as **NSFNET.** The original links for NSFNET were 56 Kbps leased lines; the same as those used by the ARPANET, but, by 1987, the implementation of a T1-carrier network that could deliver a transmission rate of 1.544 Mbps to the NSFNET was well under way.[6] Once NSFNET had a 1.544 Mbps infrastructure, the decision was made to decommission the ARPANET and transfer connectivity to the faster NSFNET. The transition was completed during 1988 and 1989, and the ARPANET was officially taken offline at the end of February 1990.

---

[4] Both networks were still under military jurisdiction and several computer hosts maintained connectivity to both networks so that information could be transferred between them.
[5] Routers were commonly called gateways in the early days of the Internet.
[6] MCI provided the T-carrier circuits for the NSFNET.

With the transition to NSFNET in 1990 and the decommissioning of ARPANET, the military jurisdiction of the Internet ended, which paved the way for a truly civilian Internet. The only problem was the NSF's acceptable use policy limited the use of NSFNET to research and academic activities. Because for-profit business activities weren't allowed, and with growing business demand for data communications services, several commercial TCP/IP networks that weren't limited to research and academic interests sprang to life, including offerings from carrier companies such as AT&T, MCI, Sprint, and numerous regional providers. By 1991, the growth of commercial data network backbones and services had expanded sufficiently to allow the NSF to plan for a smooth transition to the private sector. Under the plan, the NSF would privatize the Internet by turning over Internet service to competitive **Internet service providers (ISPs).** The plan took effect in 1994, and the NSFNET backbone was officially decommissioned in April 1995. The Internet was now a private commercial enterprise, consisting of a network of high-speed backbones and maintained by carriers and ISPs.

Internet Topology

The Internet is comprised of millions of computers and computer networks that are linked together through various Internet access locations and across various types of high-speed carrier services into a vast network of networks. The topology that supports this structure includes national ISPs, regional ISPs, local ISPs, **network access points (NAPs), metropolitan area exchanges (MAEs), Internet exchange points** (EPs or IXs or **IXPs**), ISP **points of presence (PoPs), local exchange carriers (LECs),** and, of course, the computers and networks that are located at homes and businesses all over the world. Figure 10.1 provides an example of the services that make up the Internet.

In Figure 10.1, an ISP creates a PoP in a geographic area by installing equipment that can provide Internet access and services to local homes and businesses. For dial-up connections, the ISP maintains banks of modems at its PoP to receive data streams from analog local loops that are switched through the local exchange carrier's central office and then routed across high-speed circuits to the ISP's PoP. For high-speed digital connections between customers and the ISP PoP, the ISP maintains equipment such as a digital subscriber line access multiplexer (DSLAM), Metro Ethernet switch, ATM switch, frame relay switch, cable modem termination system (CMTS), or any other connectivity equipment used for

FIGURE 10.1
Connectivity to an ISP

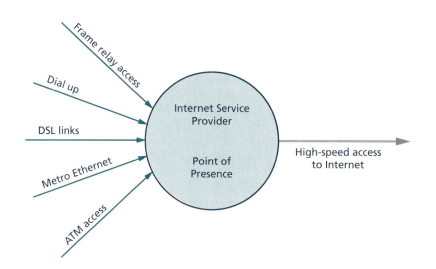

delivering and accepting specific high-speed service types to and from various businesses and residential users.[7]

Connectivity between the ISP's customers and the ISP PoP can be provided by the ISP but is generally provided by the local exchange carrier (either ILEC or CLEC). In many cases, the local exchange carrier is a local ISP as well. Connectivity between the local exchange carrier's central office and the ISP's PoP can be high-speed links such as T-carrier or optical carrier, or the ISP can rent floor space from the local exchange carrier, install its equipment at the LEC's central office, and then interconnect with the local exchange carrier's equipment. If the ISP is a cable television (CATV) company, connectivity between customer and the CATV PoP is provided across the CATV media that connects customers' homes to the CMTS located at the CATV company's main office facility.

Local ISPs connect their PoP equipment to one or more regional ISPs and if local Internet traffic volumes warrant it, to a local Internet exchange point (IXP). The connection to the regional ISPs provides ultimate connectivity to the high-speed optical carrier (OC-*x*) networks that interconnect the United States and circumvent the globe. The connection to a local IXP prevents Internet traffic that is destined for other local ISPs from being routed over longer distances through regional and national ISP networks. Connectivity to a local IXP also improves transmission times between local ISPs and reduces traffic congestion on regional and national ISP networks. The limiting factors to the success of an IXP include inducing local ISPs in a region to lease the circuits that connect their PoPs to the IXP, purchasing ports on the IXP switch from the IXP provider, and signing **peering agreements** that allow local Internet traffic to be switched onto any local ISP network that is connected to the IXP.[8,9]

peering agreement
a contract between two ISPs that allows each party to the contract to switch local Internet traffic from its own network to the other ISP's network without incurring monetary charges

Regional ISPs maintain digital services (DS-*x*) networks and optical carrier (OC-*x*) networks that span a limited geographic region. These networks provide local ISPs and organizations that can afford the high-speed access, with connectivity to the Internet without the significant costs of connecting to a national ISP. Regional ISPs interconnect with other regional ISPs through Internet exchange points known as metropolitan area exchanges (MAEs) in much the same way that local ISPs peer through local IXPs. In addition, regional ISPs lease high-speed circuits that connect them to one or more national ISPs.

National ISPs, sometimes referred to as *national services providers (NSPs),* provide access to the most extensive and highest speed communications networks that support Internet traffic. Typical bandwidths range from OC-3 to OC-192 with OC-768 available from at least one NSP as you're reading this. Future technology will allow greater bandwidths that will extend optical carrier capabilities into the hundreds of terabits per second range over a single fiber. Technology developers are already discussing how to implement multiple OC-3072 channels on a single fiber, with each channel supporting 160 Gbps.

National services providers connect regional ISPs and organizations that can afford the connection costs and operational expenses of connecting to a NSP, to the mesh of high-speed carrier services that support Internet traffic across the United States and the world. NSP networks interconnect with other NSP networks through network access points (NAPs) in much the same way as regional ISPs interconnect through MAEs. In addition, local and regional ISPs with sufficient bandwidth demand and capital budgets can connect

---

[7] You learned about DSLAMs, Metro Ethernet, ATM, frame relay, and CMTS in chapter 8.
[8] IXP providers are usually an independent company that specializes in IXP services
[9] Peering agreements are generally signed between ISPs that have similar traffic volumes. Peering agreements are not usually signed between local and regional or between regional and national ISPs because of the difference in traffic volumes.

to a NAP to provide their customers with the quickest access, fastest response, and highest available Internet bandwidth.

ISPs are also frequently categorized into Tier-1, Tier-2, and Tier-3 networks. Tier-1 networks span national and international boundaries. In the US, NSPs have Tier-1 networks. Tier-2 networks have large regional networks but don't span country or international boundaries. In the United States, regional ISPs have Tier-2 networks. Tier-3 networks are limited to a local area, such as a local exchange carrier, and must purchase Internet access from a Tier-2 or Tier-1 network provider. Small ISPs fall into the Tier-3 network category and many times simply resell the services available from regional and national ISPs.

Internet Governance

The Internet is governed by many different professional societies and organizations working to create, implement, and advance Internet technologies, applications, standards, architecture, and usability. One of the most influential organizations that works to this end is the **Internet Society (ISOC).** Officially formed in 1992, the ISOC was created to expand financial support for Internet activities and support the publication activities of the **Internet Engineering Task Force (IETF).** Today, the ISOC continues its funding efforts for IETF activities, and it provides ISOC members with the current status of technical developments and IETF standards.[10]

FIGURE 10.2   **Interrelationships among ISOC, IAB, IETF, IESG, and IRTF**

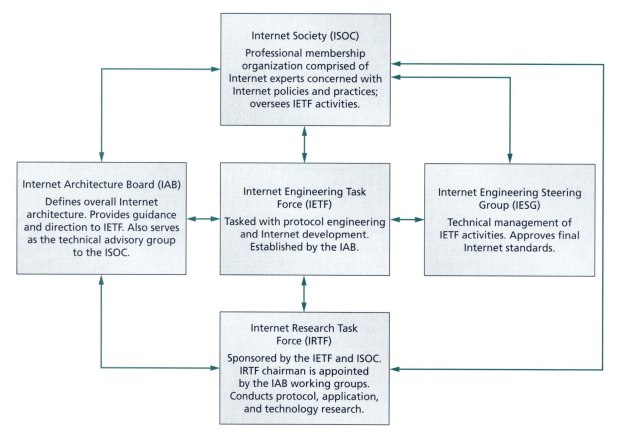

---

[10] For more information on the ISOC, have a look at the ISOC Web site at www.isoc.org. For more information on the IETF, check out www.ietf.org.

Standards are another key driver behind Internet governance. The three key organizations that perform Internet standards development work are the **Internet Architecture Board (IAB),** the **Internet Engineering Steering Group (IESG),** and the IETF. The IAB has the responsibilities of defining Internet architecture and keeping the pulse of long-range Internet issues. The IESG handles technical management of IETF activities as well as the Internet standards process and approvals. The IETF is the primary organization under ISOC responsible for Internet standards development.

Other important Internet organizations include the **Internet Research Task Force (IRTF)** and the **Internet Corporation for Assigned Names and Numbers (ICANN).** The IRTF coordinates research activities involving Internet protocols, applications, and other Internet-related technologies. The IRTF is sponsored by the ISOC and the IETF, and its chairperson is appointed by the IAB. Various working groups within the IRTF conduct the actual research in support of protocol, application, and technological advancement of the Internet. ICANN is responsible for the allocation of IP address space, assigning Internet protocol identifiers, and managing top-level Internet domains such as .com, .org, .net, .edu, and several others.[11] It also provides management functions for the domain name system (DNS) root servers that maintain the list of top-level Internet domain names. Figure 10.2 illustrates the relationship among ISOC, IAB, IETF, IESG, and the IRTF.

ACCESSING INFORMATION ON THE INTERNET

Accessing information on the Internet is a process that involves many key components, functions, and protocols. The actual data that you access is stored on mainframe computers or network servers that can be physically located anywhere in the world.[12] The mainframes run their proprietary operating systems, and the servers run network operating systems such as UNIX, Linux, NetWare, or a Microsoft Server operating system. The mainframes and servers are configured with application software that delivers content such as files, Web pages, or streaming media. Protocols such as IP, DNS, HTTP, and FTP assist in locating data. Internet domains such as .com, .edu, and .int loosely organize data access by function or geography, and DNS assists data access by resolving friendly names to IP addresses. Applications such as e-mail, instant messaging, and VoIP provide person-to-person, person-to-group, and group-to-group communication capability, while streaming media and QoS provide multisensory and content-rich combinations of audio and video. Throughout this section, we'll take a detailed look at how these components, protocols, and applications assist in information access on the Internet. As you're reading keep in mind that every time you use your favorite search engine, access your favorite Web site, or send e-mail or instant message someone, you're using the components, protocols, and applications that you're about to investigate.

The Origin of the Domain Name System

In the early days of the Internet when it was still known as the ARPANET, computers that needed to communicate with other computers required and stored a **hosts file**. The hosts file was stored on each ARPANET computer at every ARPANET site as hosts.txt, and the file contained a computer name and corresponding address for every computer that was

hosts file
a file that is stored on a computer's hard drive and which contains the names and addresses of every computer on a network. It is used to identify and locate any computer host that is listed within the file.

---

[11] You can find a list of top-level domains on the ICANN website at www.icann.org. A good website that defines the structure of ICANN is available at www.icann.org/general, and then click the organizational chart link.

[12] Workstation computers can also be configured to provide data access across the Internet to requesting users. Generally speaking, however, workstation operating systems are not designed to provide high-performance delivery of data or support large numbers of simultaneous Internet connections.

connected to the ARPANET.[13] With the information in the hosts.txt file, any ARPANET computer could locate any other computer host on the ARPANET.

As the number of computer hosts connecting to the ARPANET began to accelerate in the early 1980s, the size of the hosts.txt file grew proportionately. That is, for every new computer added to the ARPANET a new entry was added to the main hosts.txt file located at the **Stanford Research Institute (SRI).**[14] Any ARPANET site that added a new computer would send the new host information to SRI, and SRI would update its hosts.txt file on its Network Information Center (NIC) computer. ARPANET administrators at all sites could then download the updated file and replace the old hosts.txt file with the new (and larger) file.

While the hosts.txt file worked well when ARPANET was small, an ever-increasing number of hosts that were dependent on a hosts.txt file that was constantly being updated created several potential problems. First off, with every new host came an increase in network traffic—traffic to send the updates to SRI and download traffic to update a growing number of hosts. Second, the potential for name duplication was very real once TCP/IP was introduced. SRI could control IP address assignment to each host, but creation of the host names was left up to each ARPANET site. Since two hosts cannot share the same IP address in the world of TCP/IP, the potential for disrupting service on the entire ARPANET grew with each newly added host. Third, the ability to implement and maintain a consistent hosts.txt file across an expanding ARPANET decreased with each new host that was added. With centralized control of the update process, hosts could change names or addresses, or new hosts could be added to the network, and an older version of hosts.txt might not be available immediately.

All of these problems presented a serious disruptive threat to the ARPANET in the early 1980s, but the problem was not long without a solution. In 1983, **Paul Mockapetris** and **Jon Postel** of the Information Sciences Institute at the University of Southern California formulated and tested a distributed database of host names and addresses that circumvented the old system of updating a single computer with all host and address information. Originally described in Request for Comment (RFC) 882 and RFC 883, Mockapetris' and Postel's **domain name system (DNS)** technology is currently specified in RFCs 1034 and 1035 and supplemented with security, implementation, and administrative issues in RFCs 1535, 1536, and 1537.[15] With the introduction of DNS, control of host name and address information was shifted from centralized control to distributed control. When a site adds a host, DNS distributes the host's information automatically to DNS servers throughout the network. Other hosts at other locations can then access these distributed DNS servers to resolve host names to IP addresses and thereby locate and identify any computer host on the Internet. DNS added a hierarchical and distributed structure to host information updates and access that freed administrators of the issues associated with updating and distributing the hosts.txt file.

Name Servers

The hierarchical DNS database is distributed among many **name servers,** commonly called DNS servers on the Internet, and these servers are generally located in pairs at every

[13] Although the hosts file stored by ARPANET computers was called hosts.txt, modern computers store it as hosts, without the .txt extension.

[14] SRI was one of the first four computers on the ARPANET. The first ARPANET transmission took place between UCLA and SRI.

[15] RFCs were first covered in chapter 1 and as a quick review, they provide the accepted detail of an Internet standard. If you want to learn the excruciating detail of this process, you can check out RFC 2026, The Internet Standards Process—Revision 3 at www.ietf.org/rfc. If you want to look at the entire list of RFCs, have a look at the RFC Index link on the RFC page.

local, regional, and national ISP. When you enter a URL in a Web browser's address field, the client computer—also known as a resolver in DNS terminology—generates a resolve request, directs the request to the IP address of the ISP's DNS server, and the DNS server at the ISP looks in its DNS table to see if it can match the Web site name that you're requesting to an IP address.[16] If the ISP's DNS server has the specific DNS record you're looking for, it returns the IP address of the requested Web site to the client computer. If the ISP's DNS server can't find the address you're looking for in its local table, it queries other DNS servers in the hierarchy to locate the requested site. Once the site is located, the ISP's DNS server forwards the Web site address to the client computer so that you can access the Web site and your data.[17]

From an implementation viewpoint, DNS servers are configured with operating system software and DNS software, and each DNS server on the Internet stores a portion of the DNS database. Each DNS server is configured to communicate with at least one other DNS server so that all name servers on the Internet are either directly or indirectly interconnected. In addition, DNS servers have the ability to cache the Web site address information that they receive while querying other DNS servers. Cached information is stored for an amount of time known as the time-to-live (TTL), a parameter that is configurable through a DNS management utility. With cached information, DNS servers at ISPs can provide quicker responses to any client computer making a request to a site that has already been resolved by another client computer.

Internet Domains

Domain Name Space the sum of all domains on the Internet and it is also all the domain names that are part of the distributed DNS database. The domain name space includes all TLDs and the domains under the TLDs.

root domain the top-level domain under which TLDs exist. It is not used in domain naming or information access, but it does represent the starting point in the DNS hierarchy.

The information that you access from the Internet is located in various domains. **Internet domains** provide organization and a hierarchical structure to the Internet. You've probably seen many domains that use the .com, .net, .org, .gov and other suffixes, but the Internet is comprised of a vast number of domains that simply use these suffixes as their **top-level domains (TLDs).** That is, there are many more domains that exist under these TLDs. In fact, statistics collected by Whois.net (www.whois.net) place the number of registered domains in cyberspace somewhere around 40 million, as this is being written, and this includes only the .biz, .com, .net, .org, and .us domains.

The actual **domain name space** that we all use when we access the Internet starts at the **root domain**, or simply "the root," which is illustrated in Figure 10.3. TLDs exist under the root domain, but it's the domain layers under the TLDs with which most Internet users are most familiar. For example, microsoft.com is a domain that exists within the .com TLD, and support.microsoft.com is a domain that exists within the microsoft.com domain. Similarly, rit.edu is a domain that exists under the .edu TLD, and cob.rit.edu is a domain that exists within the rit.edu domain.[18] Ultimately, the number of layers in any TLD is 127, including the TLD, but it's unlikely that you'll ever find a domain with that many levels. In addition, domain names are restricted to an overall length of 255 characters, dots excluded, whereas individual portions of a domain name—the part between the dots—is restricted to

[16] The IP addresses of an ISP's DNS servers are configured on each client computer so that the client computer knows how to reach the DNS server at the ISP. The client computer can either be manually configured for these addresses or it can receive them from a DHCP server that automatically provides IP and DNS information to client computers. The IP address to which the client is directed could alternatively be a DNS server at the organization's location. Many organizations maintain their own DNS servers to resolve requests.

[17] You learned about the iterative process of resolving host names to IP addresses in chapter 5.

[18] If you want to register a domain name, you only need register the first level below the TLD. Once a domain name is registered, the owner can create numerous domains under the registered domain, and these subdomains do not have to be registered.

FIGURE 10.3   **DNS Name Space**

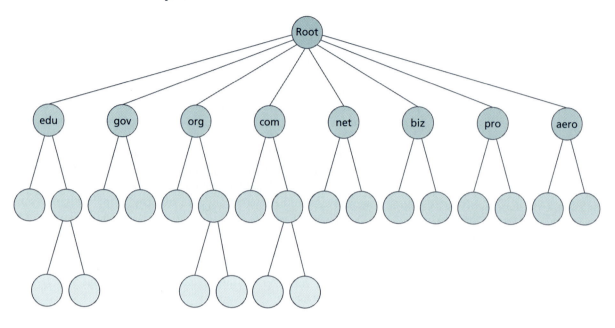

TABLE 10.1
Original Top-Level Domains

TLD	Original Purpose
.com	Commercial organizations
.edu	U.S. educational organizations
.gov	U.S. government organizations
.int	International organizations
.mil	U.S. military organizations
.net	Network infrastructure organizations
.org	Nonprofit organizations
.arpa	ARPANET hosts
New TLD	**Purpose**
.aero	Air transport organizations
.biz	Businesses
.info	Information
.museum	Museums
.name	Individuals
.pro	Professionals

a maximum length of 63 characters. Each of these restrictions further limit how many levels you would realistically place under a TLD.

With the development and introduction of DNS in the early 1980s, it quickly became apparent that a consistent domain name space that could accommodate various network types and different organizations would be required. This led to the development of the domain structure that most of us use on a regular basis and which some of us might have referred to as the dot-com world. Originally the domain name space that accompanies DNS was divided into seven **generic TLDs (gTLDs),** plus an .arpa TLD as displayed in the top half of Table 10.1. The .arpa TLD has since been relegated to technical infrastructure purposes, but the original seven gTLDs still exist. Numerous additions have been made over the years to include **country codes (ccTLDs),** new organization types, and TLDs whose

sole purpose is to accommodate the growth in the Internet. Some of these new TLDs and their purposes are listed in the bottom half of Table 10.1.[19]

Internet Protocols

The Internet protocols, such as IP and TCP, that we use every day to access data on LANs and on the Internet, were originally developed in the 1970s to provide efficient data transmission across the ARPANET and later the Internet. Once these protocols had matured in the world of the Internet, LAN administrators realized their significance for the transmission of data in smaller networks, where the protocols that were once reserved for the Internet quickly became standards for local and wide area data and voice transmissions.

Today there's an entire suite of protocols based on the TCP/IP architecture, and each of these protocols assists the transmission of data and support of various applications in some way. For example, the address resolution protocol (ARP) is a data link layer protocol that is part of the TCP/IP suite. ARP is used to map a MAC address to an IP address. IP is a network layer protocol that was split off from TCP to provide network layer functionality without the reliability that is built into TCP. DHCP is another network layer protocol that can be used to automatically assign IP addressing information to host computers. TCP was the original Internet protocol that was developed to transport data from point A to point B, and UDP is another transport layer protocol that eliminates the underlying acknowledgment of delivery associated with TCP. DNS, iSCSI, and LDAP are all session layer protocols that provide, respectively, IP address to host name resolution, data transport in SANs, and directory support and directory access to databases. And the application layer is replete with protocols that most of us use on a regular basis to access information from the Internet. These include the **hypertext transport protocol (HTTP)** and its secure relative (HTTPS), the **file transfer protocol (FTP)**, Telnet, the **Simple Mail Transfer Protocol**

---

[19] You can find up-to-date information about new TLDs at www.icann.org, and great historical information about the original TLDs in RFCs 1034 and 1035. You can find a complete listing of RFCs at www.rfc-editor.org/overview.html.

FIGURE 10.4
TCP/IP Protocols
within the OSI Model
Layers

Application	HTTP HTTPS FTP	Telnet SMTP PoP3	IMAP4 RTSP SLP	SNMP XMPP SIMPLE
Presentation				
Session	DNS iSCSI LDAP			
Transport	TCP UDP	RTP RTCP		
Network	IP DHCP			
Data link	ARP			
Physical				

(SMTP), the **Post Office Protocol (POP3),** and the **Internet Messaging Access Protocol (IMAP4),** and the **Real Time Streaming Protocol (RTSP),** as well as others that are more administrative in nature. These include protocols such as the Service Location Protocol (SLP) and the Simple Network Management Protocol (SNMP). Figure 10.4 provides an illustration of where these protocols fit within the layers of the OSI model.

Internet Applications

The application layer Internet protocols that you discovered previously in this chapter support several important Internet applications that individuals and organizations use on a regular basis.[20] Transferring files across the Internet usually involves HTTP and FTP. Remote computing may utilize Telnet as its application layer protocol. Streaming applications utilize RTSP as their application layer protocol, e-mail uses SMTP, POP3, and IMAP4 to transmit messages, and instant messaging (IM) relies on two competing IM protocols known as the **Extensible Messaging and Presence Protocol (XMPP)** or the **Session Initiation Protocol for Instant Messaging and Presence Leveraging Extensions (SIMPLE).**[21] Today we use these applications for numerous personal and business functions, and generally we have to use each application separately to accomplish the specific functions associated with an application. As we move forward through the next few years, however, the potential for all of these Internet applications to merge into a common interface is highly probable.

File Transfer

File Transfer Protocol (FTP) and Hypertext Transfer Protocol (HTTP) are the application layer protocols that allow Internet users to transfer files between locations. FTP existed

---

[20] Although the Internet protocols and applications listed in this section are discussed in terms of Internet use, most organizations also implement these same protocols and applications for use in their LANs and WANs.

[21] SIMPLE relies on the Session Initiation Protocol (SIP) that you learned about in chapter 7.

long before HTTP was developed, and it is still being used to download and upload files. Organizations implement FTP to provide remote file access to employees who need to post or retrieve files but who don't require the hyperlink browsing capability that is provided by an HTTP Web server. FTP components include a file server or mainframe that is configured with an operating system and the FTP service, and client computing devices that are configured with either an FTP client or a Web browser. To access an FTP site, the address field requires a URL with an ftp prefix, as in ftp://ftp.*sitename*.com. When the FTP site is displayed in the browser window or FTP client, the user sees a series of folders and can open the appropriate folder to access the desired file. Access through a browser requires a copy and paste, but most FTP client software provide upload and download utilities to transfer files between a user location and the FTP server.

File transfers with HTTP are also browser-based, but Web site files that are available for download are presented as hyperlinks that a user can click on to gain access. File uploads require configuration of the HTTP server application so that client devices can upload files. Common examples of file uploads are credit card numbers that you post for authorization with online purchases.

Remote Computing

Telnet is an application layer protocol that allows users to log in to remote computers and networking devices. To create a Telnet session between your computer and another computer, your computer must be configured with a Telnet client, and the target computer or device must be configured with a Telnet service, that is, the service that supports Telnet connections. When you run the Telnet program at your computer you'll be prompted for the name of the target computer. Once you supply the target's name or IP address, you'll be prompted to log in with a user name and password, if the Telnet service that is running on the target computer or device requires you to do so. After you log in, you can run applications, execute commands, or search for information on the remote computer or device.[22]

Because Telnet is not a secure program, it's generally relegated to making quick and easy configuration changes on remote devices or computers or for running programs on a remote computer where you don't want to use a browser and you don't require secure transmission channel between computers.[23] In today's security conscious networking environments, most companies instead implement secure shell (SSH) where they might have used Telnet in the past.[24] SSH behaves very much like Telnet, except that SSH encrypts the data transfer between devices.[25]

Streaming Media

To stream data from one location to another simply means that when data is accessed from a source or upon initiation of a data transmission from a source, not all of the data is delivered to the recipient before the data can begin to be viewed at the destination. Streaming utilizes underlying transport and control protocols such as RTP, UDP, and RTCP, but the application layer protocol that assists with streaming media is RTSP. RTSP is much like

---

[22] Telnet does not provide a graphical interface for the user. You run it from a command line, and you need knowledge of the command syntax in order to run programs or execute commands. If the Telnet service at the target computer is configured to deliver a menu-based application, you will be able to select from the menu choices to navigate through the presented information.

[23] With Telnet, all of the information passes between points as plain text—it's not encrypted.

[24] You'll learn about SSH in more detail in chapter 9.

[25] Telnet and SSH are not the only ways to remotely access data on other computers or networks. Graphical programs such as PCAnywhere, Microsoft's or Novell's remote desktop services, Citrix Metaframe, and X-windows for UNIX and Linux are some of the remote access programs that might be used for remote access.

HTTP, except that where HTTP will deliver a file from a Web server and then release the connection until the next file is requested, RTSP maintains the connection between a streaming server and the client that is receiving the streamed data.[26]

RTSP supports two very important application layer functions. First, RTSP provides the playback mechanisms that allow a client computer to pause, stop, start, replay, and fast-forward the streamed data. RTSP is frequently described as the VCR control mechanism of streaming media. And second, RTSP can adjust data delivery according to network conditions. If the network is congested, the media stream can be slowed to accommodate a lower bandwidth situation.

webcasting
an Internet term used to define delivery of multimedia data in streaming format across the Internet. Webcasting can deliver streaming content to employees at multiple remote locations, provide live or on-demand educational and training content, and facilitate collaborative applications such as streaming chat within an organization.

From a business perspective, streaming media has gained significant attention since its introduction in the late 1990s. Organizations use it in the form of **webcasting** to deliver streaming multimedia content to employees at multiple remote locations, to provide live or on-demand educational and training content, and to facilitate collaborative applications such as streaming chat. Webcasting requires special network device configuration so that routing devices can recognize the webcast packets and direct them to specific networks. On-demand applications require powerful streaming servers that can support numerous client connections. And collaborative applications such as streaming chat require robust applications that allow users to exchange text, voice, and video during a communications session. In addition, webcasting requires special attention to network infrastructure design and the bandwidth of WAN connections because streaming delivery of multimedia data can consume vast amounts of bandwidth.

E-mail

SMTP, POP3, and IMAP4 are the three primary application layer Internet protocols that support e-mail. SMTP is used for sending e-mails, and POP3 and IMAP4 are used for accessing mailboxes and retrieving e-mails. SMTP is utilized whenever you send an e-mail. SMTP is responsible for establishing the connection between an e-mail client and the e-mail server and for communicating with other SMTP servers. Whether you use POP3 or IMAP4 for e-mail access depends on whether you need access to e-mails when you're not connected to the e-mail server, whether you generally access e-mail from the same client computer, and the relative importance of maintaining a centralized backup of all of your e-mail versus backing up e-mails on each individual client computer.

With POP3, your e-mails are automatically downloaded to the client computer when you access your mailbox on the e-mail server. This feature gives you "anytime" access to your previously downloaded e-mails and prevents excess storage of e-mail on the e-mail server. And because POP3 downloads e-mails, you should plan on using the same client computer every time you access e-mail. If you don't, you'll have e-mail located on multiple different client machines.

If you frequently use different computers for e-mail access, you might prefer accessing e-mail through an IMAP4 e-mail server. With IMAP4, you access your mailbox on the e-mail server as if the mailbox were a local mailbox on your client computer. All of your e-mails are retained on the e-mail server, which makes it convenient for accessing e-mail from any client computer and for backing up e-mails from a single location. The only drawback to using IMAP4 for e-mail access is that your e-mail will be unavailable for access whenever the e-mail server is offline, unless, of course, you have selectively downloaded e-mails that you want to store locally.

---

[26] RTSP connections between a client computer and a streaming server are retained (stateful) so that the data can be provided in a continuous stream between server and client. HTTP connections between client computers and Web servers are called *stateless connections* because the client makes a request, the Web server responds, and then the connection is terminated.

whiteboarding
application software that allows classroom-style white board drawings and markings to be created and viewed by each participant of a videoconferencing or IM session

calendaring
the process of establishing schedules, meetings, and events on an electronic calendar

groupware
applications that allow users to work collaboratively from remote locations using network and Internet technologies

presence information
lets online users or applications know when other users or applications come online

Instant Messaging

Instant messaging (IM) has the potential to become the "killer app" of the Internet, allowing data communications across the Internet to accelerate at an even faster pace than it is today. Already IM allows users to chat using typed text, exchange files, and even exchange voice conversations of acceptable quality. In addition, video chat of equal quality is on the way along with **whiteboarding** and **calendaring** through IM, and several companies are in the process of releasing versions of chat software that incorporate these sophisticated videoconferencing and **groupware** functionalities for corporate enterprise implementations. At some point in the not-to-distant future, communications technologies such as e-mail and the telephone will even converge into a single unified data communications structure based upon IM.

Open standards will facilitate the convergence of data communications technologies such as e-mail, voice mail, group scheduling, group projects, videoconferencing, whiteboarding, calendaring, as well as text, voice, and video chat through IM. The standardized protocols that will make this happen are the Extensible Messaging and Presence Protocol (XMPP) and the Session Initiation Protocol for Instant Messaging and Presence Leveraging Extensions (SIMPLE). XMPP is based on eXtensible Markup Language (XML) and provides developers with a platform to develop feature-rich applications that can deliver near real-time delivery of data through IM. XMPP can also be used to deliver real-time presence information across the Internet. **Presence information** lets online users or applications know when other users or applications come online, that is, when they're present. When an application comes online, XMPP can automatically detect the application so that other applications can automatically connect with it and exchange information. XMPP is supported by the Jabber Software Foundation (JSF) and the XCP Consortium.[27]

SIMPLE is an extension of the Session Initiation Protocol (SIP) that is used in VoIP networks. It competes in the same space as XMPP, but SIMPLE is designed primarily for multimedia application delivery through IM. SIMPLE has the backing of IBM and Microsoft, and long-term prospects indicate that SIMPLE and XMPP might coexist in the IM marketplace with protocol translation taking place through IM gateways.

THE FUTURE OF THE INTERNET

We've already seen that the roots of the Internet were established in 1969 and that the foundation of the Internet as we know it today began with the transition from the National Science Foundation's noncommercial NSFNET to the private-sector commercial backbones that were being implemented by the major carrier companies in the early 1990s. Realizing the importance of the continued development of advanced data communications technologies as well as the future need for faster backbones than the ISPs were providing at the time of transition, the NSF commissioned MCI in 1994 to assist in the development of the **very-high-speed Backbone Network Service (vBNS).**[28] Deployed on the same day that the NSFNET was decommissioned in April 1995, the vBNS connected the NSF's supercomputing centers, government agencies, and research institutions with an OC-3 (155 Mbps) backbone that far exceeded the T1 and T3 bandwidths of the commercial Internet.[29] In 1997, the vBNS was upgraded to OC-12 (622 Mbps), and in 2000, its bandwidth was again

---

[27] The Jabber Software Foundation developed Jabber, an XML streaming technology that is being deployed through the XMPP standard as published by the IETF. XCP is the XML Control Protocol, a next-generation transmission control protocol designed to replace TCP in Web-based applications that deliver data across the Internet.

[28] The actual agreement for the development and implementation of vBNS was signed in April 1995.

[29] Research agencies and universities began calling the commercial Internet the commodity Internet to distinguish it from vBNS and other high-speed internetworking initiatives.

upgraded to OC-48 (2.4 Gbps). By this time more than 150 colleges and universities were connected to the vBNS, enabled by the federally funded **Next Generation Internet (NGI)** initiative. Announced in 1996 and implemented between 1997 and 2000, the NGI initiative assisted the NSF in getting universities, colleges, and research institutions connected to the vBNS through the High Performance Network Connection (HPNC) program. vBNS is still operated by MCI in support of the organizations that are attached to it, but it is no longer funded by NSF.

Internet2

Other future internetworking initiatives were also launched during the 1990s and continue today. In 1996, 34 U.S. universities started **Internet2** to create the next generation of Internet applications and technologies. Internet2 is not a network infrastructure like the Internet but is a consortium of more than 200 universities collaborating with private-sector organizations and government to build, test, and deploy advanced applications and technologies that will drive the Internet of tomorrow. In 1997, Internet2 was incorporated under the **University Consortium for Advanced Internet Development (UCAID)** as a nonprofit enterprise, and the following year a collaborative effort among Internet2 participants, Qwest, which provided the OC network, and several networking companies, introduced a high-speed networking backbone known as the **Abilene Project.**

The Abilene Project

Abilene is the actual physical communications network that supports Internet2 activities. It provides universities and research institutions with the bandwidth required to test and implement the advanced technologies and applications of Internet2.[30] Abilene went live in February 1999 with SONET OC-48 circuits that provided a bandwidth of 2.4 Gigabits per second (Gbps). In February 2004, the Abilene network was upgraded to OC-192 circuits that provide 10 Gbps of bandwidth. For the time being, connections to Abilene are restricted to universities and research institutions, and Abilene continues to be maintained as a separate network that is not interconnected with the commercial ISP networks that comprise the Internet. Figure 10.5 depicts a graphical representation of the Abilene network's OC-192 connections.

FIGURE 10.5
The Abilene Network

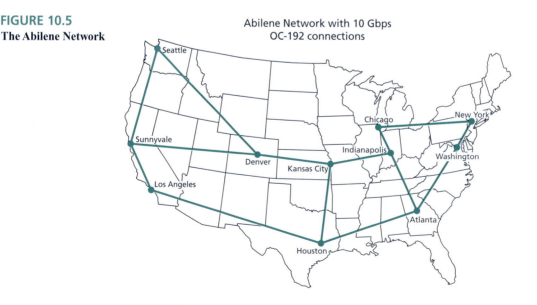

Abilene Network with 10 Gbps
OC-192 connections

---

[30] The Abilene Network Operation Center (NOC) has a great site that provides several different maps of the Abilene network at www.abilene.iu.edu/ndoc.html.

Working Groups

Since its inception, Internet2 has grown to include numerous working groups (WGs) that support advanced service, application, and technology development. The **Internet2 WGs** include Campus Bandwidth Management, Digital Video, Integrated Infrastructure for Instant Messaging, IPv6, MACE-Shibboleth and MACE-WebISO, Multicast, Orthopaedic Surgery, Presence and Integrated Communications, VidMid Video Conferencing, VidMid Video on Demand, Voice over IP, as well as several other WGs.[31] A summary of these working groups follows.

Campus Bandwidth Management   The Campus Bandwidth Management WG focuses on bandwidth and traffic management on campuses that are part of the Internet2 consortium. Toward that end, this WG can develop bandwidth strategies in support of Internet2 applications that require the kinds of bandwidth provided by vBNS and Abilene. The kinds of information collected and analyzed by this working group are used to further the efforts of QoS development and network performance solutions.

Digital Video   The Digital Video WG is chartered with advancing the capabilities of digital video among Internet2 participants. Members of this WG collaborate with other, non-Internet2 organizations that are also working on the development of next-generation digital video technologies.

Integrated Infrastructure for Instant Messaging (I2IM)   The **I2IM** WG is tasked with exploring the administrative needs of instant messaging deployments rather than developing new IM technologies. This working group considers IM technologies such as SIMPLE and XMPP as well as proprietary technologies and standards extensions from America Online (AOL), Microsoft's MSN, and the Jabber Software Foundation. I2IM works with organizations outside of the Internet2 community that are also working on current and next generation IM technologies.

IPv6   The **IPv6** WG has deployed IPv6 across the Abilene network and continues to work toward integrating IPv6 with other large networks outside of the Internet2 community. The primary goals of this working group are threefold: the continued design and operation of an IPv6 infrastructure on the Abilene backbone, network engineer training on Internet2 campuses so that they can support their own campus IPv6 deployments, and the explanation of IPv6 value to the Internet2 user community.

Shibboleth   **Shibboleth** is a working group that is creating software architectures and technologies that support the sharing of Web resources located at the numerous universities and research institutions that are part of Internet2. Shibboleth software provides user information at one site to resources at other sites and establishes levels of trust so that information can be exchanged while maintaining sufficient privacy between shared resources. Shibboleth eliminates the need for different campuses to develop separate authentication systems. Instead, Shibboleth provides a Web-based access control solution that can be used across multiple locations.

WebISO   Related to the Shibboleth project is the WebISO WG. This working group evaluates protocols, software, and architectures that can deliver single sign-on and central authentication to Web-based services. With a common platform for logging in to various services, software developers will no longer have to create their own authentication services for their applications that are accessible on the Internet. Instead, users will utilize a centralized authentication service when they sign on to the Internet, and whatever credentials are associated with the user can be used to access any of numerous Web services that participate in the standardized logon technology.

---

[31] Additional working groups and WG information, including their historical origins, can be found at www.internet2.edu/working-groups.html.

Multicast   The goal of the Multicast WG is to guide the deployment of an Internet2 multicast service. Because multicast applications can direct streaming traffic to multiple network locations simultaneously, part of the Multicast WG's deployment strategy involves the support of multicast traffic across more than one network infrastructure without any degradation in service level. That is, the next-generation multicast service must support streaming data transmissions to multiple locations across multiple networks and multiple levels of ISPs while maintaining a consistent signal to all target locations. In addition, part of the working group's charter is to identify methods for converting existing Web applications to multicast capability.

Orthopaedic Surgery WG and Radiology   The function of the Orthopaedic Surgery WG and the Radiology WG is to make the medical community aware of and get them to use high-bandwidth medical applications. Teleradiography, telemedicine, telerobotics, and interactive medical classrooms are but a few of the initiatives of these working groups. Applications such as telerobotics within the Orthopaedic Surgery WG function as a template on which future telemedicine applications might be built. Applications such as teleradiography within the Radiology WG act as a catalyst to further the development of medical imaging applications and standards and the transport of medical images across network infrastructures.

Presence and Integrated Communications   The Presence and Integrated Communications WG works with next-generation presence technologies. These technologies allow users to identify and locate other online users using protocols such as SIP and using addressing such as e-mail addresses. With the presence software loaded on their communications devices, such as laptops, wireless phones, and PDAs, users can communicate using voice, instant messaging, and video. What makes this next-generation presence technology special is its ability to automatically update user location information based on users' meeting calendars so that parties to the communications session know each other's location without asking. In addition, with wireless devices, a user's location is determined and presented to other presence information recipients via triangulation of the wireless signal.

VidMid Video Conferencing (VC) and VidMid Video on Demand (VoD)   These two video middleware **(VidMid)** working groups are collaborative efforts with the Video Development Initiative (ViDe), a member organization whose charter is to develop and promote standardized digital video technologies.[32] Both the VidMid VC and VidMid VoD working groups focus on resource discovery and resource authentication for videoconferencing, video-on-demand, VoIP, and data collaboration applications. Results from these working groups include development of new protocols such as H.350, a new ITU standard issued in September 2003 that facilitates video and VoIP resource discovery across enterprise networks.

Voice over IP (VoIP)   The VoIP WG is involved in the deployment of next-generation Internet voice technologies, which requires a close collaboration with the working groups that are working on other real-time and converging messaging and communications technologies. Some of the current projects with which the VoIP WG is involved include SIP.edu, an Internet2 project dealing with the convergence of e-mail and voice communications through Session Initiation Protocol (SIP). Another is the VoIP Disaster Recovery Trial, which seeks to provide high availability and survivability of a VoIP voice network in the event of disaster.

Other initiatives of the Internet2 consortium include the Middleware Architecture Committee for Education (MACE). This committee is composed of IT technologists from numerous Internet2 campuses with the goal of providing technical expertise and direction, especially in the areas of security and directories; that is, resource identification and

---

[32] You can find more information regarding ViDe at www.vide.net.

authentication based on a common set of stored resource attributes. The Shibboleth and WebISO working groups exist under the guidance of MACE.

The Next-Generation Internet Protocol

IPv6 is the next-generation Internet Protocol that expands the number of available addresses, known as the address space, and also provides the foundation for the next-generation Internet services you learned about in the Internet2 section. The addressing scheme that utilized four octets and 32 bits under IPv4 has been supplanted with an addressing scheme of 128 bits that can provide more than 340 trillion trillion trillion addresses.[33] That's enough addresses to assign an IPv6 address for every person on earth with enough left over to assign an IPv6 address to virtually every car, refrigerator, microwave, and just about any other conceivable device, appliance, or service. While IPv6 is not currently mainstream in most organizations and homes, it is implemented at numerous sites that utilize vBNS and Abilene, and IPv6 continues to be monitored under the auspices of the IPv6 working group within the Internet2 consortium.

The first recommendation for a next-generation Internet Protocol was published by the IETF as RFC 1752 in January 1995. Later that year they issued RFC 1884 to formalize a standards track for an IPv6 addressing architecture. Since then, two additional RFCs have been issued to update the IPv6 addressing architecture, and during October 2003, an Internet Draft was issued to update the architecture once again. By the time you read this, the latest Internet-Draft (v4-00) will very likely be the newest evolution of the IPv6 addressing standard.[34]

IPv6 Business Drivers

While most major network connectivity equipment vendors already incorporate IPv6 capability into their network devices, the implementation of IPv6 has not been widely embraced by the business community. Research organizations, academia, and many ISPs have adopted IPv6, but much of the cost associated with those adoptions has been heavily subsidized with grant money from government agencies. What will it take to get businesses to adopt this latest and greatest suite of data transmission protocols? As with most business decisions, the widespread adoption of IPv6 and the eventual replacement of IPv4 will require sound business drivers. Some of these business drivers include

- The need to provide IP addresses to a growing number of devices.
- Next-generation business applications.
- The growing use of mobile and wireless devices.
- Increased exposure of data as it is transmitted across the Internet.

One of the original incentives for businesses to adopt IPv6 was that there wouldn't be enough IP addresses in IPv4 to support a growing number of networked devices. That is, the supply of IPv4 addresses is running out while the demand for IP addresses continues to grow. This turned out to be a short-lived business problem because technical solutions other than IPv6, such as network address translation (NAT) and dynamic assignment of addresses through DHCP, solved the number-of-addresses problem for the short term, and it was relatively low cost to implement NAT and DHCP.[35] This made an implementation of IPv6 untenable, based simply on the number-of-addresses problem.

---

[33] The exact number is 340,282,366,920,938,463,463,374,607,431,768,211,456.

[34] In July 1998, RFC 1884 was made obsolete by RFC 2373. Then in April 2003, RFC 2373 was made obsolete by RFC 3513. You can find the latest information regarding IPv6 and its proposed updates at www.ietf.org/ids.by.wg/ipv6.html.

[35] You learned about network address translation (NAT) in chapter 9.

Leave it to the NAT solution to introduce another future problem, especially with the next generation of business applications that will require dedicated end-to-end connections between devices. Many of the next-generation applications will require, or at least allow, client devices to provide interactive services and connections with other end nodes as well as servers. NAT doesn't function well in this scenario because of its inability to map incoming connections and application-level services to clients' nonpublic IP addresses.[36] Even if you solve the application-level service translation problem by implementing an application-level gateway to provide the connections and service mappings to the client computers that are using NAT, the configuration and maintenance of the application-level gateway in a potentially rapid-changing world of next-generation application services could add substantial overhead to an administrator's budget. This could be a significant motivator for IPv6 adoption as businesses introduce next-generation applications.

The growing number of mobile devices and wireless devices also generates a plausible business driver for the implementation of IPv6.[37] IPv4 does not scale well with a growing number of mobile devices, resulting in inefficient routing of network traffic as the mobility of and number of mobile devices increases. IPv6 uses **autoconfiguration**, a function that automatically configures computing devices on IPv6 networks with IPv6 address information as those devices attach to an IPv6 network.[38] For mobile users, autoconfiguration eliminates the inefficient routing conditions associated with mobile devices on IPv4 networks.

Another significant business driver that could justify the implementation of IPv6 is the ever-increasing risk of tampering and theft of data as it traverses the Internet. With IPv4, numerous security measures can be implemented to protect your data as it's transmitted across a public network, including IPSec.[39] With IPv4, IPSec is an add-on security function. With IPv6, IPSec is built in. This will become increasingly important as next-generation applications are configured to automatically request a **security association (SA)** that can identify and establish security services such as data authentication or data encryption across a connection between communicating devices.[40] IPv6 with its built-in IPSec will provide configurable security parameters to protect data as it's being exchanged between computing devices across the Internet.

With these business drivers in mind, the implementation of IPv6 will very likely be tied to the deployment of next-generation applications, the increasing number of mobile computing devices, and the growing need for integrated data transmission security. With that said, you can probably expect to see IPv6 implementations in larger organizations within the next three to five years and in smaller organizations some time after that.

IPv6 Addressing

IPv6 addressing is substantially different than IPv4 addressing. IPv4 addressing uses 32 bits divided into four octets of eight bits each.[41] An example might be 128.204.15.199,

---

autoconfiguration
an IPv6 function that automatically reconfigures mobile devices as they move from network to network

security association
an IPv6 function that identifies and establishes security services such as data authentication or data encryption across a connection between communicating devices

You can keep up-to-date on the latest major deployments of IPv6 by visiting the IPv6 Forum at www.ipv6forum.com and selecting the IPv6 Deployment link.

---

[36] That's because NAT functions at OSI layer 3, and applications function within the upper three layers of the OSI model.

[37] This business driver refers to a technical standard known as *Mobile IP*, which is used in both IPv4 and IPv6 networks to provide different IP addresses and IP connections to mobile devices. Mobile IP in IPv6 is much more efficient in terms of routing data across the network than it is in IPv4. The technical details of Mobil IP in either IPv4 or IPv6 are beyond the scope of this text.

[38] IPv6 autoconfiguration makes IPv4's DHCP service unnecessary in IPv6.

[39] You discovered IPSec in chapter 9.

[40] There are two types of security associations: transport mode and tunnel mode. A transport mode security association is established between end systems and establishes either authentication or encryption for the data within each packet during the connection. A tunnel mode security association applies encryption or authentication to the entire packet, and the packet is reencapsulated with a "wrapper" that can be used for transport between end systems.

[41] You learned about IPv4 addressing in chapter 4.

FIGURE 10.6 IPv6 Generic Address Format

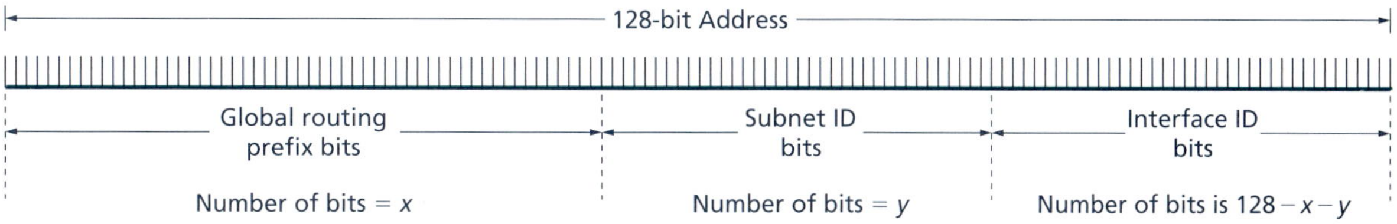

a Class B IPv4 address. In this example, the two left octets represent the network address, and the two right octets represent the node address.

IPv6 addressing uses 128 bits that are divided into eight 16-bit sections. An example address might be FE80:0000:0000:0000:ABCD:FF32:B3CC:1234. There are no address classes such as Class A, Class B, or Class C addresses that compare directly to IPv4. Instead, IPv6 addresses are comprised of global routing prefix bits to identify routing information for specific networks, subnet bits to identify a link within a site location, and interface ID bits to identify a specific node. Node bits are derived from a node's MAC address. Figure 10.6 provides a generic representation of the general address format for an IPv6 address.

IPv6 addressing also includes some abbreviations that can be used to depict addresses that have consecutive sections of zero bits and sections with leading zero bits. For example, the IPv6 address

FE80:0000:0000:0000:ABCD:FF32:030C:1234

can be represented as

FE80:0:0:0:ABCD:FF32:30C:1234

Notice that the three 16-bit sections that were each previously represented by four zeros are now each represented by a single zero. In addition, the 16-bit section that is seventh from the left was originally represented as 030C, where the two 0s are zeros. For any 16-bit section that has a preceding zero, the zero can be dropped, hence 30C. This example could even be represented as

FE80::ABCD:FF32:30C:1234

In this case, the three 16-bit sections that were filled with zeros are reduced to a double colon. That is, when an IPv6 address has consecutive sections of zero bits, you can represent those sections with a double colon. There is one caveat with this, however, and that is you can use the double colon only once in a given address.

Another IPv6 addressing convention utilizes a prefix-length notation to specify how many of the left-most bits are part of the address prefix. This can be useful to identify a specific type of address, or more generally how many bits are being used for routing in a given address. For example, the address

FE80:0000:0000:0000:ABCD:FF32:030C:1234/10

indicates that the first 10 bits of the address identify the prefix as well as the specific type of address.[42] Utilizing the syntax shortcut from previously, you could also write this as

FE80::ABCD:FF32:30C:1234/10

---

[42] In this case, the address type happens to be a Link-local unicast address.

prefix notation
the syntax used with IPv6 addresses to indicate the number of left-most bits that are used for routing. Prefix notation also indicates the IPv6 address type.

Whenever you see an IPv6 address followed by a slash (/) and then a number, it's known as **prefix notation**, and the number that follows the slash indicates the number of prefix bits.

IPv6 Address Types

Although IPv6 doesn't have classes of addresses such as Class A, Class B, and Class C that are used in IPv4 networks, IPv6 does have several types of addresses that are identified by the left-most bits, which are sometimes called the high-order bits of the address. These address types include unicast, multicast, unspecified, loopback, and six special types of unicast addresses known as global unicast, anycast, link-local unicast, unique local unicast, IPv4-compatible, and IPv4-mapped.[43]

unicast address
an address that identifies an interface on an IPv6 network.

Unicast[44]   In general, **unicast addresses** identify the individual unique interfaces on an IPv6 network. Each interface, such as a network card, switch port, router port, or even a wireless port, is assigned a unicast address, either manually or through IPv6 autoconfiguration, that uniquely identifies that interface on the network. The first three high-order bits in the address identify the address as a unicast address, and the range to look for is 001 to 111, except for 1111 1111, which is the multicast identifier.

global unicast address
an IPv6 address that is unique across the entire IPv6 address space

Global unicast addresses are unique across the entire IPv6 universe. Each address begins with high-order bits of 001, while the interface portion of the address is comprised of the right-most 64 bits. The 13 bits that follow the first three high-order bits identify a top-level aggregation (TLA) organization. TLAs are the organizations such as American Registry for Internet Numbers (ARIN) where ISPs register for their IPv6 addresses. The next eight bits are reserved for future use while the next 24 bits after that represent the next-level aggregation (NLA) identifier. An NLA is equivalent to an ISP or an exchange point at which ISPs connect to the Internet. After the NLA bits are the 16 bits that represent the site-level aggregation (SLA) identifier. These are the address bits assigned to specific organizations and can be used for subnetting their internal network. The remaining 64 bits identify a specific IPv6 interface, or node. Overall, the organization of the bits into identifiable sections provides a routing hierarchy that will be scalable for years to come. Figure 10.7 provides an example of bit organization in a global unicast address.

anycast address
a unicast address that is assigned to more than one interface

An **anycast address** is a unicast address that is assigned to more than one interface. The purpose behind anycast addresses is to allow any one of a number of like-configured devices to act as the sole provider of a service. That is, with IPv6, you can configure multiple different interfaces on different devices to have the same anycast address. By establishing this configuration, your network can provide access points or service points to multiple devices that request those access points and services. An example would be a network that had several connections to the Internet through different routers. Each router would be

FIGURE 10.7   Global Unicast Address Bit Order

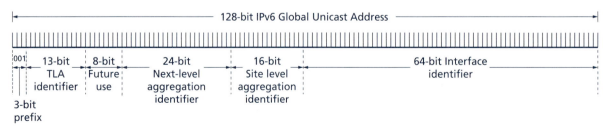

---

[43] Unique local unicast will very likely replace an older version of IPv6 site addressing known as *site-local unicast*.

[44] For those who are intimately familiar with IPv4, aggregated unicast addresses in IPv6 are analogous to IPv4 addresses in Classless Interdomain Routing.

configured with the same IPv6 anycast address. When a user required access to the Internet, the request would use the anycast address, but only the closest router would service the request. At this point in the evolutionary progress of IPv6, only routers can be configured with anycast addresses.

A **link-local unicast address** is used on networks that don't require routing. Examples include small networks that are set up temporarily to share data between a few computers and all of the computers are on the same subnet. Link-local addresses are identified by the first 10 binary bits 1111 1110 10 or by the hexadecimal notation FE80. Link-local addresses are analogous to the self-configuring IPv4 address assignments in small Microsoft Windows networks that don't use DHCP or manual IPv4 addressing. In this analogy, each computer in the small Microsoft network is configured with an IPv4 address whose first octet is 169.

The **unique local unicast address** specifies internal routing of IPv6 packets. This IPv6 addressing scheme is helpful with small to medium-sized networks that require routing within a specified site or among organization-specific sites but which don't require routing to the outside world. That is, unique local unicast addresses are not designed to work on the global Internet space. This address type also circumvents concerns that the IETF had regarding site-local unicast addresses, a predecessor to the unique local unicast address specification. While site-local addressing is still the formal standard for internal routing within an internal IPv6 address space, unique local unicast addressing is very likely to be its replacement.

Once IPv6 begins rolling out to the general Internet population and to the business world at large, IPv4 will continue to be supported until all users, devices, and networks are converted to IPv6. To facilitate the interoperability of IPv6 with IPv4, two additional types of IPv6 unicast addresses can be configured to accommodate IPv4 addresses within the IPv6 address space. **IPv4-mapped IPv6 addresses** represent IPv4 node addresses as IPv6 addresses. IPv4-mapped IPv6 addresses embed the IPv4 address of the IPv4 node in the low-order 32 bits. In addition, the 16 bits to the left of the IPv4 bits are represented as all 1s. This mapping allows IPv4 nodes to transmit their packets across an IPv6 infrastructure. Likewise, IPv6 nodes can transmit IPv6 packets to IPv4 nodes across an IPv6 infrastructure using this method. Part **(a)** of Figure 10.8 provides an example of an IPv4-mapped IPv6 address.

IPv4-compatible IPv6 addresses dynamically tunnel IPv6 packets over an IPv4 infrastructure. If an IPv6 network node needs to send data across an IPv4 network, the IPv6 node is assigned an IPv6 address that includes a globally unique IPv4 address in the right-most, or low-order 32 bits of the IPv6 address. Part **(b)** of Figure 10.8 provides an example of an IPv4-compatible IPv6 address.

link-local unicast address
a unicast address that is used in small or temporary networks in which all computers are on the same subnet. Link-local addresses are not designed to be routed.

unique local unicast address
an IPv6 address type that specifies internal routing of IPv6 packets

IPv4-mapped IPv6 addresses
represent IPv4 node addresses as IPv6 addresses for transmission across an IPv6 routing infrastructure

IPv4-compatible IPv6 addresses
IPv6 addresses that dynamically tunnel IPv6 packets over an IPv4 infrastructure. The low-order 32 bits are comprised of the IPv4 address.

FIGURE 10.8   Embedded IPv6 Addresses
a. IPv4-mapped IPv6 address. **b.** IPv4-compatible IPv6 address.

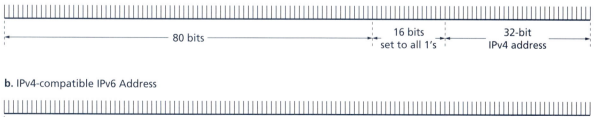

a. IPv4-mapped IPv6 Address

80 bits | 16 bits set to all 1's | 32-bit IPv4 address

b. IPv4-compatible IPv6 Address

80 bits | 16 bits set to all 0's | 32-bit IPv4 address

FIGURE 10.9 IPv6 Multicast Address Configuration

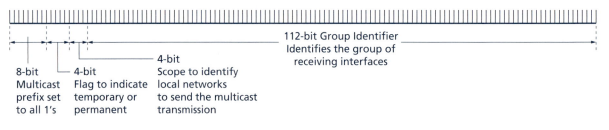

112-bit Group Identifier
Identifies the group of
receiving interfaces

4-bit
Scope to identify
local networks
to send the multicast
transmission

8-bit
Multicast
prefix set
to all 1's

4-bit
Flag to indicate
temporary or
permanent

multicasting
routes packets to groups
of end locations or
devices

Multicast **Multicast addressing** in IPv6 is specified for routing packets to groups of IPv6 interfaces. Common applications include streaming media presentations or videoconferencing that are directed to a selected group of networks for distribution to end-users. With IPv6 multicast addresses the 8-bit prefix is all 1s, followed by a 4-bit sequence that indicates whether the multicast address is permanent or temporary, followed by a four-bit scope field that identifies local networks to which the multicast transmission should be sent, and the remaining 112-bit sequence identifies the group of receiving interfaces within the specified scope. For example, the low-order bits in the 112-bit sequence could identify whether the multicast was going to all routers or all nodes within a specified scope. Figure 10.9 provides the address configuration of an IPv6 multicast address.

Unspecified The unspecified address in IPv6 is indicated as all zeros, as in 0000:0000:0000:0000:0000:0000:0000:0000. This address can also be represented as 0:0:0:0:0:0:0:0, or 0::0, or simply ::. In general, the unspecified address is used only as a source address during bootup when a device is negotiating for its address information as with DHCP. It is never configured on an interface as a source or destination address.

Loopback The **loopback address** is used in troubleshooting the IPv6 configuration of an interface. To test a configuration, a network administrator uses the ping6 command in combination with the loopback address to have a node send a packet to itself. If the ping receives a reply, the IPv6 configuration is working properly. The IPv6 loopback address is indicated as 0000:0000:0000:0000:0000:0000:0000:0001, or as 0:0:0:0:0:0:0:1, or simply as ::1.

Impact on the Organization

So how will all of this futuristic Internet technology impact our lives and the ways in which organizations conduct business? We'll see improved transmission performance for time-critical applications such as streaming digital media and VoIP. QoS will be substantially improved with the higher-bandwidth backbones that currently exist with the Abilene and vBNS networks and which will eventually be available on the regular Internet. Internet2 application development in areas such as medical imaging and multicasting promise to deliver real-time classroom instruction from anywhere and at anytime to anywhere and at anytime. IPv6 will provide greater capabilities than IPv4 and will facilitate improved support for next-generation services and applications. Application developers will be able to focus on the important features of applications rather than waste time developing authentication and Web logon specifications—Shibboleth and WebISO are building that foundation. And instant messaging, the application that is already becoming the foundation for other real-time applications, promises an Internet world of converged services; a world in which all kinds of data—audio, video, voice, and text—can be simultaneously and interactively shared in a multisensory capacity among numerous users at various and multiple locations.

The Internet is only 36 years old. When the telephone was 36 years old, the year was 1912, and the first transcontinental telephone call was not yet technologically feasible nor did the transmission lines exist to place that call. Look how far the Internet has come in such a relatively short period of time. Now consider the advances with these next-generation technologies. They're almost here, almost ready for transition to a new and faster Internet—an Internet that promises the most significant evolution in communications technology . . . ever. It will provide us with access to all the business essentials, not to mention enhanced communications with friends and families—and all of it presented in real time! And this is just the beginning. Who knows what ideas will generate from here?

Chapter Summary

- **Internet history.** The Internet was officially "born" on September 1, 1969, and it was originally called the ARPANET. The ARPANET in combination with CSNET and funding from the National Science Foundation evolved into the NSFNET in the mid-1980s, and ARPANET was decommissioned in February 1990. Growing business demand for commercial data communications services in the early 1990s led the National Science Foundation to began a transition of Internet services to the private sector. Privatization took effect in 1994, and the NSFNET backbone was officially decommissioned in April 1995.

- **Internet topology.** Internet topology consists of national ISPs, regional ISPs, NAPs, MAEs, IXPs, ISP PoPs, LECs, and the vast number of networks that are located around the world. ISPs, NAPs, MAEs, IXPs, and LECs are interconnected in various hierarchies to provide Internet access to millions of individuals and businesses.

- **Organizations that govern the Internet.** The major organizations that oversee the continued development of the Internet include the ISOC, the IETF, the IAB, the IESG, and the IRTF. Other organizations such as ICANN participate in network management, such as the allocation of IP address space and the development and management of top-level Internet domains.

- **Domain Name System and Name Servers.** The Domain Name System is a distributed database of host names that computing devices can use to resolve host names to IP addresses. Name Servers are the computers on which the Domain Name System database is stored and updated. Name servers are located throughout the Internet.

- **Top-level Internet domains.** Top-level Internet domains provide organization and a hierarchical structure to the Internet. Top-level domains include the original .com, .net, .org, .edu, .gov, .mil, and .int domains as well as newer top-level domains such as .aero, .biz, .info, .museum, .name, and .pro.

- **Internet protocols and applications.** Internet protocols span the layers of the OSI model and include ARP, IP, TCP, DNS, iSCSI, LDAP, HTTP, HTTPS, FTP, Telnet, SMTP, POP3, IMAP4, RTSP, SNMP, XMPP, SIMPLE, and others. These protocols work to support applications such as file transfer, remote computing, streaming media, e-mail, and instant messaging to name a few.

- **Internet2.** Internet2 is an initiative launched in the mid 1990s to develop the next generation of Internet applications and technologies. Internet2 is not a network infrastructure but it does support infrastructure activities such as the Abilene Project. Internet2 also oversees numerous working groups that foster the actual development of the Internet applications we'll use in the future.

- **IPv6.** IPv6 is the next-generation Internet Protocol, and it consists of numerous elements that provide enhanced functionality for data communications and networks. With its 128-bit address space, IPv6 is designed to provide many more addresses than are currently available under IPv4. IPv6 supports the next generation of Internet and business applications. It has built-in support for a growing number of mobile computing devices, and it has built-in security features that aren't available without add-on protocols in IPv4. In addition, IPv6 provides for several types of addressing so that data can be more efficiently routed between networks.

- **Internet2 impact.** The impact of Internet2 will be enormous. We'll benefit from faster data transmission speeds, enhanced security, and converged application services that will deliver real-time, interactive sharing of data among numerous users across multiple locations.

Key Terms

Abilene Project, *358*

Advanced Research Projects Agency (ARPA), *344*

Anycast address, *364*

ARPA Network (ARPANET), *344*

Autoconfiguration, *362*

Calendaring, *357*

Country code TLD (ccTLD), *352*

CSNET, *345*

Defense Communications Agency (DCA), *345*

Domain name space, *351*

Domain name system (DNS), *350*

Extensible messaging and presence protocol (XMPP), *354*

File transfer protocol (FTP), *353*

Generic TLD (gTLD), *352*

Global Unicast address, *364*

Groupware, *357*

Hosts file, *349*

Hypertext transport protocol (HTTP), *353*

Integrated Infrastructure for Instant Messaging (I2IM), *359*

Internet Architecture Board (IAB), *349*

Internet Corporation for Assigned Names and Numbers (ICANN), *349*

Internet domains, *351*

Internet Engineering Steering Group (IESG), *349*

Internet Engineering Task Force (IETF), *348*

Internet exchange point (IXP), *346*

Internet messaging access protocol (IMAP4), *354*

Internet protocol (IP), *344*

Internet Research Task Force (IRTF), *349*

Internet service provider (ISP), *346*

Internet Society (ISOC), *348*

Internet2 working groups (WGs), *359*

Internet2, *358*

IPv4-compatible IPv6 addresses, *365*

IPv4-mapped IPv6 addresses, *365*

IPv6, *359*

Jon Postel, *350*

Link-local Unicast address, *365*

Local exchange carrier (LEC), *346*

Loopback address, *366*

Metropolitan area exchange (MAE), *346*

MILNET, *345*

Multicast address, *366*

Name servers, *350*

National Science Foundation (NSF), *345*

Network access point (NAP), *346*

Network control protocol (NCP), *344*

Next-generation Internet (NGI), *358*

NSFNET, *345*

Paul Mockapetris, *350*

Peering agreement, *347*

Point of presence (PoP), *346*

Post office protocol (POP3), *354*

Presence information, *357*

Real-time streaming protocol (RTSP), *354*

Robert Kahn, *344*

Root domain, *351*

Security Association, *362*

Session Initiation Protocol for Instant Messaging and Presence Leveraging Extensions (SIMPLE), *354*

Shibboleth, *359*

Simple mail transfer protocol (SMTP), *353*

Questions

1. What is the Internet, what is its origin, what technologies comprise the Internet, and who runs it?

2. What impact did the ARPANET and the NSFNET have on the development of the Internet?

3. What was the impetus behind the transition from a research-oriented Internet to a commercial Internet?

4. What is an ISP, and what are the differences between national, regional, and local ISPs? How do they interconnect with each other?

5. What is the purpose of a peering agreement between ISPs?

6. What are some of the major organizations that govern the Internet? What does each of these organizations contribute to Internet governance?

7. What is DNS, and why does it exist?

8. What are name servers and what function do they serve?

9. What are the original purposes for each of the original Internet domains? What is the purpose of the root domain?

10. What protocols support Internet file transfer? Remote computing? Streaming media? How do organizations utilize these protocols and the applications they support?

11. What are the major differences between POP3 and IMAP4 e-mail servers?

12. What makes instant messaging a "killer app"? How do XMPP and SIMPLE assist with IM's potential to become a killer app? How does presence information fit in?

13. What is the Abilene project, and what differentiates it from the regular commercial Internet that we use today?

14. What is Internet2, and what impact might it have on businesses around the world?

15. What are business drivers that potentially induce businesses to implement IPv6?

16. In what ways does IPv6 differ from IPv4?

17. In what ways do IPv6 address types differ from IPv4 address classes?

Research Activities

1. Using the IETF Web site, locate the RFCs that relate to IPv6. Browse through the documents to discover the latest RFC or Internet draft that specifies the IPv6 addressing architecture. What is the current version of the IPv6 addressing architecture? Does the latest revision specify site local or unique local unicast addressing for small networks that require routing?

2. What alternative ways can you represent the address FE80:0000:0000:0000:FACE: AA2B:00AC:0002? How about FEC0:0000:0000:0000:AB01:000B:0000:10CF? And ::1?

3. Discover whether your school or organization is part of the Internet2 project. If it is, in what capacity does it participate? What Internet2 activities is it involved in? Are they connected to Abilene or vBNS or both? If your school or organization is not involved in Internet2, research a school that is involved in Internet2, and explain that school's involvement with Internet2, Abilene, and the various projects that are supported through Internet2. If possible, try to quantify the costs associated with Internet2 participation.

4. Using the Internet2 Web site, locate two Internet2 working groups that are not discussed within this chapter. List these working groups, and describe how they might benefit your school or organization. In addition, find at least two other organizations that have application development alliances with Internet2 and describe the projects that these organizations are working on in collaboration with Internet2.

5. Using the Cisco Systems Web site, create a list of products that support SIMPLE and XMPP for instant messaging. Briefly summarize the technical features of each of these products and describe their intended uses in the business world. In addition, locate at least two additional companies that are working on products and applications that are either currently supporting SIMPLE or XMPP or will be in the near future. Provide a brief list of IM products that each company has developed/is developing, and describe the technical features as well as the intended uses in the business world.

6. Discover the type of e-mail system used by your school of organization. In addition to the software manufacturer, make sure you describe whether the e-mail system utilizes POP3 or IMAP4 or both. In addition, describe how the network administrator established the configuration and how e-mail ties in with the overall network plan at your school or organization.

7. Locate a real-world example of a school or organization that has implemented streaming media. What technical hurdles did the implementation present to network administrators? What protocols are being used? What business benefits has the implementation provided? What future uses do they envision?

8. Discover whether your school or organization's network administrators use Telnet for any types of remote computing. Specifically, you might ask whether they use it to access routers and switches or whether they use more modern techniques such as graphical interface software to make updates and modifications to remote devices. If they're currently using graphical software, ask if they recall using Telnet in the past, and if so, how they used it and what productivity benefit it provided.

9. Using your favorite search engine and any other research tools at your disposal, discover at least three IXPs and list their peering partners. Briefly summarize the business history of each organization and describe each organization's mission. Then using the same research tools, discover at least four major NAPs and two MAEs, and describe their peering arrangements. What is the newest NAP in the world, and what connectivity does it bring to the Internet? Discover whether your school's or organization's ISP is peered with another ISP through an IXP arrangement or other peering arrangement.

10. Using the Internet2 Web site and any other related Web sites, print three or more maps of ISP infrastructures, and list the carrier service types and bandwidths for the various segments of their networks. What are the slowest and fastest carrier services currently being used within each ISP? What upgrades do these ISPs foresee in the near future?

Mini Case Study

EXCELLUS BLUE CROSS BLUE SHIELD

Excellus Blue Cross Blue Shield is a large regional health care insurance organization that currently uses IPv4. Their network infrastructure is configured for IPv4, all of their applications are built on IPv4, all of their workstation and mobile computers are configured for IPv4, and all of their customers and health care providers use IPv4 to access information from the company's mainframe-based Web server.

Recently one of their student employees was assigned the task of developing a business case for a conversion to IPv6. If Excellus Blue Cross Blue Shield is not experiencing a shortage of IPv4 addresses, what kinds of business scenarios would justify a conversion to IPv6? What will they have to consider in terms of their existing network infrastructure? What will they have to consider in terms of their network applications? What will they need to do if they want to gradually convert to IPv6? That is, how can an IPv6 infrastructure, should you be able to develop a justifiable business case, support both IPv4 and IPv6 addresses?

Appendix **A**

THE ROOTS OF WIRELESS TECHNOLOGY

The Optical Telegraph

We hear a lot about wireless devices these days. Wireless laptops, wireless PDAs, wireless networks, and, of course, the ever-so-common cell phone have become a virtual necessity in many of our personal and professional lives. But the origins of wireless technology date back to the late 1700s and have been used in various implementations since then.

The earliest means of transferring information from point A to point B would most likely have been walking to a distant point or yelling at the top of one's lungs. Impracticality aside, one of the earliest high-speed methods of information transfer from point A to point B at speeds greater than that of a person running or riding on horseback was wireless in nature and derived from the inability of the scientists, inventors, clergy, and tinkerers of the time to devise an electrical method of transmitting coded messages between two points.

Enter **Claude Chappe** (1763–1805), a Frenchman previously devoted to the study of physical sciences within the seminary at la Fleche. In the early 1790s, with his vision and a little help from the French government, Chappe was able to secure the interest of political and military officials so that he could conduct tests of his invention for a system that could transmit messages over distances of up to 10 kilometers in daylight conditions.

After two unsuccessful attempts at **encoding** and sending **data transmissions** first with audible signals between two towers and then an aborted attempt at sending encoded messages through visual means, Chappe devised a system of encoding messages for transmission between two towers that were within a line of sight of each other. This third and successful invention of an **optical telegraph** consisted of a pivoting horizontal beam with a rotating mechanical arm connected at each end mounted atop a tower. By varying the position of the rotating arms in conjunction with varying the position of the pivoting horizontal beam, the sending tower would transmit encoded messages to a distant receiving tower. At the receiving tower, the tower "operator" would watch for the encoded visual message by using a telescope, and then translate the message by using the appropriate codes as listed in Chappe's code book.

After a successful pilot implementation in July 1793 involving the construction of three towers, the French government ordered the construction of 15 additional towers, and their operation commenced in May 1794. As the French government continued its opportunistic military campaigns of the 1790s, it added to the network of optical telegraph transmission towers for transmitting battle successes and provincial activities between remote locations and Paris. Ultimately, telegraph towers and Chappe's optical telegraph connected the whole of France and continued in operation throughout France until 1846.[1]

---

[1] In 1846, France replaced the optical telegraph with the electric telegraph as the official national standard.

A Brief History of Data Communications and Computer Networks

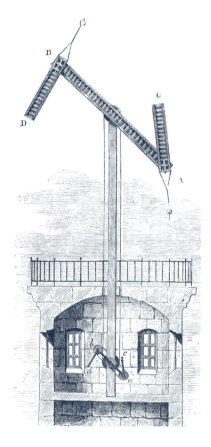

Other European countries adopted their own versions of the optical telegraph throughout the first half of the 1800s. At their peak, optical telegraph towers totaled nearly 1,000 on the European continent.

The Photophone

If you fast-forward from 1840s Europe to 1880 in the United States, **Alexander Graham Bell's photophone,** which Bell patented four years after inventing the telephone, introduced the amazing potential of light as a medium for voice or data transmission. Bell's photophone projected the sound waves created by the human voice through one receiving instrument toward a mirror, causing the mirror to vibrate. By directing sunlight toward the mirror at the same time, the vibrating mirror projected its sunlit vibrations toward another

FIGURE A.2   The Semaphore Telegraph

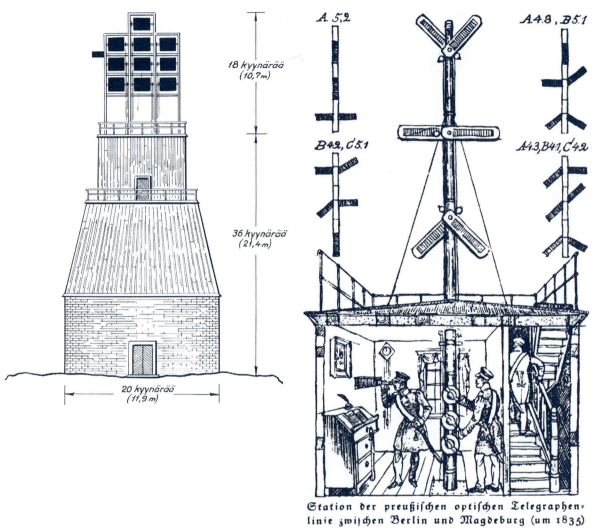

Station der preußischen optischen Telegraphen-
linie zwischen Berlin und Magdeburg (um 1835)

receiving device containing selenium that transformed the projected light waves back into sound waves.

With Bell's photophone, the world witnessed the beginnings of encoded data transmission on a beam of light. It proved impractical for its era, however, because a cloud and darkness would interrupt the light source and hence the mirror's projected vibrations. Bell's invention was revolutionary, but it was also way ahead of its time. To be practical, the photophone needed a constant light source from a technology that wouldn't be available until the 1960s.

The Impact of Radio Waves

As amazing as Bell's photophone technology was in 1880, it was the discovery and reproduction of man-made **radio waves** in 1888, by the German physicist and professor **Heinrich Hertz** (1857–1894), that led to the development of our modern wireless world. As revolutionary as his idea was, however, Hertz didn't recognize it for its commercial value. In fact, when questioned by his students about how this new "phenomenon" might be used, Hertz replied, "It's of no use whatsoever."

FIGURE A.3
Bell's Photophone

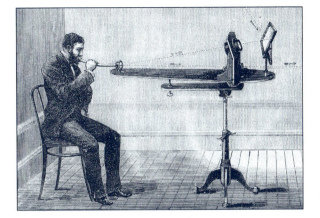

Hertz had proved the existence of electromagnetic waves in his laboratory, but it was an entrepreneurial-minded 20 year old named **Guglielmo Marconi** (1874–1937) who studied Hertz's published findings and began experimenting with how to send encoded messages using the principles of Hertz's scientific discovery. By late 1894, Marconi had invented his **spark transmitter** with antenna at his father's estate in Italy and by 1895 had successfully transmitted a wireless signal over a distance of a mile and a half. Shortly thereafter, in 1896, he headed to England, where he filed for and was granted the world's first wireless telegraphy patent. In 1897, he demonstrated his invention by successfully transmitting a wireless message across the Bristol Channel in England, and by 1901, his newly developed technology was advanced enough to send the first wireless transatlantic message.

One common use of wireless technology in the United States and other parts of the world in the early part of the 20th century was for transmitting time via Morse code to receiving time pieces. One such device, used in Paris, France, was known as the **ondophone.** It was a miniaturized crystal detector that could receive daily time signals broadcast from a radio station located within the Eiffel Tower. In the United States, a wireless radio station tower in Arlington, Virginia, broadcast a wireless time signal each day at noon for receipt by anyone who was willing to pay the somewhat hefty fee of $100 per year. Common subscribers to this service included anyone in need of accurate time, most notably jewelers selling watches and clocks. Accuracy was assured within 1/20th of a second anywhere in the United States, because radio waves travel at the speed of light.

Another potential product that never matured during the first two decades of the 20th century but which was technologically possible was the handheld **radio telephone,** not unlike the concept of the modern cell phone. The technology for the handheld phones existed, but the regulatory climate for airwave apportionment limited frequency licensing to distress signals and responses. With limited frequencies available, the potential market for wireless handheld radio telephones all but evaporated.

Building on the viability of radio waves for telecommunications, in 1917 American Telephone and Telegraph (AT&T) accomplished the first air-to-ground and ground-to-air radio communication. Fostered by the needs of World War I and the U.S. military's desire for communication with its in-flight airplanes, AT&T engineers developed a wireless radio telephone set that pilots could use to stay in two-way communication with military personnel on the ground.

Leave it to two world wars to expand communication technologies but slow commercial deployment, because the next big event in wireless communication occurred in 1946 with the introduction of the first commercial-service mobile telephone call. Bell Labs had been developing this communications technology for more than 10 years when they finally delivered it in 1946. Although this wireless service was offered in nearly 100 cities by 1948, the wireless infrastructure of that era could support only very limited call volume. In these early years, no more than three callers could be "online" in a given metropolitan area at one time. An idea that improved upon the mobile telephone, which was conceived in 1947, was cellular telephone service, but neither the grid technology nor the needed radio frequencies were available at that time. Not until the late 1970s and early 1980s would the regulatory climate be favorable or the technology practical to introduce a commercially viable wireless mobile or cellular phone service.

In 1951, the first microwave radio system was used for a coast-to-coast telephone conversation in the United States. The 107 microwave towers required for the transmission were placed about 30 miles apart and it cost about $40 million in 1951 dollars. A few weeks later, the same system transmitted the television signal for the Japanese Peace Treaty Conference being held in San Francisco.

In the early 1960s, AT&T further enhanced communications technologies by launching **Telstar,** the world's first active communications satellite. It was used for multiple data and voice communications purposes including long-distance telephone service, fax transmissions, high-speed data transmissions, and television signal transmission.

The time frame between the middle 1960s and early 1970s saw improvements in old-style mobile telephone services and the introduction of commercial cellular radio aboard passenger trains as a pay-phone service in the United States. But these really weren't revolutionary developments in the field of data communications or even minor developments that would lead toward improved data communications. Also, the political and regulatory climates in developed countries around the world simply did not have a complete grasp of the need to relinquish control of the radio airwaves for use in commercial wireless telephony. Instead, the next series of breakthroughs for wireless communications technology evolved throughout the mid- to late 1970s and into the early 1980s in Japan, Europe, and the United States. For example, in 1974, the FCC approved an additional 115 megahertz of the radio spectrum for use in wireless telephone service in the United States, and in 1975, the Bell system under AT&T began trials with its cellular system.

However, without further access to government-controlled airwaves, AT&T had little incentive to further develop a cellular network in the United States. In addition, the U.S. regulatory climate of the early 1980s prevented AT&T from deploying a commercial cellular service unless there was competition in every cellular market. Hence, the United States didn't have a commercial cellular service until late in 1983 when competition was introduced into the cellular service marketplace. At the same time, Japan had introduced commercial cellular service some four years prior, and in Europe, the Nordic Mobile Telephone System introduced cellular technology to several Scandinavian countries in 1981.

Although it took nearly 90 years after its discovery before it was commercially deployed to a vast consumer market, wireless technology is one of the cornerstones of today's rapidly growing voice and data communications marketplace. In the early days, much of the wireless communications technology was limited to telegraphy. Along the way, various devices attempted to introduce handheld or other mobile wireless to the consumer market, but most if not all were ahead of their times. Beginning in the 1940s, incremental introductions of new technologies allowed wireless to gain a foothold, but not until the 1960s did the world as a whole begin to realize the vast capabilities of wireless communications. Since the late 1970s and early 1980s, much of the technological development in wireless communications has been spurred on by worldwide governmental deregulation. Deregulation and divestiture of AT&T in the early 1980s, the privatization of the Internet in 1994, and the 1996 Telecom Act in the United States have all fostered further access to commercial radio frequencies as well as developments in wireless products. Today it is not uncommon for one person to have multiple wireless devices, and the trend toward wireless devices and wireless data communications continues. And all of these commercial radio frequency–based wireless products and services share roots with the earliest wireless technologies and devices that date to the late 1800s and early 1900s.

THE BEGINNINGS OF A WIRED WORLD

Our world is connected by wires: wires for voice and wires for data, and some that fill both roles. Trillions of bits of information cross a myriad of wired networks each second. We can send and receive information between points A and B faster and more reliably with each passing day. Yet with the vast wired infrastructure that we use in our modern world of communications, we should pause to marvel that our wired world beginnings can be traced back nearly 300 years and be awed by the developments and technological advancements made by scientists, inventors, and entrepreneurs since the early 1700s.

If you recall our simplified premise that data communications is all about getting information from point A to point B, then we really need to take a look at the early role that electricity played in driving us toward our modern wired world, because it was the transmission of electricity from point A to point B that ultimately led several innovative scientists and inventors to develop data transmission over wires. The year was 1726, and **John Wood** in England discovered that he could transmit electricity over a wire. Within two years, **Stephen Gray** and **Granville Wheler,** also in England, figured out how to send electricity over a wire to a location 750 feet away. In 1746, **Abbe Nollet** in France convinced a group of nearly 200 monks to grab hold of a long wire while he discharged a primitive electrical capacitor known as a **Leyden jar** through the wire. Each of the monks felt the electric shock immediately and simultaneously, and Nollet proved again, as had those before him, that electricity could be transmitted across a wire. Further experimenters that gained notoriety include **Sir William Watson,** also of England, successfully telegraphing electricity across a wire two miles in length in 1747, and **Benjamin Franklin** in the United States in 1748 discharging a static electricity–filled Leyden jar across the Schuykill River to ignite a spirit-soaked torch on either side of the river.

The key point in these historical examples is that the application of electricity at one end of a wire results in an almost instantaneous transmission of the charge across the wire, and these early experiments are the primitive indications that some type of transmission of information across wires might also be possible. Although the historical record doesn't indicate that these early experimenters presumed that data transmission was the next logical step, an article in *Scot's Magazine* in 1753 by an author whose unresolved initials are **C. M.**, seems to make the presumptuous logical jump that data transmission across wires was possible:

> It is well known to all who are conversant in electrical experiments that the electric power may be propagated along a small wire, from one place to another, without being sensibly abated by the length of its progress; let, then, a set of wires equal in number to the letters of the alphabet be extended horizontally between two given places parallel to each other and each of them about an inch distant from that next to it. At every twenty yards' end let them be fixed in glass or Jewelers' cement to some firm body, both to prevent them from touching the earth or any other non-electric, and from breaking from their own gravity.

C. M. went on to explain how attaching a suspended metallic ball at the end of each wire and observing the movement of the ball as an electrical charge was received on a given wire would indicate the corresponding letter of the alphabet, and, if transmitted in sequence, the series of transmitted charges across each wire would build words and an hence an entire communication. This is the first suggestion of a type of static electric telegraphic mechanism.

FIGURE A.4
From Semaphore to Satellite

Reproduced with the kind permission of ITU.

It was 1774, however, before an actual device was created that utilized the same principles that C. M. suggested in his letter to *Scot's Magazine* 21 years earlier. In that year, **George Lesage** demonstrated an electrostatic telegraphic device in Geneva, Switzerland, that utilized one wire for each letter of the alphabet and a pith ball attached to the receiving end, much as C. M. had described. As each wire was "electrified" with a static charge of electricity, the pith ball on the opposite end of the wire would move so that the corresponding letter could be recorded. Lesage was successful in transmitting a message between two rooms with his device.

Toward the end of the 1700s, a rather colorful character from Barcelona, Spain, named **Don Francisco Salva y Campillo** developed an **electrostatic telegraphic** device that at first followed the principles described in *Scot's Magazine*. His somewhat amusing, if not painful, method of electrical detection at the far end of the wire involved a person holding the wire instead of having a pith ball indicator. The person would call out the letter that corresponded to the wire on which he (or she) had just received a shock. In the last decade of the 18th century, Salva employed the recent discovery of animal electricity (by Galvani) to suggest that recently cut frogs' legs be utilized as indicators at the end of each wire. In transitioning from the 1700s to the first decade of the 1800s, Salva experimented with recently developed battery technology to transmit an electrical charge across the same wiring system, only this time the far end of each wire was connected to a small container of water. As a charge was applied to a wire, the water of the corresponding wire underwent electrolysis, which created bubbles in the water. The person watching for messages could then record each letter as it was received by watching for bubbles and accordingly assemble the transmitted message.

Several other technological breakthroughs occurred during the early part of the 19th century that provided the foundation for subsequent advancements in wired message transmission and which would lead to the modern era of data communications. In 1800, the Italian physicist **Alessandro Volta** developed a primitive electric battery that converted

FIGURE A.5
Sturgeon's
Electromagnet

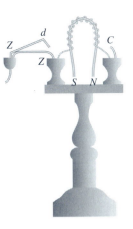

chemical energy into a steady (if not long-lived) flow of electrical energy, and in 1820, the Danish physicist **Hans Oersted** discovered the fundamental connection between electricity and magnetism. These discoveries allowed a British electrical engineer named **William Sturgeon** (1783–1850) to wrap a horseshoe-shaped iron bar in a coil of wire, apply an electric current, and create the **electromagnet,** a profound discovery that conceivably marks the beginning of the modern wired world in 1825. Sturgeon's discovery was instrumental in the development of communications because electromagnets can be turned on or off by applying an electric current. Move the electromagnet to a distant location and provide an electrical current via wire, and you can activate the electromagnet at the remote location. Activate, deactivate, activate, and deactivate via an electric current and, voila, electric signaling, the fundamental building block of data communications.

Enter **Joseph Henry,** American scientist, inventor, and lecturer (1797–1878). Where Sturgeon was interested in the nuances of electromagnetic strength, he didn't apply the remarkable mechanical potential of electromagnets as it relates to signaling. That's where Henry came in. During his lectures throughout 1831 and 1832, Henry applied an electric current at one end of a mile-long copper wire that was strung throughout his lecture hall, and to the other end of the wire he connected a powerful electromagnet of his own design. Between the poles of his electromagnet, he placed a permanent magnet so that as the electromagnet was activated, the permanent magnet was repelled from one pole and attracted to the other pole. When he reversed the polarity of the battery that supplied the current to his electromagnet, the permanent magnet was attracted to the original pole of the electromagnet. At the other end of the permanent magnet, Henry placed a bell, tapped by the permanent magnet to make a ringing sound. This is the first evidence of a long-distance **electromagnetic telegraph** and gave cause to many heated debates and court battles between Mr. Henry and Samuel Morse years later.

At about the same time that Henry was demonstrating his telegraphic method to students in his lectures, a Russian diplomat turned inventor, **Baron Pavel Schilling,** demonstrated an electromagnetic telegraphic system utilizing 72 wires and 36 deflecting needles. Borrowing from Schilling's model, several other inventors of the day developed telegraphic systems of their own. **Carl Friedrich Guass** and **Wilhelm Eduard Weber** worked together to develop a two-wire, **single-needle telegraph** in 1833, while **William Cooke** and **Charles Wheatstone** in England developed and patented a **deflecting-needle telegraph** system of their own in 1837.

The Cooke and Wheatstone telegraph was the first commercially successful **telegraph.** It consisted of several wires connected to five iron needles, the needles being controlled by the activation and deactivation of electromagnets. Two needles at a time would point to a

FIGURE A.6
Joseph Henry's Electromagnetic Telegraph

© 2004 Smithsonian Institution

FIGURE A.7
Cooke and Wheatstone five-Needle Telegraph

Reproduced with the kind permission of the ITU.

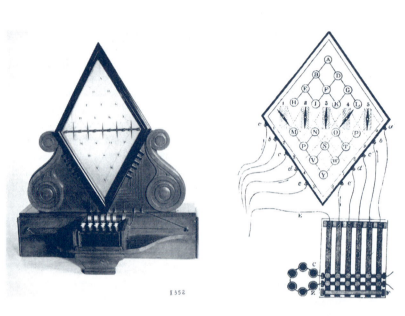

letter, and the person recording the message would note the letter and build the message from the series of needle movements. Shortly after its introduction, the Cooke and Wheatstone telegraph was improved upon so that it utilized a single needle.

No historical account of telegraphy would be complete without a discussion of the American **Samuel Morse** (1791–1872) and his impact upon the invention, promotion, and commercialization of the telegraph. On a return voyage from Europe in October 1832, Morse had the good fortune of running into **Dr. Charles T. Jackson** who discussed with Morse the electromagnetic theories and experiments of the day. For the remainder of the journey home, Morse penned his ideas for a telegraphic system in his sketch book. During the next five years, Morse conducted his experiments with a telegraphic system and enlisted the help of Professor **Leonard D. Gale.** Professor Gale, who was knowledgeable in the electrical science of the day, brought Morse up-to-date with regard to the electrical technology surrounding the battery developments of **William Grove** and the electromagnet advancements made by Joseph Henry that Morse would need to advance his telegraph.

In 1837, Morse continued to exhibit and demonstrate his invention in the hopes of engaging financial interest, and during one such exhibition, he happened to meet **Alfred Vail,** the son of an enterprising ironworks owner. Vail brought the invention to his father's attention, and Morse reached an agreement by which Vail's father would provide the financing needed to obtain patent protection, and the younger Vail would build a working model for demonstration before the U.S. Congress. In exchange for this help, the younger Vail became part owner of any patent rights that Morse obtained.

Vail turned out to be an extremely valuable partner to Morse. Not only was Vail's father's financial backing crucial, but Vail was mechanically adept at designing and building the sending and receiving mechanisms. In addition, Vail ultimately became the creative mind behind the Morse code that continues in use to this day. Vail applied his mechanical ability to Morse's early prototypes, and throughout his tenure with Morse, Vail implemented modifications and innovations that resulted in better transmitting and receiving devices than Morse had been able to devise by himself. Morse, however, took most if not all of the credit for Vail's improvements and for the dots and dashes that comprise the infamous Morse code.

Toward the end of 1837, Morse was nearly out of money and without substantial financial support, his idea might have died. However, in February 1838, Morse demonstrated his telegraphic system before the U.S. House of Representatives Committee on Commerce, and Representative **F. O. J. Smith** from Maine took an interest in Morse's invention and ideas. The following month, Smith became a partner with Morse, and by April, Smith had introduced a bill before Congress to appropriate $30,000 to build a pilot telegraph line from Washington D.C. to Baltimore. Conflict of interest notwithstanding, Smith finished his congressional term, but, in all fairness to the congressman, the funds weren't approved to build the Washington-to-Baltimore telegraph line until March 1843. The line was completed in May 1844, and the first message that Morse sent from the Supreme Court chamber at the Capitol to the B&O Railroad depot in Baltimore, Maryland, was "What hath God wrought?"

In the year that followed, Morse appointed the former U.S. Postmaster-General, **Amos Kendall,** to be the agent for Vail, Gale, and Morse for the development of additional telegraph lines utilizing Morse's patented telegraphic system through the **Magnetic Telegraph Company.** Former Congressman F. O. J. Smith developed his own lines in a business arrangement loosely associated with the other Morse patent partners. Within a very short period of time, many competitors introduced their own lines, challenging Morse's patent rights. Ultimately the courts became involved to award royalty payments to Morse.

Continued competitive pressures over the ensuing years through the 1850s resulted in the consolidation and merging of many of the telegraph companies. From 1855 to 1856, F. O. J. Smith's lines merged with the New York and Mississippi Printing Telegraph Company to form the **Western Union Telegraph Company.** Western Union ensured its growth and expansion over the next several years by absorbing many of the smaller independent lines. Three years later, in 1859, Morse's Magnetic Telegraph Company lines merged with the lines of the American Telegraph Company, and in 1866, the same year that the first successful Atlantic telegraph cable was put into service, the Western Union Telegraph Company and the American Telegraph Company merged to form one of the earliest and longest-lived monopolies in the United States.

The explosive growth of the telegraph was not limited to the United States. All over the world, the second half of the 19th century saw the development of land lines as well as underwater lines to connect countries and continents alike. **"Submarine" lines** were laid across the Mediterranean Sea, the Red Sea, and the Persian Gulf. Several attempts were made to connect Europe to the United States during the 1850s with submarine cables, and one in 1858 met with brief success; Queen Victoria sent the first transatlantic message to President James Buchanan of the United States. That cable broke, however, within a month after its first celebrated transmission, leaving the first successful and long-lasting telegraph cable connection to wait for the laying of an Atlantic cable in 1866 by **Cyrus Field** and his well-financed group of investors.

In Europe, the successful merchant **John Pender** established the **Eastern Telegraph Company** to develop and manage land lines connecting Europe to the countries of the Far East. By the late 1870s, Pender's company controlled something like 60 percent of all telegraph communications to India and 80 percent of the telegraphic transmissions to China, Java, and Australia. In other parts of the world, the Brazilian Submarine Telegraph Company began connecting South America to Europe and the United States in the 1870s at the same time that the Brazilian Telegraph Company began connecting cities along the South American coastline. The 1880s saw the connection of Europe to the African continent and as far south as South Africa, and toward the end of the last decade of the 1890s, plans were well underway for a Pacific cable to be laid between Canada and Australia. By the end of the 19th century, the world was connected by telegraphic cables that circumvented the globe. People from every continent could send messages anywhere in the world, but the beginnings of the wired world were still just beginning.

THE EARLY YEARS OF TELEPHONE COMMUNICATION

Electricity, magnetism, and batteries; these are the ingredients that made the telegraph possible, and they're also the ingredients that led to the development of the telephone. Where the telegraph relied on turning an electrical current on and off across an electrical circuit to produce an encoded message of dots and dashes, the telephone, with its transmission of the continuous flow of the human voice across an electrical circuit, required a steady and continuous current that could electrically mimic the modulations of the human voice. Telegraphy was static in nature; the current was on or the current was off to transmit a message. With telephony, a person's voice is always "on" as the person is talking, and so the current on a telephone line had to represent this flowing characteristic. This problem was the biggest to overcome in the development of the telephone, and it was solved by some of the greatest minds of the day.

On the timeline of development of the telephone, **Charles Bourseul** is one of those initial figures of interest with a thought process that allowed him to extend his thinking beyond telegraphy and suggest that electronic speech across wires was a real possibility. He was born in Belgium in 1829 and as a young man worked in France as an employee of the administration of telegraphs. In 1854, he wrote and published an article in the French journal *L'illustration, Journal Universel* describing the concept of electronic speech: "Imagine that one speaks close to a mobile plate, enough flexible not to lose any vibrations produced by the voice, that this plate establishes and stops the communications with a pile [battery]: you will be able to remotely have another plate which will carry out at the same time the same vibrations."

Bourseul was describing what Alexander Graham Bell and **Elisha Gray** would submit as patent applications some two decades later in the United States and which Bell would go on to commercially develop. Bourseul's idea was innovative for the time; however, his suggestion "that this plate establishes and stops the communications with a pile" indicates that he didn't realize the technical requirement for a continuous flow of current across a wired circuit to mimic the consistent flow of the human voice. Bourseul never pursued the concepts he outlined in his article, and had he attempted to implement his idea as described, it certainly would not have met his expectations of reproducing speech at a remote location.

Another inventor of the same era was **Johann Phillip Reis** of Germany, a mid-19th-century teacher of math and science who attempted to develop electronic speech across a wired circuit. In 1861, Reis utilized common materials such as cork, a needle, a sausage skin, and a piece of platinum to build his telephone. Basing his invention's electrical transmission technique on the telegraphic technology of the day, Reis implemented a flexible membrane in his device that started or stopped the flow of electricity through the circuit. Although his invention was able to reproduce audible clicks and fragmented sounds at the receiver, his demonstrations weren't successful in attracting the interest of scientists or

Prior to his telephone patent, Alexander Graham Bell was working on a harmonic telegraph—a device that could transmit eight telegraphic messages over a single telegraph line. And as is so common in today's world of data communications, technologies of the late 1800s were implemented only if they fulfilled a specific business need. The innovation of Bell's harmonic telegraph would have allowed telegraph companies to economize on the capital expenditures associated with adding new telegraph wires, by making more efficient use of the existing telegraphic infrastructure. Bell's harmonic telegraph might have supplanted the quadruplex telegraph, a four-message-per-line telegraphic system that was in use and which had been invented by Thomas Edison in 1874. Had Bell's harmonic telegraph technology been successfully applied to the field of telegraphic communication, it could have doubled the capacity of existing quadruplex telegraph circuits.

But as with other great innovations, work in one area frequently leads to successes in other areas, and so the historical timeline of the telephone and data communications remains intact. Bell's experiments with his prototype harmonic telegraph led to the transmission of continuous sound instead of the static clicks carried across telegraph lines, and that serendipitous moment redirected Bell's efforts away from the harmonic telegraph and toward the development of the telephone and the transmission of the human voice.

financial investors of the day. Unfortunately for Reis, his mistake was the same as Bourseul's as both men thought the movable membrane should start or stop the current flow to reproduce speech, when, in fact, a continuous circuit was required.

Many of the men who deserve credit on the telephone history timeline had backgrounds in telegraph technology. Two of these men, most notably Elisha Gray and Alexander Graham Bell, were working independently on a method to increase the number of telegraphic messages that could be transmitted simultaneously across a single wire, when each of them, independently, discovered a means for communicating the human voice electrically. To protect their ideas, both men filed paperwork with the U.S. Patent and Trademark Office. On February 14, 1876, Gray filed a caveat that announced his intention to file for a patent within three months and which described a device "for transmitting vocal sounds telegraphically." Unfortunately for Gray, Bell filed an actual patent only two hours prior to Gray's filing. Many years of litigation ensued, and although Gray's device would have worked as described and Bell's would not have (at least if it had been constructed according to the description in Bell's patent application), Gray's notch on the history timeline retained its place; and Bell was legally named as the inventor of the telephone. After Gray's death in 1901, a note was discovered among his papers, which indicated his lifelong disappointment over the development of the telephone. In it, the note stated: "The history of the telephone will never be fully written. . . . It is partly hidden away . . . and partly lying on the hearts and consciences of a few whose lips are sealed—some in death and others by a golden clasp whose grip is even tighter."

Although many inventors of the technologies that drove the telegraph also played a significant role that led to the invention and development of the telephone, Alexander Graham Bell's name is firmly etched on the historical timeline as the inventor of the telephone. Bell's contributions to the invention of the telephone and his ability to surmount the static on/off current flow associated with telegraphic communications were as attributable to his understanding of human speech and acoustics as they were to his basic understanding of electricity and his inventive prowess. Where others before him invented devices that attempted to reproduce human speech using electrical telegraphic means, Bell applied his understanding and knowledge of constantly **modulating acoustic pressure** to vary a consistently applied electrical current across a wire. His novel approach had the distinction of never having been tried, and it overcame the clicking and fragmented sound problem associated with previous attempts at telephony.

During Bell's childhood and into his early 20s, the acceptance and development of the telegraph had created a maze of wires that was very close to circumventing the world. As the demand for sending messages continued to increase, there simply weren't enough lines to carry all of the communications traffic. The common solution was to install additional telegraph lines, not an inexpensive proposition in terms of both installation and maintenance. Telegraph companies were searching for an alternative solution, and the inventive hope was to be able to send multiple messages over a single wire simultaneously, something that is accepted and expected practice in today's technologically advanced communications marketplace. But in the early 1870s it was a business proposition chasing a technological dream. However, as happens so often in modern times with technological development, inventors follow market-driven forces and focus their efforts on products to fulfill a recognized need with a potentially profitable outcome. In much the same way, inventors in 1870 were drawn to improvements in telegraph technology. Among them were **Thomas Edison,** Elisha Gray, and Alexander Graham Bell. Edison was working on the "quadraplex" system for sending two messages and receiving two messages simultaneously across a single wire. Gray was working on a device of his own design. And Bell was working on an invention that he called the **harmonic telegraph,** his own method of transmitting multiple simultaneous messages across a single wire and a hopeful contender for a potentially profitable solution to a significant business need.

Bell worked on his harmonic telegraph during the early 1870s and into the spring of 1874. Then, as fate would have it, Bell spent the summer of 1874 working on the **phonoautograph,** a device used in teaching the deaf. The phonoautograph utilized a real human ear taken from a corpse, and by applying sound through the eardrum to move a lever, Bell was able to see the wavelike pattern of the human voice re-created by the lever "writing" the wavy vibrations on a smoked-glass plate. In those reproduced waves, Bell might have made the link between his principles of acoustic pressure and a continuous electric current, but that link was displayed later on more by chance than by design. From those observations and his new understanding, he began devoting himself nearly full time to the development of the telephone.

His experimentation with the telephone would not have been possible, however, were it not for the financial backing of his future father-in-law, **Gardiner Greene Hubbard,** a prominent patent attorney and businessman, and the successful businessman **George Sanders.** Hubbard and Sanders liked what they saw with the harmonic telegraph. When a patent search determined that there were no patented competitors to Bell's proposed harmonic telegraph, Hubbard and Sanders agreed to fund Bell for continued work on the harmonic telegraph. But Bell was fascinated with his telephone experiments and so risked a potentially profitable invention in the harmonic telegraph by splitting his time between the harmonic telegraph and the telephone. Again, as fate would have it, Bell enlisted the mechanical help of **Thomas Watson** and sought consul from Joseph Henry, the man who had had such impact on the development of the telegraph. With their help and guidance, Bell continued his development on both the harmonic telegraph and his passion, the telephone, throughout the first half of 1875.

On June 2, 1875, Bell and Watson were conducting an experiment with the harmonic telegraph. Since the device was supposed to transmit multiple different messages simultaneously, Watson was at one end creating sound waves with several tuning springs of different pitches, and Bell was at the receiver, listening. He was expecting to hear the kinds of pulses associated with the on/off current generated by the batteries and electromagnets

In the earliest days of the telephone, a subscriber who wanted to talk with another subscriber had to be directly wired to that subscriber's house or business. This direct line between two subscriber locations was known as a point-to-point connection, and for each subscriber with whom you wished to communicate by telephone, you would need one of these point-to-point connections.

Early on, point-to-point connections weren't a problem as not every subscriber needed to communicate with every other subscriber. As the number of telephone subscribers increased, however, direct connections among all subscribers was simply not economically feasible. At the same time, a cost-justified connectivity solution that would facilitate communication among all subscribers was required, and that solution came in the form of the central switching office, or telephone exchange. With this new solution, commercially introduced in New Haven, Connecticut, in 1878, all subscriber lines were routed through the central switching office so that connections could be made easily between subscribers without the need to run and maintain point-to-point connections.

typical of electric telegraphs. To his surprise, Bell heard the sound of one of the tuning springs, not the expected pulse of a telegraph. It was a serendipitous moment; Bell had found what he was looking for when he wasn't looking, or listening, as the case happened to be. Apparently a contact screw had been adjusted incorrectly allowing a continuous current to flow across the wire. Quite by accident, Bell's experiment had linked his principles of acoustic pressure with a continuous electrical current and delivered to him the essence of telephony.

Attempts at re-creating the results of the June 2nd experiment eluded Bell for the next several months and even at the time he filed for his patent on February 14, 1876. Luckily for Bell, six years before, in 1870, the U.S. patent office had discontinued its requirement that a working prototype accompany every patent application; otherwise, the patent office would have rejected his application until such time as he had a working model. Requirements for working models notwithstanding, Bell was able to create a working model by March 1876, and coincidentally, it used some of the same technology as that described in the patent caveat that Elisha Gray had submitted only hours after Bell's patent application of February 14.

Bell began having modest experimental successes with telephone transmission over short distances during the second half of 1876. In August, Bell was able to hear his father's and uncle's words across a several-mile wired connection. It was a one-way conversation, but Bell had proved his concept. Then in October 1876, Bell and Watson carried on a two-way conversation across the Charles River between Boston and Cambridge, Massachusetts. These were the first conversations conducted over outdoor wires. By May of the following year, Bell had his first paying customer; a banker who wished to connect his office to his home. To further promote the use of their telephone, Bell and Watson conducted lecture-hall demonstrations in which Watson remained at a remote location and Bell appeared on stage to demonstrate his new technology. To the audience's delight, they would hear the latest musical tunes of the day. It was Watson on the remote end, singing into the telephone!

The second half of 1877 was a busy time for Bell. In July, he and Watson along with Gardiner Hubbard and Thomas Sanders formed the **Bell Telephone Company.** Two days after the company's formation, Bell married **Mabel Hubbard,** his former student and daughter of his original investing benefactor. He demonstrated his telephone to the Queen of England who found the new invention interesting, but his success in obtaining British patents met with limited success. By the autumn of 1877, the newly formed Bell Telephone Company had 600 telephone subscribers.

The patent office was not the only time that the work and legacies of Elisha Gray and Alexander Bell were to intersect. Gray had been one of the principle owners of Gray and Barton in Chicago, a manufacturer of telegraph equipment. When Gray and Barton later took on a third partner who was also a vice president of Western Union, Gray and Barton became strategically linked to the telegraph giant. A few years later, in 1872, Gray and Barton incorporated as the Western Electric Manufacturing Company with its principle investor Western Union.

Gray's fortunes continued to rise with the growth of Western Electric: By 1878, Western Electric was the world's largest manufacturer of electrical equipment. Three years later, and only two years after the fierce patent battle between Western Union and the Bell Telephone Company was settled, the **American Bell Telephone Company** (Alexander Bell's company), had a growing need for electrical hardware. So in 1881, to secure a supplier of telephone hardware, American Bell purchased Western Electric from Western Union. Elisha Gray's legacy was now part of the Bell System.

For the Bell Telephone Company, 1878 was no less busy than the second half of 1877. Early in 1878, the Bell Telephone Company brought in additional capital from private investors to facilitate expansion. With the newly added funds and a plan to license their telephone patents to numerous local promoters across the United States, the reorganized Bell Telephone Company had grown their business to more than 10,000 subscribers by June.

But their growing business was not without competition. **Western Union** had passed on buying Bell's patent rights the previous year from Gardiner Hubbard and, in the interim, had developed a better quality service based on a superior transmitter invented by Thomas Edison. Western Union was a huge and powerful company, and it was leveraging its prominent telegraphy infrastructure to rapidly expand telephone service across the United States. With patent protection on their side, the Bell Telephone Company initiated legal action against Western Union in September 1878 and reached an out-of-court settlement with their rival in November 1879. With the settlement, Western Union gave up all patents, claims, and telephone business facilities as well as the Edison transmitter and other technical innovations. In addition, the renamed **National Bell Telephone Company** added the 56,000 subscribers in 55 cities that had been developed by Western Union. In return, National Bell gave Western Union a 20 percent royalty on telephone rentals for the next 17 years. Although National Bell would be challenged in court more than once again in the ensuing years, the settlement against Western Union virtually assured National Bell of its monopoly position until 1894, the year its telephone patents would expire.

The first half of the 1880s saw two significant technical developments that fostered the expansion of long-distance communication. In 1881, a young engineer who was working on a long-distance iron-wire line that connected Boston with Providence, Rhode Island, accidentally caused two of the individual iron-wire circuits to touch one another. In so doing, he reduced the noise on the telephone circuit to such an extent as to make long-distance telephone communication technically achievable. What he had accomplished, quite by accident, was the invention of the **two-wire circuit.** But the iron wire, which was utilized in telephone communications, had distance limitations, even with the discovery of the two-wire circuit. Not until the discovery of a method to produce **extruded copper wire** cheaply and efficiently in the late 1870s and its application to long-distance lines in late 1883 and early 1884 did long-distance service become an economically feasible and commercially practical service. By 1892, these two technologies were sufficient to extend a long distance line from New York City to Chicago.

The name *AT&T* is historically linked to long-distance telephone communication, and there is a very good reason for this link. In the 1880s, as telephone subscribers wanted to communicate beyond their local exchanges, American Bell decided to build the facilities to make long-distance telephone calls a reality. But this expansion into long distance was going to require a larger corporate capitalization than had been set for American Bell by the Massachusetts legislature. To circumvent the capitalization problem, American Bell created a subsidiary company whose charter was to develop and operate long-distance telephone lines. The subsidiary was created under the less restrictive laws of New York State, and its name was **American Telephone and Telegraph.**

That was in 1885. By the late 1890s American Telephone and Telegraph's parent, American Bell, still a Massachusetts corporation, had grown so large with its local subscriber service that it was no longer able to continue expansion under the restrictive capitalization laws of Massachusetts. American Bell made a strategic decision in 1899 that gave birth to the corporate legend known as **AT&T;** all of American Bell's assets were transferred to its New York subsidiary. The child had become the parent, and AT&T became the new name for the titan of telephony.

BUILDING A TELECOMMUNICATIONS INFRASTRUCTURE

Infrastructure

All one had to do was pick up a popular business magazine or the latest tech magazine in the 1990s, and the reader would see the term infrastructure. We heard a lot about companies building their internal infrastructures for data communications during the 1990s. Companies large and small added miles and miles of twisted-pair cabling and fiber-optic cabling, as well as routers, switches, manageable hubs, and devices that connect telephone networks to computer networks as well as numerous other devices that enable connectivity between point A and point B. These are the components that comprise a data communications infrastructure. **Infrastructure** as it relates to data communications is the framework or collection of connectivity devices and transmission media that facilitates communication between a sending device at point A and a receiving device at point B. The towers that Claude Chappe built were the infrastructure that supported optical telegraphic communication. Wires, telegraph poles, and telegraph offices were the infrastructure that supported electric telegraphy in the mid-1800s and beyond. In much the same way, the invention of the telephone gave rise to a 20th-century telecommunications infrastructure that ensured voice communication around the world.

After the telephone patents expired in 1894, American Bell found itself competing with a growing number of independent telephone services that sprang up all across the United States. Over the next 10 years the number of phones in service increased from nearly 300,000 to well over 3 million, however, half of these were serviced by the newly formed competitors. Several major U.S. cities had more independent telephone subscribers than American Bell subscribers. Although the days of patent protection were gone, American Bell grew significantly during this period and benefited from the general awareness and demand for the telephone. Consumers benefited as well with increased access to telephone communication even if competing services did not interconnect.

During those early days of competition, the various independent phone services were not interconnected with each other or with American Telephone and Telegraph (as it was called after year end, 1899). If you wanted to have a phone conversation with a subscriber who was connected to a different service, you needed to have a separate phone and subscription to that service. At somewhere around $36 to $100 in 1906 for a one-year home service subscription and $72 to $125 for annual business service, having two or more phones to stay connected to more than a single service provider was at best a nuisance, at worst double the cost. Only those with substantial need of staying in touch subscribed to more than one service. If you didn't require access to long distance, you probably would have chosen an independent service. If your business or personal requirements dictated frequent long-distance communication, AT&T was your only choice because AT&T refused to connect the independent telephone companies to the AT&T long-distance lines. The era of **universal service** was a ways off.

The year 1907 was pivotal in the history of interconnecting the United States by telephone. **J. P. Morgan,** the most powerful financier of the era, took control of AT&T and appointed Theodore N. Vail as president of the newly acquired company. Together their vision to consolidate and control the telephone and telegraph communications lines in the United States, combined with significant technical advances of the era, laid the foundation for a world connected by telephones. Between 1907 and 1911, AT&T acquired a significant number of the independents, further strengthening their market presence and financial performance. In addition, during 1911, AT&T accomplished a major business takeover; they consolidated Western Union, their major rival from nearly 30 years prior, into the corporate structure of AT&T. Now they had the combined strength of both telephony and telegraphy under their corporate umbrella.

All this consolidation did not go unnoticed by the Department of Justice and the Interstate Commerce Commission. Beginning in 1913, AT&T decided to forestall any potential government antitrust action by offering a compromise solution to government officials. In a letter from AT&T vice president **Nathan Kingsbury** to the U.S. attorney general, AT&T offered to divest itself of Western Union and to discontinue buying up independent telephone companies. In addition, AT&T offered to make available its long-distance lines to all independents so that their subscribers could be interconnected with all AT&T customers.

The **Kingsbury commitment,** as it came to be known, was more of a peace offering to government policy makers and the independents than it was a commitment that AT&T would discontinue its aggressive policy toward unification of the telephone system in the United States. Even though the controlling interest of Western Union was sold, consolidations continued with AT&T absorbing independent telephone companies in the localities where policy makers approved the mergers. As part of the commitment, independent subscribers could now place calls on AT&T's long-distance lines, but only at considerable expense to the independent telephone companies; access was not free by any means and usually involved an access toll plus the physical construction of a line to connect an independent's exchange office to AT&T's long-distance access location. And although independent subscribers could now access AT&T long distance, AT&T subscribers still could not access independent exchanges. This portion of the "commitment" was very one-sided in favor of AT&T. Although frequently viewed at the time as a carrot for policy makers and the independent telephone companies, the Kingsbury commitment assured AT&T's position as the dominant provider of local and long-distance telephone service nationwide.

In addition to business policy that would facilitate telephone communications connectivity all across the United States, two major technical advances would complete a coast-to-coast telecommunications infrastructure; the loading coil and the vacuum tube triode. Between 1876 and the late 1890s, the most significant technological improvements to telephone communication were derived from the two-wire circuit and the introduction of extruded copper wire. However, the loss of signal strength over distance was a huge obstacle to high-quality communications between distant locations. Beginning in the early 1900s, AT&T introduced loading coil technology, an invention patented by Professor **Mihailo Pupin** in 1900 and acquired by AT&T that same year. The use of **loading coils** attached to a phone line every mile or so reduced the amount of signal loss or attenuation along the line so that a voice call could travel further along the wire with little or no reduction in quality. Loading coils also enabled the use of thinner copper wires in transmission circuits, which translated into large cost savings. With the use of loading coil technology alone, AT&T was able to connect New York City to Denver in 1911.

Loading coils alone could only reduce signal loss over distance, they couldn't amplify the voice signal. That's where the vacuum tube triode came into play. Invented and patented by Dr. **Lee De Forest** in 1907, **vacuum tube triodes** (sometimes referred to as *repeaters* and sometimes as *amplifiers*), provided the signal regeneration and amplification that were required to deliver high-quality long distance over even greater distances than loading coils alone could provide. By implementing both loading coils and vacuum tube triodes in 1914 on its long-distance circuits, AT&T was able to connect New York City to San Francisco, with the official unveiling of service taking place in January 1915. The United States was interconnected coast to coast and the beginnings of a telecommunications infrastructure were in place. But connectivity was not cheap; subscribers wishing to call coast to coast could expect to pay nearly $7 per minute for the first three minutes.

The first submarine cable connection was made between Key West, Florida, and Havana, Cuba, in April 1921 when President Warren Harding spoke with Cuban President Menocal. Three minutes cost $13.65. In 1927, the first transatlantic telephone connection, via radio frequency, connected the continental United States to London, England, at a cost of $75 for the first three minutes. Then in 1934, the United States connected to Japan, once again via radio frequency, at a cost of $39 for the first three minutes. Later developments included wireless microwave transmission of telephone calls between New York City and Boston in 1947 to increase transmission capacity, the first transatlantic telephone cable in 1956 to improve both transmission capacity and quality, the first telecommunications satellite in 1962, and the first transpacific telephone cable in 1964. For the second time in history (if you consider the telegraph to be the first time), consumers and businesses could exchange information electrically by wire all across the globe. The world was connected by telephone, and the best was yet to come; this telecommunications infrastructure combined with the evolving world of computers, and computer communication would provide the foundation for our modern era of data communications.

DATA COMMUNICATIONS AND NETWORKS: BEGINNINGS

semaphore signaling
a method of data communication that uses the position of dual flags, dual lights, or dual mechanical arms to represent letters and characters

We've already seen that the transmission of information between distant locations has been around for a very long time. Yelling to a friend or adversary, torches and **semaphore signaling**, optical telegraphs, electrical telegraphs, wireless communication, telephone communication; all of these technologies facilitated the exchange of information across distance. And the telegraph and telephone created global network infrastructures that allowed people and businesses all over the world to communicate with one another. The importance of these communications methods is of historical significance and underscores the human desire and business motivation to communicate. But the foundation of our modern era of data communications and networks, an era in which the transmission of text, graphics, video, and audio is as common as voice communication was to previous generations, is forever linked in history to two key events: the heightened need for national defense following World War II and the development of the interactive computer.

The Need for Better Defense

The first few years immediately following World War II are a pivotal time period that set one of the cornerstones on which our modern era of data communications and networks is built. After World War II, the Soviet Union's push to absorb small sovereign countries into

George Stibitz is credited with creating both the first electrical digital computer and the first computer network. In 1937, while working on a project for the Bell Labs division of AT&T, he created an adding circuit that could digitally represent numbers. Based on this invention, his boss asked him to create a calculator that could manipulate complex numbers and which would assist in the design of long-distance telephone communication. From that request came the **complex number calculator** in 1939, the first electrical digital computer. In addition, Stibitz configured the device to receive input from three remote teletype machines (think typewriter that has an electrical connection to a telegraph line or in this case to the complex number calculator) over a standard telegraph wire. Not only did he deliver a first in computing, he also created the world's first computer network. The complex number calculator and network functioned beautifully, fit their intended purpose, and from a historical perspective, they were the first of several ancestors to modern data communications and networks.

a totalitarian communist regime created an acute sensitivity toward national defense in the United States. As early as 1947, researchers at the Massachusetts Institute of Technology (MIT), in cooperation with U.S. defense officials began studying the possibility of a computer that could coordinate naval activities including naval aircraft, surface ships, and submarine vessels. In addition, the air force was painfully aware that the coastal radar defenses in the continental United States were inadequate for detecting a potential air threat from the Soviets, and they were looking for an advanced solution that would connect geographically distributed radar systems into a nationwide air defense system. The crowning alert came with the September 1949 discovery that the Soviet Union had detonated an atomic bomb in Siberia during the preceding month. This new nuclear threat was now just an airplane ride away from delivery on U.S. soil. The need for computer-based air defense was suddenly immediate. The ensuing decades would counter the nuclear threat with not only increased military preparedness and capability, but with computers, networks, and improved communications. But the computer, network, and communications counterattack had to start somewhere and with something. That *somewhere* was MIT and the *something* was the first **interactive computer, project Whirlwind.**

Project Whirlwind started out in the mid- to late 1940s at MIT as a project funded by the Office of Naval Research. Prior to the Whirlwind designation, the project was supposed to produce a flight simulator computer that would demonstrate the response of an aircraft to various pilot inputs and actions. By 1948, however, this original concept was modified in favor of a more general development goal—real-time computing, a type of computing that would be fast enough to provide instantaneous feedback to the computer's operator and fast enough to track the trajectories of enemy aircraft so that fighter aircraft could be dispatched and guided to the enemy's position. The original concept wasn't lost; it was only a modest leap to go from flight simulator to using real-time computing in a nationwide interconnected radar defense system. And in early 1951, after the Whirlwind computer demonstrated proof of concept (it tracked two U.S. fighter airplanes in real-time), the air force commissioned MIT to develop this nationwide air-defense system.

Launched as **Project Lincoln** in 1951, with a name change to Lincoln Lab in 1952, the air-defense project was housed at MIT, and part of MIT's mission for the project was to coordinate the design and manufacture of the high-powered computers that would drive the system. Because MIT didn't have the manufacturing expertise, it enlisted the help of IBM in 1952 to handle the high-tech manufacturing that the project would require. By 1954, the combined efforts of MIT and IBM resulted in a design effort that would ultimately begin implementation in late 1957. Named **SAGE** for **Semi-Automated Ground Environment,** the design and implementation plan called for 22 U.S. radar direction centers and one Canadian counterpart, each housing one of the IBM-built computers. In 1958, the first direction centers were brought online and connected via special modems and AT&T telephone lines. The remaining centers were up and running and interconnected by 1963. It was a huge computer network that fed data back and forth among all 23 geographically distributed air-defense direction centers. With the implementation of the SAGE computers and the connections among the direction centers, a U.S.-government sponsored project that began in the late 1940s set the first cornerstone in the late 1950s for our modern age of data communication.

The Significance of Time Sharing

At about the same time that project SAGE was getting off the ground, a young Ph.D. named **John McCarthy** spent the summer of 1955 working at IBM, and he didn't like to wait to use a computer. **Batch processing** was the standard method of computer time allocation during that era; it involved creating computer jobs on punch cards, submitting them to a card reader, which, in turn, would generate the output on magnetic tape. The data-processing staff would load the tape onto the computer at the end of the day, and the job could execute overnight. Batch processing worked under the business assumption that the computer was a scarce and valuable resource, that it was more efficient to run several jobs back to back as a batch to economize on computing time, and also by default assumed that human time was less valuable than computer time.

McCarthy, however, believed that human time, especially his own, was the scarce resource. In McCarthy's way of thinking, which was radical for the mid-1950s, multiple people should be able to access a computer and share its resources simultaneously, interactively, and from remote locations if necessary. His were the initial thoughts on **time sharing** a computer's resources, allowing multiple users to access the computer simultaneously by having the computer's central processor allocate discrete chunks of processing time to each of multiple individual users. With time sharing, he wouldn't have to wait for the computer to run his job as a batch; time sharing would make the computing experience interactive and available to many users simultaneously.

In 1957, McCarthy went on sabbatical to MIT and was confronted with the same problem he had experienced at IBM, only magnified. Earlier that same year, the relatively easy-to-use programming language called **FORTRAN** had been developed, and it gave engineers the ability to write useful programs without having to understand the idiosyncrasies of computer hardware. As a result, the demand for computing time exploded, and to handle the growth in demand, most computing environments, including the computing center at MIT, implemented batch processing.

Of course, McCarthy didn't like the fact that once again he was faced with waiting for computing time, sometimes as long as 24 hours. To alleviate the problem, he proposed a plan to the computer center management at MIT to develop a time-sharing program on their IBM 704 computer. In concept, it was a wonderful idea; he could apply the ideas he had articulated in 1955 and solve a huge resource allocation problem through multiple simultaneous access to the computer. In practice, however, his dream of developing a time-sharing computer would prove frustrating and slow to materialize; he needed a component from IBM called an **interrupt,** a device that would connect to the 704 computer and allow one computing task to be placed on hold temporarily while the central processor worked on another task. But IBM was slow to respond to MIT's request and even slower to deliver. By 1959 McCarthy still didn't have the necessary hardware to implement his time-sharing plan. In the meantime, his interests had shifted to artificial intelligence, and so he more or less handed off the time-sharing project to the MIT Computation Center's deputy director,

Fernando Corbato. Under Corbato's stewardship, by 1961, MIT had its **compatible time-sharing system (CTSS)** up and running. It utilized four terminals, which could simultaneously access MIT's newer IBM 709, and later the IBM 7090 in early 1962.[2]

So why are time-sharing systems so important in the evolution of data communications and networks? A couple of reasons make time sharing's contribution very significant. For one, providing interactive connectivity to more than one user at a time created a network of attached terminals. Although it's not the type of computer network we think of today, one that is composed of desktop PCs and various types of server computers, time-shared computers with multiple-terminal connections were the first forms of academic and commercial data networks. Second, time sharing with a central computer from a terminal required a remote connection to the computer, either through what was known as a serial connection (see chapter 2) or through a telephone line and modem connection. In either case, data was transmitted between terminal and computer. And later on, when users began exchanging files and even e-mails through connected terminals and time sharing, not only was data being transferred between terminal and computer, but information could be and was conveyed between remote users. As a result, time sharing is another of the building blocks cast in the foundation of the modern era of data communications and networks.

Satellites, Command and Control, and the Advanced Research Projects Agency

Between October 1957 and May 1958, the Soviet Union launched **Sputnik,** Sputnik II, and Sputnik III: a series of earth-orbiting satellites that would forever shape the destiny of data communications and networks the world over. Although these satellites did little if anything to transform or contribute to data communications and networks directly, indirectly they set in motion a series of political events and technological developments that have had far-reaching implications to the world of data communications and networks.

The most formidable of these political events was the formation and funding of the Advanced Research Projects Agency in February 1958. Formed in part as a response to the Soviet threat to U.S. national security, ARPA came to symbolize a shared vision to improve communication among disparate computers in support of military command and control functions. Because military command and control gives the U.S. president and other military commanders the ability to stay in contact with field operations regardless of an attack, battle conditions, or compromising military situations, the need for ARPA was exacerbated by the launching of the Sputnik satellites and paramount to national defense in the late 1950s. But support of command and control through the further development of computer technologies and data communication among various types of computers would prove to be a daunting task. By 1961, with the air force's SAGE project in full gear, ARPA was given four surplus IBM SAGE computers to use for the development of improved computer communications. However, without a focused approach to implement the vision for command and control, ARPA would soon find itself without adequate funding or insightful direction. Then came 1962, and ARPA hired **J. C. R. Licklider.**

In 1962, J. C. R. Licklider was a 47-year-old Ph.D. who had spent most of his adult working life in computing and the interaction of humans with computers. Trained as a psychologist but astute in electronics, engineering, and computers, Licklider was the right person at the right time for the needs of the emergent world of computing. He had spent significant time consulting with the air force and working on the human–machine interaction component of the SAGE project, and he instinctively saw how computers could be applied

---

[2] Simultaneous to MIT's research into time-sharing systems, colleges such as Carnegie Tech and Dartmouth and companies such as RAND Corporation and BBN were also working on their own methods of time sharing.

The **Advanced Research Projects Agency (ARPA)** provided the funding and direction for many of the key technology projects during the 1960s. Technologies such as interactive computing and time sharing, computer programming, and networked computers were developed with great success at various institutions all across the United States. In addition, computer-related and data communications–related technologies such as e-mail, word processing, packet switching, routing, the computer mouse, Ethernet, TCP/IP, windows-style graphics, and the Internet are all forever and inextricably linked to ARPA and the research projects that grew from the funding provided by this agency.

to **command and control.** So when he joined ARPA in October 1962, he saw immediately that support of command and control would best be served through interactive computing and time sharing, interactive graphics, networking, instantaneous information access, and interactive applications: all of the ingredients that military decision makers would need to make critical decisions as well as stay in contact with military field operations.

Throughout 1963 and 1964, Licklider funded time-sharing projects at Carnegie Tech, RAND Corporation, Stanford University, the University of California at Berkeley, MIT, and others. The benefits were dramatic with most locations being able to demonstrate a time-sharing system by 1964; more importantly was how the proof of concept demonstrated itself in various examples. For instance, as early as 1963, **Tom Van Vleck,** an undergraduate at MIT, created an e-mail program that worked in MIT's CTSS. Other programs at the various time-sharing locations allowed the sharing of programs and exchanging of files. These sound trivial in comparison with today's software, but in the early 1960s these capabilities were really big deals! And the truly huge outcome was that time sharing facilitated the exchange of information among users. It was data communications at its finest in those early days. Information flow in a time-shared environment was bidirectional; information could flow between points A and B—a person sitting at one location could type something at one **teletype terminal,** and a person at the remote location could receive that information. Time sharing was the latest and greatest form of data communications, and by linking multiple users together to share information, time sharing was also the ancestor of modern local area networks.

Another milestone year in the world of APRA-funded projects was 1965. The agency had 16 contractors working on computing-related projects, and they had **Bob Taylor,** a young engineer in his early thirties and eager to carry on and grow the vision begun earlier in the decade by his friend and colleague, J. C. R. Licklider. As part of the direction begun under Licklider, two very key computer networking projects were funded in 1965, one for a small network that would link three computing centers at the UCLA campus and another network that would link a computer at MIT's Lincoln Lab in Massachusetts to one of the surplus SAGE computers located at the Systems Development Corporation (SDC) in California.[3] While the UCLA project met with mixed results, the coast-to-coast network proved that data could be transmitted between two computers across a wide geographic distance using regular telephone lines. It was another first for ARPA and for the world of data communications. But Bob Taylor wasn't about to let this networking experiment sit on the sidelines. In 1966, when he became director of the **Information Processing Techniques Office (IPTO),** the office within ARPA that Licklider had pioneered, he added a new goal for the 16 contractors that were working on computer-related technologies: link them

---

[3] SDC developed the software for the SAGE project in the mid- to late 1950s. By the 1960s, SDC was one of the 16 contractors that were being funded to develop interactive computing, time sharing, and networking.

together and create a network of interactive computers that could share data all across the United States.

To execute his plan, Bob Taylor realized he was going to need a computing whiz to lead the technical design and implementation, and who better to take that lead than **Larry Roberts,** the young Ph.D. who during 1965 had designed the long-distance network that connected MIT's Lincoln Lab and SDC in Santa Monica, California.

Roberts's contributions to the creation of an interconnected ARPA community were exceptional, if not amazing. His work showed that regular phone lines were inadequate for data communication; instead they would use the AT&T leased lines that offered greater capacity and didn't require the computer to dial a phone number to connect to another computer. Borrowing from Leonard Kleinrock's 1962 Ph.D. thesis and work done by Paul Baran at the RAND Corporation in 1964, Roberts also specified a network that would segment the computer-generated digital data into smaller, more manageable chunks called *packets.*[4] By using this method, the network could include built-in error checking and higher reliability of data delivery. Finally, because all of the ARPA-funded sites would be connected to every other site by AT&T leased lines, Roberts knew that packets might have difficulty finding their destination location and the appropriate path to follow. The solution was routing: a method of directing packets that would ensure that a packet sent from any location would find the correct destination computer as well as a suitable path to get there—automatically. By 1968, Roberts had the funding to begin the first phase of the ARPA network development and implementation. He would connect four sites: UCLA, the Stanford Research Institute, the University of Utah, and the University of California at Santa Barbara.

With the design and implementation plan approved and funded, the campuses that would soon be connecting realized that their computers would need a set of common communication rules: rules that would define the data exchange application, how a data packet would be sent, how receipt of a packet would be acknowledged, how packets would find their location, how packets would be packaged for placement on the communications media, and so on. In effect they were talking about an approach to transmitting data across a network that was not unlike sending a letter through the postal system. It was a layered

FIGURE A.8
ARPANET: First Four Locations

---

[4] Kleinrock and Baran each made significant contributions to the field of networking; Kleinrock with his pioneering research into message flow across telecommunications networks and Baran with fault-tolerant telecommunications structures.

approach to data communications that would result in the development of the TCP/IP suite of protocols that is the standard for data communications on the Internet today.

The whole project came together, and the dreams and visions of the early interactive computing pioneers were realized in September 1969. On September 1, UCLA was the first of the ARPA sites to come online, and by the end of December, all of the first four sites were connected and exchanging data. The new ARPA network or **ARPANET** as it came to be called was a success; the connected ARPA contractor sites had grown to 13 by the end of 1970, and by September 1971, the number of connected sites had grown beyond the original 16. By August 1972, nearly 30 sites were connected to the growing family of ARPANET sites, and by September 1973, the ARPANET had grown to 40 sites and was international; Norway and London were online.

As happened with the electrical telegraph in the 19th century and with the telephone in the 20th century, the world was connected yet again, this time with the ARPANET, a network that could and would facilitate data communications all over the world. It continued to expand and mature throughout the 1970s and 1980s, and in 1992 it was ready to connect the population of the world, albeit with a new name, the Internet.

DATA COMMUNICATIONS AND NETWORKS—TODAY

Interactive computing, time-sharing computers, networking, and, of course, the culmination of those three as the ARPANET are the forerunner of today's modern world of data communications, high-speed data networks, and Internet technologies. It's easy to take these technologies for granted because we use them every day; they're the tools we use for everyday business and personal communication. In modern terms, data communications and networks reduce any type of information to its simplest form, bits and bytes, and convey that information over any number of media types. We can transmit text, voice, graphics, full-motion video, audio, you name it, as a series of voltage changes or optical signals. Click on a link and the information you want to see is at your fingertips immediately. If you need to send a file to a business associate or friend you attach it to an e-mail, and click on Send—your data arrives almost instantly. To make an online purchase you access the Web site, click on the items you want, provide your payment information, and you're done. But why can we do these things? What are the underlying concepts that make data communications possible? To answer these questions, you're going to need an introduction to the basic concepts of data communications and networks, and for that, you're going to have to return to the main chapters of the text.

Key Terms

Abbe Nollet, *377*
Advanced Research Project Agency (ARPA), *393*
Alexander Graham Bell, *373*
Alessandro Volta, *378*
Alfred Vail, *380*
American Bell Telephone Company, *386*
American Telephone and Telegraph (AT&T), *387*

Amos Kendall, *381*
ARPANET, *395*
Baron Pavel Schilling, *379*
Batch processing, *391*
Bell Telephone Company, *385*
Benjamin Franklin, *377*
Bob Taylor, *393*
C. M., *377*
Carl Friedrich Guass, *379*
Charles Bourseul, *382*

Charles T. Jackson, *380*
Charles Wheatstone, *379*
Claude Chappe, *372*
Command and control, *393*
Compatible Time-Sharing System (CTSS), *392*
Complex number calculator, *390*
Cyrus Field, *381*
Data transmissions, *372*
Deflecting needle, *379*

Questions

1. Who is credited with developing the optical telegraph in France in the late 1700s?

2. How did Alexander Bell's photophone transmit sound?

3. What is Heinrich Hertz noted for?

4. Who is the Italian inventor credited with developing early radio transmission?

5. In what year was the first transatlantic wireless message sent?

6. What is the ondophone?

7. What company developed the first air-to-ground wireless radio telephone?

8. In what year was the first commercial mobile telephone service available?

9. The cellular telephone service that we take for granted today was first thought of in what year?

10. What type of wireless communication system transmitted a coast-to-coast telephone call in 1951?

11. What is the significance of Telstar?

12. What limited AT&T's development of wireless communication in the United States in the 1980s?

13. What has spurred the technological development of wireless communication in the 1980s and 1990s?

14. What events in the early to mid-1700s convinced experimenters that communication might be possible across a wire?

15. What is the significance of the article by C. M. that appeared in *Scot's Magazine* in 1753?

16. What did George Lesage invent in 1774? How did his device work?

17. Whose telegraph used the electrolysis of water to convey data transmissions?

18. What events led to the development of the electromagnet? What significance did the invention of the electromagnet have on the advancement of data communications?

19. What is Henry Joseph's contribution to the advancement of data communications?

20. What inventors contributed to the development of the needle telegraph?

21. Where did Samuel Morse obtain his funding for an experimental telegraph line that ran between Washington, D.C. and Baltimore? When was the line completed?

22. What early U.S. monopoly eventually absorbed Samuel Morse's telegraph company in 1866?

23. What electrical property does telephone communication require that telegraphic communication does not?

24. What was Charles Bourseul's contribution to the development of the telephone? What about Johann Reis?

25. What were Alexander Graham Bell and Elisha Gray independently working on prior to Bell's telephone patent?

26. What company did the young Bell Telephone Company sue for patent infringement in 1878? What was the outcome of this lawsuit?

27. What discovery in 1881 made long-distance telephone calls technically achievable? What discovery made long-distance service economically feasible?

28. What is a data communications infrastructure?

29. What was J. P. Morgan's role in the development of AT&T?

30. What is the significance of the Kingsbury commitment?

31. How did loading coils and the vacuum tube triode contribute to long-distance telephone communication?

32. What method of transmission did transatlantic and transpacific long-distance telephone service utilize during the 1920s and 1930s?

33. When did transatlantic telephone communication by wire become possible? Transpacific?

34. To what two events is the foundation of our modern world of data communications and networks linked?

35. What is the significance of project Whirlwind to the evolution of data communications and networks?

36. How did SAGE fit into the development of data communications and networks?

37. How important was computer time sharing to the development of data communications and networks? Why?

38. What U.S. government agency was formed in part because of the launching of the Soviet Sputnik satellites? What are some of this agency's contributions to data communications and networks?

39. Who was J. C. R. Licklider? What are some of his contributions to data communications and networks?

40. What contributions did Bob Taylor and Larry Roberts make to data communications and networks?

41. What is the ARPANET? Where were the first four sites located?

Research Activities

1. Using the various research tools available to you, list and explain several of the business uses for which the telegraph was employed during the 1800s and 1900s.

2. Find out if your school or workplace utilizes any form of computer time sharing. How is it implemented and utilized?

3. Conduct an Internet search for the Advanced Research Projects Agency (or Defense Advanced Research Projects Agency), and identify several of the activities that this agency is involved in today.

Mini Case Studies

AMERICAN AIRLINES

Between 1959 and 1964, IBM and American Airlines worked cooperatively to develop an online flight reservation system for American Airlines. A computer system located at American's computing center near New York City was connected via modems and phone lines to teletype machines all over the United States. Known as the **Semi-Automated Business-Related Environment (SABRE),** this corporatewide computer network allowed American Airlines ticket agents all over the United States to rapidly generate flight reservations by communicating over telephone lines to a central computer. Prior to this system, ticket agents used manual and electromechanical devices to reserve seats and communicate availability of seats to other ticket agents. Toward the late 1960s and into the 1970s, American expanded its reservation network to independent travel agents so that they, too, could access American Airlines' flight information and make reservations for passengers.

SABRE required significant capital to implement and maintain. However, despite its large cost to develop and implement, American chose to take the initial leap into the relatively new world of data communications. What business reasons might have caused American Airlines to implement such a costly data communications network? What value would you say American derived from this business strategy?

AT&T AND CARRIER CIRCUITS

In the early days of telephone communication, any two telephone subscribers that wanted to talk with each other via telephone required a dedicated point-to-point circuit between the two locations. After 1878, the point-to-point connection was replaced by connecting subscribers through a central switching office so that any subscriber could be connected with any other subscriber.

As growth of the subscriber base exploded throughout the last decade of the 19th century and the first two decades of the 20th century, and subscribers demanded connectivity with subscribers connected to other central switching offices, AT&T was faced with the alternatives of installing an additional two-wire pair circuit for each additional connecting call between central offices to handle the increased traffic on its network or develop and implement new technologies that would allow multiple calls to be carried over the existing wires and cables between offices.

As early as 1902, AT&T began using two, two-wire pairs, twisted together to yield three telephone circuits between switching offices. Each of the two-wire pairs represented a telephone circuit, and the two, two-wire pairs in conjunction yielded a third circuit that came to be known as a **phantom circuit.**

But the increasing need for transmission capacity between central switching offices over existing two-wire pairs was not left to phantom circuit technology. After about 1914, with advancements in vacuum tube technology and wave filters, carrier multiplexing became a technological reality. With carrier multiplexing, AT&T could transmit multiple calls over a two-wire telephone circuit, and by 1918, with the implementation of its first commercial carrier service, known as Type A carrier, AT&T was able to achieve four two-way carrier channels over a two-wire pair in addition to the regular voice channel.

Implementing new technology is generally associated with huge development costs without necessarily knowing the potential return on investment. In the cases of phantom circuits and carrier technologies, AT&T made substantial investments in both physical and intellectual resources to achieve its strategic goals. Why do you suppose AT&T made such large investments in line-capacity technology? What added value do you think these technologies brought to AT&T? What commercial risk did AT&T make in deploying these technologies? Do you think the benefits outweighed the costs? Why?

Index